massala

Fine Indian cuisine, delicately prepared to perfection

- Authentic traditional fine Indian cuisine
- Outstanding wine list, prepared by former Claridges sommelier
- Beautifully appointed restaurant
- Cooking using traditional charcoal tandoor oven
- Signature dishes include Monkfish Malabar, Dal Makhani and Lamb Xacuti

"I have to say that it was all absolutely stunning. I don't say that very often. But it was. I just hope Cobham realises what they have in their locality. Such cooking outclasses many of the so-called top restaurants in the West End."

Pat Chapman
Editor Cobra Good Curry Guide and Founder The Curry Club

Massala | 19 Anyards Road | Cobham | Surrey | KT11 2LW
t: 01932 865005 | e: info@massalacobham.com | w: www.massalacobham.com

THREE OF THE VERY BEST
INDIAN RESTAURANTS

AMAYA

This award winning, Michelin starred, restaurant presents an unmistakable experience for lunch and dinner in Belgravia.

Halkin Arcade, Motcomb Street
Knightsbridge, London SW1

Telephone: 020 7823 1166

CHUTNEY MARY

The rich setting, interesting art and romantic candle lighting are secondary details in London's temple of great Indian food.

535 Kings Road
Chelsea, London SW10

Telephone: 020 7351 3113

VEERASWAMY

Divine dishes, lovingly prepared and beautifully served in sumptuous surroundings overlooking Regent Street.

Mezzanine Floor, Victory House
99 Regent Street, London W1

Telephone: 020 7734 1401

For details of our outside catering service, please contact our Head Office on 020 7724 2525 or email us at info@realindianfood.com.

MasalaWorld

REFRESHINGLY SMOOTH PREMIUM BEER

COBRA
कोबरा

2013 COBRA GOOD CURRY GUIDE

PAT CHAPMAN'S CURRY CLUB

THE 2013- COBRA GOOD CURRY GUIDE

Joint Editor and Database Management:
Dominique Chapman (DBAC)

Design: PCP Graphics developed from Peter Ward's design
Pat's logo and graphics by Nick Warren at www.n9design.com

Text Editor: Ronald Laxton

Statistics: Taylor Nelson, Sub Continent Publishing, yougov.com, Onepoll.com

Researchers: Shaleem Malik Alexander, Aarti Gauri Bhandari, Aftab Bhatti, Mandeep S Grewal, Jenny Guo, Gazanfer Iqbal, Sheila Jarvis, Stephen John, Ravi Makkapati, Munawar Mall, Biren Parikh, Buela Samuel, Samson Sohail, Asher Moon Tely, Kamran Tufail, Nikhil Wadhwa and Ameet Watts.
Thanks to: Roopa Gulati, Humayan Hussain, AJ Patel, Tandoori Magazine & Puja Vedi.

Good Curry Guide Frequent and Prolific Reporters:
Dave Bridges, The Wirral; N.K.Campbell, Edinburgh; Hilary Chapchal, Surrey; Bill Parkes-Davis, Kent; Rod Eglin, Cumbria; Ray & Ruby Elliot, Worcs; Tony Emmerson, Lancs; Bob Giddings, Poole; Justin Harper, Hemel; Tony and Monika Hetherington, Yorks; Andy Glazier, London; Tim & Katherine Morgan, Scotland; Paul Motley, e-mail; Steve Osborne, Bucks; Grahame and Melinda Payne, Coventry; Dr Dirk Pilat, e-mail; Nigel Thomas, Lincoln; Ralph Warrington, Hyde; Cheshire (GM); Jeanette Wickes, Kent,; Malcolm Wilkins, Gravesend, Kent; Mick Wright, Beds.
plus many hundreds of others, without whom this Guide would not exist,
and whose names appear at the end of this book.

Copyright © 2012 Pat Chapman

This eleventh edition first published in Great Britain, November 2012
by The Curry Club, PO Box 7, Haslemere, Surrey, UK. GU27 1EP,
in association with John Blake Publishers, W14 9BP

Previous Editions of this Guide:
First edition 1984, Second 1987, Third 1991, Fourth 1995, Fifth 1998, Sixth 1999, Seventh 2001, Eighth 2004, Ninth 2007, reprint of Ninth 2008, Tenth 2009, reprint of Tenth 2010

This book is copyright under the Berne Convention.
All rights reserved. No part of this publication may be reproduced, stored in a retrieval system, or transmitted, in any form or by any means without the prior written permission of the publisher, nor be otherwise circulated in any form of binding or cover other than that in which it is published and without similar condition being imposed on the subsequent purchaser.
ISBN 978-0-9537735-3-4

Printed and bound in Great Britain by Blackmore Printers, Shaftesbury, Dorset.
A CIP catalogue recommendation for this book is available from the British Library

2013 COBRA GOOD CURRY GUIDE

CONTENTS

Author's Notes ~ 6
County Index ~ 7
About This Guide ~ 8
Celebrating Thirty Curry Club Years ~ 10
The Cobra Story ~ 16
Cobra's Spicy British Classic Dishes – 18
The Currination ~ 28
Get Pickled ~ 36
The Elite A-LIST and TOP 100 ~ 40
The Hall of Fame ~ 40
A-LIST and TOP 100 Full Listing ~ 42 to 63
Map of the Subcontinent ~ 64
The Cuisine of the Subcontinent Defined ~ 65
The Cuisine of South east Asia Defined ~ 70
The A to Z of the Curry Menu ~ 74
An explanation of our Method ~ 81

THE ENTRIES

LONDON ~ **83**
ENGLAND ~ **189**
THE ISLES AND ISLANDS ~ **346**
SCOTLAND ~ **349**
WALES ~ **364**

END MATTER

What We Need to Know ~ 374
Restaurant Report Forms for your use ~ 375-378
List of Contributors ~ 379
Town Index ~ 382

Author's Notes

Sponsorship The continuing sponsorship by Cobra Beer as the Guide's sole sponsor, enables the author to finance the considerable costs of operating and producing this Guide, which include: maintaining the restaurant database on computer; subscribing to a press-cutting service and other information suppliers; printing a detailed questionnaire and mailing it to all 9,500 restaurants twice a year; mail-shotting the 1,500-plus restaurants that are selected to appear in the Guide; telephoning many for verification of information; producing, supplying and mailing the selected restaurants (free of charge) their wall certificates and window stickers; printing and mailing restaurant report forms for interested parties; collating and recording the info received (some 5,000 reports per annum) and operating the Awards Ceremony. *(see page 32).*

Accuracy The contents of this Guide are as up-to-date and accurate as possible, but we cannot be held responsible for any changes regarding quality, price, menu details, decor, ownership, health offences or even closure, following our processing of the reports.

Connections Pat Chapman, the publishers of this Guide and the proprietors of The Curry Club wish to make it quite clear that they have absolutely no financial or ownership connections with any restaurants, including those mentioned in this Guide.

False Representation Restaurant reports are welcomed from any bona-fide source. We do not pay for reports – they are sent in spontaneously and voluntarily. Our own research and restaurant testing is normally done anonymously, the bill is paid, and often no disclosure is made as to our presence. On some occasions, such as openings, we accept invitations to visit restaurants as 'guests of the house'. Under no circumstances do we tout for free hospitality, and anyone doing so in the name of The Curry Club is an impostor. We have heard of cases where people claiming to be members of The Curry Club, or Good Curry Guide 'inspectors', request payment and/or free meals in return for entry into this Guide. In such cases, we would recommend that restaurants threaten to call the police. We would also like to be informed of any such incidents and we will not hesitate to take action against people acting illegally in our name.

Discounts We used to invite all restaurants selected to appear in this Guide to participate in a discount scheme for members of The Curry Club. We have now discontinued this scheme, but we urge all readers of this Guide to request a discount from any restaurant in this Guide, and if necessary to show the restaurant their entry in the Guide.

Certificates & Window Stickers We send all restaurants appearing in this Guide a 2007 certificate, hand-signed by Pat Chapman, and a 2007 window sticker. These items are supplied free of charge. Some choose not to display them, others display them proudly and prominently. You may observe that our certificate is not displayed alone. There may well be a host of others, some bigger and flashier than ours, including the Dome Grading certificates issued by Peter and Colleen Groves, which are genuine, as are certificates issued by London's Time Out, Ronay, local council health departments and certain others. Unfortunately, some certificates are a pure sham. They are issued to any restaurant who cares to pay for them, in some cases with a promise of entry into a Guide which does not even exist. We reported last time on a scam by Good Food Guide, yet again, but this is not The Good Food Guide. There is no Guide and this is the same outfit that were sued by the Consumers' Association some time ago and have now re-emerged at a different address. Masterchef returned after being exposed by BBC 'Food and Drink' in June. Certificates are on offer for £67.50 (£10 for extra copies) and £5 for window stickers. The Asian Food Guide was caught out on Radio 4. There are others on the bandwagon. Like Peter Groves, we would like to see this scam stopped.

But how do you know that the Good Curry Guide certificate you see is genuine?

For those of you who like to follow events, we reported last time about a scam-operator called Ian Cowan of Inc Software, Paisley, Scotland. He was attempting to charge for Good Curry Guide certificates for a cost of £30. Remember, we give our certificates free of charge. -It seems that, as we predicted, he has sunk without trace. And so too has the mania to operate copy-cat websites. Infact we have become relaxed about it. If you want to read this Guide's words on some 'unauthorised' website, so be it. And if you are contemplating rewriting all the words on this Guide, I point out that there are 250,000 words to copy. Enjoy!

2013 COBRA GOOD CURRY GUIDE

County Index

See pages 382 to 384 for Town Index

London
London E	88	London EC	102	London N	106
London NW	112	London SE	120	London SW	126
London W	154	London WC	181		

England
Bedfordshire	189	Berkshire	190	Bristol	194
Buckinghamshire	195	Cambridgeshire	202	Cheshire	203
Cornwall	205	Cumbria	207	Derbyshire	209
Devon	211	Dorset	213	County Durham	215
Essex	216	Gloucestershire	219	Hampshire	221
Herefordshire	228	Hertfordshire	229	Kent	232
Lancashire	239	Leicestershire	241	Lincolnshire	244
Manchester (Gtr)	245	Merseyside	254	Middlesex	256
Norfolk	267	Northamptonshire	268	Northumberland	271
Nottinghamshire	273	Oxfordshire	278	Rutland	279
Shropshire	280	Somerset	281	Staffordshire	285
Suffolk	287	Surrey	288	Sussex	298
Tyne & Wear	304	Warwickshire	308	West Midlands	311
Wiltshire	322	Worcestershire	325	North Yorkshire	327
East Yorkshire	330	South Yorkshire	331	West Yorkshire	334

The Isles and Islands
Scottish Isles	346	Isle of Man	347	Channel Islands	348

Scotland
D & G	349	Fife	349	Grampian	350
Highland	351	Lothian	351	Scottish Borders	366
Strathclyde	357	Stirling	357	Tayside	363

Wales
Clywd	364	Dyfed	365	Glamorgan	365
Gwent	370	Gwynedd	372	Powys	373

About this Guide

The Good Curry Guide broke new ground when it was first published in 1984, by being the first restaurant guide to specialise only in the British curry. This is its tenth edition, marking its 25th year. We mark it with a special feature overleaf As usual, there there have been demotions and promotions since last time. We want continuity in each edition of the Guide, and because we do expect changes, we feel it is important that each restaurant completes our questionnaire. For one thing, it means the restaurant actually wants to be in the Guide. It also verifies its current name, address, telephone number, and above all, prices. Despite our earnest endeavours, not all restaurants reply, even if they did so last time. So if we have not received a reply from a restaurant that was in the previous edition, after it has been sent a form three times, should it be delisted? I believe it should if it cannot be bothered, for whatever reason, to talk to us. But curry restaurants are a peculiar trade; communications aren't always easy and normal rules don't apply.

A completed form from a restaurant does not guarantee entry to the Guide. We rely on various other sources of information. We can only visit a handful of restaurants each year, and do not have a team of paid inspectors. Most important to us are the opinions of the customers – you, the diners. We do not pay for such reports, though from time to time The Curry Club gives prizes for your efforts. The report itself can be a simple short note, though we have a special form (see final page) for all who want one. A report may deal with a single restaurant or several. Some reporters write to us only once, others write repeatedly. For this Guide, we received about 5,000 reports, yielding information on up to 50,000 restaurant visits. We read and record every report, although it is becoming increasingly difficult to reply to all of them. I would like, therefore, to thank all those who have taken the time to tell us where they have found the best, good, mediocre and even bad curries.

Naturally, reporting standards vary, and the The Wind of India, Puddlecome-on-the-Marsh may well be reported as the best in the world by an ardent, novice, local fan (and I want such opinions), but may not rate highly if compared with London's best. Nevertheless, it will be a competent curry house in that area, serving standard formula curry. Numerous entries in this Guide come into this category, and they are here because someone, maybe more than one person, has taken the trouble to write in and praise the place, and to exclude it would be wrong. We want to know what you know.

Answering the question *'Name your favourite curry restaurant(s)'* may not always be as easy as it sounds. It is worth again quoting Sutton Coldfield's John Brockingham, a retired college lecturer: *'My favourite restaurants,'* he wrote, *'range from opulent establishments like Rajdoot, Birmingham, where I might take the family on special occasions, to cheap and cheerful places like Erdington's Balti Express, where a meal costs £11 a head. I have a favourite posh curry restaurant, when I can afford it, and a favourite posh Balti. But I have a favourite plonk version of both, and a favourite takeaway, and then there's a favourite lucky dip. Some of my favourites are good enough to tempt me in whenever I'm in the district, but could not be nominated for the highest accolade.'*

Of course we do not receive reports on every single establishment. On occasion a restaurant we normally receive good reports about gets damned. If this is the exception, we will probably still carry that restaurant. Some will have closed, and others should perhaps have been omitted. But none get into this Guide unless we have had at least one recent good report on it, preferably several. To get into the TOP 100 we need several detailed excellent reports, including at least one by one of our elite 60 or so regular reporters. As editors we visit a top 100 restaurant anonymously whenever we can, but it's impossible to go to them all within one year. We do our best to filter out 'good' reports on bad restaurants, particularly those written by their hopeful owners. As usual, we requested that restaurants selected for entry get their customers to write to us, and many did. This way, we have almost weeded out the few restaurants who previously sent us phoney reports, purportedly from adoring customers. However, even after twenty five years in the editor's chair, it is possible that I've been conned and a 'bad' restaurant has slipped in. Equally, I'll guarantee that we've missed someone's favourite, and that there are a few faux pas too. Please let us know about these. No doubt, we'll continue to get irate letters from people who won't have bothered to read this section, telling us that, because this or that restaurant was awful when they visited, 'it casts doubt on the credibility of the entire Guide'. We certainly do not enter restaurants just because they ask us to. After twenty five years of bona-fide operations, you would imagine that curryhouse owners would clamour to be in the Guide. Indeed some do. As I have said in previous Guides, more than one restaurant has made veiled references to the benefits that would be made available to the editors if that restaurant were declared the UK's number one. The very idea is abhorrent. Besides, if one did accede to such bribery, word would soon get round risking the credibility of both author and publication. The book is paid for through book sales, ads and sponsorship, not through bribes.

So what's new in this edition? Regular readers will know that we go alphabetically by county, then within that, by town and then restaurant. We are continuing with this system, since it is easier to see at a glance what alternative choices are nearby. We also continue with the town index at the end of the book. A new idea is to put in a restaurant name index to speed up finding your favourite. At the start of each county's entry, are our thumbnail county maps, which help pinpoint the location of that particular county, along with a list of adjacent counties. It should make this Guide more informative and finding your way around it easier. And that, after all, is what this Guide is all about finding good curries easily, and nothing else.

White PEARL

THE PREFERRED CHOICE OF TOP CHEFS

Map Trading Ltd
Specialist Suppliers of Indian Foods
Rice, Lentils, Spices, Pappadoms, Flours, Pickles, Pastes, Oils, Chutney etc.

Map Trading Limited
2 Abbey Road, Park Royal, London NW10 7BW, England.
Tel: +44 208 965 0193   Fax: +44 208 963 1184   Email: post@whitepearl.co.uk

www.whitepearl.co.uk

INVESTOR IN PEOPLE

1982 to 2012

1982 — First logo. Same address as now, a shorter phone number, and in 1982 we have a recession.

A Club for Curryholics. Pat Chapman invents the word and founds the Club with this invitation in small ads in the 1982 Sunday Broadsheets.

"If you like curry join the Curry Club. Facts, fun and features, Mail order spices, events, publications, tuition, curry restaurant visits and meetings"

You join. And we've all been Currying on ever since.

P.O. BOX 7
HASLEMERE
SURREY
GU27 1EP
0428-2452

Edition 1, middle above, is published in Spring 1983, carrying news, recipes, pictures and features. It is the first of 68 editions published. The printers typeset the text from our manuscript. We placed it onto white card with scissors and glue. No home computers then, but 'cut and paste' came from those days. The chef on the left (Edition 15) is making Takatan, a Pakistani favourite curry. Edition 2 with the palm trees carries Gastronome's first Hot Gossip piece, reproduced below.

1983 Spicey goings on at Ballater

hot gossip by gastronome

We're getting used to being given a variety of names – and so are the post office. Letters arrive variously addressed to **The Curly Club, The Cure Club, The Curry Cube, The Curt Club, The John Curry Club** (the writer supposed we ran a fan club for the ice skater). Mail also reaches us under the following pseudonyms: **The Spice Co., Hot Spices Ltd., The Curry Company, The Chilli Club,** and **Curries** (copiers including Khalid Aziz please note). Thanks to the Royal Mail we recently received two remarkably addressed items, one simply 'The Curry Club UK' and the other to the editor: 'Pat Chapman, Haslemere'.

Above: One of our first Residential Cookery Courses, the Curry Cook-in is held at the Invercauld Arms Hotel Ballater, down the road from Balmoral. And yes, that's Pat, hairier and thinner than in 2012!

Photo courtesy the Aberdeen Press and Journal

Celebrating 30 Years

1983 February: Our first Gourmet Tour goes to India, the first of sixteen, the most recent being in 2009. There are no other tours like them, led and managed by Pat and his wife Dominique, who between them they have over 50 years experience of India, and over the years have become friends with many Indian chefs hotel and managers. The tours take in all the sights plus some not available to regular tourists. The destinations show you the best of historic and modern India, from chaotic cities to peaceful villages. Being a Gourmet Tour, the food is way, way better than tourist offerings and certainly not something from the buffet. In fact it is the best Indian food you can get because the chefs know Pat. Menus are carefully chosen and the chefs enjoy meeting our guests.

Right: March 1984. Chef Culinaire Satish Arora, head of all the cooking for India's most prestigious hotel group, Taj. He was also responsible for all the day to day cooking at the flagship Taj Mahal Palace Hotel, Mumbai, whether Indian, Chinese, Nouveau, Western or a room service English breakfast. The 150 chef brigade prepares 5,000 meals in the course of a day. Here we see Satish doing a bespoke cooking demonstration for our group.

*Left: April 2009: 26 years later, our 16th Gourmet Tour group, The Ma family attends a special demo/dinner at the new hi tech **Chef Studio** at the Taj Mahal Palace Mumbai, the creation of the current Taj Group Corporate Chef Hemant Oberoi. Pictured in front of Pat, he is credited with raising Indian food to world class Gourmet standards. On Pat's left is author and another good friend, Camelia Panjabi, until recently Taj Group Marketing Director. Dominque is far right.*

1984 November: We tour the country bringing Curry nights to the nation. Here we are at Nottingham's Novotel Hotel photo by the Nottingham Post. Sadly we don't have our waitress's and diners' names on record. If you know, let us know and we'll reward them.

● *Guests at the Curry Club banquet are served up a mouth-watering variety of Indian dishes*

Our 17th Gourmet Tour is planned for 2013
Visiting Delhi, Agra, Jaipur, Udaipur, Aurangabad and Mumbai.
Tracing the footsteps of Moghuls and Maharajas,
Seeing all the Sights.
Staying in Palaces.
Enjoying Indian Food.
pat@patchapman.co.uk

1982 to 2012

1984 When Pat Chapman founded The Curry Club in 1982, he asks to share curry restaurant information; you send him plenty. Others need to know the whereabouts of the best in this or that town. After a couple of years, when the scraps of paper became unmanageable, Pat conceives the idea to publish the *Good Curry Guide*. It comes out in May as a slim-line pocket book and we sell 600 copies and get a massive and very favourable press reaction. Now a collectors' item, one copy went on Ebay recently for £180.

In October 1984, Piatkus publishes Pat's first book *(left)* as a hardback at £4.95. The cautious print run of 4,000 sells out by November. It has since had 17 reprints and sold 150,000 copies. And, remarkably for a cookbook, it hasn't got a single photo in it!

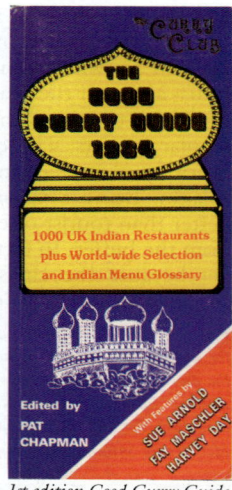

1st edition Good Curry Guide.

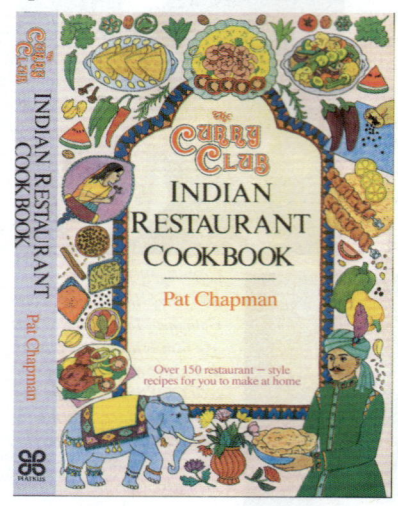

1985 March: The Curry Shop opens in Covent Garden's Piazza, rent £17.500 rates £800. We sell Curry Club branded spice mix packs and books and all sorts of curry products by other brands. We hold themed Curry Dinner on alternate Wednesday nights at the shop; a three course meal, & coffee is £6, BYO. 36 covers pack in like sardines and we book up a year ahead. It's membership only, and billed as the 'Most Exclusive Curry London'. No wonder we are always full.

In 1988 Covent Garden Piazza is bought by the Prudential Insurance company, who immediately raise our rent to what they call "market rates"; £51,000 plus a new service charge of £8,000, and as if that isn't enough new business rates are also introduced at £8,000. It was the height of a property boom and sadly this was too much for us and we had to close. The Curry Shop never had a chance to develop and is still missed by its once loyal following.

Celebrating 30 Years

1989 With dwindling funds, we seek investors and are found by a well healed company who move us to a new 6,500 factory. They get a posh London design house to design a new logo, and our unique spice packs and they engage a marketing company. They purchase Abdullah's pickles (founded 1911) and their bottling plant and they employ consultants galore and engage 22 staff. The product range looks beautiful. It includes our of 44 Spice Mix packs, now called **Blended Spices, Restaurant**-style in new smart packs on display

Second logo.

boards (*see below*), we pioneer a Balti range and there are curry pastes, poppadums, pickles, chutneys, mint raita, ghee, creamed coconut and canned curries. Add in the cookbooks and we had the fullest curry range on the market. Despite a brief recession in 1989, we get the range into Harrods, Selfridges, Fortnums, independent delis and Waitrose. In December 1990 we get our products and books into 20 Tesco stores for a three month trial, well positioned opposite the tills, and ...

Above: Our unique Balti range.

Left: Display board

Right: Tesco end of gondola unit display

1982 to 2012

1991 ... and yet another recession hits in 1991 ... and the property bubble bursts. Our investor has a huge property portfolio, and goes bust too. The Curry Club is a casualty. But help is at hand and we are bought by G.Costa, owners of the Blue Dragon brand. For the next 15 years Dominique and Pat Chapman do all G.Costa's exhibition, show and supermarket buyer demonstrations. Sadly Curry Club brand doesn't flourish; Costa's efforts centre on growing Blue Dragon with their new Thai, Vietnamese and Thai ranges. It's an ill wind however and we learn these cuisines aided by visits to those countries. Pat's vast recipe collection becomes published with a number of books, not all of them curry.

*Blue Dragon put their logo on Pat's **Noodle Book**. The book contains a full explanation*

If an author is allowed to name his favourite book it is ***Taste of the Raj***, which gives recipes and a culinary history of British India and Pat's family background.

1991 It's amazing to think of it now, with Awards ceremonies happening at the rate of a dozen a night awarding such industries and ball bearings, knickers and hairdressing, in fact any subject you can think. Hotels thrive on it. But back in 1991 they didn't happen. Certainly no one had ever run a Restaurant Awards Ceremony. The Curry Club pioneer it with curry. It's held at the overall winner,'s venue Chutney Mary's SW10 on 9th October 1991 with just ten winners.

Left to right: the late Abdul Latif of Rupali Newcastle, Sanjay Anand of Madhu's Brilliant, the late Latif Tarafder of Khyber Plymouth, Wali Udin of Verandah Edinburgh, Namita Panjabi of Chutney Mary, Hansa of Hansa's Leeds, Cyrus Todiwalla, with his first award given before he opened his Namasté, Rashmi of Jashan N8, Des Sarda Rajdoot Group (now retired), and far right John Loosemore, the our most Prolific Reporter. And that's Pat proudly seated centre.

Celebrating 30 Years
1991 to date

Cobra, just a year old, sponsors the *1991 Good Curry Guide*, our third edition. And so begins sponsorship which has continued uninterrupted for 21 years. The Cobra Guide is now as important a part of the British curry scene as is curry and Cobra themselves.

Cobra Guides, l to r:
1991 3rd edition,
1995 4th edition (pink),
8th 2004
fiery 9th 2007
10th with the chillies, 2009
and the 11th 2010.

Left: Lord Karan Bilimoria, Pat and Dominique Chapman present the 2007 *Cobra Good Curry Awards* at London's Park Lane Hilton. Above: He presents Best in the North Award to Matab Miah of Newcastle's Vujon. Below: The audience numbers 800.

Following our pioneering 1991 event *(left)* we grow the *Good Curry Awards* ceremony with our next in 1995 with 300 guests at the Park Lane Hotel. We follow this in 1998 & 99. In 2001, 2004 and 2007 we are at the Park Lane Hilton. In the last few years a number of curry award ceremonies have copied our formula. But as with many things the original is the most prestigious. It is the *Cobra Good Curry Award* which all the restaurants prize the most.

1982 to 2012

1996 to date

Pat regularly appears and cooks on British television

Below: Lorraine Kelley' discusses curry on her ITV show.

A rehearsal break on the live Good morning with Anne and Nick shown in May 1996.

1997

Cunard invites Pat Chapman to Guest chef and demonstrate curry on their 19 night Autumn Caribbean Cruise with Jilly Goolden matching the wines. Pat and Dominique go on to do a further eleven cruises aboard QE2, all around the world until this iconic liner's retirement in 2008.

Dominique and Pat demonstrating in the Grand Lounge.

CUNARD QE2 1997

QUEEN ELIZABETH 2
CARIBBEAN MASTERPIECE
HOSTED ON BOARD BY PAT CHAPMAN & JILLY GOOLDEN

1997

Hodder publish the first of Pat's Curry Bible, trilogy and the only cookery book with contents in menu order, lavish illustrations and this is followed by the Balti and Vegetable Bibles.

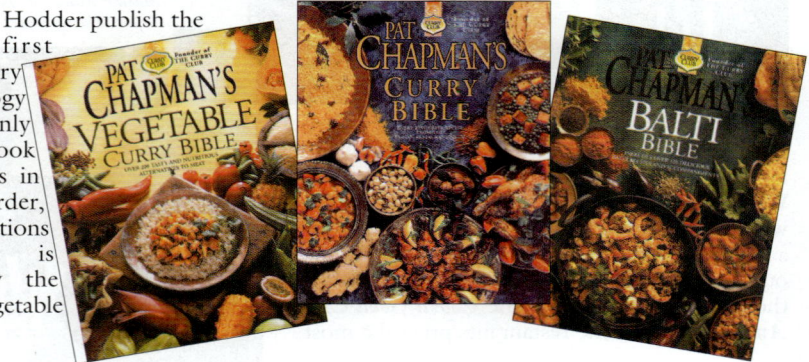

Celebrating 30 Years

2007 Time for a new logo. Pat sketches his concept of recurring 'C's and Karahi dishes. He wants a colour change too, and claret is his choice. He tracks down Plymouth graphic designer Nick Warren, whose striking theatre posters he admires.

Nick's design is simply stunning. The whiff of curry-coloured smoke snaking through the design is Nick's brilliant idea.

2008 to 2009

A gift set with the **Cobra Good Curry Guide**, a 330ml bottle of Cobra beer and a Cobra glass. Tesco purchase 20,000 for Christmas. ASDA purchase 20,000 for the next Christmas. Tesco purchase 10,000 for sale as a Fathers' Day Gift (21 June 2009). Sainsbury's purchase 12,000 gift packs for Christmas 2009
The retail price was just £8.
They all sell out in days.

2011 Cobra run a nationwide prize campaign. Buy a numbered 330ml four pack and 12 lucky winners get a 14 dish four course curry dinner for six, cooked by Pat Chapman in their own own home. 12 prizes were won from Southampton to St Ives, and Roslin to Redditch, Perth to Pershore to Penzance, and places in between.

Here's to the next 30 years!

1982 to 2012

Dig in & dig deep with The Soldiers' Charity Big Curry

ABF THE SOLDIERS' CHARITY

Every day, thousands of soldiers risk everything whilst serving on current operations in Afghanistan. At ABF The Soldiers' Charity we have helped to look after soldiers, former soldiers and their families since 1944.

Do your bit – hold a Big Curry and help us raise vital funds to benefit our soldiers.

The Soldiers' Charity BIG CURRY

Get your free pack now!
bigcurry.org
0845 504 0982

Supported by: Sharwood's

Celebrating our Royal Years

1997 November: The first **National Curry Day** is marked by many British curry houses taking part. Between them they raise £90,000 for the **Save the Children** charity.

Its President, the Princess Royal accepts the cheque on behalf of the charity. She meets us at the handover ceremony and asks Dominique who are members of the Curry Club. Did she know of knew of our Royal Navy connections? HRH has a younger brother and a husband who love curry.

2008 April: The **ABF Soldiers' Charity** comes up with a winning fund raises, the **Big Curry** and invites Pat to join the committee. This charity funds wounded troops and bereaved relatives. As our military commitments increase, so the amount needed increases year on year. Big Curry involves two subjects dear to the public's heart: curry and our troops and it raises big funds. The Lord Mayor of London hosts the biggest Big Curry event at London's Guildhall with Prince Charles as guest of honour. In three luncheon sittings, 900 city workers pay £95 each for the privilege. It has raised £1m since it began. attends which has In conversation Pat asks HRH if he likes curry. In a flash and with a wicked smile he says *"no I hate it"*.

Left to right: Academy Sergeant Major, PJ Carr the British army's most senior NCO, Major Simon Haw, Director of Music Scots Guards, Lord Bilimoria and your editor.

SPLENDIDLY INDIAN, SUPERBLY SMOOTH

drinkaware.co.uk for the facts

www.cobrabeer.co
facebook.com/cobrabee

About Cobra Beer

The Story So Far

Lord Karan Bilimoria founded Cobra Beer in 1989. He launched Cobra Beer when he realised that Britain deserved a better, smoother, less gassy lager. Not just smoother, but one which complemented food, and could appeal to both ale and lager drinkers alike. Originally imported from Bangalore, Cobra is brewed to a traditional Indian recipe with a modern twist for an extra smooth taste. Only the finest ingredients are used including rice, maize and a little less gas to create a uniquely smooth taste, quite unlike any other beer. Originally planned to be called Panther, the beer was ready to go, but the name wasn't popular with customers and was changed to Cobra at the eleventh hour.
The rest as they say, is history.

Most Celebrated Beer

Cobra Beers are also one of the most highly awarded. In the Monde Selection, one of the most prestigious quality awards in the world for beer, Cobra Beers have been awarded a total of 55 Gold medals since 2001. "*A Monde Selection award is the most prestigious award for our beer, an indisputable guarantee of high quality*", says Lord Bilimoria. "*We are proud to continue to be recognised by an award which has been synonymous with the best quality in the world since the Monde Selection was first instituted in 1961.*"

Pat Chapman on Cobra

"*I have been extolling the virtues of Cobra since 1990 when it was just breaking into Britain's Indian restaurants. Cobra was crafted in Bangalore using a traditional blend of ingredients to accompany curry as a smooth alternative to rival offerings and from the first time I tasted it I loved the beer. It had a unique, modern Indian identity, with an aroma and rounded taste I'd never encountered before.*

"*Not surprisingly Cobra took off as THE beer to drink with curry, whether at home or in the local curry restaurant. For me, getting together to share a great curry and the great social experience of sharing different dishes and accompaniments without Cobra Beer is achievable, but inconceivable.*"

Cobra's Spicy British Classic Dishes

Recipes to put a contemporary Indian twist on some British food favourites.

Curry has come a long way since the very first curry house opened in Britain over 200 years ago in 1810. In fact the dish is so popular today that a fifth of British people rate curry as their favourite meal and, as a nation, we spend nearly £400 million on it every week. This year Cobra marks its 20th consecutive year of sponsorship of the Good Curry Guide with an alternative take on curry developed in partnership with curry master chef and this guide's editor, Pat Chapman.

Pat's brief from Cobra was to take ten British favourite traditional dishes and give them a contemporary Indian twist. *"I have written many curry cookbooks totalling over 1,000 recipes, but this was one of the most exciting challenges I've had,"* said Pat. *"Fortunately, I had experienced the Anglo Indian cooking of my Raj grandmother. It was the food her Indian cooks dished up every day – spicy versions of British dishes. The results are fun to cook and fab to eat."* Try these simple recipes on the next pages and enjoy a contemporary Indian take on some of Britain's favourite dishes. And don't forget to wet them down with Cobra beer.

Yorkshire Chilli Pepper Pudding
Sunday favourite **Yorkshire Pudding** is spiced up as a delicious part of a roast or as the base for a contemporary Indian meal.

Indo-Welsh Rarebit
The simple **Welsh Rarebit** is reworked as a great snack to accompany a cold bottle of Cobra.

Lancashire Hot Hot Hot Pot
Lancashire's best-known dish, the classic Hot Pot, is given a new lease of life making it the perfect dish to share with (and surprise) friends.

Devonshire Cream Tea
And perhaps the most surprising recipe comes in the shape of the west country icon with a modern Indian twist. Afternoon tea will never be the same.

Yorkshire Chilli Pepper Pudding

Great British roasts are made all the greater by their accompaniments. What would roast lamb be without mint sauce or roast pork without apple sauce? Bread sauce and sage stuffing turns roast chicken into taste perfection as does cranberry with Christmas roast turkey. Even the humble sausage is transformed by piquant English mustard. The list goes deliciously on. By unanimous vote today's most loved Great British culinary combination is Yorkshire Pudding with roast beef. Its Yorkshire connections, if they exist at all, are unexplained. It first got its name in an early recipe by Newcastle born Hanna Glass whose 1747 cookery book was written in London. She got the recipe (then called Dripping Pudding) from an earlier book (1737) called *The Whole Duty of a Woman*, by 'A Lady' who it later transpired was a man called William Kenrick. To add to the confusion YP is neither a pudding nor a pie. It starts as a runny pancake batter made from eggs, flour, milk and oil. Today it is baked in a very hot oven so that it rises to a crisp golden outside surrounding a silky soft inside. In olden days the beef was cooked on a spit with its juices and fat dripping into the flames. Someone, somewhere thought of catching the drippings in a pan in which batter was placed. The heat of the flames cooked the batter, the drippings flavoured it. Hey presto! Britain's national dish. Or is it curry?

To get the best of both worlds, spice up YP and the result is a true Indo-Anglo fusion.

REFRESHINGLY SMOOTH PREMIUM BEER

COBRA
कोबरा

YORKSHIRE CHILLI PEPPER PUDDING

A CONTEMPORARY INDIAN TAKE ON A YORKSHIRE CLASSIC

INGREDIENTS

Vegetable oil
110g plain flour
2 eggs
250ml milk
Freshly ground black pepper
1 fresh red chilli, chopped
Garam masala
1 teaspoon salt
Handful of chopped coriander

PREPARATION METHOD

- Preheat the oven to 220°C /425°F / Gas 7.
- Put enough oil in a roasting tin to cover the bottom and lap a bit up the sides, and place in the hot oven for about 10 minutes.
- Meanwhile, sift the flour into a large mixing bowl. Make a well in the middle.
- Beat in the eggs and, gradually, the milk, using a balloon whisk to make a runny batter. An electric whisk will do this in seconds. Add the remaining ingredients.
- Take the roasting tin out of the oven, and pour the batter into it. Return to the oven for 25 minutes or until risen and browned.
- Serve cut into pieces, not forgetting a cold Cobra.

drinkaware.co.uk for the facts

SPLENDIDLY INDIAN, SUPERBLY SMOOTH

INDO-WELSH RAREBIT

CLASSIC WELSH RAREBIT WITH AN INDIAN TWIST

INGREDIENTS
SERVES 4

3 x traditional muffins, cut in half
Topping ingredients
50g soured cream or créme fraiche
250g grated Collier's Powerful Welsh Cheddar cheese
2 tablespoons Cobra beer
1 teaspoon English mustard
1 teaspoon Worcester sauce
1 teaspoon chilli powder
1 chopped chilli
Coriander (to garnish)

PREPARATION METHOD

- Preheat the grill to highest heat.
- Line an oven tray with kitchen foil to catch any cheesy drips (to aid your clean up).
- Mix the topping ingredients together in a bowl.
- Toast the muffins on both sides.
- Spread a generous layer of the topping ingredients on each muffin half.
- Place on the oven tray and grill until brown and bubbling.
- Top with Coriander to garnish.
- Enjoy piping hot with ice cold Cobra beer.

REFRESHINGLY SMOOTH PREMIUM BEER
COBRA

drinkaware.co.uk for the facts

SPLENDIDLY INDIAN, SUPERBLY SMOOTH

Indo-Welsh Rarebit

Cheese on Toast, bubbling hot, is what this dish is, served as an any-time snack. But 'Welsh Rarebit' as its name is far more alluring.

How come this name?

The derivation of 'Rarebit' is obscure. In any case should we call it 'Welsh Rabbit'? A recipe for 'Welsh Rabbit' first appeared in print in 1725. Not until 1780 did it have an alternative spelling 'rarebit'. Neither version refers to that long eared, four legged hopper, the bunny. Either way, both recipes correctly describe it as "a luscious supper or tavern dish, based on fine cheddar type cheeses and wheat breads".

To add to the etymological mystery, the very same dish was called a 'Nice Whet' by the British Raj in India. Traditionally the dish was served with good old Indian beer in the pint bottle. Cue Cobra beer in the pint bottle, and we begin to have a truly multicultural dish.

As to the Welsh connection, there is no denying, the Welsh love Cheddar Cheese, and none more than the gritty South Wales coal miners. Being simple to pack it was ideal sandwich food which sustained them as they slogged it out below ground for many hours at a time. But Cheddar is in Somerset, where it is true they originated the method for the most popular cheese in Britain. Now it is produced in many other countries worldwide, including Wales. And to prove it, Collier's Powerful Welsh Cheddar was developed in 1982 by a miner's grandson.

Whatever it all means the fact remains that this is one of the simplest, most delicious snacks around, especially here in this Collier's inspired recipe, given a Raj twist by using, amongst other ingredients, muffins, Cobra beer, Indian Spices and Collier's Cheddar.

Ha-Ghee-s (Haggis)

Haggis is regarded as Scotland's national dish. It is a kind of mutton sausage, which contains a mince of heart, liver, lungs, onion, herbs, spices, stock and salt, bound together with the Scottish staple, oats and originally stuffed into a stomach casing. Even though modern commercial haggis is prepared in an edible collagen casing rather than an actual stomach, it is, as Largesse Gastronomic says: "not immediately appealing", (though it) "has an excellent nutty texture and delicious savoury flavour". On hearing what haggis contains, one tourist was overheard saying "no wonder they refer to the country as 'Scotland the Brave". There is nothing like Haggis in India, even though the Kashmir wedding feast, the Wazwan majors on sheep and creates no less than 35 dishes using every edible part. But they missed a trick by not making a version of Haggis. We don't think we can improve on, let alone cook Haggis. So here we use a shop-bought Haggis. To this we add another Scottish favourite: curry sauce. Serve with 'tatties' – mashed potatoes to which you can add fresh coriander, chopped and chilli, and 'neeps' – mashed swede to which you can add garam masala. The recipe for this and more info can be found on **www.cobrabeer.com/blog (older posts)**.

Lancashire Hot Hot Hot Pot

At the end of the 18th century the Industrial revolution saw the emergence of coal-fired, steam machines enabling mass production and rapid transit of goods. Britain's empire was expanding as was her indigenous population. The famous Lancastrian cotton mills opened all over the county, which in those days included Manchester and employed vast number of women and children in conditions and wages, which though unacceptable today, provided them with a life time of work. The men did heavier work in places like the mines and railways.

Despite their 70 hour, 6 day week, the workers standard of living improved considerably. They could now afford meat on a regular basis. The mills provided terraced houses, which had coal fired cooking ranges which were, for their time as modern as could be. But after the daily slog, it was the women who had to do the chores and the cooking. So nourishing one pot meals which cooked themselves all day and were ready for the home-coming were ideal and Lancashire Hot Pot fitted the bill perfectly. Traditionally, cheap cuts of mutton, onion and thickly sliced potatoes were layered into tall brown earthenware pots and topped off overlapping potato roundels. The pot was placed on the range to cook slowly all day, and the cooker's embers' remained hot enough to achieve this. Hence they were 'hot pots'.

Today Lancashire Hot Pot has gone up market and is as likely to appear all over Britain in gastro pubs at gastro prices using organic produce, which you are welcome to use, if you wish. Over the years dishes' simplicity has taken it all over the world. Variations can include oysters, kidneys, Worcestershire Sauce and curry powder. Which brings us to our Indian twist. No similar dish exists there, but the original slow cooking method of placing a pot over dying embers has been used in India for millennia. We can use the oven rather than dying embers in this super tasty curry recipe.

Cornish Curry Pasty Samosa

An international icon with a distinctive hemispherical shape pastry wrap and an equally distinctive filling, including beef, onion and turnip. History tells us that the Cornish Pasty was devised as a neat lunch package for tin miners and farmers at least four centuries ago. Cornwall was not the first to wrap food in pastry. As far back as the 10th century in central Asia one such was called the samosa. Writings three hundred years later prove it had evolved in India as the celebrated samosa, albeit triangular shaped, deep-fried and with of course a spicy meat of vegetable filling. Here we combine the two concepts, the circular shortcrust pastry package together with an Indian spiced resulting in a pairing made in heaven ... the **Cornish Curry Pasty**. The recipe for this is on

www.cobrabeer.com/blog
(older posts).

Cumberland Kofta Sausage

Cumberland Sausage originated 500 years ago in Whitehaven as a spicy rolled coil with wild boar meat. Even then Whitehaven imported nearly as many spices from India, and the West Indies as did London. Over the centuries, the sausage has become a milder beast. As a tribute to Whitehaven, Pat Chapman has created a new spicy Curry Cumberland Sausage, a kind of Kofta. Here, the recipe uses garam masala plus one or two other tasty ingredients.

COBRA
REFRESHINGLY SMOOTH PREMIUM BEER

LANCASHIRE HOT HOT HOT POT

SPICING-UP THE LANCASHIRE CLASSIC

PREPARATION METHOD

- Pre heat the oven to 400°F/200°C/Gas 6.
- Heat 2 tablespoons of ghee in a karahi or wok, and stir-fry the garlic for 30 seconds. Add the ground coriander, chilli powder and turmeric and continue to stir-fry for another 15 seconds.
- Add the ginger and onion and stir-fry until translucent (about 10 minutes).
- In a mixing bowl combine the lamb, yoghurt and beetroot and mix well.
- Place a further tablespoon of melted ghee into a lidded casserole pot of 2.25 to 2.75 litre (4 to 5 pint) capacity.
- Remove the pot from the oven and place a layer of potato on the ghee covering the bottom of the pot.
- Cover with half the onion fry from stage 2 above.
- Put the meat mixture from stage 3 above on top of the onion, then the carrot, chillies and the remaining onion fry.
- Mix the salt into the stock or water and carefully add it to the pot.
- Top off with a final layer of attractively overlapping potato roundels, ensuring the surface is completely covered. Brush the potato with the remaining tablespoon of melted ghee, sprinkle with salt.
- Cover the pot with its lid and cook in the oven for 30 minutes.
- Reduce the heat to 180°C/ 350°F/ Gas 4, then inspect adding the fresh coriander and garam masala.
- Return to the oven for a further 20 to 30 minutes, or until the lamb is perfectly tender and the liquid is reduced to a thick consistency, about half its original quantity.
- Remove the lid from the casserole and cook until the potatoes on the surface are brown, remove from the oven and leave to rest for 10 minutes.
- Serve with Rice and/or Naan Bread and not forgetting a Cobra beer.

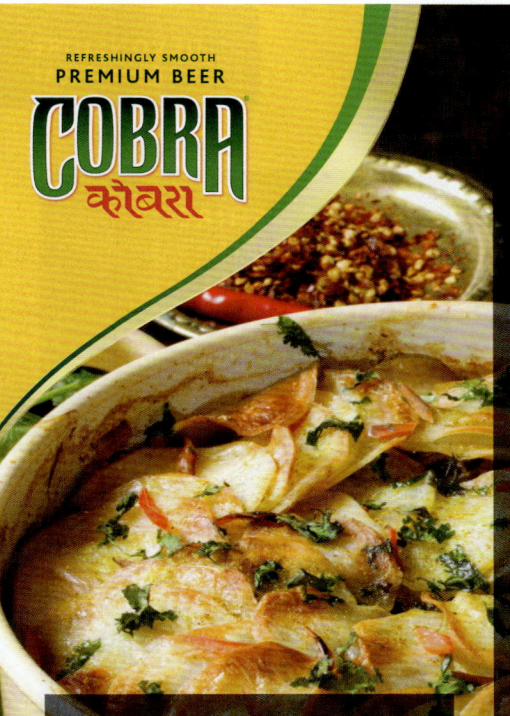

INGREDIENTS
SERVES 4

675g lamb leg or neck, weighed after divesting it of all unwanted matter, and cut into 4cm (1 inch) cubes
657g large potatoes, peeled and sliced into roundels about 8mm thick
4 tablespoons melted butter ghee
3 to 4 garlic cloves, finely chopped
2 teaspoons ground coriander
1 teaspoon chilli powder
1 teaspoon turmeric
2.5cm cube fresh ginger, shredded
225g onion, finely sliced
115g plain natural yoghurt
115g cooked, unvinegared beetroot, finely chopped or minced
1 large carrot, peeled and sliced into roundels about 8mm thick
1 teaspoon salt
300ml meat stock or water
2 or 3 fresh red chillies, shredded (optional)
2 tablespoons fresh coriander (cilantro) leaves, finely chopped
2 teaspoons garam masala

SPLENDIDLY INDIAN, SUPERBLY SMOOTH

drinkaware.co.uk for the facts

REFRESHINGLY SMOOTH PREMIUM BEER

COBRA
कोबरा

DEVONSHIRE CREAM CHAI

A DEVONSHIRE AFTERNOON DELIGHT, WITH A KICK

THE CREAM

250-300g tub of genuine clotted cream
1/3 teaspoon finely ground green cardamom seeds
- Mix the two together and keep refrigerated until use.

THE SCONES
INGREDIENTS

450g self raising flour
50g caster sugar
75g margarine
1 tablespoon finely chopped fresh ginger
Milk
Chilli jam

PREPARATION METHOD

- Mix the flour, sugar, margarine and ginger together until it resembles fine breadcrumbs and then add enough milk to make a soft dough.
- Roll out lightly and cut out scones. Bake in a medium hot oven for 15-20 minutes.
- Whilst still warm, halve and spread generously with the clotted cream. Serve with chilli jam and either an Indian fragrant Darjeeling or Assam Indian tea, Cobra or King Cobra — which goes well with any sweet dish.

SPLENDIDLY INDIAN, SUPERBLY SMOOTH

drinkaware.co.uk for the facts

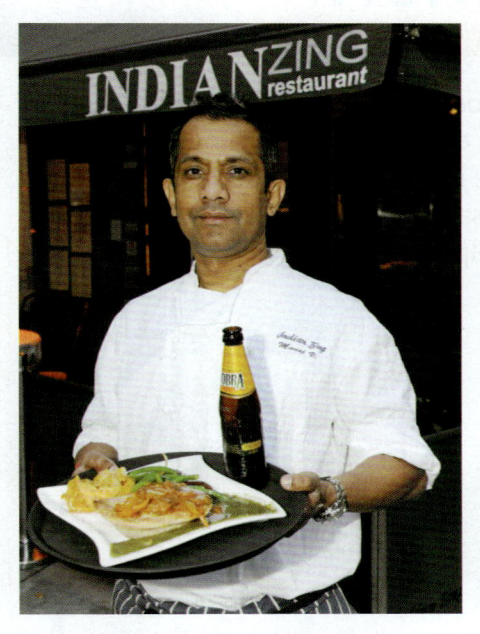

Pie Madras with Cobra beer

In the old days, it was the pie man who sold meat pies to the working class. Fillings were cheap cuts of beef or widely available, inexpensive eels, which then abounded in the Thames and when boiled in water flavoured with vinegar, lemon and nutmeg, solidifies to form a tasty jelly. As London became prosperous, To accompany their pies they sold mashed potato and a unique green parsley sauce which became known as 'liquor' containing a stock made from oysters and eel and jelly, parsley, butter, vinegar and seasoning. A pie is defined as a pastry dough which after encasing savoury or sweet ingredients is oven baked. Pies did not enter the India's repertoire until the British occupied the country. This pie filling has a Raj pedigree, including best quality meat and Cobra beer. Its 'liquor' uses India's primary herb, coriander in place of parsley, and obtains a wonderful green colour, with fish stock a quick replacement for eels and oyster.

Left: Zing, W6's chef/owner Owner Manoj made Pie Madras and Cobra beer Pie

All the recipes can be found on
www.cobrabeer.com/blog (older posts)

Left: Leicester Melton Mowbray Pork Pie

Right: Bombay Bakewell Tart (Derbyshire)

Devonshire Cream Chai

Tea originated in India, and was exported to China centuries BC where it was called Char-i-khitai. It was not until the 17th century that the British occupied India and 'discovered' tea. and established enormous plantation. They brought it to Britain in magnificent sailing ships – tea clippers, and before long it became the national beverage. Afternoon tea with scones and jam became a daily ritual with the memsahibs of the Raj. India was making cream as early as 1,500BC at a time when Devonians were worshipping Celtic gods. Long before the humble cuppa char became an institution, it seems the monks of Devon's' Tavistock Abbey enjoyed their homemade bread, strawberry jam and cream in the 11th century. Clotted cream, thick, yellow and ridiculously high in fat and cholesterol, was developed in Devon by heating milk and allowing it to thicken and clot. Quite when Devon Cream Tea became a local trademark is not clear. But today it is one of the county's main stay cottage industries. Every tourist visiting Devon, and most locals, delight in taking it. Mandatory is warm halved scones, liberally spread, not with butter but with clotted cream and strawberry jam. Delicious though the traditional Devon Cream Tea is, for a change we can give it a subtle and delicious Indian twist in the recipe on the left.

COBRA FOUNDATION

**SPLENDIDLY INDIAN,
SUPERBLY SMOOTH**

Cobra Foundation is an independent charity providing health, education and community support for young people in South Asia, especially through the provision of safe water. Our charitable objectives include giving help with Disaster Relief in the Region

COBRA foundation
FOUNDED IN 2005

Floods 2010
Pakistan

Cyclone Sidr 2007
Bangladesh

Bihar floods 2008
India

We have supported more than 175 charities and good causes since we were founded.* Three examples shown below are

Wherever the Need   Baale Mane   Thare Machi

*As at 31 May 2012

We offer financial grants and stocks of
Cobra beer to help the fundraising campaigns
of charities and good causes

Please visit the website to see our grants policy
and how you can donate
www.cobrafoundation.com

REFRESHINGLY SMOOTH
PREMIUM BEER
COBRA

Registered charity: 1111109 Company No. 5400933

The Icons

On every Cobra Beer bottle you'll find our story embossed into the very glass. It brings to life the journey we took from a brewery in Bangalore to the lips of beer lovers all over the World.

The Crossed Swords

Symbolise the army background of original Cobra founder, Karan Bilimoria, whose father was General Officer Commander-in-chief of the Central Indian Army.

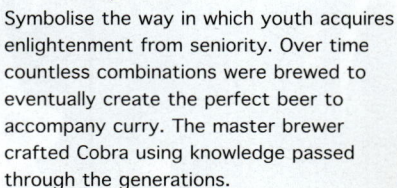

The Elephants

Symbolise the way in which youth acquires enlightenment from seniority. Over time countless combinations were brewed to eventually create the perfect beer to accompany curry. The master brewer crafted Cobra using knowledge passed through the generations.

The Snake Charmer

Symbolises the magic of the traditionally Indian Cobra recipe, blending malted barley, maize, hops, rice, yeast, water and a little less gas than other beers.

The Scales

Symbolise the way in which the odds were weighed against Cobra's success in the early days. Through dedication and determination to produce the finest beer to compliment curry, Cobra is now the preferred choice of Indian restaurants and aficionados of Indian cuisine.

The Palm Trees & Building

Symbolise Bangalore, where Cobra was crafted and first brewed, and Britain, where Cobra is now the leading Indian beer, home to some of the world's finest Indian restaurants and host to chefs who are creating new styles and flavour combinations whilst always staying true to the rich heritage and history of Indian food.

The Boat

Symbolises the journey from Bangalore to Britain also the 40 countries to which Cobra is now exported.

GASTRONOME'S CURRYNATION

Photo courtesy High

A Raita Royal Tribute

The Queen hosted a major event at Buckingham Palace ballroom to recognise the achievements of the British Indian community. Among the 700 guests were cricket's Monty Panesar, TV newsreader Krishna Gurumuthi, and **Goodness Gracious Me** stars Meera Syal and Sanjeev Bhaska. Ranjit Mathrani and his wife Namita Panjabi represented the Indian restaurant sector, by their presence and in a more tangible way. Two of their Veeraswamy chefs worked with Royal chef Mark Flannigan to make Indian canapés for the occasion. In a move reminiscent of her great grandmother, Queen Victoria, who engaged Indian servants in her close household, Queen Elizabeth has enrolled two Sikhs to join her personal body guard unit.

Curromile

Talking of Buckingham Palace, Nepalese Tharu villagers have always been plagued by rhinoceros invasions, with injuries to the farmers and severe damage to crops. Then someone happened to plant camomile plants, and the rhino visitations slowed down. Then the villagers planted camomile all around the perimeter of their village and, the rhinos never came gain. It seems the rhinos simply hated the smell. Eighty years ago, George V planted a camomile garden at Buckingham Palace. Not a lot of rhinos have been noted trampling the streets of London, but Geo V had not long since returned from a hunting trip in India where the claim was that he personally had shot 18 tigers, 48 deer a bear and yes a rhino too. Perhaps HM planted the camomile as an insurance policy incase the ghosts of those unfortunate beasts came to haunt him

Curromile

Confusion reigns on the surveys front. Problem is where and whom did they survey? Clearly not Gastronome. Were you surveyed? Whether you were of not, your lifetime curry spend is either £15,000, £30,200, £34,072, or £39,920. Metro. the free morning newspaper tells us that we spend an average £15,000 on curry in a lifetime. According to the Daily Mirror, OnePoll.com found that the average lifetime curry spend is £30,200. And they must be right, mustn't they? Well perhaps not. A few months later the Mirror published a survey by Red Tractor (a food quality assurance firm) which polled 2,000 Brits whose weekly curry spend is £8.19 – totalling £425 a year. The Mirror totalled it up to be £34,072 in a lifetime. They didn't specify what a lifetime is. Getting out the Gastronome calculator, you'll have to live to 80

Facts and Fun in the Currinary World

and start spending in your first year! But wait we're not finished yet. According to a different OnePoll.com survey 'the typical adult' [sic] spends £9.60 each week on Indian food - totalling £499 a year. And that's £39,920. So now we know. Well actually, we don't. Onepoll.com, yes them again, also did a survey of 3,000 Brits for Sharwood's finding, wait a minute, quite different figures. That study claims the average Brit spends almost £20 a month on ingredients to make their own exotic dishes at home, and another £31.44 per month eating out in restaurants. Which added together is £12.86 a week, or a massive. £53,498 in that remarkable 80 year lifetime.

But if you think that's incredible, how about this? Cardiff children's charity, Ty Hafan recently ran a fundraising dinner dinner at £200 per head at the city's 4 star Mercure Holland House hotel. Sixteen Cardiff chef were persuaded to donate their services free to cook one complete meal per table. Indian chef, Anand George was one.

After the dinner an auction was held and one prize was to nominate a chef to cook dinner for ten in your winner's home. The highest bid (anon) was for Mr George at an astounding £15,000. So if we believe the Metro that's a lifetime's budget on one meal. Hope it was good. Mr George admitted it was *"the most challenging meal of my life."*

Surveyaway

Several surveys have focused on our habits since the recession has taken its toll and energy and food prices nip at our domestic budgets. According to another survey company, YouGov, the recession hasn't dampened our need to treat ourselves to a meal out. In difficult times, it says, few things in life are as comforting as food. But we have reduced the frequency of our outings by some 50%. 73% of us regularly out at least once every three months, (down some 50%). The research found that over one in two (56%) eat out at least once a month, with most (91%) spending at least £10 per head. And it's not just Londoners who are splashing out on the comfort food – almost one in five of us (18%) nationwide spend at least £30 and half of us (50%) spend at least £20 when we eat out. The East of England, and Yorkshire and the Humber are challenging the capital (80%) as the home of dining out with both regions having 76% of their residents eating out at least once a quarter. The 'tough times' are having an impact on our tipping habits, however, with one in ten (9%) never leaving a tip and 16% leaving less than 5%. The majority of Brits do, however, give credit it where it's due with half of us who eat out (50%) leaving a tip of between 5 and 10% of the bill and (22%) leaving a tip of between 10 and 15%. 82% of the Scottish leave a tip of at least 5%, 81% of Londoners leave more as do 80% in the South East and 78% in the East of England. Young people are the worst offenders when it comes to rewarding service, with the proportion of those who eat out failing to leave a tip rising to 15% in the 18 to 24 age bracket and to 17% for full time students. Of all the UK regions, the East Midlands is the stingiest when it comes to paying the bill with almost one in five (19%) failing to leave a tip.

Not Patakularly much

Patak's was bought by Associated British Foods for £105 million in 2007. The company's founder, Shata Pathak, who once sold her hand made samosas in her husband's grocery shop on London's Drummond Street, died in 2011 leaving just £34,000 to her two daughters and four sons, the most successful of whom is Kirit, who achieved the multi million pound sale to ABF. Must have good accountants. And there's more ...

Dinner Partyak

More indeed from Patak's who want to tell us about the nation's views on the ideal dinner party. This according to the survey, is what the host should do: Invite five guests, give each guest two drinks before dinner. Spend £9 per head and guests prefer three courses. Ensure the party is all over in three hours. The survey omits to advise how many drinks should be served during the meal, nor whether most guests want curry on the menu. And there's more ...

Patake your choice

Patak's commissioned a yet another survey. This one is to discover how hot the nation likes its curry. The survey covered 2,000 curry diners and found that 7% of the nation has never tried curry (a statistic unchanged for decades – how sad is that?). On the bright side, 73% of Britons enjoy curry (up by 9% from an earlier survey – how glad is that?) It tells is that 26% like things at medium heat, 10% like it at hotter (Jalfrezi / Madras) and just 2% love Vindaloo heat. Most restaurants serve Phal, but it will be for just one or two particular regulars only, so is unmeasurable in percentage terms). In the dish ranking stakes, Korma is favoured by 20% of the Patak sample, with CTM at 18% and Jalfrezi at 8.5%. However a poll by the magazine Chaat, the house magazine of the British Curry Club (no relation to Gastronome's original and much copied Curry Club) contradicts this result. In a poll of 1058 people surveyed, more diners crave for hotter dishes than in years gone by. 21% put Jalfrezi as their favourite, with 18% voting for Madras curry and Rhogan Josh at 11%. Korma apparently only achieved 2% vote. And where is the Vindaloo? Just shows what a waste of time surveys are! That's why we love publishing them.

Eff Me Clot

Talking hot, in fact chillies so hot they can seriously hurt or even kill those not used to them. Idiots try them, like the chef you love to hate (unless you are a real chef in which case forget the love bit). It comes as a surprise to Gastronome that clot, 'Eff Me' Gordon Ramsay adjudicated at an attempt to enter the Guinness Book of Records by eating more of the world's hottest chilli, the Naga Jolokia, ghost chilli, than had been achieved before. The venue was Assam, India, the participant, one Anandita Tamuly, 26, and the achievement: she consumed no less than 51 ghost chillies She got the record, but more remarkable, given his unacceptable ,behaviour in India Mr R decided he was macho enough to eat one himself but was reported to have choked and gasped for water in defeat. Sadly he survived to cuss and swear another day, although maybe that made him more cautious when publicly tasting the fiery brute. Gastronome was invited by the self same Mr R to attend one of his TV live programmes called *Cookalong Live* in which Ramsay cooked a Tikka Masala curry with comedian Alan Carr. Ramsay's researchers wanted to discuss chilli heat on air, or so they said. So the other studio guests included Michael Michaud, the celebrated Dorset grower of the Naga Jolokia, the owners of Newcastle's Khyber restaurant, operators of a hot chilli curry challenge (eat it and get another free) and Gastronome. Apart from a brief tasting of the Khyber curry which Ramsay spat out and pronounced, live on air, as "f****ng vile", no mention of chillies took place, indeed Ramsay rudely avoided meeting or conversing with his guests, before, during or after the show, preferring instead to bask in the glory of his largely female, seemingly underage squealing audience.

Kismot Clot

Talking more hot, here's another clot, one Abdul Ali, owner of Edinburgh's Kismot Curryhouse. This barmy self-publicist, elected to serve what he called the 'Kismot Killer', to benefit a charity, and doubtless himself with the fame and notoriety his antics would achieve. The object was see who could eat the hottest curry, not an original idea and not one to be taken lightly. Because mad Ali allowed his chefs to put an undisclosed amount of Naga Jolokia chillies into a preprepared Phal sauce. OK so far, with 20 hot-headed entrants, equally barmy, having to sign a legal disclaimer absolving Mr Ali and his cronies of any responsibility. The winner one Beverley Jones ate 9 spoonfuls of the fiery concoction, and

Facts and Fun in the Currinary World

suffered no side effects. The other contestants all ended up writhing on the floor with stomach pains, vomiting, and fainting. Two were in such a bad way that they were rushed to hospital and not discharged for a couple of days. Unsurprisingly one of these wishes to remain anonymous, but the other was named as 21 year old Edinburgh Uni student Curie Kim, (yes the name's for real). Abdul Ali was not prosecuted or sued, but unremorsefully, he plans to run it all again next year, *"we'll tone it all down, heat-wise"*, he boasted. Well Ali last year a young man died following an anaphylactic attack after eating a few chillies. Our advise to all wanna-be participants of such idiocy, is to find your fifteen minutes of fame somewhere else and not in the morgue. Same advice to Mr Ali … you came next to being arrested for manslaughter. But wait, Mr Ali has a new gimmick. The chocolate Naan. *"It will replace Scotland's famous deep-fried Mars bar"*, he announce to a waiting world. Och Aye! We guess it's safer than the chilli contest.

Kismul Cool

From Kismot to Kismul, Cafe Kismul to be exact. It is in the town of Castleway on the island of Barra, population 1,200, in the Scottish Hebrides. The 24 seater is owned by Rohail Bari, 50 his wife Pauline. For years he had been a curry chef in Glasgow. In 2007 the couple settled in Barra with their daughters. Pauline said: *"I was taught to cook authentic Punjabi food by Rohail's late mother Rashida"*. Their menu is a curious mix of fresh seafood, Italian and Indian dishes, and service runs from breakfast till late. Cafe Kismul has several claims to fame. Its signature dishes are monkfish jaipuri and scallop pakora. It is the most westerly curryhouse In the entire British Isles and Eire too. It was nominated for the House of Commons' Tiffin Cup cooking contest, an annual British competition run by MPs to find the best UK curry restaurant. In 2010 it came fourth out of 74. It has many fans, including one couple who sailed their yacht from the North Atlantic paradise of Bermuda right into Barra just to eat at Cafe Kismul. Other celebrity customers include Doc Martin star Martin Clunes, chef Russ Burden and actor Tony Robinson. But its most remarkable claim to fame is that some of their home deliveries take 8 hours to reach their destinations. The neighbouring islands of Tiree, pop 800 and Coll, pop 200, are some 60 miles away across the seas. Problem is neither have a curry house. Fed up with suffering withdrawal symptoms, curry loving residents found the solution in fellow Coll resident and curry fan Tony Oliver, who works for ferry company Caledonian MacBrayne. *"We are well versed at delivering passengers to the far-flung isles of Scotland,"* he says *"and we also deliver items the islanders require, from furniture to whisky, wind turbines to groceries. Why not curries?"* He fixed a deal with Cafe Kismul for a weekly delivery for up to 30 diners. The orders are phoned over the day before delivery. The restaurant is very near the ferry terminal and the orders are placed on the 500 seat ferry Lord of the Isles on its weekly

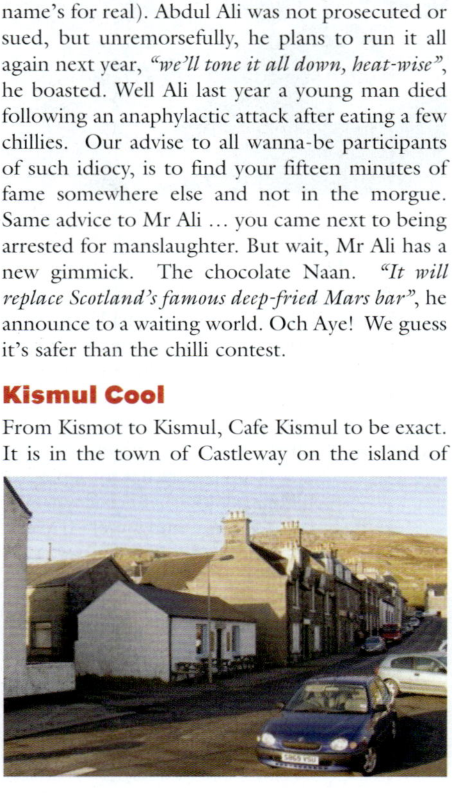

GASTRONOME'S CURRYNATION

Thursday voyage departing Barra at 3.15pm, arriving in Coll at around 7pm and in Tiree at 8pm. Once there, the orders are collected from the docks by the individual diners and by 9pm, result; 30 happy, well stuffed curryholics.

Hag Pak

Still in Scotland, Bobby Singh's popular Edinburgh restaurant Passage to India was packed out for Burns night and on the special menu for this special night came Haggis Samosa. So popular was it the Bobby's regulars got him to put it onto the a la carte menu. As to what's in it, why it's Haggis mixture spiced with Bobby's 'secret ingredients' (curry paste one imagines, Ed) and, hey presto, a star dish is born.

Weighty Suki

Coventry sales consultant Suki Burai, 42 reckons to have lost 3 stone by eating curry twice a day. She now runs a curry therapy diet group to spread the word if not the weight. She reckons to have cut out ghee, cream, deep-fried items, sugar and most oil. And almost certainly all of the fun too.

Staycation

Staycation is here and who knows, it might be here to stay. A survey carried out by Northamptonshire Enterprise Ltd (NEL) finds what is most important to Brits holidaying in UK. Good accommodation (84%) and food (79%) are the biggest priorities for either a holiday or a weekend break. Over half of those asked said how important it was for a weekend break destination to offer something for all the family and 48% said events and activities were important. The poll of just over 1,000 adults revealed that a short journey time is very important (35%), with the majority of people preferring to choose a destination within two hours drive of home. Those in London (38%) and the South East (30%) are the least willing to travel for more than 2 hours to reach a weekend break destination. The research also showed that UK holidaymakers hate having their journey time lengthened by getting stuck in traffic (62%) and road works (57%). Those from the North East find these travel hold-ups the most frustrating (56%) – over twice as many as in Yorkshire and Humber (26%).

Ich bin ein Wurst

On his visit to Berlin in 1963 the late President Kennedy thought he was ingratiating himself with the residents of that city, by saying he was one of them with the immortal words *"Ich bin ein Berliner"*. Had the city been Hamburg, one presumes he would have not have said *'Ich bin ein Hamburger'*. Everyone knows what a Hamburger is. But unlike the Germans, Kennedy and his advisors didn't know that a Berliner is a sausage roll, Berlin style, a kind of bratwürst in a bread roll, sloshed with mustard and toppings. One variety of Berliner is gaining popularity: the Currywürst has a topping of curry sauce albeit mild and sweet. If you'd like to try one, whilst in Berlin go to **Curry 36** at Mehrindamn or **Konnopke's Imbiss** on Schonhauser Allee 44a. Both venues now attract

Facts and Fun in the Currinary World

queues onto the street who pay around 2 euros for the Currywürst, plus a further euro with chips.

Small Cheese

A man who has chosen to remain anonymous has been wracked with pangs of conscience since 1996 when he did a runner from a Swansea curryhouse without paying his £10 bill. Recently he sent £60 to Swansea police asking that it be handed to Samsul Bari to apologise for the debt, with the balance of £50 being 'interest'. Bari was the owner of the restaurant back then but he is now in Pembroke. It took police 6 months and no doubt numerous curry tastings to track Bari down. And now Mr Bari would like the unknown man to come forward to be thanked. So if anyone reading these pages is that man, step up and let Gastronome know the outcome.

Big Cheese

Chicken King Ranjit Singh Boparan has acquired a controlling stake in M&S ready meals and curry supplier Northern Foods, having aggregated over 90% of Northern Foods Shares. The £342 million acquisition of Northern Foods will increase Boparan's turnover to more than £2 billion and transform the enlarged group into one of the biggest players within the British convenience foods market. Indeed, the combined Boparan Group/Northern Foods business will rival Premier Foods as the UK's largest domestic food processor.

A Pinch of Salt

CTMs from Tesco, Sainsbury's, Waitrose, the Co-op, Asda, M&S have been analysed for salt content by leading nutritionists, presumably with nothing better to do. Tesco comes high on taste with (4/5), though it's at the expense of 'health' which clocks in lowest at 1/5), (specifically because of the use of cream (34%), butter, saturated fats and a massive 3.5g salt in the 550g portion. Coincidentally, Waitrose clocks in with the same ratings and even higher salt at 3.63g in their 500g portion.

The OC Curry

Tamarind of London, sister to Michelin-starred Tamarind Mayfair has opened at the prestigious Crystal Cove Promenade Shopping Mall at 7862 Pacific Coast Highway, Newport Beach, Orange County, one of California's most beautiful and prestigious beachside cities. Known to many as the setting of TV teen drama 'The OC', Newport Beach is home to hundreds of film stars and sports personalities and is ranked as one of the richest cities in the USA. Manager is Taj trained Maneesh Rawat, who has worked at some of the best Indian restaurants in the US, including Washington DC's Bombay Club and Palo Alto's Junnoon says *"Tamarind will introduce exciting cooking a to a new audience"*

Shachi Mehra, 35 heads the cheffing, brigade having also worked at the Bombay Club and Junnoon as well as New York's Tabla. Hailed as one of America's five rising chef stars, her menus will showcase classic Indian Moghul favourites and some innovative seasonal dishes.

GASTRONOME'S CURRYNATION

Curry on Cruising

Curry is big business now and Cruising has become a big growth industry too, so It had to come ... Curry on a cruise ship. Food is a major preoccupation with cruising guests. Dining is included in the price, and three main meals a day plus frequent snacking opportunities become the cruise highlights. Most cruise ships of any stature have Indian chefs amongst their kitchen brigades, and they offer curries on their menus. The world's biggest cruise line, the-American-owned Carnival line line has recently launched its 100th cruise ship, Carnival Magic, aboard which is a number of 'original' features, including cheap balcony cabins, an AquaPark and a Curry venue. The more upmarket ships have found out that some of their passengers are seeking that little bit extra from their dining experiences. What's more, they are prepared to pay extra for it. Cunard's QM2 came up with a restaurant with food designed by American chef Tod English and James Martin consulted to P & O, one of the oldest cruise lines. One of their largest and newest ships is the Azura. According to P&O's spin office it *"offers an incredible choice of sports and spa facilities, entertainment, plus lots of exciting bars and restaurants."* P&O have joined other cruise lines in charging extra in specialist restaurants on board. One of these is Sindhus with the menu devised by Indian chef Atol Kochar. There are two menus which change over after about five days. A lunch or dinner is as much as £20 per diner per meal. *"What attracted me to working on Azura was the fact there will be a real kitchen on board."* said Kochar. Funny that ... I wonder how he thought cruise ships cooked for their 3,100 passengers and 1,220 crew without kitchens.

Kidouting

Eastern Paradise in Carlyon Bay in St Austel Cornwall do not admit children below the age of 10 after 7pm. The restaurant opens at 5pm and all age groups are welcome for that two hour period. But adults want peace and quiet later in the evening, not screaming precious brats running rampage between the vindaloos and kormas.

Naansense

Honey Top made a 40kg Naan as a headline grabber. Yes I had to Google too to find out who

Facts and Fun in the Currinary World

they are. The search didn't reveal why they did it, nor who ate it. And there's more naansense: Johnsons' Baby products have found that one in five women believe that eating curry induces labour. More than a third think raspberry leaf tea helps too. And more still: Manchester Uni's prof David McEvoy measures immigrant population since the 1960's. He states that since the number of Lebanese restaurant has reached the teens on the curry mile, the felafel will soon outstrip curry.

Swandowning

Bedford resident, Mohammed Miah, 29 was prosecuted for killing a swan on the banks of the Great Ouse river with the purpose of currying it. Prosecutors said he was caught with blood and feathers on his hands and the plucked corpse in a bag, and of course of stealing the property of the monarch. All Britain's 30,000 swans have this privilege making their capture and killing illegal.

Flyuppng

Teenager Aleem Gaffer, 18, recently took over the running of his dad's Bristol curry takeaway, Bombay Nights. Aleem, had worked there since he was 12 and his father, Bangladesh-born Abdul, 38, thought Aleem knew what he was doing. However, he was astounded to find that first thing Aleem did was to spend £5,000 on a second-hand 2 ton Hawker 800XP executive jet aircraft cockpit, which had appeared in the film, *The Da Vinci Code*, to use as the customers' seating area. Aleem's plan backfired when he realised he could not get it inside without removing the shop front. But with the help of six friends, he finally slid it into the takeaway. Asked by Dad for an explanation, Aleem said *"many customers work at the Filton British Aerospace works and I thought they would be at home sitting in a jet"*. Dad is receiving counselling.

Gourmet Society

UP TO 50% OFF

MEALS AT 1000+ GREAT SPICE RESTAURANTS

Enjoy up to **50% off meals** at 1,000+ great curry restaurants, plus thousands of other cuisines, with a **FREE** 3 month Gourmet Society dining card trial.

www.gourmetsociety.co.uk/curryguide

Call 0845 257 4477 quoting CURRY GUIDE

Restaurants Nationwide

Offers and availability may vary. Restrictions may apply. Participating restaurants subject to change. A valid credit/debit card is required to register for your free trial. There is a non-refundable charge of 49p towards postage. Membership is free for the first 3 months - you can return your card at any time during the free period and won't be charged. If you keep your card after the free period, you will become a full member and be charged the specially reduced rate of £39.95 for annual membership. For full terms and conditions visit www.gourmetsociety.co.uk.

"I have to say that it was all absolutely stunning. I don't say that very ofter. But it was. I just hope Cobham realises what they have in their locality. Such cooking outclasses many of the so-called top restaurants in the West End."

Pat Chapman
Editor Cobra Good Curry Guide and Founder The Curry Club

FREE Local Home Delivery

massala
a true taste of india

**Massala
19 Anyards Road
Cobham, Surrey
KT11 2LW
01932 865005**

**Open:
Monday to Sunday 1700 to 2300**

massala
INDIAN DINING

www.massala.cobham.com
Tel:01932 865005
"Massala Delivered"

Get Pickled

Tired of the same old Indian pickles and chutneys. Here are four superb pickles, made by small caaring producers

Mint CHUTNEY   **Mango** PICKLE   **Lime** PICKLE   **Carrot & Chilli** PICKLE   **Tamarind** CHUTNEY

The Brilliant Restaurant Range

Bottom: **Mint,** a purée which gives that savoury/tart taste of the Punjab, with chilli, mango powder and vinegar. *280g*
Top: **Mango,** finely chopped and crunched up with fennel seed and fenugreek. *280g*
Left: **Lime**, not your normal lime pickle, but slices impregnated with lime juice, salt and carom. *290g Right:* **Carrot & Chilli** in tangy vinegar *240g. Right hand jar:* **Tamarind**, the sweet and sour purée that goes so well with samosas and snacks. *290g* The recipes, created by Dipna Anand are made at Southall's Brilliant Restaurant (see page 60/1 and the entry in the Middlesex chapter).

Brilliant Restaurant, 72 - 76 Western Rd, Southall, Middx, UB2 5DZ.   020 8574 1928   www.brilliantrestaurant.com

Madhuban Honey Garden Sauces & Chutneys

Madhuban's range of ten Curry Sauces are immensely popular in the iconic yoghurt pots. Their two chutneys include their best seller, tangy **Mint Raita** *(right)*. **Y**oghurt is combined with an elusive blend of sweetness and savoury to achieve the most perfect accompaniment to your starters and tandoori items. *225g*

Madhuban's **Sweet Tomato Chutney** is a refreshing and exhilarating change to the regular mango chutney we all adore. It not only looks good, being a translucent red colour, it tastes just amazing with a perfect balance of sweet, tangy tomatoes, garlic, a little chilli heat and aromatic spices. *225g*

Madhuban chutneys and sauces are available by mail order from:

MINARA'S
Chutneys, Pickle and Pastes

Minara's family has been making Indian food since her late father, Nazir Ud-Din, opened the first Indian restaurant in Manchester, the Bombay in 1938. He went on to establish the Manzil in the late 60s as the most famous restaurant of its era and started selling his chutneys and pickles in 1968. Sauces were added to his range in 1970. The range is the connoisseurs choice!

www.minarafooods.co.uk

Minara Foods Ltd, Leestone Road, Sharston Industrial Estate, Manchester, M22 4RB Tel: 0161 491 3999 Fax: 0161 491 5999   minara@minarafoods.co.uk

BALTI CURRY SAUCE
BHOONA CURRY SAUCE
DELUXE BADAMI SAUCE
GOAN CURRY SAUCE for FISH
JHALFREZI CURRY SAUCE
KORMA CURRY SAUCE
MADRAS CURRY SAUCE
TIKKA MASALA SAUCE
THAI RED CURRY SAUCE
THAI GREEN CURRY SAUCE

MADHUBAN ®
HONEY GARDEN SAUCES LTD
Mainline Business Centre
74 Station Road, Liss
Hampshire, GU33 7AD
01730 891177
Fax: 01730 891188
www.madhuban.co.uk
sales@madhuban.co.uk

Each pot contains e485g sauce for curries for 4 or more and e2.5Kg for caterers

Chinthe Pickles

The nation's only Burmese range of pickles have been by Chinthe (pron Chintay and meaning Pagoda guardians) by the same family since 1974. The range of 15 items includes Burmese Curry Powder, Curry Byan Paste, Burmese Black Curry Paste (Amare Na), Biriani Paste, Bamboo Shoot Pickle, Lime and Mango Pickle, Mango Kasaundi, Burmese Prawn Balachaung. The entire range gives the unique and flavourful taste of Burmese curry.

Available at Amazon and on line at www.chinthe.com and at selected retailers (see Chinthe website)

Mr. Todiwala's

Available at Café Spice Namaste, 16 Prescot Street, E1 8AZ and www.mrtodiwala.com

All Mr Todiwala's 'Splendidly Spicy and Deliciously Hot Pickles and Chutneys' are hand-made in the restaurant kitchens of Café Spice Namaste, renowned Chef Cyrus Todiwala's landmark Indian restaurant in London. Inspired by Pervin – Mrs Todiwala – and the culinary tastes of thousands of loyal followers over the years, Chef Cyrus has created the ultimate condiment without preservatives except citric acid crystals. They possess certain qualities that may be lacking in more mass-produced products. These gourmet pickles include venison, wild boar, and prawn. There are also five vegetable pickles and six veg chutneys, including Beetroot.

DRUMMOND STREET NW1

+

Mithai

=

ROYAL®

Visit our Flagship store

126 Drummond Street London NW1 2PA t: 020 7388 4015

Mithai • Rassomalai • Kulfis • Snacks

Office Parties, Weddings & Celebrations all catered for.

www.royalsweets.com

Three Restaurants One Chef Patron

INDIANZING restaurant

236 King's Street
Hammersmith, London,
W6 0RF

0208 748 5959 or 2332

info@indianzing.co.uk
www.indianzing.co.uk

INDIANZILLA restaurant

2-3 Rocks Lane,
Barnes, London,
SW13 0DB

0208 878 3989 or 2480

info@indianzilla.co.uk
www.indianzilla.co.uk

INDIANZEST restaurant

21 Thames Street
Sunbury-On-Thames, Middlesex
TW16 5QF

01932 765000

info@indianzest.co.uk
www.indianzest.co.uk

"You won't get better authentic Indian food anywhere, and that includes India." **Pat Chapman Editor Cobra Good Curry Guide**

"Manoj Vasaikar blends flavours, tastes and textures like a genius artist. Everything is perfect." **Michael Winner, The Sunday Times May 2010**

Awarded Best Boutique Restaurants by this Guide since 2009

COBRA GOOD CURRY GUIDE, CHEF OF THE YEAR: CHEF PATRON MANOJ VASAIKAR

Britain's Elite A-List & Top 100 Restaurants As Chosen By You

Only one in every twelve of the nation's curry restaurants has achieved entry into this Guide, so they are all top restaurants and a cut above the norm. Put another way, all the entrants are in our **TOP 1000**. But, naturally, we are always asked to identify the best of the best, so to speak. And it is true that there is an élite number of really excellent restaurants including, by definition, those establishments about which we receive many consistently good reports. In our 1985 we pioneered a **TOP 30** list, and reflecting the improvement in standards this grew in our 1992 edition to our **TOP 100** list. As usual, this year there has been quite a lot of change. There is the usual demotion from that list because of a decline in performance or closure. Two, Le Raj Epsom and Khan's W2 have come out for neither of these reasons: they have asked to be delisted despite being in our TOP 100 list; they didn't like the minor criticisms from you. Fortunately, from the many you have brought to our attention, we have promoted a number of 'new' **TOP 100** entrants. Once again we have more than an exact 100. As ever, if there are yet others you feel we have missed, please report to us. For a restaurant to remain in our top 100 list, we also need your views. There is a further, even more élite list, the cream of the cream, winners of our **AWARDS** all of whom attend the Guide's prestigious ceremony in London to receive their awards. For the record, all our previous award winners are listed below, since they all remain at the top the tree. We describe all these as our **A-LIST** (A for Awards + Nominees).

At the request of the worldwide media, we commenced our **Best In The UK Awards** in 1992, in our third edition of this Guide. To date there have only been seven such winners, listed below. Although our judgements at the time were nearly always received with some surprise, we are proud they have all stood the test of time. Each of these restaurants continue to thrive and deliver outstanding food and service. Although so many of our best restaurants are in London, and probably most deserve the Best in UK accolade, we actively want to displace any perceived London bias, hard though this is. So in 2004 we moved a little outside London for the first time. In 2007 we went to the Midlands for our best. For 2009/10 we move to Milton Keynes to award a restaurant and its owner for his life-long persistance and eventual achievement in seeking the best.

The Hall of Fame
Our Ultimate Achievers
Best In The UK Awards

BOMBAY BRASSERIE, SW7
Lifetime Best Restaurant Award – 1982 to 2009/10

CHUTNEY MARY, SW10
Best in UK 1991-1994 – Third Edition of this Guide
Best in UK 1999-2000 – Sixth Edition

BOMBAY BRASSERIE, SW7
Best in UK 1995-7 – Fourth Edition

LA PORTE DES INDES, LONDON, W1
Best Indian and Best in UK 1998-1999 – Fifth Edition

THE QUILON, SW1
Best in UK 2001-2003 – Seventh Edition

MADHU'S, SOUTHALL, MIDDLESEX
Best in UK 2004-2006 – Eighth Edition

ITHIHAAS, BIRMINGHAM
Best in UK 2007-2008 – Ninth Edition

JAIPUR MILTON KEYNES, BUCKINGHAMSHIRE
Best in UK 2009-2010 – Tenth Edition

THE ONLY THING OLD ON THE MENU IS THE AUTHENTICITY

Savour the change at London's iconic Bombay Brasserie. A larger more spectacular setting serves up an eclectic ambience. Where authentic Indian flavours are transformed into a contemporary gourmet experience.

BOMBAY BRASSERIE

Courtfield Road, London SW7 4QH • Tel: 0207 370 4040 • Email: bombay1brasserie@aol.com • www.bombaybrasserielondon.com

2013 COBRA GOOD CURRY GUIDE

Britain's Elite A-List & Top 100 Restaurants as Chosen By You

† = One of a group of restaurants

LONDON
London East & EC

E1	Cafe Naz
	Mujib Indian Cuisine
	Shampan Sheba
	Cafe Spice Namaste
	Lahore Kebab House
	Needoo Grill
	Tayyabs
	Tiffin Indian
E12	Chennaidosa
	Saravanaa Bhavan .
E14	Dockmasters
EC2	Cinamon Kitchen
	Mint Leaf Lounge
	Kasturi

London North

N1	Delhi Grill
	Roots At N1
	Masala Zone
	Zafrani
N2	Cochin
	Majjos
	Rani Vegetarian
N16	Rasa
	Rasa Travancore

London North West

NW1	Ambala
	Diwana Bhel Poori House
	Great Nepalese
	Namaaste Kitchen
NW3	Eriki
	Woodlands
NW4	Prince of Ceylon
NW6	Elephant Walk
	Geeta
	Vijay

2013 COBRA GOOD CURRY GUIDE

Britain's Elite A-List & Top 100 Restaurants as Chosen By You

London South East

SE1	Bangalore Waterloo
	Bengal Clipper
SE13	Spice Of Life
SE15	Ganapati
SE24	Babur Brasserie

London South West

SW1	Amaya
	The Cinnamon Club
	Mint Leaf
	The Quilon
	Woodlands
SW3	Haandi
	Rasoi Vineet Bhatia
SW5	Masala Zone
	Nizam
	Star Of India
SW6	Blue Elephant Thai
	Nayaab
SW7	Bombay Brasserie
	Shezan
SW10	Chutney Mary
	Painted Heron
SW13	Indian Zilla
SW15	Ma Goa
SW17	Ambala Sweet Centre
	Jaffna House
	Radha Krishna
	Sree Krishna
	Vijaya Krishna

London West & WC

W1	Anwars
	Benares
	Carom At Meza
	Chor Bizarre
	Cinnamon Soho
	Gaylord
	Imli
	Indian Ymca
	Masala Zone
	Mooli's
	La Porte Des Indes

2013 COBRA GOOD CURRY GUIDE

Haandi Knightsbridge

Authentic North Indian Cuisine
One restaurant, two entrances

**7 Cheval Place
Knightsbridge,
London
SW7 1EW**

**136 Brompton Road
Knightsbridge,
London
SW3 1HY**

Email: haandirestaurant@btconnect.com
http://haandi-restaurants.com

Telephone:
0207 823 7373

Fax:
0207 823 9696

**Open seven days a week
including public holidays
Lunch: 12:00 to 15:00, 7 days
Dinner:
18:00 to 23:00 (Sun – Thurs)
17:30 to 23:30 (Fri - Sat)
HOME DELIVERY AVAILABLE**

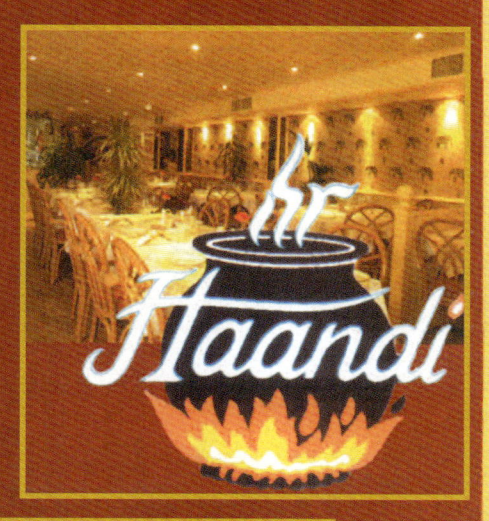

'Haandi - some kind of crazy, wonderful dream.'
Jan Moir, The Daily Telegraph

'Skilled spicing, top notch ingredients…'
Good Food Guide

New Menu!
Celebrating our fourth decade!

Cobra Good Curry Guide 2012
Nominated as one of the four Best Restaurants in London.
"Nayab is one of London's longest established Indian restaurants. It simply ouzes class and quality."
Pat Chapman, Editor

The Rough Guide
London Restaurants
'Representative of the best cooking in Delhi'
Charles Campion

Food Spy 26 January 2007
Everything was steaming hot (free of chemical colourings) exceptional and took curry cuisine to a gourmet level. Leaps and bounds better than the average curry house. The side dishes, especially the moreish baby aubergines sautéed in spices, deserve credit. Would definitely do it again – as delivery or at the Fulham Restaurant.

Food Spy 28 March 2008
This well-established restaurant delivers, colour-free and low-fat 'home-cooked-style' Indian cuisine. The food arrived piping hot and aromatic. The poussin was tender and plump, coated in a delicious sauce of plum tomato, spices and pomegranate, complemented by the zesty rice. The lamb was great, too.
The only problem is what to choose.

William Sitwell

The London STANDARD Guide
'Nayaab is a stayer as it is a cut above most Indian restaurants for the freshness of the food and the pleasantness of approach'
Fay Maschler

Collection
Call us and collect your order within 30 minutes.

Deliveries
Minimum order for delivery £12
Free delivery within 3 miles of Parsons's Green, Fulham
Place you order from 5.30pm onwards.

How Long?
Usually 45-60 minutes depending on distance and weather. Please allow extra time on weekends.

Payment
By cash or credit / debit card at your door.

Delivery Service Times
Sunday - Thursday   6pm - Last Delivery 11pm
Friday - Saturday   6pm - Last Delivery 11.30pm

Restaurant Opening Hours
To dine in or call & collect.
Monday - Saturday   6pm till Midnight
Sunday   6pm till 11.30pm
Closed on 24th, 25th, 26th of December

NAYAAB
indian restaurant
Established 1981

Cooked fresh, delivered fast.
Indian curries travel well and are still delicious when they arrive.

020 7731 6993
020 7736 9596

Celebrating 30 years!
The home of
fine Indian cuisine
since 1981

309 New King's Road
(at the Junction of Munster Road)
London SW6 4RF
www.nayaab.co.uk

**Britain's Elite A-List & Top 100 Restaurants
As Chosen By You**

London West (cont) & WC

	Rasa Samudrat
	Rasa Express
	Red Fort
	Roti Chai
	Tamarind
	Trishna
	Veeraswamy
	Woodlands W1
W2	Bombay Palace
	Durbar
	Mandalay
W5	Monty's Nepalese
W6	Indian Zing
	Potli
	Sagar
	Zaika
W11	Chakra
W13	Laguna
	Monty's

London WC

WC1	Hason Raja
	Malabar Junction
	Rasa Maricham
WC2	Dishoom
	India Club
	Masala Zone
	Mela
	Moti Mahal
	Punjab
	Sitaaray
	Amarai

England

BERKSHIRE

Cookham	Malik's
Slough	Baylis
Suningdale	Tiger's Pad
Twyford	Haweli
Windsor	Mango Lounge

BRISTOL
Myristica

2013 COBRA GOOD CURRY GUIDE

BUCKINGHAMSHIRE
- Milton Keynes — Calcutta Brasserie
- Jaipur
- Jalori
- Orchid Lounge At Jaipur
- Stony Stratford — Moghul Palace

CAMBRIDGESHIRE
- Cambridge — Cafe Naz

CHESHIRE
- Northwich — Bengal Dynasty

DERBS
- Burton-on-Trent — Anoki
- Derby — Anoki

DEVON
- Ilfracombe — Rajah

DORSET
- Wareham — Gurkha

ESSEX
- Gants Hill Gl — Kanchans
- Ilford (Gl) — Jalalabad 2

GLOS
- Cheltenham — Koloshi

HAMPSHIRE
- Fleet — Gurkha Square
- Liss — Madhuban
- Southampton — Badi Mirchi
- Kuti's Brasserie
- P.O.S.H.
- Southsea — Bombay Bay
- Golden Curry

HERTS
- St Albans — Chez Mumtaj
- Mumtaj

KENT
- Bromley — Tamasha
- Halstead — Calcutta Club
- Margate — The Ambrette

LEICESTERSHIRE
- Leicester — Curry Fever

G. MAN
- Altrincham — Dilli
- Ashton-Un-Lyne — Indian Ocean
- Manchester Central — Akbars
- This and That
- Zouk
- Ramsbottom — Sanmini

MERSEYIDE
- Liverpool — Gulshan

2013 COBRA GOOD CURRY GUIDE

MOTI MAHAL

Authentic Indian dining in the heart of London's Theatreland

- Private Dining -
- Bespoke Menus -
- Boutique Catering -
- Central Covent Garden Location -

45 Great Queen Street
Covent Garden, London, WC2B 5AA
020 7240 9329 | reservations@motimahal-uk.com
www.motimahal-uk.com

*Excellence and expertise…
with a touch of brilliance*

OFFICIAL CATERERS AT:

HILTON METROPOLE NEC BIRMINGHAM
PARK PLAZA RIVERBANK
JUMEIRAH CARLTON TOWER
LANCASTER LONDON
PARK PLAZA WESTMINSTER BRIDGE
LONDON HILTON ON PARK LANE
GROSVENOR HOUSE, A JW MARRIOTT HOTEL
INTERCONTINENTAL LONDON PARK LANE
THE GROVE
NATURAL HISTORY MUSEUM
LONDON SYON PARK A WALDORF ASTORIA

SOFITEL LONDON HEATHROW
THISTLE LONDON HEATHROW
SHERATON SKYLINE HEATHROW
RADISSON EDWARDIAN HEATHROW
LONDON HEATHROW MARRIOTT

MADHU'S

Madhu's Limited
39, South Road
Southall
Middlesex
UB1 1SW

020 8574 1897
www.madhusonline.com

There are many excellent reasons to dine at

MADHU'S

What's yours?

39 South Road, Southall, Middx. T: 020 8574 1897

Restaurant and Caterers Est 1976.

TOP 100 Rated in this Guide since 1992.

Omi's

1-3 Beaconsfield Road,
Southall,
Middlesex UB1 1BA

info@omisrestaurant.co.uk
www.omisrestaurant.co.uk

020 8571 4831
or
020 8571 7669

Upstairs private dining room seats 75

A-LIST & TOP 100 RESTAURANTS

MIDDLESEX
- Brentford — Pappadums
- Edgware — Haandi
- Harrow — Connoisseur Cuisine
- Ram's Surti
- Southall — Brilliant r
- Madhu's
- New Asian Tandoori Centre
- Omis
- Palm Palace
- Sunbury-q — Indian Zest
- Twickenham — Tangawizi
- Taste of Moghul

NORHTAMPTONSHIRE
- Norhtampton — Tamarind

NORTHUMBERLAND
- Berwick-on-Tweed — Magna
- Corbridge — The Valley

NOTTINGHAMSHIRE
- Mansfield — The Mint
- Nottingham — Anoki
- The Cumin
- Mogal-E-Azam
- Spice Takeaway

SHROPSHIRE
- Shifnall — Shifnal Balti

SOMERSET
- Bath — The Mint Room
- Taunton — Mint And Mustard
- Yeovil — Signature Viceroy
- The Viceroy

STAFFORDSHIRE
- Alton — Thornbury Hall Rasoi
- Leek — Bolaka Spice

SURREY
- Cobham — Massala
- Epsom — Le Raj   t
- Kingston — Roz Ana
- New Malden — Sesame
- Oxted — Gurkha Kitchen
- Richmond — Origin Asia
- Warlingham — India Dining
- Woking — Jaipur

SUSSEX
- Brighton — Indian Summer
- Crawley — Blue India
- Rye — The Ambrette at Rye
- Worthing — Indian Ocean Takeaway

2013 COBRA GOOD CURRY GUIDE

Brilliant

North Indian Cuisine with a Kenyan slant

The Brilliant family looks forward to welcoming you.....

Brilliant Restaurant was voted as one of Gordon Ramsay's Best Indian Restaurants

The Brilliant Restaurant and Banqueting Suite devotes itself to serving freshly prepared authentic food using only the finest and locally sourced ingredients. The Brilliant also offers 'Healthy Option' menu items and is part of the 'Just Ask' campaign encouraging consumers to ask where the food on their plate comes from. Brilliant boasts an in-house Banqueting Suite for up to 120 guests, a licence to hold Civil Marriages and an Outdoor Catering Service. The Brilliant has won many awards and accolades, including The British Curry Award as well as winning the title of Ramsay's Best Restaurant on the Channel 4 Series. The Brilliant has been visited twice by His Royal Highness The Prince of Wales and The Duchess or Cornwall. Not only does Brilliant's reputation circulate amongst Royalty but Brilliant is also frequented by Politicians, Business Leaders and Hollywood and Bollywood personalities. Brilliant's success is due to skills in creating tastes of the palette together with eminent service.

Brilliant Restaurant
72-76 Western Road
Southall
Middlesex UB2 5DZ

Tel: 020 8574 1928
Fax: 020 8574 0276
Web: www.brilliantrestaurant.com
Email: info@brilliantrestaurant.com

Brilliant

Brilliant Pickles & Chutneys
NOW AVAILABLE

- Lime
- Mint
- Tamarind
- Carrot & Chilli
- Mango

Brilliant's home-made chutneys and pickles are made using the freshest and finest of ingredients, reflecting our devotion to authentic Indian food. The name 'Brilliant' is synonymous in the UK Indian restaurant industry with quality and authenticity, and we now bring you high-grade, hand-made chutneys and pickles for you to enjoy true North Indian Punjabi flavours. All of our products are made using natural ingredients, making these chutneys and pickles *one of a kind.*

Multipack offers available at promotional discounted prices now!

Amazingly Brilliant.............

See page 38

A-LIST & TOP 100 RESTAURANTS

TYNE & WEAR
	Gateshead	The Last Days of The Raj
	Newcastle	Dabbawal
		Rasa
		Valley Junction 397
		Vujon t

WARWICKSHIRE
	Kenilworth	Coconut Lagoon
		Raffles
	Stratford-on-Avon	Coconut Lagoon

WEST MIDLANDS
	Birmingham Centre	Itihaas
		Lasan
		Maharajah
		Rajdoot
	Birmingham B66	Haweli
	Coventry	Turmeric Gold
	Meriden	Turmeric Gold at Meriden
	Sutton Coldfield	Delhi 6

WILTSHIRE
	Marlborough	The Palm
	Salisbury	Anokaa
		Hox Brasserie

WORCESTERSHIRE
	Worcester	Monsoon
		Spice Cuisine

NORTH YORKSHIRE
	Riccall	The Spice Mill
	Skipton	Aagrah
	Tadcaster	Aagrah
	York	Jinnah At Flaxton

SOUTH YORKSHIRE
	Doncaster	Aagrah
	Sheffield	Ashoka

WEST YORKSHIRE
	Bradford	Akbars
		Mumtaz
		Prashad
		Zouk
	Huddersfield	Aagrah
	Leeds	Akbars
		Aagrah
		Azram's Sheesh Mahal
		The Bird by Vineet
		Darbar
		Georgetown
		Hansa's
	Shipley	Aagrah
	Wakefield	Aagrah

2013 COBRA GOOD CURRY GUIDE

EASTERN EYE: ACCLAIMED BY MANY TOP SOURCES INCLUDING

- Best in the West and Top 30 in UK by the Good Curry Guide • Top 30 by the British Curry Awards
- Top 30 by the Real Curry Guide • Top UK Restaurant by Hardens • AA Rosette Award
- The Times Knowledge Magazine Top 10 Indian Restaurants • Top 100 Restaurant of Excellence Award UK - Asian Women

EASTERN EYE: COMMENDED WITH TOP REVIEWS FROM

- The Observer • Vogue • Eating out West • Bath Life • The Times • Heat Magazine • The Daily Telegraph
- Le Guide de Routard (France) • World Tour & Travel Guide • Michelin Guide • Rick Steven (USA)
- Lonely Planet • Itchy Guide • Fodor's Exploring Britain • Time Out

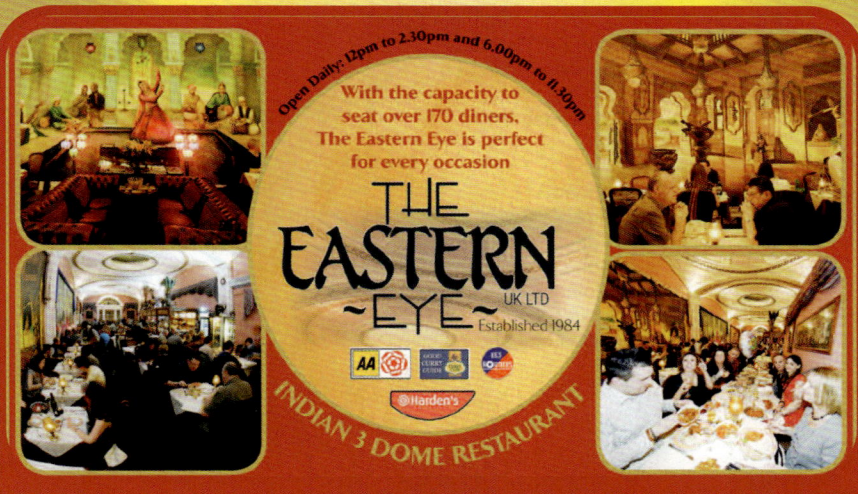

Open Daily: 12pm to 2.30pm and 6.00pm to 11.30pm

With the capacity to seat over 170 diners, The Eastern Eye is perfect for every occasion

THE EASTERN EYE
UK LTD
Established 1984

INDIAN 3 DOME RESTAURANT

Fully Air Conditioned   **3 course special lunch at £7.95**

THE MAHAL OF EXQUISITE INDIAN CUISINE
WITH ONE OF THE CITY'S MOST IMPRESSIVE GEORGIAN INTERIORS.
INTERNATIONALLY RENOWNED FOR EXCELLENCE

8a Quiet Street, Bath, BA1 2JS

Tel: 01225 422323/466401
Fax: 01225 444484/466401
Email: info@easterneye.com
Website: www.easterneye.com

Mr A.H.Choudhury (left) and Mr S.Choudhury receiving their awards at the 2005 inauguration of the British Curry Awards: Winner: Top 5 in the South West region and Top 30 UK Restaurant.

"This is the place to visit ... outstanding Indian"
[VOGUE]

"... set in the Georgian building with an incredible triple-domed ceiling ... the food far surpasses your average curry house fare, plaudits from celebrity customers ..."
[SUNDAY TIMES]

"Designer Curry House ... prices are reasonable ... food is well prepared and staff friendly and efficient ... you get your money's worth ..."
[The OBSERVER]

'A' Listed
UK Restaurant and
BEST IN THE WEST
2007/2008/2009/2010.
Awarded by
Pat Chapman's
CURRY CLUB and GOOD CURRY GUIDE

15% STUDENT DISCOUNT WITH ID
(not valid on Saturday & our lunch time special menu)

FREE ADMISSION to CLUB XL
Please check with the restaurant for further details

ELVIS NIGHTS

Contact us to find out when

See pages 254/5 for more about the Eastern Eye

Scotland

FIFE
    St Andrews   Balaka

GRAMPIAN
    Aberdeen   Cinnamon

LOTHIA
    Edinburgh   Britannia Spice   r
                        The Far Pavilions
                        Lancers Brasserie
                        Mya
                        Verandah

STRATHCLYDE
    Glasgow   Akbars
                  Ambala Sweet Centre
                  Kama Sutra   P
                  Koh I Noor
                  Mother India
                  Mister Singh's India
                  Shish Mahal

TAYSIDE
    Dundee   Dil Se

Wales

CLWYD
    Deeside   Bengal Dynasty
    Bridgend   Bokhara Brasserie

GLAMORGAN
    Cardiff   Juboraj
                Moksh
    Swansea   Juboraj
                Miahs
                Patti Raj

MONMOUTH
    Newport   Misbah Tandoori
                Juboraj

GWYNEDD
    Llandudno   Bengal Dynasty

itihaas
indian restaurant

Timeless Cuisine...

...crossing all frontiers of India

WINNERS
BEST RESTAURANT IN UK
COBRA GOOD CURRY GUIDE
2007/2008

18 Fleet Street Birmingham B3 1JL
T 0121 212 3383   F 0121 212 3393   E info@itihaas.co.uk
www.itihaas.co.uk

All aboard the award winning

BRITANNIA *Spice*

2012 BEST IN SCOTLAND 7th Time

One of the most popular Indian restaurants in the whole of Scotland, **Britannia Spice** has won a host of awards since it first opened its doors over a decade ago. Named after the Royal Yacht Britannia, which is berthed less than a nautical mile away, **Britannia Spice** has a seafaring bearing to its interior. The menus are also well travelled with options from North India, Bangladesh, Nepal, Thailand and Sri Lanka. **Britannia Spice** is renowned for its exotic multi-ethnic cuisine. All dishes are freshly and expertly prepared - with the chefs paying the highest attention to detail. Stunning spices and the freshest of ingredients combine to ensure that every mouthful is a delight. Without getting your passport out, you can skip between Thai tom yum soup, Himalayan spicy trout, and king prawns cooked in Bangladeshi style with mustard paste, green chillies and yoghurt. **Britannia Spice** has won a host of awards since it first opened its doors over a decade ago. It has been voted the **Best Restaurant in Scotland** no less than six times since 2001 by this Guide, and by the British Curry Awards and three times by the Best in Britain Awards. In 2011 it won the Scottish Curry Awards' Curry King Award – one of the most coveted accolades. That's we are one of Scotland's best loved restaurants!

BRITANNIA *Spice*
Exclusive Exotic Cuisine

**150 Commercial Street,
Ocean Drive, Leith, EH6 6LB
0131 555 2255**

www.britanniaspice.co.uk
info@britanniaspice.co.uk
Gift vouchers are available

The restaurant itself was converted from a whisky bond at the entrance to the former Leith docks back in 2000. Designed to reflect the nautical heritage of the site, the premises are light and airy during the day yet discreet and intimate in the evenings. Hosting regular charity events, functions and live musical performances, Britannia Spice is very much part of the Leith Community. But its attractions are not restricted just to the locals. With both the Royal Yacht Britannia and the Ocean Terminal Shopping Centre just a stone's throw away, the restaurant is also well placed to welcome visitors to the capital. The food never fails to impress, with many guests return time and time again.

Balaka

reservations | take-away | delivery
01334 474 825

Traditional Meal Deal

Choice of any one starter and two main courses, served with a choice of chicken, beef, vegetable, prawns or king prawn (supplementary charge 4.95).

Includes 2 popadoms & onion salad, 2 rice and any type of nan bread.

Starter
Vegetable Pakora
Chat Pat Chicken
Onion Bhaji

Main Course
Kurma
Bhuna
Madras
Pathia
Vindaloo
Malayan
Moglai
Dhansak

£17 MEAL FOR TWO

Specialty Meal Deal

Choice of any one starter and two main courses, served with a choice of chicken, beef, vegetable, prawns or king prawn (supplementary charge 4.95).

Includes 2 popadoms & onion salad, 2 rice and any type of nan bread.

Starters
Chicken Pakora
Chicken Tikka
Jinga Puri
Pakora
Onion Bhaji
Chat Pat

Main Course
Green Herb Chicken
Chicken Jalfresi
Afgani Gosht
Sag Gosht
Chicken Tikka Massalla
Sag Murghi
King Prawn Jalfresi

£20 MEAL FOR TWO

Balaka, 3 Alexandra Place, St Andrews, Fife, KY16 9XD

Delivery anywhere in St Andrews £3

Follow us on facebook.com/balakastandrews

call on 01334 474 825 or visit www.balaka.com

Juboraj
RESTAURANTS

SO MANY WAYS TO ENJOY A JUBORAJ

With one of the best Indian Restaurant experiences in Cardiff, a full menu Takeaway service and convenient Home Delivery – you'll always find a way to enjoy a Juboraj.

The comprehensive menu, contains traditional and contemporary dishes all made with the highest quality ingredients. Start with a golden Aloo Chat, diced boiled potatoes served in a rich sauce with fresh coriander or maybe a delicately spiced Shami Kebab. Follow it with a renowned Juboraj speciality of sensationally spicy Chicken Kholapuri masterfully prepared with turmeric, cumin, coriander and fresh green chillies or perhaps a traditional Northern Indian delicacy, Karahi, a rich dish cooked with exotic herbs and spices served on a sizzling karahi cast iron wok.

Many of the dishes on offer are Juboraj originals, often copied by others. One such dish, the Jamdhani Haash, a whole breast of tender duckling gently cooked in light spices, honey and lime juice giving an exquisite taste.

With an extensive wine list, irresistible desserts and high quality coffees and liqueurs you can be sure that you'll experience one of the best Indian and Bangladeshi restaurants Cardiff has to offer at the a Juboraj.

HOME DELIVERY AVAILABLE ALL OVER CARDIFF*

*CITY CENTRE & PENARTH DELIVERY (CF10, CF11, CF64): 029 2034 1114
REST OF CARDIFF DELIVERY: JUBORAJ EXPRESS 029 20 610 333
ONLINE ORDERING AVAILABLE AT WWW.JUBORAJEXPRESS.COM

RHIWBINA, 11 HEOL Y DERI, CARDIFF   029 2062 8894 | OPEN 6PM-11PM MON-SAT
CAFÉ QUARTER, 10 MILL LANE, CARDIFF   029 2037 7668 | OPEN 5PM-11PM 7 DAYS
LAKESIDE, LAKE ROAD WEST, CARDIFF   029 2045 5123 | OPEN 6PM-11PM TUES-SUN
JUBORAJ EXPRESS 290 NORTH ROAD, CARDIFF 029 20 610 333 | OPEN 5PM-11PM 7 DAYS

LUNCHTIME OPENING: 12-2PM MON-FRI
DAYS OF THE WEEK DIFFER BETWEEN RESTAURANTS
CITY CENTRE DELIVERY: 029 2034 1114
REST OF CARDIFF DELIVERY: 029 2061 0333
WWW.JUBORAJGROUP.COM

WWW.JUBORAJGROUP.COM

Juboraj
RESTAURANTS

SO MANY WAYS TO ENJOY A JUBORAJ

With one of the best Indian Restaurant experiences in Cardiff, a full menu Takeaway service and convenient Home Delivery – you'll always find a way to enjoy a Juboraj.

The comprehensive menu, contains traditional and contemporary dishes all made with the highest quality ingredients. Start with a golden Aloo Chat, diced boiled potatoes served in a rich sauce with fresh coriander or maybe a delicately spiced Shami Kebab. Follow it with a renowned Juboraj speciality of sensationally spicy Chicken Kholapuri masterfully prepared with turmeric, cumin, coriander and fresh green chillies or perhaps a traditional Northern Indian delicacy, Karahi, a rich dish cooked with exotic herbs and spices served on a sizzling karahi cast iron wok.

Many of the dishes on offer are Juboraj originals, often copied by others. One such dish, the Jamdhani Haash, a whole breast of tender duckling gently cooked in light spices, honey and lime juice giving an exquisite taste.

With an extensive wine list, irresistible desserts and high quality coffees and liqueurs you can be sure that you'll experience one of the best Indian and Bangladeshi restaurants Cardiff has to offer at the a Juboraj.

HOME DELIVERY AVAILABLE ALL OVER CARDIFF*

*CITY CENTRE & PENARTH DELIVERY (CF10, CF11, CF64): 029 2034 1114
REST OF CARDIFF DELIVERY: JUBORAJ EXPRESS 029 20 610 333
ONLINE ORDERING AVAILABLE AT WWW.JUBORAJEXPRESS.COM

RHIWBINA, 11 HEOL Y DERI, CARDIFF   029 2062 8894 | OPEN 6PM-11PM MON-SAT
CAFÉ QUARTER, 10 MILL LANE, CARDIFF   029 2037 7668 | OPEN 5PM-11PM 7 DAYS
LAKESIDE, LAKE ROAD WEST, CARDIFF   029 2045 5123 | OPEN 6PM-11PM TUES-SUN
JUBORAJ EXPRESS 290 NORTH ROAD, CARDIFF 029 20 610 333 | OPEN 5PM-11PM 7 DAYS

LUNCHTIME OPENING: 12-2PM MON-FRI
DAYS OF THE WEEK DIFFER BETWEEN RESTAURANTS
CITY CENTRE DELIVERY: 029 2034 1114
REST OF CARDIFF DELIVERY: 029 2061 0333
WWW.JUBORAJGROUP.COM

WWW.JUBORAJGROUP.COM

The Subcontinent

The subcontinent includes Pakistan, India, Nepal, Bhutan, Bangladesh, Myanmar (Burma) and Sri Lanka. Until 1947 this was one country ruled by the British. Now as independent states, each has its own unique culinary style. India has ten major regional cuisines and several minor ones, colour-grouped in the map. The main cuisines of the subcontinent are outlined in the following pages.

The Cuisine of the Subcontinent

It is a pleasant duty to enlarge this section for the fourth time in four editions. As we said before, the average overseas tourist expects to find a gastronomic desert when they visit the UK, although many it seems, are intensely relieved to find to that they can populate the proliferation of Macdonalds and its clones just as they do back home. Gourmets know better and head for culinary delights the like of which many can only dream of in their home countries. Despite our enduring reputation for boring, tasteless food, it is now several years since London has held the crown as the world's food capital. London boasts the unique and remarkable fact that every nation on the planet is represented with at least one restaurant serving its national food, and most of our bigger cities offer thirty or forty national cuisines. Their streets abound with serious cooks and restaurateurs whose mission is to produce good food and serve it well. Certainly that is the case in the 'Indian 'sector, whether it is haute-cuisine in highly-rated restaurants or simple home cooking in cosy, tiny venues. And the good news is that all over Great Britain standards are rising and authentic food is becoming more readily.

For years the majority of curry restaurants have been Bangladeshi-owned, profiting on a food style which is so alien to them they they won't eat it. In the last two decades, some have begun to 'come out' and declare their nationality, in some cases with a full menu of Bangladeshi dishes. Two do a fine job, the new Kolpata in E1 and the venerable Aziz in Oxford. There are rather less Pakistani, Sri Lankan, Nepalese and Indian restaurants. However most of these have always been true to their culinary roots, which is why we highlight as many of them as we can in this Guide.

In London you can dine in restaurants who specialise in the Indian region of their owners cooked to the highest, most authentic quality. Bengal, Goa, Gujarat, Hyderabad, Indian Kosher, Kashmir, Lucknow and Nawabi Dum Pukht, Maharashtra and Mumbai, Punjab and South India which itself has restaurants specialising in the cuisines of Kerela, Chetinad, Coorg, the Nairs, the Syrian Christians, Tamil Nadu and Udipi. They are all in London; their restaurants are all in this Guide and their cuisines and those of the subcontinent are outlined below and the next few pages. Not even India you can get such an array of good regional Indian cuisine in any one city. **The A to Z of the Curry Menu** (which follows) details every one of the items at these and all our British Asian restaurants. Outside London, regional restaurants are beginning to open up and down the country, but it remains a slow process. Sadly our sole Parsee and Rajahsthani restaurants closed, proving that they were a bridge too far even for London. It is up to you the diners to keep the others thriving and become their regular diners.

Afghani Afghanistan's location had always held the strategic key to India until this century, for it was through the solitary mountain passes that the invaders came and possessed India from as early as 3000 bc. Located between Iran (formerly Persia) and Pakistan (formerly NW India), it brought the cuisine of the Middle East to India – and that of India to the Middle East. Afghan food features Kebabs and Birianis, and skewered spiced lamb over charcoal. See Ariana 11 restaurant, London NW6. (See also Pashtoon).

Balti Balti is a Pakistani phenomenon which does not exist in India and with Pakistan and India in a permanent state of war, communications between them are limited and bitter. The reality is that in north Pakistan's high mountains is the ancient state of Baltistan, sharing its border with China and India's Kashmir, and once on the Spice Route to China. Little may have been known about Balti food outside its indigenous area, had it not been for a small group of Pakistani Kashmiris, many from Mirpur, who settled in east Birmingham in the 1960s. There, they opened small cafés in the back streets, serving curries made aromatic with Kashmiri Garam Masala, and herbs, with plentiful coriander, in two-handled pots called the 'karahi' in India, but known here as the 'Balti pan'. Eating with no cutlery, using fingers and bread to scoop up the food, is the norm to the community, but a revelation to Birmingham's white population, who made Balti their own. Bear in mind that Balti served in the average curry house bears no resemblance to the real thing. See West Midlands, Birmingham Balti Zone for information.

Bangladeshi Most of the standard curry houses in the UK are owned by Bangladeshis and nearly all of those serve standard formula curries (from mild to very hot). Bangladesh, formerly East Pakistan, is located at the mouth of the River Ganges. Before Partition, the area either side of the Ganges was Bengal. Today Bengal is the Indian state that shares its border with Bangladesh. Bangladesh is Muslim, so pork is forbidden. Unlike Hindu India, beef is eaten. The area enjoys prolific fresh and seawater fish – pomfret, boal, ruhi, hilsa and ayre, and tiger prawns – and specialises in vegetable dishes such as Shatkora (a kind of grapefruit used as an ingredient in meat/poultry dishes(and Niramish, (mixed vegeables) and some quite bitter dishes such as Shuktoni or shukti, meaning sour or bitter curry, eg using karela, bitter gourd. Until recently, true Bangladeshi cuisine was nigh on impossible to find in the UK. Now more of our Bangladeshi restaurants are serving the delights of their own country. Of these good examples are found at Aziz, Oxford, Café Naz E1, Hason Raja, London WC1, Kuti's Southampton, Shampan E1, and Spicery, Newcastle with maybe the most authentic of all at Kolpata E1.

The Cuisine of the subcontinent

Bengali Bengal is one of India's major culinary areas with Bengali cuisine India's second oldest-established. Mustard oil and seeds and the aromatic nigella seeds have been around in Bengali cuisine for thousands of years, as has the spice mixture unique to Bengal, Panch Phoran. Over time two states, East and West Bengal developed, their main difference being religion. In 1947 East Bengal was partitioned to Muslim Pakistan. In 1972 it became Bangladesh (see above). West Bengalis are mainly Hindu, and this proscribes no beef. Many dishes are common to both Bengals, for example, their adoration of sour tastes as seen in Dal Doyi Jhol – a runny lentil and yoghurt Soup, other dishes they have in common include Chachchori Morog – stir-fried mild chicken curry, Rezala Morgh – rich-tasting hot chicken, creamier curry than Korma in which green chillies are mandatory., Kalia – a thin red sauce. Aubergine (eggplant) were indigenous with Begun Shorshe, fried aubergines in yogurt and mustard sauce. while Baigan Burtha is the smoky puréed version. Niramish is another remarkable Vegan Curry. Potoler Dolma is a small wax gourd stuffed with a spicy filling. The 16th century Portuguese taught the Bengalis to make cheese (Paneer). Bengalis have a sweet tooth and they adore their sweet chutneys. J A Sharwood, a Victorian Raj merchant exported sweet Bengali mango chutney into Britain in the 1800s, and it is now a major feature at the curryhouse. It is not eaten in this form in India, but its basis was the Bengali Choti Mature sweet Mango Pickle. Calcutta is India's city of culture and in the 19th century it became famous for those wonderful, sticky sweets, such Gulab Jamun, Jalebi, Ras Malai and Ros Gulla (see glossary). When he feels like doing it, you'll find authentic Bengali dishes at Udit Sarkhel's, Mango Sweet, London, SW14.

Chetinad A style of cooking from the southern Indian state of Tamil Nadu. A meat-eating community called Chetiyars, have been resident in the Madras area since the earliest times. Under the British, they became merchants and money lenders, owning large amounts of Burmese farmland. Fish Kozambhu – sour sauce tamarind & chillies. Chetinad dishes appear on menus all over the place but Coconut Lagoon restaurants (see Kenilworth, Warks) are owned by Chetiyars so are one of the few places to do them correctly.

Dum Pukht A cooking term meaning 'containing the steam'. The technique originated in ancient Persia deriving from the Persian word 'dampukht' or baked. A pot was filled with meat and spices. A tightly-fitting lid was sealed with chupatti dough. A hole was dug in the desert sands. and hot coals were placed in its bottom. Next the sealed pot was surrounded with hot coals, buried in the sand and left undisturbed to cook for a few hours. The magical moment comes when the lid is opened in front of the diners, releasing all those captured fragrances. This was the perfect vehicle for cooking Biriani. The contemporary exponent is Delhi master chef Imtiaz Qureshi. His modern versions use pastry as the lid, and of course the modern oven. Qureshi has not ventured to London, but we have the next best chef, Mohammed Rais. He also hails from Lucknow and he too claims ancestry back to the Nawab court and Qureshi is his uncle. Rais worked at the Red Fort (W1) from 1997, but moved to Darbar, SW6. See also Kasturi, EC3 and Naresh Matta (Rias' former assistant at the Red Fort) now at Eriki NW3.

Goan The tiny state of Goa had always depended on spices, fish and coconut. In 1492 it was taken by the Portuguese who occupied it until 1962. Christianity prevails and there are no objections to eating pork or beef. Modern Goan curries are based on all these ingredients, often combined with palm todi (feni) vinegar to create a gently unique sour taste. Goans are mostly non-vegetarian. Meat is usually confined to Sundays. Fish is mandatory at least once a day in the Goan diet. Bread-making was introduced by the Portuguese and though rice is important to Goa, bread takes precedence and is eaten with most meals. Portuguese dishes, some unspiced, are to be found on the Goan menu. Many have evolved to be unique to Goa, with the addition of spices and coconut, yet have Portuguese names such as Cafreal, Xacutti and their most famous dish, Vindaloo. But it is not the dish from the standard curry house; the real thing is derived from the Portuguese dish Vino d'Alhos, traditionally pork marinated (the longer the better) in wine vinegar and garlic, then simmered until tender. To this the Goans added hot red chillies, creating a rich red curry gravy. But nothing is simple in Goa. Many dishes can appear with two different names in Portuguese or Goan (Konkani). And even same-named dishes can be cooked in different ways by the three different Goan communities. The majority of the population is Christian (Catholic) who eat everything including pork and beef and use plentiful chillies, todi-vinegar and sugar for piquancy, sweet and sour tastes. There is also a significant Goan Hindu population. Hindu Goans use less heat, tamarind or kokum for souring and jaggery for sweetening. The use asafoetida, chick peas, curry leaves, fenugreek, mustard and urid dhal. They don't eat beef, of course, and generally abstain from pork. Goa was occupied by Moslems for centuries before the Portuguese and there is still a significant Goan Moslem population. They do not eat pork or beef, mutton (goat) being their preferred meat, and the rather more complex dishes from Kashmir and the Moghals (Roghan Josh Gosht, kormas and birianis) are to be found in the Goan Muslim home. There is only one true Goan restaurant in the UK, Ma Goa in London SW15, although Goan dishes do appear at the better Indian restaurants such as Café Spice, E1 and Bombay Brasserie, SW7.

Gujarati Gujarat is a major culinary region, with a unique and abundant indigenous cuisine. It is home to more Hindi vegetarians (about 70%) than anywhere else in India, and their food is also India's least spicy. Despite her long Arabian Sea coastline, fish does not prevail. The Parsees (see entry) have lived in Gujarat for 1200 years (see below) and influenced the food with subtleties of sour and sweet. Prime Gujarati ingredients in savoury dishes are yoghurt, turmeric, gram flour, with a little sugar being added, displaying the penchant for sweet tastes. One dish exemplifying the Gujarati adoration of these ingredients is the primrose-yellow, soup-like dish called Khadi or Kari. Often served with with gram flour dumplings, this may have been the very dish which gave 'curry' its name when in 1608, the first British diplomat docked at the port of Surat in southern Gujarat, to establish the East India Company's only trading post, until Bombay was built in 1674. With plentiful rainfall, Surat is the lushest of Gujarat's several main regions, guaranteeing ample supplies of grain, fruit and vegetables. Its signature dish is Undhyoo or Oondhiya in which chopped vegetables such as sweet potato, ratallu (purple yam), plantain, brinjal, green beans (papadi) etc are marinated in a spicy coconut paste and dry-fried in oil, often til (sesame) oil. Other Surati or Surti favourites are Ravaiya (baby aubergine stuffed with paneer paste) and Paunk, the winter-time delicacy of immature, fresh green millet grains is washed down with chass (buttermilk) drink. Breads made from wheat, millet and gram flour have names like Nankhatais, Ghari and Saglu Baglu Mithai. In the south west the lands of Kathiawadi (aka Saurashtra or Sorath) benefits from annual monsoon rains. Pulses dominate, used whole, ground or sprouted. Peanuts, and sesame prevail. Kathiawadi favourites include Debra (wheat flour mixed with spinach, green chillies, yogurt, salt and sugar). Breads include Phafda, (ajowan-flavoured assorted-flour puri). Methia Masala, a dry powder made from fenugreek seeds, chilly powder and salt, is sprinkled over raw vegetables and salads giving Kathiawari food a distinctive flavour. Sugarcane from which gur (jaggery) is processed in famous sweetmeats such as Ladoo, the delectable Chhundo (hot and sweet shredded mango chutney) and Murabbo (sweet mango pickle). Central Gujarat loves its Farsan, crunchy fried snacks like Chakli, Doodh-Pak, Ghari, Nankhatai, Dhokla, and Khandvi. The famous Pakora/Bhaji also originated there, as did Dahi Vada (gram flour dumpling in a tangy yoghurt sauce), Murukus (crunchy, spicy snack nibbles made from a deep-fried spicy gram flour dough) known in Britain as Bombay Mix. Sev is the very fine vermicelli-sized version and Sevian Tamatar (wheat vermicelli noodles with tomato) is found there. North Gujarati food is non-spicy, virtually oil-free and best known for its thalis (once made of silver) consisting of rice, dhal, curry, vegetables, sprouted beans, farsan, pickles, chutney and raita. The north west province of Kutch borders Pakistan and Rajasthan in the arid Thar Desert. Specialities include Osaman (a consommée-like dhal soup flavoured with tomatoes, fresh coconut and coriander), Khichdi (rice and lentils), Dhokla, a salty steamed cake, Doodhpak, a sweet, thickened milk confectionery and Shrikhand dessert.Gujarati vegetarian restaurants are prevalent in Leicester and Wembley, Middlesex, and they pop up elsewhere, too. Not all Gujaratis are Hindus or vegetarians. As a result of ancient Moslem occupations, there remains a small group of Gujarati beef-eating Moslems, called the Bohris Community. Unique to India they like soups such as Sarka, made with toovar oily dal, peanut and coconut. Their most outstanding dishes are Gosht Tikkea Malai ke Bohris (beef cubes marinated in cream, garlic and ginger, then coated with breadcrumbs and baked) and Lagania Seekh (egg-brushed beef kebab).

Hyderabadi (Andhra Pradesh) Andhra Pradesh (AP) formerly called Hyderabad, after its major city is the fifth largest state in India, both in area and population. In the 1930s, Hyderabad's royal ruler, the Nizzam was alleged to be the richest man in the world. The state is strategically situated in the south central India and forms a major link between north and south of India. It has a widely diversified agricultural base with a variety of cash crops. It is the granary of the south and produces a surplus of food grain. Hyderabad has been south India's strongest Moslem enclave since the 14th century. Today it is 40% Moslem. Hyderabad also has a Parsee population. Consequently, it is a meat-eating cuisine, but its cuisine is also one of India's hottest, as indicated by Mirchi Ka Salan, Chilli Curry. Mirchi means chilli, 'ka' means 'of' and Salan is a type of Urdu spicing speciality of Hyderabad and we encounter it twice more in Macchi ka Salan (Fish) and Baigan ka Salan (aubergine / eggplant. Biriani is a Hyderabadi speciality and we represent it with Tahiri a Vegetable Biriani speciality. Koftas and Kebabs are popular and the Parsee Khara Soti Boti Kebab, Omelette-enrobed Meat chunks Two dishes represent yoghurt's popularity, Chowgra a Yoghurt-based Vegetable curry and Churri a Herbal Yoghurt dip. Thoran lightly spiced Coconut and shredded Cabbage, is called Thoora in Andhra Pradesh.

Kashmiri Kashmir is India's most northerly state, located in the Himalayas thousands of feet above sea level. At partition in 1947 Kashmir was split between India and Pakistan, leading to conflict. On both sides of the border most Kashmiris are meat-eaters (even Hindu Kashmiris) whose rich sauces and ghee help to combat the cold. Lotus, apples, saffron and rice but not wheat are specifically Kashmiri. The Moghuls built a summer retreat in the 16th century and brought with them aromatic spices, such as cardamom, cinnamon, clove, and aniseed. Nothing shows this off better than Kashmir's most celebrated dish, Korma. The Kashmiri Moslem wedding feast, the Wazwan at which the number of guests expected to attend always exceeds 500, is unique. Traditionally, the feast must contain exactly 36 different dishes, including chutneys and accompaniments. At least seven mutton dishes must be served. A 15kg male sheep is considered ideal. All parts are used; leg for dhaphol, ribs for tabak maz, neck for roghan josh, entrails for methi maz, quorma soured with apricots, jakhni soured with curds. Gushtaba giant meatball, with curd gravy, is traditionally the final dish, though a semolina might follow. See Chor Bizare, London, W1.

Maharashtran and Mumbai food Maharashtra is located in central India's Deccan plains. Maharashtran, or Marathi food has developed over the centuries as a minor cuisine. It is mild and delicately spiced and uses tamarind and fresh coconut. The climate is perfect for viticulture and supports two grape crops a year. One brand of method-champagne is widely exported under the name Omar Khyam. Mumbai (Bombay) is the vibrant, buoyant, commercial centre of India, with some of the highest property prices in the world, Bollywood, expensive restaurants, and home-delivery Pizza, contrasting with the appalling poverty of shanti-towns, and street-begging. Bombay was the creation of the British and as such it has never developed a large cuisine. A favourite UK curryhouse dish, Bombay Potato (see A-Z glossary) is not found in Bombay, but it is typical of Bombay tastes. Gujarat's Murukus was re-invented as 'Bombay Mix' in Southall in the 1970s. Sev *(qv)* is one ingredient of Bhel Puri, Bombay's favourite street food. It is served cold and is delicious. Restaurants such as London's Masala Zones, Bhel Puri Houses in Drummond Street, Wembley, SW16 and other places around London specialise in it. The original fishing tribes, the Kholis, however, had a couple of delicacies up their sleeve; Bombay Duck *(qv)* and Bangda (fish head) curry. Parsees migrated into Bombay after the British created their fortress trading posts there in the C18th to form India's largest Parsee community (see below).

Moghul Almost surrounded by Haryana is Delhi, the small state containing India's capital city. Delhi has no cuisine in its own right; it was during the 16th century that Indian food was taken to its supreme culinary heights in the Moghul capital city of Delhi, as well as Agrah, Lahore and Kashmir (see below). East of Delhi is the largely Muslim state of Uttar Pradesh, with Moghul Agra and its Taj Mahal in the west and the river Ganges flowing through its length. No one was richer than the Moghuls, and it was during their time, four centuries ago, that Indian food was perfected. Authentically, this style of food should be subtly spiced. The French may believe they invented 'haute cuisine', but they were pipped to the post by Moghul chefs, who did to Indian food what the French chef Varenne did to French cooking a century later; they perfected sauces using garlic, butter and cream with the addition of something uniquely Indian; a marriages of spices. They created supremely aromatics curries with sensual sauces like

The Cuisine of the subcontinent

Classic Korma, Pasanda, Rhogan Josh Gosht and Raan, roast lamb. The standard curry-house has based some of its formula on mild, rich, creamy dishes such as these, albeit lacking the subtlety of the real thing. Rather more authentic interpretations can be found in an increasing number of 'haute cuisine' restaurants around the country, spelt variously Moghul, mogul, moglai, muglai mugal, mugul, etc.

Nawabi Of culinary importance, is Lucknow, now an Indian army city, and one which is of immense historical importance especially during the time of the wealthy Nawabs, who came to royal prominence as the Moghuls declined. One inheritance is Nawabi cuisine. Lucknow, being Moslem, enjoys meat, but its cooking is unique. Flavours are spicy aromatic and subtle and the food is luxurious. One process is called Dum or Dum Pukht. It means slow-cooking by steaming the curry or rice dish, in a handi or round pot, whose lid is sealed into place with a ring of chapatti dough. The resulting dish is opened in front of the diners, releasing all those captured fragrances.

Nepalese Beautiful Himalayan mountains, the world's only Hindu kingdom, home of Gurkas, sherpas, yak and yeti, Kumari the living virgin goddess-princess, Everest, and unique food. Some similarities to north Indian, with curry (tarkari), rice (bhat), and wheat breads (roti haru). Kukhura (chicken), Khasi (lamb), Dumba (mutton), Bhutwa (pork), Hach Ko (duck), Jhinge (prawn) and Maccha (fish) are cooked in the clay oven (chula) or curried. Specialities include Aloo Achar, potatoes in pickle sauce, Momo/Momocha, keema-filled dumplings, and Tama Bodi, bamboo shoots and black-eye beans, a dish showing Tibetan/Chinese roots. More examples will be found in the entries for Great Nepalese, NW1, Gurkha Kitchen, Oxted, Surrey and Gurkha Square, Fleet, Hants.

Pakistani Until independence in 1947, Pakistan formed the north-western group of Indian states. Located between Afghanistan and India, it contains the famous Khyber Pass. The people are predominantly meat-eaters, favouring lamb and chicken (being Muslim, they avoid pork). Charcoal cooking is the norm, and this area is the original home of the tandoor. Breads such as Chupatti, Nan and Paratha are the staple. Balti cooking originated in the northernmost part of Pakistan (see earlier). In general, Pakistani food is robustly spiced and savoury. The area called the Punjab was split by the formation of Pakistan, and it is the Punjabi tastes that formed the basis of the British curry house menu (see Punjab, London WC2). Bradford, Glasgow and Southall have sizeable Pakistani populations.

Parsee/Persian This is not a regional cuisine; it is the cuisine of a religious sect, and their unique cuisine has evolved over the last 1200 years from when the Parsees fled Persia to escape persection from the newly Muslims. There are now only around 100,000 Parsees. Most live in Bombay, but there are other groups in Hyderabad and Gujarat. It is quite common to see Persian dishes listed on the standard curry house menu. Dishes such as Biriani and Pullao did indeed originate in Persia (Iran) while Dhansak and Patia. are Parsee dishes. However they are a pastiche of the real thing. Parsees have no religious proscriptions on eating, so they eat pork, beef as well as lamb and shellfish and they love egg dishes. Meat mixed with vegetables and fruit is typical of Persian and Parsee food, though the latter has now incorporated the Indian spice palette and sweet and sour combinations, typified in their Patia. The most celebrated and popular of all Parsee dishes is Dhansak, where in the real thing meat on-the-bone is incorporated with four types of lentil (polished moong, masoor, chana and toovar). Slow cooking in a heavy lidded pot amalgamates the flavours. During the cooking, a kind of ratatouille of aubergine, tomato, spinach and fresh chillies is added. Sweet and sour comes from jaggery (palm sugar) and a slight overtone of sour from fresh tamarind juice. Jardaloo Boti is lamb cooked with dried apricots and the coriander coated fish dish, Patrani Maachli is a Parsee speciality. Their roasted vegetable dish, Oonbhariu is one of the best vegetable dishes in India. With the demise of the N19 Parsee restaurant it remains to south-west London's Bombay Brasserie and Chutney Mary, who both have Parsee chefs who cook authentic Parsee dishes, and of course, Cyrus, himself a Parsee, at Café Spice Namaste, E1.

Pashtoon It refers to tribal people and their language from the rugged mountain passes of Afghanistan (*qv*) and Pakistan (*qv*) in the former North-West Frontier Province, whose name for themselves is Pathan, Pashtun, Phuktana or Pukhtun. Afghan food is pretty basic, especially at tribal level, involving hunting wild life then grilling it or slow-cooking it in pots. Grills, Kebabs, Koftas and Birianis are popular, spiced with the unique Afghan spice mix, Char Masala (four aromatic spices) and cooked mostly in their own juices. Visit Tagore, Welling Kent and Kasturi EC1.

Punjabi For the purposes of this Guide we link together India's north-central states Haryana, Himachal Pradesh, Uttaranchal and Punjab. The former have little culinary interest, though the very best Basmati rice comes from Himachal Pradesh, which as its name suggests is in the foothills of the Himalayas: Dehradun Basmati is to rice what Krug or Dom Perignon is to champagne. The Punjab, like Kashmir was another state split into two after partition, with western Punjab and the Moghul city of Lahore in Pakistan. Food knows no boundaries, and Punjabi food is a major culinary style which is identical in both the Punjabs and in Haryana (meaning 'green land') Punjabi cuisine began to evolve from early in the first millennium AD. It is perhaps the best known Indian food because the original curry restaurants in the developed world based their menus on Punjabi cuisine. Dairy farming is a major Punjabi industry and its prolific wheat and grain crops, earn it the title 'the granary of India', and Parathas and Puris are staples. Oilseeds, spices, peas and beans and much else. grows prolifically in the area. The food is very savoury and fenugreek leaf (methi) and mustard leaf (rai) are virtually staples. Robust curries like Punjabi Keema, Methi Gosht, Aloo Ghobi Methi and Sag Paneer, Mattar Valor – pea and bean curry are typical. Best Punjabi exponents are found in Southall, but look out for other Punjabi references throughout the Guide.

South Indian South India consists of three sub-tropical and very fertile states, Karnataka, Kerela and Tamil Nadu and also includes the Konkan Coast or Karavali (800 miles of rugged and beautiful Indian coastline stretching from Mumbai to Mangalore). The area was first occupied in about 1000BC by the Dravidians, who are still the largest racial group. South India's cuisine has remained virtually unmodified since that time, making it India's longest-established cuisine. When the Dravidians first arrived and cultivated the area, they encountered South India's main indigenous ingredients: ginger, coconut, curry leaves, peppercorns, turmeric and curry leaf. The food is rice-based, with no wheat. Yoghurt and tamarind provide two quite differing sour tastes. Many dishes use all these ingredients, and many dishes are common to all three south Indian states, albeit under different names, and

The Sumptuous Sadya

Labels on image: Pullisseri, Avial, Thoran, Seeni, Olan, Curd Chutneys, Erisseri, Pickles, Sambar, Payasam Puddings, Papad, Banana Chips

with subtle differences in flavourings. Common to all states is Dosa, huge, thin, crisp rice-lentil-flour pancakes, with a curry filling (Masala) and Idlis – steamed rice or lentil-flour dumplings accompanied by Sambar, a lentil-based curry, Rasam, a hot and spicy consommé and coconut chutney. Other rice-based items include Upuma and Uthappam (see A-Z glossary). Because of the intense heat and frequent high humidity, thin curries are preferred because they are more easily digested than the thick-sauced versions of the north. Day to day, much of the area's population is fish-eating or vegetarian, but most will eat meat or poultry on special occasions. Many exotic vegetables include, drumstick, mooli, snake gourd, doodi, bottle gourd, bittergourd (karela). tindoora, and long beans. Vegetable curries using them include Avial, Thoran and many others. Some specialist groups, such as Coorgs, Malabaris, Nairs, Mophlas, Syrian Christians and Jews (see below) eat meat and chicken dishes on a regular basis. Specialist restaurants have long been found been in and around London (especially East Ham, E6 and Tooting SW17). The specialist food of Udipi (a small town north of Mangalore) is to be found at Sagar, W6. The first restaurant to bring south Indian meat, chicken and sea food dishes to the UK was Chutney Mary, SW10 then Quilon, SW1. But other restaurants have developed the theme as specialisations. The best are Kerela N1, Rasa Travanvore, N19 and Coconut Lagoon restaurants (see Kenilworth, Warks). One conservation-minded, zero-cost serving method dating from 1000BC and still in daily use is the banana leaf. This fleshy, pliable, ribbed, inedible leaf serves as your plate on which is placed the traditional meal (the Sadya), all courses together, but with each item in an invariable position on the leaf, see picture above. No cutlery is needed and once you have eaten, the plate leaf is wrapped up and disposed of to bio-degrade. When will the Sadya appear in a UK restaurant as a trendy (and no doubt costly) dining experience, one wonders?

Sri Lankan Sri Lanka is the small, pearl-shaped island, formerly Ceylon, at the southern tip of India. Its cuisine is distinctive and generally chilli hot. They eat similar fare to that eaten in south India, i.e. vegetarian dishes, but they also enjoy very pungent meat, squid, chicken and duck curries. Look out for black curries and white ones, and deviled dishes. Hoppers are pancakes made of fermented rice, mixed with highly alcoholic palm toddy) and a little sugar, and are available in both sweet and savoury versions, String hoppers are rice-flour noodle nests. A festive dish introduced by a Dutch burger centuries ago is called Lampries (Longkirist). here a full meal of meat curry, kofta, rice and sambols is wrapped inside a banana leaf parcel and cooked. Samols made of coconut and onion accompany all meals. Good Sri Lankan restaurants include Palm Paradise, Southall, Middlesex, Prince of Ceylon, London N4, Elephant Walk NW6 and Jaffna House SW17.

Tandoori The ancient Egyptians created the side-entry clay-oven in which to bake their bread. Later they were used in ancient Persia where they are still called the' tonir', and their bread 'nane lavash'. A small variant seems to have been invented in India at the same time. Instead of having a side-entry, this egg-shaped vessel's entry hole was at the top, which was narrower than its centre point. It was the ancestor of today's tandoori oven. Its base had a small air-hole, below which was placed an even earlier invention, charcoal. Easily transported, this oven was probably invented to enable travelling traders to cook at their camp-sites. Corroborative evidence exists in the form of oven remains found all along ancient trade routes. By 300bc Sanskrit writings on cooking techniques describes meat spread with a honey-coloured spicy paste and cooked in the clay-oven, the 'kavan kunndu' (fire-container). Could kunndu be the derivation of the Hindi word 'tandoor'? The paste 'kunndu pachitam' (fire-paste) 'spread on meat' sounds remarkably like a marinade, the contents of which are unclear, but to achieve the colour as described, it could well contain yoghurt to assist in tenderising the flesh, plus spices, garlic, salt and indeed honey itself. For the first time we know that spiced meat, and probably poultry too was cooked in the tandoor.. The ancient Iranians also have a claim to the derivation of the word tandoor. It could have derived from their words 'tata', meaning 'hot', and 'andar', meaning 'inside'. Either way the tandoor remained on the Afghan/Pakistan border until modern times. The world's first tandoori restaurant, the Moti Mahal was established there in 1922. Partition forced its Hindu owner to move to Delhi in 1947. It remained as India's only tandoori restaurant until recent times. Even now, outside the five-star hotels, tandoori food is rarely found in India. Conversely tandoori food is ubiquitous in the UK and is some of the most popular dishes. Recently a Moti Mahal branch opened in London WC2.

BLUE ELEPHANT ROYAL THAI CUISINE
Imperial Wharf London

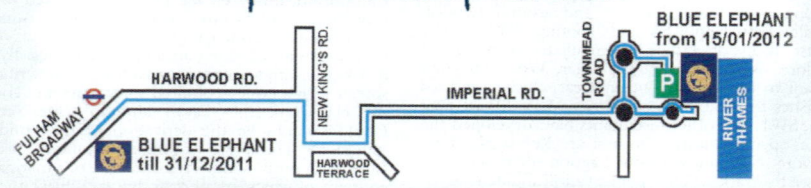

BLUE ELEPHANT ROYAL THAI CUISINE IMPERIAL WHARF
The Boulevard, Imperial Wharf, Townmead Road, London SW6 2UB
T: +44 20 7385 6595 | F: +44 20 7386 7665
E: london@BlueElephant.com   www.BlueElephant.com

Member of the Blue Elephant International Group

BANGKOK • PHUKET • JAKARTA • LONDON • PARIS • BRUSSELS • COPENHAGEN • LYON • MALTA • DUBAI • (BAHRAIN)

The Cuisine of South East Asia

INDO CHINA South East Asia, called 'further India' is the peninsula between India and China containing Burma, Thailand, Malaysia, Singapore, and Indonesia. Britain is blessed with an ever-increasing number of restaurants serving these spicy cuisines, and this Guide lists just some of the best. Here we thumbnail their cuisines:

Burmese Burma,(Myanmar), shares its boundaries with Bangladesh, India, China, Laos and Thailand. Since independence from Britain in 1948, Burma has been isolated by dictatorial communism. Our loss, because Burma is an exquisite country, with a gentle, bullied Bhuddist population, whose food is a combination of these styles. There is the spiciness of India with ghee-fried curries using turmeric, pepper, tamarind and chilli (though less than in many Indian regions). There is the fragrance of Thailand, in the form of lemon grass, (though less of this than in Thailand) shrimp paste (Ngapi), fish sauce and coconut. From China comes steaming and stir-fry wok techniques, tofu, bamboo and soy sauce. Rice (Hta-Min) and noodles (kaukswe) are is the staples. There is no wheat bread-making. There are no religious objections to eating pork (whethar) or beef (ahmai) and they enjoy lamb/mutton (seikthar) chicken (kyethar) duck (bairthar) fish (ngar) and shrimp (pazun). The only UK Burmese restaurant is the Mandalay, London W2.

Malaysian Malaysia's only border is a narrow strip at her north where the peninsula joins that of Thailand, and it shares many tastes in food. Such similarities include the love of lemon grass, shrimp paste (petis or belacan pronounced blachan) sweet lime (kaffir) and, above all chillies (the taste for really hot food diminishes in popularity as one goes southwards, away from Thailand). Differences include the use of tamarind (asam) to achieve a tart taste, turmeric for yellow colour and peanut to thicken. Instead of galangal, Malaysians use aromatic pink ginger buds with their flowers and or zedoary (cekur), both hard to obtain (ginger or galangal can substitute). Noodles are more ubiquitous in Malaysia than in Thailand, and curry with noodles is as common there as curry with rice. Try Laksa if offered it. Curries prevail, showing their Indian, Chinese and Thai influences. Thinner fragrant gravies, often based on coconut milk, also contain chillies, ginger, and lemon grass. A curry version of Satay is Inche Kabin, where curry paste is added to the sauce, which is coated onto a whole chicken, then grilled. Wet curries are flavoured with lemon grass and shrimp paste, along with the robust spices of India. Soto Ayam and Rempah are two of Malaysia's better known curries. Malaysia's population is composed of Chinese, Indians, and Malayans, and this results in a distinctive cuisine also known as Nonya. Best UK restaurants: Georgetown Malaysian, Nottingham, Stratford, Leeds and Kenilworth

Thai Thailand shares her borders with Burma, Laos, Kampuchea and Malaysia, yet her cuisine is hardly influenced by them. It is the combination of tastes which makes Thai cuisine unique. Key items are fragrance from lime leaves (markrut), lemon grass stalks (takrai) and holy basil leaves; heat from explosive tiny chillies and to a lesser extent from galangal, a peppery type of ginger. Savoury tastes come from from shrimp paste (kapi), sweet from palm sugar and seasoning from thin clear fish sauce (nam-pla) which never dominates, but enhances the other ingredients. Thailand grows dozens of vegetables which have no translation in the west. Appearance matters greatly in Thai cooking, and no where else on earth makes prettier carved garnishes than the Thai. Roses from radishes, carnations from carrots and coronets from cucumbers are examples. Chicken, pork, duck, beef, fish, shellfish are regularly in the diet. Wheat, dairy products, potato, tomato and potato are largely absent from the diet. Glutinous rice, tamarind, soy sauce, noodles and chops sticks are common to the far north. The south prefers fragrant non-sticky rice and coconut milk which gives Thai curries a creamy sauce. Indian spiced mutton is eaten in the Moslem far south, as one approaches Malaysia. The best UK Thai restaurants UK is Orchid Lounge at Jaipur, Milton Keynes, Bucks with Blue Elephant, London, SW6 and Rumwong Guildford close behind.

Singaporean Singapore is a small island country in Southeast Asia. It lies near the southern tip of the Malay Peninsula about where the South China Sea and the Indian Ocean meet. The sea is an arm of the Pacific Ocean. Singapore consists of a large island and more than 50 smaller islands. founded in 1819 by Sir Stamford Raffles, and was used by the British as their major trading post in the area, the legacy of which is today's major business centre. Singapore's population is the most cosmopolitan of the area, with Indian, Chinese, Malay, Indonesian and European influences. The Chinese or Hokkien predominate, and little wonder, so do noodles. Because Singapore, like Hong Kong were created from nothing, and then populated by such a mixture of races, there has been insufficient time for few, if any true Singaporean dishes to evolve. Fish Head Curry and Hokkien stir-fry Noodles are two.

Indonesia Adjacent to Malaysia is Indonesia, the former Dutch East Indies. It consists in excess of 13,600 islands, some of which are uninhabited. The world's fourth largest population lives on the remaining islands, which include Sumatra, Borneo, Java, New Guinea, Bali and the celebrated Molucans, the spice islands, the original home of clove, mace and nutmeg, where the cuisine never uses these spices. Indonesia likes its spicy dishes although spices, ironically earn relatively little income for Indonesia. The Chinese introduced Nasi Goreng (fried rice with vegetables), and Bhami Goreng (noodles). The Indians brought their curries and spices, the Portuguese brought chilli, peanuts and tomatoes while the Dutch brought sweets and cakes, and of course Rijstaffel (a selection of up to 40 dishes of meat, vegetables and rice served in individual bowls). Satay, meat coated in a lightly spiced peanut sauce, originated here. Rendang is a popular beef (water buffalo) curry flavoured with galangal, lemon grass. shrimp paste (terasi or trasi) turmeric leaf, and chillies

Pure Luxury

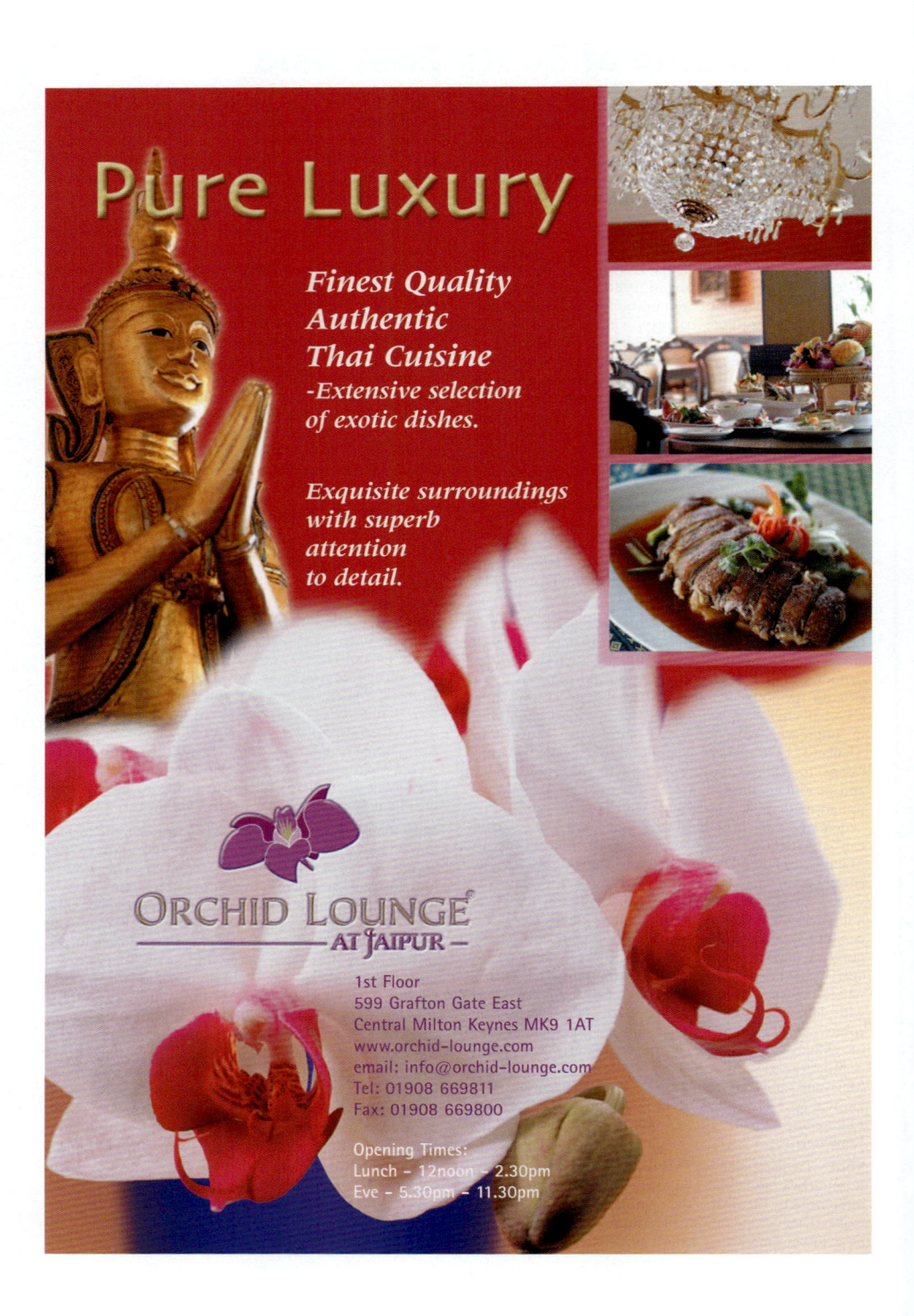

Finest Quality Authentic Thai Cuisine
-Extensive selection of exotic dishes.

Exquisite surroundings with superb attention to detail.

ORCHID LOUNGE
— AT JAIPUR —

1st Floor
599 Grafton Gate East
Central Milton Keynes MK9 1AT
www.orchid-lounge.com
email: info@orchid-lounge.com
Tel: 01908 669811
Fax: 01908 669800

Opening Times:
Lunch – 12noon – 2.30pm
Eve – 5.30pm – 11.30pm

The A to Z of the Curry Menu

To the first-timer, the Indian restaurant menu is a long and complex document. This glossary explains many of the standard, and some of the specialised, dishes and items that you are likely to encounter. See also **The Cuisine of the Subcontinent** *(psee earlier)*. Spellings of vowel sounds will vary from restaurant to restaurant, reflecting the 15 languages and hundreds of dialects of the subcontinent. *(See Masala, Moglai, Papadam and Rhogan Josh Gosht for some examples.)* Our spelling here is as near as possible to the standard accepted way of spelling, when translating phonetically from the main languages to English.

A

AAM or AM Mango.
ACHAR or ACHAAR Pickle, such as lime, mango, aubergine, etc. Achar Gohst is meat curry, curried in a pickle base, Achar Murgh is the chicken version.
AFGHANI CURRY Nuts and fruit are added for the standard curry house interpretation.
ALOO Potato.
AYURVEDIC FOOD. Ayurveda is the ancient Indian holistic philosophy from 1100BC concerning body, mind and soul, which states that each of us has one of three different body types, or 'dosha' fixed at the moment of conception, which determine everything about us – our appearance, what illnesses we are likely to suffer from and what foods we should eat. The word is derived from the Sanskrit 'ayur', meaning 'life' or more literally 'lifespan' and 'veda', 'knowledge' and is intertwined with the Hindu sacred religious works, the Vedas. Ayurvedic medicine is still widely and successfully practiced in India using, amongst other methods, herbal infusions as cures. Ayurvedic dietary rules are complex, but in outline sweet foods cool the body (ie lower its metabolism) and increase its weight; salty foods warm it and increase weight; bitter/sour foods cool it and decrease it; pungent /savoury foods warm it and decrease it. However not only is this subject to seasonal variation, the detail is confusing. For example, vegetable oil cools the body while ghee *(qv)* heats it; fennel seed cools while aniseed warms and both garlic and ginger heat it. This is further confused by the contradiction of China's ancient Yin-Yang (cool-warm) food philosophy, where garlic, for example is Yin (which decreases body heat) while ginger is Yang (which increases it). This may explain why in India today at least 25% of today's Hindus dismiss Ayurveda saying science and common sense define how your meal must be perfectly balanced. Be that as it may, some restaurants offer Ayurvedic menus, such as London's Mantra EC3 and Quilon SW1, and Altrincham's Dilli. *(see Garam Masala).*

B

BAIGAN or BEGUN see *Brinjal*.
BALTI Balti originated centuries ago in north Pakistan's Mirpur, Kashmir and Skardu (Baltistan). It found its way to east Birmingham in the 1970s, where any combination of ingredients was curried in a two-handled pot known as the KARAHI *(qv)* elsewhere, but the Balti there. Served to the table still cooking, the art is to eat the food – which should be spicy, herby and aromatic – Indian-style, with the bread as the scoop in the right hand. In the 1990s, Balti spread rapidly all over the UK and beyond. The Balti found at the standard Bangladeshi curry house, however, owes its flavours more to Patak's acidic Balti paste than to Mirpur, and unless it is cooked in its pan and served cutlery-free, it will (correctly) never convince the Brummy purist that it is anything other than hype.
BARFI or BURFI Indian fudge-like sweet made from reduced condensed milk (koya or khoa), in various flavours.
BASMATI from the Hindi word for 'fragrant' is the name for certain varieties of rice grown exclusively in the plains of northern India and Pakistan. It has a characteristic aroma in both the raw and cooked state, and a distinctive shape, which on cooking elongates to almost double its length whilst its width remains the same and it slowly releases carbohydrates (i.e. it has a low glycaemic index compared with other rice).
BATERA Football-sized fried bread puri *(qv)* becoming increasingly popular.
BATTAR Quail.
BENGAL CURRY A curyhouse chicken or meat curry with chilli, sugar, potato cubes and halves of tomato.
BHAJI or BHAJEE Dryish, pan-fried mild vegetable curry.
BHAJIA Deep-fried fritter, usually with sliced onion, mixed with spiced gram flour batter, then deep-fried. Bhajia is the correct term, meaning fried. Bhaji or Bhajee is the anglicisation. For the real thing, visit Maru's Bhajia House, Wembley, Middlesex. *See also Pakora*.
BHEL PURI This is the delicious street food snack from Bombay. It is a cold combination of those crunchy squiggles you find in Bombay Mix *(qv)*, the smallest of which is called Sev. To this is added small-diced cooked potato, puffed rice (mamra), coriander leaf, onion and chilli. It is laced with brown sweet and sour tamarind (imli) sauce, green coriander chutney (dhania) and red chilli/garlic sauce, and topped with crispy puri biscuit chippings. The result is an exquisite combination of crisp, chewy and soft textures with sweet, hot, savoury and sour tastes. Variations include differing amounts of ingredients, under various similar names, such as Sev Batata Puri, Dahi (yoghurt) Batata Puri, Chat Aloo Papri and Batata Pava. Bhel can be accompanied by GOL GOPPAS (q.v.). This delicious food is generally beyond the abilities of the average curry house, so is rarely found. Try it when you can *(see London's Drummond St NW1, Shahee Bhel SW16 and Masala Zone W1)*.
BHOONA or BHUNA Cooking process involving slowly frying out all the water content to produce a dry, usually mild curry.
BINDI A pulpy, rather sappy vegetable also known as okra or ladies fingers. Correct cooking of this dish is a good test of a chef's ability.
BIRIANI Traditionally, rice baked between layers of meat or vegetable filling, enhanced with saffron and aromatic spices, served topped with edible silver leaf – vark *(qv)*. The restaurant interpretation is a cooked rice, artificially coloured, with filling stir-fried in. It is usually heavily garnished and served with a vegetable curry sauce *(see Pullao)*.
BOMBAY DUCK A smallish fish native to the Bombay docks, known locally as bommaloe macchi. This was too hard for the British Raj to pronounce, so it became Bombay Duck. It is dried and appears on the table as a crispy deep-fried starter or accompaniment to a curry. Following a senseless EU ban a decade ago, it is now allowed. An acquired taste!
BOMBAY MIX An age-old traditional Indian snack nibble, called muruku, made from a savoury, gram-flour, spiced batter called ompadi, which is forced through a press straight into the deep-frier, to give different shapes and thicknesses of squiggly nibbles. Nuts, pulses, seeds and other ingredients are added. It should always be really crunchy and fresh. Re-invented by GK Noon, owner of Royal Sweets in Southall, under the catchy name Bombay Mix, it will keep you going at the bar.

The A to Z of the Curry Menu

BOMBAY POTATO A popular invention of the curry house. Potatoes in curry sauce with onions and tomato.

BOTI KEBAB Marinated cubes of lamb cooked in a tandoor oven (see Tandoori).

BRINJAL Aubergine, also called baigan or began. In Baigan Burtha, aubergine is smoked, spiced and mashed, in Baigan Bhaji it is chopped and curried by pan-frying.

C

CTM ~ CHICKEN TIKKA MASALA The unshakable ledgend is that it waas invented by a British curry house chef (identity unknown) c1980, as a way to exploit his already popular Chicken Tikka by adding a creamy, pink, mild sauce made tasty by 'skilful' blending of curry sauce, tomato purée, tandoori paste, cream, coconut, mango chutney, ground almonds and a surfeit of red food colouring. It is a dish not found in India (because they do not have red food colouring nor Tandoori dishes). In any case India already had a dish from the 16th century Moghuls (See *Murgh Makhani*). CTM is now ordered by 65% of all diners. Not only that, it appears in supermarket sandwiches, flavours crisps, is a pizza topping and even spices mayonnaise. If only that chef had copyrighted it, he'd be earning millions in royalties a year. See *Tandoori and Tikka*.

CEYLON CURRY Curryhouse concoction cooked with lemon, chilli, and coconut.

CHANA A yellow lentil resembling, but not identical to, the split pea, used in dhal *(qv)* and to make gram flour. Kabli Chana is the chickpea. Both can be curried or dried and deep-fried as in Bombay Mix *(qv)*. See also *Paneer*.

CHASNI CHICKEN A central Scotland Pakistani restaurant name for CTM *(qv)*.

CHAT or **CHAAT** Literally means 'snack', though often it can be a salad.

CHILLI Fleshy members of the capsicum family, ranging in heat from zero (the bell pepper) to incendiary. All chillies start green and, if left long enough, eventually turn red, the one being no hotter than the other. The chilli normally used in Indian cooking is the narrow 7.5cm (3in) cayenne. The hottest in the world are Mexican Habañeros, Caribbean Scotch Bonnets and Bangladeshi Naga *(qv)*. People build up a tolerance to chillies, but they should never be inflicted upon the novice, not even in fun.

CHUPATTI A 15cm (6in) flat disc of unleavened bread, cooked dry on the Tava *(qv)*. It should always be served hot and pan-fresh. The spelling can vary – Chupati, Chapatti, etc.

CHUTNEY The common ones are onion chutney, mango chutney and tandoori chutney. There are dozens of others that rarely appear on the standard menu. See *Sambals*.

CURRY The only word in this glossary to have no direct translation into any of the subcontinent's 15 or so languages. The word was coined centuries ago by the British in India. Possible contenders for the origin of the word are: Karahi or Karai (Hindi) – the wok-like frying pan used all over India to prepare masala (spice mixtures); Karhi or Khadi – a soup-like dish made with spices, gram-flour dumplings and buttermilk; Kari – a spicy Tamil sauce; Turkuri – a seasoned sauce or stew; and Kari Phulia – Neem leaves, which are small and rather like bay leaves, used for flavouring. The Dutch, who were in India in the 17th century have their own derivation. They say it was used in Malaya for their Malay curries, and that it derived from the word Lekker meaning delicious, or in colloquial Dutch, Lekkerie.

CURRY HOUSE See *Formula Curries*.

D

DABBA or **DHAABA** The subcontinent's version of the transport café, it's a ubiquitous roadside eatery usually made of tin sheets and thatch or tarpaulin. Millions exist. If packed with truckers (their lorries parked all around) it's good. A limited menu offers dhals, spicy omelettes, mutton and vegetable curries, tea (chai) and soft drinks at truly low prices. Seating usually a charpoy or rope-strung cot in the open air in front of the eatery. Primitive kitchen fully visible. Vertical neon tubes are its night time symbol. Dabba dishes are appearing on some London chi-chi menus, at rather more expensive prices.

DAHI or **DOHI** Yoghurt, used as a chutney (see *Raita*) and in the cooking of some curries. Most curry houses make their own, and it is delicious as an accompaniment to curry, being less sharp than the shop-bought equivalent. Incidentally, Dahi, not water, is the best antidote if you eat something that's too hot for you.

DAHI VADA South Indian savoury gram-flour doughnut, deep-fried, cooled and dunked into cold, spicy yoghurt (see *Vada*).

DAL or **DHAL** Lentils There are numerous types of lentil in the subcontinent. They contain carbohydrates and protein and being inexpensive, they are the staple much of village India. The common restaurant types are massor (red, which cooks yellow), moong (green), chana (also used to make gram flour) and urid (black).

DEGCHI or **DEKHCHII** Brass or metal saucepan without handles.

DHANIA Coriander leaf, India's main herb or seed, her main spice.

DHANSAK Traditional Parsee meat dish cooked in a purée of lentils, aubergine, tomato and spinach. Curryhouses use dhal and methi, and sometimes chilli and pineapple.

DOPIAZA Traditional meat dish. Do means 'two', piaza means 'onion'. Onions appear twice in the cooking, deeply caramelised and second fried. This gives the dish a sweetish taste.

DOSA South Indian pancake made from rice and urid (lentil) flour, which, when made into a batter, soon ferments to give a superb sour taste. The batter is ladeled onto a hot plate and spread thinly to achieve a pancake shape. **MASALA DOSA** is a Dosa filled with mashed potato curry spiced with onion, chilli, turmeric, curry leaf and mustard seed.

DUM Cooking by steaming in a sealed pot, invented by the Royal Nawabs (see *The Cuisine of the Subcontinent*), e.g. Aloo Dum, steamed potatoes. Also called Dum Pukt or Pukht (pron 'pucked')

E

EKURI Curried Scrambled Egg. Spiced scrambled eggs are the speciality of the Parsees

ELAICHI Cardamom. Can major in curries – for example, Elaichi Murgh is chicken curried with a predominance of green cardamom

F

FOOD COLOURING Unlikely to appear on the menu except to state that the food excludes it. But if your food turns up in lurid, bright flourescent reds, yellows or greens, it does include it and it ain't natural! The ingredient is Tartrazine, which is coal extract and which can cause asthma attacks and hyperactivity. Despite endless attempts to get it banned in the UK, it is sadly still permitted in small doses. See *Pullao Rice, Tikka, Tandoori and Sheek Kebabs* etc.

FOOGATH Lightly cooked vegetable dish found in the Malabar area of South India. Any vegetable such as gourds or plantain can be used.

FORMULA CURRIES Many of our 'Indian' *(qv)* restaurants operate to a formula which was pioneered in the late 1940s. In those days, a way had to be found to deliver a variety of curries, without an unreasonable delay, from order to table. Since all authentic Indian recipes require hours of cooking in individual pots, there was no guarantee that they would even be ordered. So cubed meat, chicken or potatoes, dal and some vegetables were lightly curried and chilled, and a large pot of thick curry gravy, a kind of master stock, was brewed to medium-heat strength. To this day, portion by portion, on demand, these ingredients are reheated by pan-frying them with further spices and flavourings. At its simplest, a Medium Chicken Curry, that benchmark of middle ground, is still on many menus, though sometimes disguised as 'Masala', and requires no more than a reheat of some gravy with some chicken. For instance, take a typical mixed order for two. Chicken Korma (fry a little turmeric, coriander and cumin, add six pieces of chicken, add a ladleful of curry gravy, plenty of creamed coconut, sugar, almonds maybe and a little cream – result, a mild dish, creamy-golden in colour), with Vegetable Dhansak (fry some cumin seeds, dry methi leaves (*qv*), chopped onions, a little sugar, tomato, red and green capsicum with the gravy, add cooked dhal and some cooked veg – result, colourful, and still medium-strength). Meat Korma (as for the chicken, using meat), and Prawn Vindaloo (fry spices and chilli powder, add the gravy which at once goes red and piquant, then cooked peeled prawns, fresh tomato and potato, simmer and serve). Maybe also a Sag Paneer (fry cumin, some thawed creamed spinach and pre-made crumbled paneer together, add fresh coriander – done). The curry chef can knock all these up, simultaneously, in five pans, within minutes. Rice is pre-cooked, breads and tandoori items made to order by a different specialist. And, hey presto, your order for two! The curryhouse menu can be very long, with a huge variety of dishes, sometimes numbered, sometimes heat-graded, mild, medium and hot, hotter, hottest, and any dish is available in meat, poultry, prawn, king prawn, and most vegetables, too. That's the formula of the standard curry house. Just because this is not authentic does not make it bad. It can be done well. This Guide is full of many such restaurants, which are listed as **You Say OK**.

G

GARAM MASALA 'Garam' means 'hot' or 'warming' but not in the coincidence of Ehglish 'hot' meaning piquancy. Rather, it refers to temperature, and specifically to Ayruvedic (*qv*) philosophy, where certain foods 'warm' the body, while others 'cool' it. 'Masala' means 'mixture of spices', in this case a combination of whole, aromatic spices including pepper which the mixture must coincidentally contain to achieve a little piquancy, (but never chilli or turmeric). It is much-loved in northern Indian cookery, which originated in Moghul (*qv*) Kashmir (*qv*) and is added towards the end of cooking in certain curries. It can also be used in curry masala mixes, and as a sprinkler on, say Onion Bhajis. Balti (*qv*) also originating in Kashmir, uses a type of Garam Masala to achieve its fundamental aromatic taste. There are as many recipes for Garam Masala as there are cooks who use it. Some Kashmiri recipes use up to 20 spices. However to get the best from Garam Masala, heat must be applied and the spices should be roasted, cooled and ground to release the essential oils (the analogy being roasting coffee). All factory Garam Masalas, ergo those used at most currryhouses are not roasted, thus depriving the diner of a fine home-made taste. *See also Ayurvedic Food and Masala.*
GHEE Clarified butter used in high-quality north Indian cooking.
GOBI Cauliflower.
GOL GOPPA (*see Pani Puri*)
GOSHT Meat, usually referring to lamb or mutton.
GULAB JAMAN An Indian dessert of cake-like texture. Balls of curd cheese paneer, or flour and milk-powder, are deep-fried to golden-brown and served in light syrup.
GURDA Kidney. Gurda Kebab is marinated kidney, skewered and cooked in the tandoor.

H

HANDI or HAANDI A traditional round-bellied earthenware or metal, narrow-necked cooking pot used in many parts of India, and especially Gujarat. Pottery shards have dated the design to 2500BC.
HASINA KEBAB Pieces of chicken breast, lamb or beef marinated in a yoghurt and spice (often tandoori) mixture, then skewered and barbecued/baked, interspersed with onions, capsicum and tomato. Turkish in origin. *See Shaslik.*

I

IDLI Rice-and lentil-flour steamed cake, about the size and shape of a hockey puck, served with Sambar (*qv*) a light lentil curry. South Indian in origin. (*Pictured top of next page*)
IMLI Tamarind. A very sour, date-like fruit used in cooking or chutney which is of purée consistency, sweetened with sugar.
INDIAN In 1947, the subcontinent of India was partitioned. To cut a long story short, in Britain and the West we still generally erroneously refer to our curry restaurants as 'Indian'. In fact, over 85% are Bangladeshi, with only around 8% run by Indians and 8% run by Pakistanis. There is a smattering of Nepalese and Sri Lankan restaurants, and only a couple of Afghan and a single Burmese restaurant in Britain. *See Formula Curries.*

J

JALEBI An Indian dessert. Flour, milk-powder and yoghurt batter are squeezed through a narr--ow funnel into a deep-frier to produce golden, curly, crisp rings. Served in syrup..
JAL FREZI Sautéed or stir-fried meat or chicken dish, often with lightly cooked onion, garlic, ginger, green pepper and chilli.
JEERA Cumin or cummin seed or powder, hence Jeera Chicken, the signature dish at Madhu's Southall.
JINGRI or CHINGRI Prawns of any size.

K

KALIA Traditional Bengali/Bangladeshi meat, poultry or fish dish in which red-coloured ingredients are mandatory, especially red chillies and tomatoes. *See Rezala.*
KARAHI A two-handled hemispherical Indian kitchen dish. Some restaurants reheat curries in small karahis and serve them straight to the table with the food sizzling inside. *See also Curry and Balti.*
KASHMIR CHICKEN Whole chicken stuffed with minced meat. *See Kurzi.*
KASHMIR CURRY Curryhouse pastiche where cream, coconut and/or lychees, and/or pineapple and/or banana are added to a medium curry bse.
KEBAB Kebab means 'cooked meat' in ancient Turkish, traditionally cooked over charcoal, in a process over 4,000 years old. It was imported to India by the Muslims centuries ago. Shish, incidentally, means 'skewer'. *See Boti, Hasina, Nargis, Shami and Sheek Kebab.*
KEEMA Minced meat, e.g. as used in curry. *See also Mattar.*
KOFTA Balls made from ground meat, poultry or fish/shellfish or vegetables, then deep-fried and/or simmered in a curry sauce.
KORMA Probably derived from the Persian 'Koresh', a mild stew. The Moghuls made it very rich, using cream, yoghurt and ground almonds, fragranced with saffron and aromatic spices. But, traditionally, Kormas need not be mild. In Kashmir a popular dish

The A to Z of the Curry Menu

is the 'Mirchwangan Korma', red in colour because it is full of Kashmiri chillies. To the curry house, Korma is terminology for the mildest curry, sometimes made sickly by the overuse of creamed coconut block, cream and nuts.
KULCHA Small leavened bread. Can be plain or stuffed, e.g. Onion Kulcha.
KULFI Indian ice cream. Traditionally made in cone-shaped moulds in vanilla, pistachio or mango flavours.
KURZI Leg of lamb or whole chicken given a long marination, then a spicy stuffing, e.g. rice and/or Keema (q.v.), then slowly baked until tender. This is served with 'all the trimmings'. It is many a curry house's Special, requiring 24 hours' notice (because of the long preparation) and a deposit to make sure you turn up to eat it). Often for two or four, it is good value. Also called Khurzi, Kasi, Kozi, Kushi, etc. *See also Murgh Masala*.

L

LASSI A refreshing drink made from yoghurt and crushed ice. The savoury version is Lassi Namkeen and the sweet version is Lassi Meethi.

M

MACCI or MACHLI Fish. Today, fresh exotic fish from India and Bangladesh are readily available and, when a restaurant offers them, you have the chance of getting a truly authentic dish.
MADRAS You will not find a Madras Curry in Madras. It does not exist. But the people of the south eat hot curries, firing them up with as many as three different types of chilli – dry, powdered and fresh – added to the cooking at different stages. As the Brits got used to their early formula curries *(q.v.)*, they began to demand them hotter. With no time to add chillies in the traditional way, one of the pioneer curry house chefs simply added one teaspoon of extra-hot chilli powder to his normal sauce, along with tomato and ground almonds, and ingeniously called it 'Madras'. The name stuck. *See also Chilli, Phal and Vindaloo*.
MAHARANI DHAL Classic north Indian dish, held in such respect that its name means 'lentil queen'. It obtains its gorgeous dark golden brown colour by the use of urid (dhal (black lentils), its flavour from butter-ghee and cream, and its texture by slow-cooking in a heavy pot for at least three hours.
MAKHANI/MAKHNI/ MAHKNI Butter. *See Murgh Makhani and next entry*.
MAKAHANI DHAL The invention of this dish is claimed by Moti Mahal *(see WC2)*. It is a development of

Maharani Dhal *(qv)* with the same black lentils, cream and cooking time. In place of ghee, butter itself (makhni) is used and tomato purée provides its distinctive taste and chestnut-brown colour. The dish is a real test of a chef's skill. It is never seen at curryhouses, but when it is on a menu, try it.
MALAI Cream. So Malai Sabzi Kofta, for example, means vegetable balls in a creamy curry gravy. *See Rasmalai*.
MALAYA The curries of Malaysia are traditionally cooked with coconut, chilli and ginger. In the Indian restaurant, however, they are usually based on the Korma *(q.v.)*, to which is added pineapple and/or other fruit.
MASALA A mixture of spices which are cooked with a particular dish, e.g. Garam Masala *(q.v.)*. It can be spelt a remarkable number of ways – Massala, Massalla, Masalam, Mosola, Moshola, Musala, etc.
MASALA DOSA *See Dosa*.
MATTAR Green peas. So Mattar Paneer is peas with Indian cheese, Keema Mattar is mince meat curry with peas, etc.
MEDIUM CURRY S*ee Formula Curries*.
METHI Fenugreek, pronounced 'maytee'. Savoury spice. The seed is important in masalas. The leaves, fresh or dried, are used particularly in Punjabi dishes eg Methi Gosht. At the curry house, the flavour of these leaves predominates in their Dhansak.
MOGLAI Cooking in the style of the Moghul emperors, whose chefs took Indian cookery to the heights of gourmet cuisine centuries ago. Few restaurateurs who offer Moglai dishes come anywhere near this excellence. Authentic Moglai dishes are expensive and time-consuming to prepare. Can also be variously spelt Muglai, Mhogulai, Moghulai, Moghlai, etc.
MULLIGATAWNY A Tamil vegetable consommée (molegoo pepper, tunny water), adapted by the Raj to create the thick, meat-based British soup.
MURGH Chicken.
MURGH MASALA/MURGH MASSALAM Whole chicken, marinated in yoghurt and spices for hours, then stuffed and roasted. *See Kurzi*.
MURGH MAKHANI A 16th century Moghal dish. Chicken is cooked in butter ghee, in a creamy, lightly spiced red sauce, nowadays using tomato. This was the derivation of CTM *(qv)*.

N

NAGA Until 2000, the hottest known chilli was a Mexican Habenero variant, Red Savina. Well known for centuries to Bengalis and Bangladeshis was the Naga aka Bhut Jolokia or Tezpur chilli growing in the Indian Assam and

Bengali hills, which had never measured for heat-level. It took British growers to confirm the chilli's status as the world's hottest. Scientists found Red Savina measured half the heat level of Naga. Put into perspective, Tabasco measures 25 times less and those fat chillies at the supermarket, 200 times less. Nagas and other chillies can be bought from <www.peppersbypost.biz>. Naga curries are increasingly available at the UK curryhouse, and have a totally different characteristic to Phal, and should be avoided by those not used to 'heat'. Ask at the Asian stores for the new Bangladeshi pickle called Mr Naga, though this is 'diluted' with onion, etc and is less hot then the actual chilli.
NAN/NAAN Pronounced 'narn', it is flat, leavened bread, usually made from plain white flour (maida) dough, but sometimes from wholemeal flour (atta). After the dough rises, it is rolled out and baked in the tandoor *(q.v.)*. It is teardrop-shaped and about 20-25cm (8-10 inches) long. It must be served fresh and hot. As well as Plain Nan, there are many variations involving the addition of other ingredient(s). Keema Nan is stuffed with a thin layer of minced, spiced kebab meat. Peshwari Nan is stuffed with almonds and/or cashew nuts and/or raisins. Garlic, onion, pineapple, tomato, indeed anything, can be added. Double- or treble-sized Karak, Elephant or Family Nans are offered at Balti houses to share to scoop your food up with.
NARGIS KEBAB Indian scotch egg – spiced, minced meat around a hard-boiled egg.
NIRAMISH A Bangladeshi mixed vegetable, often cooked without garlic, and spiced only with Panch Phoran – Indian Five Spice mixture.

O

OOONBARIOU/UMBERIO/OBERU Parsee vegetable dish which evolved from Undhui *(qv)* Gujarat baked vegetables using root vegetables slow-baked for several hours in a charcoal-lined pit..
OOTHAPPAM *See Uthappam*.

P

PAAN Betel leaf folded, samosa-fashion, around a stuffing of aniseed, betel nut, sunflower seeds, lime paste, etc. and eaten in one mouthful, as a digestive after a meal. The leaf is bitter, the mouth-feel coarse and the taste acquired; but more acceptable (to Westerners) small spices and seeds (supari), sometimes sugar-coated in lurid colours, are often offered by the curry house after the meal.

PAKORA The true pakora is a whole piece of vegetable, lightly coated in gram-flour batter and deep-fried, although at the curry house it is to all intents and purposes the same as the Bhajia (q.v.).

PALAK See Sag

PANI PURI or GOL GOPPA are one and the same things, the latter name used in Bengal and the East and the former in Gujarat and Mumbai. They are mouth-sized puffed-up crispy biscuits, served with Jeera Pani (water spiced predominantly with chilli, black salt and cumin water) and Aloo Chaat (potato curry) at Bhel Puri (qv) houses. To eat the correct way, gently puncture the top of the biscuit, pour in some Jeera Pani, and pop into the mouth in one. Chew and then add some Aloo Chaat.

PANEER Cheese made from milk by separating the whey (liquid) from the curds (solids) which, when compressed, can be crumbled, chopped, fried, tandoori-baked and/or curried (see Mattar). In Bengali, Paneer is called 'Chhana', not to be confused with the lentil 'Chana' (q.v.).

PAPADAM/PAPAD Thin lentil-flour wafers. When cooked (deep-fried or baked) they expand to about 20cm (8 ins). They must be crackling crisp and warm when served. If not, send them back and deduct points from that restaurant. They come either plain or spiced, with lentils, pepper, garlic or chilli. There are many ways to spell papadam, using any combination of the vowels 'a', 'o' and 'u', and double 'p' and double 'd'. But, despite many people calling it so, it should never be referred to as a pampadom.

PARATHA Brown-flour dough combined with ghee (q.v) thinly rolled out and folded over itself to create a layered disc, like puff pastry. Pan-fried to create a soft unleavened bread.

PASANDA Meat, usually lamb, which traditionally is thinly beaten, then cooked in a creamy curry gravy to which some chefs add red wine. The dish and wine were both true treats of Moghul emperor Jehangir who, though Muslim, blessed the wine to make it 'holy water' thus circumventing the rules of Islam. Then he and his court proceeded to drink themselves legless while enjoying this dish.

PATIA Restaurant curry with a thick, dark, red sweet and sour sauce. Based on a Parsee prawn or fish dish.

PATRA A Gujarati speciality, in which colcasia (patra) leaves are rolled in gram-flour paste, like a Swiss roll, then steamed, sliced and deep-fried.

PESHAWARI NAN See Nan.

PHAL The hottest curry, also known as a Bangalore Phal, invented by the British curry house restaurateurs. See Naga.

PICKLE Pungent, hot, pickled vegetables essential to an Indian meal. The most common are lime, mango, brinjal and chilli. Though rarely seen at the restaurant, meat and game are made into traditional and very delicious Rajasthani pickles.

PODINA/PUDINA Mint. A fresh chutney, puréed from fresh mint, chilli and onion.

PRAWN BUTTERFLY Usually a large or giant king prawn, cut so that it opens out and flattens, butterfly-shaped, marinated in spices and immersed in gram-flour batter, then deep-fried. A curry house invention, whose name could also have derived from 'batter-fry'.

PRAWN PURI Prawns in a hot sauce served on a Puri (qv) bread. Although sometimes described as Prawn Purée it is not puréed prawn or anything esle.

PULLAO Ancient Persia invented Pollou, with rice and meat and/or vegetables, cooked together in a pan until tender. Following Muslim invasions it evolved into Turkey's Pilav, Greece's Pilafi, Spain's Paella and, of course, India's Pullao. In many curry houses, the ingredients are mixed after cooking, to save time. (See Biriani.) There are many other ways to spell it: Pillau, Puloa, Pillar, Pilaw, Polaw, etc.

PULLAO RICE The restaurant name for rice fried with aromatic spices, usually with rice grains coloured with yellow and/or red and/or green food colouring.

PURI Unleavened wholemeal bread: rolled out flat to about 10cm (4 ins) in diameter, it puffs up when deep-fried, and should be served at once.

Q

QUAS CHAWAL/KESAR CHAVAL Rice fried in ghee (q.v.), flavoured and coloured with saffron (kesar).

QORMA Non 'u' Kashmiri translation.

R

RAAN is an absolute Moghul delight. Leg of lamb or beef is pared of fat, then marinaded in a paste made from yoghurt, oil, lemon juice, garlic, ginger, red chillies, fresh coriander leaves, ground almond and aromatic spices for at least 12 hours. It is then slow-roasted until so tender that the flesh literally falls off the bone. See Raan restaurant, SE10

RAITA A cooling chutney of yoghurt on its own or with a vegetable, e.g. cucumber or mint (sometimes called Tandoori Sauce) to accompany papadoms, the starter or the main course. See also Dahi.

RASGULLA Walnut-sized balls or ovals of paneer (q.v.), or semolina and cream cheese, cooked in syrup (literally meaning 'juicy balls'). They are white or pale gold in colour and served cold or warm. See Rasmalai.

RASHMI KEBAB Kebab of minced meat inside an egg net or omelette.

RASMALAI Rasgullas cooked in cream, served cold. Very rich, very sweet. They are the white spheres in the picture. To their right is Gulab Jaman, below is Rasgulla. Above are Indian sweetmeats, Burfi and Halva, In the bowl is Shrikand, the Bombay yoghurt sweet syllabub (all qv).

REZALA Bengali/Bangladeshi speciality. Lamb cooked in evaporated milk, rich and subtly spiced, it would be milder than Korma except that green chillies are mandatory. Traditionally no red- or orange-coloured ingredients should be used. See Kalia.

RHOGAN JOSH GOSHT Literally meaning 'lamb in red gravy'. Traditionally, in Kashmir, lamb is marinated in yoghurt, then cooked with ghee, aromatic spices and natural red colorants. It should be creamy but not hot. The curry house version omits the marinade and the aromatics, and uses tomato and red pepper to create a red appearance. There are many ways of spelling it – Rogon, Roghan, Rugon, Rugin, Rowgan, Ragan, etc, Just, Joosh, Juice, Jash, etc, Goosht, Goose, Gost, etc.

ROTI Generic word for Indian bread of any type, rolled out into thin flat discs. Often if you ask for it you will get a chupatti (qv).

S

SABZI Vegetable.

SAG/SAAG Spinach, also called 'Shak' in Bengali, Palak in Punjabi and Rai, although the latter is mustard leaves. Lalshak is delicious red spinach.

SAMBAL/SAMBOL A Malaysian and Sri Lankan term describing the chutneys accompanying a meal. Sometimes referred to on the Indian menu. Malaysians also refer to Sambal as a dish of various ingredients cooked in a hot sauce, e.g. prawn sambal.

SAMBAR A hot and spicy, runny, almost consommé-like south Indian vegetable curry made from lentils and exotic vegetables, such as the drumstick. In the Manchester/Merseyside area, the curry houses have a dish called 'Samber'. It bears no resemblance to Sambar, except that lentils and a lot of chilli powder are added to meat, chicken or prawn curry.

SAMOSA Celebrated triangular, deep-fried meat or vegetable patties, supreme as starters or snacks.

SHAMI KEBAB Round minced meat rissoles.

SHASHLIK KEBAB Shashlik in Armenia

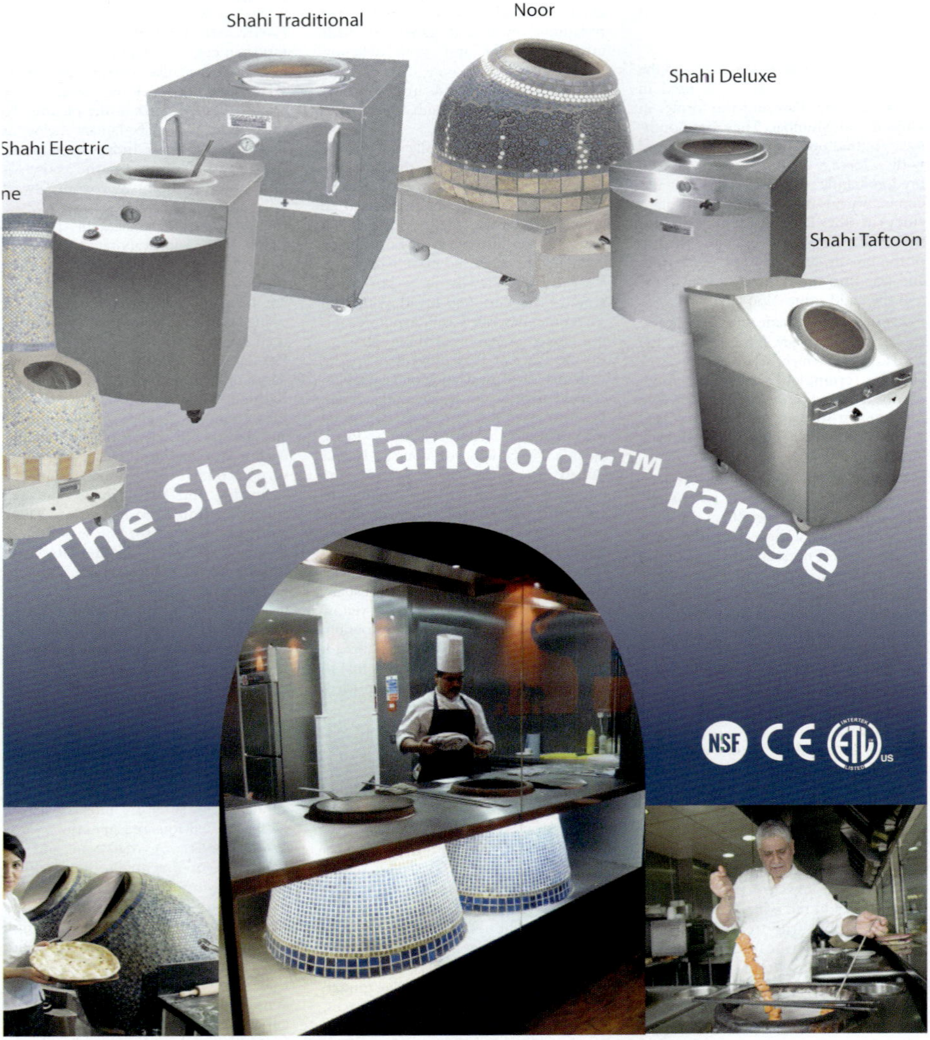
Shahi Traditional
Noor
Shahi Deluxe
Shahi Electric
Shahi Taftoon
The Shahi Tandoor™ range
NSF
CE
ETL LISTED US

The A to Z of the Curry Menu

means 'to grill'. Cubes of skewered lamb or chicken are marinated (in an oil, garlic and chilli mixture) then grilled. *See Hasina*.

SHATKORA A Bangladeshi citrus fruit, the size of a grapefruit but sharper in flavour. Can be eaten fresh or used in cooking.

SHEEK/SEEKH KEBAB Literally means (from Turkish 'shish') a skewer. Spiced minced meat, usually coloured lurid red at the curry house, from proprietary tandoori/kebab paste irradiated with chemical food colouring *(qv)*, is moulded onto the skewer, then baked in the tandoori and grilled.

SHRIKAND A yoghurt/cream syllabub from Mumbai, infused with saffron, nuts and cardamom.

SINGARA Bengali Samosa *(qv)*.

STANDARD CURRY *See Formula Curries.*

T

TANDOORI An ancient style of cooking, which originated in the rugged north-west frontier of India (now Pakistan). It gets its name from the cylindrical clay oven, the tandoor, with its opening at the top, fired with charcoal in its base. Originally the ingredients were chicken and lamb, marinated for many hours in a spiced yoghurt-based sauce, traditionally slightly reddened with red chilli, then skewered and baked in the tandoor. Now the curry house product also includes fish, prawns, paneer *(qv)* and vegetables. But its lurid red or orange colour is created by the unnecessary use of tartrazine food colouring *(qv)* in proprietary ready-to-use pastes. *See Boti Kebab, Nan Bread and Raita and Tikka.* TARKA South Indian 'tempering' technique, whereby items are fried and placed on hot, wet dishes at table to create a sizzle. The ingredeints vary from recipe to recipe and can include onion, garlic, curry leaves, dry lentils, spice seeds such as cumin and mustard seeds, dry red chillies and coconut shards.

TARKA DHAL A tasty, spicy lentil dish, the Dhal being massoor (red) lentils, cooked to a purée, to which the Tarka (in this case crispy, fried caramelized onion and/or garlic) is added. It should taste very slightly burnt (from the Tarka), and be subtly, yet decisively, spiced, neither too thick nor too thin.

TAVA A heavy steel, rimless, flattish frying pan, used to cook items such as Parathas.

TARTRAZINE *See Food Colouring.*

THALI/TALI A round tray with a low rim, averaging about 34cm (12in) in diameter. It is a plate on which an entire meal is served. Dry items (rice, bread and even dry curries) are placed directly on the thali. Wet portions (curries, dhals, soups and sweets, etc) are placed in matching serving bowls (tapelis), and they too reside on the thali. They were made of gold for the Moghul emperors, silver for the Maharajas, and stainless steel for the rest of us. To be found at certain restaurants serving 'special' meals.

TIKKA Literally, a small piece. For example, Chicken Tikka is a filetted chunk of chicken, marinated (see Tandoori), skewered and baked in the tandoor. Traditionally, the marinade is identical to Tandoori marinade, and cooks a naturally russet brown colour. Proprietary Tikka paste, as used in the curry house, is lurid orange or yellow because of the tartrazine *(qv)* it contains.

TINDALOO *See Vindaloo.*

U

UNDHUI/OONDHIYA Gujarati signature dish in which chopped vegetables such as sweet potato, ratallu (purple yam), plantain, brinjal, green beans (papadi) etc are marinated in a spicy coconut paste and dry-fried in oil, often til (sesame) oil.

UPPUMA South Indian dish. Lightly fried semolina with onion & spices.

UTHAPPAM/UTHAPPAM/OOTHAPPAM South India pancakes made of rice and urid *(qv)* dhal which is soaked and ground, then allowed to ferment. The rice should be sambar (south Indian) rice, a small oval-grained variety, available at the Asian store. Traditionally the batter contains dried red chilli, ginger and onion. Recent developments include Pizza-style toppings of garlic, tomato, onion and green chilli

URID A type of lentil, with a black husk, when whole, and cream when split or polished. Available as a dhal dish in some restaurants, e.g. Maharani Dhal *(qv)*.

V

VADA/VADAI Lentil-flour spicy, savoury doughnut, enjoyed in Gujarat and south India. *See Dahi Vada.*

VARK Edible silver or gold leaf, made today in Hyderabad, but a Moghul speciality, said to be an aphrodisiac.

VINDALOO This fiery dish from Goa (pronouced vin–dar–-oo) which derived from a Portuguese dish, uses pork marinated in garlic, Goan vinegar and cooked with many chillies. At the curryhouse it is pronounced vindaloo means the second hottest dish (three spoonfuls of chilli powder), never pork and no vinegar marination. The curryhouse pastiche is always served with a chunk of potato because the Aloo (meaning garlic in Goan) means spud at the curryhouse! Also sometimes called Bindaloo or Tindaloo (even hotter). *See also Chilli, Madras and Phal.*

W

WAZWAN Kashmiri wedding feast, described in the Cuisines pages.

X

XACUTTI Pronounced Sha-cute-ee, it's a popular Goan curry, Mutton, chicken, fish or crab is cooked with grated, roasted cashew, coconut paste, red chilli, tamarind and spice masala, including one of Goa's unusual spices, dargaful (poppy petals).

Y

YAKNI A spicy mutton, or meat-based stock, also called Akhni.

Z

ZAFFRON Saffron, also known as Kesar or zafron. The stigma (stamen) of the crocus flower. Though never as expensive as gold (2008 prices are $1000 per oz gold and $180 per oz saffron) it is world's most expensive spice, because picking is is laborious and expensive.

ZEERA Alternatively called Jeera, which is cumin.

The Entries   –   An explanation of our method

There is no perfect system for laying out a nationwide restaurant Guide. Many Guides simply list their entries in town alphabetical order. The problem here is that there is no geographical relationship between each town. Cheltenham, Glocs to Chelmsford, Essex via Chelsea, SW3 is 180 miles. The method we have adopted in our Guide is to record the entries by county since most people know their British counties. We list them alphabetically. Unlike some Guides, we do not group the counties in National Regions (such as 'The Midlands' or the 'West Country', etc), since this too lacks logic. Counties are not without confusion. In some cases, their once sacrosanct borders have been altered by frequent local government tinkering. Greater Manchester is one example. When it was established as a 'Unitary Region' in 1965, it nibbled away parts of Cheshire and Lancashire. Many residents prefer to stick to these counties in their addresses, though we have adopted 'Greater Manchester' as a 'county' in this Guide. Other bodies, such as the Post Office, add to the confusion of recent years. Their postcodes are far from logical and do not follow county borders. BT also have their own system of geographical reference. It is because few people understand postcode logic, and even fewer understand phone codes, that we use the counties. Following London, we cover the English counties. With the demise of Avon (which was in any case, not a county, but a Unitary Region), we now start with Bedfordshire. Within each county, we record the relevant towns alphabetically, and within each town, we record each restaurant alphabetically. In Bedfordshire, for example, the first town we record is Arlesey, and its first restaurant is Raj Villa, and so on. Following England, we then look at the Isles and Islands, Northern Irelaand, and after some years of absence, Eire returns to this Guide. Then it's Scotland and finally Wales. We start with London, as is explained overleaf.

REFRESHINGLY SMOOTH PREMIUM BEER
COBRA
कोबरा

2013 COBRA GOOD CURRY GUIDE

THE ENTRIES

PAT CHAPMAN'S CURRY CLUB

CENTRAL LONDON

Area: British capital
Postcodes: E, EC, N, NW, SE, SW, W & WC
Population: 6.125,000

For the purpose of this Guide we define Central London as its 1870 postal districts, now known as postcodes. We run them alphabetically as follows: E, EC, N, NW, SEW, SW, W and WC. Within each individual postcode, we run numerically, starting with E1 and ending with WC2. As with all postcode logic, this is not in any geographical order. For example, W5 Ealing, shares its borders with W13, West Ealing and W3, Acton. For 95 years these postcodes comprised all of London. In 1965 Greater London, (GL) was established. It includes these postcodes and expanded its borders, absorbing Middlesex and parts of Essex, Hertfordshire, Kent and Surrey (shown in lilac in the drawing below). For GL (Greater London) towns/boroughs in these areas, please see the relevant county (Essex, Herts. Kent, Middlesex and Surrey) – see list on page 9.

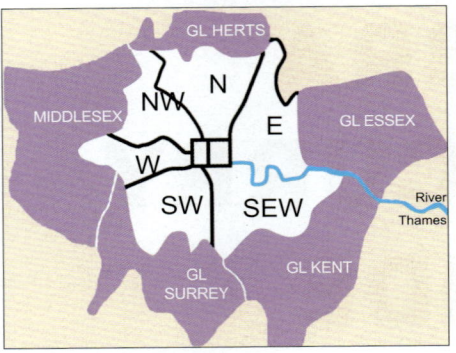

Greater London covers 1579 km² (609 sq. mi) and had in 2006, an estimated population of 7,500,000. The highest point is Westerham Heights, in the North Downs on the Kent / SE London border, at 245 metres. The River Thames flows west to east through central London, and forms the natural boundary between E and SE London and Essex and Kent

London E

Area: East London
Postcodes: E1 to E18
Population: 1.150,000

London E1

Brick Lane – Banglatown

Once predominantly Jewish, and bustling with tailors, salt-of-the-earth street markets and cab drivers, (to emphasise its roots you'll still find a 24 hr fresh-baked bagel shop at 159 where cabbies queue for sustenance) the long and narrow Brick Lane, has, since 1971, become home to the country's largest Bangladeshi community. Running north between Shoreditch and Aldgate East tube stations, it is now called Banglatown, indicating its proliferation of cheap and cheerful curry cafés, snack bars, restaurants and provisions shops, run by the thriving community. Some of these establishments have remained fairly spartan, and unlicensed (you can BYO). Others have redecorated and become licensed. We're not convinced that a Balti house is PC on the street, but there is one. But the curry-hungry can get breakfast from 8am here (Sweet & Spice, no 40). The late arrivals can get into Shampan until 2.30am. Many other on the Lane are open all day. Here are your favourites:

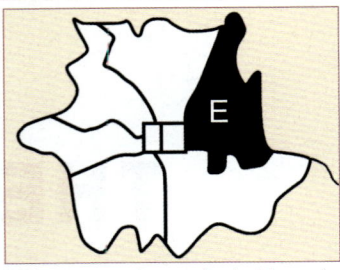

SPLENDIDLY INDIAN, SUPERBLY SMOOTH

BENGAL CUISINE
12 Brick Lane, E1 6RF
020 7377 8405   www.bengalcuisine.net

'Continues to be my favourite on the Lane. Buy Rahid's privilege card and you get a 10% discount on all meals, and notes of functions, special evenings etc.' BF. Onion Bhaji £2.50.Curries from £6.95. Popadoms 50p Delivery: 3-mile radius. Noon - Mdnt non stop, daily. *Branch: Taja, E1.*

CAFE NAZ   TOP 100
46-48 Brick Lane, E1   020 7247 0234

Naz, or 'pride in Urdu. Café Naz occupies the 1930's Mayfair Cinema building which became the Naz Cinema in the 60s, showing Asian films and visited by Dilip Kumar, the Clark Gable of the Indian film industry. Muquim Ahmed, Brick Lane's first millionaire, bought the failing cinema in 1974 shortly after arriving in Britain from Bangladesh. Attendances declined as home video gained popularity and he was obliged to close it down. It lay dormant until Muquim opened Café Naz on the site in 1993. Its immediate popularity was anchored by good cooking and service with very experienced crew including Chefs above average chefs from the top hotels in the subcontinent. The modern decor was new to Brick Lane (though now the norm) and Naz became a hit with city workers at lunch and dinner. The menu provides a wealth of unusual choice. Starters include Handni Chicken Tikka (spiced morsels of chicken cooked in tandoor), £3.95; Panni Puri (crispy, hollow wheat balls, served with chick peas and tamarind sauce), £4.25; Paneer Tikka (cubes of cheese marinated in tikka sauce and prepared in clay oven), £4.95 Mains include: Garlic Chilli King Prawn (cooked with green chillies and fresh garlic, blended with onion and capsicum), £12.25; Chicken Shaslick (diced chicken grilled in tandoor with capsicum and onions), £9.50; Dhal makhni (lentils slow cooked overnight on top of the clay oven, finished with tomato and cream), £7.25 (expensive for dhal. But a real test of skill to get right and the reason why this dish is not seen on the curryhouse menu); Gosht Kata Masala (lamb with chopped onion, sliced ginger, a touch of garlic and mild garam masala), £9.50; Fish Mahikli (cod fish filled with mustard and coconut sauce), £14.95; Veg Dosa (a large crispy rice-batter pancake filled with mutton / chicken served with coconut chutney & sambar), £12.25, a Café Naz signature dish, again not seen on the curryhouse menu because, 1 it is south Indian and 2 it needs specialist cooking gear and skill. Hyderabadi Achar Ghost (chunks of lamb slow-cooked on the bone and served in a rich curry sauce with limes and spices). Takeaway Service. Free Delivery over £12 within 2 miles. Mon to Weds: 12 - 12/ Thur & Fri: 12 to 1am; Sat: 6 - 1; Sun: 12 - 3 & 6 -12. *Branch: Cambridge.*

Welcome to the 2013 edition of the Cobra Good Curry Guide.

We trust it will enhance your curry dining.

We need your opinions for our future editions.

Check out our new website for the latest, most up-to-date reviews.

www.thegoodcurryguide.co.uk

CINNAMON
134 Brick Lane, E1 6RL
020 7377 5526   www.cinnamonbricklane.co.uk

The refurbishment has gone down well with its followers. Magnolia walls, brown chairs, white cloths red artwork, red carpet, air-conditioning and downlighters, and a costly sound system,. It's all a far cry from the utilitarian style of the Brick Lane of yore. .And to their surprise there's more. The rather large basement has been added to the assets with magnolia walls, red and white chairs and wooden floors, so the capacity has more than doubled. All the standard Indian dishes are available on the menu, at sensible prices and there are some interesting specials all at £8.95... Lamb Bhuna Naga is the immensely popular ultra hot Bengali chilli in "chef's special sauce".Mr Naga pickle is the base, and if you like very hot, this is for you; Lamb or Chicken Shatkora the special citrus vegetable, available in Bangladesh in the Sylhet region, cooked in a medium thick sauce; Modhucash Chicken is a unique mild, combination of chicken, cashew nuts and honey. Takeaway orders taken online. Noon - Mdnt daily.

CITY SPICE   TOP 100
138 Brick Lane, E1 6RU
020 7247 4222   www.cityspicebricklane.co.uk

Heading north up the Lane you have to pass by all the rivals until you are just short of the brewery bridge. On the corner of Brick Lane and Woodseer Street is the fully licensed City Spice. Brick Lane's ever popular Sunday market is held in the former Truman's Brewery building between 10am and 5pm every Sunday and Sheeba is open all day, making it just the place to enjoy your post or pre market curry. You can enjoy a high quality, good value meal whatever their budget. City Spice was formerly Shampan 2 and it retains that incarnation's dark blue exterior. In daylight the ground floor room benefits from twin aspect windows. Decor is magnolia walls with loads of interesting artwork. Chairs are a dignified classic look and the day we were there owner Abdul Ahmed was proudly showing off his new bar in the corner. More seats (brown and modern) are downstairs, along with more artwork. The menu is formula with some nice specials. Starters include Stuffed Capsicum, (with curried vegetables) £3.50; Paneer tikka (tandooried), £3.50. Tandoori Lamb Chops marinated in yoghurt, garlic, ginger, fresh lemon leaves & grilled), £4.50. Garlic mushroom (fresh garlic and mushroom mixed with olive oil, salt and pepper), £4.50; Tandoori Duck Tikka (marinated with herbs & spices, cooked in the tandoori oven), £5.25. Unusual mains include Nargise Kufta (India's Scotch Egg with boiled egg and Keema mincemeat cooked with light spices, fresh herbs, onion and green pepper), £10.50. Ginger meat (slices of lamb tikka shallow fried with sliced onions, green chillies, ginger paste and special herbs), £10.50. Tandoori Duck Tikka Shashlick (duck marinated with freshly mixed herbs and spices, barbecued with onions, green pepper and tomatoes), £11.50. There are always Bangladeshi fish dishes on offer but you may have to ask for them. Ask too for your discount if you show them this Guide. Booking is advisable at peak times. Mon - Thur: 12 - 3 & 5:30-12.30. Fri: 12-3 & 5.30 - 2am. Sun: Noon - Mdnt.

YOU SAY OK BRICK LANE
Standard Curries at fair prices

ALADIN 132 **BRICK LANE** Basic curry house with funky red tables. Sun to Thur: 12 - 24/ Fri & Sat: 12 - 01 .

EASTERN EYE 63A Brick Lane, E1 6QL 020 7247 8643 Sun - Wed: 12 - Mdnt. Thur -Sat: 12 - 01.

NAZRUL 130 Brick Lane, E1 6RU 020 7247 2505 Sun to Thur: 12 - 11pm. Friday to Saturday: Noon - Mdnt.

PAPADOMS, 94 Brick Lane, E1 6RL 020 7377 9123 www.papadomsbricklane.co.uk

SAFFRON 53 Brick Lane, E1 6PU 020 3551 2350/ 020 7247 2633 no website.

STANDARD BALTI HOUSE, 71 Brick Lane, E1 6QL 020 8166 2649 www.standardbaltihouse.co.uk 180 seater opened 1989. Mon & Tues 1130 -2.30/ 5.30 -Mdnt. Wed - Sun 11.30 - 24.

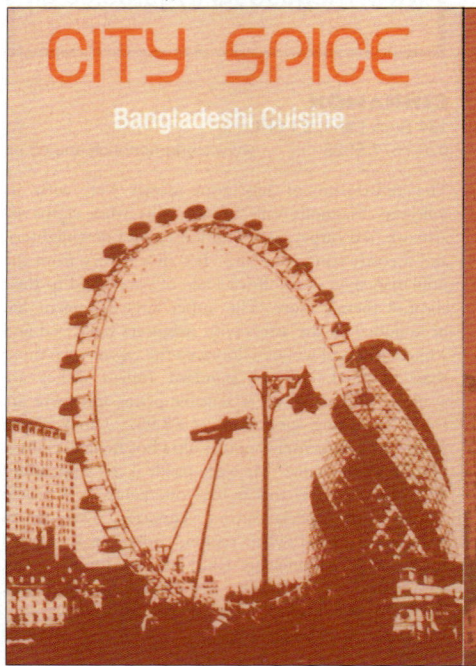

CITY SPICE
Bangladeshi Cuisine

CITY SPICE
138 Brick Lane
London E1 6RU
T: 020 7247 1012 / 4222
F: 020 7247 3330

Opening Hours
Mon-Thur 12 Noon-3pm / 5.30pm-12.30am
Fri 12 Noon-3pm / 5.30pm-2am
Sat 12 Noon-2am & Sun 12 Noon-12am

Private Party Room Available
For 70 People

www.cityspice.co.uk

SPLENDIDLY INDIAN, SUPERBLY SMOOTH

MUHIB
INDIAN RESTAURANT
EST 1992 — BRICK LANE

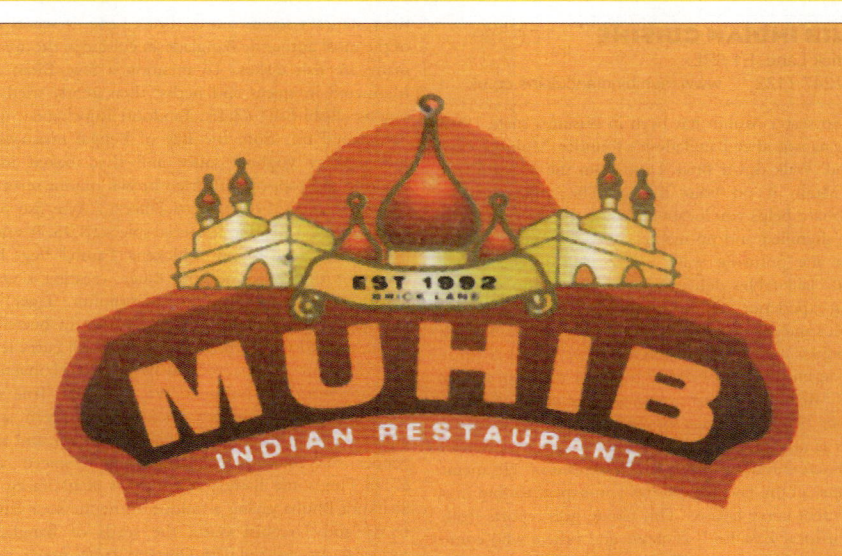

UP TO 92 PEOPLE CAPACITY, FOR YOUR EVENT REQUIREMENT PLEASE CALL US FOR FURTHER INFO

WE PROVIDE OUTDOOR CATERING FOR FUNCTIONS AND EVENTS

TRY OUR FAST AND EFFICIENT HOME AND OFFICE DELIVERY SERVICE

FOR ALL ENQUIRIES PLEASE CALL
T: 020 7247 7122

MUJIB INDIAN CUISINE   TOP 100
73 Brick Lane, E1 6RL
020 7247 7122   www.muhibindiancuisine.co.uk

The 86 seater Muhib has been in business since 1992 and is named after Bangladesh's founder. Muhib is easy to find. Walk down Brick Lane from the Aldgate end and Mujib is on your right. The canary yellow headboard helps you locate it. Inside the atmosphere is calm, dignified and up-market. Gold framed pictures adorn the primrose walls. The elegant chairs and smartly laid tables deliver a comfortable and relaxing dining experience. Owner Elias Miah is usually on hand to greet and advise his guests about the menu. Service is gracious and efficient. Chef Tonjob Ali takes great pride in ensuring his brigade turn out the best quality food. *"We use the freshest ingredients and the finest spices"*, he said, *"but it is how you use them that counts. I want my diners to taste the individual flavours in our secret recipes Unlike others we don't use any artificial colours."* His menu contains all the favourite dishes you expect to find in a competent curry house. This Guide gets reports from regular local East End clientele and others who come from as far away as Kent, Essex and Surrey. There are 26 starters, including the unusual Nargis Kebab £3.95, a kind of spicy Scotch Egg and Diana Vegetable £4.95, spicy mixed vegetables stuffed in a pastry case and deep-fried and served with an omelette. The range of Tandooris and Baltis is extensive, and Bangladesh Fish appears in a number of dishes from £6.95. Curry dishes range from mild to hot and from just £4.50, and the chefs can make you any dish on request. There are some unusual gems amongst the specials, which the chefs especially enjoy cooking. Try Shahi Mogul £10.95, Tandoori Chicken cooked with Keema (mince) in a creamy curry sauce with Vegetable Mint Korai £7.95, or Lamb Juliet £10.95 with brandy. Then there is Lamb Chop Shatkora, £9.95, the latter being a gentle citrus vegetable. *"Muhib House Biriani at £10.95 with Chicken, Lamb and Prawn Tikka goes well with Deshi Dal £3.50, lentils with fried black chillies and garlic. And Muhib's Stuffed Paratha £2.95 shows off the skills of the bread cook."* DBAC. House wine is £8.50, a pint of beer is £4.50. They allow BYO. No cheques accepted and Credit card min £15. Takeaway service. No home delivery. Mon to Sat 12 - 3 & 6 - 12. Sun 12 - 11. 365 days a year.

SHAMPAN
PREVIOUS AWARD WINNER & CURRENT TOP 100
79 Brick Lane, E1 6QL
020 7375 0475   www.shampanbricklane.co.uk

We rate Shampan very highly. It is a mature venue run by 'old hand' Shiraj Haque. Tthe Shampan is on the corner of Brick Lane and Hanbury Street. Way back it was once a pub (though now no name survives) so it is apt that it is fully licensed. A Shampan is a Bangladeshi canvas fishing boat. And so we have the clues to why the restaurant stands out on Brick Lane. It serves some of the most authentic Bangladeshi cuisine in the area and many are fish dishes. To mention a few: Biran Mass Marinated in spices and herbs, then gently fried with onions (Rohi fish) £3.45. Tandoori Rupchanda, whole flat shaped fish from the Bay of Bengal marinated in special spicy yoghurt sauce and then baked in the tandoor and topped with fried brown onions served on a sizzler, £9.95. Fish Sylhetti Jalfrezi, Ayre fish pieces cooked with aubergine & special spices £8.95. It's not all fish. Tetul Tanga Bujon (Chicken/ Lamb/ Veg) Kofta cooked with a picy and sour sauce, creating a unique flavour, £7.95. King Prawn Cornofuli, Tiger King prawns from the Bay of Bengal, tossed in butter and garlic, cooked with herbs, onions and fresh curry leaves, £12.95. Lamb Acharia, pickled-flavoured dish in a tangy, medium hot rich sauce, £7.95. Chicken Tofa Goa, roasted pieces of chicken cooked with green spices, tamarind, fresh mint, green chilli, coriander and green pepper. Served with aromatic medium spiced sauce, £7.95 Plus some Bangla veg such as Shatkora eg Beef Shatkora Bhuna giving a unique authentic sour flavour, £8.95 and Ureebisi Gatta the seeds of Bangladeshi runner beans, cooked with Chicken, lamb, prawn or fish cooked with green chilli, coriander and spices. *"I spied Aloo Chop on the menu. It's a breadcrumbed rissole made from lightly spiced mashed potato filled with tender curried lamb or chicken mince. You don't come across that very often."* RL. As well as its Bargaldeshi specials, a full range of popular curries is on the menu. Shampan is also noted for really cheap eats. Express Lunch (2 course) from £5.95. Naan wraps (Sheek Kebab, Chicken Tikka and Mixed Veg £2.99. And an Eat-in-Naan topped with CTM, salad etc for just £3.99. Branches Clifton, E1 & E14. Shampan is also noted for its long hours: 12am - 2.30am non stop, daily.

SHEBA
136, Brick Lane, E1 6RU
020 7247 7824   www.shebabricklane.com

Established in 1975, Sheba is run by Sultan Miah and family and accommodates 110 diners across two floors (street level and basement). Both floors can be booked for parties or corporate events and have a widescreen TV for presentations etc. Appetisers range in price from £3.10 to £8.95 for a mixed grill for two. Main courses run from £4.95 to £14.50. An extensive selection of vegetarian main courses and side dishes is also available. House specials include Shatkora dishes (Banglandishi citrus veg), Naga dishes made with Bangladeshi naga chillies, Sylheti seafood dishes such as Roopchanda (queen fish from the Indian ocean marinated in lemon juice with coriander sauce, tomatoes and garlic), Shim Machli with Bangladeshi green beans and Special Sylheti Jalfrezi. Among Head Chef Gulab Miah's Specialities are classic Goan Chicken Xacutti, Lobster Bengal Special and – for the very brave - the fiery hot Bollywood Blast

COBRA — SPLENDIDLY INDIAN, SUPERBLY SMOOTH

93

Real Indian Cuisine
SHEBA
Brick Lane

Family run since we opened our doors in 1975 making us one of the longest serving and most popular Brick Lane restaurants.

**Opening Times
7 days a week**
(Including bank holidays)
**Monday - Sunday
From 12 noon to
12 midnight**

See our website for our **SPECIAL OFFERS**

- Winner 2006 /7 – Chef of the Year – Brick Lane Curry Festival
- Tandoori and Balti Specialist
- The best selection of seafood dishes in Brick Lane

**SHEBA
136 Brick Lane,
London, E1 6RU
020 7247 7824**
www.shebabricklane.com

(with naga chilli, Mexican chilli, African chilli and green chilli). there is Raja Jhinga Nizami £12.95 - with mustard, green chillies, garlic, yoghurt, spring onion; Lamb Lucknow £12.50 - lamb shank or nalis as they are called in India, with its rich thick gravy and spicy carrots with aromatic herbs, cardamom essence or kewra, screw pine flowers and saffron; King Prawn Malabar £12.50, cooked with fresh green chillies, curry leaves, mustard seeds, mixed spices and coconut cream. An extremely generous 20% discount is to be had on meals if prebooked. Price Check: Popadom 80p, CTM £8.95, Pullao Rice £2.70, Plain Naan £2.40. Licensed: House wine £13.95. Service: 12.5%. Hours: Noon to Midnt.

SWEET AND SPICY
40 Brick Lane, E1 6RF
020 7247 1081   www.sweetandspicylondon.co.uk

One of the Lane's oldest (1968) seating 40 diners in a simple clean cafeteria. It's Punjabi Pakistani cuisine which is more robust food than cooked by its Bangledshi neighbours. Choose from the counter. Favourites such as Seikh Kebab or Aloo Bora for £1.45p each. Chicken Karahi or Vindaloo or Korma for £4.25 or £6.50 (large). Karahi Gosht or Madras £7.25 Chuppatis, Puris and Popadoms are all 50p each. A favourite is the CTM Roll £2.35. Specials: Halwa Puri and Chana. Set lunch, set dinner, delivered to your table. Sunday Buffet: £4.50. *'What a great restaurant. It comes across as a simple restaurant for the city commuter. It was busy when I visited. I ordered a chicken madras, with chapatti and plain rice, and it was one of the best madras curries I have eaten. The flavouring, plenty of cardamom in the dish. The restaurant was clean and lived up to the great reviews I had read prior to visiting London. £7 for everything - unbeatable prices for central London. Will return.'* DW, Keele. *'P.S: Rest assured you will continue to get my report as long as I am consuming good curries!'* Sun-Thur: 11-11. Fri-Sat: 11am-Mdnt.

Elsewhere in E1

CAFE SPICE NAMASTE   FINE DINING
AWARD WINNER & CURRENT   A LIST
16 Prescot Street, E1 8AZ
020 7488 9242   www.cafespice.co.uk

Cafe Spice Namaste (CSN) is more like a club than a straight restaurant; there's always something going on. Owners Cyrus and Parvin love it and they make every visit welcoming (Namaste means welcome) and enjoyable fun. The listed building is impressive and the warm blue, cream and brown murals create a kind of native pueblo atmosphere. The welcome is equally warm with knowlegable, informed long term staff. Cyrus himslf has boundless energy and loves talking about food. He very energetic and inventive. Easlily bored, Cyrus fills his 'spare time'(!) making the most divine pickles, see page 44, and appearing at food shows

here there and everywhere. On my last visit, on a midweek evening, CFN was buzzing. Cyrus was hosting a Slowfood group of 100 in the one room. At the same time, the restaurant was heaving in the main room. Despite it being packed, no one was hurried and Cyrus and Parvin found time to talk to us and all their diners, most of whom are clearly regulars. We spent most of the evening there, and some tables had two or more sets of diners. Such is CFN's popularity. Slowfood had ordered canapés and Cyrus sneaked samples over to us. They were inventive and delicious. They weren't on the menu, of course. In any case, the menu is frequently changed, allowing Cyrus to bring in new dishes. You will not find food like his anywhere else; nor the names of dishes. We can just give you an idea of the unusual items you might expect (with Cyrus' descriptions), eg: Beetroot & Coconut Samosa, a south Indian-style filling of diced Cheltenham beetroot blended with diced potato, tossed with freshly grated coconut and sizzled with mustard seeds, curry leaves, cumin and chilli, £5.75; Squid Dynamite, baby squid rings, marinated in fiery Goan peri-peri masala, dipped in a spiced coating of wheat, rice and white lentil flour, fried & served with a really hot red Goan style masala, £7.75; Duck Tikka a la Mrs. Matthew, breast of Barbary duck marinated Keralan-Syrian-Christian style* as created by one Mrs Matthew. It is marinated in yoghurt with tamarind extract, crushed red chilli, toasted fennel, ginger & roasted cardamom, chargrilled to medium rare, £7.95/ £15.50. [*From the

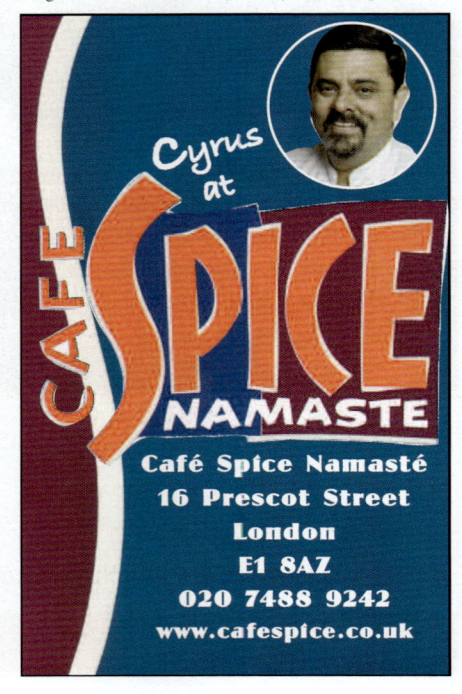

Café Spice Namasté
16 Prescot Street
London
E1 8AZ
020 7488 9242
www.cafespice.co.uk

3rd century Jews from Syria and Baghdad and Christians have traded in Kerela]; Venison Sheek Kavaab Maharaja Sailana, influenced by the late Maharaja of Sailana in Rajputana, an avid cook who created great kebabs and wrote a cookbook. It is one of the best ways to cook venison (from the Denham's estates in Suffolk) flavoured with a dual hit of fennel and star anise, £7.95 / £15.50; Springbok Bhuna: not native to India or Britain, it's lean and low in saturated fats, cholesterol & calories. Steaks are cooked 'Bhuna style', served with pullao & chunks of fried potato, £15.95; Dhaansaak: the authentic version is derived from two words "Dhaan": rice and "Saak": puréed vegetable /lentil slow-cooked with lamb on-the-bone. It is served with kachumber onion salad, with and a meat kebab placed in the brown onion rice, £14.95; Vindalho de Carne de Porco: the real Goan vind-a-lho is not the mind-blowing hot formula item, but a rich, hot, slightly sweet & sour gravy with pork (organic British Lop – rarest of the rare British breeds), served with rice, £14.95; Beef Curry A' La Dada: "Dada", Café Spice's late grand tandoor master chef, created this beef curry using Aberdeen Angus, in the Darjeeling style. It stings a bit on the tongue but is full of the flavours of blended spices combined with yoghurt and puréed onions. So popular, it's impossible to remove from the menu, served with steamed rice. £15.50. *'We were expecting great things and we were not disappointed. The building, a large Victorian red brick edifice, is impressive, very different from the nondescript street it is in, the entrance is covered with certificates and awards, as impressive. The decor reminded me more of Mexico than India. I was very pleased to see that most ingredients were free range, organic or from a named source. The descriptions were helpful as well as amusing. Wonderful light, warm Popadoms served with four excellent relishes, one was so good we bought a jar to take home'.* [We never leave without a carrier bag of at least four jars. Ed.] *'Our choices came on plain, white, modern style china, well presented. For example the Dynamite Squid was served in a tall, square dish with fried strips of one of the Indian breads, super. Desserts were rather disappointing, mostly variations on Kulfi and ice-cream with Indian flavours. Both Cyrus and his wife chatted to us for a long time. Prices higher than average Indian restaurants, but worth every penny.'* HJC. Service charge: 12.5% Takeaway service; delivery service (within 2-mile radius). Mon-Fri: 12-3 & 6.15-10.30. Closed Sundays & Bank Hols. *Branch: Mr Todiwala's Kitchen, Hilton Heathrow Airport Terminal 5, SL3 0FF.*

CHAAT — AUTHENTIC BANGLADESHI
36 Redchurch St, Shoreditch, E2 7DP
020 7739 9595   www.chaatlondon.co.uk

Newly trendy Shoreditch has a newly trendy small – 6 tables –Bangladeshi restaurant. But it's not your usual formula. It's real Bangladeshi food, albeit to a limited menu, 5 starters, 5 main dishes, 3 "moppers", rice/bread, 6 accompaniments, and finally a dip or chutney, including Naga Morich, which the menu states carries a health warning, though it's rater diluted. It's not your usual male-run venue either; Chaat (pron chart and meaning snack) is owned by a young female, Shanaz Khan. She enjoys a chat (scuse the pun) and will tell you her parents owned a curry house and she didn't understand why the food on the menu was totally different from that eaten by the family. [something this Guide's been banging on about for years. Ed]. Inexpensive. Licensed. Cards OK. Mon-Sat: 6-11.

CLIFTON
1 Whitechapel Road, E1   020 7377 5533

The iconic Clifton closed in 1997 when its owner passed away. Though unable to build on the original site, current owner Shiraj Haque of Shampan fame, wanted to resurrect the name and recreate the fine cuisine and great reputation that Clifton once had, and he found a site virtually at the entrance to Brick Lane. It opened in 2005. With its beautiful Indian and Bangladeshi art in a variety of mediums adorning the walls on both the ground and lower ground floors, the eatery has a simple but modern feel and seats 200 covers. Chef Musavir Ahmed and his kitchen team have designed an extensive menu. The open-plan kitchen on the ground floor entices passers by and customers can see and understand how the dishes are prepared. Puja Vedi, Tandoori Magazine. For menu see Shampan above. 12am to late, non stop, daily. *Branch Clifton E14.*

MERAZ CAFE   BYO
56 Hanbury Street, E1 5JL
020 7247 6999

Est 1974, just off Brick Lane so is one of the old boys, with its loyal regulars. Daily Specials. No alcohol sold but allows BYO Daily: 11 - 11.30.

EMPRESS TANDOORI
141 Leman Street, E1 8EY
020 7265 0745

Owned by Mr Islam since 1992. Good Bangladeshi choices here, including the restaurant's most popular dishes: Skiandari Lamb – marinated and roasted. Cox's Bazar Crab – soft crabs cooked with ginger, garlic, coconut and fresh herbs, garnished with cucumber and lemon. Annan's Haash – succulent roasted breast of duck, cooked in aromatic spices, served with pineapple and cherry tomatoes, fairly hot. Takeaway: 10% discount. Minimum charge: £12. Delivery. Lunch to 3pm weekdays. Dinner to 11.30pm.

HALAL RESTAURANT
2-6 St Mark Street, E1 8DJ
020 7481 1700   www.halalrest.co.uk

Established way back in 1939, making it the second oldest Indian in London and the East End's oldest.

Mahaboob Narangoli is proud of the fact there are no *"gimmicks, no fancy names and no plates made to look like works of art."* So no Baltis, no bull. Just a straightforward curryhouse in very experienced hands. *'Better than the trendy places in Brick Lane with their freebie inducements. Have been going there for over twenty years but am still regarded as a newcomer. Plenty of city retirees of older vintage still go for old time's sake. Good value for money, quiet in the evening.'* CC. Fully licensed. Mon - Fri: 12-11.30 (Sat & Sun 12 - 10.30).

LAKSHA BAY
83 Wapping Lane, Wapping. E1
020 7481 07777   www.lakshabay.co.uk

Laksha is a group of tiny islands off the south cost of India, and the restaurant's name has nothing to do with its cuisine which is mainly north Indian. The menu includes all the old favourites that we love and know, plus some items with unique names such as starters: Bangla Salad, mixed salad dressed with mustard oil, fresh chilli, coriander and lime juice £3.25; Duck Tikka, £5.60; Calamari, marinated in herbs and spices deep fried; Spicy Sardines, Lightly spiced and fried in olive oil served with mixed salad, both £4.25; Chicken Momo, a Nepalese favourite with minced chicken cooked in butter with fresh onions and coriander served with Chapati £3.95; and Mushroom Chahath, Mushroom with minced meat, mildly spiced and deep fried. £3.35. Mains at £9.95 include Pasta with Spicy King Prawns; Duck Tamarind and Lamb Shank marinated with mustard, yogurt, lemon juice, green mango powder and spice, and baked in the oven. Fish Tikka Harialy - spicy Scottish salmon charcoal roasted and cooked with coriander, chilli, garlic, ginger, fresh mint and mustard seed is £8.25; Mains at £7.95 include Captain Pathila (mild), Marinated chicken cooked in creamy sauce with nuts; Katmundu (hot - chicken or lamb), A semi dry dish prepared from our special recipe of tender meat pieces, cooked with ground onion, green peppers, fresh herbs, shredded ginger, crisp red naga chilli. Sehjani (chicken or lamb), Grilled chicken or lamb cooked with fresh cream, cheese lightly spiced. Rajeswari (chicken & lamb or prawn), Cooked Kashmiri style, in a rich onion and roasted tomato sauce. Owner Fareed Nabir and Mngr Jebu Miah will give you a discount at quieter times if you show them this Guide. Home Delivery: 5 miles, £15 minimum. Price Check: Popadoms 60p, CTM £8.50, Pullao Rice £2.10, Plain Naan £2.10. Licensed: Cobra £4.10, House wine £13.95. 12 - 2.30 (Friday lunch closed) and daily 5.30 to 11.30.

LAHORE KEBAB HOUSE   A-LIST
TOP PAKISTANI RESTAURANT
2 Umberton Street, E1 1PY
020 7488 2551   www.lahore-kebabhouse.com

Not likely to win the Location Award, Mohammed Sidique's venue has expanded onto the corner site of the ever-congested A13 Commercial Road and the rather scruffy Umberton Street. It doesn't serve alcohol so BYO (offie on the other corner sells Cobra). LKH is now an enormous 350 seater on two floors and is jointly managed by his sons Emran and Asif. It serves Pakistani food, which is gutsy and tasty and if you've not been to either Pakistan or to Sparkbrook, the LKH is what it's all

COBRA
SPLENDIDLY INDIAN, SUPERBLY SMOOTH

about. Despite Brum's claim to be the inventor of the currinary world, this gaff has been doing Balti, under what some say is its true name, Karahi – or Karrai (sic.) – since it opened in the seventies – serving darned good food, geared to Asian tastes, without compromising it for Westerners. At least that's what it used to be. But its relatively new-found glory as a lunchtime dive for the money boys and girls from the City has permeated into the evenings, and it's had an effect on management. There is no doubt the menu reflects this and items like lamb trotters, steam roast (Choosa) and quail have been taken off the menu. Shame. It's still halal though and if the squeamish can't take all this they should go elsewhere. In fact it's time for the age old caveat. If you expect curry house food, this ain't it. And expect limitations if you're a veggie. Halal mutton, chicken and quail are in the karahi, from the tandoor as tikkas or kebabs, or as, with robust lentils and fragrant rice. Lamb chops are very popular, laced with the Hot Chilli Raita, followed by their gorgeous Kheer rice pudding. Service is swift though sometimes things arrive in the wrong order, and don't expect pampering, and don't expect to pay much more than a tenner, including tip. It has a different atmosphere at different times of the day, different again at the weekend, depending on who's eating when. *'Please, please delist this restaurant from your Guide. It's already too busy, and we don't need you piling in more people.'* anon. Credit cards OK. BYO. 11.30-1am non stop, daily. Branch *Streatham High St, SW16 3QL.*

MALA
Marble Quay, St Katherine's Dock, E1W 1UH
020 7480 6356   www.malarestaurant.co.uk

Super location at one of London's oldest marinas just down the road from the Tower of London and Tower Bridge though not overlooking the latter. Mala restaurant was established in 1987 by clothing and property tycoon brothers, Charanjit and Malkit Roy Sandhuis as a place to wine and dine their clients. In 1996 they expanded the restaurant from 80-covers to 120 and built a large bar area. Today, Charanjit's son, Vinnie has taken the reign. Head Chef, Madhur Sheel gained a vast deal of experience in some of India's most respected five-star hotels, and with Bharat Singh Panwar and Kirti Singh cook dishes from across India. Familiar names are on the menu, but try the unusual, such as starters: Mullingatawny Soup, £5.50; Warm Tandoori Chicken Salad, warm tender ripped tandoori chicken, served on a bed of lettuce, red onions and olives drizzled with a tangy cocktail dressing, £6.95; and Delhi Aloo Tikki Chaat Pan grilled mashed potato cakes, stuffed with mango, served with yoghurt and chickpea chutney, £5.95. Mains include Malabari Prawn Curry from Tamil Nadu at £18.50 and Goan Fish Curry (Pomfret) at £14.95 and Dal Makhani, black lentils, simmered overnight with garlic, cream and tomatoes, £5.95. The four Nawabi Biriyanis are *"amazing"* RL from £14. The wine bar is run by Portuguese Fernando Lopes, *Restaurant Manager and Sommelier. "Exquisite murals and paintings and antiques imported across Asia give Mala a certain charm that veers towards traditionalism, making the restaurant a perfect melting pot of culture".* P V.
Sun-Fri: 12 - 3 / Daily: 6 - 11.

NEEDOO GRILL   PUNJABI   A-LIST
87 New Rd, Whitechapel, E1 1HH
020 7247 0648   www.needoogrill.co.uk

Former Tayyab's (see below) manager Mr Ali the opened Needoo with an almost identical Punjabi Pakistani menu/concept, and now an equally packed house, so espect a queue but a darned good, inexpensive meal. Cards OK. 11:30-11:30.

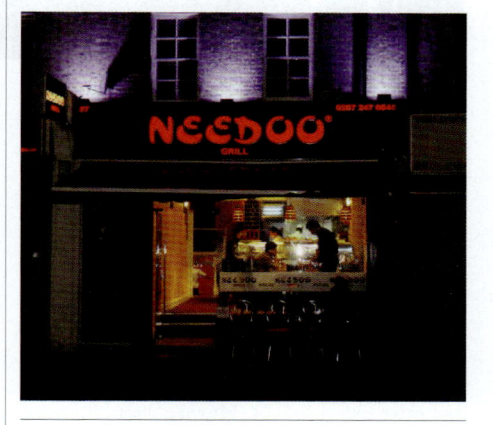

SCARLET DOT
4 Crispin Sq, Crispin Place, Spitalfields, E1 6DW
020 7375 0880   www.scarletdot.co.uk

Scarlet Dot is in the famous indoor market. "It's as much drinking-den as restaurant." PV. The Scarlet Spice Bar is 30 feet of tropical wood, dark blinds and marble floors and walls, providing a popular place to meet for lunch or after-work drinks. Neon floor-lights lead up to the bar where chill-out music plays by day and the tempo picks up by night. The adjoining 120-cover restaurant is boosted by a further 125 seats outside on a modern terrace under an impressive glass and steel canopy. Nothing on the menu will surprise the curryholic, except perhaps the prices. Lagosta Lobster, for example is £28.95 (cooked in Xacuti [Goan] sauce, accompanied by crisp okra and red onion salad). Lamb Wala Chops at £14.25 give you Goat (nice change from lamb) chops with a fresh green salad & chutneys. scarlet Crab Cakes, £8.95, fresh crab seasoned with herbs, lime juice, sweetcorn and chilli, then breaded with garam flour. Opens early at 9am - noon (drinks and snacks); Lunch 12 - 3 12 - 11pm (Main menu and drinks).

Always packed, elbow to elbow, Tayyabs, with its neonic decor.

TAYYABS   PUNJABI   A-LIST
83-89 Fieldgate Street, E1 1JU   UNLICD   BYO
020 7247 9543   www.tayyabs.com

Rivalling the Lahore Kebab House and Needo (see entries above) in popularity and exquisite Punjabi Pakistani food is the long-standing family owned Tayyabs now run by the owner's three sons, Saleem, Aleem and Wasim. In the beginning (1972) it was a simple caff in a scruffy street which before long became a haven of good food. Today Tayyabs extends to three huge consecutive shop frontages, painted in British Racing green complete with blue neon lights and three snazzily decorated floors and own labled bottled water and never ending lines of chattering diners. To quote the Randomness Guide *"Tayyabs inspires a degree of cultish fandom and as such is a London institution."* And it copes with this remarkably well. Asians, whites, the aged and babes and anyone who loves good food are all welcomed and well served. Many come for the renowned mixed grill and sizzling lamb chops, but anything on the menu is worth having, be it starters: Tikkas, Tandoori, Paneer, Kebabs, (Shais on Wes only), Fish, and King Prawn or mains: curries and karahis. *"I adore their Chicken Keema; is it unique to Tayyabs?"* HEG. Daily Specials include Nihiri-lamb trotters (Mon), Batera – Quail (Tues) through to Haleem (Sun). Though, as with all Pakistani cuisine, it's meat, meat, meat, there are about 8 vegetarian dishes, equally delicious. Everything is inexpensive, and you can BYO (they don't sell alcohol). There is always a queue but you can book and they are accurate about it so you do get your table; but not if you're late. Top up with Indian snacks and sweets from the counter on your way out. Daily: Noon-Mdnt. Closed for Ramadan (apart from takeaways).

And here's what many queue for ...

... the renowned mixed grill and sizzling lamb chops.

SPLENDIDLY INDIAN, SUPERBLY SMOOTH

TIFFIN INDIAN   TOP 100
165 Cannon Street Road, E1 2LX
020 7702 3832   www.tiffinindian.com

Abul Kalam's father owned The Nisshan in the 60s in the commercial Road. From a very early age, he watched chefs cooking different styles of Indian cooking. He left the trade for a decade and went into running social clubs and then came back to what I was good at. In 1992 I he decided opened Tiffin Restaurant, then became very successful. Tiffin chefs Faruk Miah, Dinar Ahmed and Aaman Uddin cook all the old favourites and ysome unusuals too. Bathara is quail in a spicy garam masala sauce, £9.95; Boti Kebab is Chunks of lamb marinated in lemon and yogurt with mint and other fresh herbs. Served with rice and a keema naan. £10.50; Bangladeshi fish steak Ayre, Ruhu or Bohal cooked with 100% mustard oil, with rice, £10.95. BYO. aily: 12-3/5:30-11:30.

YOU SAY OK, E1 to E4

E1: EASTERN SPICE 2a Artillery Passage, Bishopsgate, E1 020 7247 0772. A full range of Tandooris, Baltis, Kebabs, Samosa. Bhajis and Curries are available at this well-established City curry house. Mon - Fri: 12-3/6-11.30. Closed Sat & Sun.

E1: MIRCH MASALA   PUNJABI/KENYAN ASIAN BYO
111 Commercial Road, E1 1RD   0207 377 0155 One of seven branches with identical meat, fish and veg menu. See SW16 for full details.

E1: PRIDE OF ASIA 207 Mile End Rd, E1 4AA 020 7790 1600 A bog-standard, 65-seater owned and managed by Abdul Habiz. Chef Amir Uddin continues to provide all the favourites at prices made all the better with the Curry Club Discount. Delivery: £10 min, 3 mile radius.12-2.30pm. Dinner to 12 daily.

E1: TAJA 199a Whitechapel Rd, E1 1DE 020 7247 3866 no web. This 80 seater can get busy at times. Ask about their loyalty club for instant savings, which will ensure you get your fill for under a tenner. Daily: 11am to mdnt. Branch: 1 Brick Lane. E1.

E2: AL AMIN 483 Cambridge Heath Rd, E2 9BU 020 7739 9619. Abdul Noor's 2 room 39-seater pleasing standard curry house , with all the trimmings, including Balti. Daily: 12-2/6 - 12.

E4: PURBANI 34 The Avenue, Chingford, E4 9LD 020 8531 8804. Est1983. Owner Tony Turu Miah's air conditioned 54-seater is a regular in the Guide does all the usuals. Try Bamboo Shoot Bhajia for something different. 12- 2.30 / 6 -11.30 daily.

London E6

LAZZAT KAHAR   NO ALC ALLOWED
18 Plashet Grove, Upton Park, E6 1AE
020 8552 3413

Busy, cheerful, basic, friendly, buzzing, friendly ... these are your words, and above all cheap! We add to that Punjabi so expect meats, savoury flavours, no holds barred on the chilli front, al denté-perfect rice. You watch them cook, and you know it's fresh. The lettuce, onion, tomato, and chilli salad is free. With main courses c£5 and starters much less, it's hard to spend a tenner here, so cash is best here. Alcohol not permitted. Noon-midnight daily.

CHENNAIDOSA   SOUTH INDIAN
177 High St N, Manor Park, E6 1JB   020 8552 2430

See E12 below for details.

London E7

MOBEEN'S VILLAGE   PUNJABI
224 Green Street, Forest Gate, E7 8LE
020 8470 2419   www.mobeensvillage.co.uk

From humble beginnings in 1981, it's now a 450 seat giant. The mainly Punjabi food is churned out by a battery of cooks, in view and female servers. It is busy, busy with Asian families high on the attendance list and they love Nehari (lamb shank), Haleem (wheat and meat) and Paya (lamb trotter) all at £7.50. Bliss if you love Indian food. But for those who play safe, there are many more familiar items on the menu. A good range of Indian puds. 11-10 daily. *Branch Ilford, Essex.*

VIJAY'S CHAWALLA   GUJARATI VEG
268 Green Street, Forest Gate, E7 8LF
020 8470 3535   www.vijayschawalla.co.uk

And just down the road is another all-day caff which takes credit cards. More bliss! Again, it's a non-nonsense value-for-money caff, but with a different food-style from Mobeen. It is Gujarati pure vegetarian, apt considering its address. There is an abundance of gram flour, used in rissole form, sauces, curries et al. Yoghurt also prevails in the cooking, as does the typically Gujarati sweetness in savoury dishes. Sev Khaman, is gram-flour dumplings with topped gram flour squiggles (sev) with yoghurt and sweet and sour imli (tamarind chutney). Ragada patties, balls of mashed potato stuffed with curried chickpea are deep-fried and served in a tangy sauce. *'I started with that delightful Bombay street snack Bhel Poori'* (see glossary) *'and it was sublime. Then I went on to a fab thali'*. HEG. They dosh up good Indian desserts here, and someone, not sure if is VJ himself, makes Indian tea as it should be made (bring milk to the simmer with green cardamoms. Add too much sugar and serve in a large cup. Well that's what Chawalla means – tea maker!) If you've not had it before, this is the place to indulge. Main courses £4 - £7. Thalis from £7. Unlicensed. BYO allowed. Corkage no charge. 11 - 9 daily.

London E11

CHANDNI   SOUTH IND VEG
715 High Rd, Leytonstone, E11 4RD   020 8539 1700

Vegetarian food here including South Indian in this licensed café. *I thought hang it, money is no object today ignoring the £5 thali, I splashed out on the top-priced version (£6.50). I enjoyed a platter of mixed vegetable pakoras (very fresh, very tasty) while I pondered whether I would regret this impulsive act. The rather bumbling but amiable waiter eventually ambled up with my thali, and placed it in front of me with a flourish I never suspected he had in him. Now I've had salutations all over India, and I have to say this one was worth every penny of the extra investment. I'll be back! And I have been.* HEG. House wine: £8. Credit cards OK. 11-11

London E12

CHENNAIDOSA TOP 100   SOUTH INDIAN/SRI LANKAN
353 High Street North, Manor Park, E12 6SA
020 8552 4677   www.chennaidosa.com

339 High St N, Manor Park, E12 6PQ
020 8470 6566   www.chennaidosa.com

Since 2006, the High Street between Manor Park and East Ham stations is a new curry mile and we take an in-depth look at it on the next page. Of particular note are two large south Indian café chains, Chennaidosa and Saravanaa Bhavan (next entry). Both have multiple branches in India and and between them they have opened not two, but three within yards of each other on this same street and in Tooting and Leicester too. Overview: Chennaidosa (literally Madras pancake) own a rapidly expanding world-wide chain of 38 vegetarian caff/restaurants, the first of which opened in Chennai in 1981. They opened their first UK branch in 2003, and now have 11 branches (see below) and plan to open more, with the claim to be the largest dosa maker in Europe. They are clean and basic with caff-style plastic tables, metal cups and jugs of tapwater. These two venues, though close together, with are packed with Asian families all day long. They specialise in South Indian dishes such as dosai, idli, and vadai (see next entry for descriptions) and all but two (Wembley & E12) sell non-vegetarian dishes, from fiery chicken Chettinad curry, through dry mutton dishes to whole fried pomfret. There are also a few Sri Lankan dishes, such as mutton kothu parotta (chopped flatbread fried with mutton and hot spices). Many dishes are served thali-style, in stainless steel trays with recessed compartments to contain the sauces. There's a sweet counter in the front section, with various fresh sweets laid out on trays behind a glass guard and packets of savoury snacks piled on top of the counter. No alcohol but though credit cards are accepted, be prepared to pay cash. Main courses £5-£14. Daily: 9am-11pm.
Branches: E6, E12 (2); SW17; E'hm B16; Harrow; Ilford; Leicester; Mcr M16; Reading; Croydon; Wembley (2)

SARAVANAA BHAVAN   SOUTH IND VEG
300 High Street North, E12 6SA   TOP 100
020 8552 4677   www.saravanabhavan.co.uk

Following on from the Chennaidosa entry above, this is the second large south Indian café chain to spread its wings from India to the UK. Overview: 'Sarvanaa' is a son of Hindu god Shiva, a name often used in businesses. 'Bhavan' is a house or store. Put these words together and you have Saravana Bhavan, a chain of south India vegetarian cafés founded in 1981 by P. Rajagopal (Annachi) and his sons, Shiva Kumaar and R. Saravanan. Today the group has 25 outlets in India, and 16 more in places like USA, Canada, UAE, Oman, Singapore and Malaysia, including 5 in the UK. All serve a vegetarian menu with south and north Indian cuisine and some Hakka dishes (Indian-style Chinese - uniquely spicy and worth a try). Saravana first opened in the UK at in May 2005 in a distinctive corner site. The 110 seat space has a semi-open kitchen linked by dining areas. With prices ranging from £2.45 to £3.95 the south Indian items include Hot Idly, rice & lentil patties served with varieties of chutney, sambar & chilli powder; Rava Kichadi / Uppuma, roasted sooji cooked with onions, tomatoes, carrots, green chillies & green peas, sauteed with flavoured herbs served with chutney & sambar; Ghee Pongal, steamed raw rice smashed, sauteed with ghee, pepper, jeera, dal, garnished with cashew nuts; Adai Avial, pancake made of pulses & lentils, served with Kerala style sauce made of vegetables, coconut paste & spices; Curd Vada (Lentil flour doughnut immersed in yoghurt garnished with carrots & coriander. Bonda of the day, deep fried urid balls stuffed with the day's special. Dosas (rice crepes) with a choice of fillings such as Masalas Dosa, stuffed with spicy potatoes & onion. Rava Dosa is made from wheat Uthappam (a thick rice & lentil pancake) comes with various toppings inc onions, green chillies & tomatoes. Bagalabath is rice mixed with yogurt, cashews, grapes, mustard seeds served with pickle. Bisibelabath is rice cooked with lentils & mixed vegetables served with Appalam. The Hakka Chinese menu includes Vegetable Hot Garlic (Gravy), slices of mixed vegetables fried & seasoned with strong garlic sauce; Hakka Vegetables, in red chilli oil & red pepper sauce; Chilli Paneer, batter fried cottage cheese sauteed with onion, green chillies, chilli paste & Chinese herbs. Paneer Fried Rice; Hakka Noodles, sautéed with red pepper sauce. Cash preferred. Not licensed.10am to 10:30pm.   *Branches: Harrow Middx, Ilford Essex, Leicester, Tooting SW17.*

COBRA
कोबरा

SPLENDIDLY INDIAN, SUPERBLY SMOOTH

101

FOCUS on High Street North, E6 / E12

In the last five years or so certain parts of East London have become a centre for South Indian and Sri Lankan food, pure veg and non veg. Nowhere beats East Ham High Street North (and South) between East Ham and Manor Park Stations for its concentration of café-style venues; it's a new Curry Mile. On the adjacent page we examine the 'big two' in detail. Below in Street number numerical order, we list the others:

CHUTNEYS TAKEAWAY 90 High St S E6 3LR 020 8548 8282

SHUJON CURRYHOUSE 105 High St N, E6 1HZ 020 8472 1956

ORENTAL GRILL INDIAN 135B High Street North, E6

LAHORLAHORE LAHORE EH 155 High Street North, East Ham, E6 1 JB 020 8471 7691 Photo by my village.com

CHENNAIDOSA SOUTH INDIAN 177 High St N, Manor Park, E6 1JB 020 8552 2430 (see adjacent page)

VASANTA BHAVAN PURE VEGTN 206 High Street South, East Ham, E6 020 8475 8986. Photo, bottom right by Kake.

SUVAI CHETTINAD S.IND / SRI LANKAN 207 High St N, E6 1JG 020 8471 5777

PRIYA S.IND / SRI LANK 209 High St N, E6 1JG 020 8471 5552

MOBEEN TAKE AWAY 229 High St N, E6 1 JG 020 8470 9365

ROYAL SWEETS SWEETS & SNACKS 237 High St N

ANANDA BHAVAN 240 High St N, E12 6SB 020 8586 7537

DEEPAM SRI LANKAN 240 High St N, E12 6SB 020 8586 7537

THATTUKADA KERELAN 241B High St N, E12 6SJ 020 8548 8239

KABUL AFGHAN 264, High St North, London , E12 6SB

EASTERN EYE TANDOORI 269 High St S, E6 3PG 020 8475 0932

THAYKAM S IND VEG 286 High Street North E12 6SA 020 8470 6644

TASTE OF INDIA PURE VEG 293-295 High St N, E12 6SL 020 8472 9779 www.restauranttasteofindia.co.uk Owner Mr Sarbadine. Non veg Branch at 340 and Barking and Kerela

SARAVANAA BHAVAN SOUTH IND VEG 300 High St N, E12 6SA 020 8552 4677 Photo, 2nd from top, courtesy myvillage.com.

MADRAS S IND VEG 305 High St N, E12 6SL 020 8503 5255

HYDERABADI SPICE 309 High St N, E12 6SL 020 8472 0255 www.hyderabadispice.co.uk Branch: 47 Spring Grove Rd TW3 4BD 020 8570 5535 Desc by www.yel.com as Hyde Rabadi – shows what they know. Photo opposite by Kake.

CHENNAIDOSA SOUTH INDIAN/SRI LANKAN 339 High St N, Manor Park, E12 6PQ 020 8470 6566 (see adjacent page) Photo, top by Kake.

TASTE OF INDIA NON VEG 340, High St N, E12 6PH 020 8471 2122 (see details above)..

CHENNAIDOSA SOUTH INDIAN/SRI LANKAN 353 High St N E12 6SA 020 8552 4677. (see adjacent page)

SATHIYAMS SOUTH INDIAN SRI LANKAN 379 High St N, E12 6PG 020 8552 0777 opened 2006 www.sathiyams.com

KEBANA KEBABISH 385 High Street North E12 6PG

RUSKIN 386 High Street North, E12 6PH 020 8470 7114

SABRAS SWEETS & PURE VEG SNACKS 400A High St N, E12 6RH 020 8470 2700

APNA PAN SHOP SWEETS & PAN 402B High St N, E12 6RH

LAHORE GRILL 427 High Street North E12 6TL 020 8472 0202

SACOR RESTAURANT 538 High St N,E12 6QN 020 8514 5825

Sri Lankan & Indian Grocers on High Street, North:
Station Superstore 5 (East Ham) Station Pde; **Judiya** 242; **Shakthi** 245 (Biggest); **Ali** 301; **Swathi** 306 ; **KSP** 318; **Seelans** 332; **JBK** 387 (inc offie); **B.B. Fatima** 394, (near Manor Park Station).

A hugely satisfying pure vegetarian Thali by Saravanaa Bhavan is typical of the south Indian Cuisine delivered up and down the High Street.

Photos courtesy and © copyright Kake at kake@earth.li / myvillage.com / Saravanaa Bhavan

London E14

DOCKMASTERS TOP 100
Dockmaster's House, West India Dock Gate,
Hertsmere Road, E14 8JJ
020 7345 0345   www.dockmastershouse.com

For a century this 1807 Georgian building was the home of the all-powerful London dockmaster. Then it survived life as a low level pub, the blitz, a grubby government office, a demolition threat and finally restoration in the dwarfing surrounds of Canary Wharf's sky-tech towers, with the overhead tracks of the Docklands railway snaking between them and the surrounding drab, gloomy overparked streets. The movie 'Batteries Not Included' springs to mind, but such is progress. The rear glass framed extension looks as though it was an afterthought but from the inside it is stunning with its pine floor, smooth chairs and chic furnishings. There are three elements. Jewel in the crown is the 100-seat a/c restaurant with a satisfying range of Indian regional dishes Oberoi trained Chef Navin Bhatia produces the likes of Scallops with spicy anise squids and apricot sauce £9.95; Green Spice Crusted Tandoori Salmon with quinoa leaf salad, roasted tomato and pepper sauce £7.95; Duck Seekh Roll (Duck Samosa) and pear-ginger chutney £7.95; Prawn Balchao Traditional Spicy Prawn Curry from Goa £14.75; Kofta Alubhukhara (V) dumplings of Indian cheese with prune served with garlic spinach and tomato fenugreek sauce £15.50. Tasting menu £55 or £80 with wines. A 200-seat bar is down in the former cellars, offering a range of spicy pub grub. Outside the garden seats 100 and in good weather serves BBQs of Indian kebabs, grills and tandooris on platters alongside pitchers of beer. Discretionary 12.5% serv ch. House Wine: £14 Weekdays: 11:30-3/6-11. Weekends: 6-22:45.(bar 5pm - late).

YOU SAY OK, LONDON E14 to E18

MEMSAHEB ON THAMES 65 Amsterdam Road, E14 3RU 020 7538 3008 www.memsaheb.net Mridul Kanti (Moni) Das runs it and the service is amiable, the food curryhouse but competent. "We could sort of see the Thames".DBAC. Mon-Fri: 12- 3/6-11. Sat:6-11. Sun: 12-4/6-10.

SPICE MERCHANTS 38 Salter Street, E14 8BH 020 7987 8779 www.thespicemerchants.com Managed by Mr Uddin, previously of the Tale of India (below). *A very pleasant environment, with most tables on the first floor and a good value fixed price 2 course lunch menu, all dishes not presented on their à-la-carte. Recommended.'* SH.*'Nothing was to much for them. The popadoms were fresh, thin and crisp. Starters and Main dishes all excellent. A very pleasant experience'* IC.

TALE OF INDIA 53 West India Dock Rd, E14 8HN 020 7537 2546 www.thetaleofindia.com Seats forty diners in air-conditioned comfort. Interesting starters include: Uribeesi Baja £3.50, specially flavoured Bangladeshi beans fried with onions and coriander, and Fish Bora – salmon, mixed with fresh coriander and onions, lightly spiced and deep-fried with egg and breadcrumbs. Main courses include Lau Tarkari, £6.95, chicken or lamb cooked with red pumpkin in a rich, thick, sauce blended with onions, coriander and capsicums. Millawat £6.95, chicken and lamb cooked withonions, tomatoes, capsicums and fresh coriander. Delivery: 3 miles, £10 min. 12-2.30 & 5.30-11.30.

SPICE INN 22 Romford Road, Stratford E15 020 8519 1399 *'Swift and polite service, but lacks interpersonal skills. Mixed Kebab – sheik kebab, chicken and lamb tikka, reshmi kebab, all very well spiced and delicious, but lukewarm. Methi Gosht – best I've had since the untimely demise of the Shish Mahal in Dumbarton, but again warm. Nevertheless very, very good. £17 for food plus 2 pints Cobra.'* DP.

MECHNA GRILL 219 Woodford High Rd, E18 020 8504 0923 Siddiqur Rahman's long-established (1971), competent Bangladeshi curry house. It's one of those places which is always busy. Says it all really. For those who don't eat curry (they won't be reading this then) let them eat chips, as Marie Antoinette didn't say. But the Meghna serve them and Roast Chicken. But I'd plump for the Tikka Trout £6.90 or Bangladeshi Fish-on-the-bone £7.80, myself. Half price Mondays if you book. Daily: 12-2.30 / 6 - Mdnt.

London EC

Area: The City of London
Postcodes: EC1 to EC4

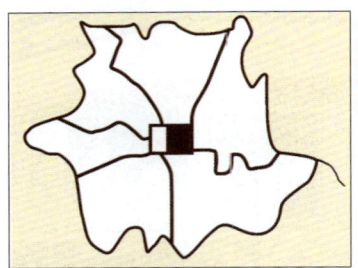

See page 88 for key to this map

London EC1

CHAWOL
5, Clerkenwell Road, Barbican EC1M 5PA
020 7490 4468   www.chawol.net

'Decor is pleasant, plain and modern with rattan chairs. Shame about the dead, pre-holiday rose on each table. Only two other tables occupied, but did roaring trade in takeaways and deliveries. Very light and crispy Popadoms, excellent relishes. Very good Tandoori Salmon and King Prawn Butterfly. Butter Chicken was very almoady and good. King Prawn Dhansak, also good, but not very 'dhansak,' hardly sweet, lentils not very evident but with black eye peas or beans. Would have been fine under a different name. Broccoli and Mushroom Bhaji and Brinjal Masala - both very good. Exceptionally good with lots of large pieces of mushrooms and very well seasoned. Full marks for serving espresso coffee. £63.40 for two including drinks and service.' HJC. Popadom, 60p, Duck Bhuna, £9.95. Buffet Mon to Fri: 12 - 3. Daily: 6-11..

CURRY LEAF
20 City Road, Old Street, EC1Y 2AJ
020 7374 4842   www.curryleaf.co.uk

The attractively named Curry Leaf opened in 2004 and is owned by S. Rehman, T. Ali, P. Chowdhery, and S. Sohail who between them for the past 30 years own twelve other top-end restaurants across London. There is a 15-seat bar/lounge area, with comfortable bar stools and dim lighting and a basement private 35-seat room. The main dining area has a 25-seat balcony and 70 seats on the ground level. *"The walls are noticeably bare embellished with arched Burma teak beams, which coordinate with the curved-back chairs. The illuminated glass panel at the back of the restaurant enhances the generous space between tables and minimalism, while allowing the diners privacy to a backdrop of Indian classical music. to create a cool atmosphere for diners."* PV. Though the curry leaf is a southern Indian spice, the menu here is mainly north Indian, with some specials from across India. Exec Chef, Ramu Sharma trained in Dehradun's School of Food and Arts and worked for Delhi Moti Mahal group (see London WC2) before moving to London. Try Sikandari Raan, £14.95, leg of spring lamb soaked overnight, simmered in coconut milk with shredded ginger soured with raw mangoes and Lamb Hyderabadi Biryani £11.95. Price Check: Popadoms 80p, CTM £8.50, Pullao Rice £3.95, Plain Naan £2.50. Mon-Fri: 12-3 / Daily: 6-11-30.

SEMA INDIAN BALTI   UNLIC BYO
141 White Cross Street, EC1   020 7253 2927

Proprietor, Abdul Khalique Choudhury says he'll provide the glasses, you just BYO at his friendly 25 seater. He tells us Chicken Jalfrezi Balti £5.75 including a Nan bread is his most popular dish, probably because all Balti dishes come with a free Nan bread. Interesting starters : Liver Hazri £2, I can hear screeches of 'yuk' but liver curries very well. Semi Balti Soup £1.75. Main courses: Ginger Chicken, Chicken Tikka Pepper Balti and Nan around a fiver. Set lunch: £5.50, set dinner: £6.40. Delivery: 1 mile, £10 minimum Takeaway: 10% discount. Lunch to 2.30pm. Dinner to 11.30pm.

SONIA BALTI HOUSE
1 Lever Street, EC1   020 7253 3398

Brisk takeaway trade. Service is very homely and friendly. Very tender and tasty Sheek Kebab £1.95, with a cool crisp salad and very yellow and garlicky yoghurt sauce. Lamb Taba Gosht £5.95 – rather tough lamb in well spiced and appetising, but thin gravy. Very doughy Garlic Nan £1.40.' rw. No credit cards. Takeaway: 10% discount. Delivery: £10 minimum. 5.30 to 12.

SMITHFIELD TANDOORI
12 Smithfield Street, City of London,   EC1A 9LA
020 7248 4000   www.smithfieldtandoori.co.uk

Very popular curry house right opposite the meat market, from where, surprise, surprise, they buy their meat. Floor to ceiling plate glass windows iallow you a full view of the pale wooden floors and tall brown chairs which contrast with the crisp white table cloths. Reliable menu, service and food. *"Full marks – they had several Indian sweets ?– I had Gulab Jamun, served warm, lovely. This Indian meal turned out to be a real pleasure."* HC. Mon-Fri 12-2.30/6-11.30 /Sat 6-11.

YOU SAY OK EC1
RAVI SHANKAR INDIAN VEGETARIAN RESTAURANT
422 St Johns Street, London, EC1V 4NJ 020 7833 5849

London EC2

CINAMON KITCHEN & ANISE BAR
FINE INDIAN   TOP 100   9
Devonshire Square, EC2M 4YL   020
7626 5000   www.cinnamon-kitchen.com

This is the second restaurant from Cinnamon Club's Vivek Singh. He has singled out the rich pickings of the City to aims at a more casual dining experience, notable for some remarkable Singh innovations combining modern Indian cuisine and British ingredients. The bright and spacious 110 seat dining room rather aptly located in the former East India Company warehouse is managed by Shane Lee Sa. The conversion paints the high ceiling, beams, and pillars in ivory white. Glossy a/c ducts and pipework add character. Ample windows allow lots of light in the day and hand-fretted Indian lamps and downlighters create the night time atmosphere. Rich brown, intensely grained wooden round and square tables need no cloths and punctuate the room with inviting wine glasses and cinnamon coloured chairs. Some of the grill cooking is on view, with an almost Tepinyaki style seating arrangement. The western courtyard is extends the dining room, with its outdoor terrace for alfresco open all day and all year round. The adjoining Anise cocktail bar operates from 4pm. Vivek's menu is adminstered by Head chef is Abdul Yaseen (below). Portion sizes are small, so order several dishes if you have a large appetite, and even

Chef Yaseen in Cinnamon's outdoor area

LONDON EC2

Cinnamon'Kitchen and, below, their Chef's Table.

if you don't ... they are all delicious. Ten All day snacks (11-11) include this editor's favourite Indian breakfast dish, Masala green chilli omelette on toasted brioche £5.70; Vivek's cutely named Naanza - Indian pizza £5.00; and the traditional Haleem (wheat and meat) with saffron pao [bun] £4.80. Lunch includes 5 starters such as Bengali style vegetable cake, beetroot & raisin £7.00; 6 'grills' include fat chillies with spiced paneer £ 5.50 or a platter of all six (for two) £25.00. Seven Mains include pan seared sea bass, kokum [sour] curry sauce £15.00; and Rajasthani roast red deer, stir-fried mushroom £32.. One Vivek innovation is 'All Balls! (complete with exclamation mark!). They are all cherry tomato size, batter dipped and deep-fried: Crab Cakes balls, Potato Bondas, Vegetable Shikampur, Beef Shammi Kebab balls, Bangla-Scotch Quail Egg balls. Tiny balls, large price: £3.80 each, £9.00 for a selection, albeit served with home-made chutneys. Then there are Brit-style pies, suc as Roganjosh Shepherd's Pie and Keralan Mooli Seafood Pie, both traditional curries topped off with a pastry lid, £12 . Other British influences includes Curried Cullen Skink, £5.80 a Scottish staple spiked with ,Indian spices and Punjabi-style Fish and Masala Chips or Herring roe on toast £6.20. The adventurous will try Bheja fry-lamb brains in mince curry £6.50, Coorgi pork stir-fry £6.00, Vindaloo of ox cheek £15.50 or Lucknow-style Black Leg chicken biryani £14. Mon-Fri:12-2:45. (Anise: 4-Mdnt) Mon-Sat: 6-10:45 (Anise-Mdnt). *Branches Cinnamon Club and Cinnamon Soho, both W1.*

MINT LEAF LOUNGE & RESTAURANT
FINE INDIAN　　　　　　　　　　**TOP 100**
12 Angel Court, Bank, EC2R 7HB
020 7600 0992　　　　www.mintleaflounge.com

The other west London giant to open a branch in the City (see previous entry) is this stylish 90 seater. Gerard McCann manages both this and the original SW1 Mint Leaf. The bar is 16m long and presided over by Lara. A

COBRA

SPLENDIDLY INDIAN, SUPERBLY SMOOTH

Mint Leaf's Chef's Kitchen

mezzanine overlooks the main room and contains a champagne bar. Head Chef Dhayalan Paul ex Dubai's Madinat Jumeirah Hotel and Cinnamon Club (SW1) head the brigade. Starters include Tandoori Duck Breast Kebab and Chilli chutney £10; Tandoori Paneer Stuffed With Pickle with Chilli mango and tomato mustard relish £7.50 Potato Cakes with curried chickpea, tamarind and yoghurt (aka Aloo Tiki) £7.50; Tandoori Guinea Fowl Tikka wioth Pineapple raita and chilli mango, £12.50. Mains include: Tandoori Chicken Supreme with stir-fried pak choy and Dhal Makhani, £18; Tandoori Broccoli and Cauliflower with Sesame tamarind sauce and pulao rice £15; Tandoori Venison with Kadhai Sauce with cumin mash potatoes and crispy okra £23; and Grilled Beef Fore Rib with Masala potatoes £26.00. Wines here are from £22 to £890 (1998 Chateau Latour. Taj introduced Chef's Tables to Delhi and London (BB SW7) Mint Leaf's overlooks the open kitchen and groups of max 4 watch a 5 course menu being cooked and taste it for £85 pp with matched wines and £65 without. 12.5% service charge. Bar: Mon-Tue: 11.30am-12am (Wed-Fri: to 1am), Bar food:12-12. Restnt: Mon-Fri:12-3 & 5.30-11. *Branch: Mint Leaf SW1.*

London EC3

KASTURI TOP 100
57 Aldgate High St, EC3N 1AL
020 7480 7402   www.kasturi-restaurant.co.uk

Nur Monie's Tanjore, Welling, Kent has been in our TOP 100 for ages. In late 2002 he teamed up with Bashir Ahmed (owner of five popular Kohinoor restaurants in Holland) to open their 80-seater Kasturi. It has the current look of blonde wood floor, bright lights, colourful walls and pot plants. Management tell us, Kasturi means 'the strong scented secretion found in rare musk deer, used in expensive perfumes'. Phew! I don't know about that, but the scent of the tandoor is more likely to be encountered. Kasturi has an ace up its sleeve – Chef Rajandra Balmiki, head chef at The Tangore. He trained at the Delhi's Mauyra Sheraton Hotel, under chef Imtiaz Qureshi of Dum Pukht fame and former training chef, the highly respected C.P Rahman. Maurya has the best Tandoori restaurant in the world. What a background for Balmiki. Kasturi claims to specialise in Pakhtoon cuisine. It's a far cry from Delhi and Welling. It refers to the tribal people of Afghanistan from the rugged mountain passes in the former North-West Frontier Province, whose name for themselves is Pathan, Pashtun, Phuktana or Pukhtun. Afghan food is pretty basic (see pages 66 & 73), especially at tribal level, involving kebab-skewer cooking and slow-cooking in pots. Grills, Kebabs, Koftas and Birianis are popular, spiced with the unique Afghan spice mix, Char Masala (four aromatic spices) and cooked mostly in their own juices. Try the Kebab Ke Karishma, a selection of kebabs. It includes Chicken, Lamb and Minced meat kebabs. Served as a starter for two persons: £14.95. Kandahari Paneer Tikka £5.95 home-made cheese wrapped in yoghurt, marinated and stuffed with fresh herbs and spices in olive oil and cumin, grilled in the tandoor. Lal Maas £10.95, Rajasthan's favourite red hot lamb dish; Lazees Pasllan £10.95, lamb chops cooked in a cashew nut & yoghurt-based gravy with cardamom & saffron flavour. Any of the Biryanis will *'blow you away'.* HEG. Our benchmark Dal-Dera Ismail Khan – *'A harmonious combination of black dal and herbs, simmering on slow charcoal fire'* (aka Dal Makhani) is just £5.95. Kasturi has attracted rave reviews from our reporters But such a menu and such a skilled Indian chef will of course bring adverse comments from what Monie calls *'those with their brains closed'.* He's prepared for it, and he offers them formula curries.
Mon-Sat: 12-3 & 6-11. Closed Sundays.

YOU SAY OK EC3
RAJASTHAN 49 Monument St, EC3 8BU 020 7626 1920
www.rajasthan1.co.uk Sadly not a Rajasthani dish in sight, because it's a formula Bangladeshi curryhouse. *'Duck Pineapple, very nice, enjoyably unusual. Obviously priced to reflect that it's in the city, although not bad.'* NP. Mon-Fri only: 11.30-3/5.30-11.

TASTE OF INDIA 76 Aldgate High St, EC3 1BD 020 7481 4010
The deft service at this Bangladeshi formula curry venue. And it is a favourite haunt of many a city regular, of which VW-P and LD-W are two. 12-11 daily.

LONDON N
Area North London
Postcodes: N1 to N22

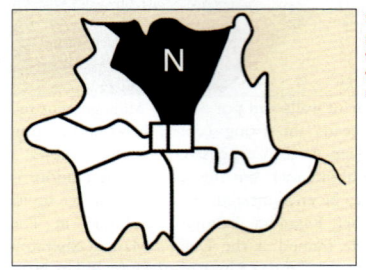

See page 88 for key to this map

London N1

Delhi Grill's quirky decor, below, and tasty thalis. Photos courtesy Saff and Ade. Visit their entertaining and foodie website www.welovefood-itsallweeat.com

DELHI GRILL   TOP 100
21 Chapel Market, N1
020 7278 8100   www.delhigrill.com

With Indian Street Food gaining ground all over the trendier parts of London, Delhi Grill says it's a 'dhaba' or an *"informal canteen where people from all walks of life sit together and enjoy spicy, delicious street food"*. The equivalent of our greasy spoons, Indian dabbas are roadsde shacks with crude alfresco benches for the diners, mostly truckies, and a rudimentary kitchen under a leaky canvas roofs. There are millions of them in India. Forget hygiene and running water, and for that matter, cutlery ... this is India. They generally serve outstanding food at rock bottom prices and your editor has on a few occasions actually taken British tourists to such venues where not even middle class Indians dare to dine, when the coach drivers take their chai break. Believe me judging by the incumbents' expressions, that never happens. So forget Delhi Grill's spin, *"all walks of life"* don't use the Indian dabba and for rock bottom prices, expect London suburbia prices, and yes, the EHO has ensured the place is up to British standards. Polished pine floors, simple chairs and tables with large menus. Enjoy the carefully placed posters and newspaper clippings on the walls; read them if you can squeeze past the ever-full crowd, made to look larger by large mirrors. Managed by the affable Ashik DG serves wraps, £2.95, on good weather lunchtimes from a BBQ stall outside, or try the thalis *"reasonably priced and cooked well."* RL. Rogan Gosht, £8.95, lamb, tomatoes and spices slow-cooked for over 2 hours.and spices slow-cooked for over 2 hours; Chicken Karahi, £8.95, spicy chicken dish (boneless or OTB); Fish Special, £9.95, atch of the day cooked in chef Prakash's masala base. Veggy curries at £4.95 eg: Aloo Gobi, potato and cauliflower in cumin, coriander and ginger or Channa, chickpeas slow cooked in a coriander, garlic and tomato masala. Price Check: Naan, £1.75, Pop 50p, Pilau Rice £1.95.Takeaway available in the evenings. Tue-Sun: Noon-2:45/6-10:30.

ROOTS AT N1   FINE INDIAN DINING TOP 100
115 Hemingford Road, N1 1BZ
020 3589 2751   www.rootsatn1.com

From time to time a group of restaurant professionals form a partnership and open their own venture. Harsh Joshi, Bhola Kunwar and Rohit Bisht, ex Ritz London, Benares Mayfair and Oberoi Delhi are one such and in 2011 they have chosen to stylishly refit a former pub in fashionable Barnsbury. Hanging beaten-copper lamps look down on beechwood flooring, leather banquettes and bentwood chairs whilst on the wooden tables, huge long-stem wine ballons simply wait to be filled, with an inviting international choice from the wine list. The partners make a point of pairing wines with the food, which is Chef Kunwar department, ensuring expert

COBRA
SPLENDIDLY INDIAN, SUPERBLY SMOOTH

cooking in the haute Indian hotel style. The menu, is not burdeningly long. Some descriptions are in English only – others include Indian dish names amongst its collection of dishes, familiar and original. Pops are not on the menu, thus creating a potentially long period of inactivity whilst awaiting order delivery, though a demi-tasse of spicy soup as a gratis amuse-bouche off sets this a bit. Starters include samosas, chicken tikka and seekh kebabs. Pan seared scallops on cauliflower purée are in the original category. Mains include Butter chicken masala (which Roots dub *'the real thing!'* and recommend it with a Bourgogne wine, or Roast duck breast, in a chetinad sauce or Lamb shank `roganjosh' coupled with a 2010 Argentinian Malbec Mendoza. The chef test is their Black lentils with kidney beans (Dhal Makhni), which is beyond curryhouse skills, requiring long and careful cooking. Desserts include 'Roots carrot pudding' (aka Gajjar Halva) which is another test of slow cooking and good ingredients, such as pure butter ghee.

Carrot pudding with pistachio Kulfi

Roots suffers from criticism from the vindaloo brigade, who wouldn't understand subtlety if you tatooed it onto them. So let's be clear ... the food is Mayfair not curryhouse. Despite being a roti throw from the aforesaid, prices (under £20 per meal) are suburban, not Mayfair. Sat & Sun: 12-3. Tues-Sat: 6-10 (Sun to 9).

INDIAN VEG BHEL POORI HOUSE
92 Chapel Market, N1 9EX   020 7837 4607   n/w

One of the two London pioneers of vegan (plus yoghurt items) Indian Street food, it remains unpretentious and inexpensive. For £4.50 you can buy the all-you-can eat buffet. *"The quality is always consistent. Occasionally there is a superb mashed potato and onion curry. Always a friendly welcome and my half lager is now brought automatically.'* TN. *'All the dishes are superb, and I'm no veggie. The Bhel Puri is still my favourite though.'* ME. Hours: 12-11.30.

MASALA ZONE   STREET FOOD   A-LIST
80 Upper Street, N1 0NU   020 7359 3399
www.masalazone.com/locations_islington.php

The 2nd of the chain. A clever idea. Briefly it is basic food, but cooked as if it is at the Indian food. You can't reserve, and it is inexpensive. Hard in fact to exceed £15 per head (more with wine). You won't find better real Indian food at such prices. 105 seater plus outside pation for 24. Mon-Fri 12.30-3 /5.30-11.30; Sat:12-11, Sun to 10.30 . See entry in W1.

PARVEEN
6 Theberton Street, N1 0QX   020 7226 0504
www.parveenrestaurant.co.uk

Established 1977 and seating 100 diners on two floors. It's an air-conditioned, contemporary restaurant, decorated in reds and yellows. Polished blonde wooden floor, spot lights and marbled bar. You'll find the curry formula done well here. Here are the opinions of some of Parveen's many friends: *'Great decor and food that tastes authentic!'* HN. *'Faruk and staff are so amazing, makes everyone feel special. Food lovely and decor fantastic.'* JO'B. *'Great food and service.'* HM. *'By far the best Indian in Islington, highly recommended.'* CR. Sea bass, £10.25, fresh sea bass grilled with lemon juice, crushed peppers and finished with ground mustard sauce, served with salad and Lamb Pasanda £8.50; Duck Mirchiwalia, £8.95, duck marinated in herbs then cooked with chillis and peppers are popular favourites. Set dinner £33.95 for two. Sunday / Monday all day special offer. Any starter, any main meal, any rice or nan, Ice Cream and a Free 330ml Bottle of Cobra beer. See their Special Offers web page for details. Takeaway service. Hours: Mon-Fri: 4-12.30am / Sat - Sun 1pm - 12.30am.

Parveen
Indian Restaurant
London. Est 1977

6 Theberton Street, N1 0QX
020 7226 0504
www.parveenrestaurant.co.uk

Opening Hours:
Mon - Fri: 4pm to 12.30am
Sat - Sun: 1pm to 12.30am

Orders Over £20:
10% Discount on Collection.
or
Free delivery 2m radius,
6.30 -11.30

RAJ MONI
279 Upper Street, N1 2TZ   020 7354 1270

This small venue, about fifty covers, is *'pleasantly decorated; prompt service.; standard menu – Silsila Masala Chicken and Afgani Chicken new to me. Started with Rajmoni Special which was basically Chicken Chat – good portion, nicely spiced with tender chicken, OK, but nothing special. Main course – Chicken Tikka, good portion, 10 pieces, served on sizzler; Madras Curry Sauce – nice and hot; Plain Rice – generous portion, light and fluffy. Standard formula curry house.'* DB. 6-mdnt daily.

ZAFRANI
47 Cross Street, Islington, N1 2BB   0207 226 5522
www.zaffrani-islington.co.uk

On a corner site its attractive, cool frontage invites you in to a minimalist but friendly feel. Inside you will find a comprehensive menu with all the old favourites and some interesting specials. Starters include: Tandoor Ki Gazak, 5.95, For two 8.95, a medley of char-grilled kebabs consisting of marinated pieces of chicken breast, tenderised pieces of lamb, minced chicken, and minced lamb. Served with mini-nan bread. Mains Specials include: Badak Naranghi, 8.95, Pan-roasted duck supreme, served in a creamy orange sauce enriched with

a selection of spices. Amshetikshe, 7.95, strips of chicken sauteed with onion, tomatoes, and green chillies, and enriched with tamarind, chilli and cumin. Patrani Machli, 14.95 halibut fillet marinated in green herbs and grated coconut, and baked in a banana leaf, served with sauteed spinach and lemon & lime flavoured rice. *'This is fresh clean Indian cuisine: forget your 'brown' sauces and think delicate pure spice. I read an old guide (2008) and was shocked not to have found it listed. Loving curries and living in Islington I can assure you this is better than any other mentions. The staff are also knowledgeable and efficient and well managed. Costs: normally less than £25 per head with drinks.'* PS-C. 6.30-11.

London N2

COCHIN   SOUTH INDIAN
111 High Rd, East Finchley, N2 8AG   020 8444 5666

This South Indian restaurant serves all the vegetarian dishes you'd expect at around £5 to £6. Thali set meal from £10.95. The also serve many familiar formula non-veg curries including tandoori items. 12-2.30 / 6-11.30.

MAJJOS   KASHMIRI, PAKISTANI & INDIAN
1 Fortis Green, N2 9JR   020 8883 4357

Established in 1993 by Mrs Ashraf. Manager S Mogul. A shop with a seating area for just 10 diners, so you can enjoy some spicy dishes while shopping for your Indian groceries. Kashmiri, Pakistani and Indian food. Great prices: Meat curries £5.50 or £4. Veg curries £3.50 or £2.30 Hours: 10.30am-10.30pm (10pm on Sun.).

London N3

RANI VEGETARIAN   GUJARATI
PREVIOUS AWARD WINNER   **TOP 100**
7 Long Lane, Finchley, N3 2PR   020 8349 4386
www.rani.uk.com

Established in 1984, it proudly and correctly bills itself as the longest established Gujarati restaurnat in London. Jyoti Patni is front of house in this venue tastefully decorated in shades of turmeric and red, with Georgian chairs and glass-topped tables. Rani means Queen, and the term could as well refer to the cooks, Jyoti's wife and his mother, because their mainly Gujarati vegetarian food cannot be bettered anywhere with items tasty enough to please all but the most obdurate non-veggie. India's most western state, Gujarat, is the home of mild, slightly sweet dishes, with a love of yoghurt and gram flour. The soup-like curry Khadi is one dish showing Gujarati adoration of both. The famous bhajia (pakora) also originated in Gujarat, as did the lesser known Dahi Vada, a gram flour dumpling in a tangy yoghurt sauce.

SPLENDIDLY INDIAN, SUPERBLY SMOOTH

photo: Kake Pugh

Kachoris – Spicy mashed potato and peas spicy ball, coated in batter and deep-fried. Bombay Bhel Puri is there along with Gujarati curries e.g. Undui – five vegetable stew, and a Gujarati national dish; traditionally the five vegetables are beans, aubergine, red pumpkin, sweet potato and a further vegetable. These are cooked in a sauce made from gram flour, asafoetida and yoghurt. It is often served with besan kofta balls in it. Another superb dish is Lasan Bateta, literally garlic potato, but it's not that simple, it is baby new potatoes, and the stuffing includes spices and red chilli.the whole is dipped in gram-flour batter, deep-fried and served in imli (sweet tamarind chutney). Wow!!! *'The menu has some cold starters which are "to die for". Rashia Vall, great. Rice and breads as good as usual.'* CT. Says the highly critical rl: *'Menu includes unusual and tasty dishes. Recommended to me by so many people. Aloo Shai Poori (crispy pooris, potatoes, onions with yoghurt) and Vall Papri (spicy beans and onions on pooris with tamarind and yoghurt), both a taste of heaven. This restaurant is pure quality. It's world class.'* RL. Rani's daily eat-your-fill buffet spread consists of eight starters (hot and cold), nine main course items and a variety of accompaniments to compliment the selection. To finish Shrikhand and fresh fruit salad. The ever popular Bhel Puri and Masala Dosa are always included in the spread. The buffet is clearly labelled and indicates if food contains onion, garlic, wheat, diary, nuts or sugar. Licensed. Hours: 6-10 daily / lunch: Sundays only 1-2.30.

London N4

JAI KRISHNA   BYO   VEGETARIAN
161 Stroud Green Road, Crouch Hill, N4 3PZ
020 7272 1680

North Indian vegetarian food and the quality is good. 'The set-menu feast (£6.75 for 2 courses) s home-style, plentiful and wonderful.' RL. An added advantage is that it is BYO. Try the set luch in a Bento Box for £5.95. Cash only and the WC is accessed from outside of the venue. Hours: Sun-Thur: 12-10.30 to 11 Fri & Sat.

London N8

JASHAN
19 Turnpike Lane, N8 0EP   020 8340 9880
www.jashan.co.uk

Welcome back (by popular request) to the Guide to this long-standing (1989) venue. Jashan meaning 'celebration', specialise in real Indian food. It's not bog standatd. They do all the favourites and few things more and 'they do it really well, so please reinstate it' RL. [done, Ed]. Stters include: Aloo Tikkiya Chaat £3.50, Deep-fried potato cakes stuffed with spiced lentils and green peas; Makkai Paneer ke Pakore £3.50, Golden corn kernel and cottage cheese fritters; Hare Bhare Kabab £3.50, Minced vegetable cakes stuffed with cottage cheese and Macchi Chatpati £4.25, batter-fried traditional fish Koliwada. Mains incude: Desi Chooza Curry £6.95, joints of chicken marinated with fresh ginger, garlic, green chillies, spices and cooked in homemade-style curry; Elaichi Raan (min 48 hours notice) £34.00, Leg of lamb marinated overnight with yoghurt, cardamom and fresh herbs, pot-roasted and served sliced with pulao rice and spiced vegetables. It's enough for 4 or more. Their Rogan Josh £6.95 uses the authentic From Kashmir recies – tender pieces of lamb gently cooked in a mild curry with almonds and Ratanjot (kashmiri root spice used to achieve dark red colour) and

Jashan's appetising Starters and Mains

far from the curry house paastiche as you can get; Kofta Malmali £4.95, is delicate cottage cheese and vegetable balls simmered in a gravy, enriched with nuts. Their Dal Makhani £3.95, black lentils really slowly cooked with cream and butter is always a supreme test of cooking skills, which is why it is absent from curry houses. Puds include Kulfi, Gulab Jamun and Rasmalai all £4.50. Hours: 6-11 daily / lunch Sun only.

London N10

TASTE OF NAWAB
93 Colney Hatch Lane, N10 1LR   020 8883 6429

Established in 1996 the comfortable air-conditioned Nawab has all the old favourites plus exciting dishes. Owner Abdul Rahman says it all. *'If you as customers are happy, then I'm happy. If I'm happy the waiters and the cooks are happy'*. And it seems Abdul's customers really are happy. Won the local area Curry Chef Award. Roshun Specials snapshot: Agni Hash Duck £10.50, strips cooked with a special spice mix, garlic, pepper, carrot, red cabbage, onions, fresh mint and coriander. Paneer Sabji Roshun £6.95, home made curd cheese and steamed vegetables. Korak Bagon Bortha, £8.35, pieces of chicken or lamb cooked with grilled aubergine paste, fresh mint, coriander, garlic and lime juice. *'All dishes are large, reasonably priced and tasty. Service great!'* SM. Delivery: £10 minimum, 3 miles. Hours: 5.30-12am.

London N12

FINCHLEY PAN CENTRE
15 Woodhouse Road, N12 9EN   020 8446 5497

A tiny, unlicensed Indian snack bar, frequented by Indians. Kebabs, samosas, veg rissoles, etc., very inexpensive. Friendly service. Cash please. Oh, and as for Pan or Paan, it's not a cooking vessel, it is a collection of edible ingredients, ranging from very bitter to very sweet wrapped in the paan or bright dark green paan or betel leaf. Paan is an acquired taste, used as an aid to digestion. The observant visitor to India will have noticed very busy street kiosks dispensing paan all hours. We only know of a few other Paan houses (in Asian communities such as Southall). See page 81 for more about Paan. 12-10pm (Fri:3.30-10); closed Tues.

You say OK London N.

N3: GURU 12 Long Lane, Finchley, N3 2PT   020 8346 0530
N7: INDIAN OCEAN 359 Holloway Rd, N7 0RN   020 7609 9953
N8: JAI SHRI KRISHNA PURE VEG BYO 10 Turnpike Lane, N8 0PT   020 8888 7200
N11: BEJOY 72 Bounds Green Road, N11   020 8888 1268
54 seater, est 1995. Owner Abdul Sukur & chef M Rahman.
N13: BOMBAY SPICE 396 Green Lanes, Palmers Green, N13 5BD   020 8245 6095

N14: BEKASH 6 Hampden Square, N14   020 8368 3206.
Owner Nazrul Miah & Harun Ali (chef). 55 seater. 5.30-11.30 (Sat. to 12).
N16: PUNJAB 58 PUNJABI 58 Church St, Stoke Newington, N16 0020 7254 5021   www.punjab58.co.uk
14 hour marinated grills, curries cooked for 7 hours, and a selection of deliciously baked breads to choose from.

London N13

DIPALI INDIAN
82 Aldermans Hill, N13 4PP 020 8886 2221 www.dipali.co.uk

This popular long-established (1972) restaurant has appeared in all our Guides. It delivers all the old favourites plus some unusuals, eg: Starters: Chotpoti, tamarind sauce with chickpeas, potato, egg, herbs and spice. Chicken Pakora Pieces of chicken coated with spiced bhaji batter, deep-fried and served with salad. Both £3.55. Specials: Murghi Shassle, chicken marinated in mint sauce, cooked with selected spices and topped with salad. Murghi Tamatar, £6.95, chicken cooked in fresh green chilli and coriander ginger, very spicy hot. Achar Murghi, cooked with pickle. Shathkora Gosht, traditional Bangladeshi lamb dish, with citric fruit, both £7.95. Mishti Gosht lamb cooked with pumpkins and cardamom, also £7.95. Sunday buffet. Over 14 dishes, eat-all-you like. £7.95 (veg £6.95. Kids halpf price. Mon-Sat: 12 2 (Sun to 3) Sun-Th: 6-11.30 (Fri & Sat to 12).

Akbar Ltd.
TANDOORI & BALTI HOUSE
INDIAN TAKEAWAY

Free Home Delivery

Tel 020 8888 3865

Delivery: N4, N8, N10, N11, N13, N15, N17, N22
Minimum order for Delivery £7.00
£1.00 Delivery Charge under £7.00
Delivery between 6.00 - 11.30

Open Daily
5.30pm - 11.30pm
13 Salisbury Road,
Wood Green,
London N22 6NL

Established 1988

COBRA
SPLENDIDLY INDIAN, SUPERBLY SMOOTH

London N16

ABI RUCHI — KERALAN VEG & NON VEG
42 Church Street, Stoke Newington, N16 0LU
020 7923 4564   www.abiruchi.com

Recently taken over by the Kerela Group (see below) the authentic Kerelan cuisine, remains as constant as ever. Parippu Soup £2.75, from lentils, garlic, shallot onions and black pepper. Vazhudananga Porichethu, sliced aubergine coated in batter with coriander leaves and deep-fried, served with pineapple chutney, both £2.75. Chicken Kizhi, £3.75, a deep-fried dumpling filled with grated chicken, spinach, potato and herbs. Mains include: Bekal Meen Kootan, £6.30, kingfish curry with smoked tamarind and Koonthal Masala, £7.25, spiced baby squid, stuffed with tomato, pepper, coconut and chilli. Upperikal Stir-fried Side Dishes include: Cheera, spinach cooked with garlic, mustard seeds, chopped onions and curry leaves and Pacha Payar, long beans cooked with garlic, onions, grated coconut, mustard seeds and curry leaves, both £2.95. '*Friendly helpful service.*' BD. Hours; 12-3 & 6-11. *See Rhada SW17.*

RASA — KERELAN VEG   A-LIST
55 Church Street, Stoke Newington, N16 0AR
020 7249 0344   www.rasarestaurants.com

Shiva Das Sreedharan's and his wife Alison's first restaurant. He worked at a Delhi hotel before coming to England to manage a small restaurant. Believing he could do things better, he set up this restaurant in 1994 in this then unfashionable street serving then unfashionable south Indian vegetarian food. Thanks to enthusiasts like Das, we know that there is so much more to Keralan food than Masala Dosas. Rasa chefs are expert vegetarian cooks. Cooking uses coconut, mustard, curry leaves, curds, chillies, lentils and rice. Exotic vegetables include plantains, drumsticks, gourds, sour mango, and beans. The differences between the cooking of the five Kerelan groups is intensely subtle, *Below: All Rasa's nine restaurants are coloured this distinctive pink.*

including the names of the similar dishes. But differences there are, so try it out. Ask managers Usha or Bhaskar or the staff for advice. Favourites include Nair Dosa – a Keralan speciality, usually eaten during festivals and celebrations. A rice and black gram flour pancake filled with a mixture of potatoes, beetroot, carrot, onions and ginger, served with sambar and fresh coconut chutney, c£6. Chef Narayanan's signature dish is the Rasa Kayi, a mixed vegetable speciality from the Southern State of Karnataka. A spicy curry made of beans, carrots, cauliflower, potatoes and simmered in a sauce of garlic, ginger and fennel, c£4. Cheera Curry is Paneer and spinach cooked with garlic, peppers and tomato in a creamy sauce, c£3. For pudding, if you have room, try Banana Dosa, the Palakkad Iyer (Brahmin) speciality with a difference. These tiny pancakes are made from bananas, plain flour and cardamom. Lots of reports. Most love the food and are happy with the service. An added extension has not really helped its being crowded. Like adding a lane to the M25, it simply fills up again. It's the problem of being popular. Sun to Thurs: 6–10.45. Fri, Sat to 11.30. Saturday/Sunday Lunch: 12–3. Service: 12.5%. Branches: next entry, and London NW1, W1, WC1 & Newcastle.

RASA TRAVANCORE — KERALAN NON VEG
56 Church St, N16 0NB   020 7249 1340

This Rasa is nearly opposite the original at 55 (see above). You can't miss it. The colour is the key. Das just loves pink – the hue that is blackcurrant yoghurt. It's the colour of his venue frontages, decor, menu and his web site. So why this new venue? We normally think of Kerala as a vegetarian state. In fact there have been passionate non-vegetarians – Muslims, Jews and Christians – living there side by side for centuries, each with a distinctive cooking style. As for the latter, St Thomas the Apostle landed in Kerala in ad50 and made many converts to Christianity. His language was Syriac Armenaic, his converts known as Syrian Christians. To this day they eat offal, chicken, duck, fish, shellfish, beef, and wild boar. Dishes with very unfamiliar names crowd the menu. A great introduction is the Travancore Feast, where you get a good selection of dishes for £20. Chicken Puffs, spicy chicken masala stuffed in puff pastry are frankly Anglo Indian Raj stuff, but they're great stuff, £3.50, and eat them with Meen Achar – Chicken pickle. More traditional Syrian Christian specialities include Kerala Fish fry, £3.95, kingfish marinated in a spicy paste made of ginger, green chillies and coriander, then shallow fried in the traditional fashion. Chicken Stew, £5.25, chicken cooked in fresh coconut milk, with finely chopped ginger, green chillies and flavoured with cinnamon, cardamom, cashewnut and raisins. Erachi Olathiathu, £6.95, cubes of lamb and dry cooked in turmeric water, then stir-fried in an open kadai with an abundance of black pepper, curry leaves, and finely sliced fresh coconut slivers. Tharavu roast, £6.95, duck cooked in a thick sauce with ginger, garlic, onion and coriander. Rasa in Sanskrit means amongst other things, taste, flavour, liking, pleasure, delight and essence. There is so much more. The venue is managed by Jinu and Mustafa. Let them and the staff guide you. Hours: as Rasa above. Branches: see previous entry.

JOGINDER'S SUPPER CLUB Secret venue, N19
http://jogindersupperclub.wordpress.com/

Secret supper clubs are plentiful in the US and are now they're over here. They bridge the gap between restaurants and dinner parties. A number of diners, (no kids allowed) who may or may not have met, book and pay for a home-cooked meal. At Tuffnel Park's Joginder Supper Club, for instance, the food is cooked by retired teacher Rani Ranjit and her daughter Saira for up to 12 guests who are invited to donation £25 to dine on Punjabi food around one large dining table. Guests are encouraged to BYO. *"People wander into the kitchen to watch us cook. They take away spices and ask for recipes,"* says Baker.

AKBAR TAKEAWAY
13 Salisbury Rd, N22 6NL   020 8881 7902

Chef Proprietor - Mostakin Miah (Mintu) has been running this takeaway since 1988 and his Chicken Korma and Chicken Tikka Masala literally runs out of the door, he says they are just so popular. His set dinner for £7 a person is also a favourite and consists of a Popadom, Onion Bhajia, a Chicken Curry, a Vegetable Curry, Pullao Rice and Onion Salad - good value I know we will all agree! Delivery: 2.5 miles, £7 minimum. Price Check: Popadom 30p, CTM £3.80, Pullao Rice £1.50. Is this STILL the cheapest popadom in the Guide? Hours: 6 - 11.30.

LONDON NW
Area: North West London
Postcodes: NW1 to NW11

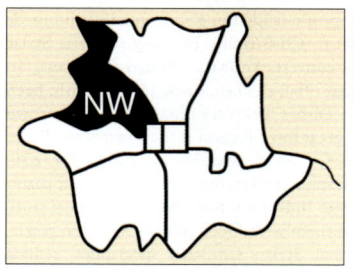

See page 88 for key to this map

London NW1

Drummond Street, Euston, NW1

Drummond Street is a mini little India. West of Euston station, it will not win any beauty awards, and it lacks the ethnic glamour of Southall and Wembley, or the intensity of purpose of Brick Lane. Its assets are a concentrated selection of extremely good, inexpensive Indian greengrocers, a Halal butcher and ingredient stores, such as Viranis (where Pataks began trading in the 60s).

Viranis is open all hours for all things Indian including Cobra (useful for the nearby BYOs), a dozen or so takeaways and restaurants. Here in alphabetical order are your Drummond Street favourites:

AMBALA   VEG SWEETS & SNACKS
112 Drummond Street, NW1 2HN   020 7387 3521
www.ambalafoods.com

Ambala started trading here in 1965. It specialises in takeaway-only savoury snacks (Pakoras and Samosa, etc.), Indian sweets (Halva, Jalebi, Gulab Jamun, Barfi, etc.) and a few vegetarian curries such as chickpea. Established initially for Asians, it now has branches in London (8 inc this one also at Brick Lane E1, E7, E10, E17, N8, SE18, SW17, also Birmingham (3), Bradford, Derby, Glasgow, Ilford, Leicester, Luton, Manchester, Slough, Southall, Surbiton and Wembley. All branches serve identical items at identical prices. The quality is first-class and the prices are always reasonable. Be prepared to queue, and pay cash. Daily 10am-11pm.

CHUTNEYS   VEG
134 Drummond Street, NW1 2PA   020 7387 6077

Good vegetarian food at good prices. Lunch and dinner daily.

DIWANA BHEL POORI HOUSE
VEG STREET FOOD   BYO   TOP 100
121 Drummond Street, NW1 2HL   020 7387 5556

It's a café-style, unlicensed, open all day, still very cheap, highly successful 100-seat restaurant, divided into two ground-floor sections plus a further floor. The food is all vegetarian, with much vegan, and above all, it's all fabulous, and it's most certainly all authentic. Diwana pioneered Bombay pavement kiosk snack food in the UK and is undoubtedly still the best of its kind. The ownership change could have dethroned Diwana, but it has remained one of London's iconic eating-holes. 'Not to be visited for the decor, nor for a long and relaxing meal – sitting on the floor would be more comfortable than sitting on the bolted-down benches, so opt for chairs if you can. I have the same thing every time I visit, Papadam with Coconut Chutney, Rasam, a soup, whose chillies without fail give me attention-drawing hiccups, then a Dosa £3 to £4.60 depending on type, with more Coconut Chutney, with its mustard seed and chilli and Sambar. If Pat and I share, I try to get all the drumsticks before him. And of course I never miss out on one of their adorable Bhel Puris, their masthead and their most ordered dish.' dbac. Bhel Puri, or Poori, is defined on page 81. Diwana offers several types – Batata Puri, Dahi Batata Puri, Chat Aloo Papri and Batata Pava, all £2.10. Bhel can be accompanied by Gol Goppas (see pp 73 & 79). A super alternative starter is Dahi Vada (see page 80). By now you've spent £6 or £7, and you're probably full. But try to leave a little space for the Diwana's

COBRA — SPLENDIDLY INDIAN, SUPERBLY SMOOTH

desserts. Their legendary Kulfi, perhaps, or 'the highlight of our meal, the Falooda – an Indian knickerbocker glory – probably the best in London. The quality of the food outweighs the numbness in your backside!' db. 'All first class. Reasonably priced.' mw. 'Consistently good quality and low prices. Never changes.' jr. ''On one of the hottest days in July, I needed lunch in Drummond Street. I chose Diwana because of the jug of water that is automatically provided. It was too hot for alcohol and lassis is too filling when there is serious eating to be done.' bs. 'Will certainly go back, but not for buffet.' np. 'The back of the bill has a questionnaire. I was pleased to tick excellent for everything.' hc. Booking is hit and miss, and they won't even try on Fri. to Sun. so expect a queue (especially at peak hours). Great value and don't forget to BYO (no corkage charge). Off-license with chilled Cobra available at Viranis up the street. Thali from £4.00 to £6.00. E-a-m-a-y-l lunch to 2.30pm, £4.50. Hard to exceed £12 for a good veggie blow-out! It remains very high in our TOP 100. Hours: 12-11.

GUPTA — VEG SWEETS & SNACKS
100 Drummond Street, NW1 2HN 020 7380 1590

A very good, long-established, less flashy vegetarian snack and sweet takeaway. Samosas and Pakoras, plus their unique, delightful, and often still-hot Pea Kebab, a Gujarati speciality, are freshly cooked in the kitchens behind. Their sweets achieve a lightness of touch, and seem to avoid the taste of tinned evaporated milk that sometimes spoils those made by others. Cash or cheque. Branch: Watford Way, Hendon, NW4.

RAVI KEBAB HALAL — PAKISTANI NON V E G
125 Drummond Street, NW1 2HL 020 7388 1780

Opened 1978. 'Kebab' tells you it's very much a meat place, Halal that there's no pandering to Western tastes, as one can tell by its local mostly Muslim patronage (so no alcohol permitted). Grilled and curried meats are all there at bargain prices. There are some vegetable and dhal dishes but this is no place for the veggie. '*One of my favourites. Cheap and cheerful. Food superb. Sheek Kebabs amongst the best anywhere.*' RE.

RAVI SHANKAR — VEG STREET FOOD
133 Drummond Street, NW1 2HL 020 7388 6458

Vegetarian restaurant similar to the Diwana which it followed into Drummond Street. Prices are still very reasonable and it is usually busy at peak hours. Recommended are the two Thali set dishes, the Mysore and the Shankar, and the Shrikand dessert. '*Every dish was excellent – flavoursome, spicy and delicious. Prices are extremely reasonable.*' MW Daily specials at under £4. Hours: 12pm-11pm. Branches: Chutneys, and Haandi, both on Drummond Street.

Elsewhere in NW1

CAFE INDIYA
71 Regents Park Road, NW1 020 7722 5225

Seats 28 in two rooms. We hear of Goan Fish Curry with coconut milk, £9, and Chicken Xacutti £8.50, fairly hot. Sabziyon Ki Shaslick £6.50, fresh vegetables, marinated in a special tandoori sauce and grilled in the clay oven. Paneer Simla Mirch £3.75, medium spiced stir-fry of homemade cottage cheese, green peppers and fresh tomatoes. Service: 10%. 5.30-11.30 / Sat only 12-2.30 Sat only / Sun: 12-11.30.

GREAT NEPALESE www.great-nepalese.co.uk
NEPALESE AWARD WINNER TOP 100
48 Eversholt Street, NW1 1DA 020 7388 6737

Opposite Euston Station Gopal P Manandhar's Everest pioneered Nepalese cuisine in London in 1982, and it has stood the test of time, Chef is son Jeetendra, whose charming wife Mandira also adds her culinary expertise, especially with Nawari (an Nepalese ethnic group) food, for example the starter, Momo – steam-cooked veg-filled pastries, and Masco Bara, black lentil pancakes with curry sauce both £4.50, Kalezo Ra Chyow (chicken liver) £4.75. Main courses include Dumba (mutton), Pork Bhutwa (the Nepalese have no proscriptions of either pork or alcohol) and Hach Ko (duck) curries. There is also a range of eleven Nepalese vegetable dishes. Add those to sixteen 'standard' curry house vegetable dishes and the vegetarian will be spoilt for choice. In addition, the Great does all the standard curries and tandooris, from Phal, 'very very hot', to Shahi Korma, 'very very mild', though why you'd go there for these is beyond me. Go for Nepalese food, and if virgin to it, ask the staff to explain. Ask Ghopla for a shot of Coronation rum. Brewed in 1975 in Katmandu, its bottle is kukri-shaped, its contents lethal. Set Veg Nepalese meal £14.50. Service 10%. Takeaway: 10% disc. Del: £12 min 5-miles. 5.30 - 11.30. Sat. to 12.

NAMAASTE KITCHEN TOP 100
FINE PAN-INDIAN DINING
64 Parkway, Camden, NW1 7AH 020 7485 5997
www.namaastekitchen.co.uk

Don't let the down-market street and Namaaste Kitchen's unremarkable interior put you off. Get stuck in and you are in for some of the best cooked Indian food in London. It isn't owner Sabir Karim's day job, he's a senior BA steward. But it's the Indian chefs who do the cooking and their spicing is subtle and masterly. They specialise in Indian and Pakistani grills, using the three core methods of the tandoor clay oven, the sigri over a coal flame and on the tawa, a hot iron griddle plate – all in full view of customers at two chefs' tables by the grill area with their perfect seats for those who want a ringside view; they can take parties of eight apiece.

Namaaste's grill area.
Photo courtesy: www.theupcoming.co.uk

Namaaste Kitchen's o Owner Sabir Karim.
Photo courtesy: Tandoori Magazine

Starters range from just £3.95 to £5.95; main courses run just £7.50 for tandoori chicken in sizzling peri peri spices or £7.50 to £18.95 for the fabulous lobster in Malabar spice.; Mangalore crab (dorset brown crab cooked with mangalore sauce served with plain rice), £12.90; From the special grill menu Tandoori Rubyian Duck, Sea Bass marinated in raw coastal spices, and Peshawari Lamb Chops Lamb barra kabab (afghani style lamb cutlets marinated with kachri, in ginger, black pepper & spices slow cooked in tandoor), £5.50. TMon-Thur: 12-2.30pm, / 5:30-11:30. Fri-Sat; 12-11.30 (-11,Sun) Branch Salaam Namaste. WC1N 3EF.

RASA EXPRESS   KERELAN NON VEG
327 Euston Rd, NW1 3AD   020 7387 8974
www.rasarestaurants.com

Rasa Express is a simple, inexpensive, no fuss brand. It's lunchtime only takeaway fast food with just eight items on the menu at prices ranging from £1.50 to £3.50. In the latter category are Mysore Bonda – Potato balls laced with ginger, curry leaves, coriander cashew nuts and mustard seeds, dipped in besan batter and crisply fried. Fish Cutlet, spiced cassava and tuna breadcrumbed and Veg Samosa, all served with coconut chutney. Chicken Biriani is £3.50. Top of the bill is the Rasa Lunch Box, two curries, a stir-fried vegetable dish, bread, rice and a sweet. Mon to Fri: 12-3. Credit cards: over £15. Branches: Rasa London N16, W1, Newcastle and Rasa Express, 5 Rathbone St, W1T

London NW3

ERIKI   FINE PAN-INDIAN   TOP 100
4 Northways Parade, Finchley Road, NW3
020 7722 0606   www.eriki.co.uk

Entrepreneur Sat Lally opened here in 2002 in a former Italian restaurant. It's a 75-seater with a modern Indian look with orange and magenta walls, Indian cushions, carvings and chairs and a huge bar. Sat requests that you don't nick the trendy cutlery imported from Rajasthan; it's for sale if you fall for it! The place has a homely yet upmarket feeling. It is a place which could well become your local. The welcome is certainly one for regulars and newcomers alike: friendly, swift and sure-footed. Lally has recruited serious talent here: Naresh Matta was for many years one of Amin Ali's Indian chefs at Jamdani then the Red Fort, W1, working under Mohammed Rias, a Dum Pukht practitioner (see pages 72 & 80) and more latterly at Soho Spice. Matta learned Goan cuisine from former head chef Jude Pinto (ex Goan specialist at

COBRA
SPLENDIDLY INDIAN, SUPERBLY SMOOTH

Veeraswami and Chutney Mary). This gave Matta a very wide Indian palette to work from. He says *"The menu offers a tour of India, with dishes starting from the northern regions of Hyderabad, Punjab, midway through Delhi and Bombay (Mumbai), moving south to the coastline of Goa" Starters include:* Murgh Haryali Kabab £6, rchicken breast marinated in a paste of mint, coriander, garlic, yoghurt & spices, cooked in the tandoor, Camalari Mirch Fry, £7 rings stir-fried with onions and keralan spices served on a leafy salad' Scallops Hariyali £7, steamed with a hint of garlic and served in a curried green herb sauce, Baigan Tikki. £4.50, liced aubergine stuffed with cottage cheese, potatoes, sesame seeds served with a garlic and tomato sauce. Mains include: Murgh Xacuti, £11 Rich chicken curry from , Saag Gosht, £12 tender lamb pieces cooked with fresh baby spinach and methi (fenugreek) leaves, Lukhnowi Lamb Chop Masala, £13 Tender lamb chops in a spicy masala with denghi pepper, ginger and fresh lime, Kadai Methi Paneer, home-made cottage cheese tossed with kasturi methi, mixed peppers and kadai masala Bhindi Masala, okra with sauteed onion tossed with carom seeds, tomato, ground spices and coriander leaves, both £7.50 Fresh . No cheques. Service charge: 12.5%. Hours: 12-3 Mon-Fri & Sun. and 6-11 daily. Branch: Crowne Plaza Hotel, Heathrow, Junction 4 / M4

GUGLEE — INDIAN MEAT & VEG
7 New College Parade, Finchley Road ..NW3 5EP
020 7722 8474   www.guglee.co.uk

In Cricket, the restaruant tells us, a googly is a type of delivery bowled by a right-arm leg spin bowler. We're not sure what this means in culinary terms, but you like it, so here's a bit more about it. Starters include Tandoori Broccoli. £4.25, marinated with yogurt & tandoori spices then roasted or Mini Masala Dosa £4, with Coconut Chutney – south Indian crepe made of rice & lentils batter, stuffed with curried potatoes. Crab Cake, £5.49, pan fried crab meat tikki mixed with potato and spices. Sev Puri Chaat £3.75, 4 puffed hollow pastry filled [gol goppas] with chick peas & mashed potato topped with yoghurt and home made chutneys. Mains include: Butter Chicken on the bone, £8.50; Makhmali Duck Breast, £11.99, tossed with red onion & sage leaf finished with star anise & orange juice; Lamb Curry Indian Railway Special, £10, cooked in the style you'd find at all raiway station. Desserts include Phirni, saffron flavoured rice pudding' Gajar Halwa, carrot Pudding and Kulfi, all £2.99. Thalis from £12. Set meals from £18. Daily, all day. *Branch: Gulgee, NW6 1QS*

WOODLANDS — VEGETARIAN
102 Heath Street, NW3 1DR   020 7794 3080
www.woodlandsrestaurant.co.uk

Branch of the veteran chain. It has branches in India, Singapore, London and the USA. See SW1 for details. Daily: 6-10.45, Tues-Sun: 12-3.

Bhel Puri as served the traditional way in Mumbai, in newspaper. Elf and Safety won't allow newspaper to be used in this country (remember fish & chips in the good-ole-days?) Guglee's Bhel is served on plates. It's crispy rice puffs and sev with chopped onions, coriander leaf, tomatoes & chutneys £3.99

London NW4

LAHORE ORIGINAL KEBAB HOUSE
PAKISTANI/PUNJABI   150 Brent Street NW4 2DR
020 8203 6904   www.originallahore.com/hendon

Lahore Kebab House E1 was, of course, the original venue of its genre, its food being pure, unadulaterad, Pakistani / Punjabi food, geared to Asian tastes, without compromising it for Westerners. It still is. Several copycats have popped up here and there but this branch is for real. Meat is the main player; Halal meat is a given, with dark, thick-gravied, pungent, savoury curries served in the karahi, or with items from the tandoor in the form

Woodlands Exec Chef Raj Gopal displays a dosa and chutneys

of succulent tikkas or kebabs. But the observant tell of a seed change here. The menu has a Kenyan Asian twist with an emphasis on vegetable dishes such as Paneer or Chilli mogo, cassava stir-fried with garam masala and a heap of fresh coriander and chillies, then combined with tamarind sauce. The lentil dishes, a great test of the cook's skills. are to die for. Try the Mung Makhani (a green lentil version of black urid makhni dhal, makhni being butter). Prices remain excellent, eg: Main courses from £7. Takes some credit cards. Takeaway service. 11am-11.30pm daily. See menu details on E1 branch.

YOU SAY OK – London NW1 to NW5

NW1: BONGO RAJ INDIAN TAKEAWAY, 162 Agar Grove, NW1 9TY   020 7267 1530

NW1: SHAH TANDOORI, 159 Drummond Street, NW1 2PB 020 7383 5677

NW2: KHANA, 68 Cricklewood Bdy, NW2 3EP   020 8452 4789

NW3: FLEET TANDOORI 104 Fleet Rd, NW3 020 7485 6402
Good prices enhanced by a 10% discount if you show them this Guide

NW4: GUPTA CONFECTIONERS 262 Watford Way, NW4 4UJ 020 8203 4044 See Gupta Drummond St, NW 1 for details.

NW5: CHAMELI, 56 Chetwynd Rd, NW5 1DJ 020 7482 2833.

PRINCE OF CEYLON   TOP 100
SRI LANKAN AWARD WINNER
39 Watford Way, NW4 3JH   020 8202 5967
wwwprinceofceylon.co.uk

Abdul Satter has been here since 1979, during which time it has grown to 150 seats split over five rooms. The Prince's standard menu of tandooris, kebabs, curries and all the business, all perfectly competently cooked, are not what you go there for. It is the Sri Lankan specials. And if these items are unfamiliar, ask the waiter's advice, but be patient if explanations are unclear at first. It is a rice (Buth) cuisine. Jaffna Thossai, soft pancake made of soaked and ground urid dal, served with coconut chutney. Devilled curries are there, including Squid curry. Fried Cabbage with onion £3. Coconut Chutney £2. Hoppers or Appas are rice and coconut-flour pancakes; String Hoppers, like string made of wheat or rice flour dough, but resembling vermicelli nests, from £6.50; or Pittu – ditto dumpling, £3.85. These or straight rice are accompanied by pungent watery curries, in which coconut, turmeric, tamarind, curry leaves and chillies feature. But they can be mild, too. Look out for aromatic black curries and fragrant white ones. Fish dishes, such as Ambul Thial, £5.50 (a Sri Lankan national dish of sour, spicy mckerel fish dish) and the Ceylon Squid (Dhallo) £5.25, curry are both popular. Mon & Weds - Fri: 6-12; Sat - Sun 12-12; Tues closed.

London NW5

LIBERTY KEBABISH   PAKISTANI
56, Chetwynd Road, Kentish Town. NW5 1JD
020 7267 2000   libertykebabish.co.uk

Formerly Indian Lancer, it was taken oven by owner: M.Y.Hashmi in 1990. *"Old hands, and smooth service of good gutsy food"*. RL. Chicken Afghani stuffed with paneer, mixed with herbs and spices and grilled in a clay oven £4.95; Garlic Nan £2.00; Lamb Biryani £6.96; Cucumber Raitha 95. Sunday Buffet: 12 to 5 - £4.95. Home Delivery: 3 miles, £12 minimum spend. Credit Cards accepted. Discount - a very generous 10% on evening meals from Sunday to Wednesday - booking advised. Licensed: £4.50 pint of beer. Price Check: Popadom 50p, CTM £5.50, Pullao Rice £2.20, Plain Naan £1.20. Hours: Tues - Sat: 5.30-11.30. Sun: 12-11. .

COBRA
SPLENDIDLY INDIAN, SUPERBLY SMOOTH

London NW6

ARIANA 2 — AFGHAN BYO
241 Kilburn High Road, NW6 7JN   020 3490 6709
www.ariana2restaurant.co.uk

Afghani food is Halal. Yoghurt always accompanies a meal. Try Dogh, £1.50, Savoury Yoghurt with mint, and the Tourshis or chutneys. The food is less spicy than Indian, (see also p 71) but some names are similar. Bread isn't Naan, it is Nane Lawash – thinner, glazed and basket-shaped. Qurma is Korma, etc, etc. Considering our long term relationship with Afghanistan it is surprising how few Afghan restaurants there are. Owned by Wali and son, Ariana 2 is simply furnished and service is friendly though reportedly slow at times. Starters include Aushak, boiled dumpling filled with leeks, spices and topped with ground meat and yogurt. S £4; L £8.

Aushak

Kadoo Buranee, mashed pumpkin in oil and mixed herbs and spices, topped with yoghurt, with Naan, £4; Aush Soup, homemade noodles with mixed vegetables, £3. Bolanee (a fried pastry turnover) four types Gandana, with leeks seasoned with herbs, served with yogurt sauce; Katchalou with mashed potatoes; Kadoo with pumpkin; Buranee fried aubergines in olive oil each £ and served with Afghan with nan. Afghans love Kebabs and the menu has many. Some have familiar Indian names, eg: Tikka Kebab, or Shish Kebab. Afghan kebabs include Koubideh (ground lamb), Joojeh, poussin marinated in garlic & saffron, Sultani Kebab, ground lamb and chunks of lamb, with tomato and onion; Kebab E Barg, skewer of baby lamb fillet marinated with garlic. Mains include Kabuli Palow, lamb shank with basmati rice, topped with carrots, raisins, almond & pistachios and a side dish, £9 Quorma Chalow, chicken or lamb sautéed with onion and green pepper served with rice and salad; Mantu, lamb mince wrapped in steamed pastry, served with yogurt and topped with meat sauce and lentils, both £8. Dessets include Firnee, homemade with almonds and pistachio, £3. Nuckel, sweet coated almonds (best served with tea). Dinner for Two £25. Dinner for Four £50: Starter around the table, Kabuli palow, chicken kebab, Lamb kebab and kofta kebab, drinks and desserts. BYO (offie opposite) no corkage, in fact no corkscrew so BYO that too. Credit cards OK. 12-12

ELEPHANT WALK   www.elephantwalk.co.uk
98 West End Lane, NW6 2LU   020 7328 3308
SRI LANKAN AWARD WINNER

Specialising in Sri Lankan and South Indian food, with a sprinkling of Pan-Indian items such as Sheekh Kebab and curries, it opened in 2005, fronted by Kannan Rajapakse, with his Head Chef wife, Deepthe. Located a stone's throw from Lord's Cricket Ground, it seats 42 people in the main dining area, with an additional function room on the lower level that can hold up to 30 people. The front patio opens its French folding doors every summer for outdoor dining (2 tables). The charm is the fact that the Deepthe's dishes are ones that her own mother prepared for her in their family home. So Deepthe guarantees authentic dishes prepared in a traditional method. Typical Sri Lankan treats include String Hoppers, steamed noodle made of rice flour and Kotthu Rotis, a flatbread that is shredded and chopped in a wok with vegetables and other ingredients and served with sauce on the side. Devil Dishes, mainly served the clubs in colonial times – dry dish served on a hot plate. One outstanding dish on the menu, which is hard to find even in Sri Lanka is Lamprias (Lampries), which is several curries and rice wrapped in a banana leaf parcel (one per diner) and steamed until cooked. It is a

Lamprais parcels after cooking.

complete meal. Tradtionally (see below) it contains aromatic yellow rice, a meat fish or vegetarian, a kofta rissole, two veg curries such as plantain and aubergine, red onion aambal (chutney) and a deep-fried boiled egg, though the contents do vary chef to chef.

The banana leaf is unwrapped and the meal is ready to eat.

LONDON NW6

Lampries are great fun. But they must be pre-ordered for sseveral diners. It isn't worth Deepthe making just one. The Dutch introduced some European vegetables to Ceylon, as it was then known. Try Deepthe's curries lusing them: Beetroot & Potato Kari, Green Cabbage stir fried with coconut, Green Beans kari, Swede kari, Leaks stirfried with coconut, Turnip kari. There are some unusual exotic karies on the menu such as Breadfruit kari, Manioc kari, Drumsticks & Potato kari, Bitter Gourd kari, Pumpkin kari, Snake Gourd kari, Aubergine kari and Green Banana kari. Thali's and masala dosa's are other specialties coming out of the kitchen. Mon - Sun: 5-11; Sat & Sun Lunch 12.30- 3.30.

GEETA   MAINLY SOUTH INDIAN   TOP 100
57 Willesden Lane, NW6 7RL   020 7624 1713

It's mainly south Indian veg food with some meat dishes as well, at which Geeta excels, and has done since the 70s, with never a decline in standard.. Geeta and son work front of house and a safe-hands, elderly male chef commands the kitchens. Try his Dosa, Idli, Sambar, Upamas Karela (bitter gourds), drumsticks (long pithy marrow which you suck to extract the tender flesh), Ravaiya – baby aubergine and plantains stuffed with a coconut spicy filling Rasam – and more. And with most of these around the £2 mark, and providing you keep off the carnivorous items, you'll fill up for less than a tenner, with drink. You can get standard meat (inc beef) and chicken curries, et al, and from the reports I get, the thoroughly devoted following adore it. *'It's all fine stuff, served in less than glamourous, but typically Indian surroundings, to a thoroughly devoted following. This and Vijay (below) are different and should not be missed.'* DMW. Hours: 12-2.30/6-10.30p, Fri & Sat: to 11.30.

KOVALAM   KERELAN MEAT & VEG
12 Willesden Lane, NW6 7SR   020 7625 4761
www.kovalamrestaurantonline.co.uk

Kovalam is a rather good government-run (Ashoka Group) beach hotel at the town of Trivandrum, just 30 miles north of India's southern most tip. Actually it's probably the best hotel in that chain. Coconut palms, temple elephants, white dotis, sea, sun and sand. Their restaurant is called Sea Shells and it serves a range of south Indian dishes, protein as well as vegetable. I digress; Trivandrum is a far cry from Willesden, but Kovalam restaurant opened there in 2001 and you'll get the picture from the pictures on the wall. And as at Sea Shells, the food is spot on. It offers south Indian dishes such as Dosas, Idli, Sambar, Upamas and Vaadia. Pazham Pori Plantain Pakora makes an unusual starter. Try the Keralan seafood and meat dishes, such as the traditional Lamb Fry where the meat is dry-fried with pepper, coconut and curry leaves. Though we cannot imagine why they do it, the south Indian chefs offer curry-house dishes. But why order these when you can have a plateful of south Indian delicacies such as those

Below: a south Indian vegetarian meal is traditionally served on a banana leaf, see page 75. Kovalam have translated this to a large dinner plate. Top bowl Rasam soup, clockwise from one o'clock: Spinach curry, red coconut chutney on white rice, popadum, tomato curry, sambar, mango pickle, and yoghurt curry in the centre bowl.

pictured above. Takeaway service; delivery (3-mile radius on over £15). Daily: 12-2.30 / Sun-Thur: 6-11 Fri & Sat: to 12. Branch: Nila, Sutton-In-Ashfield Notts.

SURYA   GUJARATI VEGETARIAN
59 Fortune Green Road, NW6 1DR   020 7435 7486

Mr (front of house) and Mrs Tiwari (chef) really pack 'em in at this tiny, 34-seat vegetarian, licensed restaurant – there's no room to move, almost literally – it's always full. The dish of the day (it changes daily) excites several of our regulars. We hear well of Gujarati dishes such as Patra and Kaddu Kari and inexpensive prices. Hours: 6-10.30pm, and Sun. lunch. Branch: Shree Ganesha, 4 The Promenade, Edgwarebury Lane, Edgware, Middx.

VIJAY   S. INDIAN VEG & NON VEG   TOP 100
49 Willesden Lane, NW6 7RF   020 7328 1087
www.vijayrestaurant.co.uk

Vijay was founded in 1964, was the earliest to provide south Indian food in the UK, and its menu contains all the vegetarian items listed in Geeta's entry, at much the same prices. Indeed my remarks are the same, since Vijay like Geeta does carnivorous dishes too. Vijay has its own clan of loyal regulars who know they'll get *'very nice tasty food.'* B&WW. Prices are perhaps just a tad higher here, but again, you'll only spend a tenner if you stick to the scrumptious vegetarian delights.
12-2.45/6-10.45 (Fri-Sat to 11.45.

SPLENDIDLY INDIAN, SUPERBLY SMOOTH

London NW9

LAHORE KEBAB HOUSE PAKISTANI
248 Kingsbury Road, NW9 0BG   020 8905 0940

No longer connected to the celebrated London E1 original, but identical menu. (See E1) It's licensed, and the food is good. No credit cards. Daily: 1pm to midnight.

TANDOOR, GREAT EASTERN PUNJABI
232 Kingsbury Rd, NW9 0BH   020 8205 1450

One of those divine venues where the food is better than aerage and, being Indian-owned, it is licensed so 'An impressive place that opened in late 2003 in a barely converted pub, where instead of serving overpriced gastropub nonsense, here you get authentic Indian food, as evidenced by the high proportion of Indians actually eating here. Pops are free (remember those days?). The food has that authenic Punjabi taste, whether its favoutite curries or specials. When a venue can make Romali Roti, (aka handkerchief bread), the thinnest Indian bread made on a very hot steel hemisphere of their own kulfi you know it isn't a curryhouse. And to prove it, their chef has cooked for over 2 decades in various Indian hotelss meal as well. Av £25'. AH. AndyHayler.com Daily: Midday-Mdnt.

KOSHER INDIAN CUISINE

There are, it seems, 1,000 Indian-born Jews in the Hendon/Golders Green area. One of these is Nathan Moses who was born in India, lived in Israel and came to Hendon in 1978, where he runs a kosher and Indian bakery in Vivian Avenue, Hendon. Moses felt sure there was a demand for a kosher Indian restaurant, and Kavanna opened in 2005, though it has since closed. However its place has been taken by several others, and we list them below. Any food style can be kosher if it is prepared and supervised in accordance with certain laws and supervision. Kosher and halal rules have in common meat slaughtering rules and a proscription on pork. Kosher goes further with stating no shellfish can be eaten and that meat cannot be cooked or eaten with yoghurt, butter, ghee, milk, cream or yoghurt. According to some fish cannot be mixed with meat. Moses employs Indian chefs, who adapt traditional Indian recipes to be kosher. At the restaurants below, non-Jews are welcome.

BEIT HAMADRAS 105 Brent Street, Hendon, London, NW4 2DX   020 8203 4567 www.beithamadras.co.uk Sun - Thur: 12-3; 5:30- 11. Sat:open 1hr after Shabbat to 12am in Winter.

BIRIANI EXPRESS 198 Brent Street, NW4 1BE branch of Moses Tandoor, offering quick take-away Kosher Indian meals

MATTANCHERRY RESTAURANT 109a Golders Green Road, NW11 8HR   0208 209 3060 www.mattancherry.co.uk

MOSES TANDOOR 168 West Hendon Broadway, NW9 7AA 020 8203 501 www.mosestandoor.com

London NW10

GALLE CAFÉ SRI LANKAN
91 Dudden Hill Lane, Dollis Hill, NW10 1BD 020 8459 7921

Named after the town (pron Gaul) in south Sri Lanka, it's an unpretentious café with unpretentious prices, very popular with local Asians. And look at the hours. Fancy breakfast? There is the typical British greasy spoon stuff: eggs, bacon, beans et al, but why not try String Hopper (steamed noodle) with a thin curry or Egg Hopper (ditto with an egg) The dishes of the day are on the board. Main stream curries may include, Cashew, or tuna fish, or beetroot. Meat might be beef or it might be lamb. Sambols (chutneys) add to the fun. Cash only (and not much of that either). You can exit with filled tummy for a fiver! Mon-Sat: 8-8.

KADIRI'S KENYAN ASIAN
26 High Rd, Harlesden, NW10 2QD   020 8459 0936

Run by the Kadiri family since 1974. Jamal Kadir (founder) is either out front or in the kitchen, Mo Kadiri manages day to day running and Azam Kadiri maintains the quality control. The family is proud of their redec and space-age kitchen, which includes the Rolls Royce of ovens, the Rational Combination, a pricey computerised oven, which decides when items are cooked to perfection. It results in the tenderest of meats and freshest of vegetables. Tue-Thur: 12-2.30 / 5 - 11. Fri: 2 to 11; Sat: 12-11; Sun: 1-11.

SARAVANAS N & S IND VEG
77 Dudden Hill La, Dollis Hill, NW10   020 8459 4900

It is vegetarian, and inexpensive.(even so it does take credit cards) and popular with the local Asians. Say no more, well a bit more ... There are two dining areas, the formica tabled café and the cane-seating 'smarter' room with bar. Rasam soup and Sambar are competent, as are the curries, and the Thalis (£7 to 9) are a splendidly filling, economical meal. Tue-Sun: 12-10.30.

YOU SAY OK - London NW7 to NW10

NW7: DAY OF THE RAJ 123 The Broadway, Mill Hill, NW7 020 8906 3477 www.dayoftheraj.com Est 1989 by S Miah, who tells us that he changes the wallpaper every six months *to 'maintain standards'*. It is very smart indeed and is a place to go for an enjoyable meal out. Service 10%.

NW7: DAY OF THE RAJ EXPRESS 36B Bittacy Hill, Mill Hill, NW7 1LB   020 8371 9696 www.dayoftherajexpress.com Takeaway/del only branch of above. Min order £12. Daily: 5-11.

NW10: RAJ: 43 Chamberlayne Rd, NW10 ~ 0208 960 7090. Misbah's smart and popular venue. Del min £10.00. 10% disc on collected orders over £15. Hours 12-2/6- 11.30.

LONDON SE

Area: South East London
Postcodes SE1 to SE28

See page 88 for key to this map

London SE1

The unique seating arrangement along one wall of Waterloo's Bangalore Express. The upper deck is the most popular. Even though you can't stand up, diners queue up for as much as 45 minutes to sit up there.

Tell us about your favourite curryhouse or your least favourite. We need to know what you know!
pat@patchapman.co.uk

BANGALORE WATERLOO TOP 100
INDIAN FAST FOOD www.bangaloreuk.com
103 Waterloo Road SE1 8UL 020 7021 0886

This Guide's Top Chef 2004 and 2007, Yogesh Datta and partner Charles Hill continue to achieve acclaim with their the Painted Heron, SW3. In 2008 they decided to venture into the realm of Indian fast food with this location, right opposite Waterloo Station. Hill gave the design project to Outline, a newish company, who, faced with a high ceiling and narrow room looked for inspiration from Japanese pod hotels and came up with this elevated / alternative seating. . Six four-seater booths line one wall. An identical line is directly above accessed from bunk-bed style ladders. I am surprised that the dreaded Health and Safety Department didn't squash this idea. Myself, I prefer the ground floor and not in the heaven's. High heels, short skirts and a bottle of wine, are not recommended for climbing a ladder to reach tables on the upper deck. However, it is an interesting idea, though I am sure that the waiting staff find it a pain. The concept is popular with the younger element who also like the free wi-fi. Weather permitting, there is a wee outdoor seating area. The menu is a brief one-page on-the-table document with what they call 'tapas-style' items – starters include tandoori chicken, duck cashew nut and raisin roll, fenugreek-marinated chicken drumsticks, dosa. Mains include 'build-your-own-rice-and-curry-plates' of items such as chicken curries, lamb jalfrezi, sweet potato salad, sag rice & tamarind rice. Menu Snapshot: Tapas - to mix and share - £4.25 each - Golden Fried Tiger Prawns with lentil dumpling; Spicy Chicken fillets with chilli-yoghurt cake; Duck, cashew nut and raisin roll; Minced Lamb Kebab Roll with red onion and tomato salsa; Yoghurt Cakes with green chillies, red onion and feta cheese; Spicy Minced cauliflower and Pea Curry with a bap. *'The decor is very geometric, mostly green, modern and not geared up for a long comfortable evening. It is designed for a quick meal or for (mostly) young office groups. One half has bench seating made of scaffolding and the other half has tables for four in two layers, the upper reached by a scaffolding ladder, rather like bunk beds. glasses and flatware are plain but good quality. The menu on the place mats appear to be unchanging with no specials. Spicy Minced Cauliflower - bought in error, tasted good. Broccoli and Cauliflower Heads, really very good. Dosa with Prawns £4.25, very good. Bengal Fish Curry £8 - beautifully cooked, good Korma style sauce. (I asked what fish they used and was told it was haddock, it certainly didn't look like haddock). Yellow Peas with Spinach - weird, never tasted anything like it, waitress changed it to Pea and Mushroom Curry £3 instead - good. It is possible to have a very well cooked meal for very little money. Staff, smart and efficient and the food was attractively served on large white rectangle or square plates. I wouldn't be at all surprised if they don't spread, the concept is really good and a bit different'* HJC. Fully licensed to 11.30. Food: 11am-12pm.   Branches: Bangalore City, EC3; Painted Heron SW1. More planned.

BENGAL CLIPPER
Cardamom Building, 31 Shad Thames   SE1 2YR
020 7357 9001   www.bengalclipper.co.uk

Finding it is the problem. It's a fair walk from the tube! Taxis will find it (it's behind Conran's). If you're driving, squeeze through the narrow one-way s. Once inside, you'll find owner Mukhit Chouhury's 150 seater is sophisticated and expensive and complete with grand piano (played Tues to Sat eves) and original paintings by Christopher Corr and Brian Grimwood. The menu reads like a standard curryhouse, but in the hands of ex Taj hotel Delhi Chef Mohammed Asrar itis way above average. And there are bargains to be had with the Suday buffet at £9 amd weekday meals from £12. Average a la carte meal price: £30.   Mon to Sat: 12-2:30 (Sun to 4) Daily: 6-11.30. *Branches: Bengal Trader, E1, Bengal Mangrove, Halstead, Kent, and the original Bengal Lancer, Chislehurst, Kent.*

LOVAGE
15 Queen Elizabeth St, SE1 2JE
020 7403 8886   www.lovagerestaurant.com

Opened in 2007, it is is set on two floors, with the 80 seat restaurant on the mezzanine level overlooking the stylish bar. Located in Butler's Wharf 200 guests can be accommodated for pre or post-dinner drinks before dining. Designed by Europe's famous Zoran Zafaria, the bar front is fitted with a translucent marble pieces sourced from Rajasthan and finished in Italy. Modern European furniture and a mixture of dark brown leather seating and elegant stools are scattered round the bar. Curries average £11, with Squid, scallops, mussels, duck curries at £14.95. Two course set menu 6pm -8, £12.95. 12-2.30; 6-11.30 (to 12 Fri & Sat).

SILKA
6 Southwark SE1 1TL   www.silka.co.uk
                              0207 378 6161

Abdul Mushahid form chef at Tamarind, Chutney Mary, Three Monkeys and the Red Fort, opened his own venture in 2003 as the Silka. Managed by A. Hannanin, it is in a Grade II listed building between London Bridge and Tate Modern. Located in the basement, the entrance has a Tardis-like doorwaopening ont the staircase down to the 80 seater, where the eye leads to Mushahid's window kitchen. *'Our starters included Baked Lemon Sole £5.25, wrapped in a banana leaf, Stir-fried Baby Squid, £5.75, and Mixed Sprout Lentil Soup, £3.95 lotus leaves coated with white sesame seeds and spiced gram flour batter is refreshingly innovative and served with a typically tangy tamarind chutney. Other gems include Wild Duck braised with delicate spices, Roasted Cauliflower marinated with cheese, yoghurt and cashew nuts and fiery Peri Peri Prawns.'* RG. *'The service was polite, attentive and helpful. One dish immediately struck me – Bombay Duck!! The portion £was hardly substantial (two very thin slices) but my friend enjoyed it very much. I have to say I was not so sure. The rest of the food was very good. One aspect worth a special mention is the toilets – you enter via a completely wall-to-wall mirrored room, which totally confused me (not difficult). Though the mirrors were not in the toilet itself, I still have an aversion to seeing myself in the mirror I'm afraid. Very enjoyable ... food and service good.'* AG. Lunch platter c£9. Dinner av £26. Valet Parking. 12-3; 6-11. *Branches, SW*

SIMPLY INDIAN   PAN INDIAN   BYO
25 Tabard , SE1 4LA
020 7407 5005   www.simply-indian.co.uk

Est 1998, it has a far from simple menu, where the adventurous can try unusual dishes, such as (starters): Sundal, £3.50, chickpea and coconut salad cooked in mustard seeds, gram flour, curry leaves, lemon zest, garnished with mango slices, fresh plum and coriander, served warm; Baingan-e-bahar, £3.50, baked aubergine ring stuffed with edam cheese, ginger, coriander and toasted sesame seeds with blended tomatoes and mustard sauce; Goan king prawn baza, £3.95, wrapped in fresh spiced leaf spinach, coated with rice flour rolled onto a wooden skewer and crisply fried; Kalegi Masala, £3.90, sliced chicken liver and heart sauteed with cumin seeds, onions, mushroom and tomatoes; Momos, made from plain flour and stuffed with chicken mince, chilli and coriander powder with chopped basil leaves, onion and lemon, served with sweet tamarind chutney; calamari, fresh cut squids stir fried with onion, capsicum and curry leaves, both £3.50. Mains: Stuffed baby aubergine, £3.50 (side) £5.10 (main) roasted, stuffed with fried onions, almonds, shredded sultanas and cumin seeds cooked in mild masala sauce; Goan crab curry, £6.90, cooked in its shell with thinly sliced onions, ginger garlic paste, red chilli, ground coriander, tamarind pulp and coconut milk; Stuffed chicken bhona, £6.90, whole breast stuffed with chopped mushrooms, ginger, coriander, garam masala and topped with black pepper and onion sauce, served with a pulao rice; Duck Xacutti, £6.90 the most complex of all great curries boasts over twenty ingredients, each roasted prior to being ground with onions and coconuts; Mamsa Ishtew, £5.80, lamb slow-cooked with coconut milk, aromatic whole spices and potatoes until the meats are very tender. They also do Masala Dosa and Uthapam, both £7.25. Desserts include Gulab Jaman, Gajjar Ka Halwa and Mini Rasamalai, all £2.90. BYO. Daily: 12-2:30; 6-12.

YOU SAY OK, SE1

SE1: CAFE NAWAZ BYO 92 Snowsfields, SE1 3SS 020 7403 9905. Salmon samosas Memsahibs lacy cutlets (£3.15 for 2)

SE1: CHILLI CHUTNEY EXPRESS PAKISTANI 47 York Rd, Nr Waterloo Stn, SE1 7NJ. 020 7021 0202 See SW16 for details.

SE1: THAMES TANDOORI 79 Waterloo Rd, SE1 8UD 020 7928 3856. Opposite W'loo Station and DRC's favourite.

SE1: TOWER TANDOORI 74 Tower Bridge Rd, SE1 4TOP 020 7237 2247. *'8 mins walk from the bridge. Prices very favourable.'* NB.

London SE13

GREEN CABIN   SRI LANKAN
244 High , SE13 6JU   020 8852 6666

40 seater opened in 1996 by SE Jebarajan and serving Sri Lankan and some south Indian food as well as the safe-bet Korma-through-Vindaloo range. Forget all that and go for the real stuff – you won't be disappointed. Meat Roll (diced lamb, onions, chillies and potato wrapped in a pancake, bread crumbed and deep-fried, served with spicy sauce), Potato Kulambu (deep-fried cubes of potato cooked in coconut milk with dry roasted chilli), Cabbage Mallung (shredded cabbage stir-fried with mustard seed, turmeric and spices), Kotthu Roti, soft and thin as a silk cloth sliced into pieces and mixed with shredded chicken on a hot griddle and blended together). Delivery: £15 min, 2m. T/a 10% disc, £15 min. 12-3 / 6-11; closed Mon.

PANAS GURKHA   NEPALESE
318 Lee High Road, Lewisham, SE13 5PJ
020 8852 9891   www.panasgurkha.co.uk

Nepalese chef-owner Sujan worked with Atul Kochhar and Das Sreedharan (Rasa, N19). Panas serves a full gamut of formula curries, *"but their Napalese specials are the best bet"* GM. For example, staters: Momo lamb or veg, five dumplings served with tomato chutney. Sadeko Kukhura, BBQ chicken marinated with mustard oil, fenugreek seed, both £4.85. Mains: Choyola Chicken £9, dry dish popular, BBQ chicken seasoned with traditional spices & mustard oil; Jhaneko Masu £9.55, a very dry dish of lamb pieces cooked in tandoor & then pan fried with fresh spring onions, ginger, garlic, dry chilli, fenugreek, with touch of lemon; Pole Ko Khasi £10, from Eastern Nepal, lamb marinated with Nepalese spices, crushed black pepper & tandoored; Bhutwa £7, chicken or lamb cooked with green peppers, spring onions with Nepalese herbs; Jogi Tarkari £5, seasonal vegetables cooked Nepalese style. Daily 5.30-10.30 (to 11.15 Fri & Sat / to 10 Sun).

YOU SAY OK, SE 8 & SE 13
SE8: TANDOORI XPRESS PUNJABI 111b, High Road, Deptford SE8 4NS 020 8320 2555. Punjabi-style takeaway with a couple of tables Cooking in view and c£5 for a good fill. No frills, no toilets & no credit cards. Mon-Sat: 11.30-11; Sun:12-3/6-10.30.

SE13: ARRU SUVAI SRI LANKAN 19 Lee High Rd Lewisham, SE13 5LD ~ 020 8297 6452. Sri Lankan caff complete with Bollywood telly, fruit machine, Devilled dishes, Kotthu Roti, Pittu, Tuna Curry. Cash only, but you can fill for a fiver. 10-11 daily.

SE 13: BENGAL BRASSERIE 79 Springbank Rd, Hither Green, SE13 6SS ~ 020 8461 5424. Syed Ahmed's 60-seater *'The Lobster Sagheeis a fine dish.* £8.75' ES. 5.30-11.30 (12 Sat).

SE13: EVEREST CURRY KING   NO ALC SRI LANKAN 24 Loampit Hill, Lewisham, SE13 7SW 020 8691 2233 Don't be fooled by the name, Everest is 1500 miles N of Sri Lanka, but it's the food which counts. It's a typical caff with no menu, just items on display. Fill up, pay up (and not much of that and by card if you wish). Superbly tasty, & authentic. No alc allowed. 11-11.30 daily

SPICE OF LIFE

Opening & Take Away Hours:
Sunday 6pm to 11pm
Monday 6pm to 10pm
Tuesday CLOSED
Weds & Thurs 6pm to 11.30
Fri & Sat 6pm to Midnight
Sorry we don't deliver!
Join our Key Fob Club for 15% Discount

TOP 100 in this Guide since 2007

**020 8244 4770
260 LEE HIGH RD
LONDON SE13 5PL**

SPICE OF LIFE   TOP 100
260 Lee High Road, SE13 5PL   020 8244 4770

Owner, Mahmud (Moody) Miah's fully licensed, a/c venue seats 58. It has its devoted following although we did get a rather critical report saying the food was just average, and 'enhanced' by food colourings. But the general flow is: *'Well above average.'* C&GM. *'Moody was his usual charming self and was delighted to see us. He didn't need to ask if we wanted popadums. He just bought them over with the exceptional, as ever, pickle tray. Why can't other restaurants do these simple but important things as well as this? What caught my eye was just how much effort this restaurant makes. They have a 'specials board', something one so rarely sees in an Indian restaurant, which listed some real gems. After the pops we shared bhajis, samosas etc. Although it was nowhere to be seen on the menu he said I must try the tilapia dish. It was firm but soft and retained all its flavour whilst still being well spiced and just beautiful. We also ordered my old favourite, the garlic chilli vegetables, although this too wasn't on the menu – the smoky garlic flavour was just as prominent, he had added just the right amount of extra chillies and it was bursting with flavour and fresh vegetables. None of the food remotely disappointed – the rice continues to be light and beautifully presented, the naan soft and the dhal just the right texture. Places like this, and people like this are very, very, hard to find.'* AG. No del. T/a: 10% disc. Mon: 6-10; Wed-Th to 11:30; Fri-Sat to mdnt; Sun to 11pm. Closed Tuesdays.

London SE15

GANAPATI — KERELAN MEAT & VEG — TOP 100
38 Holly Grove, Peckham, SE15 5DF
020 7277 2928   www.ganapatirestaurant.com

Ganapati (aka Ganesh) is the the elephant-headed god and the bringer of good luck. Peckham's good luck is that Claire Fisher's passion for south India was so passionate that she opened Ganapati South Indian Kitchen in 2004. She first visited India in 1992, and fell in love with the food, as one does. On returning home, she got a job cooking at Rasa Samudra, N16. In 2000 she cooked at an Islington pub with Keralan chef K.P.Sukumaran. This led to opening her own venture in 2004, in Peckham. Forget images of graffiti, high rises and Delboy, Ganapati is located in a leafy of unique, attractive terraced houses, which AT describes as *'the posh bit of Peckham (yes that does exist!) ... it's a gem'* AT. Ganapati seats 40 at wooden tables, and simple chairs amid colourful, leafy decor. Seating is augmented in good weather with 4 outside tables and 4 more in the 'garden'. *'Simply wonderful staff. The young lady who served us knew everything about the food and also about what went well together.'* HD. Starters include Idli, Chaat or Dosa or 'Vegetarian Snacks', £4.75: Mysore Bonda, spicy potato balls fried in chick pea batter, Parippu Vadai, ground chana dal with ginger, curry leaf & green chilli shaped into patties and fried. Or Sardine Fry £5.50, south Indian style, marinated in chilli & lemon &pan fried. There is choice of just twelve main course dishes. Snapshot: Tamil Nadu Fish Curry £12.50, King fish steak cooked in tamarind, onions, chillies, tomatoes, spices. Lamb Dal Cha with Neychoru Rice,£12.75, Tamil Nadu style dish of lamb cooked with chana dal + spices with Kerala style pilau rice, cooked with onions, carrot, curry leaves, a touch of ghee, cloves, cardamom & cinnamon; Vendakka & Green Mango Curry, £9.95, Okra & green mango in spicy tomato, fennel, fenugreek & chilli masala with raita, thoran & poppadoms; Baby Aubergine Masala £9.95, aubergine cooked in tamarind, jaggery, chilli, tomato, coconut with thoran, raita & pickle. Masala Dosa, £6.75, served with sambar & chutney. *'I chose Vegetarian Banana Leaf Thali, the classic south Indian meal served on a banana leaf, £13.25. He chose Fish, but could have had Lamb or free range Chicken £14.25. It gave us a real all round taste of the menu'*. DC. Sweet-lovers, including Ganesh, will not be disappointed. Desserts, such as made-in-house Ice-cream £4.95 or Sorbets £4.75 in various flavours catch the eye, as do Gulab Jamun, £4.75 because they are homemade 'dumplings' in rose syrup with creme fraiche. In fact everything at Ganpatti is home-made. Lunch £5.50 to £6 with 7 items on the menu. *'Simple decor, super service, stupenous food'*. HEG. Seats 4 outside tables (4 more in the 'garden').Takeaways, available at non peak times. No del. Licensed. Credit cards accepted. Service: 12.5%. Tue-Fri: 12-2.45; 6-10.30 / Sat:12-10.30 (Sun -10). Closed Mondays.

Ganpatti Restaurant
38 Holly Grove
Peckham,
London
SE15 5DF
020 7277 2928

www.ganapatirestaurant.com

Kerelan Cuisine

Hours: Tuesday to Friday
12 — 2.45pm
& 6 — 10.30pm
Saturday 12 — 10.30pm
Sunday 12 —10pm

ganapati
south indian kitchen

CHANDNI PUNJABI
134a Thurlow Park Road, West Dulwich, SE21 8HN
020 8761 9738   www.chandnirestaurant.co.uk

All the favourites cooked Punjabi style. Restaurant & Sweets. 12-2.3- /6-11.30 daily.Branches: Dagenham Essex, Southall Middx.

SURMA CURRY HOUSE 020 8693 1779
42 Lordship Lane, SE22 8HJ   www.the-surma.co.uk

Give me a place like the Surma. It is exactly what is says it is – a Curry House. Muzazid Ali's been running it since 1976, and it's a gem: no pretensions, no frills, a heap of happy regulars and a regular entrant in our Guide. It serves the standard menu with all your favourite starters: Bhajis, Samosas, Kebabs and Chaat. Tandooris and Tikas, and curries, side dishes and accompaniments. All are cooked just as they should be – perfectly. And there's more eg: Quail, squid and dosa, for starters at under £4. Rajastan Reshmi chicken £8.95, tandoori chicken in garlic, olive oil, fenugreek, cumin and nutmeg; Calamari 9.95, a Goan Portuguese delicacy, marinated with coarsely ground spices and then slowly stir fried. *'We just love going here. We go with our parents and with our kids. What more could you ask for'* AAR. The picture shows owner Ali receiving a local Award from customer Angela Burgess. Show Mr Ali this Guide and he might give you a discount. Eat-all-Sunday buffet of 17 dishes £6.95, under 12: £3.95. Daily:. Sun 12-11.

London SE24

BABUR BRASSERIE A LIST
HAUTE PAN INDIAN CUISINE
119 Brockley Rise, SE24 1JP
020 8291 2400   www.babur.info

Babur established the Moghul Empire in 1483 through his courage and daring in capturing Delhi. This restaurant captured Forest Hill in 1985, though its ownership by the dynamic Rahman brothers did not occur until 1992. Quite simply, it's in our AWARD-WINNING category because everything the Rahmans do, they do well. The restaurant was completely rebuilt in 2006 by architects, Glas. Art is integral to Babur. The Kalamkari by Ajit Kumar Das in the entrance lobby uses Sanskrit words written in Bengali characters. Two suede and leather triptych wall hangings are by Sian Lester. The entire restaurant is most elegant. Babur say of their menu *'it has been evolving since we opened ... so it's a work in progress'*. Formula curries are not on offer. The menu is realised by Head Chef Jiwan Lal, from the Punjab, Basant Lal who cheffed at Simla's Oberoi Cecile Hotel and Sous Chef Praveen Kumar Gupta who cheffed at Jaipur's Oberoi Rajvillas. This very strong kitchen team enjoys offering contemporary Indian dishes, some with unusual ingredients, whilst maintaining the accurate tastes of traditional regional cooking. At once you can tell this is not your ordinary venue. The Papadom basket comes with with home-made pickles and chutneys and is well worth it at £1.25 per person. Starters include South Indian-style mussels with rice flour croutons, £7.25, steamed in a coconut milk, mustard seed and curry leaf broth; Ostrich Soole, £8.50, passanda cuts, clove-smoked and marinated in Rajasthani spices; Tamarind-glazed quail breast £6.95, from the tandoor, with bubble 'n' squeak boneless leg meat; Venison Chapli, £7.95, spiced minced patties wrapped with mixed peppers and spring onions; Goat patties with tamarind and raisin chutney, £7.95,ibrantly spicy with star anise, coriander and black pepper. And non meat: Beetroot cutlet, papaya chutney, £6.75, in crispy sago, warm masala spicing, bit of heat and sweet or Vegetable beggar's purse, £6.75, pastry filled with paneer, cashews, organic potato and peas, seasoned with chat masala. Each of the dozen Main dishes is matched to both a red and a white wine inc by the glass. For example, Chicken Chettinad, £13.75, is cooked in a peppery Chettiyar masala from South India, and served in a rice dosa 'fool's cap' [an edible cone, see picture, right] and is matched to Alsace Koenig, Pinot Gris 2008 and New Zealand Green Stone Point Pinot Gris 2009. Chicken Lababdar, £12.95, traditional Mughlai chicken in creamy tomato with fenugreek (OK it's Haute CTM) is matched to the Pinot Gris and an Italian Corvina. All the main courses have interesting matches and space

SPLENDIDLY INDIAN, SUPERBLY SMOOTH

> A smart, comfortable, space with fantastic food

babur

119 Brockley Rise, Forest Hill SE23 1JP
020 8291 2400
www.babur.info   mail@babur.info

preclude us mentioning them all. Pot-roasted mustard rabbit, £14.25, is cooked in a sealed pot with mustard and ginger in rabbit stock and served with garlic roti. Khata-meetha spiced duck breast, £14.95, seared Gressingham breast, served with sweet and sour plum sauce and carrot masala. Steamed spice crusted shoulder of lamb, £14.95, is marinated for 100 hours in a spice-rich Punjabi masala then baked and served with beetroot khichdi and lamb jus. Laverstoke Park Buffalo Lal Maas, steamed rice, £15.25, is clove-smoked buffalo cooked in a Rajasthani-spiced hot masala. Interesting dish this because Lal means Red and Maas means meat and buffalo is a very common India domestic animal. For the non meat eaters, the Vegetarian Thali, £14.50, includes Paneer Makai Tawa Masala, Green Bean Fogath, Dal Makhni, Sondhi Gobi, Pachari, Pulao Rice and Mini Nan Bread. It is matched to the Pinot Gris and Italian Amano Primitivo, 2009. Dal makhni, £5.25, slowly cooked, creamy – rich black lentils is the real test of chefs' ability. Paneer Makai Tawa Masala, £6.50, stir fried cottage cheese, corn, organic green peas, kadai spices. Crispy fried potatoes, £4.95, thinly sliced and seasoned with tart dried mango powder. Desserts are hybrids mixing East and West. Babur's Sunday lunch buffet changes each week and is £11.95 for adults and £7.95 for children 7 to 12 years – under 7s   free. 12-2.30 (Sun to 4) and 6-11.30 daily. *Branch: Planet Spice, 88 Selsdon Pk Rd, Croydon, Surrey.*

Babur Deliveries and takeaways:

A LA CARTE AT HOME. 020 8291 2400. Home delivery of the full Babur menu (and wines) part listed above call.

BABUR-TO-GO 020 8291 1853 or 020 8291 4266.
It has a different menu which includes the formula favourites as well as some specials, all at a much lower price point. The kitchen is in the very capable hands of chef Enam Rahman, who was head chef at Babur for many years.

Free delivery on orders over £15, within a 2 mile radius. Open 7 days, 6pm to midnight (last orders for delivery by 11pm). Usually delivered within 1 hour.

LONDON SW

Area: South West London,
Postcodes: SW1 to SW20

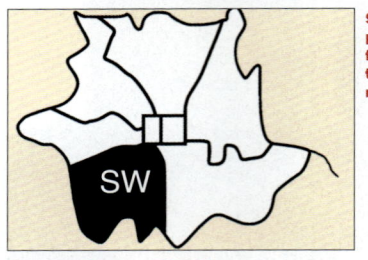

See page 88 for key to this map

London SW1

AMAYA
INDIAN GRILL FINE DINING   TOP OF A-LIST
Halkin Arcade, 19 Motcomb , Knightsbridge, SW1 8JT
020 7823 1166   www.amaya.biz

Amaya is one of a continually growing portfolio of superior Indian restaurants, including eight Masala Zones, Chutney Mary and Veeraswamy. It makes a formidable portfolio; Masala Zone for the quick in-and-out dining experience; he other two for Indian regional fine-dining. The owners call Amaya the India Grill. But this is no ordinary grill. Amaya is at the higher price range. The equivalent of a three course meal with wine will cost about £70 per head. And the clients flock in. And this is what they find. The decor is stunning. First there is a most attractive bar, encased in rosewood and vibrant red panels. The private dining room seats 14; the main room 100. Colourful, bright art sparingly decorates the walls in this sleekly dark restaurant. Day time provides a totally different atmosphere to night where the moody crystal chandeliers, spotlights and candles do the work. I don't know which I prefer. Statues, dark wood fittings, Indian sandstone and rosewood panelling; tasteful use of colour, subtle table settings, separate areas yet it is all one. And above all, a view of the kitchen running full-length at the end which where on view are a wide range of cooking implements used in India for thousands of years such as Sigrhi (open fire grill), Tawa (griddle), Mahi Tawa (walled griddle), Kadhai (wok), Lagan (steam pot) Shilajit Stone (special stones from Hyderabad, said to have aphrodisiac properties) and of course the Tandoor. Expertly positioned spotlights illuminate the equipment and the food, but not the chefs, discretely dressed in black creating a culinary spectacle. Other dishes are seasoned with subtle marinades. These sit alongside fragrant light soups and exotic salads. The food is designed to be shared and is served as it is prepared. There are no conventional first courses or main courses. The staff warn you of this but can lead to complaints from those who like to get things in the order they believe they should be served. This is also how items are served at Masala Zones. Others complain that this is not 'curry' as they know it. The owners explain this very tactfully. *'Our restaurants are very different from the inexpensive neighbourhood curry restaurants started in Britain by enterprising non-Indian entrepreneurs who developed their own brand of curry totally different from the tastes of real Indian food.'* Put it another way, curryhouse they are not. And of course we hear about it being pricey with small portions to boot. DBAC says: *'Portions can be on the small side, but that's what makes it really lovely, you can share all those deliciously delightful little dishes, with your closest friends. The bar area is just perfect for a light lunch of perhaps, The Amaya Platter - eight little wonders, beautifully presented - all for £16.25. However, if you have a little more time on your hands and wish to linger over a longer lunch or perhaps dinner, retire to the main dining room with comfortable leather chairs and watch the chefs prepare kebabs and salads. Main course dishes are superbly presented on plates of different sizes and designs.'* Food presentation, like the venue's design is seductively striking. But that alone is not what makes Amaya one of the most highly rated restaurants in this Guide. It is attention to detail in all departments, originality, careful service, cleanliness, immaculate food and sheer excellence. It is also only the fifth Indian restaurant anywhere to get a Michelin Star, though why Veeraswamy and Chutney Mary are still waiting years later for theirs, only Michelin can explain. As to those prices, you can pay two or three times more for higher-rated Franco-British restaurants in town, but you won't get better quality. Main courses £10 to £28. Dinner with wine c£65 pp. Many desserts are light, and some are sugar-free. A favourite is plum compote with chilli custard and rose sorbet. Amaya Platter for a quick lunch. Offering the equivalent of 3 courses - 6 tasting portions served on a platter and a dessert for £19.50 per person. Set lunch menu offering the equivalent of 3 courses for £29 per person. Average à la carte price: £60 per head for the equivalent of a 3 course à la carte meal including wine and service for dinner, and £35 for lunch. Mon-Fri: 12.30-2.15 (Sat to 2.30); Sun: 12.45 - 2.45; Mon-Sat: 6.30-11.15 (10.15 Sun).

COBRA
SPLENDIDLY INDIAN, SUPERBLY SMOOTH

BUKHARA
Sheraton Park Tower, 101 Knightsbridge, SW1X 7RN

We reviewed the original Bukhara at Delhi's luxury hotel ITC Maurya Sheraton in our xxxx edition of the Cobra Guide. Opened in the 1977, it is in our view, the best Tandoori restaurant in the world, where you need to book months in advance. A 'pop-up' ran at the London's Sheraton in May 2012 for just 15 days, complete with Gingham bibs to avoid spilling on your clothes and to wipe fingers (no cutlery is served). The menu (£79), devised by the Group's Indian Corporate Chef, Manjit Gill, included favourites like slow-cooked Black Lentil Dal, and Sikandri Raan (marinated spring lamb cooked in a tandoor) with superbly sweet-and-sticky Gulab Jamun to finish the meal. There was also a vegetarian option (£50) with tasters of the stuffed capsicum skewers, aloo and tandoori salad. It was fully sold out and is entered here in case Sheraton decide to repeat the operation. Who knows, it may one day herald a permanent London Bukhara.

Chef Majit Gill

THE CINNAMON CLUB
FINE INDIAN INNOVATIVE DINING   A LIST
Old Westminster Library, 30 Great Smith Street, SW1P 3BU 020 7222 2555 www.cinnamonclub.com

The Cinnamon Club celebrated its 10th birthday in 2012. A decade ago it broke ground by reinventing Indian food, by its conservative decor in its Grade 11 listed building, by refusing to serve popodums and by reverential service from young waiters with black waistcoats, white shirts, long white aprons and black trousers. None of that has changed today. The food is, if anything, even more innovative, but gone and best forgotten, thank heavens, are some rather dodgy combinations. What is served today has been honed by trial and error and by the approval of the 100,000 diners they serve each year. Such innovation is not universally popular. But while Cinnamon Club's spin that it is unlike any other restaurant in India is true, less so is their spin that it changed people's perception of wines with Indian food. Chutney Mary was doing it in 1991 and 25 years before that Chateau la Tour was available (at £100 a bottle) at the long-gone, up market Chelsea Tandoori. Cinnamon Club's founder was Iqbal Wahab (now written out of the Cinnamon picture) who had the dream of opening an Indian restaurant with food that would break with convention. In Vivek Singh, then Exec at Japur's Oberoi Hotel he found a chef capable of fulfilling the dream and brought him to Britain. Today it is Vivek, now CEO whom everyone knows. Head Chef Rakesh Ravindran Nair and his team of 18 chefs is talented enough to produce rule-breaking combinations of spices and ingredients. large enough to change the menu almost daily, and to serve food from

Above: Vivek Singh used Naga chillies in his 'Bollywood Burner' lamb curry setting the new world record for the hottest curry, sponsored by Richard Branson to promote one of his media products

early morning to dinner. It is one of the very few Indian restaurants to serve breakfast (from 7:30am). Try Uttapam – South Indian rice pancake with toppings of onions, green chilli and/or tomato. £8; or Kedgeree with smoked haddock and poached egg £7.50 or Bombay scrambled eggs on cumin 'pao' £7.. Examples of their a la carte lunch and dinner offerings include: Tandoori breast of red leg partridge with pickling spices £14.50; Crisp zucchini flower with royal cumin, tamarind glazed vegetables £8.50. Main courses: Fillet Wagyu beef with stir fried morels, saffron sauce £95; Char-grilled halibut with Bengali 'dopyaza' sauce, ghee rice £25; Roast saddle of 'Oisin' red deer with sesame tamarind sauce £32. Side dishes: Tandoored aubergine crush £5; Rajasthani sangri beans with fenugreek and raisin £5.50; Pilau rice £3.00; Garlic Naan £3. Set menu (table d'hote) £22 2 course, £24 3 course. Available: any lunchtime and 6-6:30pm and from 9:30pm onwards. The changes are rung monthly with such offerings as (at the time of writing) an Indo-Nepalese Festival menu at £50 per diner it consists of an Appetiser of Hans Choila, duck salad with toasted rice flakes, a Starter of Kukhura Momos, steamed black leg chicken dumplings with peanut chutney; a 'Rest Course': Maacha Fry, batter-fried grey mullet with garlic and chilli, cucumber relish; Main course: Khasi Sekwa, grilled Herdwick lamb, curried bamboo shoots, potato raita and rice and a Dessert: Gajar ko Hulwa & Chawal ko Kheer, traditional carrot fudge with rice pudding. Alternatively there is the Tasting Menu: £75 per person, £115 with premier wines, £150 with premium wines. And as for those wines, they are on a 33 page list with a huge price range. Reds, for example, range from £28 per bottle to £625.00 (1990 Solaia, Antinori). More booze is available in the ground floor Library Bar, seating 24 or downstairs, the Club bar, capacity 60, has Overseesing the three Cinnamon branches (here, EC2 & W1) is Group General Manger Jean-Luc Gique. Hari Nagaraj is Cinnamon Club Manager. Mon-Fri: 7:30-9:30 / Mon-Sat: 12 -2:45 & 6-10:30.

MINT LEAF
FINE INDIAN DINING   A-LIST
Suffolk Pl, Haymarket, SW1 4HX
020 7930 9020   www.mintleafrestaurant.com

This 4,000 sq ft basement 140-seater is simply gorgeous. The decor is breathtaking. It is intensely dark, created by dark American wood panelling and sexy downlighting. You enter downtairs to the bar, said to be the longest in Europe, in the charge of cocktail mixologist Lara Zanzarin. Bar-snacks include: chicken Tikka Roll £8.50, Duck Kebab £9.50, Crab & Mackerel cake £10, or for the vegetarian Paneer Tikka £8. When you do move into the main dining area, it is in fact several areas, expertly divided, yet all in vision. There are intimate spaces and semi-private areas for groups You'd never guess it can seat 220 diners. Chef is Ajay Chopra, ex Marriott, Bombay and his menu is quite short and includes seafood and game, including Rabbit and Guinea Fowl. As always there a high proportion of vegetarian dishes, giving the option to experience more variety and flavours at one sitting. The new menu also encourages more sociable dining where patrons can order multiple dishes to share. Sharing Menu £40: Start with: Potato Cake, Lamb Seekh Kebab, Tandoori Salmon Tikka. Mains: Tariwala Chicken, Thigh Braised with brown onion, tomatoes and spices, Goan Tilapia Curry, simmered in coconut and Tamarind Sauce, Potato and Spinach, tossed with garlic, Yellow Lentil, tempered with cumin and Garlic, Steamed Basmati Rice, Naan & Roti. Then Date and Carrot Pudding. The £50 and £70 versions contain more dishes. A la Carte Menu Snapshot: Starters include: Bombay Spiced Vegetables, with Buttered pao (Goan bread roll) £8; Achari Guinea Fowl Tikka with Pineapple Raita, £12.50; Rabbit Seekh Kebab, with honey and mustard drizzle, £12. Mains include: Nihari, diced lamb braised with onion, tomato £19.50; Paneer Butter Masala, tandoor-grilled paneer onion and tomatoes finished with cream £18; Venison Pepper Fry with onion, curry leaf and black peppercorn £18; Pan Seared Black Cod, in a Goan curry sauce with stir-fried beans, £28.00. Wines from £24.50 to £295 a bottle. Prices are not for the faint-hearted, but this is Haymarket. We were asked to recommend a venue for a pre-Christmas office party for 6 senior execs of a multinational US company. They wanted a venue where they could arrive at lunch time and relax until evening. We suggested Mint Leaf. *'We enjoyed the pre-lunch drinks and lunch, then we returned to the bar sofas and enjoyed our drinks. Next I knew it was midnight and they were closing. Our bill £1200 +Tip. Worth every dime!'* GR. Service charge: 12.5%. Mon- Fr: 12-3 Mon to Sat: 5:30-11.30 (Sun to 11).Bar: Mon-Weds:12-12 (Th-Fri: to 1am; Sat & Sun from 5pm.   *Branch*
Mint leaf Lounge, EC2.

COBRA
कोबरा
SPLENDIDLY INDIAN, SUPERBLY SMOOTH

Mintleaf Restaurant
Suffolk Place
Haymarket
London
SW1Y 4HX
Tel: 020 7930 9020

mint leaf

Mint Leaf Lounge
12 Angel Court
Lothbury
Bank
EC2R 7HB
Tel: 0207 600 0992

mint leaf lounge

Mint Leaf restaurants are synonymous with fine Indian food complemented by friendly and attentive service in elegant and sophisticated surroundings.

With striking design and a professional team, Mint Leaf restaurants provide the perfect setting for fine dining, private and corporate entertainment or just cocktails in one of the lounge bars, with both venues offering a range of versatile areas.

For enquiries please contact the restaurants directly.
www.mintleafrestaurant.com - www.mintleaflounge.com

THE QUILON
AWARD WINNER
KERELAN COASTAL FINE DINING
St James Court Hotel, 45 Buckingham Gate, SW1 6EF
020 7821 1899   www.quilon.co.uk

Taj Hotels Group operate the elegant St James's Court Hotel and one of its 'house' restaurants is the adjoining Indian restaurant, The Quilon, though not accessible, from the hotel but from the . It is, like the hotel, a luxury venue at luxury prices. It opened in 1999 and in 2012 it underwent its first redec. Taj wanted more sophistication, so out went the sparkly mosaics and the monkey mural. Like the public rooms and restaurants of the Taj Mumbai flagship, the redec removes any trace of its Indian heritage. Nice though the redec is, it could be anywhere on the planet. For those who wonder these things, Quilon is an unremarkable working town on the coast road in south Kerala, not far from India's southernmost tip, so it came as no surprise to find The Quilon specialising in authentic south Indian cuisine; nothing unusual about that in London. However Taj had an ace to play, a USP: its menu delivered Karavali food, recipes from the southwestern coastal regions. To understand the significance of this we need to go back in time. In the late 1980s, the Taj Group was not known for fine Indian cuisine, let alone authentic regional dishes, despite employing chefs bursting to deliver it in Taj's rapidly expanding chain of up-market hotels being built all over India. Chef Aylur V Sriram was one of those chefs. He originally learned his trade working under his father at the family-owned Karntaka Hotel Sriram, in Udipi, home of the dosa. Feeling there was a bigger world out there, he went on to work in some of India's top hotel restaurants, ultimately with Taj. His timely suggestion that a new kind of Indian restaurant was needed in the Group, and he would be its chef, focusing on the food dearest to his heart, south Indian coastal food, fell on the sympathetic ears of Camelia Panjabi then Taj marketing director. In 1988 she proposed he piloted his restaurant at a new Taj hotel, the Gateway in Bangalore, which would bear the name Karavali (meaning coastal food) with cuisine specifically inspired by that of the Bunts of Mangalore, the Coorgies, the Malayalees, and the Goan Portuguese using local spices, red chillies, coconut, pepper, fresh

Chef Sriram

fish, meats and vegetables of the coast. Karavali and Sriram soon attracted comment. The New Statesman described him as *'One of the top five chefs in India.'* Karavali remains one of the city's favourites. With the acquisition in 1999 of St James hotel, Taj took the opportunity to bring Sriram to London with his mission to recreate Karavali in London, albeit called The Quilon. Chef Sriram is a master; his spicing lyrical; his balance of flavour dreamlike; his menu a super choice of meat, fish and vegetable dishes. Unlike others in town, Sriram proves that there is no need for flamboyance, spin or new wave, *'Do not take a traditional dish and mess around with it'* he says. In typical understated Taj style, he simply and quietly goes about his business of producing perfect Indian cooking (others please note). His reward is that he is now Quilon's General Manager as well as Chef. Change of decor there maybe but fortunately Taj management have left the menu decision is Sriam's hands. And the cuisine remains firmly Karavali. The new 'Q bar enhanced with a wall of flickering tea-lights, inspired by Hindu temples is well stocked and enhanced by Chef Ramesh Ganiga's canapés eg: Tamarind Glazed Chicken Winglets £4; Crispy Fried Silver Fish £4 or Semolina Chips with Tomato Onion Chutney £3.50. The a la carte three course meal averages £50 and consists of 13 starters, from £5.50 including Lotus Stem and Colocasia Chop With mango and mint sauce, Cauliflower Chilli Fry Gobi Kempu Bezule, crispy fried cauliflower tossed with yogurt, green chili and curry leaves to Crab Cakes, claw meat tossed with curry leaves, ginger, green chilies and cooked on a skillet or Char-Grilled Scallops with mango chilli relish £8.25. Between courses, comes a complimentary shotglass of Tomato Rasam. Main Courses include Seafood Moilee, cubes of halibut, grouper, tiger prawns and potato gently poached in a light coconut sauce; Lobster with Kokumand Mango Fresh lobster cooked with raw mango, ginger, kokum and curry leaves; Crispy Fried Squid with Spice Pounded Shrimps Crispy fried squid with spice pounded shrimps; Malabar Lamb Biryani, £18, lamb cooked with traditional malabar spices in a sealed pot, with basmati rice. Game includes Quail Legs stuffed with quail mince, chilli, ginger, brown onion and spices, roasted and served with mustard sauce. Manglorean Chicken Kori Gassi is a typical Karavali dish, of chicken cooked in finely ground fresh coconut with spices; Venison Coconut Fry, strips of venison fillet tossed with onion, tomato, ginger and spices with coconut slivers. Vegetable dishes include Crispy Okra, thinly sliced, batter fried, tossed in onion, tomato and crushed pepper; Spinach Poriyal, shredded fresh spinach cooked with mustard seeds, whole red chillies, and freshly grated coconut; Mango Curry, cooked with yoghurt, green chillies and tempered with mustard seeds and curry leaves. Pachadi, £3, pineapple and pomegranate mixed with yoghurt, ground coconut, cumin seeds and mustard. Quilon is one of the few places where you can try Bibinca and Dodhol, Goan speciality pudding. Three Course set lunch: £24. Sriran loves his beers and he has devised a unique eight course menu matching beers as follows: Popadums and Tomato Chutney with Ceilidh Lager, Scotland 4.7%; Lotus Stem Chop and Oysters with 312 Urban Wheat Ale, Chicago 4.4% ABV; Grilled Scallops with Mango and Chilli, and Peppered Batter-fried Shrimps in a fiery masala Pietra, Corsica, 6% ABV; Mini Masala Dosa served with Sambhar and Coconut Cream Chicken with Brewsters Pale Ale (England, 5% ABV); Quilon Salad and Baked Black Cod with Chimay Red, Belgium 7% ABV; Kerala Chicken Roast and Cauliflower Chilli Fry (Gobi Kempu Bezule) with Duvel, Belgium, 8.5% ABV; Lamb Biryani and Coconut with asparagus and snow peas with Chalky's Bark, Sharp's, Cornwall 4.5% ABV; Lentil Cappuccino and Cardamom Shortbread with Liefmans Fruit, Belgium, 4.2% ABV. Cost £85. Quilon's private dining room is a restaurant within a restaurant for special occasions or private dinners, with its own entrance, glass top bar complete with 'wine wall' (a floor to ceiling glass wall displaying the wine cellar), on-view show-kitchen, and specially commissioned dining table seating up to 16 people. In conclusion, a restaurant of this calibre means its quality remains rock-solid. It won our Best UK Restaurant award, which means what it says. Though this award goes elsewhere this time, it remains in the Best in the UK category. Service: 12.5%. Mon-Fri: 12-2.30 & Mon-Sat: 6-11.

SALOOS — HAUTE PAKISTANI — A-LIST
62 Kinnerton Street, SW1 8ER
020 7235 4444   www.salloos.co.uk

M Salahuddin's Saloos is a Pakistani institution. This 1st floor restaurant been around since 1976 as has its chef Abdul Aziz. As you enter into the first floor venue, *'you are greeted by the warm orange glows, floral glass oil lamps and music in the light bar. You have stepped into an oasis of calm and beauty. Upstairs the seductive chandeliers twinkle in the dimly lit restaurant surrounded by fettered windows. Pakistan's famous artist Mashqoor adorns the cream walls with his abstract paintings. The theme is women and horses. The eye catching red feature wall, in the far distance, covered in arched frames, is in fact, a series of small paintings, giving the illusion of intricate embroidery. Flame coloured banquettes sit brightly against the dark chairs and crisp white linen.'* So says Salloos about Salloos. The elegant Farizeh Salahuddin (daughter of the house – she can be heard out of hours on the answer machine) handles bookings with considerable aplomb. Being Pakistani, meat, meat and more meat predominates ('*A vegetarian-free heaven'* says RA who, like Bernard Shaw, despises vegetables). He's not quite right, there's Bhindi Okra, thick Dhal, Baingan sweet aubergines, crisp vegetable kebabs, a spicy mash of mixed vegetables coated with bread crumbs to add a finishing crunch when fried crisp and golden and Chana Chickpeas all at £10.50. But it really is the meat dishes which make Salloos stand out. Their signature dish is Tandoori Chops, £24, (chops of tender lamb marinated in spices and herbs and barbecued in the Tandoor). All their Tandoori items are cooked to order and are *'divine'*. DBAC. Chicken Karahi £18.50, a speciality from the Khyber is diced and de boned chicken, cooked with spices, tomatoes, chopped ginger, coriander and green chillies. Hard-to-find, acquired taste Haleem Akbari, £19, shredded lamb cooked with whole wheat germ, lentils and spices, cooked over a day until all the ingredients melt into one; an original dish from the Mughal emperors. Another hard-to-find dish and an equalt favourite of the Mughals is Nargasi Kofta £18, (the Asian Scotch Egg), hard boiled eggs, coated with kebab meat finely ground to paté texture, named after the Narcissus flower due to the yellow yolk and the surrounding white of the hard boiled egg. It is sered with a tasty gravy. Gosht Khara Masala £19, is lamb cooked with whole fragrant spices and julienne ginger. Salloos is still much hallowed by my Pakistani and Indian friends, well-educated wealthy citizens, who ignore politics when it comes to conviviality. The last time we were there seemed to be family day. There were kids all over the place (well behaved ones, Asian and white), thoroughly enjoying themselves as were their parents, the staff and us. An unmissable treat for the aficionado. High in our A-LIST. Cover charge £1.50. Service 12.5%. Mon-Sat 12-3 (last ord 2) & 7-11.

SEKARA — SINHALESE SRI LANKAN
3 Lower Grosvenor Place, SW1
020 7834 0722   www.sekara.co.uk

A combination of Indian and Sinhalese Sri Lankan cuisine. Go for the latter, and if you like it hot, ask the helpful personnel for it done as it would be back home. Menu snapshot: Sri Lankan Starters, mutton Rolls or Fish Rolls £3.50 two deep-fried crispy pancake rolls stuffed with a mixture of lightly spiced savoury lamb or fish and potato; Vadai £2.50, two deep-fried crunchy, spicy lentil cakes. Some mains: Hard-to-find Mutton Lamprais £15.95, deep-fried pieces of mutton mixed with basmati rice flavoured with saffron and spices and served with mutton curry, aubergine and seeni sambola (fried onions). Lampreys or Lamprais (from the Dutch word, 'Longkirist') was a festive dish introduced to Sri Lanka by a Dutch burger centuries ago:a full meal of meat curry, kofta, rice, and sambols is wrapped inside a banana leaf parcel and served like a hot picnic. It is rare to find this dish even in Sri Lanka. Chicken Koththu Roti £9.95, soft home made roti bread chopped up and stir-fried with chicken, fresh leeks, tomatoes and carrots to a historic recipe. String Hoppers £8.95, ten rounds of steamed Sri Lankan noodles, served with potatoes in a coconut milk sauce infused with cinnamon sticks, curry leaves and turmeric and freshly grated coconut mixed with sweet paprika, red chilli, red onion and fresh lime juice; Devilled Wild Boar served with Steamed White Rice, £14.95 cooked with sweet green and red capsicums, onion and fresh green chillies in a very spicy sauce of tomatoes and crushed red chillies. Dessert: Wattalapam £4.95, coconut milk, sweet jaggery, cashew nuts and pure kithul treacle and spiced with cinnamon and nutmeg. Sunday Lunch buffet £12.   12-3 & 6-10.

WOODLANDS — TOP 100
JAIN & SOUTH INDIAN VEGETARIAN
37 Panton Street, SW1Y 4EA
020 7839 7258   www.woodlandsrestaurant.co.uk

Long-established (1985) licensed, vegetarian, south Indian 65-seat restaurant, just off Haymarket and recently refurbished as a casual restaurant with wenge (rich brown) coloured tables, beige walls and wooden flooring. There are 30+ branches in India, Singapore and LA, each serving an identical menu. Bhel £4.95, Dosa, Idli £5.25, Vada £5.50, Samosa £5.75 , Paneer Pakora, £6.50, Utthapam, the Indian Pizza £6.75. They do a range of veg Tandoori items and veg curries. They also uniquely do Jain Food (which excludes onion and garlic). *'I particularly like southern Indian food, and find the menu so appealing, it makes choice difficult. We chose one exceptionally good-value set meal, Thali, £18.50, which was quite generous, with good variety Also glad to have a choice of Indian desserts. Good value.'* HC. *'Gulab Jamun, slightly chewy cardamom-scented fried milk balls in a sticky syrup, Kulfi, Indian ice-cream in a variety of flavours and Carrot Halva, a dense pudding that has the consistency of fudge, are enough to satisfy any sweet tooth. And, if you missed out on a Dosa for your main course or want to continue the pancake theme, you could always end the meal with a butter dosa with sugar'*. TY. Lunch from £4.95; Dinner c £20. Service 12.5%. 12-11.

Branches: Hampstead NW3 & Marylebone Lane W1.

YOU SAY OK, SW1 to SW3

SW1: KHAN'S 24 Brixton Water Lane, Brixton, SW2 1PE 020 7326 4460

SW1: KUNDAN PAKISTANI 3 Horseferry Road, London, SW1P 2AN 020 7834 3211

SW2: PUKKA BRASSERIE 89 Streatham Hill SW2 ~ 020 8671 1171. Kebabs good. Tues Banquet Night.Hours: 5.30 (Sunday from 12) to 12.

SW2: RAJ POOT 67 Streatham Hill, Streatham, SW2 4TX 020 8674 9151

SW3: RASOI 10 Lincoln St , South Kensington, SW3 2TS 020 7225 1881

London SW3

HAANDI   PUNJABI KENYAN   A-LIST
136 Brompton Rd, Knightsbridge, SW3 1HY
and 7 Cheval Place, SW7 1EW   020 7823 7373   www.haandi-restaurants.com

One restaurant with one bar, two addresses and two entrances. One at the rear on Cheval Place is at level, the other, on Brompton Road is down a generous staircase, leading to a bright, clean and tidy reception and the bar, which serves snacks, and on the left is the restaurant. The lemony-yellow decor, with inviting tables and chairs, give a cheerful sunshine welcome. It is managed by Henry Muriuki and owned by Ray Bangra *'We propped up the bar on High Roadools, and sipped glasses of red wine, and chatted with Ray the owner about India, its food and his Kenyan connections (Ray has a highly regarded restaurant there). All dishes cooked properly, presented carefully, served professionally and in generous portions.'* DBAC. Starters include Aloo Chaat £5.90, crispy fried potatoes tossed with onions, tomatoes and chillies topped with chutney; Mogo, £6.70, crispy fried Cassava, with or without chillies; Haandi Paneer Tikka £9.70, Tandoored skewers of home-made curd cheese onions, peppers and tomato; Kaju Till Rolls £7.10, fried croquettes of mixed veggies coated with cashew nut powder & sesame seeds. Tandoori Lobster £26.50, slices of barbeque lobster in shell laced with garlic tomato chutney; Chilli Chilli Fish £11.75, sliced haddock tossed with red and green chillies; Heera Panna £14.50, slices of Calamari and Monk fish lightly tossed in butter, ginger, garlic, cumin and fresh coriander; Chicken Tikka Chettinad, £9.95, tandoored boneless chicken with South Indian spices. Mains include Tawa Chicken Rara £13.80, cooked on an iron griddle with onions, crushed peppercorns and coriander; Kake-Di-Lamb Curry £14.10, lamb on the bone in a curry with lots of onions, tomatoes and spices; Chandni Chowk Ka Keema £14.50 spicy minced lamb with fresh peas, onions, tomatoes and chillies; Prawns Vindaloo £18.50, classic chilli-hot Goan dish with the addition of coconut milk and fresh herbs. Veg dishes incude: Punjabi Aloo Baigan £9.10' whole Baby aubergines and potatoes prepared in special onion masala; Jeera Aloo Banarsi £7.80, a spicy potato dish with methi, cumin and dry red chillies; Dal Bukhara £8.50, creamy black lentils simmered overnight on charcoal embers; Choley Masaledar £8.50, chickpeas made the authentic Punjabi way; Traditional Egg Curry £9.90, Chef's special for eggytarians. *'Excellent menu, food and presentation with a warm welcome. A wonderful restaurant.'* RB. *'Chakula Mzuri Sana is Kenyan for Good Food!'* NH. *'Absolutely gorgeous, good food, wine and service.'* JH. *'A great experience, not only the place was relaxing, the atmosphere and the staff really helpful. We had one of the best Indian meals we have ever come cross. We'll definitely go back.'* NM. *'I have become a regular. Absolutely amazing food, a great ambassador of Indian cuisine.'* AB. *'Absolutely love Haandi. Food so flavourful, spicy and delicious. Courteous staff are welcoming.'* CM. Lunch Menus: from £10. Bar: drinks served between 12-10.30, light meals and snacks available all day. 12-3 & 6-11 (5.30-11.30 Fri & Sat). *See page 51.*

RASOI VINEET BHATIA   A-LIST
CONTEMPORARY INDIAN FINE DINING
10 Lincoln , Sloane Sq, SW3 2TS
020 7225 1881   www.rasoi-uk.com

Vineet Bhatia is no ordinary chef. He tells you he *'came to London with nothing but ambition and a love of Indian food.'* He worked his way up via the Star of India to Zaika, Chelsea then South Ken, where he gained his Michelin Star. He finally settled for a tiny venue (38 seats) where he now cooks, as he calls it *'properly, with a more hands-on approach rather than for a 300 cover factory'*. Rasoi appropriately meaning 'kitchen' is located in a 100 year old house which was previously Richard Corrigan's English Garden restaurant. Vineet and his wife Rashima revamped the

COBRA
SPLENDIDLY INDIAN, SUPERBLY SMOOTH

Vineet Bahtia

Chelsea property into a mini-Indian palace. It is divided into two floors; the lower is the main dining area and bar and the upper level is split into two private function rooms and named after Rajasthan's twin cities – Udaipur and Jaipur, seating 8 and 15. V and R globe-trotted to source many of their furnishings and crockery. Chic chocolate brown dining tables are imported from Turkey, plates (there are over 50 types) have been brought in from countries like Spain and America, the silverware is from France and the Rosenthal glassware is German. A glass covered wall adds depth to the modest space and overlooks the teak wood surface of the bar. A myriad of rich eastern treasures creates a regal air. Rajasthani jharokas, - beautifully crafted wood frames, wedding saris draping the walls, a stunning Kashmiri rug, vibrant Benares saris framing the windows and antiquated Indian chests placed throughout the restaurant. All embody the rustic charms and colourful culture of India. FOH is managed by Gopi Ketineni, Kenny Kurian and Parag Rane. In the kithen Vineet is aided by Head chef Manmeet Bali, and his dedicated brigade. As you would expect Vineet varies his menu and he experiments with ingredients we do not normally associate with Indian food; items like broccoli, chestnuts, beetroot, pine nuts, Stilton (in the Naan) and honey. A fine way to explore the menu is to take the 7 courses 'Prestige' menu at £87 per person. It consists of Crab lolly, crab chutney-mustard caviar; Lime-coconut soup; Banana wrapped mustard Tilapia; Aubergine Achari cous cous; Spice grilled foie gras with green apple chutney wild mushroom naan; White Tomato Chicken Makhni with Goan Cafreal rice. A refresher is Champagne-rose petal sorbet and this is followed by the main course of Smoke cloud- herbed lamb rack, cobnut-saffron upma, Sauce Rogan Josh, Stilton Lamb tikki. Dessert is Pista delice, 'Varqi' 24 carat Chivas Regal truffle, Chocolate with rose heart. There is a veg alternative at the same price. A la carte menu is £49 for 2 courses and £59 for 3. Lunch is from £22. Frequently reported is the *'delicately explosive individual spicing'* RCF countered with *'rather bland. but enhanced with some green chillies'* JGS. There is a carefully selected and extensive range of wines, in addition to spirits and cocktails. Service: 12.5%. Mon-Fri: 12-2.30 Mon-Sat: 6-10.30. *Branch: The Bird, Leeds, W.Yorkshire.*

London SW4

MAHARANI
117 Clapham High Road, SW4 7TB 020 7622 2530 www.maharaniclapham.co.uk

The 104-seat Maharani was established in 1958, at which time there were under 200 curry houses in the whole of the UK. It was not only Clapham's first curry house, opened long before Cla'am became trendy ma'am, it was one of the first to open in a London suburb. It has always earned its keep by providing good, bog-standard, formula curries; indeed, owner SU Khan was one of the pioneers of the formula. Under the same ownership for all these years, Khan has kept up with the trends, though, and everything is as it should be. Hours: 12-2.30 & 6-12; 12-12 Sun.

London SW5

MASALA ZONE   INDIAN CASUAL
A-LIST
147 Earl's Court Rd, SW5 9RQ 020 7373 0220
www.masalazone.com

London's most exciting chain. Its distinctive decor and food make it stand out. From a simple selection of food dishes from £4, to a thali – a complete meal on a plate, from c£9 to c£12 noodle bowls, curry & rice plates such as butter chicken, prawn malai (flavoured with coconut), dhaaba roghan josh (intensely flavoured lamb curry), and undhiyo - the celebratory Gujarati vegetarian dish., tandoors & grills and Masala burgers. Most meals served within five minutes of ordering. *'Quality Very good Quantity Adequate Decor Minimalist Service Prompt and pleasant Comfort Adequate and very clever*. G & MP. Mon-Fri 12 -3 & 5.30-11 (12.30-11 Sat & Sun. More details see page 2 & London W1 branch.

RARA KENSINGTON   NEPALESE
152 Old Brompton Road, SW5 0BE 020 7373 0024
www.rarafood.co.uk

Because they need to pay the rent Rara do formula tandooris, tikkas and kebabs, and curry-house staples ranging from chicken dhansak and lamb bhuna to king prawn jalfrezi. So if that's you, enjoy it. But Rara is Nepal's largest lake which give us a clue that it serves Nepalese food. And that's what the discerning diners go for. The menu has some 20 authentic items including spicy steamed momo dumplings, £7.75, spiced and steamed chicken dumplings served with chutney. (ten per serving) with chutney, as a starters and Mains including Lamb Sekuwa £10.95, lamb pieces spiced with ginger, garlic & yoghurt cooked in a clay oven. Chicken Bhutuwa £10.95, cooked in rich gravy and green herbs. Rara Rasilo Pieces of lamb or chicken simmered in a reduce sauce and flavoured in ginger, garlic, nutmeg & green herbs, all at £10.95, or the south Indian special: Crab Kofta Curry minced Crabmeat mixed with potato and herbs, cooked delicately with curry leaves in an aromatic sauce at£14.95, Rara proudly to tell us their chefs 'have a low threshold for chilli', which is rather alarming.' So tell them to spice it up if you have a high threshold. Lunchtime thalis are great value, while a 30-dish buffet (£8.50) is the served on Sundays. . Daily: 12-3 & 5-11. *Branch Rara, Ruislip, Middx*

THALI   NORTH INDIAN
166 Old Brompton Road, SW5 0BA
020 7373 2626   www.thali.uk.com

Formerly Bar Asia this tidy restaurant with its oriental carvings ornate gold-framed mirrors is no ordinary curry house. Owner Vikash Dhawan brings to Thali a three generation family background of restaurateurs spanning 50 years, and he is usually on hand. Chef Dila Ram worked for the Taj Group since 1997, including a spell at the Bombay Brasserie. In Taj tradition he respects traditional dishes but enjoys innovations, and it is this combination which makes Thali stand out. The bar offers canapés such as Tandoori Wild Boar, marinated in Indian spices, served with a mint sauce, Amritsari Fish, Cod fish simmered with malt vinegar, garam masala, battered in flour & herbs and Vegetable Hara Kebab, Green chickpeas, infused with spinach, green chilli & masala. A la Carte Starters include: Prawn Balchao £6.50, Tiger prawns seasoned with a Goan masala, Grilled Scallops £7.50, seasoned in light spices & a cherry tomato cream sauce, Achari Quails Eggs £5, marinated with Indian pickle & spices Shallow (tala) fried; Squid Bezule £6, baby squid marinated in chilli lemon juice & masalas, Crab Patties £7.50, snow crab meat coated in mint, coriander & spices. Tandoori items start at £6.50. Thali Seafood £20, Non-veg £18 and Veg £12. Mains include Keema & Kidney Masala £9 lamb mince & kidney morsels cooked in onions, herbs & garam masala; Chicken Hara Curry £11.50, breast cooked in a mint coriander, chillies & coconut cream sauce. Dahl Makhani £5.50 creamed black lentils tempered & seasoned with mild spices is our chef-test because it takes skill and overnight to cook and isn't found in the curryhouse, and Dila Ram's version is excellent. As is the pudding dish, Beetroot Halwa £5, beetroot simmered to a fudge-like consistencey with almonds, nuts, milk & sugar. Service charge 12.5%. Daily: 12-3 & 6.30-11.30 (Sun-10)

NIZAM   NW FRONTIER/MOGHUL   TOP 100
152 Old Brompton Rd, SW5 0BE   020 7373 0024

The Nizam was the former ruler of Hyderabad. Until partition he was the richest man in the world, and his dining table seated 101 guests, yes, at one table! On it was a silver model railway which chugged around the table dispensing whisky et al to the distinguished guests which included the Viceroy, European monarchs, the Duke of Windsor, Maharajas and heads of state. The table is still in the Durbar Hall at Hyderabad's Falaknuma Palace, now restored by Taj to luxury hotle status. M Mian's 1989 vintage Nizam is rather smaller, seating 65 on several tables in two rooms. '*Attractive appearance and warm reception. The food was varied and excellent, especially the smoked aubergine. Service was superb throughout.*' RH. Service is exemplary, with smartly waistcoated waiters, exuding expertise with cooking by chef M Riaz. Specialities include smoky Baigan Burtha, (charcoal-grilled aubergine, its flesh then mashed to a purée), Prawn Piri Piri, (coconut milk & chilli). Cover charge £1. Takeaway 10% disc. Del: £12 min. 12-2.30 & 6-11.45.

STAR OF INDIA   TOP 100
154 Old Brompton Rd, SW5 0BE   020 7373 2901

Reza and Azam Mahammad run this startling restaurant. I say startling for two reasons. One is because Vineet was once chef here. (see Rasoi Vineet Bhatia, SW3, earlier). Vineet is a larger-than-life character, but he fades to insignificance alongside Reza. Get him talking to you and you'll see what I mean. It is startling too because the decor is a dead-ringer of Michael Angelo's Sistine Chapel. Starters include: Galouti Kebab, smooth mince lamb patties, served with onion and cumin relish. Samundri Ratan, Saffron infused chargrilled scallops served in a creamy sauce. Chenna Samosa crispy parcels filled with a trio of goat, buffalo and cow's cheese, mixed with leeks, ginger and green peppercorns, served with a spiced tomato and chive chutney. Main courses: Murghabi Tawe Wale, escallops of mallard marinated with garlic, nutmeg, lemon and chilli oil, pan fried on an iron griddle. Raan Mussallam (serves two), roasted leg of baby lamb marinated in a mixture of spices then cooked over a gentle flame in a rich onion and tomato gravy, flavoured with nutmeg and flambéed with rum. If you can spare room for a pudding, try either the Dum Malai Chikki, steamed milk pudding scented with nutmeg and cardamom, topped with caramelised jaggery and carom seeds, served chilled, or the Phalon Ka Muzaffar, home made seasonal fruit compote, served with cardamom ice cream, or have both! Lunch and dinner daily. Some say the Star has passed its zenith. Tell that to its regulars! 12.30-2.30 & 6-11.45.

YOU SAY OK

SW4: CLAPHAM TANDOORI 10 Clapham Common S ~ SW4 020 7622 4470. Clapham's 2nd oldest (1971); 72-seater owned by Abdur Rhaman Choudhury. Del: 3m £10 min. Hours: 12-2.30 &6-12.
SW6: LILY TANDOORI 86c Lillie Rd, W. Brompton SW6 020 7385 1922 '*The original Bengali cuisine, the one I was brought up with, the old fashioned taste. And the people so friendly. We were working at the Ideal Home Ex, erecting stands. I'm in my 50's now and was pleased to get that authentic taste. We need more old fashioned restaurants like this, not the fancy types which we are getting now.*' PC. Peter, you are not alone with this comment.

London SW6

BLUE ELEPHANT THAI A-LIST
The Boulevard, Imperial Wharf, Townmead Rd SW6 2UB   020 7751 3111   www.blueelephant.com

The group, which includes La Porte des Indes W1, is headed by Belgian Karl Steppe, and his Thai chef-wife Nooror Somany Steppe and has branches world-wide, including in Bangkok and Phuket. London's huge Fulham Broadway Blue Elephant has always been the group's flagship, and in our view consistently the Best UK Thai restaurant. When their 25-year lease came to an end in early 2012 the challenge was to maintain the standards despite relocation. Though smaller, the new venue has its charms: the view over the river Thames for one through the floor to celing windows. The decor is sumptuously Thai *'I can't think of many better views to enjoy over a summer night's dinner. Blue Elephant basks in the warmth of a setting sun and diners watch the dusk fall over the River Thames. The quality of light changes inside the restaurant as well. The striking dragon bar is transformed into a shimmering swathe of richly tooled gold. The dark polished wood of windows and doors reflect the low lights. Outside has become a sophisticated night-time cityscape.'* The bar retains as much magnificence and sense of theatre as its predecessor, and all diners should allow time to enjoy its delights. The mixologists know their job and turn out a wealth of cocktails, familiar and otherwise. Wanting something not too sweet, I was drawn to their Thai take on Bloody Mary – Tom Yam Mary (Sputnik vodka & tomato juice with piquant red chilli jus) my companin chose Mai Thai, a melange of cool refreshing exotic fruit juices with a hint of alcohol, both £10. With tastebuds tingling, one is all-set to explore the restaurant proper.Ther dark wood floor and furniture competes with tea lights, ceiling fans and whicker baskets. Huge plants; and bunches of redolent orchids, freshly imported from Bangkok's famous floating market and displays of fresh fruit and vegetable carvings fill the light and airy interior. Friendly and efficient staff are at hand to recommend and advise from the unique selection of menus, categorised into Thai cooking past, present and future ('tomorrow'). There is even a vegetarian menu. If the choise is a tad bewildering, the answer is to go for the Tasting Menu, containing many of Nooror's signature dishes. It begins with Foie Gras Tamarind Sauce, pan fried French goose liver from "Landes" with Thai tamarind sauce, pomelo salad and crushed peanuts add a new and delectable Thai flavour. Emerald Chicken is jewels of marinated chicken wrapped in pandanus leaves and accompanied by a ginger and sesame sauce. Khang Khao Phuak is a Thai recipe from the past of minced prawns, chicken and sweet spices stuffed in a golden taro pastry, Dim Sim is steamed parcels of Thia-flavoured minced pork, shrimps and crab meat. Middle Course is Grilled Lobster marinated with garlic butter, green peppercorns and fresh coriander; Black Cod Rad Prik, deep fried black cod topped with chilli, garlic, sweet basil and red curry paste. Drunken Beef: Stir-fried Scottish rib eye with home-made chilli paste and sweet basil; Lamb Shanks Yellow Curry, lamb shanks simmered in coconut milk, yellow curry paste with fresh turmeric, sweet potato, served with roti. This is accompanied with Stir-Fried Morning Glory, Thai water spinach stir-fried in low fat rice bran oil with crushed chillies and oyster sauce and Benjarong Rice, a combination of steamed wild rice with lotus seeds and black sesame seeds wrapped in a banana leaf. If you can still move, there's an umissable dessert of Black Sticky Rice Pudding With Longan. The The spectacular Sunday buffet Brunch includes entertainment for children and unlimited servings for £30 and is another good way to experience many dishes. The relocation has not changed our view that Blue Elephant delivers the finest Thai cuisine anywhere. This is why we continue to rate it the Best Thai restaurant in the UK. *See page 76.*   Mon-Sat: 12-2.30 & 6-11 (to 3:30 & 10.30 Sun).

Below: Chef Patron Nooror Somany Steppe at Blue Elephant's new riverside venue.

NAYAAB FINE PUNJABI PAKISTANI A-LIST

309 New Kings Rd (jnct'n Munster Rd), SW6 4RF
020 7731 6993   www.nayaab.co.uk

The Nayaab is one of London's longest established Indian restaurants (est 1981). Praveen Rai is from the old-school of owner-management. He is gracious, articulate, witty and thoroughly good company. Nayaab simply ouzes class and quality, from the smart Nehru suits worn by Praveen and his staff as they welcome clients, to the superior Pakistani/north west Indian cooking cooked by chef Akeel Ghani and his brigade. The menu is a balance of popular all time favourites and genuine, authentic dishes *'some dishes you won't recognise and some that you will'*, he says. At the beginning it was all the latter but though he has to keep the 'old curryhouse favourites' on the menu ('to pay the rent'), for the if-you-must-brigade, he is delighted that the former dishes, the unusual are becoming more demanded. It is these dishes we urge you to try. For example: Starters: Peshawari Champen, a Nayaab signature dish: succulent lamb chops marinated in a marinade of yoghurt & chilli garlic paste, £4.95 or Main Course £8.95; Baigan Pakoras £4.95 - gram flour coated aubergine roundels filled with cheese and herbs, crispy fried; Dhingree Chicken £6.95 - supreme breast of chicken stuffed with delicately spiced garlic mushrooms, rolled in gram-flour batter and deep-fried; Amritsari Masala Fish, sole goujons seasoned with a unique blend of selected herbs and spices, deep fried.Starter £6.95, Main Course £12.95. Other main course examples: Nihari-Kohi-Avadh – Shank of Lamb, it is sautéed then slow cooked in a pot with a special spicy sauce. The enables the bone marrow to gently infuse the dish with additional flavour ,£8.95; Haleem, broth of lamb & lentils, spicy, £6.95; Paya a saucy & spicy delicacy made from lambs shin & feet, £6.95; Barrahan Kadi Murg Chicken Twelve Kadi. Kadi Sauce is a unique blend

Below: Champen, left and Kadi Murg Chicken Twelve Kadi.

Above: The Murgh Biriani Dum by special arrangement

of yoghurt and besan enhanced by twelve seperate spices and herbs, subtly added at various stages of cooking. Breast of chicken stuffed with spiced mushrooms, simmered in the sauce. Besan Wali Punjabi Kadi Pakora Twelve "Kadi" is the vegetarian version with vegetable dumplings, £6.95. Either way this is a rarely found Punjabi speciality, and at the Nayaab, it is as good as it gets. So too is Dumba Lamb cooked in it's own juices on the bone as in all parts of India, £8.95, or £7.95 for chicken on the bone. Punjabi Maa Cholleyean Di Daal is a mixture of black & white urad, gram pulse & red kidney cooked on a low flame, £3.95. By special arrangement, (pre-ordered and prepaid on his quieter days, min 6 diners) they will make you a properly oven-cooked authentic Biryani Dum (not a stir-fry) and it is *'to-die-for'* to quote DBAC. Pictured below featuring lamb or chicken cooked on the bone, it is not on the menu because it is time-consuming to cook. So, telephone him a few days before to book it. We did and we were not be disappointed! We cannot recommend Nayaab highly enough. And the added advantage is the discount: Show Praveen your copy of this Guide and receive a generous discount on food bill, reservation essential for this. Del: 3m £10 min. Hours: 6-10.45 (to Midnight, Fri & Sat). See page 52.

Below: Praveen Rai

seasoning
RESTAURANT | BAR

84D - 86 Lillie Road
Fulham, London, SW6 1TL
T: 020 7386 0303
F: 020 7386 5888

www.seasoning-restaurant.com
info@seasoning-restaurant.com

For further information, please contact Mr Bhatia
07956 3783000

INDIAN SEASONING

86 Lillie Road, Fulham, SW6 1TL 020 7386 0303
www.seasoning-restaurant.co.uk

Indian Seasoning launched in 2009 and is owned by Nitin Munglanai and New Delhi-born Salal Bhatia. who worked in the Oberoi group, then as a director of London's famed Gaylord restaurant. The venue has a bar, function rooms, a DJ booth and an outdoor terrace. The 100 seat dining room has white walls and wooden flooring. Outer walls have long coffee coloured banquettes, a "wall" of bottled wines, square tables with white cloths and Kings cutlery, stemmed wine glasses and a fresh flower. Smart and elegant and not unusual, then you spot the chairs ... clear perspex arm chairs. But this brave mix of modern and traditional works amazingly well. Head Chef, Mumbai-born Nirmal Save cooked at the Mumbai's JW Marriott hotel. Unusually, he is trained in that rarity, Haakan Indian Chinese cuisine, and a selection of these dishes are on the menu along with Indian dishes. Start with the likes of Walnut Kebab, finely minced vegetables mixed with crushed walnuts and herbs and spices; Drums of Heaven, chicken drumsticks coated in a medium-spiced Chinese sauce, both £4.25; and Mussels Rasam £5.95, mussels simmered in tomato and tamarind broth, flavoured with ginger and curry leaves. Main courses include the old favourites, CTM, Butter chicken, Vindaloo, Madras, Rogan and Dhansak all at £7.25. But there is also Chicken Kalimirch, £7.25, boneless chicken with black pepper and aromatic spices); Lamb Shank £8.95, braised in a sauce of poppy seeds, onions and ginger; and Duck Chettinad, £7.95 Barbary breast in Chettinad spices, roasted coconut, mustard seeds and curry leaves, or Chinesse King Prawn in Pepper sauce £13.95. Sides feature Baingan Bharta, freshly minced baked aubergines; Pindi Channa, medium-spiced chick peas served dry; Malai Kofta, cottage cheese dumplings in a mildly spiced rich gravy all at £4.25; A fascinating rice dish is Lemon and Ginger Rice, rice cooked with peanuts, lemon juice and curry leaves. For the sweet-toothed, there are home-made traditional desserts such as Firni, traditional Mughal rice pudding and Kulfi Falooda £3.25. Service is quick and efficient. 12-3 & 6-11.30. Sunday Buffet: £9.95, 11.30-4pm.

London SW7

BOMBAY BRASSERIE
LIFETIME BEST RESTAURANT AWARD
14 Courtfield Close, Courtfield Road, SW7 4QH
020 7370 4040   www.tajhotels.com

The Bombay Brasserie (BB to its friends) pioneered Indian regional cooking in this country, in fact in the world when it opened in 1982. It hadn't even been done in India It is now the 50-strong Taj Hotel Group's flagship restaurant, the most star-studded, most profitable, most awarded (we were the first) venue. It is an icon. Sadly its original director Adi Modi no sooner retired than he unexpectedly passed away. He is greatly missed. The BB is fortunate in that Arun Harnal had worked with Adi for many years. He is now in charge assisted by Shailesh Pandya and Sidhartha Oberoi, and the management is as ever, exemplary. Staff turn-round is minimal. Locals and regulars, of which there are very many, greet the same staff faces year after year. Of our many thousands of reports received each year, we typically get around 100 about the BB. It way out does any other venue. Despite seating a considerable 265, you are advised to book. Some nights they serve 400 guests. It's nothing to see Madonna on one table, Hugh Grant on another, and the odd politician or peer on a third. None of this phases the waiters. Not everyone likes the redec of a year or two back. Current Taj management have a penchant for undertaking time-consuming and ginormously expensive and utterly tasteless refurbishment schemes. Inexplicably their brief is to remove all traces of India. They did it first in their Mumbai flagship and just recently at Quilon SW1. Quite why they feel every property has to look like an international hotel lobby, or a footballer's wife's lounge, I am at a loss to explain. I am not alone. Metro's Marina O'Laughlin says. ... *'the recent revamp seems to have as its "blueprint the Heathrow branch of the Radisson Edwardian ... looks like the Taj Group has squandered squillions.'* The Independent's Terry Durack says *'The word mausoleum springs to mind, but perhaps museum is kinder ...'* Hardens: *'OMG, what have they done to it? Perhaps there should be some sort of law that London hotels just aren't allowed substantially to refurbish their restaurants? ... and the more cherished the restaurant, the more crass redevelopment seems to be. ... feel is now Travelodge de luxe'.* For sure this vandalism would not have taken place under the previous Taj management, and the proof of this is to look at any of Camelia Panjabi's ventures, (the outsted former Taj Group marketing director and brainchild of none other than the BB), such as Amaya, SW1. The BB's conservatory survives and one asset dominating it, is the show kitchen, with seats for an audience of eight, dreamt up by Taj Group Corporate Chef Hemant Oberoi. All Taj chefs are Taj-trained in India and it takes years, and no chef is better trained. Leading by example, Oberoi encourages his chefs to display this expertise in public, to the obvious

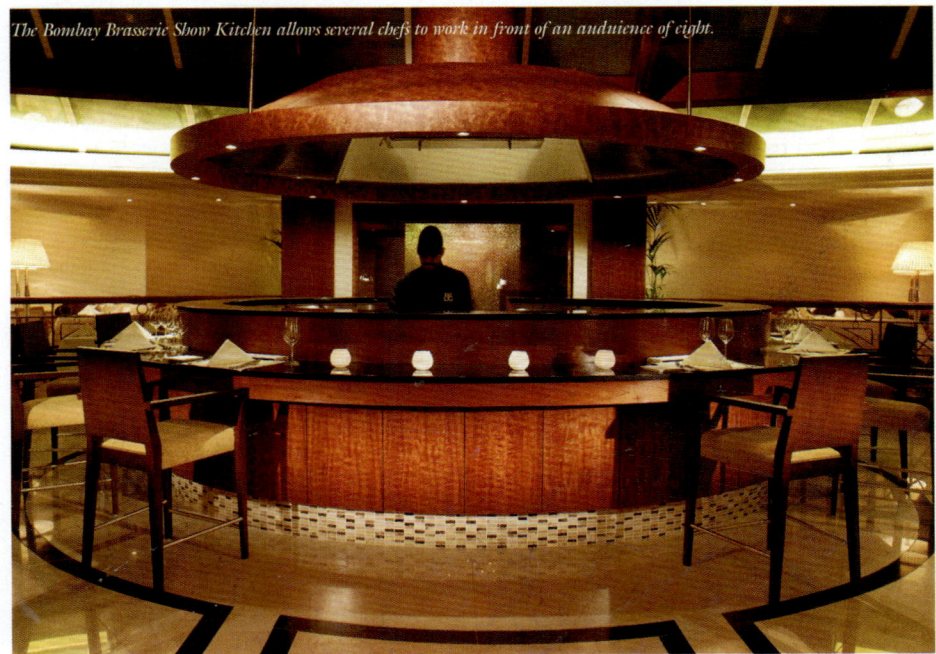

The Bombay Brasserie Show Kitchen allows several chefs to work in front of an audience of eight.

COBRA

SPLENDIDLY INDIAN, SUPERBLY SMOOTH

Taj Corporate Chef, Hemant Oberoi

delight of his clients. He doesn't want show-offs; he wants his chef's love of food to shine. He has piloted similar kitchens in Delhi and Mumbai. Only the cream are posted to London. Head Chef Prahlad Hegde worked at Taj Mahal Hotel Mumbai and Goa. In 1991 he joined the BB. His bar menu (which Oberoi called tapas, now much copied) includes Sev Batata Puri Paneer Tikka, Ragada Pattice, Potato cake with chickpeas and chutney; Seekh Kebab £5, skewered minced lamb kebabs. Authentic 'old'recipes sit alongside modern innovations on the a la carte menu, while traditional tiffin boxes make an excellent lunchtime treat. Current starters include the highly popular Sev Batata Puri £8.50, crisp mini puris topped with a spiced potato mix, gramflour straws and chutneys; Bhatti Ka Asparagus £8.50, char grilled spiced asparagus tips; Malabari Soft Shell Crab £11.50 spiced soft shell crab. Main Courses include Tandoori chargrilled King Prawns, £23.50, or chicken and salmon £18. Oberoi signature dishes include Dum Ki Nalli £18.50, slow-cooked lamb shanks in a delicate saffron curry; Scallops on Peppered Crab £11.50, curry leaf scallops on a peppered crab with tomato chutney; and Paperwail Machchi - monkfish fillets drizzled with freshly ground peppercorns enveloped in parchment paper, chargrilled in an open pit and served wrapped in a Bombay Brasserie newspaper! Lamb Chops with Ginger and Green Herbs £19.00, is a Chef Oberio special. French cut, English lamb cooked Indian style. Another of his dishes is Kashmiri Chilli Curry Leaf Fried Lobster £28.50, fresh whole lobster, cut, spiced and pan-fried, as is Chicken Khorma Lucknowi, £17.50 an interesting take on classic Korma. Traditional dishes still are in demand such as Prawn Balchao £20.50, cooked with goan vinegar and chillies and Lamb Roganjosh £18.50, tender pieces of lamb cooked in a traditional masala. And no self-respecting restaurant would dare to operate without Chicken Tikka Makhani £17.50. An Oberoi vegetable dish is Chilgoza Falli £9.00/£5.00, haricot beans with pine nuts, and his unique bread is Piri Piri Olive Naan £3, with chillies and a very non-Indian ingredient ... olives. The BB pioneered Indian regional restaurant cooking. Now it has stiff competition. But for sheer style and competence, it is a hard act to beat. Daily: 12-3 & 7-11:30. Bar: 5:30-11.30 (from 6.30 Sat & Sun). *See page 48.*

SHEZAN   FINE PAKISTANI   TOP 100
16 Cheval Pl, off Montpelier St, Knightsbridge
SW7 1ES   020 7584 9316   www.shezan.co.uk

This long-established (1966), very traditional 120-seat Pakistani restaurant, is in a residential a block north of Old Brompton Road. The downstairs dining room, past the bar, is elegantly oppulant, from the to the wall decor, the pewter plates, long-rolled napkins, traditional Pakistani chairs, all made theatrical by strategic lighting and candlelight. Chef Khan's food is as sophisticated as the service. It's traditional authentic Pakistani food done as it would have been for the royal courts. No innovation, no nonsense. Not even CTM (but its originator dish, Murgh Makhni) £12. The prices are Knightsbridge, but it's worth every penny just for regal service and care. Taka Tak, £15finely chopped kidneys and liver in a thick masala curry. Keema Bharay Keralay, £17, bitter gourd stuffed with spicy minced lamb; Raan Masala, £69, whole leg of lamb marinated and slow roasted Dumm Pukht (24 hours notice required £300, whole young lamb marinated and stuffed with Basmati Rice and other exotic spices cooked in the Pashtun Style. Mini charge dinner £25. Service 10%. Cover charge £1.50. Takeaway 20% off. Daily: 12-11.30. Branches in New York and Riyadh.

Shezan Hare Murgh Tikka (Green herbal chicken Tikka)

You say OK

SW7: DELHI BRASSERIE 134 Cromwell Road, SW7 .020 7370 7617 Owner Mr A Jabber's and Chef Ram Singh's comfortable spacious 60-seater. 12-11.30.

SW7: KHAN'S OF KENSINGTON 3 Harrington Road, South Kensington, SW7 3ES   020 7584 4114   . 60-seater, est. 1991. Malabar Fish in a coconut sauce £10;Lamb Chilli Stir-fry, thin-sliced lamb with capsicum & chillies. £9. 12-2.30 & 5.30-11

SW9: OLD CALCUTTA 64a Brixton Road, Oval, SW9 020 7582 1415. Old-hand Abdul Mazid's curryhouse has been in this Guide since 1984. Del: 3m,£12 min. Hours: 12-2.30 / 6 -12. Go on the web site to hear some lyrical Ravi Shankar music. www.calcutta.co.uk

London SW8

Battersea, South Lambeth, Vauxhall

CAFÉ ZIA
811 Wandsworth Rd, SW8 3DH   020 3202 0077
www.cafezia.foodkingdom.com

In 2002 chef and restaurateur, Manju Choudhury took leave of his successful group of over 20 restaurants (the Hawelli Group) to open a new restaurant, Café Zia. Manju's brother, Mosru co-owns and manages the 100-seater. The contemporary design is fresh, with curtained windows and natural lighting offering a homely setting. Head Chef Govinder Prasad-Gurung, joined the restaurant after ten years as Head Chef of Battersea's Bombay Bicycle Club. He offers signature dishes like Bhuna Gosht Khybari, tender lamb flavoured with a hint of coriander and ginger cooked in a garlic and onion sauce; Chicken Aishwarya, slices of tender butter chicken breast marinated in lemon and methi leaf and cooked in a rich almond sauce; and Mala King Prawns, simmered in wine, garlic & almond sauce. 5:30- 11.

HOT STUFF   PAKISTANI BYO
19 & 23 Wilcox Road, SW8 2XA   020 7720 1480
www.welovehotstuff.com

In London's SW1 you'll find the most expensive, haute decor restaurants in the UK. Not so far away, you'll also find a gem like this one which has been around since 1988, It's a well-loved caff on a parade of shops at Lambeth's Wyvil Estate Decor is not a consideration here, and in that respect it's like India which means 'it's *'cheap and cheerful, totally lacks location factor and hi glam. Formica tables and plastic chairs and plastic chilliies dangle amongst the bling from the fairy lights in the ceiling.'* And that is the beauty of this Guide. We love them at any level so long as they deliver. And the food is the thing. The menu looks like standard curryhouse but , it is far from it; everything is top notch. *'Pat, everyone is raving about it. And when you find it don't give up because it looks so drab – go in, but not before you've stocked up at the offie next door. It's BYO.'* JGS. Owner, waiter (and for all I know chief bottle washer too) is Raj Dawood. Let him guide you to your meal. Whatever he suggests is good. I had bhajis for starters, £2.50, followed by. hot chilli chicken and Raj told me to have the Magic Mushroom Rice with it. What a trip! Here it's hard to spend a tenner for good gutsy Pakistani food. In between his multitasking Raj is a raconteur too. He'll tell you that 'My Beautiful Launderette' was filmed nearby, implying that the crew all ate there. Lucky them, It is packed at times. Price Check: CTM £6.75, Pullao Rice £2.25, Plain Naan £2. Unlicensend. BYO No corkage (offie next door). Free del over £15.00, cards taken. Mon- Sun: 5-10. Daily:11-10

OVAL TANDOORI
Contemporary Asian Cuisine

- Fully licensed
- Take away and home delivery service
- Highly recommended by food critics and celebrities
- Newly refurbished with private party rooms
- Open seven days a week inc bank holidays
  12pm to 2.30pm & 6pm to 12am

THE FAMOUS INDIAN RESTAURANT

TRADING SINCE 1971

**64a / 66 Brixton Road
Oval
London SW9 6BP
020 7582 1415 / 020 7793 0311
www.ovaltandoori.co.uk**

London SW9

ELEPHANT CAFÉ   BYO   PAKISTANI
55 Granville Arcade, Brixton Village Market,
Coldharbour Lane Brixton SW9 8PS   07590 389684
www.elephantcafe.co.uk

Cheap and cheerful, no frills food in Imran Bashir's weeny caff in a small arcade. Seating inside and on the . Curries and thalis. Tue: Noon-5:30 / Wed-Sat: Noon to 4pm (Tue-5:30/Sun-5)/Thu-Sat: & 6-10pm.

OVAL TANDOORI
64a / 66 Brixton Road, Oval, SW9 6BP   020 7582 1415   www.ovaltandoori.co.uk

Established in the 1970's, this is a typical and much-loved curryhouse with an experienced team front and back in an intimate, comfortable atmosphere. All the old favourites are there. Fish dishes include Telapia £7.95 and Salmon, £8.95 cooked in any curry sauce a, hot or mild; Kali Mirch Gosht. £7.95 is hot and is lamb cooked with ginger & crushed black pepper. Duck Sag, £9.95, cardamom, turmeric, cloves, cumin, cinnamon etc, with cream, garlic, ginger, coriander, capsicum, onion, green chillies and spinach. Daily: 12-2.30 & 6-12.

London SW10

CHUTNEY MARY — FINE INDIAN DINING
BEST UK RESTAURANT, 1992, 1999 & 2013
535 Kings Road, SW10
020 7351 3113   www.realindianfood.com

Chutney Mary opened in 1990 with a policy to present food from at least six different regions of India, and they reasoned, such foods are best be cooked by the chefs from that region. Tonaccomplish this they recruited a brigade of specialist chefs directly from India. The BB (see earlier) was the first to do this, but Chutney Mary did it in rather greater depth, albeit at first publicising the food as Ango-Indian. We are proud of the fact that we gave Chutney Mary the first ever Best Restaurant Award back in 1992. And we did it again in 1999. Owners Camellia and Namita Panjabi and Ranjit Mathrani have since become well-established in the restaurant industry and have become renowned for their high quality Indian restaurants currently numbering twelve (see below), all Award winners in this Guide. One, Amaya, SW1 was awarded the most sought-after Michelin star in 2007. Michelin are totally confused whrn it comes to awarding stars to Indian restaurants, and as we have stated time after time, no one can iunderstand why Chutney Mary is not similarly recognised. Everything is highly professional, from the decor (Michelin score decor highly in the rating sytstem, but you can;t eat the decor). Much more important is a venue's cleanliness; there is no point in spending £1m on a refit, as Chutney Mary recently did if you don't clean and maintain it. The decor, in any case, is Mich Star quality as are the all-important front-of-house staff who glide each diner through their experience, from the cloakroom receptionist's friendly greeting to the floor staff's knowledgable and discreet service. At entrance level there is a bright and airy private dining room seating up to 28 or 50 standing. Downstairs the dining room is in three areas. The Club Section on the left, in the lower area seats 50 andcan be sectioned off to take private parties. The central area also seats 50 and on the right is the legendary conservatory, decorated with its forest of Indian greenery and admitting much needed light in the day In the dark, hi-tech lighting gives a moonlit effect to the conservatory, its tree and sparkling fairy lights. A sumptuous, thickly woven carpet and dark wood furniture swathed in silk cushions helps to create a luxurious yet relaxed atmosphere. Wines have always been taken very seriously at Chutney Mary. It is unthinkable that when they opened back in 1991, the notion of drinkng fine wine with Indian food was an absolute taboo to most celebrated wine critics. CM's glassed-in, temperature-controlled wine room remains the central feature in the restaurant permitting customers can see the ideal conditions in which their wine is being kept. The wine list featuring over 100 definitive wines, is by wine writer Mathew Jukes is , and would do justice in any restaurant.

Jukes promises relatively low mark-ups on the more expensive wines – 'to encourage experimentation'. Presentation has always been Indian food's downfall, but at Chutney Mary it is given the highest priority. Some years ago, Mathrani asked me how presentation could be improved at Indian restaurants. I recall blubbering some inconsequential answer. I know now that the Panjabis already had the issue in hand. When introduced it was revolutionary and unique in the Indian market. Though copied now, CM still lead the way with. Each dish has its own bespoke high-quality white platter or handmade glass plate chosen for shape and utility. on which it is plated with its own food-layout by the chefs. We do receive a few complaints about plated food, but we commend the detractors to admire the skill that plating requires, besides not all dishes come plated. CM prefer not to publish their menus because they like to make frequent changes, and the staff are on hand to explain all items on the menu to the last detail. Starters are priced between £8.50 and £11. One of the most demanded starters is Tokri Chaat, £8.50, and is the epitome of presentation. Centre piece is a golden edible, crisp, deep-fried potato straw-lattice, dominating the plate in a peacock fan display. A combination of moong lentils, tamarind, onion, amchur and chilli are anchored in brilliant white home-made yoghurt, drizzled with imli (tamarind jus) and studded with fresh green coriander leaves and red pomegranate seeds. The Kebab platter (illustrated below) is equally appetising.

continued overleaf

CHUTNEY MARY

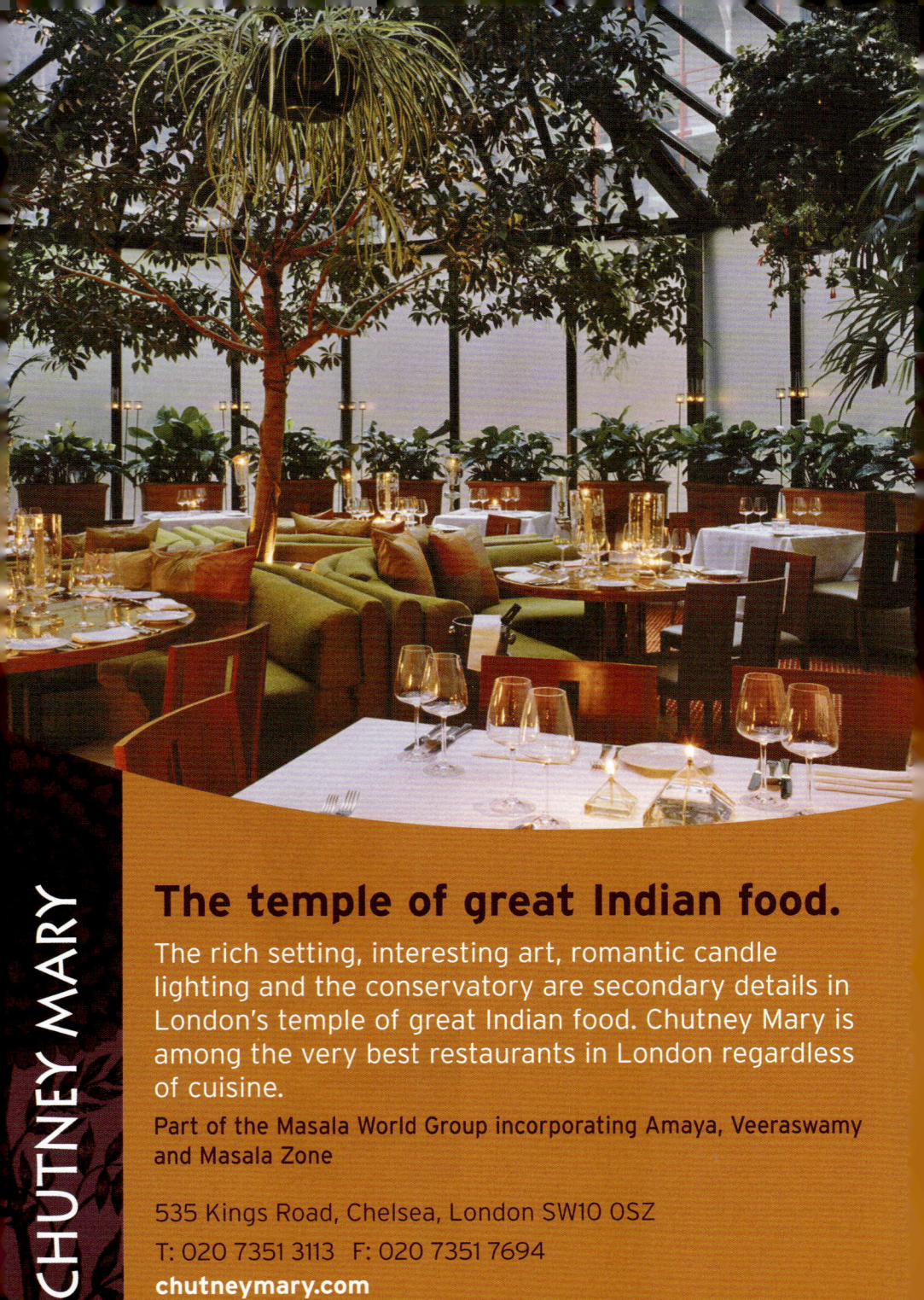

The temple of great Indian food.

The rich setting, interesting art, romantic candle lighting and the conservatory are secondary details in London's temple of great Indian food. Chutney Mary is among the very best restaurants in London regardless of cuisine.

Part of the Masala World Group incorporating Amaya, Veeraswamy and Masala Zone

535 Kings Road, Chelsea, London SW10 0SZ
T: 020 7351 3113   F: 020 7351 7694

chutneymary.com

COBRA
SPLENDIDLY INDIAN, SUPERBLY SMOOTH

CHUTNEY MARY *Continued from previous page.*

Main courses, from £16.50 to £26 (more for lobster!) cover the gamut of Indian cooking techniques, tandoori, sigri grill, tava pan-frying, slow cooking curries and deep-frying. Spice mixes are wet-stone-ground in house achieving smooth textures and fine mixes. Examples of what to expect: Meat curries using lamb sourced from farms in Essex; Chandini Tikka (cornfed chicken breast tikka using white spices); Duck with apricots (Jardaloo), a Parsee favourite – fanned slices of pinky duck breast, drizzled with a spicy minced sauce with halved apricots; Konkan Prawns with asparagus; A fab Tandoori Crab; Wild Sea bass Allepey (pan-grilled in a coconut and coriander sauce with green tomato salsa) or Mangalore prawn curry (with chilli hot sauce with tamarind and coconut). Vegetarians have two choices, a traditional North Indian platter of vegetables and daal, or seven southern vegetarian dishes such as stir-fried banana flower with coconut, baby courgette masala, okra and water chestnut. There is a good selection of sides and breads, including Black Urid Dal (Maharani) [DBAC's favourite] dark, rich, creamy, aromatic spices, and swirl of cream, cooked for 24 hours on embers and as good as it gets at CM. Innovative desserts, unusual for Indian restaurants, are priced at about £7 and include the legendary Dark Chocolate Fondant with orange blossom lassi. One way to try it all is to order the Tasting Menu of seven courses at £75 per head. Chutney Mary deserved its 1992 and 1999 Awards and it deserves it again. Nobody does it better. The Panjabis are the most innovative restaurateurs in the Indian sector. They stick to their beliefs, which is to offer Indian food done exquisitely well. Chutney Mary, their first venture got off to a slow and timid start. But that was years ago. It is now a huge success and a visionary pioneer. The team are now as confident as can be, and we can only await their future ventures impatiently. Meanwhile Chutney Mary remains my all-time favourite Indian Restaurant. Service: 12.5%. Sun to Fri:; 6.30 11 (Sat to 11.30); Sat & Sun: 12.30-2.30.

Group restaurants: Amaya SW1, Veeraswamy W1 and eight Masala Zones, (see W1). See also p2 and p55.

PAINTED HERON FINE INDIAN DINING
BEST UK CHEF   112 Cheyne Walk, SW10 0DJ
020 7351 5232   www.thepaintedheron.com

It's between Albert and Battersea Bridges, on a corner site. Parking is difficult; there are few single yellow lines. The restaurant has been refurbished. Tables are simply laid, white linen cloths, napkins, contemporary cutlery and a single wine balloon. Rounds of moulded glass contain coloured oil with wick to light each table inadequately. Chairs are painted black wood, seated with leather and comfortable. Lumber floors are polished and the large plate glass windows are dressed with wooden slatted blinds. We perused the menu and sipped Shiraz (£17), over a large oval platter, generously piled high with fresh Popadum strips, accompanied by three chutneys – Beetroot, Coconut and Mango and Chickpea with Chilli. All handmade and all fabulous. Staff are smilers - smart, clean and very willing. The Painted Heron's owner decided in 2003 to get into the Indian restaurant business. He's in property and owns the building, and he seems to have an instinct for it. His ace card is his choice of chef – Yogesh Datta. He's Taj-trained, and readers of this Guide know how good Taj chefs are. Yogesh has absolutely no ego (others take note). He is totally dedicated to hands-one cooking. He enjoys a challenge and he's very much hands-on. His menu, which changes every few days, has no long, meaningless narrations, just short, concise definitions, or perhaps the best explanation, honesty! And Yogesh runs the kitchen with Kansili Brahmanand (ex ITC Sheraton India) and just one other chef. (others take note). The food sometimes has an innovative signature, but it is glorious Indian food, all carefully crafted and accurately spiced. With an ever-changing menus we can only talk about typical dishes. Starters: Squab pigeon breasts in tamarind, tandoor grilled, £8; Quail, tawa fried with Pakistani "taka tak" spices, £7; Tandoori lamb chops with nutmeg flowers, £7. For £20 you can sharing a starter platters: seafood with crab dosa, monkfish, tiger prawns & sea bass, or meat with keema naan fingers, chicken tikka, duck tikka & lamb chops, or vegetarian with spicy sprouting lentils, paneer tikka, baby aubergine, pineapple & crispy onion bhajis. Back for a retest, main courses remain a quarrelsome choice, with so many delectable dishes. We agreed on Corn-fed chicken stuffed with pickled lime, £13.50, (the breast flattened and rolled in a cylinder then baked) in a karahi masala with chick peas & fried green chillies and Lamb Shank with aromatic spices, served in a impressive, round, shiny, white metal bowl with a wide flat rim. The portion was so large it could have generously fed two and was so tender it literally fell of the bone. I choose 'Creamy Black Lentils' urid dal, well cooked, indeed creamy, with a whirl of fresh cream decorating it surface; quite chilli hot, but with a full, rounded flavour, not raw. Pat requested a Mint Parantha. He thought it would harmonise his meal well and he was right. It was delivered in a basket, rolled very thinly and sprinkled with finely chopped, dried, mint leaves. Pat's words *'VERY nice.'* Full to the gills, we tried Gulab jamun with iced candied fruit nougat, £5. We were delighted to give Yogesh our Best Chef Award. Nobody anywhere does it better. Discretionary 12.5% service charge. Garden seats. 6-11 daily. Brunch: Sat & Sun 11-5. *Branches: Bangalore City EC3 & SE1*

BATTERSEA RICKSHAW NORTH INDIAN
15-16 Battersea Square, SW11 3RA
020 7924 2456   www.battersearickshaw.com

Battersea Rickshaw is in London's trendy and cobbled Battersea square, home to several other restaurants, pubs and bars. Popular, we're told for celeb-spotting [wow], it's a stone's throw from the river Thames and ten minutes walk from Clapham Junction station. The Chefs are from North India have recipes from their home towns. Appetisers feature spicy crab cakes £9 and Duck Samosas £7. Mains include Tilapia Masala, £10 Nalli Gosht £13, lamb shank and a variety of prawn, lamb, Kadu £4 pumpkin and Saag Makai, £4 stir-fried spinach and corn with red chilli flakes. During the summer, their outdoor seating and Indian Barbeque are avaailable. Mon-Sat: 5.30-11.30. (Sun 5-11) Sat & Sun: 12-3.

NOIYA INDIAN KITCHEN AND BAR,
62 Lavender Hill, SW11 5RQ
020 7228 7171   www.noiya.co.uk

A formula menu is there, presumably as a safe bet for the won't-try-something-new brigade. More intriguing is its range of interesting specials eg: Mezai Chicken Spring, on the bone, marinated in spices with mango, cinnamon and bay leaves skewered, slowly grilled in the tandoor, then cooked in a medium rich sauce; Jawabi Chops, seasoned with garlic, cumin seed, crushed coriander then gently grilled in the tandoor, then sautéed with potatoes in a tomato base, both £8.25. Mehel Ka Sabji, potatoes & Mushrooms, marinated in crushed mint leaves and garlic, sauteed with ground herbs, garnished with a spicy tomatoe and coriander sauce; Rajnee Ka Paneer, Goat's cheese cooked with cauliflower florets in a mild cream sauce, garnished with garden peas, both £7.25. Para Ka Matchli £8.95, fish cooked with a selection of spices in a thick creamy honey sauce garnished with cashew nuts and sultanas. Toak £3.75 is char-grilled tomatoes, sautéed with garlic & bay leaves with a hint of green chillies. Mon-Sat: 12-2.30 & 5-12 (to 1am Fri & Sat). Sun: 1 to 12.

HOP & SPICE SRI LANKAN
53 Bedford Hill, Balham, SW12 9EZ
020 8675 3121   www.hopandspice.com

Once upon a time on one of my tour groups, the ones I take to India, we called in to the Bangalore Cobra brewery. I know the owner well, and he suggested the group took b & b there. I assured him I had booked bed and breakfast at a nearby 5 star hotel. *'No, no'* he said giving me a withering look, as if I had just failed my English GCSE. *'I mean beer and biriani'*. And believe me, he laid on the most sumptuous feast complete with newly brewed Cobra. With a name like Hop and Spice I was reminded of this story and on my visit, I wondered how Sri Lankan owner Bahi Sivalingam would combine the two. His corner site is very distinctive. He runs a very family-friendly house. You are greeted profusely by him and his staff and the golden Buddha statues that inhabit the interior. And he chats on about his Welsh upbringing and how his mum curried leeks in his childhood. In Sri Lanka starters are known as 'short eats' I started with Devilled Chicken, £6.15, coated in a sweet and spicy marinade and fried with caramelised onion and chilli. My companion had Spicy Tuna Fish Cakes £6.20, spiced with chilli, curry leaves and garlic before being crushed with masala potato, crumbed and fried to create delicious crispy spheres. Bahi suggested we try the set Thali with coconut lamb, chilli chicken, batticaloan salmon, fried aubergine salad, spinach and coconut milk, spiced green beans with spinach rice, paratha or chapati. In fact using the clever two-priced menu we chose single dishes: Jaffna Fried Pork Curry (Hot) Main £15.75/Thali £4.95, cubes steeped in home-roasted masala overnight before being slow cooked with cardamom, and curry leaves, then flash fried and finished with a touch of cider vinegar. The menu suggested we chose Old Speckled Hen, a rich ale with a sweetness that balances the spice in this dish; Beef Berruwella Main £16.55/ Thali £5.55, slow cooked in our home roasted masala with fresh tomato, ginger, garlic and chilli to create a melt in the mouth curry. Suggested beer St. Peter's bitter; Crab Varal white crab meat with fresh shredded coconut, green chilli and curry leaves, finished with a squeeze of fresh lemon. Suggested beer Summer Lightening the citrus notes in this ale blend beautifully with this dish. Plain rice accompanied this. We each chose a different pudding: Raspberry Eton Mess (fresh raspberries, meringue and cream) and Wattilappam (set custard with palm sugar, mango, and cashew nuts). Hop and Spice has 12 carefully chosen beers on its menu. 2 Course meal £20 per person, 3 course £30. Service charge 12.5%. Sun-Tu: 6-10.30; Wed-Sat to 11pm.

London SW12

LIGHT OF GURKHA NEPALESE
88 Balham Hill Road, SW12 9AG
020 8673 4160   www.lightofgurkha.com

Name change from Banglo and still highly popular and still one of the few Nepalese restaurants in the country actually serving authentic Nepalese food, which you should try, rather than the unnecessary curryhouse items. Modern decor invites you to tread the blonde boards and observe the bright pink banquettes. The menu invites you to try all sorts of goodies. Starters include Alu Patty, £3.75, potato rissole laced with herbs and spices, deep fried or Thukpa Soup £4, freshly made noodles delicately spiced and cooked with lamb served in a savory broth. Main course specials include, Nepalese Chicken £8.25, cooked with mild cream and cashew nuts. served with sliced mangoes; Khursani (meaning chilli) Chicken or Lamb £6.50, fiery dish withginger and yes fresh green chillies; Nepalese Sam Chicken or Lamb, £8, noodles spiced and cooked with avegetables served with side sauce; Phewa Fish £9.45, west Nepal is famous for fish; salmon deep fried fillets cooked with coconut milk; Pahelo Pharsi £4, pumpkin, tomato and onion; Aloo Tama, £4, potatoes cooked with bodi black eye beans, bamboo shots and fried spices, fresh chillies and coriander; Paloong Sag with spinach said to 'popular with Kathmandu farmers'. *'I am a retired Major - 6th Gurkha Rifles, who lived in Nepal for 5 years. The food we had was authentic Nepalese, very tasty, large portions. Service excellent. A clean, fresh and modern decor (no garish painting of Mount Everest! All staff Nepalese. Head chef is Anand Kumar Gurung who is cultural secretary of the Yeti Nepal Association in the UK.'* JT. 12-2.30 & 6-11.30 to 12 Fri & Sat to 11 Sun.

London SW13

INDIAN ZILLA   BEST NEWCOMER 2013
2-3 Rocks Lane, Barnes, SW13 0DJ
020 8878 3989   www.indianzilla.co.uk

Chef proprietor Manoj Vasaikar explains that *'a Zilla is a small district, and that's what we're looking to create with Indian Zilla in Barnes'*. The former Chutney Mary / Veeraswamy opened his Indian Zing to much acclaim and this branch followed later. The menu is the same as Zing. Mon-Fri: 6-11, Fri & Sat: 12-3 & 6-11. *Branches: Indian Zing, W6 &Indian Zest, Sunbury Middx. See p 46.*

YOU SAY OK SW11 to SW14

SW11: AKASH TANDOORI, CLAPHAM, 70 Northcote Road, Battersea, SW11 6QL 020 7228 6324 www.akashtandoori.com

SW11: HOLY COW 166 Battersea Park Road, SW11 4ND 020 7498 2000 www.holycowonline.co Popular curryhouse

SW11: KHAN'S TAKEAWAY 159 Lavender Hill, Battersea, SW11 5QH   www.khans-sw11.co.uk   5.30-12.

SW12: VIJAYA KRISHNA 43 Balham High Road, SW12 9AN 020 8675 5522 SOUTH INDIAN See Rhada Krishna SW17.

SW14: LAL BACH 467 Upper Richmond Road West, SW14 7PU 020 8878 0010 Run by Choudhury family since 1998.

SW14: TASTE OF RAJ 130 Upr Richmond Rd, SW14 8DS 020 8876 8171. tasteofraj-restaurant.co.uk Owned by the charming and personable Shawkat Ahmed since 1986. 5.30-11.30.

London SW15

MA GOA   UK'S ONLY GOAN   TOP 100
244 Upr Richmond Rd, SW15   020
8780 1767   www.ma-goa.com

Opened in 1993 by the Kapoor family. Deepak looks after the diners, while Sushma is the chef. In fact she's his mum, so easy on the Ma Goa gags! The restaurant seats 50 and has a discrete modern-look. We describe Goan food in some detail on page 73, but here is the place to taste it authetically and correctly cooked. Goa is one of India's 24 states, not a country in its own right, as some think. It is on the western coast of India and, because it was Portuguese for nearly 500 years, inherited different characteristics from the rest of India, including a small pork-eating, Christian population. Goan cooks were prized in the Raj (because they would handle beef and pork and could cook well). Until a few decades ago, Goan cooks were frequently to be found in merchant ships. In the 1960s Goa was 'discovered' by hippies, and more recently, it has been 'discovered' by holiday companies offering the cheap package at formerly beautiful, exclusive, caring hotels. Goan food is rarely found in Britain. And what of Sushma's food As a regular visitor to Goa, I can vouch that it's as near to home-cooking as it gets. Goan food is unique, having that Portuguese influence – any meat goes and pork is the favourite, as is the chilli. Good menu examples are Goa Chorizo, £6.50, traditional spiced

Goan chouriço (Chorizo) sausage

pork sausage, stir-fried with with potato & onion or Balchao & Sanna, £5.55, shrimps in tomato and a hint of spicy "balchao" pickling masala served with Goan steamed bread (Sanna). Sorpotel is a Goan favourite using lambs liver & kidney with pork belly in rich a zesty Goan roasted spice masala, starter £5.65 main £9.95. Other mains: Porco Vindaloo £9.75. This is the real thing, based on the Portuguese dish, Vinho d'alhos. In the Goan version, pork is marinated with palm (toddy) vinegar, garlic and roasted spices and plenty of red kashmiri chillies. It is then slow-cooked to achieve maximum penetration of flavours. Ma Goa serve it in traditional earthenware; Aunty Bella's Lamb Kodi, £9.75, slow cooked with tomato, palm vinegar, whole garam masala, Goan red masala & curry leaves;

Gallina Cafrael, £11.95, quarter free-range chicken in a fresh green masala with crushed garlic, coriander, green chili & mint marinade, slow cooked in the tandoor & served with a light sauce, served with coconut & curry leaf rice. Ma's Fish Caldin, £11.75, swordfish in a coconut, mustard & fenugreek sauce. Konkan Style Gallina, £9, diced chicken in a piquant sauce with curry leaves & ground Goan red masala. Goa Prawn Kodi, £11.95, cooked in a kashmiri chilli, tamarind and ground coconut sauce. as found in the many Goan beach hut restaurants. Nariyal Gosht £9.75, lamb on-the-bone in a "dry masala" with coconut, curry leaf, green chilli, fennel & mustard seeds There are several veg dishes. Notable is Sabzi Amo-tik, £8.25, an assortment in a traditional Goan hot & sour sauce.The daily specials board makes this restaurant an adventure. Goan delights, with unique names such as Xhacutti, Balachao, Assado, Temperado, Buffado, and Recheiado all appear at one time or another. If these dishes are new to you, advice is forthcoming. Also they do cook regional dishes other than Goan, but our advice is to stick to Goan. *'If you ask for Goan heat, you'll get it hot! For loonies like Pat, look under side orders and accompaniments for Taliwi Mirch £1.85 (fried green chillies in mustard oil)'.* There are even Goan puds, such as Bebinca, a heavily

Bebinca

sugared egg layer-cake, with cashew nuts, *'fantastic but sickly!'* DBAC. But a word of caution. Please be patient. Sushma will not be hurried in the kitchen. Relax with their chilled Portuguese Vinho Verde wine, or Ambari beer, brewed in Goa, £3.25 and nibble something while you wait for your order to be cooked. *'Had one of the best evenings we have ever had. Definitely the sort of restaurant to enjoy the whole evening. Interesting food, good portions, well presented and fabulous. Faultless service and atmosphere. Mature clientele. Not cheap, but uperb for the value.'* HC. Service 12.5%. Takeaway: 10% discount. Tue-Fri: 12-3. Mon - Sat: 6.30 -11 (to 10 Sun)

MUNAL   NEPALESE
393, Upper Richmond Road, Putney. SW15 5QL
020 8876 3083   www.munaltandoori.co.uk

Khem Ranamagar established his 65-seater in 1991. As with so many restaurants with specialised cuisines he is obliged to sell formula curries or close down. You'll find at least 100 of them here. But this is Nepalese and the 'always-polite' crew would love you to try some of chef Bijaya Thapa's few Nepalese items on the menu, such as the starter Momo, £3.95, steamed minced meat dumplings served with Nepalese tomato chutney ; or Fried Squid, £4.25, marinated and fried Nepalese spices; or Chicken Chhoyela, £3.95, pieces of chicken cooked in the tandoor and mixed with herbs, spices and chopped onions, served on a fresh salad base. Nepalese mains include Duck £8.95, lamb £8.50, or Chicken £8.25, Bhutuwa, a dry-fried dish in a thick gravy. Fish Masala, £8.90, marinated cod fillet deep-fried & cooked in a special masala sauce. *'This restaurant is where I took my wife on our first dinner date together. A frosty evening but welcome was as warm as ever,'* says RAC. *'I just thought to tell you about my daughter's wedding reception for 45 people. Starter and ample main course. Dessert was a wedding cake provided by us but fruit salad and coffee was available. The cost of this was £650 which included all drinks from the bar and seven bottles of champagne.'* DAB. Min charge £10. Del: £12, 3m. Price Check: Popadom 50p, CTM £7.95, Pullao Rice £2.50, Plain Naan £1.60. Pint of beer £3.30, House wine £9.95. Delivery: 3 miles, £12 min. Mon - Th: 5-11 (Fri - Sat to 12, Sun to 10.30). Sat & Sun: 12 to 2.30. Branch: *Munal, 76, Central Road, Worcester Park, Surrey. KT4 8HX.*

London SW16

CHILLI CHUTNEY   LAHORI PAKISTANI
20 The High Parade, Streatham High Road,
Streatham, SW16 1EX   020 8696 0123

Neelofar Khan is young and energetic and his mission is to make authentic and contemporary Lahori food accessible to the European and young Asian palate. Deciding that what was needed was as they put it ' a thoroughly modern and vibrant ambience'. Following, they say, frequent visits to India and Pakistan to develop the concept, and source qualified Lahori chefs, the 130-seat restaurant opened in late 2003. It very soon became the official caterer for the UK Pakistan High Commission. 11-10.30.pm. Branch: *Chilli Chutney Express, 47 York Rd, Waterloo, London SE1; Chilli Chutney at Alders Mall Croydon, Surrey*

MIRCH MASALA
PUNJABI / KENYAN ASIAN   **BYO**
1416 London Rd, Norbury SW16 4BZ
020 8679 1828   www.mirchmasalarestaurant.co.uk

Mirch Masala, 'pepper mixture' is a pleasant, light and bright, 70 seater caff serving sumptuous Punjabi meat, fish and veg food, with a Kenyan Asian slant, such as Cassava chips (fried mogo) , Tillapia (African Queen) fish or Karahi Corn-on-the-Cob. It is all the more highly rated for being cheap and cheerful, unlicensed, and it's air-conditioned. It is a pleasure to see the group has expanded from this Norwood first (1995) to seven branches, see below. It is in part in the style of the ever-popular Lahore Kebab house and Taayabs (E1). Cutlery is out (OK, limpets can have cutlery) and BYO is in, no corkage charge. The open kitchen buzzes with owner Raza Ali's brigade, who delight in bringing their own cooking straight to the horse's mouth – yours that is. Great theatre, enhanced by high decibel Bangra and lively diners. There's Garlic Mussels amongst the starters as well as samosas, tikkas and chops. Wide selection of dechi (saucepan) or karahi dishes, kebabs and all the trimmings. Main courses: Karahi Methi Gosht/Murgh (lamb/chicken with fenugreek leaves) – can't imagine a Punjabi restaurant without this dish. Whole Leg of Lamb Cooked on Order, and a group of you can enjoy a whole lamb with 36hrs advance notice. Good veggie stuff, too. How about Karahi Valpapdi Baigan Masala Karella, the bitter gourd, or Karahi Egg. Set lunch: c£6 for veg, c£7 non-veg, served from 12-4. Credit cards accepted. 12-12 daily. *Six other branches, identical menus at E1, SW17, Croydon Surrey, Hounslow & Southall Mdx, Ilford Essex.*

SHAHEE BHEL POORI   JAIN VEGAN
1547 London Road, SW16 4AD   020 8679 6275
www.shaheebhelpoori.com

Moshahid (Shahee) Miah opened his licensed 75-seater, opposite Norbury Station in 1988. Drummond 's Diwana Bhel Poori restaurant pioneered Bombay food in London. Ubaydur Rahman, was chef there from 1980. He joined Shahee in 1988. Ubaydur brought Bhel Poori to the venue, but more than that, he added Keralan food to the menu. Being a strict vegetarian, a Vegan, the menu contains dishes vegetarian without any animal products such as dairy products and honey. There are many goodies in this style of cooking. But there are non vegan vegetarian dishes too, involving dairy produce, for example Paneer Pakora - homemade cottage cheese battered and deep-fried £3.25; and yoghurt: Aloo Papri Chat - chickpeas and potatoes served on Indian savouries blended with spices, topped with spicy yoghurt £2.50; Bhel Poori £2.50; Pani Poori - delicate hollow crispy balls (like egg shells) served with special spicy water sauce and chickpeas (good for weight watchers) delicious £2.50; Vegetable Cutlet, crispy vegetables laces with herbs and spices, served on a bed of salad £2.50; Vada, Pakora, Samosa, Tikkis and Chana starters cost £2.50. Masala Dosa - crispy pancake stuffed with spiced potato mixed and served with coconut chutney and vegetable sambar sauce £5.75; Idli Sambar - steamed spongy rice cake dipped in vegetable sambar sauce and served with coconut chutney £6.75; Uthappam - a south Indian version of pizza made from rice and lentil flour with a topping of chopped onion, green chillies, tomatoes, curry leaves and ginger, served with a special chutney £6.75; Poori - small delicate deep-fried bread puffs, four to a serving £1.60; Coconut Chutney £1.30. Thalis range from £7.50 to £9. There are Indian desserts. Weds set meal. Children under 7 years, half price. Takeaway: 10% discount. Wheelchair access. Price Check: Popadom 60p, Pullao Rice £2.20. Set Weds Dinner: £7.50. Sunday Lunch Buffet: 12.30-5, £5.50. Sunday Dinner Buffet 5-10, £5.95. Licensed: Pint of Beer £3.95, House Wine £7.95. Hours: 5.30 (12.30 on Sunday) to 11.Mon-Sat: 5.30-11. Sun open: 12.30-11.

SHAMYANA   BYO   PAKISTANI PUNJABI
437 Streatham High Rd, SW16 3PH   020 8679 6162

Another good value Pakistani Punjabi caff, opened by Mohammed Tanveer in 1998. No frills. Seats a huge 130 in two black-and-white tiled floored rooms. Enormous menu, some 130 dishes, cooked in an open kitchen. Starters: Masala Fish (white fish in spicy sauce), Dhal Bhajia (spiced lentils deep-fried in chicken pea dough), Zeera Chicken Wings £3 (wings marinated in spicy sauce). Main courses: Masala Karela Gosht (lamb cubes cooked with bitter gourd), Ginger Chicken, Lamb Biriani (lamb with stock flavouring the rice). BYO. Daily specials. Service 10%. 50 space car park at rear. Set lunch: £6. Sunday buffet £7, 12-6,12-12.

YOU SAY OK SW15 to SW16

SW15: BANGLADESH CURRY MAHAL 294 Upper Richmond Road, Putney, SW15 6TH   020 8789 9763

SW15: MIRAJ INDIAN TAKEAWAY 123 Putney Bdge Road, SW15 2PA   020 8871 2806

SW15: TAJ MAHAL RESTAURANT 150 Upper Richmond Road, Putney, SW15 2SW   020 8788 5941

SW16: DATTA TAKEAWAY 235 Streatham High Road, SW16 6EN   020 8696 0063

SW16: TAJ MAHAL 11a Leigham Ct Road, Streatham, SW16 2ND   020 8677 7818

SW17: ACHAR, TOOTING 2 Church Lane, Tooting, SW17 9PP   020 8767 7377   www.acharonline.co.uk

SW16: AL MIRAJ   PAKISTANI 215 UT Rd, Tooting, SW17 7TG   020 8772 4422   www.al-mirage.co.uk

SW16: RAJAH ROWING TEAM 238 Balham High Road, SW17   www.rajahrowingteam.com

Moshahid (Shahee) Miah proudly displaying a Thali.

FOCUS on Tooting High, SW17

Upper Tooting Road (UT Rd) and Tooting High Street (TH St) has for years, the area has reflected the varied roots of its Asian population. In the half a mile, between Tooting Bec and Tooting Broadway tube stations, there are restaurants serving nearly every style of authentic food from the subcontinent; it's an all-day curryholic's theme park. Nowhere else in the world has such variety cheek by jowl. Below in street number order, we list them: *(E&OE)*

UT Rd begins at the Northern Line's Tooting Bec Tube Station
(numerical order southwards from the station)

ZAYTOON 14 UT Rd, SW17   020 8672 6680

CHATKHARA GENERAL CURRIES 15 UT Rd, SW17 7TS

NAMAK MANDI 25 UT Rd, SW17 7TS

SPICE VILLAGE TANDOORI & PAKISTANI CURRIES 32-36 UT Rd SW17 7PD www.spicevillageltd.com Branch: 185 The Broadway, Southall. See p 150 *Two top pics.*

CHENNAI DOSA SOUTH INDIAN 33 UT Rd, SW17 7TR South Indian. Meat & Veg. One of a chain of 14. See London E12 for menu & details. No licence. 10:30am-11pm.

AMBALA SWEET/SNACK TAKEAWAY 47 UT Rd, SW17 7TR. See review alongside.

LAZEEZ 47 UT Rd SW17 7TR

ROYAL (SHABAB) SWEET/SNACK TAKEAWAY 50 UTR, SW17 7PE 020 8767 8907 www.shahabsweets.com

KOLAM SOUTH INDIAN 64 UT Rd, SW17 7PB.   See p 150

ALAUDIN SWEET/SNACK TAKEAWAY 98 UT Rd SW17 7EN 020 1682 3033. Branches: 72 Brick Lane, E1 7 148 Green Street, Forest Gate, E7.

CALCUTTA INDIAN 116 UT Rd, SW17 7EN 020 86727447

MASALEDAR BHEL POORI & MEAT CURRIES 121 UT Rd, SW17 7TJ.   See p 150

MILAN VEGETARIAN GUJARATI 158 UT Rd, SW17 7ER   See p 150

HANDIS PAKISTANI 164 UT Rd SW17 7ER.   See review alongside.

DIANA AFGHAN 166 UT Rd, SW17 7ER

POOJA SWEET/SNACK TAKEAWAY 168-170 UT Rd, SW17 7ER, 020 8672 4523 poojasweets.com   Branch 487 Kingsbury Road, NW9 9ED

PUNJAB PUNJABI 174 UT Rd, SW17 7EJ

RAJA CURRY HOUSE 169 UT Rd, SW17 7TJ 020 8767 4425

LAHORE DREAMS PAKISTANI 200 UT Rd, SW17 7TG 020 8682 9777. See p 150.

MIRCH MASALA PUNJABI/KENYAN BYO 213 UT Rd, SW17 7TG 020 8672 7500 www.mirchmasalarestaurant.co.uk   One of seven branches with identical meat, fish and veg menu. See SW16 for full details.

AL MIRAGE PAKISTANI 215 UT Rd, SW17 7TG

ROTI PAKISTANI 225 UT Rd, SW17 7TG   020 8696 1269.   Early opening: 9am to 11pm.

SARAVANAA BHAVAN SOUTH INDIAN 254 UT Rd, SW17 0DN 5th (7/2011) of a new chain of 5 south Indian vegetarian cafés. Capacity 1200. See London E12 for menu & details. Cash pref. No licence. 10am to 10:30pm

The road changes name to Tooting High Street after c 600m.
(numerical order southwards from this point)

LAHORE KARAHI PAKISTANI 1 TH St, SW17 0SN   See p 150

DOSA N CHUTNY SOUTH INDIAN 68 THSt, SW17 0RN 020 8767 9200 www.dosanchutny.co.uk)

SARASHWATHY BAVANS SOUTH INDIAN 70 TH St, SW17 0RN

RADHA KRISHNA BHAVAN SOUTH INDIAN 86 TH St, SW17 0RN

JAFFNA HOUSE 90 TH St, SW17 0RR 020 8672 7786.   See review alongside.

SPICE LOUNGE 102 TH St, SW17 0RR 020 8767 5012

TOOTING SPICES 115 TH St, SW17 0SY

KHANI CUISINE FUSION/CHINESE/INDIAN 168 TH St, SW17 0RT

APOLLO BANANA LEAF 190 TH St, SW17 0SF.   See review alongside.

SREE KRISHNA SOUTH INDIAN 192 TH St, SW17 0SF

ONAM SOUTH INDIAN 219 TH St, SW17 0SZ

YHAAL HOUSE 1 London Road Tooting ,SW17 9HW

Best Indian and Sri Lankan grocer, Dadus at 210 UTR. There are many others, plus utensils shops, sari boutiques and halal butchers all displaying their wares on UTR and TH St, and many until late, 365/7.

Photos courtesy and © copyright Spive Village / Kake at kake@earth.li / myvillage.com

AMBALA SWEET CENTRE TOP 100
47 UT Rd, SW17 7PD   020 87671747

Takeaway-only savoury snacks (Pakoras and Samosa, etc.), Indian sweets (Halva, Jalebi, Gulab Jamun, Barfi, etc.) and a few vegetarian curries such as chickpea. Branches in London (8 inc this one also at Brick Lane E1, E7, E10, E17, NW1, N8, SE18 also B'ham (3), Bradford, Derby, Glasgow, Ilford, Leicester, Luton, Manchester, Slough, Southall, Surbiton and Wembley. The quality is first-class and the prices are always reasonable. Be prepared to queue, and pay cash. Daily 10am-11pm.   *Above: An Ambala display counter.*

APOLLO BANANA LEAF BYO SRI LANKAN
190 Totting High Rd, SW17 0SF   020 8696 1423

Tamil decor (dysfunctional) and Sri Lankan Tamil food highly functional and you can't eat the art'. No regard is paid to the Scoville scale and if you like mild, it's hot, hotter hotter. Dosa, Rasams, Hoppers, Black Curries, Devilled dishes ~ it's all here for a minimal cost made even nicer with BYO (it's U) and no corkage. Hard to spend a tenner yet credit cards OK. 12-3 & 6-10.30.

HANDIS PAKISTANI
164 Upr Tooting Rd, SW17   020 8672 6037

A 60-seater Pakistani restaurant owned by Mrs S Sheikh and managed by Mr J Sheikh. Cooking is down one entire side. Dishes are served either in Handis (cooking pots) or in the karahi. It's kebabs, tikkas, tandoori meat and chicken dishes in which this type of venue excels. There are a number of Punjabi-style vegetable dishes, such as Aloo Sag, and well cooked side dishes. One correspondent loves their chupattis. CT. Hours: 11-11.

JAFFNA HOUSE SRI LANKAN & TANDOORI
BEST SRI LANKAN 2007/8
www.jaffnahouse.co.uk
90 High Roadreet, SW17 0RN   020 8672 7786

K Sivalogarajah and M Sivanandan established their Jaffna House on a corner site in 1991. On the High Road is a bright and modern café/take away area with 20 or so seats and a display cabinet. On the side road, Coverton Road a bar and a 36 seat dining room, with black Bentwood chairs and tables with blue and red cloths. The two rooms are distinctively different and Jaffna house will never ever win a Michelin Star for decor. It's too homely for them. That's Michelin's loss because who cares so long as the service and food is good. Good service is guaranteed by one or both owners always being there. As for the food, the restaurant takes its name from the captial city of north Sri Lanka, Jaffna. Its population is mostly Tamil. The restaurant's owners are Tamil and so is their cuisine. It has subtle variations from the Sinhalese cuisine of the south and is cooked by Aziz and Kannan is good and their Jaffna cuisine is particularlty accurate, and for that reason we restate that they can cook better than-90% of the UK's Michelin-starred chefs. In theory you get Tandoori items in the dining room and Sri Lankan in the caff. Actually you can get both in each, but the rooms don't interconnect. For those who must have meaty tandoori items and north-Indian curries, you won't be disappointed. I've no idea how good they are; but do enjoy (and tell us about it, if you like). Where the serious palates boldly go for authentic, no compromise, chilli hot (as-it-should-be) Sri Lankan and south-Indian dishes with its particularly popular different Friday, Saturday and Sunday specials. Tastebud-tantalising stuff like Vadai – gram flour doughnut, drenched in home made yoghurt and sprinkled with garam 45p and (if you are lucky) chopped fresh green chilli, Masala Dosa £1.75 – must be one of the cheapest in the country. Sri Lankan specials are delightful, with Pat's benchmark crab curry £4 scoring really high because it was searingly hot, and used fresh crab. 'Wow!! this was the second TOP 100 restaurant in 24 hours. lucky or what !' [Yes] 'and we didn't break £50! I have LOVED this restaurant/cafe for years, eight or nine at least. It remains magnificent value for wonderful food. Potato Bondas and Onion Bhajia simply the best, and this before we got to Mushroom Curry, Chana Curry, Coconut Rice – fragrant and so light, almost floated off the plate! Vegetable Kottho – substantial, full of fresh vegetables. Curries clearly freshly prepared, very chilli-hot, just beautiful. We were stuffed full, long before we finished the food. all for £9!! Wonderful!!!' AG. 'We holidayed in Sri Lanka and were longing to try the food again. Starters were the best – delicious Masala Dosa and lovely spicy Devilled Chicken which was very reminiscent of the food we had sampled in Sri Lanka. Chicken and String Hoppers, but they came all mixed together, which made it taste a bit like vermicelli or chow mein – anyway I shall definitely try again.' NP. Set lunch: c£5 from 12-3. Hours: 12-12.

KOLAM   TAMIL NADU, SOUTH INDIAN
58 Upper Tooting Rd SW17 7PB   020 8767 2514

Sathyan Rajakumar (Raja) established his Kolam (a rice flour pattern decoration laid outside homes) in 1982. It seats 52 in one long thin dining room. The food is authentic South Indian, as they have it in Tamil Nadu, plus standard north Indian items. Speciality meat dishes include Fried lamb – marinated spiced pieces of lamb, stir fried with onions, or the Kolam Bhoona – lamb or chicken cooked in a medium spicy sauce with fresh tomato, capsicum and fenugreek leaves. Fish dishes include Meen Varuval – masala marinated king fish steaks fried, and served with saladService is very friendly, albeit at freeze-frame slowness. Mañana is far too fast, which reminds one greatly of India. Patience will reward you with a good inexpensive meal, and, as ever, go for the South Indian delights, which is what they know best. BYO allowed: £1 corkage. Hours: 12-2.30 Tues-Sun / 6-11, daily (12 Sat).

LAHORE DREAMS   BYO   PAKISTANI
200 Upper Tooting Rd SW17 7EW   020 8682 9777

This is quite an upmarket restaurant (for Tooting) which adds to the super local mix. The food is Pakistani and the decor evokes the Moghul Lahori atmosphere (Lahore was one of the emperors' four major fortress-cities). So none of your minimalist décor, hard surfaces and and lurid dayglow colours. Here it is olde-worlde Indi-pics on the walls, carved chairs and lamps and good old sensible service. But it is Tooting, so expect ridiculous prices; cheap that is! Buffet lunch £6 / £9 dinner eat your fill. Even a la-carte won't set you back more than c£16, and it's unlicensed with BYO with no corkage. 12.30-11.30.

LAHORE KARAHI   BYO   PAKISTANI
1 Tooting High Street, SW17 0SN   020 8767 2477

This was the first Karahi-house on Tooting Broadway opening in 1995. It has been copied a fair bit so the formula is now quite well-known; stand at the counter and order your takeaway – or if you plan to eat in, sit down and wait to be served, with the cooking on view. Typical Pakistani Kebab House menu. Starters include: Masala Fish, chunks of marinated fish, fried. Sheek Kebabs. Main courses: Chicken Jalfrezi. Veggies might try the Karahi Karela, bitter gourd, Methi Aloo or Saag Paneer. Cash only. No credit cards. Unlicensed, BYO, no corkage. Average meal £10. Hours: 12-12.

MASALEDAR   NO ALCOHOL ALLOWED
121 Upper Tooting Rd, SW17 7TJ   020 8767 7676

Halal mutton, on-the-bone, slow-cooked in a metal-waisted cooking utensil without handles. Strict Muslim rules apply: no alcohol permitted so BYO is not permitted. Credit cards accepted. 5-11.30.

MILAN VEGETARIAN   GUJARATI
158 Upper Tooting Rd, SW17 7ER   020 8767 4347

Taj Mehta's vegetarian café is just the sort of place we like to recommend. It's unpretentious, unexpectedly licensed and air-conditioned. Ask for popadums and their adorable fresh home-made relishes. Next I'd ask for their fabulous Bhel Poori then I'd go for its subtly-spiced Gujarati curries, made largely from besan flour and yoghurt, spiced with turmeric and curry leaves. If it's new to you, ask for help. The dish of the day is always a good option. And do try the fresh Rotla (millet bread). Leave some room for the terrific Indian sweets on display. And buy some fresh 'Bombay mix' items. For a complete filling meal, try the Thali – a good selection of vegetarian curries including something sweet for pudding. 'Another good one' SM. Minimum charge still a Average meal under £10. Takes no credit cards so cash needed. Sunday lunch £5.75. 10-10.

RADHA KRISHNA BHAVAN   TOP 100
86 Tooting High Street, SW17 0RN   020 8682 0969
www.tootingsouthindian.co.uk
www.keralagroup.co.ukkerelan

Passionate Kerelan H.K.Haridas has been a major force in promoting his home state as a tourist destination and in the establishment of south Indian restaurants in the UK. He was involved in setting up Sree Krishna (see alongside). When he split from that partnership in 1999 he opened Radha Krishna Bhavan on the same street. It is also now the head office for his group of 12 restaurants (see below) all specialising in South Indian Keralan cuisine, with dishes from the cities of Cochin, Malabar and Travancore. RKB it is now run by son, T, Haridas. A fine starter is Spinach Vadai £3.50, fried crunchy doughnut of Chana dal, green chillies, onion,

COBRA
SPLENDIDLY INDIAN, SUPERBLY SMOOTH

ginger, curry leaves and fresh spinach served with chutneys. Rasam, £2.95, a hot and spicy soup, with floating slivers of garlic, curry leaves and a red chilli! – this is a DBAC benchmark, which if she doesn't get hiccups, it's not hot enough for her!). Masala Dosa, Sambar and Coconut Chutney are as good as it gets. Some have that choice for starters and go on to curries. They offer formula curries, and they are given the south Indian touch. For example, Chicken Kurma is creamy, with coconut and ground almond, £4.95. But it's the Kerelan specials you have come for. You can stay vegetarian if you like. All their vegetable curries are spot on. However, contrary to popular belief, meat, chicken and fish dishes are commonplace in Kerela. Cochin Prawn Curry. £7.50, cooked with crushed coconut, garlic, green chillies, ginger, turmeric, cumin, shallots and curry leaves flavoured with cocum (tart fruit). Vellappam, fermented rice pancake with ground coconut and coconut milk, is has a lacy egg appearance meat or chicken or potato malabar - malabar is a curry with spices, tomatoes, fresh coconut milk and curry leaves, £6.95. Chilli Fried Chemmeen, £7.50 king prawns cooked with onion, chillies, curry leaves, tomatoes and capsicum; Erachi Ulathiyathu, £5.95, lamb cooked with coconut. It's dry, spiced with pepper, coriander and chilli. And if you have any room left Payasam, £3, is a traditional Keralan delicacy of roasted vermicelli, sugar and sago slowly simmered in milk and garnished with cashewnuts and raisins.

Service 10%. Licensed. House wine: £9.95. Credit cards OK. Hours: 12-3 & 6-11; (to 12 Fri & Sat).
Branches: London: Abhi Ruchi N16; Cocum SW20; Ragam W1; Malabar Junction WC1. Krishnas Inn Bristol; Cocum, Cambridge; Pallavi, Twickenham, Middx. Surrey: Kerala Bhavan Croydon; Cocum, East Molesey, ; Tandav Sutton.

SPICE VILLAGE   020 8672 0710
32-36 UT Rd SW17 7PD   www.spicevillageltd.com
TANDOORI & PAKISTANI CURRIES

It opened in 2004 in a small way and expanded in 2008 to 200 seats, offering Authentically cooked Lahori Pakistani items such as: Peshawari Chapli Kebab (minced mutton), Karahi dishes, such as Chicken Tikka Karahi, Lamb Kebab, Paya Curry (goat feet), Lahori Nihari, Shahi Haleem, (traditional lahori dish prepared with lentils, wheat, lamb & spices), Chops, Nihari, Biryanis and the popular Masala Fish Tikka. It took off because of its smart surroundings (See top two pics on 148) and good service. Spice Village won the MP's Tiffin Cup award in 2009. following a cook-off held in the House of Commons. Daily: 12-12.
Branch: 185 The Broadway, Southall.

SREE KRISHNA   KERELAN   TOP 100
192 Tooting High Street, SW17 0SF   020 8672 4250   www.sreekrishna.co.uk

Pravin Pillai's Sree (pron Shree) was the first south Indian restaurant in London; was established in 1973!. And now there a couple of dozen, not counting the Asian-style cafés in Asian areas such E6 and here, SW17. Indeed there are three with Krishna in their name in SW17 alone (see Radha left and Vijaya below). So you'd be forgiven for thinking south Indian food is taking off. Sadly, even after all these years, it isn't and most of the nation know nothing about this delightful cuisine. For this reason even a veteran like Sree Krishna is obliged to sell formula curries to the dunderheads who don't appreciate a good thing when it's under their nose. Leave the Krishna to do what they do best, which is anything South Indian, and preferably vegetarian. It's more satisfying than any carnivore realises. Their menu includes all the generic south Indian items you'd expect from a Kerelan restaurant, meat and veg. However, aficionados look for clues which reflect the owners' backgrounds such as, in Sree's case, regional specialities from Karaikkudi and Chettinadu. Karaikkudi Chicken Stir Fry, £7.50, Chicken marinated in combination of medium hot spices & stir- fried. King Prawn Chettinadu Curry, £7.50, cooked in Chettinadu curry sauce. Or there's Appam & Meat Curry, £8, a south Indian 'crumpet' with a special meat curry. Despite a redec Sree retains all the old charm which lets you pretend you are in India while you indulge in no-nonsense, efficient and friendly service, and they're used to full houses (120 seats). Sun lunch thali, veg £7, non veg £9. Credit cards OK. Daily: 12-3; Sun-Thu: 6-11 (to 12 Fri & Sat).

VIJAYA KRISHNA   KERELAN   TOP 100
114 Mitcham Road, SW17 9NG   020 8767 7688

At Tooting Broadway tube, go a couple of hundred meters down Mitcham Road and you'll find the third Krishna in the trilogy. Locals in the know place their orders at the Vijaya, then take a pint or two at the nearby Selkirk pub, and then get called when the foopd is ready. What a service. The 40-seater, decorated with scenes of south India, was opened in 1995 by Vijayan Mullath who also manages front of house and keeps a watchful eye on the kitchen, where he poached the sous

Tooting's Krishna Restaurant trilogy. Rhada, Sree and Vijaya. Krishna, the ultimate Hindu god, is much revered in Kerela.
Photos courtesy and © copyright Kake at kake@earth.li / myvillage.com

chef from Sree Krishna at the time of the partnership row. The menu is the same as Sree though the prices are are a tad higher, though considerably less than places other than Tooting. All the anticpated pleasures are on offer: Tandoori, formula curries, Dosai, Vadai et al. We had Avial, a fluid curry made with yoghurt and mixed vegetables, and Sambar, that hot, spiky runny lentil curry *'containing, if you are lucky, many drumsticks, with which you are to scrape the flesh off with your teeth – lovely'* says DBAC, who also enjoyed Kozhi Varutha Curry, chicken in garlic and coriander sauce. Green Banana Bhajia are served. PS, she adds: *'please ignore the curryhouse favourites and enjoy Kerala!'* Del: 2m, £12 min. Serv: 10%. Daily: 12-3 & 6-11; (to 11.30 Fri & Sat.

London SW18

KATHMANDU VALLEY   NEPALESE
5 West Hill, Wandsworth, SW18   020 8871 0240
www.kathmanduvalley.com

Owner Uttam Basnet, took over the reigns of this very cosy 38-seater in 2005 and serves Nepalese delights. Remember that Nepal boarders India and China, so don't be surprised to see Spring Rolls £2.75 on the menu. Menu Snapshot: Kalejo Puri £3.95, chicken livers fried with Nepalese spices on a puri bread - a favourite of mine; Lamb Sekuwa £6.50, Nepalese spiced tandoor lamb chops; Chicken Chitwan £6.95, spicy hot; Gurkha's Lamb £7.50, with tomatoes; Nepalese Murgh Masala £7.50, spicy sauce, mushrooms and peas. Aloo Tama is the celebrated Nepalese veg dish with bamboo shoots, £4.10. Katmandu Beer, 660ml £4.75 a bottle, house wine c£10. Del: 3m, £7 min. Mon-Sa:t 5:30-11:30 (Sun to11

NAMADA
197-199 Replingham Road, Southfields, SW18 5LY
020 8870 5538   www.namada.co.uk

It was a blow when Sarkhel's closed some years back. And it is sad to record that its founder, Udit sarket passed away in 2012. The good news is that two of his former chefs have opened their own restaurant, Triphal, right next door. See next entry. Meanwhile, Saif Alom and brother Munjir have opened Namada in the original Sarhel's premises. Saif's tells us his goal is to achieve the "real" taste of authentic Indian food, rather than the British Indian food in the UK, claiming to be "the real McCoy". Saif embarked on a culinary journeys to India to further his understanding of what truthfully defines a perfect curry. and to select a chef who could cook authentic curries with a contemporary twist. M.A Bari is that chef. It's a tall order, given the skill of the neighbours. Namada's menu is adventurous. Yybari Baby Squid, £4.50, with ginger, garlic, green chillies, curry leaves and aromatic spices; Spicy Crab cake, £4.75, fresh crab meat, mashed potatoes, fresh coconut & spices; Aloo Chop, £3.45, ashed crispy potato made into patties topped with yoghurt and tamarind sauce and there are mussels and scallops, £5.95. Mains include Lamb shank, £12.95 or Raan Mussallam, £11.95, leg of lamb, marinated, cooked over a gentle flame in a rich onion and tomato gravy, flavoured with nutmeg. Formulas protein curries come in at around £8, and veg at £6. Dall Makhani £6.25, black lentils cooked in tomato, fenugreek & light butter sauce is always a test of cooking skills. Sunday lunch £9.95 (12:30-5). 5:30-11. Sun: 12 -11. *Branches: Silka SE1, Indian Moment SW11 and Indian Room SW12.*

TRIPHAL   INDIAN FINE DINING
201 Replingham Road, Southfields, SW18 5LY
020 8870 0188   www.triphalindianrestaurant.com

For those who like to know these things, Triphal is a spice, and one rarely used in Indian cooking. All will be revealed. As for Tripha,. the restaurant, some of the staff from Sarkhel's have opened their own next door to the old Sarkhel's. That places them alongside Namada (previous entry). This doesn't concern the two main chefs: Premsing Rathod has cheffed at Taj Goa and for Michelin-starred Rasoi and Urbun Turban. Bammu Ponde previously cheffed for Sarkhels as a chef. Their remit is to combine ancient traditional Indian recipes with modern British ingredients to create a light, contemporary menu. And there is no doubt that it fills the gap for regulars who mourn Sarkhel. It's small which makes it hard to make profits. We've said it before and we say it again, here you can get Indian Fine food as good as any London venue, but at suburban prices. Starters include Crispy Squid £4.50, battered in spiced rice flour, and pan-fried; Amritsari Machee £4.50, crispy tilapia with carom seed (ajwain) and garlic. Haryali Murg Tikka £4.50, chicken pieces in a fresh green herb (coriander, mint, chilli & garlic) marinade, and Tandoori-cooked. Mains include Chicken Kurma £6.95, buit a galaxy away from the crude curry house variation. This is a south Indian authentic recipe where onion is slow-fried and introduced to a cashew nut and saffron gravy. As for that rare spice ... it appears in just one dish ... Karwari Fish Curry £7.95, from the west coast of India with that unusual flavour of the spice,Triphal. So what is it? None other than one of the Chinese Five-spice ingredients – Sichuan pepper. And yes, it is grown in India, particularly in the Marathi west coast region and it is used occasionally. Booking essential. 12-3 & 6-10.

London SW19

SUVAI ARUVI   SRI LANKAN
96 High Road, Colliers Wood, SW19 2BT
020 8543 6266

For such a small venue, the range of Sri Lankan food on offer is impressive. Devilled dishes (prawn, meat and chicken are suitably hot, and the Kotthu Roti (slices of Sri Lankan flatbread, chopped up with curry), is light and moreish. Sambols, such as Sambol (coconut or onion chutney) are a must, as are Hoppers (noodles). The takeaway trade is brisker than the sit-in. No credit cards. Cash needed. 12-3 & 6-11 (to 12 Fri & Sat).

London SW20

COCUM   MALABAR SOUTH INDIAN
9 Approach Rd, SW20 8BA
020 8540 3250   www.cocumrestaurant.co.uk

Cocum or Kokum is a plum-like, dark, purple-black fruit, dried by wood-smoking. Also called Fish Tamarind, Kodam Puli, Kudam Pulli, etc. the words Kodam Puli are Malayalam (language of south India) for 'fish' and 'tamarind' (puli). However it is neither, but it gives us the clues that it is sour and used with fish. It is used by Kerala's small Syrian Christian community at Travancore Unlike most Keralans they eat offal, chicken, duck, fish, shellfish, beef, and wild boar. So what do we find at Cocum, SW19? *'As ever a friendly welcome and swift seating and advice to try the fish and prawn pickles with Achappam (flower-shaped wafers made of riceflour and coconut with black sesame, soonf and cumin seeds).'* RCF. Their fish dishes include Alleppy Meen Vevichadu, £7 red in colour and approriately flavoured with cocum and chilli. Kingfish Curry (Vevichathu Surmai), £7 also uses cocum. There is a good selection of vegetable dishes all at £4.25 eg: Cheera Parippu, toor, yellow mung and masoor dhals cooked with spinach, green pepper, garlic and cumin-flavoured thick, tempered with black mustard seeds, shallots & curry leaves, Mango Pulissery, a sweet and sour curry crushed ripe mango, plantain, garlic & ginger cooked in fresh cumin -flavoured paste. Aubergine Thiyal, chopped fresh aubergine cooked in tomato, onion and coconut milk with south Indian spices. Okra Ullipoo, a paste of deep fried onion blended with blanched tomatoes and simmered with a powder of roasted coriander is combined with spring onion and okra taste. *'We were toern between our ususal choice of Payasam, vermicelli pudding boiled with coconut milk and jaggery and garnish with fried cashew nuts. Banana Dosa botrh £2.95, sweet pancake made from the mixture of ripe bananas, rice flour, cardamom and sugar. Served with ice cream.'* DBAC. Service charge: 10%. Sat-Th: 12-2.30 & Mon-Th: 5:30-11 (to 11:30 Fri & Sat, and to 10:30 Sunday).

YOU SAY OK, SW18 to SW20

SW18: AKASH TANDOORI 9 Granville Road, Wandsworth, SW18 5SB   020 8875 0860   www.akash-tandoori.com

SW18: AROMA MAHAL 493 Garratt Lane, Earlsfield, SW18 4SW   020 8870 8969

SW18: RAJNAGAR SPICE   103 East Hill, Wandsworth, SW18 2QB   020 8870 2468   www.rajnagarspice.co.uk

SW19: SPICE OF RAJ 26 Christchurch Road, Colliers Wood, Merton, SW19 2NX   020 8542 6545

SW20: DABBAWALLA TAKEAWAY Worple Road, SW20 0LR www.dabbawalla.co.uk

SW20: HOUSE OF SPICE 507 Kingston Road, SW20 8SF 020 8542 4838   www.houseofspiceonline.co.uk

LONDON W

Areas:
West End of London
Postcode W1

Outer West London
Postcodes W2 to W14

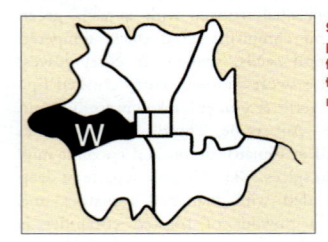

See page 88 for key to this map

London W1
The West End

ANWARS PAKISTANI BYO TOP 100
64 Grafton Way, Tottenham Court Rd, W1T 5DP
020 7387 6664

Treat Anwars as the forerunner to the numerous successful Lahore Kebab Houses. It opened in 1962 as a 52-seater to serve local Asians, drawn to the area to buy spices next door at the then renowned Bombay Emporium, which later closed and went on to become BE International (Rajah brand), which is now owned by ABF. Anwar's itself was taken over in 1985 by Muhammad Afzal Zahid. who keeps to the old ways. It serves gutsy, spicy Pakistani food. You walk in, make your choice from the dishes of the day (no menu as such) on display in the serving counter, pay – they do accept credit cards – then carry your tray to a formica table, jugs of water in place, and enjoy it. *'Everything, including bhajis and naan bread, is microwaved. Seekh kebabs, Karahi Gosht was really tasty. ambience and, more importantly, the food all remain unchanged. Set lunch, , £6 for Chicken Curry, ladle of mixed vegetables, ladle of Chana, ladle of Sag Aloo over a mound of rice, with a Puri and a cup of tea.'* MW. Unlicensed, BYO no charge. 12-11, daily.

BENARES INNOVATIVE INDIAN TOP 100
12 Berkeley Sq, W1J 6BS
020 7629 8886   www.benaresrestaurant.com

The nightingale didn't sing for Benares when a fire forced a four month closure for refurbishment in 2010. Benares is located amid Mayfair's dearest properties. ; it is, after all, financed by one of India's richest tycoons. So expect expensive decor, (much the same as pre-fire) but with an increased capacity to a hefty 140. Expect an equally hefty bill (over , £75 pp). The Michelin star remains. If that's what it takes to impress Michelin, so be it. Me, I prefer to be wooed by food and service. The entrance next to the Rolls Royce/Bentley showrooms takes you upstairs and into the bar. On the night we went, it was full of shouting business persons, yelling into iphones. We were drawn to the Mumbai Martini cocktail: Wyborowa vodka shaken over muddled curry leaves, fresh root ginger, fresh lemon juice and sugar, helped along withbar snacks such as Fried Squid, Sweet & Sour, or Stir-fried masala lambs liver kidney on skewers are , £7 each. The rebuild has produced four private dining rooms off this area. The smallest, for six diners has its own on-view kitchen, unorignally called the 'Chef's Table', aping Taj, whose Hemant Oberoi thought of it first (See Bombay Brasserie SW7). Pay enough and you'll get media darling, Chef Atul Kochhar in attendance. It is also where they hold regular master classes, for groups of between up to six for two hours at a time, *'where they can be privy to Atul's kitchen secrets'*. PV. Kochhar started his career at the Oberoi Delhi, from where he was hired by the aforesaid Indian magnate when he opened Tamarind in 1994. His boss was happy to allow Atul to flourish and it paid off when Tamarind was the first Indian to get a Michelin, which followed Atul when he was transfered to Benares. His menu changes frequently, so we won't try to list it. Rather, we show you right what it takes to present Indian dishes in a modern style. It is very pretty, but it isn't to the taste of those who like traditiona Inidan cooking. So is there CTM? Yes of course there is, but this is how you ;describe it if you want that star: *'Murgh Makhani: Tandoori black leg chicken stuffed with forest mushrooms, spinach & wild garlic,'* [with a] *'spiced yoghurt croquette'*. Atul is involved in Ananda Dublin and Sindhu on P&O's cruise ship Azura *(see page 38)*. Benares service ch 12.5%. Mon to Sat: 12-2.:0 & 5:30-10:30 (6-10 Sun).

COBRA

SPLENDIDLY INDIAN, SUPERBLY SMOOTH

Above and left, Examples of Benares presentation. It may please Michelin, but is it Indian? What do you think?

CAROM at MEZA — FINE PAN INDIAN
100 Wardour Street, W1F 0TN
020 7314 4002   www.caromsoho.com

Almost every major rock band of note played on this site. It was once home to the long-gone Marquee Club. Note the adjacent red brick arch with the black doors. This was the entrance. Look top right and you'll see Keith Moon's blue heritage plaque. Music of a different kind now plays here; DJs play from 9pm Weds to Sat in the busy bar, Meza. Once a Conran venue, it is now owned by D&D along with 30 top London restaurants including Bluebird, Quaglinoes and Skylon at the RFH. Carom, named after an Indian spice [ajwain/lovage] opened in November 2011 as their first Indian restaurant whilst the Meza's central curving cocktail bar serves a menu of Indian-inspired cocktails using spices and exotic ingredients. Carom seats 250 including 44 in the private dining room and 50 under the glass-roofed atrium, used for functions. GM is Max Rhodes. From Madras, Exec Chef Balaji (Bala) Balachander worked his way up to become sous chef at Southern Spice the feature restauarant at the city's top hotel, Taj Coromandel. In 2005 Atul Kochhar suggested that he joined him at Benares (see previous entry) as sous chef. From there he came to Carom with some cute ideas but a feet-on-the-ground approach to curry cooking with a Madras slant. Starters include: Vegetable 'Potli' parcel's, mint & tamarind chutney, , £3.95; 'Tilapia Amritsari' crisp fried carom-spiced batter, roasted tomato & garlic relish, , £5.75. Mains: Pork 'Coorgi style', fresh black pepper, fennel & tamarind, , £7.95; Chicken 'Chennai' a home delicacy, , £8.95; Beef 'Sukha', pepper & coconut, Goan spiced, , £8.50; Sea bass 'Kerala', curry leaf & mango, coconut ginger sauce, , £8.95; Dal Makhani', black lentil specialty, , £3.50; Green Beans & chestnut Poriyal, crushed peanut and coconut, , £4.50. Two lunch innovations are 'Carom Wraps' a roti filled with tandooried salmon or chicken tikka or paneer, served with avocado, tomato chutney and salad, , £5.50. Chef Bali is a real chef, a hands-on worker, not a poser. He talks passionately about food and his love for cooking. Another of his innovations is in our view one of the cleverest. It is what Bali privately calls his 'Love Box', served in a Bento Box. The menu calls it Caarom Lunch Box, a curry, lentils, salad, raita, bread, mini poppadams, steamed rice and a dessert. Vegetarian , £ 7.45, Chicken , £ 7.95, Lamb , £ 8.45. Discr 12½% sc. Mon-Fri: 12-3 & Mon-Sat: 5.30-11 (bar to 2am).

CHETTINAD   TAMIL NADU CUISINE
16 Percy Street, London, W1T 1DT   020 3556 1229

Chettinad is a district of southern Tamil Nadu known for its culinary delicacies. Chettinad food is spicy, with meat and vegetables predominating. The menu contains over 50 items to choose from:. 3 soups, 8 types of dosa,and many meat / fish /veg items. Starters such as eg: Aadu chuka , £4.95, is dry lamb pieces cooked with south Indian spices and served with salad., curries such as Vendaya Kozhi Curry, , £7.85, cubes of chicken with Chettinad spices and savoury taste. Chettinad Kozhi Curry , £8.25, our head chef uses 23 different ingredients to make this headline chicken curry. Avial, , £5.95, mixed fresh vegetables put together in thick gravy. Breads include Paratha, , £1.95, layered bread unusually made with white flour and various sweets,. *"A good way to taste this food is to order one of the 3 thalis from , £14.95.. Delicious"* HEG.(Avg Price per person for two courses, coffee, half a bottle of house wine and tip/service) Lunch: , £15,   Dinner: , £25, Mon- Thur: 12- 3 & 5:30 - 11 (Fri -Sat: 12- 11; Sun 11-3.

CHOR BIZARRE   KASHMIRI   A-LIST
16 Albemarle St, W1S 4HW
020 7629 9802   www.chorbizarre.com

Delhi's Chor Bazaar is a kind of permanent car-boot-sale, where you can buy anything at knockdown prices. Meaning 'thieves' market' it was originally the place where the villains pushed stolen goods. Entrepreneur Rohit Khattar, owner of Delhi's 32-room Hotel Broadway, hit on the idea to exploit this image. The hotel restaurant needed a revamp, and he cannily renamed it 'Chor Bizarre' exploiting the linguistic twist from 'Bazaar' to 'Bizarre'. The spin told Delhi it was furnished from the real Chor Bazaar. No two chairs or tables are the same. An aged car is the salad bar, and it took Delhi by storm. Mr Khattar set his eyes on Mayfair. When Mahendra Kaul's 85-seat Gaylord site became available, in 1997, it was perfect. There is so much to look at in this fabulously interesting restaurant. 'Antiquities' abound. As in Delhi, everything is mismatched, all the chairs and tables are different; one, for example is encased in an *'18th-century four-poster bed'* from Calcutta. Sadly Mayfair is bereft of the car. Chefs Deepinder Sondhi and Manpreet Ahujas cook dishes from all India but specialise in Kashmiri dishes. It is the only UK restaurant where you can get Goshtaba. *'It's one of the Wazwan wedding feast dishes where velvety spheres of finely minced lamb are flavoured with cardamom and cooked in a yoghurt sauce.'* DBAC. Menu Snapshot: Pakoras , £6, assortment of batter fried spinach, aubergine, cauliflower, onion and potato served with strawberry chutney and tomato and white radish salad; Dakshni Crab cakes , £8, white crab meat flavoured with South Indian spices served with salad and chutney and Shikampuri Kaba , £6.50, melt in the mouth ground lamb kofta kabab flavoured with cinnamon & cardamom stuffed with spiced curd prepared on an iron griddle served with mint yoghurt chutney and tomato and white radish salad; Aloo Tikka Chaat , £5.50, pan fried patties of mashed potatoes filled with spiced lentil and green peas, served warm, topped with yoghurt, and mint chutney. However, if you feel like a slightly more substantial starter then go for the Keema Tak-a-Tan Kaleki , £7.75 from Pakistan; after the chef starts frying the dish, in this case chicken liver tossed with coriander-flavoured masala, he takes the two steel, flat-edged spatulas and rapidly bangs them one after the other on to the pan to chop, mash and mix the ingredients. The dish gets its name from the noise made – taka-taka-taka-tan. It is served with a flaky Reshmi Parantha. The Tandoori items are also very good, especially the Adraki Chaampen , £22, tender lamb chops marinated with fresh ginger and tandoori spices. Now for the main courses. Do try the Baghare Baingan , £10, a Hyderabad favourite, sautéed aubergine simmered in piquant peanut, and sesame-seed sauce. Main course Chicken Chettinnad , £14.50 turns up on many a menu, usually cooked totally incorrectly. But here it's perfect, cooked in a hot sauce with a predominant flavour of pepper, aniseed and curry leaves. It comes from Tamil Nadu and is wonderful eaten with a Malabar Parootha , £3, a south Indian layered paratha (good for mopping up the sauce!). Other Kashmiri dishes include Nadroo Yakhani, lotus stem in spiced yoghurt gravy. Marz Wangun Korma, lamb cooked with loads of Kashmiri chillies (yes chillies in a Korma) with cardamom and cloves; Haaq, spinach cooked with aniseed and Rajmah, red kidney beans and Chaaman, (lotus stem). A neat way to try Kashmiri dishes is to order the Tarami, , £30 pp, 2 diners min: a copper platter with Kashmiri specialities Roghanjosh, Rajmah kidney beans, Nadru Palak and Chicken Dhaniwal on a bed of rice. Our benchmark Dal Makhni, thick black lentil flavoured with tomatoes and cream, immersed overnight on the tandoor; here it's masterly. *'We probably spent more time standing outside deciding whether or not we could afford to go in than actually eating! Once inside, it didn't disappoint. Food, it has to be said, was fantastic but expensive so baked beans for a week.'* AR. *'Friendly service, cheerful and efficient. Absolutely superb food, well spiced, good initial ingredients in good portions. A first class lunch – lucky that my new office is in the same street! , £97 for two, very typical for lunch in Mayfair.'* DRC. Wines matched to each dish by Charles Metcalfe, available by the glass. Private room downstairs, seats 30. Serv 12.5%. 12-3 & 6-11.30 (10.30 Sun).

CINNAMON SOHO
5 Kingly Street, W1B 5PF
0207 437 1664   www.cinnamonsoho.com

This is the third restaurant from Vivek Singh of The Cinnamon Club (see SW1) and Cinnamon Kitchen (see

COBRA कोबरा   SPLENDIDLY INDIAN, SUPERBLY SMOOTH   157

G·A·Y·L·O·R·D
RESTAURANT

Est 1966
London   and   Mumbai

79-81 Mortimer Street
London, W1W 7SJ
020 7580 3615   020 7636 0808
Email: Info@gaylordlondon.com
www.gaylordlondon.com

review overleaf

Gaylord offers the best Mughlai and North-Indian fare in London.
Served in relaxed surroundings
with an all-ivory interior and minimalist glass frontage.

EC2). Located near Carnaby Street in the former Red Bar, Nicolas Digard manages the venue's two floors, ground and a basement. The former is light and airy with Dainius Kazlauskas' bar at one end, producing such concoctions as 'Bhangra Bubbles' – rum, Chambord, homemade spiced syrup and champagne. Downstairs, the ceiling and walls are dark teak wood panelled inset with chrome yellow lighting strips under which is cobalt blue banquette seating. The open style chairs are with Indian red squabs stand on a hard white flooring. At the far end diners can watch chefs preparing those remarkable Singh innovations of modern Indian cuisine and British ingredients. Head Chef Ramachandran Raju has worked in the kitchens of both Cinnamons for more than a decade. Being from south India his expertise is shown in Tanjavore and Chettinaad specialities. Dishes including Sticky desi pork back ribs; Seared sea bass with aubergine-potato crush; and Vindaloo of ox cheek. The showstoppers, however, are the cheeky range of Indian-inspired 'balls', such as the crab cakes and Bangla-Scotch eggs, as well as exotic pies, such as Keralan seafood and rogan josh. The menus are identical to Cinnamon Kitchen (See EC2 for details). Discr s/c 12.5%. Mon-Sat: 11-11/ Sun: 11-3pm. Branches Cinnamon Club W1 and Cinnamon Kitchen EC2.

COLONY BAR and GRILL
8 Paddington Street W1U 5QH
020 7935 3353   www.colonybarandgrill.com

Restauranteur Carlo Spetale and Atul Kochhar of Benares fame opened it in April 2010. Spetale's spin is that *'the cuisine is inspired by that of the British colonies from colonial Asia, East Africa, the Caribbean etc. but is mainly inspired by Indian street food, specifically "the marinades, aromatic flavours and grilling methods" of the street traders of colonial Asia'*. GM John Lacombe, formerly of Harvey Nic's 5th Floor Restaurant is also responsible for the wine and cocktail lounge menus. The restaurant is said to be a favourite of Simon Cowell's when he is in London and in September 2010 Liam Gallagher stormed out of the restaurant after the staff refused to make him a bacon butty. Kochhar has also walked saying he wasn't in control. Make of all that what you will.

GAYLORD   CLASSIC NORTH INDIAN   TOP 100
79 Mortimer Street, W1W 7SJ
020 7580 3615   www.gaylordlondon.com

The name is a play on the names of the original owners Gai and Lamba, who had opened one of Delhi's very first Indian restaurants called Kwality in 1940. By the 50's there were Kwalities all over India. But they were little more than caffs. Having made a fortune producing ice-cream, the pair decided to go upmarket, with and London's Gaylord opened in 1963 Gaylord. It was not only Britain's first upmarket Indian restaurant, it also pioneered the Tandoori oven in Britain. Today, 70 years lKwality is headed by Sunil and Dhruv Lamba, who operate numerous food and beverage outlets in Delhi and Mumbai including brands: Angeethi, Chopsticks and Tonic. *'We enjoy excellent quality curries and the dining experience is very important as we make a night of it. All four of us agreed it was a wonderful curry with such different tastes. We started with tandoori fish, onion pakora, vegetable samosa and chicken chat. The starters were good quality with the chicken chat being made up into a salad, very interesting and quite spicy, but not too spicy. Chutneys were good with an especially hot green 'harassi like' substance the favourite of us all, though to be used with caution. Diane had to wait for her starter of samosa a bit longer than the rest of us because according to the waiter the chef had discarded the first lot because they were not up to standard!!! (A good sign I think) Main courses were superb, sag chicken – the best we've ever tasted! Chilli chicken tikka had an excellent char grilled flavour, chilli lamb was some of the tenderest lamb ever in a curry and my Chana Kabuli was stunning, very hot with lots of taste and small pieces of raw chilli – all excellent. The side dishes were good too, with Aloo Zeera being our favourite'*. KW. Serv 15%. Cover ch: , £1.20 – includes pops & pickle. Delivery. Takeaway: 10% disc. 12-3 & 6-11.30 (to 11 Sun). *See previous page.*

GOPALS OF SOHO
12 Bateman Street, W1
020 7434 1621   www.gopalsofsoho.co.uk

Gopal, real name NT Pittal, was Amin Ali's exec chef first at the Lal Qila, then at the celebrated Red Fort whose names he helped to build by cooking superb food. Feeling his career was going nowhere, he opened his own restaurant in 1988, and the accolades poured in. Mr Pital jnr, Gopal's son, now runs the place. It's a standard menu, with the full range of starters from bhaji to kebabs, tandoori and curries, but a closer look reveals specials from Goa to Kashmir, Lucknow to Hyderabad: *'Gopal's was very good indeed, helpful with the menu, and very tasty indeed.'* JRG. 10% serv ch. 12-3 & 6-11.30 (11 Sun).

IMLI   CASUAL DINING   A-LIST
167 Wardour St W1F 8WR
020 7287 4243   www.imli.co.uk

'Imli' in Hindi means 'Tamarind' and this gives you the clue that Michelin-starred Tamarind (see entry) has an interesting branch – a casually sophisticated eatery in London's West End. Spread across 2,000 square feet over two floors, Imli is a 124-seater casual and informal all-day diner. The decor delicately blends the simplicity of the modern world and combines it with traditional Indian elements including an eclectic mix of Indian art and artefacts. Modern characteristics of bold form, colour and scale are mixed and layered with traditional Indian elements of craft, pattern, and textureto create a unique and inspiring culinary experience. Tamarind's Sous Chef, Samir Sadekar was promoted to the role of Executive Chef at Imli. Originally from Goa, Samir

COBRA

SPLENDIDLY INDIAN, SUPERBLY SMOOTH

imli

'carefully prepared fresh food, friendly service and exceptional value for money'
Time Out

'A godsend to Soho'
Faye Maschler, Evening Standard

Imli offers *Indian tapas* food with innovative cooking that is both accessible and affordable.

Imli
167-169 Wardour Street, Soho,
London W1F 8WR
Closest tube: Piccadilly Circus/Tottenham Court Road
www.imli.co.uk

For reservations, venue hire or information
please call **020 7287 4243**
or e-mail info@imli.co.uk

FREE glass of wine or Cobra beer on presentation of this voucher* *when ordering from our regular menu.

studied Hotel Management at India's prestigious Institute of Hotel Management in Bombay, and then spent two years training at the Maurya Sheraton, where he cheffed at the world-class Dum Pukht and Bukhara restaurants. Samir has created an exciting menu, taking influence from the dabbas (roadside stalls) mainly of the coastal areas of southern and western India. The 'light and refreshing' dishes are the ultimate in snack foods Papdi Chat, £4.95, whole wheat crisps and bean sprouts with vermicelli, sweet yoghurt and mint chutney; Bhel Puri, £4.85, a medley of puffed rice, cucumbers and roasted peanuts tossed with assorted chutney. Tandoor Grilled Paneer and Broccoli £9.50, Fish Nimbu Walli, £13.50, nile perch marinated with lime leaf, mint & fresh coriander; the highly popular Amritsari Fish £7, batter-fried, with mint chutney (podina). If you feel you can manage a little more then choose dishes Palak Methi Chicken Curry, cooked with spinach & fenugreek and blend of freshly ground aromatic spices or Lamb Roganjosh, from kashmir, lamb cooked in aromatic spicy sauce, flavoured with saffron, both c£9. Vegetarian Tapas include Punjabi Kadi Pakora, £6.50, fritters cooked in yoghurt sauce with aromatic spices or Daal sMakhni, , £4, black lentils, slow-cooked with butter, cream and tomato, a specialty of the north west frontier. Desserts include Saffron and Cardamom rice pudding, , £4.50 or Carrot Fudge (Jajjar Halva) with melon seeds and raisins, served with ice cream, , £4.65. Formidable value are the 'tasting' menus starting at c£25. At affordable prices, even with the service charge of 12.5%. Imli proves that London's west end need not break the bank. Takeaway available. They claim max wait time, if any, is 10 minutes. Group CEO Rajesh Suri's cocktail bar continues to thrive.' Here are three of DBAC's favourites, Bollywood Bash, gin, whisky and triple sec, topped with orange juice; Bombay Crush, white rum, orange curaçao, topped with lemonade and Sunrise in Goa, vodka, white rum, topped with lychee juice and grenadine syrup, fabulous! All cocktails are priced at c, £7. 12-12, Sun to 10. (On Fri & Sat nights bookings are only taken for 4 or more people.) *Branch Tamarind, W1*.

INDALI LOUNGE INDIAN 'HEALTHY' EATING
50 Baker Street, Marylebone, London W1U 7BT
020 7224 2232   www.indalilounge.com

Owned by Dr Kartar Lalvani (who according to the media is India's answer to Heston Blumenthal), Indali doesn't use butter, cream or ghee in its cooking, while the naans are made with flour, oats and barley to maximise fibre and minimise starch, and the only oils used are sunflower and olive - both sparsely. Dr K says of it 'This is a smart, sophisticated curry house with a modern edge and a unique philosophy. The food is cooked slowly and gently to retain its freshness and flavour (making for extremely tender mouthfuls) while no artificial colouring is used (so bright orange chicken tikka is off limits)'. Downsides: the portions are not huge and sometimes the choice of overhead music can be a bit clubby. There's a separate bar area with a contemporary feel and an extensive wine and cocktail list. A new buffet lunch is available during the week 12pm-3pm for , £8.90.Starters , £4-, £9, Mains , £9-, £12. Set Menu – , £35.50: Mixed Platter of Starters Amritsari Fish and Prawn Grill, Hydrabad Grill Fish in Green Herbs, Crisp Konkan Coconut Crab, Mushroom Crispy Masala, Chicken Tikka. Main: Goa Fish Curry, Prawn Konkan Fusion, Original Butter Chicken, Shredded Cabbage bake, Yellow Dal, Bangalore Aloo, Sindhi Sai Bhaji, Rice and Naan. Dessert: Mango Kulfi, or Carrot Halwa Gulab Jamun with Vanilla Ice-Cream or Kheer (Rice Pudding). Mon-Sun: 12-3 & 6-11.30 (Sun-11)

INDIAN YMCA CHEAP CANTEEN CURRIES
NO ALC   INDIAN BREAKFAST   TOP 100
45 Fitzroy Street, W1 6AQ
020 7387 0411   www.indianymca.org

Like this place this entry hardly changes since it was founded in 1920, though the acceptance of credit cards, a longer lunch time and non-resident access to dinner, wi-fi (chargeable) and a website are new, as is the price rise – up by an inflationary 10 pence per curry. To find it, follow your nose north up Fitzroy Street – the hideous large modern block on your right may already be permeating curry smells from its basement kitchen. Enter, and out of courtesy, please ask at reception, (manned by gentle young Indians) if it's OK to use the canteen. It's on your right, clean, with functional formica-topped tables. It's deserted 5 minutes before opening time, then as if the school bell's rung, it's suddenly packed full with Asians, many of whom are students, and this is their residence. (Like all YMCAs, residency is open to anyone, though officially this one is subtitled Indian Student Hostel.) All students of good curry, should visit here before they can graduate as aficionados. These are the rules: Be punctual, (opening and closing times and rules are as sharp as the Post Office); no bookings, no smoking, no license, no alcohol, so no BYO, and no nonsense! *'If the food runs out, tough! So get there early.'* Bec. Unlike the Post Office, everything else works, and the staff care. Take a plastic tray, join the always-busy queue at the stainless-steel servery. It's basic, and unsophisticated but authentic expertly spiced and cooked Indian school-dinner-style – food, like you get at streetside Dabbas the length and breadth of India. Chicken and fish curries, lamb curry from , £2.50, vegetable curries all , £1.50 and lentils , £1. Your choice handed to you in bowls. Top up with chupatties, tea or coffee, and pay at the till. It's absurdly cheap – hard to exceed a fiver, and it's remarkable that they now take credit cards. Then jostle for space at a shared formica table. The food may not be five-star but the company can be, when you share your table with talkative, friendly students. Men in white coats tidy up after you. *'Marvellous.'* MW. Set lunch , £5 two course. One of the very few venues where you can get an Indian breakfast: 7.30am-9.15. Lunch: 12-2 Dinner: 7-8.30pm. (Sat-Sun & Bank Hols: 8am-9.30 / 12.30-1.30/ 7-8.30pm).

MAHARANI SOHO
77 Berwick Street, Soho, W1F 8TH   020 7437 8568
www.maharanisoho.com

Maharani Soho, founded in 1971 by Abul Kalam is now run by Kalam, Imran, Mohamed, Ali and Inayat. It has been completely refurbished. Head of Tandoor Dinesh Chand Sharma and Head Vegetarian Chef Mohinder Singh Bisht, both ex Oberoi Delhi have created an diverse menu structured around the cuisine of their native North India with new dishes,such as Lobster pepper fry, , £20; Begum-e-Samundar, whole sea bass marinated in coconut and a spice paste, wrapped in a banana leaf and steamed, , £13. Try a traditional Chat Ki Jinga – four king prawns, garnished with lime pickle, , £13. There is a selection of tandoori items, , £7.95/, £19.95.Bhuni Duck, , £12.95. Heerni Ki Chops Venison chops marinated in fresh Indian green herbs and finished with sweet chilli, , £19.95. A wide choice of vegetarian dishes are also available. 11am to 1am.

YOU SAY OK, W1

W1: THE KERALA SOUTH INDIAN 15 Great Castle Street, W1W 8LT   020 7580 2125

W1: LAL QILA 117 Tottenham Court Road, W1T 5AL   020 7387 5332

W1: NEW TAJ MAHAL MAYFAIR 2 White Horse Street, Mayfair, W1J 7LD   020 7493 0024

MASALA EXPRES,
400 Oxford Street, London W1A 1AB

Masala Zone (see next entry) have created a new brand for its first concession in someone else's venue. Masala Express has an outlet at Selfridges fourth floor Café Food Garden. It's the upmarket name for a food court and the downside is that Masala 'competes' with six other cuisines (pretzels, Chinese, British pub grub, pastries and cakes, juices and smoothies and a salad bar) and lacks control over the central table area and staff. On the day we visited there were an unsmiling till person and clearing staff who took ages to clear tables. They do soups from , £2, help yourself salads from , £4.75, asnd there is Bhel Puri, Veg or Chicken Samosa, Gol Goppa & Onion Bhajia, each , £5. Dosas served with chutney & Sambar from , £7. Tikkas and kebabs from , £5, Curries, Thalis & Biryanis all from , £10. Gulab Jamun too. To reflect Selfridges Arab customer base, Mas does Shawarma & Falafel platters & wraps at , £10.25 & , £8.25. Selfridges opening hours: Mon to Wed: 9.30-8pm; (Th; to 9pm; Sat: 9-9; Sun 12-6.

MASALA ZONE   STREET FOOD A-LIST
9 Marshall Street, W1F 7ER   020 7287 9966

This, the first of seven Masala Zones was established in 2001. The concept, totally original at the time, was to serve real Indian food cooked by a fresh new wave of young Indian chefs at a price point of around , £15, to appeals to a new young wave of customers. The concept has been widely copied, but as with Hoover, Biro, Ford and Dyson, the first is usually the best, having been thought out in detail. Masala Zone is one of those

As you approach the interior is revealed behind full-length, full-width plate glass windows, through whichyou'll see the 160 seats, some at street level, and the remainder a few steps down on a lower lever. Check in at the door and be shown to your seat. Chairs and tables are light and modern, on a wooden floor. Wall decor is inspirational, and deserves your attention. It was painted on a mud-like terracotta background by Indian tribal artists, who paint cartoon-like line-drawings in white with sticks. They'd never been outside their village, let alone to London. Doing what the tribe has done for centuries, they tell the history of mankind, in a series of episodes. The drawings carry humour, pathos and perception. And the artists were so awe-struck with their first flight (India to LHR) and the capital, that they added a new penultimate episode – scenes of London, including some things they'd not seen before – Buck House, some guardsmen, the Tower, and their favourite – a stretch limo. Their final episode is drawn around the restaurant's bar servery hatch and depicts mankind getting drunk and falling over. There's not much chance of that at Masala Zone, only soft drinks, wines and beers are sold, and customer turnround is fast. This is because service is fast, from smartly uniformed young men and women and the kitchens are fast too. But this is no criticism. It's fast if you need it, but if you want to dwell, we've never noticed pressure on you to leave, no matter how busy it gets. The actual cooking takes no shortcuts – curries are slow-cooked to maximise flavours in the large kitchens behind, which includes a completely separate vegan kitchen, with its utensils coded so that they never touch meat. There is a further kitchen in view, with a series of smallish warmers containing ready-cooked food, which are constantly refilled by the chefs behind. Cold food emanates from one side of the kitchen, hot on the right. Your order is immediately doled out to the waiter. This leads to dishes arriving at your table as soon as the chefs issue them. Some things take longer than others, and your order may arrive mains first, starter last, in any order. If it bothers you, order your starters first and then further food later. A few other aspects of Masala Zone already noted: price, queues, youth and fun may be likened to Wagamama But the resemblance is skin-deep. Service, rather than self-service is an obvious difference, as are comfortable chairs. Most importantly, Masala Zone's food is much more complex. Wagamama's is noodle nosh doshed out by non-skilled cooks. All Masala Zone food requires very high skill levels to cook. Snacks (or starters) include several types Bhel – Bombay street food. Chicken Samosas, lightly spiced, finely minced chicken with green peas; Shikampuri Kebab, melt in the mouth, aromatically spiced, minced lamb croquettes. Malabar Seafood Bowl, prawns, calamari, fish kofta with flat noodles in a richly curried soup. Everything is available a la carte, but one way-to-go is with the chicken, meat and vegetarian Thalis, there's even a weekend children's Thali. Caramel or Mango Kulfi, Shrikand with Fresh Fruit, Gulab Jamun with ice-cream, Caramelised Carrot with ice cream all priced at , £2.50 each. *Fantastic*

concept. *A top quality Indian meal cooked in front of your eyes for less than a tenner in a prime West End location! It is a large split-level, modern café-style restaurant with the cheerful and confident chefs practising their art with a flourish in full view at the back of the establishment, as you dine. A nice piece of theatre for the West End! Food quality was first class. Good-sized portions and outstanding value for money. Service was efficient. Overall opinion – very good and factor in the prices and location as well and it would be daft not to return (and I will!). Would highly recommend. This establishment truly is a gem.'* SO. Lunchtime treats also include spicy sandwiches. Spend between , £8 and , £15 plus drink. No reservations, so queuing is possible at peak times. Takeaway menu offers a good selection of street food and curry and rice dishes. Delivery free over , £10 and covers the many central and west London postcodes. 25% discount is also available for delivery lunch orders over , £40. Service: 10%. 12-11 Sunday: 12:30-10:30. *Masala Zone Branches: Islington N1; Camden NW1; Earls Court SW5; Fulham SW6; Battersea, SW11; Covent Garden, WC2.*

MOOLI'S   INDIAN WRAPS
50 Frith Street, W1D 4SQ
020 7494 9075   www.moolis.com

Mooli's opened in 2009 as the brainchild of two former city workers, Sam Singh and Mathew Chady, or S&M. As a brand it has achieved great success. However it went into administration in 2012 and has been bought in a prepack, by Iqbal Wahab. More on that later. Because of its potential we are giving Mooli's a lot of space here. S&M decided to open a restaurant in London selling what they claimed was a USP: wraps, *Pic by Saff & Abe-www.we love food.com*

Indian style. Hm! Nice one; wraps of all styles, Indian or otherwise are not original British chow. None the less the lads wanged a , £2m from the Bank of Baroda. The clean and bright venue features a continuous timber table-top along the northern edge with high bar-stools. Now in my dictionary a mooli is that long white tusk-shaped Chinese radish or Japanese daikon. But according to S&M, it means a tasty flatbread wrap, with spicy fillings, and is found on the streets of Delhi and Bangalore. As a frequent traveller there, I have to say that's news to me. Maybe I'm not looking in the right places, maybe I'm not hip enough. Because hip is what Mooli's branding is all about. So too is fun. It is reminiscent of that stellar brand, Innocent who make humdrum drinks and smoothies into must-haves with innovative humour on their packaging and website with the strap line *"we're here to make it easy for people to do themselves some good, whilst making it taste nice too"*. It could be Mooli's strap line, because it has become an instant success with younger workers, who like the short menu with nothing over , £6 and quick service, a simple license (it sells Cobra), sensible hours opening early enough to serve breakfast (Goan sausage and Mysore coffee) and late enough to satisfy most night owls. S&M needed the right chef and got him in Raju Rawat, ex Oberoi Delhi and Benares. And he had just skill needed; he could create the wrap (sorry mooli!). Nothing new needed, just the age-old Romali Roti, the thiniest of Indian unleavened breads, aka the Handkerchief Bread. It involves years of skill learning to throw it. Only six fillings were needed, each rolled in an absolutely fresh, hot romali, served like a burrito or wrap (sorry Mooli). Raju used traditional recipes. Keralan Beef, £5, inspired, by Olathiya Erachi, (see page 74) dry-cooked with pepper and coconut, wrapped with cucumber raita and salad. Goan Pork, £5, is based on Portuguese Vinha d' Alhos, pork marinated in wine vinegar, chillies and garlic, then slow-cooked and wrapped with red pomegranate salsa. Chicken, £5, comes with lentils and pickled turnips, fenugreek and raita. Scrambled Paneer, £4.80, is mixed with panch puran and served with grated carrot, salad and *'Raju's secret tomato chutney'* [Forget that spin, a recipe for it is in Pat Chapman's cookbook, published 1984. Punjabi Goat, £5.50, spiced with dry mango and roasted cumin potatoes served with red onions, tomatoes, fresh coriander and lime juice. Chickpea: £4.80, with tamarind and spring onion salsa. Is Mooli's hip? My favourite food writer Tony Naylor is no more convinced than I am. *'"F*ck the chicken tikka," runs the provocative slogan painted on the wall in the toilet.'* he wrote in The Guardian. *'It is typical of Mooli's unconvincing attempts to portray itself as all hip and rebellious.'* He goes on to say *'it all has the feel of somewhere that has been conceived, with cool corporate logic, as a novel fast food concept that could easily be rolled-out as a chain.'* Well spotted Tony. S&M aren't the first to claim they pioneered the wrap hybrid, what ever name they invent for it, and they won't be the last. As we write, Moolis has been acquired by Iqbal Wahhab founder of The Cinnamon Club and Roast. *'We have the ambitious plan*

SPLENDIDLY INDIAN, SUPERBLY SMOOTH

to open in new locations' says Wahhab. 'I see it as the Indian Pret A Manger. The chef team remains intact - led by Raju Rawat - but the menu will undergo some slight tweaks. New sites in London are already being investigated. The creators of Moolis did a fantastic job in creating a new space in the casual dining arena. People in Soho love Moolis and we intend to spread that love." I'll second that. Mooli's in one to watch. 8.30am to 11.30pm. Closed Sundays.

LA PORTE DES INDES   FINE DINING
OUTSTANDING RESTAURANT
32 Bryanston Street, W1H 7EG
020 7224 0055   www.laportedesindes.com

La Porte is one of two Indian restaurants owned by the Blue Elephant Group (see SW6). The other is in Brussels. It was given a French name because 1) La Porte des Indes sounds better than India Gate, 2) the owner is Belgian Karl Steppe, and 3) the Franco-Indian connection was, and is unique in the industry, if a bit tenuous. The spin links La Porte to the former French-governed Pondicherry, a state in eastern India, with little distinctive Indian cuisine, though this has not prevented La Porte from inventing some truly creative dish names, as we shall see later. La Porte opened in 1996, since when it has been under the direction of Taj-trained Sherin Modi Alexander with her husband, Mernosh Modi, in charge of cooking. Once a ballroom which blossomed in the wartime 1940's, and lying derelict by the 1980's, Steppe applied his Blue Elephant decor yardstick here, and went all-out with a £2.5m spend. . Fortunately, unlike Taj with their woofter bland international foyer redecs, La Porte's all Indian decor remains in tact and long may it do so; when I go to an Indian restaurant I want to experience India. No where has more colourul and fascinating decor, and none more than La Porte. Features include a sandstone arch, a 40-foot waterfall, a sweeping staircase made of white marble with pink sandstone balustrades, imported especially from India's pink city, Jaipur. Airy, domed skylights enhance La Porte's daytime atmosphere, making it a different place in darkness. There is a forest of jungle plants, a wealth of Indian artefacts and antiques, and a range of eating areas, including two tiny private dining rooms seating 12 and 24 respectively, bringing the total seating up to 300. The food is as good as it gets. The e-a-m-a-y-l Sunday Buffet lunch is a fine way to explore for £30. Accompanied by a jazz band, starters are demonstrated and served by chefs at food stalls. Main dishes are presented in opulent and attractive copper salvers. These are some of the items you might choose, with their a la carte prices. Starters: Pepper Crabs, £12, soft shell crabs with garlic and black pepper with a ginger and green mango sauce; Chard Pakoras, £7, crunchy green and red chard and water chestnut pakoras with gramflour, green chillies, coriander, turmeric and caraway seeds. There are three soups, eg: Dakshin, £7, a southern lentil soup, enhanced with roasted spices, curry leaves & fresh lime. King of the Tandoor is Lobster Peri Peri, £35, a whole lobster marinated in yoghurt, garlic & chilli flakes. And there's Chef Mody's speciality: Parsee Fish, £11, fillets of sole encased in a mint and coriander chutney and lightly steamed in banana leaves. There are four Thalis at c£25. With the main courses, La Porte's inventive use of French steps into overdrive. Cassoulet de Fruits de Mer, £19, a rich seafood stew simmered with local 'Vindai' spices equivalent of the French bouillabaise, with rice; Policha Meen, £25, grilled sea bass marinated with green pepper, garlic and shallots, enveloped in banana leaves and served with tomato 'rougail' which according to the menu is *'a recipe from the house of Mme Blanc, the "Grande Dame" of Pondichèry'*; Poulet Rouge, £18, shredded chicken marinated in

Pat Chapman and Chef Mehernosh Mody in the La Porte Kitchens

yoghurt and red spices, grilled and served in a creamy sauce [it's CTM, really]; Kari de Mouton, £18, home style goat meat curry spiked with robust spices and laced with coconut milk. *'Mme David Annuswamy's cherished family recipe'* [sic]. There's duck, guinea fowl and monkfish, lamb shanks and a fine Hyderabadi Biryani, £19, lamb marinated with mint, coriander and pomegranate seeds, cooked with basmati rice in an earthenware pot with fried onions, saffron and quail egg. Vegetables are represented. Stars are Coorgi Mushroom Curry, earthy mushrooms in a green herb curry from the Coorg region and Rougail D' Aubergine, smoked crushed aubergine with chilli, ginger and fresh green lime and Red Rice, £3.50, Steamed organic husky red rice. *'My all-time favourite restaurant.'* SO. Ours too, Steve. La Porte's ambience, decor, service and food is all

Your editors at La Porte. It's hard work testing all that food! Says Dominique Chapman (DBAC) 'I love this restaurant. From the welcome at the door to the presentation of the bill. The food, is just superb. Murgh Makhani (CTM) is just how it is in India. Flavoursome chicken pieces from a whole chicken – not the usual chunks of tasteless chicken breast – are smothered in a delicious, creamy, delicately spiced crimson gravy. Potato-stuffed parathas are buttery and light. You will want to eat them even if you are full to bursting. Big, fat, juicy King prawns floating in a light, mustard seed, turmeric coloured, coconut milk sauce.'

as good as it gets and has become an Indian's Indian, with an ever-increasing clientèle from the subcontinent. We gave it our Best in UK Award in 1998. This Award is a permanent accolade, and does justice to Mehernosh's fabulous food and Sherin's tight management. Average spend £60. Service 12.5%. Cover charge £1.50. 12-2.30 (to 3.30 Sun) & 6.30-11.30 (6-10.30 Sun & BH). Branches: La Porte, Brussels, Blue Elephant Thai, SW6, and others in Europe. See page 27.

RAGAM   SOUTH INDIAN
57, Cleveland Street, Fitzrovia, W1T 4JN
020 7636 909   www.ragamindian.co.uk

Established in 1984 and now of the Kerela group. See Rhada Krishna Bhavan, London SW17 for full menu details. 12-3 & 6-11.

RAJ TANDOORI
72 Berwick Street, W1F 8PD   020 7437 2897.

You're in Soho. There are restaurants all around you. Many are Indian, many are in this Guide. Many have introduced real authentic food, not just from the many regions of India, but from all the countries of the subcontinent. Many have lifted the bar way above what was the norm four decades ago. They have helped London obtain its culinary crown as Gourmet capital of the world, and there is no stopping the innovation, investment and culinary achievements of some of them.

RAJ
TANDOORI RESTAURANT
72 Berwick Street, London, W1F 8TD
Tel: 020 7437 2897
020 7439 0035
Open 7 days a week

SPLENDIDLY INDIAN, SUPERBLY SMOOTH

Who would have thought that mighty Michelin, even with their lack of understanding of this food, would deign to award their coveted stars. That's now. Bur go back 40 something years and there were no fine Indian dining restaurants then. But there was Raj. Established in 1969 by Abdon Noor it is exactly what you expect from a well run curryhouse. All the favourite dishes are on the menu. There's no pretention and no fuss. Service, cleanliness, facilities and prices are spot on. Sometimes you just need a fix. Your editor has no problem telling you he has enjoyed his stonkingly good curries here for many a year. Show them this Guide and you may get a discount. 12-2.30 & 5.30-12.

RASA SAMUDRA   KERELAN SEAFOOD   A-LIST
6 Dering Street, W1S 1AD
020 7629 1346   www.rasarestaurants.com

In Feb 2012 the Rasa group consolidated a little by moving their Rasa Sumadra seafood operation here to Dering St, and combining the two menus. They also closed their Rasa Mudra E11 branch after just over a year since it opened. Sadly Leytonstone just wasn't ready for Kerrelan food. Glad to say the remaining Rasa restaurants are fully operational andnothing on the menus has been lost. Dering Street opened in 1998, following the success of Shivadas (Das) Sreedharan and his wife Alison's two Stoke Newington N16 restaurants. Now that Samudra is in house the menu features many of the vegetarian delicacies of that eatery, but includes some lamb and chicken dishes from northern Kerala and superb cooking by Chef RS Binuraj and his team.The very chatty menu is without doubt one of the most informative and well written menus in the business. It gives the origin of the dishes and a description which simply makes you want to try everything. Here is a snapshot. Pre-Meal Snacks, £4, a snack tray consisting of crisp: flower shaped Achappam, Pappadavadai, pops dipped in batter and fried to give them extra "crunch and crackle", regular Pappadoms, Banana Chips and Murukku, crunchy sticks, with home made Pickles: £3.50, Lemon, Mango Pickle, Mixed Veg, Garlic, Konju Achar (Prawn pickle), Meen Achar (Fish Pickle) and Podina. Follow with Parippu, £4.50, a soup made from three different lentils, tomato, garlic, coriander & pepper. Starters: eg Seafood Karumuru,£7.50, tilapia fish and prawns, green chillies, shallots & curry leaves. Mysore Bonda, £4.50, potato balls laced with fresh ginger, curry leaves, coriander, cashew nuts and black mustard seeds, dipped and fried in besan batter and crisply fried. Served with coconut chutney. Main Dishes include Konju Manga Curry, £13, king prawns with turmeric, chillies, green mango and coconut. Crab Varuthathu, £13, crab cooked dry with ginger, curry leaves, chilli and mustard seeds, chef's speciality. Meen Molly, £12, a speciality of Travancore Christians. Lightly fried King fish cooked with coconut, green chillies, curry leaves and ginger. It's not all seafood: Varutharacha Kozhy Curry, £10, is chicken in dry roasted coriander, grated coconut, dried red chillies, fresh curry leaves and tomatoes ; Malabar Erachi Chaaru , £10, is aromatic lamb, turmeric, red chillies and onion (this dish is great eaten with a Paratha). Of the three Rasa's Dosas at £11 Chilli Onion Rava Dosa is unusual with a filling of ginger, green chillies and cumin seed. Served with sambar coconut chutney and spicy potato masala. Vegetable curries at £6.50 include Moru Kachiathu, sweet mangoes and green bananas cooked in yoghurt with green chillies, ginger and fresh curry leaves. Beet Cheera Pachadi, a wedding feast dish. Fresh beetroot and spinach are blended together in a yoghurt sauce with roasted coconut, mustard seeds and curry leaves. Cabbage Thoran, £5.50, is made from shredded cabbage, tossed with onion, fresh coconut, mustard seeds and freshly ground turmeric. Keralan rice specials, £3,75, include Coconut Rice, Tamarind Rice or Lemon Rice, And then there is Uzhunappam, £2.50, a bread madeから rice, roasted coconut, shallots and cumin seeds. Appam, £2.50, the Kerelan crispy, spongy rice pancake, 'essential for mopping up moist curries'. In the unlikely event that you have room for a dessert, Pal Payasam, £3.50, is the celebrated Kerelan rice pud cooked in sweetened milk flavoured with cardamom, cashew nuts and raisins, or Banana Dosa, £3.50, aka Palakkad Iyer, a Brahmin speciality of tiny bananas pancakes flavoured with cardamom and served with a scoop of Banana Ice Cream. Two set meals are good value and give a varied selection of Rasa specials: Vegetarian Feast £22.50 or Seafood Feast, £30. The place is very tiny with seating on two floors packed into the narrow rooms. It does two full sessions every night, plus a full weekday lunch trade. So book and go early. Service 12.5%. 12-3 not Sun & 6-11. *Branches: Rasa, N16 Rasa Express NW1 & N16 & Rasa Newcastle*

RASA EXPRESS   KERELAN TAKEAWAY
5 Rathbone Street, W1T 1NQ   020 7637 0222

NW1, was so successful at serving busy office workers inexpensive lunchtime e tasty, spicy, take-away treats, that a sister takeaway was called for. The menu is the sam, just eight items on the menu from £1.50 to £3.50,. See Rasa Express NW1 for details. Mon-Fri: 12- 3

RED FORT   FINE MUGHAL CUISINE   A-LIST
77 Dean Street, Soho, W1D 3SH
020 7437 2525   www.redfort.co.uk

The very capable Amin Ali opened his Red Fort back in 1987. In 2001, a controversial fire closed this iconic venue until a £2m rebuild took place and it reopened in late 2002 to a fanfare of publicity, something Amin is livened with three small tables and some six seats, enhnaced with umbrellas and foliage. Inside 85 seats reside in a modernist Mughal setting of natural materials. The Jaipuri red sandstone is imported from

Rajasthan. The walls are a mixture of inlaid sandstone and Mughal arch motifs with images of Delhi's Red Fort. The opulence of the Mughal Court is evoked by the deep brown silk and leather banquettes, antiques and objets d'art sourced from the Mughal centres of Delhi, Hydrabad and Lahore. Rare 'shattered glass' hangings with intricate detail adorn the restaurant. The Welsh slate floor with a red path is dotted with mosaics leading you to the back where a copper mosaic-tiled water feature, based on classical Mughal garden designs drizzles elegantly down the wall. At the rear, a skylight provides natural light. The drama continues in the toilets, where no expense has been spared. Neither is it backstage where there is a space-age, rarely-found air-conditioned kitchen. Syletti-born Chef Azadur Rahman has been with the Red Fort since 1992. The team of seven chefs, includes Surindra Sing from Delhi's Bukhara whose tandoors are on view behind glass adding theatre in the open-plan kitchen. Breads specialist Shispal Negi offers over twenty different varieties, including 'Peshawari naan' to 'Makkai roti' (maize flour bread), as well as six different homemade chutneys ranging from 'Mango with curry leaves' to 'Banana with orange and cinnamon'. A la carte specialities include Scottish lobster with saffron, garlic, cinnamon and nutmeg; Jumbo Prawns marinated with saffron, chilli and garlic and Stone Bass fillet with mustard seed, coconut milk and curry leaf sauce. Hyderabadi bhuna gosht (with Herdwick lamb), roast rabbit with mustard & fennel, & tandoori Gressingham duck breast. The front is designated as 'the Brasserie' 12 -4 Monday to Friday, serving a casual dining experience, or just a quick snack of small plates, such as crispy coated soft shell crab with curry leaf and chilli or Tandoori Fruit Chaat, a charcoal-cooked selection of fruits with sweet and tangy spices. Small plates of chaat & kebabs from £4.25 or larger plates of chicken shashlik, prawn malai & grilled sea bass £8.50-13.50 or baby aubergines stuffed with tangy spices, with textured peanut & tamarind or The Red Fort Biriyani, which combines aromatic rice, tender lamb slow-cooked together in sealed clay pot. The restaurant has plenty of focus and charisma, just like its owner. 'The food is really superb, service good and the whole lunch a very enjoyable experience. I did notice the the menu is very small but I am sure all diners would be delighted

chairs, candles, oriental rugs, soft leather and plush blue velvet stools. Its hours are 5 till late, Tues to Sat and its operation and entrance is separate from the restaurant where. table d'hote lunch and pre-theatre specials from c£22 for 3 courses.Dinner average from £42. Dress smart casual. Service 12.5%. Mon-Fri: Lunch 12-2.15; 'Brasserie' 12-4. Dinner Mon-Sat: 5.45-11 (6-10 Sun).

YOU SAY OK, W1

W1: PALMS OF GOA NOT GOAN 12 Charlotte St, W1T 2LT 020 7636 1668

W1: THE RAJDOOT 49 Paddington Street, Marylebone, Mayfair, W1U 4HW 020 7486 2055

W1: REGENT TANDOORI 16 Denman Street, W1 – 020 7434 1134. Good for a fix at sensible prices. Lunch and dinner daily.

W1: TASTE OF MUGHAL 29 Great Windmill Street, W1 020 7439 8044. Long-standing 50-seater which *'never varies after all these years of visits.'* RW. Takeaway: 10% disc. Hours: 12-11.45.

ROTI CHAI
3-4 Portman Mews South, W1H 6HS
020 7408 0101   www.rotichai.com

Roti Chai (literally meaning bread and tea) operates as two venues under the same roof with different menus, price points, décor and independent kitchens. Street Kitchen has a very casual feel and guests are happy to pop in any time of day for a quick bite or a more substantial meal. Dining Room is what it says on the tin and is downstairs in a more formal room. It is still relaxed but the menu has more complex dishes. Street Kitchen is the ground floor snack eatery. It specialises in what is now called 'Street Food', which is served from carts, dabbas (roadside shacks) and railway stations all over India. In Britain the few venues capable of making such food correctly are only found in London. Despite having been has exemplified by Masala Zone (see W1) street food is still little known inside the capital and is virtually unknown outside it. So it never hurts to have a new contender, particularly since that contender is Rohit Chugh, formerly MD of Cinnamon Club (see W1). It's a fascinating change from the 'hautest' of 'hauts', to 'rustic'and 'earthy' (at least that's how he describes his Chettinad Chicken – a *'rustic earthy Tamil Nadu*

Casual dining outsde The Red Fort's red sandstone-coloured frontage

with anything they choose.' DC. The venue's basement with its steep staircase and low-lit alcoves never worked well in its previous incarnations. Now a cocktail bar named Zenna, it is decorated with silk-upholstered gold

Roti Chai's Bhel Puri is 3.9

speciality'). Street Kitchen achieves its casual look courtesy of its art-style and Rohit's carefully planned placement of props Time out's Rupa Gualati says it all: *'The pared-back decor - a quirky mix of industrial chic contrasted with cleverly presented Indian groceries - is laden with nostalgia appealing to wistful Indians.'* [and all lovers of real India, Ed] *'Cartons of mango juice, glucose biscuit packets, retro advertising logos and bottles of rose-scented squash add an air of corner-shop-cool to this trendy and spacious all-day café.'* RG. But it's the food that counts. Street Kitchen's menu is a delightful combination of items sold by India's street cart vendors. And the prices are exactly how Mr Chugh lists them, not our typos in this instance! And no they aren't rupees. Here are some starter examples from the ten listed: Bhel Puri is 3.9; Chicken Lollipops, batter-dipped drumsticks using the pared bone as the stick, 4.8; Hakka Chilli Paneer, fiery speciality from Kolkata's Chinese Indian community, 5.2; Dhokla, Gujarati steamed chickpea cake, 3.9. Roti does serve Roti of course, a selection at 4.5; Kitchen's mains are described as *'Road & rail rustic dishes from the roadside 'dhaba' cafes & bustling train stations of the subcontinent.'* Railway Lamb Curry, with potatoes and two chapatis 8.5; Pulusu Chicken, chicken curry Andhra Pradesh style with steamed rice, 7.9; Chicken Kola Urandai – Chettiar style chicken 'kofta' (balls) kari served with rice, 7.9. Dining Room's menu is mostly different. Three interesting starters are Chicken 65 (South India's answer to KFC) – fiery deep-fried chicken originated at Chennai's Buhari Hotel, and is priced appropriately at 6.5; Chicken keema kaleji with chicken livers 5.8. Mains include: Pork vinha d'alhos, the classic Goan dish of slow -ooked pork belly with a hot tangy sauce, 9.0; Kozhikode prawns subtly spiced Malabar coastal kari with tiger prawns, mustard seeds & curry leaves 15.8; the aforesaid Chettinad chicken, 15.5. Street Kitchen: Mon-Sat: 12-10.30 (Sun12.45-10.30). Dining Room: Tues-Sat: 6-10.30.

SAGAR — SOUTH INDIAN VEGETARIAN
Sagar, 17A Percy Street, Off Tottenham Court Rd, London, W1T 1DU 020 7631 3319

See Sagar W6 for menu details. Mon-Th: 12-3 & 5.30-10.45 (Fri & Sat: 12-11.30; Sun: 12-10.45).

SILK at COURTHOUSE DOUBLETREE HILTON
19-21 Great Marlborough Street, W1F 7HL
020 7297 5555   www.courthouse-hotel.com

If we were to make an award for quirkiest decor this might be it. Hilton have taken over a Grade II listed former magistrates' court building just off Regent Street. Around the hotel, glimpses of its former use can be seen – such as the iron bars that separate the lobby lounge from the Bar, original Robert Adams fireplaces in some of the suites, and the bar's tables inside three of the original prison cells. was once the Number One court, where Charles Dickens worked as a reporter for the Morning Chronicle in 1835. Napoleon was a witness in a fraud case between attempts to establish a second empire in France. Oscar Wilde's 'Queensbury' case was heard. Mick Jagger Marianne Faithful and Keith Richards were tried here possession of marijuana. John Lennon's case regarded the sale of sexually explicit drawings. Now it is the home of Silk, the hotel's destination restaurant. It is lit by a stunning vaulted glass ceiling and framed in English Oak panel walls. The Judges bench, witness stand and dock have been thoughtfully retained. Silk's menu is a fusion of Thai and Indian cusines, more Thai than Indian, which according the the spin is *'a comestible cruise down the old Silk Road'*. Exec Chef Rajesh Parmar's rotating menu includes starters such as Konkani jhinga, £9.50, king prawns with ginger, curry leaves and kokum; a galette of chick peas, £7; or a selection of mini starters on a platter, £13. Main courses could entail a paneer and broccoli kofta, £13.95; tiger prawns in curry paste, , £19.95; or an 8oz fillet of black peppered beef with curry leaf, £22.95; while those with a sweet tooth conviction can indulge in banana and raisin five spice spring rolls, £6.95; or a Silk dessert platter selection, , £12. Tues-Sat: 6-10:30.

TAMARIND

"Let us change your perception of Indian Dining"

Tamarind offers the ultimate in authentic Indian cuisine exploring an unprecedented variety of the subcontinent's culinary traditions using the highest quality ingredients to create unforgettable dishes.

Set Lunch Menu
Fresh and seasonal produce are used to create all menus by chef Alfred and his team.
2 Course & 3 Course menu available Monday to Friday
Tasting menu – Lunch on Sundays

Early Dinner
An additional 2 Course menu has been crafted which is perfectly balanced, delicately spiced and never too heavy, the frequently – changing menus are ideally suited for pre or post theatre dining.

TAMARIND FINE MUGHAL DINING A-LIST
20 Queen Street, W1J 5PR
020 7629 3561   www.tamarindrestaurant.com

Opened in 1994, this Guide gave it Best Newcomer Award in 1995 & 97, Best Indian, 1998-9 and and best Chef 1999-2000 becoming the only Indian restaurant to be so awarded It won its first Michelin star in 2001 which it continues to retain. General Manager Rajesh Suri (formerly with Red Fort and Veeraswamy) joined in 1998 and is in no small part responsible for this success. Atol Kotchar was the original chef, and when he left in 2002 (to open Benares, W1), Sous chef Alfred Prasad (ex Delhi Sheraton and Veeraswamy) took on the mantle of Head Chef. He graduated from the Institute of Hotel Management, Madras in 1993 and completed his advanced chef training at the Maurya Sheraton in Delhi, working at the legendary 'Bukhara' and 'Dum-Pukht' restaurants then to the Madras Chola Sheraton where he was Executive Chef at 'Dukshin'-one of India's premier south Indian restaurants. Alfred finally moved to London in June 1999 where he worked as Sous Chef at Veeraswamy. The restaurant is downstairs (no wheelchair access). A structurally essential central pillar dominates the room, but its gilt covering matches the browns and golds of the tasteful decor in the room with 26 well-spaced tables seating up to 90. A well laid out bar also features. Tamarind specialise in matching Indian food and wine. Rajesh says, *'Over the years we have learned to change 2-3 different wines each month. Every fortnight we have a wine tasting for the staff. We have a really good sommelier, so the customers can trust his judgement'*. He is Tobias Gorn, who can draw on a choice of 140 different wines, mainly from France and the New World. Prices range from £20 to £1300 per bottle. As for the menu, it features Moghul and North West Indian cuisine and has no innovative surprises, thank heavens. In fact it looks quite ordinary, and not too long either. But the cooking is far from ordinary. Pappads, £3.95, served with a trio of home made chutneys; date & ginger, tomato & nigella seeds and spiced gooseberry. A la carte starters include: Tandoori Khumb, £10.95, Tandoor grilled portabella, shiitake and oyster mushrooms with pickled onions in a curry leaf dressing; Gilafi Reshmi, £9.75, Skewered kabab of ground chicken with ginger, green chillies, cheese and spices; Pudhina Chops, £11.75, lamb cutlets with ginger, turmeric, dried mint, malt vinegar and peppercorns and chilli yoghurt dip; Kabab Selection, £26.50, an assortment of tiger prawn, kingfish, chicken supreme and lamb chop. Mains include Lobster Masala, £32.00, diced lobster tail tossed with browned shallots, tomatoes and spices, finished with crushed pink and black peppercorns; Murgh Makhni, £18.75, Chicken tikka in puréed fresh tomatoes flavoured with ginger, green chillies and crushed fenugreek leaves (CTM!); Vegetables: Masala Dal, £7.15, Yellow lentils simmered with ginger, tomatoes, green chilli and fresh coriander; finished with juice of lemon Dual priced for Side or Main: Tarkari Handi £8.95 £11.95, broccoli, shiitake, asparagus, baby corn, red peppers and spinach tossed with cumin, red onions and crushed peppercorns; Gucchi Kofta £9.85 / £12.85 Stuffed morels in minced vegetable dumplings in a creamy sauce of browned onions, melon seeds, tomatoes and spices; Achari Bhindi £9.25 / £12.25, okra tossed with ginger, red onions, turmeric and fresh coriander; finished with pickling spices; Naan £3.95. Gajjar Halwa £8.50, Pistachio Kheer £7.50, Gulab Jamun £7.75. *'Our benchmark dal Makhni, low-cooked black lentils was perfect. Romali Roti was handkerchief-thin and soft.'* DBAC? 'We had been waiting a long time to have an opportunity to dine here. It was a very enjoyable evening, but not as outstanding as we expected, definitely one notch below Moti Mahal, Benares and The Cinnamon Club. I give it full marks for the young woman who took the reservation, polite, friendly and efficient and welcoming, very different from the officious and, 'you will fit in with us' type of attitude so often encountered at top restaurants. On arrival we were very nicely shown to our table and graciously moved when we requested a table further into the room away from the bar. The decor is attractive, not specifically Indian and the atmosphere was great. Wine list is wonderful, a large selection with many real prestige wines. My husband much enjoyed reading it and chose a Stag's Leap Zinfandel, which was a vinous treat. Menu is of average length and mostly Tamarind's versions of the classic Indian dishes. I had expected more unusual ingredients. We started with Lamb Chops and Scallops, both excellent. Chicken, sea bream, side dishes are rice all marvellous. Small pieces of Popadom with very good relishes were brought to the table when we sat own. Gajar Halwa with vark for dessert. Flavours of every dish were delicious, but not any better than many of the other Indian restaurants we frequent. For a restaurant with Tamarind's reputation and classification we expected to be 'wowed'. The presentation of the curries was the biggest let-down, and descriptions of dishes weren't very helpful. Service OK, reasonably efficient, but impersonal. The room was full and atmosphere buzzing. However, smart and elegant, a large proportion of diners turned up in jeans, a very great shame. £165 for two, including £64 for wine.' HJC. Tasting menus: £56 or £68pp, Min order of 2 diners. Set lunches: 2 course £18.50 (with wine £28.50); 3 course £21.50 (with wine £31.50) Service: 12.5%. Sun-Fri: 12-2.45 Mon-Sat 5.30-11 (Sun: 6-10.30). *Branches: Imli W1, Tamarind of London,, CA, US.*

TRISHNA FINE KARAVALI CUISINE
Blandford Street, Marylebone Village, W1
020 7353 3633 www.trishnalondon.com

Trishna Mumbia is so much of an institution that its Indian aficionados (who still call Mumbai Bombay) include captains of Industry, shop owners, Bollywood stars, and tourists (who call Bombay Mumbai) blindly directed there by Guide books, and who wouldn't know a Bollywood star from a black hole, let alone appreciate Trishna's food. It's in the old Fort district, between Ballard docks and Taj. Decor never rates highly in India, and here, it's caff-style, pack-em-in, but above all, it's clean with fast service. And it is always packed. Trishna's London outpost opened in 2008, with the brief to go upmarket. and the designers, B3, who probably haven't vistited Trishna Mumbai, say *'the 80 seater has a minimalist feel offset by tumbled marble, smoked oak flooring, brickwork and glass* [to create] *a casual, informal and sociable dining atmosphere with*

Trishna Mumbai

great buzz and energy.' Fortunately, as with the mother ship, Trishna London's menu focuses on Karavali cuisine of coastal south west India, specialising in seafood, crab being the star dish. Whole Crab, cooked in butter, black pepper and garlic is Mumbai's signature dish costing c350 rupees (c£5) and won the 2010 Mumbai 'Best Eats' competition with the boast that the crabs are caught that day and are alive when ordered in Trishna. It's £20 in London. Sadly Marylebone Village doesn't have live crabs on the doorstep. They claim the next best thing : *'seafood and crustaceans are supplied daily from the Cornish, Dorset and Scottish coasts, from high-quality, sustainable sources.'* The good news is that Rasoi of Chelsea's former Head Chef, Ravi Deulkar is in charge of cooking. Proprietor, Karam Sethi says, *'Ravi's come up with an absolutely delectable selection of dishes. His cooking is in tune with Mumbai Trishna but has its own style.'* Apart from the mandatory crab, Ravi rings the changes on his menus, so these are examples only. He has a selection of cooking methods: char grilling on the 'sigri' for such dishes as Fish Tikka £10.75, Hariyali Sea

Trishna London

Bream, £13 with green peppercorn spice paste, and Lobster Goan Masala with spiced mustard dressed cucumber. The steel tawa (flat frying pan) produces dishes like Razor Clams, with white beans and Goan sausages and Mussels and Clams are stir-fried in a Mangalorean roasted coconut and garam masala paste. Bombay Duck is coated in rice flour, turmeric, fried and sered with and kokum chutney. And there is a further selection roasted in the tandoor. For those not fishily inclined, there's Salt Marsh Lamb Chop and Neck with black peppercorn and poppy seed masala, or Pork Rib with red chilli and goan 'toddy', palm vinegar masala and spiced crackling or Whole Baby Chicken, Karavali marinade roasted on cedar or Aylesbury Duck Salad, with whole masoor lentils & sautéed wild mushrooms. Keema and Quail Egg Pilau with sautéed spinach & fresh mint. Sommelier Suniana Sethis offers a full and diverse range of fine wines, champagnes and beers. Trishna's 5 Course Koliwada tasting menu is £38.50 incl. wine £74, each 100ml. Lunch from £15.50. 12-2:45 (Sun- 3:15) & 6-10.45. Sun:6:30-10. *Branch: Trishna, Birla Mansion, Sai Baba Marg , Kala Ghoda, Fort, South Mumbai*

LONDON W1

VEERASWAMY
FINE DINING
OUTSTANDING RESTAURANT AWARD
99 Regent Street, W1   020 7734 1401

Veerswamy opened on 21 April 1926, which coincidentally happens to be Queen Elizabeth 11's birthday. Its founders were an Indian princess and her husband, the great grandson of an English General in the Bengal Army. Customers included Edward V111, then Prince of Wales, King Gustav of Sweden, Pandit Nehru, Indira Gandhi, Charlie Chaplin, King Hussein of Jordan, and Marlon Brando, and for that matter your editor's mother, who saved up her nurse's money for an occasional visit in the 1930s to satisfy the fix she had acquired in the Raj. She would have decidely recognised picture above which shows it in all its early glory. For many years it was Britain's only Indian restaurant, and is therefore our longest survivor. By the 1990s, Veeraswamy was, after several rebuilds, faded and neglected, and it very nearly got the axe. Fortunately salvation was at hand. Visionaries Ranjit Mathrani, Namita and Camellia Panjabi, the trio behind Chutney Mary, Amaya and Masala Zone purchased it. It was a high-risk venture. The rebuild exceeded £1.5million. Their aim was to restore its pedigree and reputation as it entered its ninth decade with 21st century decor and decent food *letting it reflect the Maharajah-style glamour and glory it exuded in the 1920s'*. They reopened the entrance from the aptly-named Swallow Street, and more recently returned the doorman (Darwan which translates as an "imposing gentleman with a turban") to greet arriving guests and direct them to go up the stairs one floor or take the lift. You will notice pictures of the rich and famous devotees of Indian food, whose rendezvous it has always been. As you enter the main room, the wall-to-wall picture windows at first dominates with their great view of Regent Street. But you are soon spellbound with the interior. The ten foot high ceiling is sparkley silver panels, countered by a dark wooden floor, handmade Moghul floral design carpets and Indian black granite speckled with gold. On one wall, vividly coloured turbans evokes the Indian Maharajas who once trod the boards at Veeraswamy. Century-old Kalighat-style Bengali paintings adorn the restaurant. A tiled mirror wall is at the cute booth called the honeymoon table. The lighting combines primary-coloured glass shades redolent of handis, exorbitant chandeliers, and LCD lighting colour-changing the fretwork screens. The short menu includes classics from throughout India and

SPLENDIDLY INDIAN, SUPERBLY SMOOTH

contemporary creations produced by a brigade of specialists from different Indian regions. Items from bhel to dosas and lamb shank to lobster, and dishes from Hyderabad to Chowpatti and Goa to Delhi are produced with regional accuracy. This is not to everyone's liking, since it's far removed from curry house stuff and it's in the higher price range. Caveats issued, let me now tell you why this restaurant is so high in our estimation. We have always found the starters to be par-excellence, sometimes delectable, sometimes transcendent and the protein dishes too. On our recent visit we had Raj Kachori (a giant pani-puri filled with dahi and bhel street food, quite divine and much better than its description in the menu) and green vegetable kebab. Our mains were a delectable Lamb Biriani with a smooth pink Mirchi Salan sauce (chilli curry – delicious but very mild) and Syrian chicken stew, pink sauce again, but spicier and quite outstanding. Desserts at the Panjabi establishments have always been way above average, partly because they are made on site and not bought in. I am indebted to Sejal Sukhadwala, whose Time Out Indian restaurant reports are always perceptive and very witty, and who wrote of US food writer Jeffrey Steingarten, *'he once memorably described Indian desserts as tasting of face cream., but here the own-made kala jaam (semolina and milk dumplings in rose-scented syrup) and rasgollas (poached paneer dumplings) were fabulous.'* I can add to that: for it was at Veeraswamy that I first had hot Gulab Jamun, flambéed in Cognac. Some face cream! One more thing: the wine list is an exemplary selection. Mr Mathrani is a connoisseur, and it shows. If ever there were a time to convert from beer to wine, this is it. Upstairs the Palmer room (named after the founder) takes 36 seated and 60 standing. When we started the Curry Club in 1982, we used this room to hold our monthly meetings. It was then rather tatty. Not now: it is transformed with more turbans and is invitingly laid out for dinner for 18. And there are a number of framed prints up there which deserve attention. As for price: it's not always out of reach. There a number of attractive set meal options: Lunch Mon to Sat: £17.75 for 2 courses, and £20.75 for 3 A La carte Lunch prices are about 10% less than Dinner. Business lunch offering a selection of light starters, salads and grills; £27 for 2 courses. Pre theatre menu from 5.30 Mon to Sat and Post theatre menu after 10 pm Mon to Fri: £17.75 for 2 courses, and £20.70 for 3 courses Special Sunday lunch of Indian Favourites: £24 for 3 courses. A la carte dinner £50. Service 12.5%. Mon-Fri: 12-2.15; (Sat & Sun to 2.30). Dinner: 5.30-10.30 (Sat to 10.45; Sun 6-10. See page 1.

WOODLANDS   SOUTH INDIAN   TOP 100
77 Marylebone Lane, W1   020 7436 3862

A branch of Mr Sood's well-liked, small chain of southern Indian vegetarian restaurants. The menu and prices are the sameSee SW1 branch for details.

ZAYNA   PUNJABI
25 New Quebec Street W1H 7SF
020 7723 2229   www.zaynarestaurant.co.uk

Punjabi Chef/Proprietor Riz Dar has achieved his dream to own a restaurant and to name it after his daughter. It's no secret that this Guide's editors love the gutsy, savoury tastes of Punjabi food. And if you do, seek it out it behind Marble Arch tube. Starters include Pakoras, £4.75 Meat Samosas, £5.75 with chickpea sauce and Lahori Mucchi, £6.50, fresh cod fillets deep-fried in gramflour batter. Mains include Mukhun Murgh, £16, OK it's CTM but adorable when cooked Punjabi Moghul style. Baati Ghosht, £17 is a traditional Punjabi market dish of lamb cooked in a piping hot wok with tomato, ginger, onion, garam masala & a whole host of spicy goodness. Ishtu, £17 is a Zayna signature dish named after the word 'stew', but if you imagined it was public school canteen stuff, try it for a surprisingly tasty, savoury delight. It's slow-cooked lamb in a yoghurt, onion, garlic, ginger & mixed herb source. Paya, £19 separates the sheep from the goats ... this traditional street food from Delhi to Lahore is lamb trotters, slow cooked overnight, garnished with fresh diced ginger, coriander leaves & sliced lemon. Gurda Qeema, £17.50 is typical Punjabi market food, combining lamb kidneys & mince with ginger, garlic, fenugreek & caraway seeds. Kapora Taka Tak, £17, is a Lahori delicacy of lamb sweet breads cooked with yogurt, ginger, chopped onions, tomatoes & fresh herbs. It gets its name from the tak tak tak noise made when the ingredients are chopped on a steel tawa frying pan. Though Punjabis love their meat, never forget the Punjab is the vegetable garden of the area. And these dishes are typical: Aloo Gobhi, £9, is cauliflower in a lightly spiced batter & cooked in a tangy garlic & tomato sauce with potatoes, cumin, coriander & home made red chilli. Shahi Palak, £10, is fresh spinach leaves and sautéed paneer cooked in ground spices Bhindi Karahi,,£12.50, is fresh okra mixed with sliced onions & dried pomegranate seeds. Shipketa, £9.50, a home-style dish combining cauliflower, carrots, garden peas, potatoes & turnips to create one of Kashmir's most popular dishes. 2 half portions of any vegetarian dish for £13. Daily: 12-2:30 & 5:30-11 (to 11:15 Fri & Sat).

London W2

BOMBAY PALACE   FINE DINING   **TOP 100**
2 Hyde Park, 50 Connaught Street, W2 2AA
020 7258 3507   www.bombay-palace.co.uk

In the late 1970s, Mr SS Chatwell was a successful Indian restaurateur in Ethiopia. Then a regime-change left him fearing for his life. He packed his bags and left for the USA. Luckily he'd packed his many bags full of dollars, and I mean FULL. I know because I met him in NY and he told me. It was not long before he opened Bombay Palace London opened in 1983. The elegant 135-seater is entered via a lounge. Current Head Chef Harjeet Singh worked at Delhi's Maurya Sheraton Bukhara (See W1) and Dum Phukt restaurants, arguably India's top restaurants, so unsurprisingly his menu is composed mainly of Northern Indian dishes. Menu Snapshot: Starters: Onion Bhaji £6, nion coated in a mildly spiced gram flour batter, deep fried and served with tamarind chutney; Kheema Potli £8, spicy lamb mince cooked with chopped celery, stuffed in a savoury pastry fried until crisp; Murgh Kaleji Masala £8, chicken liver sauteed with onion, tomato, cumin seeds and coriander. Mains: Meen Pollichathu, £ 17.95, whole white pomfret marinated in spices, wrapped in a banana leaf and pan fried; Nalli Gosht, £17.85, a speciality of Lucknow, slow cooked lamb shanks in a delicate saffron curry; Chicken Kolhapuri, £15.95, a fiery preparation with whole red chillies, from the west coast of India; Anda Masaledar, £12.50, hard boiled eggs simmered in a country style spicy curry; Karela do Pyaza, £ 10.95, fresh bitter gourd sauteed with onions, herbs and spices. Roomali Rotihi £3.40, paper thin bread. *'Top notch restaurant, impeccably appointed in bright and airy single room. Smart polite and efficient staff. Real tablecloths and napkins. Engaging, not extensive menu. Complimentary Popadums and small tubs of sauces. The food is distinctively different and very tastyBalouchi Raan £23- outstanding, exquisite, beautifully tender cut of lamb leg, partially sliced of the bone. Had been marinated and slow cooked, with a hint of char – fabulous, subtle, varied flavours, a little sauce.'* RW. Service 15%. Cover charge £1 Takeaway: 10% discount. 12-2.45 & 6-11.30 (11 Sun). Branches: Beverly Hills, Kuala Lumpur, Montreal, New York, Toronto, Brampton, Hyderabad.

DURBAR   TOP 100
24 Hereford Road, W2 4AA
020 7727 1947   www.durbartandoori.co.uk

Opened when time began in 1956, by Shaimur Rahman Syed. Seats 60 diners – wicker chairs, arches, plants, Indian art, brass coffee-pots. Specials include: Chicken Xacuti, very hot with dry chilli and coconut and Chicken Silla, shredded chicken tikka. Good-value are the Thali set-meals from c£10; Southern Indian recipe for Kholopur Chicken – very hot with chilli, ginger and lime; Mughlai Badami Chicken steam cooked in a delicate bland of spice with pistachio & cashew nut sauce £8; Nihari Lamb shank marinated with yoghurt, garlic & ginger. Slow cooked with wild lemon £9; Chicken Malaber Mango and coconut milk with mustard seeds & jeera sauce £8; Lime Chicken With onion, coconut milk, lime juice, lemongrass, chilli and ground spice £8; Lamb or Chicken Tikka Masala Tikka morsels in exotic masala sauce. Mild spice £8; Gosth Hindustani Lamb with Roasted spice, garlic, ginger & ground almonds £8. There is a good range of veg dishes and 13 varieties of bread are baked daily in the Tandoor. Tandoori fish and meat dishes are cooked in true northwest Indian style. Biriani, Parsi, Kashmiri and Thali set meals, from £15. All give the diner a chance to sample a wide variety of dishes influenced by regional home cooking. Co-owner Chef Shamin Syed won the International Chef of the Year Contest in Feb. 2000. He says of his winning dish – Oriental Chicken (diced chicken cooked with onions, yoghurt, tomato, ground almond, and coconut in hint of spice cream sauce, served sizzling £7.95) *'it's been on the menu for over 30 years'*. What more can we say about one of London's most stable and experienced venues Well there is a bit more. RCF says *'it's one of our regular haunts. Whenever we go it is without fail packed full of Indians and Arabs. That says quality.'* Takeaway: 10% discount. 12-2.30 (not Fri) & 5.30-11.30 daily, including bank holidays.   Branch: Greenford Tandoori, Ruislip Road East, Greenford, Mddx.

DURBAR
24 Hereford Road
(off Westbourne Grove)
London
W2 4AA
020 7727 1947
020 7727 5995
www.durbartandoori.co.uk
Top 100

Established 1956   One of the oldest family-run restaurants in London

MANDALAY — BURMESE — A-LIST
444 Edgware Road, W2
020 7258 3696   www.mandalayway.com

Located in the unfashionable end of Edgware Road, this restaurant will never get a Michelin star, thank heavens – it's far too scruffy and in the wrong location! But for an utterly honest, non-rip-off, inexpensive, hard-working, sensibly operated, clean and simple gaff, this is it, above all reeking with care from top to bottom and sumptuous food. It is an absolute favourite of mine not just because it has the distinction of being the UK's only Burmese restaurant, but for its unpretentiousness, for its friendliness, for the owners' love of food and for always being constant – and since the menu never changes, apart from a minor price rise from time to time, there is no reason to change my review. Mandalay seats just 30 and is run by the Ally brothers, Dwight (front) and Gary (cooking) Burmese-born and Norwegian-educated. Mum and Dad were on duty when I dropped in for lunch. She was busy cooking, and he busy chatting to a regular customer. I asked for a beer and got it at once, suitably cold, from the Fanta-packed cabinet, as much part of the décor as the oil-cloth table covers. This place is a must for foodies. Burmese food is a cross between Chinese and Indian cuisine with a slight influence from Thai food.

The location, frontage and decor aren't Mich star stuff, thank heavens. Pictures couresy of Bellaphon.com (a most interesting food blog site).

Rice and noodles are the most important staples. Fritters, soups, salads, stir-fries and curries are eaten every day. Ingredients such as garlic, turmeric, tamarind, coriander, mint, tamarind and chilli show the Indian influence; fish sauce, shrimp paste (which comes in a very strong smelly block, shaped rather like a small house brick, very dark brown in colour called blachan) dried shrimps, lemon grass and coconut milk, its Thai influence and soy sauce, noodles, rice flour and ginger, Chinese. Pork and beef are eaten. Menu Snapshot: Popadoms (Papara) £1.40 Prawn Crackers (Nga-Moak-Kyam) £2.10. For starters choose from three different Spring Rolls (Kaw Pyant Kyam), vegetable, shrimp and vegetable, or chicken and vegetable, all are £2.10 for a portion of two. Samosas (Samusa), vegetable, egg and potato or minced chicken, £2.50 for a very generous portion of four. Shrimp & Vegetable Salads (A-Thoat), feature strongly on the menu. I rather liked the Raw Papaya and Cucumber Salad at £4.30; Chicken and Cabbage Salad £4.50; Shrimp and Lettuce Salad £4.50. Soups (Hin-Cho) all £3.20, are eaten as a digestive (just like Thailand) and there are some interesting choices: Bottle Gourd Soup; Dozen Ingredients Soup (Sett-Na-Myo Hin-Cho) (sounds intriguing!). Let's move onto the main course lamb, chicken and seafood dishes and my favourites are - Spicy Lamb Curry (Seit-Tha Hin) £7.50; Chicken with lemongrass (Kyet-Tha Zabalin) £8.50; Crispy Fried Fish in Season Sauce (Nga Kyaw) £8.50. Noodle and Rices dishes are also very good like the Rice Noodles in Fish Soup (Mokhingar) £7.50; Noodles with Coconut and Chicken (Kyet-Tha Ohn-No Khauk-Swe) £7.50 and Spiced Rice with King Prawns (Bazun-Kya Dan-Bauk) £8.50. If you can manage a pudding, I recommend the Banana Fritters at £2.50, if you really can't manage another mouthful, take them home and eat for breakfast! Or Coconut Agar-Agar Jelly and Faluda (milk, ice cream, jelly and Rose syrup £3.90. Dad told me to try the Tea-leaf salad. It uses leaves he says are imported from Burma (I didn't ask how) which Mum had made that morning just for him. I protested saying I couldn't eat his lunch. He said *'no worries she's made enough for an army.'* It consisted of fried moong lentils with the texture of rice crispies, loads of chilli (great) something fishy and salad and tea leaves. Amazing! *'All dishes were excellent, each tasting very distinct, fresh, lively, and agreeably flavoursome. Wonderful food, value tremendous. Highly recommended.'* MW. That was MW's first visit. Here's what he has to say three years on, now as a regular: *'Had one of my regular visits last week. As always, wonderful food. It's certainly my sort of place, and as it's always good there's little to add'.* MW. Licensed. Despite being inexpensive, they sensibly take credit/debit cards. Essential to book evenings. Takeaway service. Babies & children welcome: with high chairs on offer. Mon-Sat: 12-2.30 & 6-10.30 (Closed Sun and bank hols). *Just round the corner is the Ally family's hotel, called the Mandalay Picton House (£75.per double/twin En-suite room inc Eng breakfast).*

YOU SAY OK, W2

CONNOISSEURS INDIAN 8 Norfolk Place, W2 1 LQ ~ 020 7402 3299. 46-seater. *'Excellent value, good quality, nicely presented and very filling.'* Del: 5m. Hours: 12-2.30 / 6-12.

GANGES 101 Praed Street, W2 ~ 020 7723 4096 It's been with us since our first Guide. 12-2.30/5.30-11.

MAHAL 138 Edgware Road, Paddington, W2 2DZ 020 7723 7731 www.mahal-w2.co.uk

MAHARAJA TANDOORI 50 Queensway, Paddington, W2 3RY 020 7727 1135

NOOR JAHAN 2 26 Sussex Place, W2 2TH 020 7402 2332. MD Aziz Ahmed's 90-seater on two floors . Av with wine £30 pp. 12-2.30/6-11.30.

SITARA 228, Edgware Rd, W2 ~ 020 7723 1101. Indian /Arabic entertainment, on dance floor to 6am.. Av with wine £50. Hours: 5.30 to late Mon-Fri; from 6 Sat. Closed Sun.

London W5

Monty's Nepalese Cuisine TOP 100

There are enough Monty's in Ealing to form a Gurkha regiment. Three Nepalese chefs Hari Thapa, Bisnu Karki and Mahanta Shrestha, set up originally in Ealing Broadway venue in 1980. They relocated to South Ealing. After that, the original group split, but they all still use the original name, logos, spin and menu and they all have Nepalese cooks. So because we have as many raving reports about any of the four venues, what we say is that all the Monty's do all the formula curries (which they cook well). And they all have a Nepalese specials list with items such as: Kathmandu Dal £5, lentils with ginger, onion, green chillies, tomatoes and cumin; Aloo Bodi, £5, potato with black-eye beans; Chicken Dilkhoosh £12, chicken breast in a creamy sauce with rice and mushrooms to mention just three. Moglai Dal £6 (Hot, medium or mild), black and yellow lentils with spinach and egg. Nepalese Khukhura Masala £10.20, chicken on or off the bone cooked with special sauce. There is a full menu of 'standard formula curries, all cpmpetently cooked, but our advice is that you go for the Nepalese items. *'Monty's provides excellent value for money and are a haven of quality cuisine, exquisite Nepalese spicing and caring service.'* AIE. Take your pick.

MONTY'S NEPALESE CUISINE
4 Broadway Centre, 11 High St, W5   020 8579 4646

Young blood Dipender (Bishnu's son) converted an Italian restaurant next to the Post Office and Club Boulevard in 2000, and refurbished it to be the most spacious, and most modern Monty's. It's a light and airy restaurant with wicker furniture, layers of fresh linen and attentive, smiley waiters. *'We are named after Sir Montgomery'*, he says, but doesn't expand on this elusive explanation. 12-3 & 6-12.

MONTY'S NEPALESE CUISINE
1 The Mall, Broadway, W5   020 8567 5802

Mahanta Shrestha took on this 68-seater venue, *'Monty's came from my name, Mahanta'*, he says. 12-3 & 6-12. *Branch, Monty's 53 Fife Rd, Kingston, Surrey. Run by Kishore Shrestha.*

MONTY'S NEPALESE CUISINE
224 South Ealing Road, W5 4RP
020 8560 2619   www.montys-tandoori.co.uk

The first Ealing Monty's opened here years ago. Still going strong with Hari Thapa in charge. *'The name Monty's,'* he says, *'is a tribute to Field Marshal Lord Montgomery, of WW11 Romell and Tobruck fame, and many Gurkhas fought under him.'* 12-3 & 6-12.

MONTY'S TANDOORI
54 Northfields Avenue, W13
020 8567 6281   www.montysrestaurant.co.

This is up the road in West Ealing but we detail it here alongside its stablemates. *'My curryholic daughter moved to Ealing and sussed Monty's out pretty quickly and invited me their on my previous visit. Lovely decor, swift service, fresh salad and yoghurt dip. Pops and picks were served while we ordered and this immediately relaxed us for a pleasant evening. Spicing and quality subtle and superb. We were stuffed, enough left for a meal for two in the freezer. Why black ceilings in the toilet?'* AIE. *'Highly recommended.'* SO. 12-3 & 6-12.

YOU SAY OK, W3 to W5

W3: JUBRAJ Gunnersbury, W3 9BD

W4: ANAPURNA Chiswick High Road. W4 2ED 020 8995 4431

W4: GEETANJALI 470 Chiswick High Road, W4 5TT 020 8994 0702

W4: TASTE OF RAJ 18 Fauconberg Road, Chiswick, W4 3JY 020 8742 0881

W5: ZAYKA INDIAN CUISINE 8 South Ealing Road, W5 ~ 020 8569 7278. Opened in 1990 Sunday e-a-m-a-y-l. Hours: 12-2.30; 3 /6-11.30; 12 Fri & Sat.

W5: ZEERA, 34 Hanger Lane, W5 3HU ~ 020 8997 0210. *'Always excellent. My girlfriend is veggy and she gives it a thumbs up too and it is very friendly.'* JR.

London W6

INDIAN ZING BEST UK
AUTHENTIC REGIONAL INDIAN CUISINE
236 King Street, W6 0RF
020 8748 5959 www.indianzing.co.uk

Manoj Vasaikar wanted to pilot Indian Air Force jets but he failed the tests and catering college was close to his Mumbai home and there he discovered he had talent as a chef. He cut his teeth at Taj and Oberoi Hotel's celebrated Kandahar restaurant. In 1990 the Panjabi sisters were head-hunting chefs for their upcoming venture, Chutney Mary. Manoj became a chef de partie there, working his way up to head chef at Veeraswamy. *'I learnt a lot from the two sisters'*, admits Manoj *'they are very astute in the intricacies of spicing and selecting quality ingredients.'* After a decade, like so many other Indian chefs, Manoj decided to branch out on his own opening – India 2000 in Esher, Surrey, it didn't last, nor did his other venture which followed in 2002 – Just India, SW14. He opened Indian Zing in 2005, and it too nearly folded. But the seeds were sown, and public and critics alike loved his style. *'For the first three months of opening'*, states Manoj, *'I was losing money and almost regretted launching another restaurant. But then the reviews started to come out and I was bowled over, not only by them, but also the public reaction. I was just getting packed out and that's still happens'* So booking is advisable. Indian Zing is comfortable, simple and elegant. The food, whilst being inventive, fresh and healthy, strictly has its roots in classical Indian cuisine. *'Im a great believer in taking ingredients from anywhere and using them for Indian cooking,'* says Manoj. *'I don't think there should be any barriers so long as the strength of the saucing and the right balance of spicing are there in the food. I also like talking to customers and gradually take my restaurant to a new level each year.'* You start with a free amuse-bouche which in our case was roast pumpkin, swede and parsnip rasam. For starters you can tTry melt-in-the-mouth green peppercorn Malai Tikka with cheese, £7.25, or Vasaikar's signature Vegetable Bhanvala, £5.75, a flat bhaji-style snack of onion and spices baked and then griddled. Mains include Lobster

Manoj shows off his Lobster Balchao with Vegetable Foogath, Lemon and Ginger Rice topped with deep-fried dry red chillies.

Balchao, £22.00, Lobster tails seared with a full flavoured hot sauce and balanced with Goan jaggery and spices. An all time Goan favourite; Chicken Miravna, £9, a dish from the earliest Mumbai settlers (The PatharePrabhu) using natural green fresh herbs and spices; Khyber-Pass Raan £11.50, made with lamb shank, poppy seeds, ginger, onion and spices; Tandoori Artichoke and Paneer, £12.50 in a cashewnut and tomato sauce; Ghatti Lamb, £9.75, from the Sahyadri Ranges with herbs and black pepper; Nilgiri Lamb, £9.75, a hill station lamb curry, made using stone ground spices, coconut and fresh green herbs. *'I was taken by a business friend, therefore have no idea how much the meal cost, but what ever the cost it was worth it. This was Indian food of the highest quality and imagination. The decor is modern and elegant and the service is excellent and extremely friendly. Definitely service with a smile and helpful advice. We both started with scallops in Hirva Masala and it is almost impossible to describe just how sublime there were. The delicacy of flavours and the richness of the marinade were just stunning and although the remainder of my meal was superb this was definitely the highlight. My host followed with Jumbo Prawns in Pomegranate seeds and Dill and was most enthusiastic about this dish. My main course was Gymkhana Lamb Chops with were absolutely superb. Excellent quality lamb, very gently spiced with a superb smooth lamb gravy. We had basmati rice (my host) and mushroom rice, both of which had just the tight texture and we added some Baingan and Makai Bhartabrinjal as well as the Vegetable Bhanavia, which is Indian Zing's version of Onion Bhajia as side dishes and both were quite delicious. By now I was beyond a dessert but my host treated himself to the Tandoori Figs and Organic Muesli Crumble and was so impressed that he insisted I try a little and indeed it was quite delicious ... A truly excellent experience, well worth the journey - highly recommended.'* DRC. Most items have been on the menu from the start, showing that Indian Zing has all judged its customer's wishes correctly. Add great service and arelaxed atmosphere and it is somewhere I would visit for a light Indian lunch or for a relaxed evening with friends. 12.5 % serv ch. 12-2.30 & 6-1030. Branches: Indian Zilla Barnes, SW13 & Indian Zest, Sunbury Middx .See page 26.

POTLI TOP 100
319-321, King Street, Hammersmith, W6 9NH
020 8741 4328/ 020 8741 5321   www.potli.co.uk

The website listings magazine Londonist.com brought more than a smile to my face when they launched a series of restaurant reviews entitled 'Dining Beyond Zone 1'. (It's the innermost of nine tube fare zones). Most of the places in this Guide are beyond Zone 1. Most Londoners rarely venture into any zone which is devoid of concrete and as for north-of- Watford (Zone 8). Londoners are concrete dwellers and anything green and countryside is seriously to be avoided. Anyway, the Londonist's Ben Norum ventured into Zone 2, with the tongue in cheek comment *'who'd have known that a westbound District line service could take you so far east?'* He was of course referring to the rare atmosphere of Hammersmith's King Street with its multi-Asian choice of eateries, his target Potli. Jay Ghosh and Orissa-born Uttam Tripathy decided to set up a restaurant as chef and manager. The once highly rated Tandoori Nights premises was available. Despite the competition on this highly competitive street, and they chose to open there in 2011 with the unique name of Potli meaning 'small pouch'. The inside is cool (in both senses of the word). White walls are lined with green-backed banquette seating with scatter cushions above which are placed Indian paintings and Salvidor Dali-like face masks of beturbaned sages. Dark wood tables are surrounded by chairs with alternate red and green squabs. After sunset a series of attractive hanging ceiling lights spill their own colours into the room. Jay and Uttam use the strap line *'an Indian market kitchen'*, not just to emphasise the freshness of their produce, but in a clever unique way, of which more later. The menu offers some 22 pan Indian main course dishes, dishes, with twelve Non Vegetarian Curries such as Goan Prawn Balchao £9.50, flavoured with vinegar, clove, chillies and pepper. Prawn Narkel Diye £9.50, cooked Bengali style in coconut water milk flavoured with mustard paste and fresh coriander. Chooza Khas Makhani £8, a Delhi favourite is tender pieces of char grilled chicken tikka in a creamy fenugreek flavoured tomato sauce. Yes, it's butter chicken or CTM with a fancy name. *'It's absolutely divine. If only my local curry houses made it like that'*. RCF. Hiran Laal Maas £19, a spicy Rajasthani national dish, here with venison haunch simmered in an aromatic chilli yogurt sauce. On-the-bone chicken £9.50 or mutton curry £8.50 is rarely found and is one reason you may well find Indian clientele loving it. Eight vegetable curries include some beauties at two price points, side or main. For example Mirchi ka Salan £4.50 or £6.50 is a Hyderabadi signature dish of mild chillies cooked in a gravy of coconut, peanut and yoghurt with curry leaves. Desserts include Shrikhand, yogurt flavoured with saffron, pistachio and green cardamom and Mango Crème Brulée with a caramel top, both £4.50. *'We felt spoilt for choice, so we left it to them, and everything was divine'*, JGS. So what's unique? It's their spin on their starters which they divide regionally into six street market areas. OK it's spin, but it's fun too and it's fairly accurate. Chowpatty: Mumbai's famous beach noted for its night time street food kiosks, eg: Bhel £3. Chandni Chowk: once the Mughal emperors' Oxford Street, meaning moonlit square, now known for the best street food in Delhi eg: Piazi (onion bhajee) £4.25; Samosa & Chickpea Masala £4.50; Methi Gota £4.25, fresh baby fenugreek leaves fried in a seasoned batter; Chicken 65, £6.25 originated in Chennai in 1965, a kind of Kentucky Chicken here coated in a gram flour batter spiced with crushed black pepper and fried curry leaves. Chowrenghee Lane: Calcutta's roadside kiosks serving items such as Aloo Tikki with Chole £4.25, potato cakes served on a with chickpea masala. Pather ke Gosht £7.50, piccata escalope of lamb double marinated and slowly cooked on top of limestone. Aminabad, Lucknow: the Old town's market, famous since the Nawab ruler's love of kebabs and Tandoori dishes. Potli's from £6.50. Charminar Market: at old Hyderabad's old four tower building is the home of Nizami cuisine with biryani and delicious kebabs , Potli's from £5.50. Fountain Chowk, Ludhiana: the Punjab's largest city serves baked-to-order breads. Potli's Naan £2; Stuffed Tawa Paratha (wholemeal) £2.50. Barely a year old, Potli deserves to become a national treasure. Set lunch from under a fiver (wraps), 1-course curry lunch, £6, 2-course, £9. Served in under 30 minutes. Service charge of 12.5%.   Mon-Sat: 12-2.45 & 6-10.30 (Sat to 11). Sun: 12-10.30.

SAGAR KERELAN (UDIPI) VEGETARIAN TOP 100
157 King Street, Hammersmith, W6 9JT
020 8741 8563   www.sagarveg.co.uk

It is a pleasure to see the first South Indian in Hammersmith thriving. And you can tell it is because it is now open all day. Sagar and the other 'new' boys on the street are a pointer to the way things are heading. The public are tiring of formulaic curryhouse food and once they taste the real thing, there is no going back.

SPLENDIDLY INDIAN, SUPERBLY SMOOTH

There are two pavement tables on the outside dark wood frontage. By contrast Sagar's interior is modern with pale floor tiles and furnishings, featuring a modern spiral staircase to a similarly decorated upper floor. The pale walls have the right amount of south Indian knickknacks inset. Owner S Sharmielan cooks food from Udipi, a small coastal town, north of Mangalore in the south-western state of Karnataka, celebrated for Bramin temples and cuisine. Masala Dosa originated here. By the sixth century AD, they were being made as temple feedings for thousands of worshippers. Udipi dosas are made from a thin batter cooked very thin and crisp in Karnataka and thick and small in Tamil Nadu. Also on the menu are Rasam, Sambar, Uppuma, Uthappam ranging in price from £3.45 to £6.45. And if it intrigues you, try the accompaniment Mulaga Podi (gun powder} a combination of lentils ground together with spices and served with ghee, £1.55. Curries range from £3.75 to £5.45 and include Kootu, a typical Madrassi dish as found in the local homes, where it is slow-cooked in a mud pot over wood fire. It's a hot and sour curry, containing gourd, chilli, tamarind, sesame and coconut. Traditionally it's served with Kazhani meaning 'rice-washed water'. Kootu is traditionally served with it. Try Bakabhat, a yoghurt-based rice, or Lemon rice, with cashews and curry leaves. The menu is a glossary in itself. Two temple puddings traditionally served to the public (by the thousands) at festival time are Payasam, made with vermicelli, sugar, condensed milk and cashews and Sheer, a wheat-based pudding with ghee, raisins and nuts. The staff are ever-helpful if you need menu translations. Hours: 12-11. (to 10 Sun) *Branch: Sagar, 17A Percy Street, Off Tottenham Court Rd, W1T 1DU 020 7631 3319. Sagar, 31 Catherine St, Covent Garden, WC2B 5JS 020 7836 6377.*

Pictured above: a huge Sagar Dosa, is it the world's largest? Below: a Thali with a Dosa and right, Popadom. On the side plate: Potato Bonda with coconut chutneys.

SHILPA KERELAN NON VEG
206 King Street, W6 0RA
020 8741 3127   www.shilparestaurant.co.uk

2006 saw Jay Nambiar open the second south Indian opening on this well endowed street. He engaged Chef Sunny Kuttan ex Taj group and Biju Monbillai. It is part of the Kerela Group see below. *'The menu is mostly Keralan, with a few token north Indian dishes – quite why chicken tikka masala was felt to be necessary is beyond me.*
 The room is a fairly narrow rectangle, with one set of tables on each side. Decor is a little eccentric, with sparkly blue lights and a couple of plasma screens showing Bollywood films.' AH. AndyHayler.com See Radha Bhavan Krishna SW17. 12-3 & 6.-11 (Thu-Sat: to 12).

YOU SAY OK, Hammersmith, W6
AKASH TANDOORI 177 King Street, W6 9JT 020 8748 4567
ANARKALI 303-305 King Street, W6 9NH 020 8748 1760
CHARCOALS 286 King Street, W6 0SP 020 8563 2233
HAWELI 357 King Street, W6 9NH 020 8748 7408. *'Excellent. Friendly staff, fronted by ebullient owner. Lamb Kalia £6.95 - brilliant, light sauce, almost Thai-style, loads of spring onions, ginger, garlic, suffusion of tender pieces of lamb with oodles of taste. Chum Chum Chicken £4.95, marinated chicken breast, stuffed with special chutney, barbecued in tandoor. Great glass of Lassi too!'* RW.
LIGHT OF NEPAL 268 King Street, W6 020 8748 3586. Est 1979 by Jaya K Tamang & KC Druba with mostly curryhouse favourite items. Hours: 12-2.30/6-11.
W6: RAFIQUES 291 King St, London, W6 9NH 020 8748 7340
NEW MAHARAJA 10 Greyhound Rd, W6 8NX 020 7385 4521
RAJ OF INDIA 46 Shepherds Bush Rd, W6 7PJ 020 7602 9112
RAJPUT 144 Goldhawk Road, W12 8HJ 020 8740 9036

London W7

AFGHAN KHAYBER BYO
205 Uxbridge Rd, Hanwell W7 3TH 020 8579 5111

We include Afghan because it is a deriviative of Indian food. But is is quite different, and not to everyone's liking. The small menu contains items like Aushak steamed scallion dumplings topped with yogurt-mint sauce; with or without meat sauce, Baunjaun Bouranee eggplant slices layered over mint yogurt; vegetarian or with meat sauce. Skewered charcoal-grilled meat (Halal) items such as Chelow Kebab-E-Barg £9.50, lamb fillet, served with basmati rice and grilled tomato. They take no credit/debit cards, but unlic, allow BYO.

BAWARCHI
102 Uxbridge Rd, Hanwell, W7 3SU
020 8567 8013   www.bawarchi-restaurant.com

Regular menu with specials. Bawarchi Special Potatoes, Chefs Special Masala, Ginger Chicken and Bawarchi King Prawn Special to name a few in his time at Bawarchi. Tu-Sun: 12-2.30 & 6-11:30. Closed Mon.

London W8

MALABAR NORTHERN INDIAN
27 Uxbridge Street, Notting Hill, W8 7TQ
020 7727 8800   www.malabar-restaurant.co.uk

Jo, Sophie and Tony Chalmers' and Anil Bis's three-floor 56-seat Malabar has quietly gone about its business since 1983. and it is a Notting Hill fixture, largely enjoyed by its clutch of locals. For necomers, the team want you to know it is located behind the Coronet CinemaIt is not expensive, and the care is comfortable and assured, from the cooking to the service. Despite its name, it has nothing to so with south India. It's distincly northern. Chilli Bhutta starter £4.70, sweet corn kernels mixed with fresh gree chillies and green pepper, is unusual. Murgh Makhni, butter chicken, Gosht Masala – plenty of fresh mint, both c£9, and delicious. Five Lentil Dhal £5. *'A likeable restaurant with food quite different in spicing and presentation. I wish this were in my home town, Berlin.'* BH. Sunday buffet lunch £12 with variety of curries and tandoori dishes, the Sunday papers and the kids eat for free. Mon-Sat; 1-2.45 & 6.30-11.30 Sun.

UTSAV
17 Kensington High St, W8 5NP   020 7368 0022

Entrepreneur owner of Malabar Junction, WC2, Ashok Modi launched Utsav, meaning 'festival' in 2003. It has 150 seats on two floors, almost opposite the Royal Garden Hotel. Architects Astore Harrison designed contemporary decor, outside (striking glass and blues, and a cute use of the first floor bay window. Inside an attractive wooden bar, white walls, creative lighting, theming blues and blondes. The food by chef Gowtham Karingi, ex Zaika sous chef (see next entry) is pan-Asian, a bit from here and a bit from there. Ok if the chefs understand regional spicing immaculately, and that they can get difficult ingredients. We felt perhaps the Goan Prawn Balchao lacked that sourness only achieved from toddy vinegar, while Kashmiri chilli would have helped the Roghanjosh. And there were too many squiggly dots and squirls (a Ziaka trick, passée in our opinion). That said, the Tirangi Chicken Tikka, marinated in saffron, cheese and coriander, was masterly. The Chicken Varutha in tamarind, red chilli, shallots, curry leaves & tomato sauce had spot on south Indian tastes, as did the fine Dosa and chutneys. The Paneer was fresh and juicy. Service charge 12.5%. Daily: 11.30-3 & 6-11 Mon - Thurs; 11.30 Fri & Sat; 10.30 Sunday.

ZAIKA FINE MODERN INDIAN   A-LIST
1 Kensington High Street, W8
020 7795 6533   www.zaika-restaurant.co.uk

Zaika translates quite literally as sophisticated flavours. This was the first Indian venture (with Vineet) for Claudio Pulze and Raj Sharma (owners of SW1's celebrated Al Duca and Fiore Italian restaurants). Under

SPLENDIDLY INDIAN, SUPERBLY SMOOTH

General Manager Luigi Gaudino it is in a former bank, which bestows on it carved high ceilings and double height windows, with their crimson swag curtains. The interior is elegant with ivory and buff paint scheme and wood panelling. Seats have various coloured backs. Delhi-born Sanjay Dwivedi is probably the brightest star to have qualified as a chef via the celebrated Ealing's Thames Valley Catering College's Asian course. At first he practised his continental skills, but his Indian roots soon came to the fore and he joined Zaika when it first opened in 1999 as Vineet's deputy. becoming head chef when Vineet departed to open his own venue (Rasoi Vineet Bhatia). Head Barman Davide Farchica residing in his 'Bedouin-style' 25-seat cocktail bar has cocktails from £9 to £40 and if you think that's expensive, how about the Louis Roederer "Cristal" 1989 champagne at £700.00, Starters include: Talawa Kedka £11.50, soft shell crab dusted with onion seeds, smoked chilli and mustard seed jam, black salt & tamarind mayonnaise & salad; Subzi Ki Vinyaas, £8.75, medley of grilled aubergine steak, vegetable samosa, tandoori broccoli flavoured with paprika; Khargosh Tikka, £9.75, Tandoori Rabbitmarinated in fennel seeds & whole grain mustard, 'San Marzano' tomatoes, rabbit juices & olive oil. Mains incude Samundari Machl, £26, monkfish marinated in red chillies and garlic, fired in the tandoor, accompanied with cauliflower rice, sun-dried cauliflower, shellfish emulsion, & cocoa powder; Murghabi Mussalam, £19.50, breast of duck, garlic & chilli mash, crispy ladies fingers, duck juices infused with cloves & black cardamom; Tandoori Titar, £17.50, Tandoori Guinea fowl, marinated in mustard seeds and curry leaves, withsmoked aubergine mash, guinea fowl jus, fresh fennel salad; Tandoori Murg Makhanwala, £17.50, [CTM] corn fed breast & off the bone leg, gently poached in a buttery tomato sauce flavoured with fenugreek, cumin tempered spinach, pulao rice.' *I have for some time had my eye on the Jugalbandi Vegetarian Tasting Menu, my colleague choosing the omnivorous 6-course Jugalbandi Tasting Menu (both £47 per head) My colleague was equally complimentary about the omnivorous menu by the way. Suffice to say the food at Zaika that is the real star of the show. Zaika was excellent in pretty much every way and certainly worthy of the many accolades it has received since it opened.'* AG. A la Carte menu prices range from £7.50 to £12.95 for starters and £15 to £19.50 for main courses. Should diners wish to sample a broad scope of cuisine the six-course 'Jugalbandi' menu is available at £47.00 or alternatively why not treating yourself with a journey into the nine-course Gourmet menu at £62.00. Dwivedi's continental hand and his time with Vineet shows through with flavours and ingredients which are not Indian. Ingredients such as rosemary, basil and olive oil are distinctively European and do not sit easily on my Indian palette. That said Zaika is a well-oiled, competent venue, usefully placed for the Royal Lancaster Hotel and Albert Hall. If you're going there, the Swadwala Menu available between 6 & 7pm is £22.50 for 2 course &£27 for 3. Lunch 1 course, £12, 2 £18.50, 3 £22.50. Service 12.5%. Sun-Fri: 12-2.45 & Mon-Sat: 6.30-10.45 to 9.45 Sun.

London W11

CHAKRA ROYAL INDIAN FINE DINING
157-159 Notting Hill Gate, W11 3LF
020 7229 2115   www.chakralondon.com   **A-LIST**

Brothers Arjun and Andy Varma are an institution on the London Indian restaurant scene. Recently, they've had a few turbulent years with failed partnerships through no fault of their own. After the success of Chelsea's Vama they have once more teamed up with Shomit Basu, this time in trendy Notting Hill. We wish them every success and the permanency they deserve. Chakra means vortex or spinning wheel. The logo depicts this. Designer and A-List Club owner, Dezzi McCausland (Kingly Club) has come up with an original design evolving from his use of Chesterfield buttoned leather sofas and walls at his City venue McQueen. From the street, Chakra's large plate glass windows with white Venetian blinds offer a view inside. White is the theme, Chipperfield and Chesterfield, the latter as white buttoned leather padded wall cladding echoed by similar banquets along the walls and comfortable white leather armchairs at the tables. Roof lanterns let in daylight and it's warm gold lighting at night. The inner room is similarly attired though in contrasting dark mahogany walling and armchairs with a wall to wall mirror adding depth and wall to celing dark leather cydinders cladding the end wall. Flooring is varnished mahogany wood.

Taimur Khan is G.M leading a front of house team of twelve *"enhanced by long legged, high heeled pretty gals in short cerise dresses"* HEG. Menu Snapshot: Yam Chaat, £8.50, salad with roasted cumin & lemon-flavoured sweet potato (Jimikand) drizzled with tamarind chutney; Curry Patta Burrata, £12.50, dusted with a special spice blend with curry leaves, tempered cherry tomatoes & grilled aubergine. From the Chulha or char-grill: Patiala Chaap £16.50, English lamb chops cured in a garam masala & lemon yoghurt marinade with a hint of cardamom; Venison Kakori £15.50, a Royal hunt special with venison mince imbued with specially roasted masala & grilled, both favourites from the Royal Kitchen of Maharaja Bhupinder Singh of Patiala; Jaipur Seekh £12.50, star anise and fenugreek-flavoured courgette mince vegetarian seekh served with sweet tomato chilli chutney. From the Griddle Tava or flat frying pan: Garlic Scallops £16.50, roasted with carom & garlic chilli; Lucknow Plate £10.50, a vegetarian delight of delicately spiced lentil & mint kebab, red kidney bean mince patty & spinach & nutmeg kebab, served with coriander chutney; Tava Machli £12.50, carom-flavoured tilapia fish sautéed with leeks, spring onions & roasted garlic; Chakra Black Cod £26.50, marinated with lime juice , cracked pepper and yoghurt, roasted in the tandoor; Murgabi Tandoori £18.50, smoked Gressingham duck breast tenderised with papaya,& marinated with robust spices grilled in the tandoor; Roasted Quail £17.50, crushed chickpea flour-coated roasted quail marinated in a chilli& onion paste, smoked in the tandoor; Jalandhar Chicken £14.50, Chakra's version of the Punjab classic.– tandoor grilled chicken simmered in a fine tomato & cream masala [CTM really!]; Garlic Pepper Kekra £16.50, crispy coriander & chilli marinated soft shell crab with a garlic pepper cream sauce. From the Veg Pan: Crispy Okra £9.50, Rajhasthani-style sprinkled with dry mango powder & roasted carom seeds; Palak Paneer £9.50, fresh nutmeg-flavoured spinach & home-made paneer cheese flavoured with ginger. Try the weekend lunch menu, eat as much as you like for £16.95 (under 12s £8.95). Of the puddingd, Shahi Tukra with Berries and Rabri is by far the best choice. Wines start at £24 to £92 for 2005 Château Gruard Larose. Disc Serv charge 12.5%. Sat-Sun:12-3; Mon-Sat: 6-11 (Sun -10:30)

LONDON WC

Area: West End
Postcodes WC1, WC2

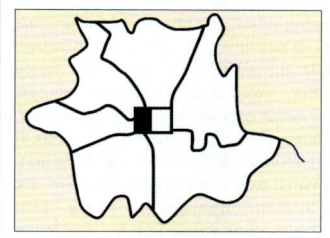

See page 88 for key to this map

London WCI

HASON RAJA   A-LIST
84 Southampton Row, Holborn, WC1B 4BB
020 7242 3377   www.hasonraja.co.uk

Hason Raja stands out on Southampton Row, despite its comparatively small plate glass window frontage. A comfortable waiting area greets you with a substantial purple and cream striped sofa, with matching arm chairs and a wonderfully grand portrait of the restaurant's namesake, the mystical Hason Raja a 19th century Bangladeshi poet-playboy who led a life full of drama, colour and romance. The bar is well organised with sparkling crystal reflecting on the mirrored wall and glass shelving. It is also well stocked, with spirits, wines and Kingfisher on draught. The main dining room is on the ground floor and seats 70 diners. It is stylishly decorated with white walls, white table linen and pretty, bright turquoise suede chairs. There are two further dining areas downstairs. The restaurant is run by the owner's two sons, Nurul and Ruhul Noor, who despite having degrees in mathematics and business studies respectively, have decided to manage and run the family business. Chef Prasun Saha is from Calcutta and has worked at the celebrated Oberoi. Sadly, some of the unusual items they used to offer have gone including

London W13

LAGUNA   TOP 100
1-4 Culmington Pde, 123 Uxbridge Rd, West Ealing, W13   020 8579 9992

You cannot miss the huge frontage, decorated with individually planted conifers in square wooden tubs. And you should not miss going in to this 120-seater restaurant with its stylishly decorations in pastel shades, with arches and ceiling fans. Established in 1984 by Sunil Lamba, (with relations to London's Gaylord) and it's been in this Guide since then, serving competent north Indian formula food. It's built up a large local following, and in its time it's seen so many new Indian restaurants come and go in Ealing, and even now it stands out above the 25 or so competitors, a chupatti-throw away. Laguna Special Butter Chicken £5.95 is the most popular dish. Service 10%. Sun. 12-12. www.lagunarestaurant.com Branch: Mr Lamba is proud of his outside catering department, and what a party with a difference it will make when you use the service. at Laguna Banquet Hall, North Acton Road, NW10.

MONTY'S TANDOORI   NEPALESE   TOP 100
54 Northfields Avenue, W13   020 8567 6281

First opened in 1980 and seats 64 diners. Menu Snapshot: Aloo Chat, Spicy Potatoes £3.50; Lamb Chop, Charcoal grilled (3 pieces) £4.50; Lamb Chop HOT, five pieces of lamb on the bone cooked in a dry fry sauce, green chilli £8.90; Chicken Safarkan, with mild sauce with peas and minced lamb £10.75; Chicken Shajani Masala - Chicken breast cooked with spring onions and thick sauce £10.90; Kathmandu Dal Chicken/Lamb, cooked with a mixture of lentils, ginger, onions, tomato and jeera spices £8.50; Moglai Dal, Black and yellow lentils, spinach & egg £5.95. Home Del: 2 miles, £20 min.12-3 & 6 -12. *Branch: Monty's W5. (and more menu details).*

the unique Goose Ki Parchy. What remains is formula items, but look carefully and you will be rewarded with such specials as Tandoori Phool, £4.25, fresh broccoli lightly marinated with cheese & cracked peppers, then tandoor-grilled; Malai Kofta, £9.95, vegetable dumplings containing potatoes, sultanas, pistachio nuts and cashew nuts, served in a rich, mild, creamy sauce; Chicken Chasnidargh, £10.95, in a unique sauce consisting of honey, fresh lime & balsamic vinegar giving a distinctive sweet yet sour flavour; Fish Kasundi, £12.95, Tilapia fillets cooked in green paste of fresh ground black mustard seeds & coriander; Lamb Paslion, £14.95, rack marinated with whole spices, grilled in clay oven and served in a saffron sauce; Top of the bill is Lobster Adraki, £24.95, fresh whole Lobster steamed in a creamy ginger & celery sauce. Nominated as Best UK Bangladeshi restaurant by this Guide. Lunch: from £6 to £12. Hours:12-11.30.

MALABAR JUNCTION   KERELAN   TOP 100
107 Great Russell Street, WC1 3NA
020 7580 5230   www.keralagroup.co.uk

Along from the British Museum is this light, bright and airy restaurant with Victorian-styled glass skylight giving good light, bamboo chairs, palm trees in polished brass pots, original paintings, a marble fountain. The bar and further dining facilities are downstairs. Owned by Ashok Modi it specialises in Keralan cuisine was described as Britain's first up-market south Indian. Its prices reflect this and its location. Masala Dosa, for example is £8.50, double that of its Tooting sister. (It's now part of the Kerela Group (see Rhada Krishna Bhavan, London SW17). That siad, it is still reasonably priced. It has extended its menu to include Tandoori items and formula curries (because that's what you order, so I'm told). What we say is order the Kerelan items. That's what they do best. If you are new to it, the smiling Keralan waiters will explain the menu. They will tell you that meat and chicken is eaten by most of the population in south India; but being expensive, it's mainly on festivals and weddings, and that fish is loved on the coastal and river districts. There are a number Kerelan starters eg, several Dosa, Uthappam £8.50, Iddly £5, Cashew Nut Pakora, £5, cashew Nuts dipped in spicy gram and rice flour batter mixed with ginger and green chilli and deep fried, Vada £5, Garlic Mogo £6, cassava (Tapioca) marinated in turmeric and tossed with ginger, garlic and herbs into a dry serving. Chilli Paneer £7.50, cubes of homemade cheese cooked with onions, capsicum, tomato, curry leaves, chilli sauce, soya sauce in a very dry preparation; Fish Fry £10.95, whole Pomfret marinated in a special masala and deep fried; King Prawn Poriyal £10.95, fried and tossed in brown sliced onions and a lightly spiced Masala; Spicy Lamb Chilli Fry £9, pieces of lamb marinated in spices cooked and fried with black pepper, onions, tomatoes, curry leaves and coriander. Interesting Mains include:

Chicken Malabar, £10.95, cooked with spices, tomatoes, and fresh Coconut milk and curry leaves; Kozhi Varutha Curry, £10.95, chicken breast marinated in spices and made in to a curry with coconut milk; Kerala Mutton Curry, £10.95, cooked with turmeric, coriander, chillies and a hint of black pepper; Cabbage Thoran, £6.50, cooked with onions, fresh coconut, fresh coriander, Green chili, and mustard seeds- dry preparation. And if you have any room left Banana Leaf Cake £5, rice with sweet filling of coconut, banana and jaggery wrapped in banana leaf and steamed – divine. *'We love this place so after a visit to the British museum, we couldn't wait for lunch there. But we found a dullness in the food, a lack of love in it, which disappointed. Bad day; bad time or what?'* DBAC. Restaurant: 12-3 & 6-11.30.

RASA MARICHAM   KERELAN   TOP 100
1 Kings Cross Road, WC1 9HX
0871 0757217   www.rasarestaurants.com

Located in the 405-room Holiday Inn is, of all things a 160-seater Kerelan restaurant and it's part of the Rasa restaurant group (See N16 and W1). Maricham means black pepper, and pepper, particularly Keralan pepper is India's king of spices and her biggest spice export. This major spice was the heat-giver before chillies arrived from Brazil in the 16th century. Keralan food had been developed centuries before Christ, and pepper was and still is a big player in recipes. Take Mulligatawny. It literally means 'pepper water'. Das's spin told us that the menu would be 'showcasing' black pepper'. Pepper, the menu tells *'is used to cure digestive problems such as wind, constipation, nausea and diarrhoea.'* Hmm! Just what we need to read before eating. But if it hasn't got you on the run (to the exit), stay. The venue lacks atmosphere, reminding one of many an Indian hotel restaurant, which would not matter except for the fact that the food, in gargantuan portions, on the evening we went was just ordinary, as if the chefs are just going through the motions, though inexpensive at £50 inc wine for 2. Vegetarian Feast (per head), £17.50, veg starters, curry selection, side dish, rice, bread and a traditional Keralan rice pudding. Maricham Feast, £22.50, non-veg starters, veg curry selection, side dish, rice, bread and a Keralan rice pudding. Reports please. Service: 12.5%. Hours: 6-10.30. *Branches and menu details: See Rasa London N16.*

COBRA

SPLENDIDLY INDIAN, SUPERBLY SMOOTH

London WC2

DISHOOM PARSEE & STREET FOOD
2 Upper St. Martin's Lane, WC2H 9FB   **TOP 100**
020 7420 9320   www.dishoom.com

Once upon a time in far distant Bombay, there were hundreds of cafés opened early last century by Parsees. At their peak in the 1960s there were almost 400. Now, fewer than fifteen remain. Your editors have been to one or two, Leopold's and the 90-year-old Parsee Britannia Restaurant in Mumbai's Colaba and Ballard Estate.

Mumbai's hubby, but packed Britannia Restaurant with its 90 year old owner pointing to his picture of QEII. Note the writing in the background, enlarged below and copied by Dishoom. Picture courtesy Britannia.

respectively and a similar venue in Calcutta. On our first such occasion our friend said it was *'a great place to people watch.'* He was right; *'spy with chai'*, he called it. The cafés are a dying breed of faded elegance and memories. Yet the few that remain are heaving with custom, often located in large, high ceilinged rooms with round dark wood tables, surrounded by Bentwood cane chairs. The ceilings are decorated in ornate plaster work in desperate need of repainting, and huge colonial fans, turn slowly with disapproving croaks and alarming wobbles, having absolutely no effect in cooling the room. "*stained mirrors hang next to sepia family portraits; students had breakfast; families dined; lawyers read briefs;*

writers wrote. Each café wallows in faded sophistication." So say three brothers who have opened a so-called Bombay Café in London calling it Dishoom. *"We aren't trying to recreate faded elegance"*, they declare. What they have created is tasteful decor; clean paintwork, working fans, oak floor boards, and optical illusion cube linoleum [Necker cubes], sepia prints, 'Indian' paraphernalia and a great atmosphere on two floors, ground and basement each floor with a bar and room for 100 diners. A sense of humour abounds. The owners describe the spaghetti trail of overhead lighting cables as *'playfully drooping'*. Note the replica station clock and do find the house rules copied form the Britannia by the entrance. *"no talking to the cashier", "No discussing gambling", "No talking loud"," No telephone"*, displayed for fun not enforcement judging by the number of mobiles being texted and tweeted. The list continues with *"No fighting"* (Dishoom's name incidentally means the sound of a large fist punch.) They could add *'no bookings'* to the rules because you can't. As for *"no credit"*, you bet they do take credit cards, and re *"no change,"* they do give change though they are not adverse to it being given as a tip, and they are licensed. Being just one of two London venues where you can get an Indian breakfast expectations ran high. But it was disappointing on the day I visited: stained A5-size paper menu, slightly sticky table, one manager 3 waitresses, attentive but with a customer: staff ratio of 2:1 they should be. Newspapers good idea, but no hot towels offered to clean up sticky fingers blackened from newsprint; orange juice not freshly squeezed. Chilli omelette, £5.90 was cold, 6 cherry toms on the vine were piping hot; plate too small and cold; toast warm but no marmalade available. Musac irritating. Avoided the Bombay Sausages Nan Roll (or the bacon variety), £3.70, but others seem to enjoy them. One item on the main menu is unique – Chicken Berry Biryani, £7.50, cooked in a pot sealed with atta dough and opened on the table in front of you. Pictured right, its USP is dark red, tart and sweet tasting dried barberries or Persian zereshk. The original ,an Indianised version of the Iranian Zereshk Polow, was invented 50 years ago by the Parsee owner of of the Britannia. It's the only place in India that you'll find it and Bombayites in the know squash into the Brit two or three times a week just for that dish alone. At 250 rupees (£3.50) it is a bargain And now, unique to GB, here it is at Dishoom, and it is a must. *"There are many photographs of the owner's family. It reminded me*

DISHHOOM, CONTINUED: *of a French brasserie. The restaurant was full and the noise level very high, but superb atmosphere. The whole place is very casual and the menu very different - no curries! Wine is served in chunky water glasses and food served tapas style, with plates and cutlery piled in the centre of the table. Dishes arrived at different times and were all absolutely wonderful. We also ate Desi Fish Fingers £3.90; Dishoom Calimari £4.50 - with zesty lime and chilli; Pau Bhajia £3.90 - mashed veg with hot buttered bread, Chowpatty Beach style; Spicy Lamb Chops £7.20 - rubbed with crushed black pepper and chillies; Dill Salmon Tikka £8.50 - with lemon zest and light spices; Grilled Masala Prawn £8.90 - with lime, tomato and fresh coriander; Grilled Vegetables £6.50 - peppers, red onions, portobello mushrooms and aubergine with a tangy dressing; Plain Naan £1.70 - fresh from the tandoor with/out butter, the Naan was the thinnest and crispest I have ever had. Wraps are made with Romali roti, the thinnest of white flour flat bread."* HRC. 8am-11pm.

INDIA CLUB   A-LIST
143 The Strand, WC2R 1JA
020 7836 0650   www.strand-continental.co.uk

The India Club is the second oldest Indian restaurant in Britain. It opened in 1946 and management is proud of the fact that they have hardly changed a thing since. *'Hidden up a flight of stairs, India Club is one of London's best kept secrets. Enter a timewarp, with portraits of the Independence era on the walls, bottle-green leather chairs, red lino flooring and wooden laminate tabletops. It is a British curry house of the first generation. Authentic 'home cooked' South Indian cuisine at extraordinary value makes India Club an unforgettable dining experience.'* So says the India club on its website. To find it turn right from Waterloo Bridge onto the Strand and between two shops, you will notice a door-width entrance with a gold on black sign, saying 'India Restaurant and Hotel'. Look up at the upper floors and you'll see the sign 'Hotel Strand Continental.' To set the scene there's conspicuous wealth on show all around. The iconic 260 room Savoy hotel down the road has just spent £220m on a refit. Nearby Dishoom, one of the newest arrivals on the Indian scene, spent a cool £2m to create a mock shabby India, a manufactured image of 'faded Indian café', trendy enough to make it a darling of the media and the 20 somethings. Decor is not an issue at IC. Nor is

helpful signage. There are no frills, and if tourists, fledgling journalists and newcomers are put off by the Tardis-like entrance and no idea about what lies up that flight of stairs, tough. In IC's own words it was *'originally established as a members'-only club with bedrooms, a bar and a dining room by Krishna Menon, India's first High Commissioner to the UK, with founding members including Pandit Nehru, Lady Mountbatten and Indian diplomats from the new High Commission. In 1947, India independence took place, and over 60 years later, little has changed. With features untouched by time, and portraits of Gandhi and Dadabhai Naoroji adorning the walls of the restaurant, it is easy to mistake that you are back in 1940's India. The modern world has passed India Club by, and we now invite you to experience this miracle of steadfastness. With its rich history and faded colonial atmosphere, the charmingly eccentric India Club Restaurant has become something of an institution.'* What did change was the decline in membership. Rather than close IC became a 26 room hotel with bar and restaurant, open to all. Today's customers are a mix of Indians (including generations from the High Commission on a 3 year posting) and white aficionados, devotees of real Indian food.

Enter through the narrow door, noting a lack of menu. Climb the stairs. On the first floor is the hotel reception. Note the b & b room tariff: at singles £50 and doubles £70 it's cheaper than many Delhi hotels. Proceed up to the second floor. In front of you is the door to the L-shaped restaurant. In fact it did undertake a refurb a few years back, but it was hardly more than some new light fittings and a lick of paint *'Hadn't been here since the redecoration – phew, what a lurid yellow the walls are now. Everything else unchanged – menu is the same, still good value, service still efficient.'* HC. *'Not sure about the repainted walls, glad about the retained pictures and ancient stair carpet!'* GM. It still has a canteen feel about it. It's clean and functional. Table number disks are superglued to the tables ... this is no Michelin joint. Their inspectors would

SPLENDIDLY INDIAN, SUPERBLY SMOOTH

need counselling, if they made it past the first floor. It's friendly. The crew are all old hands. Waiters wear white tunics, Maurtania-style. Don't expect to be sychophantly ushered to a table. Just sit down, preferably at one of the tables opposite the large kitchen hatch; the chefs will wave at you, even if you don't wave at them. *'Some people will undoubtedly be put off by the funny decor and the almost stand-offish nature of the waiters. They don't keep you waiting for that long but don't go over the top in trying to please you either like they do in your average high street tandoori'* BB. If anyone is looking for fine dining and prices to match, thumping Garage music, or Dishoom-style manufactured decor, India Club is not for you. What you get is fabulous, uncompromisingly Indian food, served in unpretentious surroundings at super cheap prices. Head chef Puroshot-haman is from south India, and it's that food at which the kitchen surpasses. If it's curry house formula you want, then go somewhere else. The restaurant is unlicensed so you can BYO – no corkage. This is just one of IC's idiosyncrsities because *'on the first floor there is a well-stocked 'residents' bar. If you have neglected to BYO, and ask the waiters about booze, you're likely get a one-liner "downstairs sir" (or madam)'. So proceed downstairs to stock up from a 'cackling' bar maid'* HEG. The Daily Telegraph's Mathew Norman cites it rather neatly: *'perhaps the single most charming aspect of eating here is the question of drinks. The restaurant has no licence, so diners are encouraged to walk down a flight of stairs to the bar [inexplicably named] the Calcutta Rowing Club - presided over by Doris, the barmaid here for the past 42 years, and beginning to get the hang of pulling a pint. Before buying the Cobra beer, or whatever, according to Doris, it is technically necessary to obtain life membership by joining the Calcutta Rowing Club - something I have done eight times over the years (all I need is a cox and I'll be ready to race). The last time I joined a few years ago, life membership was £1. Now it is £4, so it was a relief when Doris turned a blind eye to the sign on the wall reading, proof of membership may be required.'* MN. She never issues any paperwork, or proof, nor a receipt. She welcomes a tip though, Ed. India Club, like India herself, is one big excentricity. It leads to some laughable comments by some junior restaurant critics. One claimed *'there is no hotel'*, another complained about *'dry Naans and disappointing Korma'*. A third was confused about the drinks routine. A fourth finds it *'apallingly downmarket'*. So, just for those who don't get it, let me spell it all out again. 1) It IS a hotel. 2) Don't buy the northern Indian food, it's never been their forté. 3) Their drinks operation is as unfathomable unless you're in the know. 4) Down market? Get a life. And don't even think of visiting India. Because that's what IC is; a little India in London. *'My husband takes visiting colleagues from India to the India Club for dinner and they say it is most authentic. They are also surprised that such a place exists in central London, a stone's throw from the Savoy.'* Demon Cook. *'What can you say about The India Club. Neither the ladies nor the gents had lights, there was still no Lassi (there never is!),* the chutney and onion salad were both served piled up in saucers, there was no attempt at presentation but the food was sublime and what value for money with the quantities just right.'* G&MP. *'Another good meal! Chilli Bhajis predictably hot. Prawn Pullao excellent and enormous portion, Masala Dosas delicious as ever. Still excellent, wonderful no-frills ambience, and still the same elderly lady in the bar to have a quick word with (she was a dolly bird when I first went there – I'm sure she's the same one!).'* [She is, Ed]. MW. *'Even better this time around! Chilli Bhajis are not for the faint-hearted, but then neither is the decor ... the waiters must keep the pictures deliberately crooked!! We were absolutely stuffed and still had food left over. – has to be a winner!'* AG. *'Hi, I would like to add some comments of my own which may be of interest to you and your readers. I first came across this restaurant in the early 1970s when I worked for the London offices of an Indian newspaper chain in Carmelite Street, London. The India Club was a regular haunt of the Indian journalists based in London and home to an institution called 'the India League' an organisation that promoted Indian business and cultural interests in Britain. I first dined there at a reception held for the Indian statesman Krishma Menon a contemporary of Jaharwal Nehru the first prime minister of Independent India. On crossing the threshold again in 2004 was just like being in a timewarp; everything seemed to be the same. No-one could ever remember a time when the lift was in use. It had worked once apparently but the management had forgotten to renew the guarantee and the parts were all out of date, even in the 1970s. Up the steps past the hotel reception desk. One hotel manager in the 1970s had installed his entire extended family in half of the rooms. It turned out he'd been fleecing the place for years before someone actually checked the books and sacked him. I peeked into the same bar and the same lounge and then walked up the same stairs to the same restaurant. The woman at the bar has to be called Doris and has been there since forever. There used to be a legendary eastern european woman called Christine who waited at tables in the restaurant. I first took my fiancée to eat there in the early 1980s and it hadn't changed in ten years and I suppose I had got used to the slow service and taken the luke warm food for granted but my fiancee was very keen on hot food and trying to impress her I asked Christine if she would mind heating it up a bit. Christine gave me a look of daggers and said 'I try' and emerged ten minutes later 'wiz warmed plates - okay is better? It made absolutely no difference of course. As you rightly say probably not the place to take someone you are trying to impress. It worked for me though as my fiancée became my wife and we have been married for 30 years.'* BB.

If you really want to know what a real Indian eating dive is like, this is it. Decor, presentation, smiling and saying please and thank you are not what matters. Cooking super food and getting your order to your table at affordable prices, is what matters. Not a Michelin-star formula (M's loss), so virtually devoid of posers. Despite its eccentricity, no because of it, the Indian Club decidedly remains high on our A-LIST. BYO no corkage charge. 12-2.30 & 6-10.50 (closed Sun). The last words, as always, go to PD: 'Long may the Club remain open.'

MASALA ZONE A-LIST
48 Floral Street, Covent Garden WC2E 9DA
020 7379 0101   www.masalazone.com

SSummer 2007 saw the launch of this branch located opposite the now-disused old stage door and tall scene-dock doors of the Royal Opera House. For aficionados of opera, ballet and decent Indian food, this branch cannot be better placed. In fact, we had a backstage tour of the House in the morning, popped in to Masala Zone for lunch and enjoyed all our usual Bombay Street snacks, went back to the House for a show and returned to Masala Zone in the evening for a Thali dinner before going home! It's a large restaurant, seating 200, but it doesn't feel like a barn, due to the clever location of the kitchen, which is in the middle of the main dining room. A bright and colourful display of Indian puppets hanging from the ceilings make for interesting decor, but I wouldn't like to have to dust them! There is a no booking policy, you just turn up, sit and eat. If it is full, you never have to wait long, as a table will become empty soon. We have only ever waited a maximum of 5 minutes. Items ordered arrive when they are ready, so your starter may arrive after your main. If that upsets you, (as it does some) order the starter only. When that arrives, order your main. Simple isn't it! *'Agree with all the comments about the concept, the convenience and the good standard of food. I did have to complain at one that my order seemed to have been overlooked - it was rustled up very quickly - I was impressed.'* MW. 12-11 (1230-1130 Sun). *For full menu description and list of branches, see Masala Zone, W1.*

MELA FINE PAN INDIAN TOP 100
152 Shaftesbury Av, WC2H 8HL
020 7836 8635   www.melarestaurant.co.uk

Kuldeep Singh, Sanjay Singh Sighat and Surinder Kumar Mehra (all Taj-trained chefs) opened Mela (meaning 'festival') in 2000. The restaurant is open all day but it changes atmosphere in the evening, becoming less hurried. Kuldeep says *"ingredients here in England are much better than back home. This is a chef's paradise."* And he proves it with dishes such as: Tiger prawns marinated in saffron, caraway seeds and coriander, £15. Lahsooni whitebait (marinated in garlic and caraway seeds, gram flour batter & fried), £5.95 Murg Malai Kebab (chicken supremes matured in a delicately spiced marinade, chargrilled), £12.95 Kheer (traditional Indian rice pudding with saffron & raisins), £3.25. Main courses £9 - £15. Set lunch £3 - £6. Set dinner – veg £15 non-veg – £18.50, Set meal (5.30-7pm, 10-11pm) £10.95, 3 courses. *'Mela is a lovely restaurant, with cheerful waiters, serving lovely Indian food.'* DBAC. This is echoed by HC: *'Charming and authoritative person in charge. Whole place was running well. Food, again outstandingly good, definitely a very good restaurant – amazing menu.'* HC. 12-11.30; 10.30pm Sunday. Branches: Chowki W1. Mela Redhill Surrey.

MOTI MAHAL FINE NORTH INDIAN
45 Great Queen Street, WC2   A-LIST
020 7240 9329   www.motimahal-uk.com

London's Moti Mahal (Pearl Palace) opened in 2005 with a remarkable pedigree. The tandoor, the ancient clay oven, and its offspring tikka, meaning 'a little piece', had been an unintentionally well-kept secret in its place of origin, the rugged, inhospitable, mountainous area of Pakistan/Afghanistan for centuries, When Kundan Lal Gujral opened Moti Mahal to serve tandoori dishes in 1920 in Peshawar it was the only such restaurant in the world. Partition in 1947 caused the separation of one nation into the states of India and Pakistan. It cause an upheaval to those of the 'wrong' religion who feared persecution. Hindus fled from what became Pakistan into India and vice-versa. Gujral, a Hindu, fled from Peshawar taking his tandoors with him. In 1948 he established Moti Mahal in Daryaganj, Delhi making it not only India's first tandoori restaurant, but one of India's very few restaurants of any kind. It remained the place to go for decades. I was taken there in 1984 by a Delhi friend of mine, who remarked, *'Visiting Delhi and not eating at Moti Mahal is like going to Agra and not seeing the Taj Mahal'*. Tandoori in Britain was in its infancy at that time, and I can truly say I had never tasted Tandoori items as good as there. So successful were they that Moti Mahal embarked on the franchising route and now have over 30 franchise Motis, many in Delhi and they are looking for more franchisees all over India. So Moti Mahal finally opened in London under the ownership of the founder's grandson. Monish Gujral. You will be forgiven for finding it hard to find. Its signage is tiny and high up and the full-length, full-height glowing window display of bottles looks like an extension of the pub next door, but it is the Moti. The 85-seat restaurant spans two floors. Guests can join the bustling ground floor bar and dining area. The main interior is raw-stone-walled, while natural linen and cotton cloths and upholstery give the Indian feel. Dark heat-treated oak floors are offset against the orange silk wall hangings. The copper-backed open kitchen is busy with chefs at their the tandoors. Candle lanterns lead you downstairs to a more intimate dining room and another bar where 80 different whiskeys are displayed on illuminated glass shelves. (There is a 10 page whisky menu with prices fromCameron Brig £7 to Glenury Royal 1971 £93. Moti selected Anuirudh Arora, formerly at Oberoi's Hotel Udaivilas then sous chef at Benares. With TV presenter stand-up comic Hardeep Singh Kohli he recently co-authored **Food of the Grand Trunk Road**. It features the ancient trading route between Calcutta, Lucknow, Delhi and the Punjab. Kolhi wrote the travelogue, Arora the recipes, some of which are on Moti Mahal's menu. Inevitably CTM is there since Moti claim it as theirs: *'this butter chicken recipe was created by a chef at the first Moti Mahal restaurant in New Delhi. Here, we faithfully recreate our namesake's recipe'*. Murgh Makhani

£21, chicken tikka simmered in a creamy tomato sauce; The menu notes are fun. For example: Maghz Masala £12, lamb's brain stir fried with coriander, green chillies and served on masala pao bread. The menu notes say *'lamb's brain has been used as an aphrodisiac since the ancient Indian times, where it was believed to have special powers'.* [reports please]. The main ingredients are diverse: Barra Peshwari, £21, tandoor roasted lamb chops with kashmiri chillies, tomato salad, avocado chutney; Bateyr Ka Kofta £17, quail mince 'Kofta' dumpling stuffed with quail egg, cooked in a sealed pot with yoghurt, saffron and lanzan seed (charoli) paste; Malai Saunfia Paneer £10, tandoor-glazed homemade fennel paneer; Multani Khubani Gosht £19, goat meat cooked with garlic, apricots and dried red chillies, cooked in a sealed clay pot. Katli £8, Punjabi pan-fried aubergine steak stuffed with seasonal vegetables, pear and clove chutney; Torai Aur Wadi £12, ridge gourd (Torai) with (Wadi) seasoned lentil dumplings simmered in a yoghurt tomato sauce with potatoes, tomato and green peas; Kararee Subziyan £12, crisp-fried okra with carom seeds with lotus stem, peanut and coriander; Dal Makhani £10, black lentils slow cooked overnight on the tandoor's charcoal. *'To see the chefs in their open-kitchen preparing the breads, kebabs etc and using the tandoor was fascinating. The food was outstanding. Our starters included wonderful tandoori-baked stuffed new potatoes which were so delicate and soft you wondered whether they were potatoes at all! The main courses however were the stars of the show, particularly the paneer simmered in a rich, tomato sauce. The mixed vegetable curry was very dry, beautifully spiced and contained almost no sauce at all; a welcome change as vegetable curries can often be all sauce and nothing else! We had mint paratha, which was just sublime and gave everything an unusually refreshing edge!! Just fantastic food. The coup de grace however, was the outstanding malt whisky menu. As one would expect from a restaurant like this, the prices were approx double what they really should be, but the range was superb. I had an 18 year old Caol Ila 43%. (£16) Beautiful. A wonderful experience.'* AG. *'This is as good at it gets. Having recommended this restaurant. I was taken there by a business friend and although the restaurant was superb on previous visits this time it came as near as heaven as one can reasonably expect. For starters we shared a Scallop Dish and Chicken Skewers which had three different types of chicken The waiter asked us which was our favourite. What a question, they were all three perfect and each more interesting than the previous one. For main course I had Murgh Makhani, absolutely miraculous and Lamb Biriani which was equally spectacular. We also had Pullao Rice and a side dish of Spicy Fried Potatoes. The staff insisted on giving us, on the house, a small portion of Dal Makani...my favourite black dal! ... and on hearing that we were celebrating my birthday, also brought us a Kulfi each. To the famous Dudley Moore question, "is this heaven Pete?" the answer would assuredly have been 'Yes!' £150 for two.'* DRC.   12-3 & 530-11.30; Closed Sun. See page 55.

PUNJAB NORTH INDIAN PUNJABI   A-LIST
80 Neal Street, WC2H 9PA
020 7836 9787   www.punjab.co.uk

The Punjab opened in 1946 in Aldgate and moved to its present site in 1951, making it the oldest UK Punjabi restaurant. For its entire life it has been in the capable hands of just two men, the late founder and now his son Sital Singh Maan. The venue has several areas. Some prefer the rear room with its more modern looks. Others prefer the side room which seems to retain its Indian looks. The Punjab was one of the original pioneers of the curry formula. Only here it is done as it has always been done, and as it should be. The result is unlike the newer Bangladeshi clones, and is probably what old farts think they remember when they say *'curry isn't like it used to be'.* CT is a bit suspicious if the redec; *'the wooden tree is quite striking. Seems not to have weakened the food.'* CT. The food is meat-orientated, spicy, savoury and very tasty. Specialities: Punjabi Aloo Croquette, £3.35; Kadu Puri £3.35, golden pumpkin on a crispy puri (bread); Chicken Wings £3.80, roasted in the tandoor for 20 mins; Tandoori Vegetables £9.20, marinated mixed vegetables roasted in the Tandoor; Chicken Tikka Special £11.85, served flaming at your table with a shot of brandy, we are notoriously known for this historic flambé dish; Methi Gosht £9.75, lamb cooked with fresh fenugreek, a favourite Punjabi herb. *'Chicken Methia – beautifully flavoured and chicken was real quality. Linda had Chicken Tikka flambéed with brandy at the table – spectacular.'* MG. Regulars have their own club, the 'Punjabbers'. Service 10%. Hours: 12-11.30 (10.30 Sun).

SAGAR SOUTH INDIAN VEGETARIAN
31 Catherine Street, Covent Garden, WC2B 5JS
020 7836 6377   www.sagarveg.co.uk

See Sagar Hammersmith W6 branch for full details.

SITAR BALTI
149, Strand, WC2R 1JA
020 7836 3730   www.sitarstrand.co.uk

Their all day opening is useful for theatregoers. All the favourite items are on the menu and some unusuals. Whitebait, monk fish and salmon feature among the crab and swordfish among the mains. It's not all fish, and chicken, lamb and vegetables starters and mains feature as do Tandoori items. Despite Balti in the name, only five dishes are offered. The special 8 item set meal is £9.95, Pop, Bhaji, Chicken, Lamb and Veg curries, Pillau rice, Naan and Raita: from 12-6.30. *'Tempting menu, particularly good for fish lovers. Decor is attractive and uncluttered. Average wine list with an Indian wine, which we tried, a first. Quite acceptable, opened and poured slightly more professionally than is usual. Starters attractively presented, both very good. Monkfish Pudina, Chicken Xacuti, Mushroom Rice (well above average), Baigan (particularly good flavour, I rarely eat them, apart from a taste nibble, but really enjoyed them, had several forkfuls) - all really good. Obviously a lot of attention is given to side dishes. Gulab Jamun for desert, served at right temperature. Attentive and friendly service.'* HJC. Mon-Fri: 12-12, Sat-Sun: 3-11.

SITAARAY   TOP 100
167 Drury Lane WC2B 5PG
020 7269 6422   www.sitaaray.com

Sitaray means stars, galaxy type, but its other English meaning is celebrity type stars, such as inhabit the movies. Rohit Khattar owns the quirky Chore Bizarre W1 & Delhi. It is surely no coincidence that he chose this play on words to name this venture. Its reds, golds and over-the-top decor, and intimate booths give you full-on India. Dozens of framed pictures line the walls depicting Bollwood stars, giving diners, according to the spin *'an upclose look atfaces of heroes and heroines,* *villains and vamps, legendary romantic couples, icons and comediens through the ages'.* LCD screens installed in each booth show popular Bollywood scenes and clips. At lunchtime Sitaray serves street food like papri chaat, platters of seafood (Lasooni Prawns and Ajwaini Monk fish), lamb (Chicken Lamb Makhmali Tukre and Adraki Booti) and a large vegetarian selection. A big feature is all-you-can-eat Kebabs, Tandoor to table with pops and chuts, lentils, curries and accompaniments. 2 course £14.50. 3 course: , £16.50. £22.95 dinner. Serv 12.5% 12-3 & 5.30 -11.30.

TAKARI
22 Drury Lane, Covent Garden, WC2B 5RH
020 7836 1628   www.takarilondon.co.uk

Formula curries and a range of low calorie dishes and no relation to the other similarly named venues on this page.

TAMARAI   TOP 100
167 Drury Lane, Covent Garden, WC2B 5PG

Tamarai means Lotus flower and that is the clue that Chef Manish Mehrotra's 'pan Asian' menu is more oriental than Indian with influences of China, Hong Kong, Singapore, Thailand, Malaysia and Vietnam. Located in the basement under Sitaaray and in the same ownership it's a 110 seat restaurant and bar from 5.30 to 11 after which it's a night club complete with DJ, VJ (Video Jockey) and a late night license till 2am Mon to Thur and 3am on Friday and Saturday.

YOU SAY OK WC2

BHATTI 37 Great Queen Street, WC2 5AA 020 7405 5222. Owned since by 1990 by N. Ruparel. Seats 95 in 2 rooms. Del: £25 min, 4m. Hours: 12-2.45; 2 Sun / 5.30-11.45; 10.30 Sun.

ST MARTIN'S SPICE 92, St Martin's La, WC2 ~ 020 7379 9355. *'One of our guests has always been very anti-Indian restaurant. Luckily it passed with flying colours. Service efficient and friendly, all the food very good and prices are reasonable. £116 for 4 inc two bottles of wine and liqueurs.'* HC. T/a: 10% disc, £10 min. Delivery: 5m, £10 min. Hours: 5.30-1.30, 12 Fri & Sat.

TANDOORI NIGHTS 35 Great Queen Street, WC2 ~ 020 7831 2558. Owner Mrs Yasmeen Rashid opened here 1993. Service 12.5%. Lunch and dinner, daily.

ENGLAND

The entries in this Guide are recorded in alphabetical order: first the county then, within that, the town, then the restaurant. We start with Bedfordshire, Bedford, Blue Ginger.

BEDFORDSHIRE

Area: East of England.

Adjacent Counties: Bucks, Cambs, Herts and Northants.

Bedford

BLUE GINGER
116, Bedford Road, Kempston MK42 8BG 01234 856 800 bluegingerbedford.co.uk

Blonde wooden floors, alternate white and paprika coloured walls, cream leather high back chairs, white linen place settings, abstract art on walls. Menu Snapshot: Mass Biran £4.50, fillets of fish spiced and cooked on a chargrill; Ostrich Tikka £5.50, Chicken Momo £3.50, shredded chicken cooked with medium spices, wrapped in a puri; Jalshah Duck, £10 - breast of duck, medium hot masala; Broccoli Bhaji £3; Saag Naan £1.90. *'We're regulars. Owner and staff always welcoming and the loos spotless. Decor is modern and the chairs are comfortable. The restaurant is small. The food is always freshly cooked, tasty and nicely presented. Portions are such that we never get beyond starters (to share) and mains. A good restaurant, one we do recommend to friends.'* S&MR. Takeaway: 10% disc.12-2 (resvn only)/5.30-11.30.

MAGNA TANDOORI
50 Tavistock St, Bedford MK40 2RD 01234 356 960

Mostly good comments about this previous entrant to this Guide.

CHOUDHURY'S OPEN KITCHEN
2 The Broadway, Bedford 01234 356162

'We have travelled quite extensively in India and Sri Lanka and Indian restaurants in the south of England and we have come to the conclusion that Choudhury's is best. It's the largest in Beds and has been beautifully refurbished. Its menu with has tasty and exciting dishes including fish. You can watch your meals being prepared hence the new name.' PE.

SAAGAR
71, Tavistock Street, Bedford 01234 400026

'The food is brilliant, King Prawn Korma and Salty Lassi is my favourite. The staff are all charming and extremely attentive - nothing is too much trouble and the food is great.' SF. email your reservation to: saagarindian@hotmail.co.uk

Leighton Buzzard

THE INDIAN LOUNGE
57 Lake St, Leighton Buzzard LU7 1SA
01525 851 257

'My friend recommended to me your 'Cobra Good Curry Guide'. I haven't put it down since. I'm a self confessed curryholic, well known for it and spend many hours in the gym each week paying recompense for my addiction. (Sure, it's not all bad for you but weight watchers don't recommend papadoms and naan you know!) My local restaurant is called 'The Indian Lounge', which about a year ago took over what was for many years 'The Indian Pavilion'. Now I have to tell you, The Indian Lounge is 200 yards from my front door. They refer to me as family. So you'd be quick to call me bias in my opinions and forgiving in certain areas because it's right on my doorstep. However, this is one of the finest restaurants you could wish to eat at. I whole heartedly believe it would rank in your top 10 if you were to try it. It's sensational. I convert people weekly to this place. What can I do to get these guys on your 'radar'? RW.

Luton

ALANKAR
276 Dunstable Road, Luton LU4 8JL
01582 455189 www.alankarrestaurant.com

'Took advice from the Guide and was very impressed. Looked, from outside rather peculiar for a curry house. However, the food was of excellent standard. Reminded me of Madhu's, Southall. Not quite as good but the menu was vast. Had Kebabs and Lamb Chops, all came sizzling. Fish Masala very enjoyable. I must also say the spicy Popadums were the best I've had, full of flavour. Well worth a mention, would go again without a doubt. Nearly forgot, they served a beautiful dish called Begun Bortha, which is mashed aubergine. It was wonderful, trust me'. LH.

YOU SAY OK
You may get a discount if you show them this Guide.

ARLESEY: RAJ VILLA 27 High Street, Arlesey ~ 01462 835145. 70-seater owned by Akthar Ali since 1996. Branches: Raj Gat, Bedford St, Ampthill, and Raj Moni, London, N1.

ALAMIN TANDOORI 51 Tavistock St. Bedford ~ 01234 330066. Gulzar Miah's 42-seater. Hours: 12-2 / 6-12; 12.30 Sat.

GULSHAN 69 Tavistock St, Bedford ~ 01234 355544. Owners: Mrs BK Nijjer and Pakistani food by Chef Shanu Miah. *'Try Lamb Sharab,*

BERKSHIRE

Area:
South East England
(west of London)

Adjacent Counties:
Hants, Surrey,
Middx, Oxon,
Wilts

Cookham

MALIK'S **TOP 100**
Royal Exchange, High St, Cookham, SL6 9SF
01628 520085   www.maliks.co.uk

Set in a former country pub, complete with clinging ivy, and olde beams, this restaurant takes its name from Malik Ahmed, who, with partner Mujibur Rahman, runs front of house. He promises to give you food cooked to the highest standards, along with good wines, elegant surroundings and a wealth of atmosphere. Maharaja Banquet (min 8) £40 pp. Appetisers: Stuffed Chillis (stuffed with soft cheese), Pancake Kebab (stuffed with delicious spicy lamb), King Prawn Suka (King prawns cooked in sweet and sour tamarind sauce). Chicken Chat (Chat Massala used on diced chicken, sweet and, savoury), Nazakat (succulent chicken skewered and grilled in Tandoori), Tandoori King Prawns (marinated in spices and cooked on a skewer over charcoal). Main Courses: Sulemani (Whole leg of lamb marinated for 48 hours and oven roasted), Patan Para (Spring chicken cooked with medium spices and fresh herbs), Chicken Tikka Massala, King Prawn Jalfraizi (cooked in hot spices with onions, peppers, shallots, fresh herbs, green chilli and coriander), Dall Tarka, Motor Ponir (Cheese and peas in a mild sauce), Sag Aloo (Spinach and seasonal potato wedges cooked with subtle spices and herbs), Pilau Rice, Special Rice and Naan. Dessert: Rice Pudding or Kulfi (Indian Ice Cream) 12-2.30 & 6-12. *Branches: 14 Oakend Way, Gerrards Cross, 101 High Street, Marlow, Buckinghamshire SL7 1AB   01628 482180s.*

YOU SAY OK
You may get a discount if you show them this Guide.

CAVERSHAM: THE GURKHA INN 64 George Street. ~ 0118 948 3974. Popular 42-seater. Car park nearby. Del: 3m £12 min. Hours: 12.30-2.30/6-11.30.

CROWTHORNE: VILLAGE TANDOORI 204 Dukes Ride. ~ 01344 780118

HUNGERFORD: MOONLIGHT 43 High St. ~ 01488 685252

ETON: GOLDEN CURRY   46 High St. ~ 01753 863961. *'Still there and very good.'* BT.

READING: GULSHAN TANDOORI Wokingham Rd ~ 0118 966 799799. *'Owner Mr Raja always eager to hear our views with a view to improve. Our answer is always same, food is nice - keep it that way.'* HBR. *'The best in Indian Cuisine.'* SSJ.

Eton

TIGER GARDEN
47 High Street, Eton, SL4 6BL   01752 866310
www.tigergarden.co.uk

Situated in 'The Cockpit', built in 1420, where Charles II was a spectator. Note the stocks outside for ancient punishment. Menu Snapshot: Dhal Pakora £4.50 – lentils mashed with onion, coriander, battered and fried. Enda Bhunjon £6 – spiced egg halves in aromatic onion sauce. Mass Biran £17 – boal fish steak, pan fried with green chillies. Good weather al fresco in the Beer Garden. New is their selection of handmade Indian Savouries and Indian cakes and sweets with a cup of spiced Masala Tea, Darjeeling tea or Mango Lassi. £4.95.T/a: 15% disc. Hours: 12-2.30 (High Tea 12 -4) & 6-11. *Branches: West Street, Marlow. 01628 482211. Tiger Cub: 29 Station Rd, Marlow. 01628 482020.*

Reading

CINNAMON TREE
The Street, Mortimer, Reading RG7 3NR
0118 933 2428   www.cinnamontreemortimer.co.uk

'I had the pleasure of dining there on Saturday night and was impressed again with the warm welcome, tasteful decoration and comfortable furnishings. Our reserved table was available immediately and drinks and Pops/chutney orders were taken straight away. A couple of branded lagers were on tap (Stella & Carlsberg from memory), it would have been nice to also be able to order Indian beers on tap, however we consoled ourselves with bottled Cobra. Our Pops were hot, well drained and crispy and the chutneys were passable, the lime pickle could have had a bit more zing for me. On this occasion we opted to skip starters in favour of a few more main dishes. The star of the show for me was the Ghust Shahjanee at a reasonable £7.95, really tender pieces of lamb and rich ginger & spicing made for a dish to savour. We also really enjoyed Jhinga Chilli Massala; fat, juicy prawns with a gently delayed kick. Sag Bhaji still had texture and a bit of iron to help offset the richness of the lamb, Onion Bhaji were sizeable, tasty and very crisp, bombay aloo was reasonably spiced and cooked but was outshone by the other dishes. Chapatis were well prepared and generous. On this as in occasion as previously we were also pleasantly surprised to be offered any liqueur or spirit on the house to round off the meal. Keen to go back and try some of their Bangladesh dishes such as the Rezalla, Rosuni or the intriguingly names Misty Lau, chicken or Lamb cooked with red pumpkin.' TS, Hartley Wintney. Large Car Park. Business lunch, Takeaway service, Special Sunday buffet e-a-m-a-y-l, Adults: £9.95. Children: half price. Mon-Sat: 12 -2.30 & 6-11.(Sunday : 1- 5 & 6-11).

KATHMANDU KITCHEN   NEPALESE
59, Whitley St, Reading, RG2 0EG   0118 986 4000

This 90 seater opened in 2001 and changed ownership to Nikul Patel in 2005, after which we received several favourable reports on Manager Navib Thapa's service and Chef Purja's food. True it has only a few Nepalese dishes on the otherwise standard menu. Try the Momo, or special Noodles, or the underrated Shak-Sukha, a Nepalese mince dish. Our our Indian friends like the place. *It fairly recently changed hands and you can see a great deal of improvements in the service at this big restaurant. You will notice that the restaurant is getting fuller every week. By contrast, the owner, Nikul Patel, is a young chap and he is equally dedicated to this new business, enthusiastic and eager to improve. Although he appears new in the business and in the area, with his talent, he is learning the ropes pretty quickly. You see constant improvement inside and outside and a great deal of improvement in the taste of food with the same chef working there. I wrongly judged him first by his lower prices but then realised that he has to do that, being right in the middle of the most deprived ward in this country! We all admire the food, service and personal touch at this restaurants and would like to recommend you to feature it in your Guide.'* HBR. Good Gimmick: If you live within 3m, and spend £90 or more (max 4 diners) you get a chauffeur service. Hours: 11-2.30 & 5 -11.

SPICE OVEN
4 Church Street, Caversham, RG4 8AT
0118 948 1000   www.spiceoven.co.uk

Fully Licensed. Air conditioned 215 seater in a listed building. Every night is World Cuisine Buffet Night at The Spice Oven where you can eat to your heart's content. The modest price for Sunday Lunchtime is £10.99; On Sunday Evenings, Mondays & Tuesdays it is £12.99, Wednesdays and Thursdays at £13.99; with Friday & Saturday at only £14.99 per person and Children 10 and under eat ½ Price - infants under 3 are FREE. *'The food tends to be on the spicy side and not for the faint hearted. The restaurant is large, luxurious with wood carved fittings. The Taj-trained Indian chef produces authentic regional food. The prices reasonable. One of the best. A great addition to the Reading scene.'* GP. 12-2.30 & 6-11.

STANDARD   TANDOORI & NEPALESE
141 Caversham Rd, Reading, RG1 8AU
0118 959 0093   www.standardtandoori.co.uk

Est 1980. Seats 140. 8 parking places at front. Pond and fountain as centrepiece. Nepalese specials include Kathmandu Aloo. *'Three of us descended on this very spacious restaurant at 6pm on a Wednesday evening; by 8pm it was packed and queuing! Delicious spicy hot carrot chutney. Chicken tikka cooked in a specially prepared mild tomato sauce was out of this world. Chicken shashlick was brilliant. Absolutely nothing standard about this restaurant.'* MB. T/a: 10% disc. Free del. 12-2.30 & 6:-11. Sun: 12.-11.

Slough

BAYLIS HOUSE   NORTH INDIAN TOP 100
Stoke Poges Lane, Slough, SL1 3PB   01753
555555   www.baylishouse.co.uk

Baylis pronounced Bay-lees opened in 2003 and is an exciting venue. The main house is quite old. Set in a five acre garden, it was built in 1697 by Sir Christopher Wren. It lay derelict for decades until it was bought in 2002 ago by an enterprising team. At once they restored the house and built a huge modern conference and banqueting suite which can hold more than 400 guests alongside. This marriage of old and new is striking and exciting. Alongside is a 16-bed hotel with en-suite bedrooms, and there is also a restaurant and bar, called Club Baylis, open to all. But the beauty of Baylis is that it is Indian-owned, Indian-managed. The food is gloriously cooked the brigade of Indian chefs. The venue handles a large number of Indian weddings. Service is as you get at 7-star Indian hotels – discrete yet attentive and very accurate. Menu Snapshot: Starters:Aloo Mint Tikka, £3.25 mash potato pattie delicately spiced and topped with a mint, yoghurt & tamarind sauce. Main courses: Chicken Dum Malai Korma, £6.75, simmered in a rich sauce of almonds and cream infused with saffron; CTM, £7.25; Saag Gosht £6.95, diced lamb leg braised in yoghurt sauce; Dal Makhani c£6 - black lentils in tomatoes and garlic. *'I regularly visit here and there is no doubt that this restaurant has maintained its level of service with the ever-excellent food quality as good as we experienced at the opening.'* HBR. *'Overall opinion – excellent, would definitely recommend and I really must make the effort to return.'* S.O. Desserts: Gajar ka halwa with ice cream, carrot grated and cooked for a long time with milk and sugar, finished with rabri & nuts. Bar Menu: small portions (and prices!) of snacks including: Cocktail Samosas; Vegetable Pakora £2.95; Malai Kebab; Prawn Chilli - wrapped in filo pastry. Lunch Buffet: 12-3, Mon-Fri, £15. Dinner, 6 - 10.30. Sun Dinner Buffet: 12-3 & 7-11, adult £9 and children £5.

HAVELI   PUNJABI
93, Stoke Poges La Slough SL1 3NJ
01753 820300   www.havelirestaurant.com

This is the kind of restaurant that never blows its own trumpet yet is packed with Asians who adore good food at good prices, a la carte or self-served from the buffet. It has a banqueting suite that seats up to 500. Reasonable prices. The venue is adorned with antiques from India and the chefs prepare Northern Indian or Punjabi, Chinese and European cuisine. 12-3 (Lunch Thali & a la carte) 6-11 (A la carte). Sun – 12-10. (All day buffet, a la carte and Set Menu's).

Suningdale

TIGER'S PAD   TOP 100
3 Station Parade, London Rd, Sunningdale, SL5 0EP
01344 621215   www.thetigerspad.co.uk

Richard Green's Tiger's Pad is set in expensive, minimalist, open-plan decor with satisfying tables. They have Indian chefs, led by Chef Ajoy Sachdev and it is great to find the real delicious thing, rather than another formula curry house. We get many satisfied reports on the place, for example AF has consistently commented the likes of: *'Gets better and better. They continually refine and change their menu. Sikadari Badi Lamb is out of this world. I'm convinced it is the "find of the decade".'* AF. DBAC says: *'it is a gem of a place and the sort of pad anyone would wish to find as their local.'* And then we got this poignant note from Alan: *'We moved to the curry desert of Devon from Berkshire and can find no equal to the Tiger's Pad in Sunningdale, a great exponent of the skills of cooking great Indian food.'* Sun Buffetc £12 from 12-5. Mon-Thur: 12-2 & 6-10.30 (11 Sat & 7-10 Sun).

Thatcham

KAILASA
35 High Street, Thatcham, RG19 3JG   01635 862228

'There are some restaurants which give you a good feeling as soon as you walk in - the Kailasa is one. Inviting eatery with white wood tables, royal blue napkins and fan shaped wall hangings - flock wallpaper enthusiasts would probably have a fit! Chefs Specials include: Boal Kofta, Sabji Bangla, Shatcora Gost, Sylheti Akni, Chingri Anana. Tandoori Chicken - seriously tender and seriously large. Excellent King Prawn Puree - juicy, tender, well spiced beasties. Chingri Ananas - chicken with pineapple, served in half a shell, with loads of fresh coriander - delicious. Sylheti Akni - kind of mixed meat biryani with a proper vegetable curry. A special mention to Sag Bhajee, obviously made from fresh spinach - a really nice change. Nan and Popadums were, respectively, light, moist and warm, non-greasy. All in all a very pleasant lunch.' S&ZM.

Twyford

HAWELI   TOP 100
15 Church Street, Twyford, RG10 9DN
0118 932 0939   www.hawelitwyford.co.uk

Raj Sattar runs a very good establishment. It is an bog-standard menu, but you like it. We like the amazing table viewer on-line. Like booking your seat in a theatre. as is recorded by our reporters. *'I telephoned for a collection as my wife wasn't feeling up to going out. The telephone*

manner was very friendly (I think they are beginning to remember me) and the food was ready when I arrived. The friendly greeting at the door made me feel like a sultan! The meal was carried to the door for me and contained two Popadums and a rose for my wife. The food was excellent as usual. ' RT. Menu Snapshot: Reshmi Kebab c£4- minced lamb burger spiced and cooking in butter served with a fried egg; Sulimoni Kebab £4.50 - served with melted cheese; Aloo Bora c£5 - potato cake made with mashed potatoes, seasoned with mint and ginger, served with tamarind sauce; Mr Bhagisa, fresh baby lobsters cooked in a spicy sauce using garlic, ginger and green chillies. Hot or very hot. *'the increase in the number of naga chillies nearly blew my head off! It was very nice once my internal chillimeter had readjusted itself.'* R&NT. 12-2.30 & 5.30-11.30.

Windsor

MANGO LOUNGE   A-LIST
9 Datchet Rd, Windsor, SL4 1QB   01753 855576
www.mangoloungewindsor.com

It's opposite Windsor Castle, and near the Theatre Royal and the stations. Parking is tough. Decor is modern and exciting. The first floor meeting / dining room holds 25. The secret weapon is is chef Ashwani Kumar from Baylis, Slough [qv], as are his backers. He is one of the best Indian chefs in the UK, and further more he is one of a rare breed – he just loves cooking and he gets on with the job without blowing his own trumpet. (others please note). His menu changes frequently, and is one of the signs of good cheffing. They get bored without

Chef Kumar, right and his talented brigade

SPLENDIDLY INDIAN, SUPERBLY SMOOTH

challenging changes, At the time of writing, starters include: Spinach and Feta Cheese Samosa £5.50, spiced with roasted cumin and chilli; raisins add a fruity note. Tilapia in spiced batter £6.95, coated in gram flour batter and spiced with carom seeds, ginger, green chillies and lemon juice. Served with plum chutney; From the tandoor is Venison Tikka Tandoori Guinea Fowl and Tandoori Monk Fish Marinated each £7.50. Allo superb, but this is the favourite of many regulars: Tiger Prawn Martini £8.50, giant warm water prawns wrapped in rice flakes and deep-fried and presented in a shot glass layered with a trio of chutneys and topped with a dash of martini. Notable mains include Rabbit Tikka Lababdar £16.25, tandoor-cooked rabbit infused with onion and tomato based semi sauce, fenugreek, butter and a dash of cream; Lal Maas £13.75, literally meaning 'red meat' in Rajasthani, it is a fiery curry where lamb is steeped in a spice-laced yogurt marinade and cooked with a generous amount of chillies and spiced with cardamom and cumin; Miloni Vegetable Handi £9.50 nine types of fresh vegetables in a silky smooth sauce with subtle aromas; Black Chickpea Curry with aubergine £4.25, cooked with cumin, ginger and hot chilli, all mellowed by lashings of tomatoes.Desserts include Rosemary Poached Pears, served with a fruit compote and an organic chilli-chocolate sauce and Mango and passion fruit brûlée An Indian twist on a classic French recipe served with mango kulfi, each £5.50. The wine list is equally thoughtful, with prices from £15 to £55. Tucked into the reds list amongst international classics are two of interest: Shiraz, Sula 2007 India £25.00, Indian full-bodied wine said to *'go well with rich food'* Windsor has 110 restaurants, of which most are mediocre troughs for tourists. We doubt that few will realise how good the place is. But you will, so reports please. Service 10%. Sat & Sun: 12.30-2.30; Daily: 6-10.30 (to 10 Sun).

YOU SAY OK
You may get a discount if you show them this Guide.

TWYFORD: THE MITA'S 37 London Rd. ~ 0118 934 4599. M.Quayyum & Chef Shilu Miah's 38-seater opened in 1994. T/a: 15% disc. Car Park . Hours: 12-2.30/6-11.

WINDSOR: RED ROSE, SHARMIN & VICEROY PREMIER are *'Still there and very good.'* BT

WOKINGHAM: ROYAL INDIAN TANDOORI 72 Peach Street, Wokingham ~ 0118 978 0179. 70-seater est 1978 by T Ali. T/a 15% disc. Hours: 12-3/6-12.

WOKINGHAM: SULTAN BALTI PALACE 7 Market Place, Wokingham 0118 977 4397 www.sultanpalace.co.uk Good Pakistani cooking. Branch Originasia, Richmond, Surrey.

Email your opinions to
pat@patchapman.co.uk
from a one-liner to
an essay! All welcome.

BRISTOL
Area: South West England

Adjacent Counties: Glos, Som

Bristol

AAGRA GRILL PAKITANI & SNACKS
386 Gloucester Road, Horfield, Bristol, BS7 8TR
0117 9232190.   www.aagrah.com

The renowned chain of West Yorkshire restaurants expands to its 14th branch in new (for them) west country territory. Gutsy Pakistani tastes are side by side with snack items such as Nanwich Tikka in a naan, wraps and Paninis. Modest prices and really useful hours. See Aagrah Shipley West Yorkshire for details.11.00am to 1.00am 7 days a week

KATHMANDU NEPALESE
Colston Tower Colston St Bristol, BS1 4XE   0117 929 4455   www.kathmandu-curry.com

Ashok Mali's family-run 100 seater opened in 2003. Menu snapshot: Nepalese Kancha Mali's repertoire: Kancha Kukhura Special. Tandoori chicken cooked in Nepalese spices; Chhoyla Lamb cooked on charcoal with ginger and garlic and served in a 'hot' sizzler; Chicken or Lamb Kritipur, with whole spices in the curry; Sea Bass Nani, fillets cooked in a creamy Nepalese sauce, served with butter beans and asparagus; Chicken or Lamb Natapole, with tomato, coriander and ghee; Duck Makalu, strips of duck breast cooked with coriander, peppers and onions – truly Nepalese style. *'Ashok suggested we try his Nepalese specialities. Boy, are we glad we glad we did! They were right up there with the very best food we have enjoyed, ever.* 'DS. Your editors visited with Janis Leibart long-time a backing singer with Michael Bolton. OK – explanation: she bought a number of my cookbooks and we got a freebie to the show at the Colston Hall, which was GRRREAT by the way. Anyway in return we hosted her to a pre-show curry and since the Kathmandu is almost opposite the stage door, we went there to find most of the crew and musicians were already trunking in! Set Lunch c£10, Set dinner from £16. Hours: 12-2 & 5.45-11 to 12 Sat; 10.30 Sun.

KRISHNAS INN   SOUTH INDIAN
4 Byron Place, Triangle South, Clifton, Bristol, BS8 IJT
011 7927 6864   www.keralagroup.co.uk

See Rhada Krishna Bhavan, London SW17.

MYRISTICA — PAN INDIAN — TOP 100

51 Welshback, Bristol, Avon BS1 4AN
0117 927 2177   www.myristica.co.uk

Myristica (translated as nutmeg or spice) was opened a listed building by brothers Amit and Tosh Lakhani in 2006. The chefs under Bhaskar Cokkalineam ex Taj and Mela, are on show cooking the curry sauces to order and naan breads and tandoori dishes straight from the oven. A fresh seafood counter offers a marinated selection of fish that customers can choose and request the chefs to cook as they like. For example, pick the marinated prawns on display and have them served as a starter, in a mixed salad, with your favourite curry sauce, or just as they are! a plasma screen in the window gives passers-by a taste of the action! Menu snapshot: Starters include: Baby Squid £5.95, rings tossed with bell peppers, chilli flakes and honey; Mussel Fry £5.9. stir-fried in the tawa with mustard seeds in a spicy tomato masala; Rabbit

Mysterica's Tiffin lunch box

Varuval £6.95, a South Indian speciality tossed with onions, chillies, curry leaves & ground spices. Mains include Organic Black Cod £13, marinated with crushed chilli flakes, dry coriander, chopped ginger, garlic, garam masala and chargrilled; Achari Venison £13, in a pickling marinade, cooked in tandoor served with potato & spinach mash; Guinea Fowl Stir Fry, a stir fried boneless breast with dry red chillies, roasted spices, shallots and curry leaves; Vermicelli Mysore Chicken £12 cooked with roasted coriander, chillies, curry leaves served on bed of India's thin rice pasta. Desserts include Chocolate Samosas, filled with chocolate dipped sponge & shredded pista served with ice cream and Shrikhand, made with cream, milk, saffron, nutmeg, and crushed pistachios.Tiffin lunch boxes aavailable £5 for t/a to enjoy at work or picnic at the harbourside. Mon-Fri: 12-2 & Mon-Sat: 6-11.30; 10.30 Sun.

THALI CAFÉ

1 Regent Street, Clifton, Bristol, BS8 4HW
0117 974 3793   www.thethalicafe.co.uk

Following succesful operations at music festivals like Glastonbury, the first Thali Cafe opened in 1999 and now there are three in the area, serving authentic Indian street food. They are what the say on the tin, or in it being that thalis are metal containers. There are four thalis from £8 to £10, eg Southern Thali – incorporating a Goan fish curry, dahl, vegetable dish, chutney, rice and salad, or a Northern Thali – incorporating a Tarka Dahl, Saag or Mutter Panner, chutney, rice and salad. There is also a 'Kid's Tiny Thali' of rice & dahl with a choice of fish pieces, chicken or pakora at £4.25. They aslo do street food. When it comes to takeaway the Thali Café's system is unique and clever. You buy your own Tiffin box (a stack of four stainless steel food containers) for £25 (the first takeaway is free), you then keep taking it back whenever you fancy saving on waste. Refills from £8.50. The two branches below do Indian breakfast (from 10am). eg Dosa, Sambar and Coconut Chutney £7 or Aloo Parantha withan yogurt, hot lime pickle and a large glass of chai, £3.50. 12 till close. Branches: 66 St. Marks Road, Easton BS5 6JH 0117 951 4979. 10am till close and 12 York Road, Montpelier BS6 5QE 0117 942 6687. Week days: 6pm to close. Weekends: 10am to close.   *Below*

A Thali Café dosa and venue. Above: A Thali Café Tiffin box.

YOU SAY OK – BRISTOL

You may get a discount if you show them this Guide.

BRITISH RAJ 1 Passage Road, Westbury-on-Trym: BS9 0117 950 0493. www.british-raj.co.uk   Respected in the area.

CASSIA   79 Gloucester Road, Patchway, BS34 0117 969 0907
A favourite Bristol Balti House.

SPLENDIDLY INDIAN, SUPERBLY SMOOTH

CHILLI'S TANDOORI 39 Park St, Bristol, BS1 5NH

CURKAS TANDOORI NEPALESE 403 Gloucester Road, Horfield, BS7 0117 942 2898 46-seater with some Nepalese dishes. Hours: 12-2 & 6-12.30.

LAL JOMI 2 Harcourt Rd, Bristol, BS6 7RG 0117 942 1640 JS likes the beezer, the man in costume who greetsy and she likes the cosy booths and *'the best curry house in Bristol'*.

OH CALCUTTA! 216 Cheltenham Rd, BS16 5QU 0117 924 0458 www.ohcalcutta.co.uk T/a 20% disc 6-7 & 10-11, 10% 7-10. Hours: 6-11.30.

OLD INDIA 34 St Nicholas Street, Stock Exchange Buildings, Bristol, BS1 1TG www.oldindia.co.uk

RAJ MAHAL 8 Frome Valley Rd, Bristol, BS16 1HD 0117 958 6382 www.rajmahalbristol.co.uk 12-2 & 6-11.30. Branch: Raj Mahal City Indian, 69 Clarence Road, Redcliff, Bristol, BS1 6RP 0117 929 0516

SITARA TANDOORI 3a Regent Street, Clifton Village, BS8 4HW 0117 973 9937 www.sitaratandoori.co.uk

BUCKINGHAMSHIRE

Area:
South East England
(west of London)

Adjacent Counties:
Beds, Herts,
Middx,
Northants, Oxon

Amersham

LEMON GRASS **BYO**
17 Hill Avenue, Amersham, HP6 5BD
01494 433380   www.lemongrasscuisine.com

Golam Sarwar opened this 38 seater in 2005. Its name might make you think Thai not Indian, but in fact it is a regular curry house with all the favourites. It is BYO making it attractive, price-wise. Some of chef Islam's specials have curious names too: Flamingo is not, presumably, that pink bird (though it might make a great alternative name for CTM), it is chicken or lamb cooked with herbs, yoghurt and, yes, lemon grass!. Juliet Roman sounds like a Shakespearean TV police series, but is in fact Chicken Tikka with minced meat, capsicum, tomato and saffron, both £9.25. Chicken Sandeman is not to do with wallpaper, it is Tikka cooked with garlic, yoghurt, cheese and mushrooms, etc at £8.25. Good fun, eh. And good prices and BYO. If only they all did that. 5.30-11.

YOU SAY OK - BUCKS
You may get a discount if you show them this Guide.
AMERSHAM: SANTHI 16 Hill Ave, Amersham ~ 01494 432621. www.santhirestaurant.co.uk 90-seater established by Rashid Miah & Chef Shotul Miah in 1992. 12-2.30/6-10.45.
ASTON CLINTON: SHAAD, 132 London Rd ~ 01296 630399. Opened in 2004 in a former pub with large conservatory at rear

and car park. *'Clean toilets.'* CL. T/a: 20% disc £15 min. Sun Buffet: 12-3 - £9 adult, £5 child. Banquet Night: £10.95 Th. Hours: 12-2.30/5.30- 11.30.
AYLESBURY: THE CHADNIS 43 High Street, Waddesdon ~ 01296 651255. 70-seater est 1999 by Mr Shah. *'All super, couldn't be faulted. Plenty of staff, service attentive.'* DL. Hours: 12-2.30 / 6-11; 11.30 Fri & Sat.
BOURNE END: ALY'S TANDOORI, HEART IN HAND, Cores End Rd, Bourne End ~ 01628 531112 Mohammed Hussain's 70- seater est 1999 in former pub, with a pretty front 'awning' and hanging baskets. Hours: 12-3/6-11.30. Sun: 1-1.
COOKHAM: SPICE MERCHANT NEW ENTRANT High Street, SL6 9S. ~ 01628 522584. Est 1983 as Cookham Tandoori in a 500 year old building, with low ceilings and original beams, all of which contribute to a cosy and intimate atmosphere.

Beaconsfield

BASMATI
43 Aylesbury End, Beaconsfield, HP9 1LU
01494 671500   www.basmatibeaconsfield.com

'We love Basmati, the menu, food and service is always outstanding. Food is a modern twist on a traditional menu and always served with flair by charming staff. We have visited many times and have never been disappointed and are always greeted like old friends. I love the tandoori king prawns and apparently the chicken dishes are superb. Parking is usually available outside, I would suggest booking as they get busy in the evening.' GW. 12-2.30 & 5.30-11 (11.30 Sat). See overleaf.

SPICE MERCHANT
33 London End, Beaconsfield, HP9 2HW
01494 675474   www.spicemerchantgroup.com

The flagship of four venues estin 1994 by Bashir Islam and his wife Aysha. Alfresco dining is fun in a garden complete with waterfall and a pond spanned by a wooden bridge. Group chef is Vijay Anand. Menu Snapshot: Starters: Bataki Nazrana, Tandoori duck & cumin-tempered potatoes, wrapped in filo pastry, served with onion & mango chutney; Murgh Nazakat, skewered chicken flavoured with garlic and nutmeg; Chat Masala, tangy masala sauce cooked with chicken or potato or chana (chickpeas). Mains: Dum Ka Murg. Baked flattened chicken breasts stuffed with a mixture of spinach and cheese, cumin and mashed potatoes; Sunehri Jalpari, Pan fried sea bass, marinated in lime and mustard, crusted with gramflour and served with kadhai vegetables; Sikendari Badi Lamb, shank marinated then roasted in the oven. Avg Price: £43. 12-2.30 & 6-11. Branches: Cookham, Henley-on-Thames, Uxbridge.

Buckingham

DIPALEE TANDOORI
18 Castle St, Buckingham. MK18 1BP

'I highly recommend that you pay it a visit! The staff are extremely friendly and helpful and the food is delicious and extremely reasonably priced I am a very satisfied, regular.' PT.

BASMATI

Indian Restaurant

Order & Book Online!
www.basmatibeaconsfield.com
T: 01494 671500 / 676806
43 Aylesbury End, Beaconsfield, Bucks, HP9 1LU

Free Home Delivery
On orders over £20
4 mile radius
10% discount on collection

- Fully licensed & air conditioned restaurant with extensive, specially selected wine list
- Extensive menu with innovative new dishes
- We cater for small and large parties
- Up to 110 covers
- Home cooking style dishes as well as traditional Indian dishes
- Fish dishes as well as vegetarian dishes
- Outside catering available

indigo BAR & GRILL

The Finest Indian Cuisine brought to you by our hand picked chefs from the best 5 Star Hotels all across the Indian subcontinent

Why not try our new Grill or Pan Asian Menu

Lunch Special Menus Start £6.99 per person

The Indigo Bar & Grill
Indigo House

Oxford Road,
Gerrards Cross,
Bucks
SL9 7AL
01753 883100
www.indigobarandgrill.co.uk

Gerrards Cross

INDIGO BAR & GRILL
Indigo House, Oxford Road, Gerrards Cross, Bucks SL9 7AL   01753 883100
www.indigobarandgrill.co.uk

Indigo is bright & modern with wooden floors and slick black furniture, efficient relaxed service. Chefs from the finest 5 Star Hotels across the subcontinent cook refined food such as Makhmali Seekh, lightly spiced fine chicken mince cooked in clay oven, Kurkuri Batak, shredded duck spring onion, carrot & ginger wrapped in filo pastry. Delhi Chilli Chicken, thigh cube tossed with soya, fresh green chilli, ginger & garlic. Nalli Ka Khallia, lamb shank cooked with brown onion, ginger and garlic. Fish Moily, Tilapia fish with ginger, coconut milk & curry leaf. Some Thai dishes. Lunch Menus start at £6.99. 12-3 & 5-11

Haddenham

HOUSE OF SPICE
19 Fort End, Haddenham HP17 8EJ   01844 299100   www.houseofspice.uk.com

Agna Choudhury's 'House' is situated in a former public house, with a varied menu showcasing some interesting new dishes. *'Offers a varied menu, showcasing some interesting new dishes alongside some old favourites.*

Nicely appointed with good ambience. Very good quality food and service during each visit. Didn't disappoint this time either. Benchmark dishes passed with flying colours along with some new offerings. Overall opinion: very good.* SO. 12-2.30 & 6-11.30.*Branch:* 59, Lower Rd, Chinnor, Oxon.

YOU SAY OK, High Wycombe
BOMBAY PALACE   6 Crendon St, High Wycombe, HP13   01494 531595   Owner:Hannah Miah   07888 672 129 bombaypalacehw.com

CURRY CENTRE 83 Easton Street, High Wycombe, HP11 1LT   01494 535529. www.thecurrycentre.co.uk Same family owners since est in 1970.

ELAICHI 188 Cressex Road, High Wycombe, HP12 4UA   01494 510710/510810 elaichiofhighwycombe.co.uk

LITTLE INDIA Cross Roads Hazlemere High Wycombe HP15 7LG   01494 717351

MR INDIA, High Wycombe 01494 465999 Owner: Kazi Islam (Mngr Mr Khan)

Marlow

MALIKS
101 High Street, Marlow, SL7 1AB
01628 482180.   www.maliks.co.uk

Always good reports about the three Maliks. Booking is advised. Menu Snapshot: Special Stuffed Calamari £13, it's stuffed with spiced minced prawns and chicken, and cooked in a tasty sauce. Red Mullet Biraan £14.50, marinated with light spices & herbs, pan-fried with mushrooms & cayenne peppers. Cox's Bazaar Crab £13, soft shell crab served over a bed of aromatic sauce. Meat: Lamb Jalfraizi £8 cooked in hot spices with shallots, capsicum, fresh chilli, fresh herbs and coriander. Tetul Lamb £7.50, simmered with tamarind. Haash Shugunda £8, breast of duckling with onion, ginger and garlic, in a creamy coconut milk with garam massala.Green Chicken Curry £8, cooked with broccoli, baby aubergine, coconut milk and aromatic ground spices. '*Just to let you know, my favourite curry house in the UK For takeaway. You can see you curry being cooked on live stream.Track you order on google maps, their cars have tracker fitted. They also do the Hottest curry in the world. Chicken Lava.*' SW. Special Banquet £17.00 pp minimum of two. Sunday Buffet e-a-m-a-y-l – 12 to 2.30, £10 Adult £7 Child. *Branches:* Cookham, Berks, 14 Oak End Way, Gerrards Cross, Bucks, SL9 8BR   01753 880888.

Milton Keynes
(Includes Bletchley, Stony Stratford, Woburn Sands and Wolverton)

CALCUTTA BRASSERIE   TOP 100
7 St Paul's Court, High St, Stony Stratford, MK
01908 566577   /www.calcuttabrasserie.co.uk

The former Moghul Palace recently changed ownership to Mo Abdul and is renamed the Calcutta Brasserie. The decor is the same, though and one has to say it is

BUCKINGHAMSHIRE

Above: Part of Calcutta Brasserie's amazing decor. Inset : Mo Abdul displays his Cobra Good Curry Guide TOP 100 certificate.

Welcome to a unique culinary experience in MK

BRITISH Curry Awards — FINALIST 2010
MKNEWS CURRY COMPETITION — WINNER 2010

The number one Indian Restaurant in Stony Stratford, Milton Keynes

Calcutta BRASSERIE

Calcutta Brasserie - 7 St Pauls Court, High Street, Stony Stratford, MK11 1LJ

Calcutta Brasserie - St Pauls Court, High Street, Stony Stratford, MK11 1LJ

SPLENDIDLY INDIAN, SUPERBLY SMOOTH

outstanding. *'It's an old monastery school where monks once beat knowledge into the sons of local gentry.'* says LT. Now the local curryholic gentry beat a path through its Gothic arch, complete with wrought-iron gate, beyond which stands the imposing clerestoric building. In 1994, the previous owners converted this Victorian former cigar-factory-cum-orphanage-cum-school into their 100-seater Palace. And impressed you will be, with the spacious reception area with its armchairs and comfortable sofas where you wait to be seated, and the scale, height, tiled floor, stonework and wood panels of the dining room. *'Original wood panelling still in place, very high domed ceiling over half of restaurant - with mock stars in the deep blue sky and a mural copying Michael Angelo's Sistine chapel ceiling at the non-smoking end, which is raised up two or three steps. Food superb. - delicious. Service good and friendly - I'll go again.'* MS. *'we perused the menu in the lounge, where the conversation ranged from church to curry.'* DL. Starters: Talli Kekra £6.95, Crispy fried soft shell crab with tamarind chutney; Manglorean Scallops £6.95, Pan seared king scallops with mustard and curry leaves; Dakshini Mussels £6.95, fresh steamed bantry bay mussels in allepy sauce and fresh cilantro leaves. Served with naan bread; Seafood Tomato Rasam £5.95, mussels, baby octopus, clams stewed in south Indian tomato shorba. Served with naan bread. Lollipop Chicken £4.95, herb crusted chicken wings spiced with paprika and peppers served with green salad and podina. Mains: Tharavu Roast £11.95, pan-seared spiced gressingham duck breast cooked with orange zest and tomato sauce; Chicken Chettinad £7.95, classic south Indian dish created by the chettiyars of tamil nadu, chicken simmered in a sauce of black pepper roasted coriander and tomatoes; Dhaba Chicken £8.95, a truly punjabi favourite, home style chicken cooked on the bone with hot spices and fresh green chillies and lots of fresh coriander; Nalli Korma £10.95, slow-cooked shanks of lamb braised in hyderabadi korma sauce; Kosha Mangsho £8.95, low cooked, lamb in its own juices with aromatic hot spices and caramelised onion and ginger. Vegetables: Panjabi Chole, Side £3.95/Main £5.95, chick peas cooked traditionally like a north Indian style with yoghurt and special chana masala; Urulai Vatakal £6.95, famous south Indian style potato wedges stir-fried with mustard seeds and curry leavesT/a: 10% disc. 12-2 & 6-11 (12-10 Sun – all day Sun Buffet, £9.95).

JAIPUR   AWARD WINNER
Grafton House, 599 Grafton Gate East, MK9 1AT
01908 669796   www.jaipur.co.uk

Owner Ahad has built his name in MK, running a series of successful restaurants with the help of his equally successful brothers. Here's the background: Known only by his surname, Ahad had a dream to construct a new fantastic new restaurant, in white marble – a Taj Mahal complete with dome. We all have dreams; few of us realise them. He spent years planning and once he decided to proceed he took a financial risk the like of which is no dream ... nightmare rather. Even his banks were dubious.

But Ahad started to build. MK's residents thought he was building a mosque, which Ahad thought hilarious, as he is firmly a restaurateur. It was opened in 2004. Even now, the resulting free-standing restaurant is unique in the world. The inside is just as plush and it cost Ahad a cool £4m. You can spot the Jaipur from some distance away, it really does stand out. Through double glass doors is a large circular reception. A young man takes coats, umbrellas etc. Photographs and awards adorn the walls, a sweeping staircase or a lift takes you upstairs to Ahad's new Thai restaurant, the story of which appears below. There is a sign on the restaurant door, which politely requests smart dress, no trainers or jeans. (Hooray for that). A grand, well-stocked bar, is located on your right and is for drinks service only. If you have arrived early or are waiting for a table, you on the side of the main eating arena, behind very beautiful and high, turquoise glass screens. The dining area has been divided into three spaces. The main area is encircled by more turquoise screens, which in turn encircle a lavish, four-faced, three-tiered waterfall, made from beaten copper cubes. Sparkly glass coins, in different hues of blue share the tiers with fresh orchids. The walls of the other two dining spaces have huge, tasteful, hand-painted murals of Maharajas in howdahs on elephants. Menu Snapshots: Dahi Papdi Chat - tangy mix of flour-crisped, potatoes, chickpeas tossed with yoghurt and tamarind sauce. Squid and Avocado Salad , served on a bed of sliced mango. King Prawn Puri sweet'n'sour spiced prawns rolled into a spinach flavoured bread. Sula Salmon c£8, smoked Rajasthani speciality, marinated with honey and dill leaves. Dum ki Nalli , delicately spiced Avadh's lambshank. Lal Mas, lamb cooked with red chilli. Ahad has a huge following of sophisticated diners, who love it. t's a massive 250 seater, yet, you need to book '... *the whole place wass throbbing, as you might expect in a town where economic growth is meant to be three times the national average.'* Mark Palmer, Daily Telegraph. As last time, we've had loads of reports about the Jaipur and there isn't a bad one amongst them. Indeed have had more delighted reports about the Jaipur than almost any *'Hi Pat, Looking forward to your new good curry guide, take old copy where ever we go. Tried at least 35 restaurants from it. Our favourite is Jaipur in Milton Keynes. We stay in the Hilton for the weekend and always visit the Jaipur Sat night. A place to dress up for.'* DV-W. *'I have visited this restaurant on many occasions and aside from the outstanding quality of the food, the other most noteworthy element of this establishment I would like emphasis is its consistency. The ambience of this restaurant and service is also spot on. It is probably my most visited restaurant; whilst by no means the closest to home (it takes between 45 minutes and one hour to get there). The reason that I keep coming back is that the quality of the food is outstanding and it has never let me down. I have taken friends, clients and overseas visitors there on numerous occasions and it has always consistently been exceptional. Overall – an excellent top quality restaurant! They'll have to change the locks of the door is they want to stop* me coming back! I will continue to recommend it.' BP. Dinner for two, including cocktails and wine, £85. T/a: 10% disc. Sun Family Buffet: 12 to 4 – £12 adult, £6 child. Hours: 12-11.30 (10.30 Sun). Snacks and beverages only between 3 and 5pm, except Sun. *See also inside front cover.*

LA HIND
502 Elder Gate, Station Sq, MK
01908 675948   www.la-hind.com

La Hind, formerly Mr Ahad's Jaipur, is now run by Suhel Ahmed. It is a fairly standard menu, with Duck appearing here and there. Specials include Duck Tikka Jalfrezi. Sun Buffet: £9 adult, £6 child, 12-4. Hours: 12-2.30, not Fri & 5.30-11.30; 12-11 Sun.

JALORI   BYO   TOP 100
23 High St, Woburn Sands, Milton Keynes,
MK17 8RF   01908 281239   www.jalori.co.uk

Abdul Hai (Ahad's brother – see Jaipur, above) is known to all simply as Hai, and like his brother he is a very successful restaurateur. He established the the 80-seater Jalori in 1994. It's bigger than it looks, and has a loyal following. It is really pretty inside and out. Chef Abdul Quayam prepares food that is *'First class.'* BG. Starters include Kebab-e-Aloo Palak £4.35, a crisp rissole of potato and spinach served with sweet & sour sauce. Spicy Tandoori Wrap £4.25, barbecued spicy sweet and sour chicken served in a pocket of thin Indian bread. Some mains: Elaichi Duckling c£10, roasted duck breast cooked with spices, dried apricot, pepper, tomato and fresh herbs. Chicken or Lamb Peri Peri £8.45, chicken or spring lamb cubes, spiced with peri peri sauce, (chilli) and finished with Sun-dried tomatoes. One English dish roosts uneasily on the menu: Roast Chicken with chips peas and mushrooms. £8.95. After all these years Hai still hasn't got rid!. If your diners don't like Indian food, why are they there? You do not often find Indian Desserts at Indian restaurants (no demand they tell us) but at the Jalori you will get Gulab jaman, small cake-like fried spheres in sweet syrup and Rasmali, ditto, not fried, in a milky sauce with pistachio nuts, both c£4. They are divine ! Try them, or else it will be 'no demand!' *'I'd like to tell you how much we always enjoy eating at Jalori. Mr Hai and his staff are always very welcoming, the restaurant is* always immaculate and popular with other diners. They have a wide range of choices, all well described on the menu and altho ugh there is always something we haven't tried before, the Onion Bhajees always get my vote as the best I've ever tasted. We do try other Indian restaurants, but the Jalori is the one we keep coming back to.' M.A. Licensed but, unusually you may BYO, corkage charge £2. Every restaurant should do that. Indeed the Jalori deserves its TOP 100 rating for that alone, but it also deserves it for Hai's attention to detail and care. Min charge £15 per person, but no service or cover charges, and the prices are reasonable. Hours: 12-2.30 / 6-11.30. (Sun e-a-m-a-y-l buffet till 3pm, c£10).

ORCHID LOUNGE AT JAIPUR
THAI CUISINE   AWARD WINNER
599 Grafton Gate East, MK9 1AT
01908 669811   www.orchid-lounge.com

It is a sumptuous, astonishing venue, not bettered by anything in the west end. The cooks and waiting staff are Thai and the food is authentic and served beautifully. We have had several reports which cannot fault the place. *'Situated upstairs in the excellent Jaipur restaurant in Milton Keynes, this restaurant oozes class from the moment you get through the door. The interior is exquisite and the ambience was excellent, a bright and airy outlook with access to balconies which boasted 'stunning' (I quote) views of Milton Keynes. The waiters / waitresses also looked the part, being dressed in regional costumes, and there was a lady playing traditional dulcimer as you entered.'* SO. Menu Snapshot: Orchid Lounge Mixed Starters £1.95, A selection of Spring Rolls, BBQ Chicken Wings, Chicken Satays, Prawn Toasts and Fish Cakes. (for two people), Hoy-Ob (Mussels) 9.25 Steamed mussels with chillies, sweet basil and lemongrass; served with traditional Thai chilli dressing. Salads Yam Neua Yang £9, Spicy grilled beef salad with vegetables and chilli dressing. Tom Yam Goong, £6 raditional spicy prawn soup with mushrooms, lemongrass, chillies and lime juice, garnished with chopped coriander. Curries: Panang: Neua, Gai, Ped Lychee from £8, Choice of beef, chicken or duck (lychee) in smooth Panang curry flavoured with coconut milkand Kaffirlime leaves. Vegatable Dishes: Phad Hed Gratium £5, stir-fried seasonal mushrooms with garlic sauce. Phad Phak Ruam-Mit £5 assorted vegetables with oyster sauce. Gaeng Gra-Ree Tofu Lae Phak £8 yellow curry with fresh tofu and vegetables in coconut milk. 12-2.30 & 5.30-11.30; (10.30 Sunday). *See page 78.*

THE SILK ROAD   INDIAN & THAI
151 Grafton Gate E, MK9 1AE
01908 200522   www.thesilkroadrestaurants.co.uk

This is first venture of owners, Adbus Samad, who also lectures on Pan-Asian food at Birmingham City College and Subhojit Chakravarty, who is also Head Chef, who trained as a chef in Calcutta then worked at Delhi's Orchid hotel. The menu is largely Indian regional cuisine, rather than curryhouse, with Thai and fusion in some dishes. Presentation is plated rather than served in a pot or karahi. Many diners dislike this style, because it determines your portion size and it makes sharing difficult – a technique done at a number of trendy London westend Indian restaurants. Some menu snapshots: Rajasthani laal maas £7.95, lamb braised with aromatic spices, chilli, ginger and garlic. Chennai ka Chettinaad, £7.95, fried with spices crushed pepper and curry leaves. Thai Red Curry (Gaeng Phet) flavoured with bamboo shoots, coconut cream, lime leaves and fresh chillies, from £7.95. Malaysian King Prawns £12.95, simmered in coconut milk, lemongrass, chillies and roasted mustard with cucumber and mange tout. Vegetable dishes can each be ordered as side £3.50, or main £5.95. Notable is Dhal Panchmel, a mixture of five different lentils cooked slowly in a pot and then tempered with whole cumin. Indian Banquet £14.95 pp (min 2) and Oriental Banquet £15.95 pp (min 4). Hours: 12-2.15 & 6-11. All day Sun Buffet 12-9.30.

Newport Pagnell

MYSORE   TOP 100
101 High St, Newport Pagnell, MK16 8EN
01908 216426   www.the-mysore.co.uk

Another high-standard goodie from the Ahad stable, this one operated by brother M Abdul Odud. *'The dining room, cleverly housed within two cottages, seats 98, yet provides a number of secluded areas, which give a good feeling of privacy'* HG. *'Lamb Dhansak with Sag, Mixed Raitha, Pullao Rice and Paratha, all very good. The complete meal and decor (small corners and niches, then a large area with skylight, a bit colonial and glorious at full moon) to be recommended.'* BG. *'Colleague prefers the Mysore to Jaipur. He had Chingri Puri – KP's served in a thick sauce on thin deep-fried bread. I had, Jhinga Puri – KP's in a sweet and sour sauce, served on a puffed bread. Both went down a treat. Followed by Chicken Zallander, Chicken Delight, Vegetable Pullao, Bhindi and Naan. I have to admit that it was better than the Jaipur, which is not exactly a slouch in the curry stakes. I guess when you are choosing between very good restaurants, personal taste has to come into it. I have been to the Jaipur and had just about the best meal I have had, but it is a bit formal. I like places that are more cosy fand laid back and the Mysore is that'* MW. T/a:10% disc. Hours: 12-2.30 & 6-11.30.

Princess Risborough

COCO TAMARIND
Aylesbury Rd, Askett, Princes Risborough, HP27 9LY
01844 343111   www.cocotamarind.co.uk

Opened in 2005 in the former Black Horse pub, this classy restaurant seems to have got it right. The parking is sorted, the decor is modern and stylish with elegant, high backed chairs, white tablecloths, recessed spotlights in the ceiling and a pretty blue teardrop-shaped oil lamp and a rose bowl containing a contemporary flower on each table. There is a wooden display cabinet at the far end of this 62-seater restaurant, housing traditional Indian-themed ornaments including wooden elephant bookends, spice collages and a pestle and mortar. The effect is finished off with solid, nicely weighted cutlery next to large, square, white 'welcome plates' which remain on the table during popadums. Being just a couple of miles from Chequers, the Prime Minister's country residence, you never know who might drop in for dinner. David and Samantha Cameron do, it seems. Owner Mohammad Hasan looks after front of house. Chef Anwar Hussain is in charge of cuisine with Asab Ali. The menu offers North Indian standards, including some luxury items, such as mussels, duck, salmon & monkfish; plus a few dishes from Goa – all carefully cooked. Starters weigh in at around £6 to £8. Main courses: eg Tandoori Monk Fish, £17and Goan Fish Curry £14. *'I visited Coco Tamarind twice in the last week and although the food is still excellent (possibly moving towards Top 100 standards in fact), they have reduced the size of the onion bahjis, so they are not the size of bowling balls any more (you now get two cricket ball sized pieces instead). They still represent an excellent execution of this dish though, but I wouldn't want folks to feel cheated if they are expecting huge ones!'* SO. 12 -2.30 & 6 -11.

YOU SAY OK
You may get a discount if you show them this Guide.

PRINCESS RISBOROUGH: JAFLONG 16 Duke Street ~ 01844 274443. *'Reasonably priced, very friendly, welcoming staff. Best in the immediate local area.'* SO.

WINSLOW: MAHABHARAT 25 Market Square 01296 713611. 44-seater est 1979, taken over by Nurul Islam in 1990. T/a: 15% disc. 6-11.30; 12 Sat.

CAMBRIDGESHIRE

Area:
East of England

Adjacent Counties:
Beds, Essex, Herts, Rutland, Lincs.-

Cambridge

CAFE NAZ   TOP 100
47 Castle Street, CB3 0AH
01223 363666   www.cafenaz.co.uk

One of the very successful restaurants in the bright, well-run chain. It is in our A-LIST as Nominated Best Bangladeshi and Winner Best Chef Award. *'One of the* best meals that I have had.' JP. Party room 30 Del: 2m £12. Hours: 12-3 & 6-12. Menu details and branches at Cafe Naz, Brick Lane London, E1.

COCUM KERELAN
71 Castle St, Cambridge, CB3 0AG
01223 312569   www.keralagroup.co.uk

Good Keralan food plus they do formula curries as well. See Rhada Krishna Bhavan, London SW17.]

THE RICE BOAT KERELAN
37 Newnham Road, Cambridge CB3 9EY
www.riceboat.com

Identical to Cocum's Kerelan menu above and similar pricesbut no formula curries.

YOU SAY OK
You may get a discount if you show them this Guide.

GOLDEN CURRY 111 Mill Road, CB1 2AZ 01223 329432 www.thegoldencurry.co.uk 12-2.30 & 6-12.

GULSHAN 106 Regent Street CB2 1DP ~ 01223 302330. *'Polite staff - handshakes by five of the staff!* The flavours overlapped.' DW

INDIA HOUSE 31 Newnham Rd, Cambridge ~ 01223 461661

PIPASHA 529 Newmarket Rd ~ 01223 577786. Mngr: Abdul Hye's 60-seater in 2 rooms. Del: £2.50 ch, 3m £10 min. Hours: 12-2 / 5.30-11.30; 11 Sun. www.Pipasha-restaurant.co.uk

KOHINOOR 74 Mill Road, CB1 2AS ~ 01223 323639. Used by generations of dons and students.

TAJ TANDOORI BYO 64 Cherry Hinton Rd CB1 7AA ~ 01223 248063 www.tajtandooricambridge.co.uk

ELY: SURMA TANDOORI 78 Broad Street, Ely ~ 01353 662281

PETERBOROUGH: BOMBAY BRASSERIE 52 Broadway ~ 01733 565600

INDIA GATE 9 Fitzwilliam St, P'brough ~ 01733 34616

TAJ MAHAL 37 Lincoln Rd, P'brough ~ 01733 348840

ST NEOTS: JONONI 12 High St, St Neots ~ 01480 219626

Wisbech

CHESHIRE
Area: North West

Adjacent Counties:
Clwyd, Derbs,
Greater Man,
Mers, Shrops, Staffs

MOGHUL
13A North Street, PE13 1NP   01945 466228

'We visit this newly refurbished restaurant every Friday night and have done for the last six years. Everything is clean and welcoming! There is always a very friendly welcome. Every table is laid and complete with fresh flowers. Menu is quite extensive – but they will cook things that are not on the menu and will offer "new" dishes. We've watched them advise those who have never visited a curry house before. Portions are generous and service is with a smile and a quip. Food quality is always good. There is quiet background music and comfortable seating, including for those waiting for T/as. We have a lot of curry houses to choose from in the King's Lynn and Wisbech area but always return to the Moghul. They cope well with large parties and still look after the individuals on their own. Toilets are clean and well looked after. We recommend the Moghul to everyone !' JRF

Chester

GATE OF INDIA
25 City Road Chester CH1 3AE   01244 327131

64-seater in 2 rooms, est 1973 by Moinuddin Ahmed from from 1992. T/a: 10% before 11. Hours: 6-2 (2.30. Sat & 1 Sun).

Ellesmere Port, Wirral

The Wirral is neither a town nor a county and until 1965 part of Cheshire. Since then the northern part (a small, (15 miles x 7) digit-like, curry-rich peninsula between the rivers Mersey and Dee) has been part of Merseyside. Ellesmere Port remains in south Wirral but is in NW Cheshire. See also Merseyside.

THE TAJ OF AGRA FORT   TOP 100
1 Cambridge Rd, Ellesmere Pt CH65 4AE
0151 355 1516

A wide green and red frontage invites you into a spacious, clean and welcoming restaurant owned by Shams Uddin Ahmed. *'A couple of nice touches set it apart – the waiters, in their Agra Fort jackets, ask you how long you want between starters and main courses and give you the time requested, and slices of orange were delivered with the hot towels after the main course, whether desserts were ordered or not. Pepper stuffed with small pieces of tandoori chicken and lamb, as mentioned in the guide, was excellent. Paratha was one of the best I've had. A very good evening and I look forward to visiting again.'* OC. 'Heartily recommended.' RW. *'We totally recommend this restaurant to you.'* MB and friends. *'Decor and service top drawer. Popadums – warm and crisp, lime pickle needed replenishment, garlic and ginger chutney (a new one to me) was excellent. Tikka melt in the mouth, Bhajia size of tennis ball. CTM – too red, Jalfrezi – drier than normal, both excellent. Naan warm and moist. Top rate.'* DB. 12-2 & 6-11.30 (Sat 12.30am; Sun buffet 1-11.30.

YOU SAY OK, Ellesmere Port
You may get a discount if you show them this Guide.

HOLDI SPICE LOUNGE 331-Chester Road, Ellesmere Port, CH66 3RF 0871 9695165 www.holdispicelounge.com

LIGHT OF INDIA 11 Whitby Road, Ellesmere Port, CH65 8AA | 0871 963 0614

MUJIB Viscount Hotel, Whitby Rd, Ellesmere Port CH65 8DN 0151 357 1676 www.mujibrestaurants.co.uk Chef Proprietor Nazrul Ali has created a fusion menu plusclassics like Korma, Madras and Vindaloo. *Branch: Harrogate, N Yorks.*

SAFFRON Whitby Road, Ellesmere Port, CH65 6RT 01513555277 www.saffronellesmereport.co.uk. In large premises with eye-catching conservatories.

Knutsford

SHAMOLI
73A King Street, Knutsford WA16 6DX
01565 652735

It's in a basement which puts some of its critics off. But it's so popular that you need to book to be sure. Good natured experienced staff handle things with aplomb.

Neston

BRITANNIA SPICE
18-19 The Parade, Parkgate, Neston, CH64 6SA
0151 336 1774   www.britannia-spice.com

Being located on the 'seafront' with spectacular views over the Dee estuary, with the Welsh hill as the backdrop, especiallly when the sun is setting, All the buildings on Parkgate are painted white; many with black beams. Brittania Spice is the only 'Indian' in the area, and it has parking facilities. Inside is '*a maze of a place, spread over two floors with a couple of tables tucked into nooks and crannies*'. BT. Get (or book) a window seat to enjoy the views. Competent and friendly service. Food is standard formula items. Starters range from £2.50 to £4. Notable is Whole Pepper £2.95 stuffed with chicken, lamb, prawn or vegetable curry. Notable Mains: Dilqush £5.50-roasted chicken fillets simmered in coriander and garlic; Murgh Batwaar £5.80, created for the Royal Indian Cavalry, chicken tikka and minced lamb in a medium sauce. As well as CTM £5.95, there's DTM (Duck) at £7.95. Boal Bangladeshi fish £6.90 Set meals (£19.50 for 2) non Veg Thali £11 (Papadom, Tandoori Chicken, & Balti, Keema Mottor, Pilau Rice & Naan. Veg Thali £9.50 (Papadom, Mix Veggie Starters, Vegetable Dopiaza, Bombay Aloo, Dal Sag, Pilau Rice & Naan). 5-11 (Sun: 1 -10).

YOU SAY OK, Cheshire

CHESTER: GATE OF INDIA 25 City Road, Chester 01244 327131.

CREWE: EVENING SPICE Poolside, Madeley, Nr Crewe 01782 750088 Est 1998 in a former pub. Prop Nasir Miah with chef GA Choudhury. T/a: 20% disc. Hours: 5-10.30, Mon closed, except Bank Hols. www.eveningspice.co.uk

MIDDLEWICH: SPICE GARDEN 338 Booth La. ~ 01606 841549. '*Strange location - you need a car to get there! Quite surprised to see a number of people eating at 5.45pm. Madras curry sauce thick and spicy. Service pleasant.*' DB.

SANDBACH: THE TASTE OF THE RAJ 11 High Street. ~ 01270 753752. Anam Islam's 38-seater.

WINSFORD: KESAAN 23 Queen's Pde. ~ 01606 862940. 'Scruffy but excellent'. DB.

TARPORLEY: RED FOX NEW ENTRANT Four Lane Ends, Tarporley. 01892 733152. Owner, AK Jilani's former public house, nicely decorated in white and orange, with heavy dark wood tables and chairs, upholstered in yellow and orange stripes and soft lighting.

Northwich

BENGAL DYNASTY TOP 100
Hall Lane, Wincham, Northwich CW9 6DG
01606 351597   www.thebengaldynasty.com

The interior of this 150-seater is an absolute dream. with white walls, blonde floor boards, original hanging art and suspended lights over each table. Running down both sides of the restaurant, are comfortably upholstered, semicircular booths, encasing round tables, very stylish and enough space for six. Square tables, two lines of them, run parallel to the booths, giving great flexibility for dining. '*Impressed.*' DBAC. This is the third of a small chain of excellently managed restaurants. For more information see Bengal Dynasty, Deeside, Clwyd, Wales.

Warrington

JAHAN
Chester Rd Walton Warrington   01925 86086

Previously 'The Ship Inn.' '*Just happened to be driving past, noticed this relatively new restaurant open for lunch. Out of the way for passing custom, so surprised to be joined by a group of twenty others. Nicely decorated, modern style, light and airy. One of the best Birianis I've had over the last year. I'll give it another try.*' DB. Sun Buffet adult c£12, child £7. Secure parking. Hours: 12-2.30 & 5-11; 12-11 Sat & Sun.

CORNWALL

Area: West Country

Adjacent County: Devon

Bodmin

VIRAJ
50 Higher Bore St, Bodmin, PL31 1JW
01208 74664   www.virajbodmin.co.uk

After opening as a take-away in about 1996, it expanded to a fully fledged restaurant some four years later under new ownership as a fairly standard, well produced venue. *'The food was surprisingly good. Three round Onion Bhajias as starters came with riata and a salad garnish and were crisp, nicely spiced and a good curry house standard. Chicken Chat was very good and as it should be with small pieces of chicken in a hot and tangy sauce. Main dish of Tandoori Chicken was extremely well marinated to get the flavour ingrained, very tasty and plenty of it so got high marks, while the Chicken Dhansak was also of a good standard - lots of large pieces of chicken in a thick sauce with a nice, underlying hotness which came through during the eating. Mixed Vegetable Bhaji a little greasy but had a nice, peppery flavour to it and a good variety of vegetables. Prices about average, portions ample and service good. All in all an unexpectedly good formula curry meal and one of the better Indian restaurants in the area.'* Malcolm Wilkins. No cheques. 5.30-11.

Padstow

THE JOURNEYMAN
Mellingey Mill, Mellingey, St Issey, PL27 7QU
01841 540604   www.journeymanrestaurant.co.uk

Situated in a picturesque 17th century mill house a former tea house owned by Christine Old, it is up a narrow lane where the chances of attracting casual passing trade are zero. In 2004 Brummy Steve Lloyd approached the owner with the concept to feature Indian and Oriental cuisine as well as traditional English fare at this tiny 20-seater. Though not a professionachef, he had travelled extensively in the Far East and lived for a while in Hong Kong and India, where he developed his love of their cuisine. He said *'I just got fed up with not being able to get a decent curry after years of coming here on holiday from the midlands and so decided to do something about it'*. Pat Chapman's balti cooking book was the first curry recipe book I bought'. In 2008 it underwent a refurbishment, *'although I am delighted to say that it hasn't lost its 'olde-worlde' charm. I understand that there is further seating downstairs which can accommodate private functions.'* MW. Dr MO says *'First impressions: very friendly, cosy, tasteful decor, original features in keeping with the buildings original function as a watermill. Friendly welcome, homely, felt comfortable straightaway. Well presented and varied menu - including Beef Wellington. Good quantities, excellent Balti Jalfrezi - very tasty. Very impressed all round.'* Dr MO. OK so it does English food. but in the curry desert of Cornwall, it makes a change not to be a Rick Stein fish operation. *'I have eaten in Jamie Oliver's 15 at Watergate Bay, Rick Stein's Seafood Restaurant, Margots and Paul Ainsworth No 6 in Padstow. All have been good to varying degrees, but I have to say that for a balance of ambience (the best), quality of food (superb) and price (the most reasonable), then the Journeyman is well ahead.'* MW. Starters from £5.25-£7. Balti Chicken/Veg £8.50; Lamb/Prawn/Quorn/Paneer, £8.95; KP £11. Steve loves his chillies. *'Make Chef's Day!'* says the *menu challenge: 'Any style of curry can be cooked as our very hottest dish with 7 types of chilli, including naga & habaneros, some of trictly for experienced curryholics! This dish will be a lot hotter than anything you may have previously tried so please order with care!!'* Reports on this any anything Journeyman welcomed. Large onsite car park. Two Bed Cottage available. Hours: In season: Mon- Sat: from 6. Booking essential.

Penzance

BABAS   BYO
The Promenade, Wherrytown, Penzance TR18 4NP
01736 330777   www.babapenzance.co.uk

Opened in 2004 by Sazzadur Rahman in the last remaining fisherman's cottage on the picturesque seafront promenade between Penzance and Newlyn. The 43 seater is managed by Lucy Thorogood. It's a well appointed restaurant on the . *'The menu (which must be the biggest I've seen in a restaurant - a heavy tome of about 2ft x 1 ft in pseudo leather) has all the usuals plus a few different names. Its tsister restaurant is in Truro, in which I've eaten and which provides a good curry, and has a good pedigree. And so it proved. The Onion Bhajias (3 round type) were crisp and well spiced, and very attractively presented with 4 slices of cucumber and 4 slices of radish neatly arranged*

SPLENDIDLY INDIAN, SUPERBLY SMOOTH

around the edge of the plate (In fact, all the plates were similarly artistically garnished). The Balti Dhansak was really no different from an ordinary Dhansak except that it was served in a karahi, but it had a nice flavour and was pleasantly hot. The Vegetable Bhaji was good, dry with a nice spicy/peppery flavour and contained a good selection of vegetables. The service was good and friendly, the portions perfectly adequate, but the prices were distsinctly higher than average. However, it was a good standard formula curry, well presented in pleasant surroundings' MW. Sun-Th 3 course Meal £15. Parking opposite. T/a 30% discount. 12-2 & 5-10.30. Branch: Baba Truro.

St Austell

NEPALESE GURKHA   NEPALESE
9 Grant's Walk, St Austell

'Waiters are in traditional costume with a small fez, and the whole dining area is light and airy with plenty of space between tables. It seats over 100 in two dining areas separated by a glass partition and there is an open kitchen. Décor is modern, with wipe-down tables, light-coloured walls and a splash of greenery. The menu contains Nepalese dishes in addition to many of the more common Indian dishes. There is also a 'Specials Board'. We started with the traditional Nepalese Momo, 5 small stuffed dumplings: the inside meat was very tasty. and Choyala (diced lamb spiced with 'aromatic spices' and ginger): excellent – well marinated tender lamb with a good taste of ginger and an underlying perfumy flavour that we couldn't quite place. For mains we had Choudary Haans (duck breast with 'Nepalese herbs') and Chitwan Bazaar (their Nepalese chef's version of a Nepalese dish combining of lamb and chicken with spinach and vegetables), accompanied with Aloo Tama (a bamboo shoots with potato. All were very good, with a mysterious underlying perfumed herb/spice flavour. Not only was it a good meal, but it was all well presented, and the service first class. In fact some of the friendliest of staff I have come across. The head chef - Mr A - walks the tables towards the end to enquire about the food and engage any customer who wants to talk about the food. Prices might be slightly higher than ordinary high street Indian restaurants in other parts of the country, but on par with the better ones in Cornwall, and the portions plentiful. marks all round.' MW.

YOU SAY OK
You may get a discount if you show them this Guide.

LISKEARD: EVEREST TANDOORI   NEPALESE   Pike Street, Liskeard PL14 3HW 0871 5287809. All the old favourites with Nepalese items.
LOOE: MOONLIGHT TANDOORI Fore Street, Looe PL13 1AE 01503 265372. This family-run venue has been going for decades and has a devoted local following. No tourist jokes about Vindaloo and the other thing please; they've heard 'em all.
PENZANCE: GANGES BALTI 18 Chapel St. ~ 01736 333002. 'A large restaurant. Huge chunks of chicken, the largest I've ever seen. Many different flavours in the meal, top quality stuff.' GGP. 'Chicken Karahi, cooked with black pepper, attractive sour taste. Very prompt, efficient service.' MP.
PENZANCE: TAJ MAHAL 63 Daniel Place Penzance. 'Excellent. Quantity generous. Service prompt and polite. We always enjoy this little gem. Good quality food at reasonable prices. 8/10' G&MP.
ST AUSTELL: TAJ MAHAL   57 Victoria Rd, Mount Charles 01726 73716. Est 1985. 'Bhajias, crisp and tasty. CTM well-spiced, generous portions. Looking forward to visiting once more.' N&JG. 5.30-1.30.
ST IVES: RUBY MURRIES TAKEAWAY   PUNJABI   4b Chapel Street. ~ 01736 796002. T/a only. 'Punjabi cuisine. Have arrangement with pub up the road you can eat your T/a with a pint – an admirable arrangement.' MW.
TRURO: GANGES   St Clement St. ~ 01872 24353. Truro's first (1987) and biggest (100) owned by Mohammed Udin. 'Good sized portions, average prices.' MW. T/a: 25% disc, min £10. Hours: 12-2.15 / 6-11.15; 11.45 Fri & Sat.
TRURO: SHANAZ   1 Edward St. ~ 01782 262700. Karim Uddin's popular Shanaz is in its 12th year. 'Our Truro favourite. Food extremely well done and well presented.' GP.

St Ives

RAJPOOT   BYO
56 Gabriel Street, St Ives, TR26 2LU   01736 795307

The Rajpoot is a long term entrant in this Guide. It is a typcial curry house serving formula food, The locals tell us how much they like it. St Ives is a pretty vibrant tourist town and it has generally received good reports from the tourists too. 'Were we impressed ! Nice clean surroundings, very approachable staff and excellent food cooked freshly while we waited and if you were on a budget you could even take your own wine' [get it at the Co-op opposite] 'although they did have a full licence! Who could ask for more? Highly recommended.' DC.

Email your opinions to
pat@patchapman.co.uk
from a one-liner to
an essay! All welcome.

CUMBRIA
formerly Cumberland and Westmoreland

Area: North West England (Lake District)

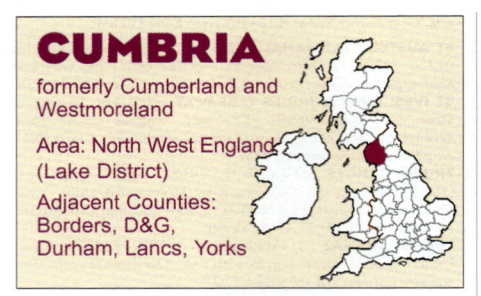

Adjacent Counties: Borders, D&G, Durham, Lancs, Yorks

Barrow-in-Furness

MITHALI
252-254 Dalton Road, Barrow-in-Furness, LA14 1PN
01229 432166   www.mithali.co.uk

'Drove around town and discovered Mithali by accident. Met a man outside, carrying his T/a, said it was his regular haunt and the curries were very good. So, in we went! Two elderly waiters seemed to know all their regular diners. (Show them this Guide and you may get a discount). Mushroom Pakora - dipped in a light besan batter, slightly spiced, then deep-fried - very, very good. Sheek Kebab - OK. Mithali Special Curry - lamb and chicken in hot sauce with huge lightly battered (unshelled) King Prawn on top eaten with Nan bread - couldn't fault it. A little on the expensive side, but we came away extolling the virtues of the place.' T&MH. Takeaway: 2 Meals, 2 Portions of Rice and a Naan for £9.95. 5-12 (to 12.30 Fri & Sat).

Carlisle

DHAKA TANDOORI
Carleton Rd, Carlisle, CA1 3DS   01228 523855

Off at J42 of the M6 and you'll find y Mahmud Ali, Fazul Karim and Abdul Harid's 100-seater smart, upmarket restaurant. Est in 1985, the 100-seater has car parking for 100 at rear and a new large front conservatory. *'Comfortable seating and pleasant decor. Good, friendly service. Large portions of lovely food reasonably priced. Much better than motorway services!'* IB. *'Consistently good. Try Chef M Ali's Kebab Kyberi, diced chicken in mild spices with fresh tomatoes, onions, served sizzling in iron karahi.'* AY. Show them this Guide and you may get a disc. Del: £12 min. Hours: 12-2 (not Fri) & 6-12.

TEZA
4a, English Gate Plaza, Botchergate, Carlisle
CA1 1RP   01228 525222   www.teza.co.uk

Contemporary restaurant, full name Teza Indian Canteen and Bar. Uncluttered, clean lines, decorated with white walls, spot lighting, dark veneer floors and bar, tubular steel chairs with leather seat and back (you know, those iconic German designs from the 1930's) no tablecloths, white linen napkins. Fantastic cocktail bar. Extensive wine list. Head chef, Sanjay Mohakud's Menu Snapshot: Chicken Malai Tikka ; Punjabi Chilli Chicken Tikka both £4; Salmon Tikka £5 - cubes of salmon marinated in English mustard, honey and cream cheese, grilled; Aloo Tikka £4 - pan fried patties of mash potato filled with green peas, served warm, topped with yoghurt tamarind and mint chutney; Chicken Chettinad £8.50 boneless chicken, South Indian spicy masala with black pepper and mace; Lamb Shank Rogan Josh £12, braised slowly in a chilli infused broth, flavoured with fennel and ginger powder, served with Vegetable Pullao; Mushroom & Jeera Rice £3; Alloo Kulcha £3. Thursday night: all-u-like buffet £9.95pp, from 5.30. Tue-Sat: 12.30-11; Sun-Mon: 2-10.

Cockermouth

THE SPICE CLUB
25 Main Street, Cockermouth, CA13 9LE   01900 828288   www.thespiceclubcockermouth.co.uk

Six brothers set it up in 2006, with one, Abul 'Jimmy' Haidur as manager *'Recomended to me by a friend who drives miles to here for a takeaway. ignoring all his local curry houses. A very modern design in the spotlessly clean restaurant. Very nice welcome and good table settings very well laid out and a pleasure to sit at. Menu had many stylish dishes as well as the usuals. Service very good and professional. Food was superb. I had Chicken Tikka 'Delight', a dish made with the addition of Cointreau (the Cointreau was a bit heavy and appeared to have been added at the end of cooking, careful if you are driving. This did not spoil the dish but it almost did). All served in white dishes/bowls and plates. Onion rice was very good and the Garlic as was Cheese Naan. Toilets were emaculate.'* RE. T/a: 15% Disc. 12-2.0 & 5.30-11.30.

THE MANGO TREE
Market Square, Kirkby Stephen, CA17 4QT
017683 74959

'Opened 2009. Was well impressed, new and very clean, very welcoming. Described as contemporary Indian cuisine, their menu is interesting, including plenty noted by 3 chillis (very hot !) Seats around 30 - 35 max. After the obligatory (for me anyway !) 2 pops & pickles, I opted for a King Prawn Chilli Fry (2 chilli, hot) as starter. I wouldn't argue if they upgraded this to 3 chillis, a long time since I had such a hot starter. West Indian Chicken (3 chilli dish) for my main course accompanied by Lemon Pilau Rice, Garlic Naan and a side order of Jeera Alu. All very nice, tasty and filling. Food cost £25.25. Service was very good too, waiters asking me between courses whether I was ready for the next. Despite the place being half-full...quite a turnround of customers, some leaving, others coming....I was impressed by the speed and efficiency of service. Booking a table might be advisable. Overall, very favourable. Didn't try the toilets but, as the restaurant is very clean, I expect them to be likewise. Will be going back, it is my local,

SPLENDIDLY INDIAN, SUPERBLY SMOOTH

Penrith

RAJINDA PRADESH
Centre Parks, Whinfell Forest, Penrith CA10 2DW

This restaurant has been there for yearsalong with other outlets the likes of Hucks US Diner, Bella Italia, Café Rouge. Rajinda Pradesh is quality Indian and we have to make it clear that only booked-in resident holidaymakers can enter the Park, let alone dine there.There are four parks (listed below) all in 400 acre forests. The spin says *'Nestled in a stunning landscape on the edge of the Lake District, it's a wildlife haven, home to one of the few remaining colonies of Red Squirrels'. 'Rajinda is nicely decorated, light and airy, and has a lovely relaxed atmosphere. The food is excellent. Pops and chuts excellent. Menu has changed since my last visit but there is plenty of variety. I ordered Kodi Vepudu, chicken marinated in spices and vinegar and deep fried, very like a spicy chicken tikka, excellent start to the meal. Jacs had the onion bhaji, crisp, light and moist. My main course was Chicken Chattinadu, chicken cooked in a tamarind sauce with 10 different spices, from South India. Again a good portion of chicken, plenty of sauce beautifully spiced. Pillau rice was light and fluffy. Jacs had the Methiwale Scallops, we asked for the sauce to come separately as Jacs wasn't sure whether she would like it. After deliberation with the chef she was told that yes they would do it that way but the flavours would be totally different. Huge portion of scallops arrived (at least 10) and a well spiced fenugreek sauce. Again the food in this restaurant never fails to impress and is up there in my top 5. It's a pity that we only visit once a year. Food & Drink: £50'.* DB. Also at Centre Parks Sheerwood, Notts, Elveden Suffolk and Longleat, Wilts. NB: There is another outlet called 'Dining' which also includes Indian in its offerings. Reports please.

TASTE OF BENGAL
61 Stricklandgate, Penrith, CA11 7NJ 01768 891700

Established 1994. Fully licensed and air-conditioned. *'Sun night at 7.45pm: waiters not geared up for a rush, because two other parties arrived at the same time. Nice to see families with children enjoying a curry experience. Parking difficult, fairly good 'chippy' across the road. Drinks served promptly, but waited for starters. We shared a Mixed Kebab - not really big enough for two, too much for one. Friends ate Onion Bhajia £3 and Sheek Kebab £2.70, OK, enjoyed. Naga Curry Masala chicken version £7, marvellous. Lamb Tikka Roghan Josh £6.50, lamb slightly chewy, but not gristly bits. Lamb Pathia £7.50, definitely the hottest dish between us, enjoyed it nevertheless. Chicken Tawa c£11, expensive, but Nan included, very impressed, very tasty, slices of chicken, served on griddle. Our friends, Julia and Peter, have a spoilt Jack Russell, they always take a couple of pieces of lamb or chicken back it him - but not today, they didn't. Highly recommended.'* T&MH. Thursday Night: choice of starter and main course set meals for £10.95, including Pops & Chuts. T/a: 20% disc. 5-11 (11.30 Fri & Sat).

STARLY'S AT STAVELEY
47 - 49 Main Street, Staveley, LA8 9LR
015398 21807 www.starlys.co.uk

Steven Higginson (self-taught cook) and Carly Jones (front) (=owners of Starly's (get it?) met selling timeshare then moved to Cumbria in 2007. They decided to sell curry spice blends and currently have 14 in total, with recipes so they say *'unique to us'*. [deja vu for the Curry Club - we had 44 blends in 1982, see page 13]. The also have a bistro by the entrance to the Mill Yard, and near the celebrated Hawkshead Brewery. A bistro is defined in Wikipedia as *'a small restaurant serving moderately priced simple meals in a modest setting. Bistros are defined mostly by the foods they serve; home-cooking with and slow-cooked robust earthy dishes, foods are typical'.* So often this word is misused, but not at Starlys. It's spot-on. The small venue has simple pine tables and chairs, and the equally small menu delivers Bistro dishes as defined. Starters: Chana Chaa £4.75, Chickpea's and potato salad with flakes of corn (contains yogurt); Keema Paratha..£4, Paratha bread lined with spicy lambs mince. Main Courses: Matter Paneer £8.50, Indian Cheese in a spicy tomato sauce with peas; Gujerati Dhal £6.50, lentils with onions, chillies & ginger; Goan Coconut Chicken..£8.50, coconut cream & yoghurt with mild spices; Mumbai Pork £9, Slow cooked pork in a garlic & ginger sauce; Kashmiri Beef (house special) £9.50' cooked for 7 hours in a balsamic vinegar & garlic sauce. Thu-Sat 6.00 - late.

YOU SAY OK
You may get a discount if you show them this Guide.

KESWICK: LAKELAND SPICE: 81 Main Street, Keswick CA12 5DT 017687 80005

THE ROYAL BENGAL Central Car Pk Rd, Keswick, Cumbria CA12 5DF 017687 75086

COCKERMOUTH: TASTE OF INDIA 5 Hereford Ct, Main St ~ 01900 822880. F Rahman's Chef NI Khan's 60-seater in 2 rooms + 44-seat private room. *'Excellent flavours / use of spices.'* AY. Hours: 12-2.30 5.30-12. Branches: Red Fort, Keswick *'excellent meal.'* DH, and Emperor of India, Bowness.

KENDAL: FLAVOURS OF INDIA 20 Blackhall Rd, Kendal ~ 01539 722711. Yaor Miah's 95-seater.

PENRITH: CHUINI'S 19 King St, Penrith ~ 01768 866760. Hours: 5-12.

WHITEHAVEN: AKASH 3 Tangier St.~ 01946 691171 Owners Abdul Karim, MK Rayman and chef Nurul Hoque. T/a 20% disc. Hours: 12-2.30 6-12.

ALI TAJ 34 Tangier Street, Whitehaven 01946 693085. *'Long-est curryhouse gets better with age. Best in the area.'* RE

Email your opinions to
pat@patchapman.co.uk
from a one-liner to
an essay! All welcome.

DERBYSHIRE

Area: East Midlands

Adjacent Counties: Cheshire, Leics, Greater Manchester,

Alfreton

NEW BENGAL BALTI & TANDOORI
3 King Street, Town Centre, Alfreton DE55 5PU
01773 832824   www.newbengalrestaurant.co.uk

We hear of warm welcomes from manager Mr Rahman and his cheerful crew. Standard menu and some *'tasty unusuals'* RCF such as Starters: Spicy Fish Cake, Bengali style £3.95, cooked with aromatic spices and served with salad; Garlic Mushroom Puri, £3.65 lightly spiced mushrooms, garlic and fresh herbs served on a deep fried leavened bread. Five spicy Soups, £2.45, Chicken, Dall, Mulligatawny, Tomato & Vegetable. Mains: Tandoori Jalfrezi Cocktail, including Chicken & Lamb Tikka and Sheek Kebab prepared with ghee, green chillies, red pepper, tomatoes, hot spices, fresh herbs and thickened to a savoury flavour; Fish Chilli Mosolla, marinated in garlic, flavoured with Dhania leaves, cooked with tomatoes and ground spices, thickened to give a rich taste. Sat -Thur: 6-12; Fri & Sat to 1am.

Burton-on-Trent

ANOKI BURTON   TOP 100
A38 Burton Road, Eggington, Burton   DE65 6GZ
01283 704888   www.anokiburton.co.uk

One of the three Anoki restaurants in the east Midlands. It's just a mile or so north east of this famous brewing town and home of Cobra the ex Mumbai Blue is now in the capable hands of this well-praised restaurant group. The unusual address on the A38 between Derby and Birmingham means a large car park which fills quickly, despite the restaurant's capacity of over 170. *'It's a premium car thief's Mecca! a sign of good clientele dining there'* AS. Advisable to book. The decor is 'plush maharaja's palace' *'The dining room is a stylish and sophisticated affair with a rich colour scheme, soft lighting and exquisite attention to detail. As with all three of the Anoki restaurants, the experience to be had when dining here is unique, indulgent and totally memorable with male and female serving staff in traditional costume.'* GD. The menu carries all your favourites. Menu snapshot: Tandoori Garlic Mushrooms £6.95, coated in a special spicy garlic mix and cooked with cheese, peppers and onions; Lamb Chop £7.95, in a spiced marinade and cooked until tender and slightly crisp over charcoal; Hot Chilli Fish £6.95, cod tossed in a piquant chilli sauce; Balti Special Mix £15.95, chicken, lamb and king prawns prepared together Balti-style fresh, fast and spicy; Lamb Haandi £16.95, cooked slowly in a sealed pot, on the bone for maximum flavour, in a spicy aromatic sauce; Chicken Makhani £13.95, aka CTM which Anoki describe as chef's signature dish. Vegetables as mains £11.95, sides £5.95, such as Achari Aubergines in a pickle sauce. Set meal with 4 starters and main of 5 curries, Breads & Pilau Rice, £28pp; with Dessert & Coffee £33. Min 2. A la carte not cheap with the average food price c£25 plus drinks. Wines from £13.50 to £44. So it tends to be a place for that special occasion and for the well-healed patrons. Look out for deals, half price before 7pm and BOGOFs at the time of writing. Mon-Sat: 5.30-11; Sunday 3.30-9.30.   *Branches: Derby & Nottingham.*

The elegant interior and service and customers too at Anoki Burton

Mouthwatering curries by Chesterfield's India Blues

Castle Donnington

CURRY-2-NIGHT
43-45 Borough St, Castle Donington, DE74 2LB
01332 814455   www.c2n.co.uk

'The service exceptionally polite and attentive. Food far more tasty than the insipid offerings that is made at other establishments. Has become a favourite. Recommended.' N&JG. *'All Tandoori Special Masala dishes, Karahi dishes, f and House Specialities are all served with Pulao Rice, making for good value meals. Balti Dishes, are served with a plain Naan Bread - delicious!'* N&JG. T/a: 10% disc, £10 min. Del: £10 min, 5m. 5.30-11.30; (to 12 Fri & Sat)

Chesterfield

INDIAN BLUES
7 Corporation St, Chesterfield, S41 7TP
01246 557505   www.indianblues.com

Curries the way we love them, as mouthwateringly depicted below. *'Colleagues had praised it. Fairly busy, bar with a handful of drinkers looking as though they had no intention of moving to a table. Usual versions of everything,;not a modern style menu. The candle on the table was lit when we asked but blown out when the food arrived! Brinjal Bhajee, disappointing, very undercooked, all other dishes good. Nan, excellent, light, crisp and well charred underneath. Food was very good, very reasonable and we really enjoyed the meal.'* hc. *'Recommended by 'locals'. Despite not booking, were shown to an excellent window table, offered drinks and popadums straight away - fresh and excellent. Very good and hot Shami Kebab. Chicken Pasanda - enjoyed. Mama Halimas Biriani c£9 (lamb tikka, chicken tikka, king prawn served with chilli and tomatoes, hot and spicy) - served on a silver platter, really excellent, hot, spicy - fabulous! (garnished with enough salad to feed a platoon.) Not exceptional service.'* DL. *'You are immediately struck by the 'accuracy' of this restaurant's name when you enter and are faced with the striking red walls! Mixed Kebab starters very good as was Tandoori Trout. Prawn Puree was slightly odd though with a creamy coconut Korma style sauce, although I think this dish seems to be popular in this region (see also Kaash, Chesterfield). Service was good. Overall opinion – very good, would recommend and return here.'* SO. 6 to Late.

Derby

ANOKI   TOP 100
Old Picture Hall, 129 London Rd, Derby, DE1 2QN
01332 292 888   01332 292888   www.anoki.co.uk

A uniformed beezer *(see inset picture left)* greets you at the entrance. Ascend the stairs, adorned by rose petals and enter the dining room where you are warmly welcomed by your host in It is in 'The Old Picture Hall', with a marvellous barrel-vaulted ceiling and modern chandeliers, though the only nebulous link to its cinema origin is the playing of Bollywood musicals on the end wall plasma screen. Menu details on the Burton branch. *'A cut above your average curry house with expensive designer furniture and turbanned waiters of the old school, starched tablecloths and napkins. Marvellously equipped toilets, where hands are dried on individually laundered and rolled white linen towels - top notch stuff. Pops and chuts appeared automatically. Stunning starter. Outstanding Haandi no cloying stewiness, rather an aromatic fusion of quality meat and a well thought out blend of spices. Perfectly accompanied by a light and fluffy Naan covered with plenty of fresh garlic. Very highly recommended and worth missing the train for!'* RW. *'Uses high quality tableware and crockery which would not look out of place in any Michelin star establishment. Luxurious and very tasteful surroundings, very comfortable high backed chairs with beautifully decorated tables including white linen. Complimentary Popadums are served, neatly cut into triangles, with a selection of pickles. Menu quite limited, but varied enough, daily specials add variety. Thoroughly enjoyed starters of Paneer Kebab – excellent; Prawn Puri - best I've tasted. Lamb Haandi, Dal Makhani, Pullao Rice and Nan - perfect presentation and exceptional taste. Extensive but pricey wine list.'* D&VH.   5.30-11.30.

SHALIMAR

2 - 3 Midland Road, Derby, DE1 2SN
01332 366745   www.shalimarderby.co.uk

Mahmood Akhtar's decribes his specialities with original language: Chandani Malai Tikka is white as moonlight, soft and mild tender chicken marinated in cream, cheese and light spices. Vindaloo is related to madras but involving a greater use of garlic, tomato, lemon, ginger and black pepper. We love his menu challenge. *'Have you ever wanted to cook the finest mouth-watering Indian cuisine with some of the world's finest chefs? We invite you to cook your own meal (if you dare) alongside and under the watchful eye of our highly talented and professional kitchen staff.'* Any takers? Please let us know. *'What a fantastic find! A delightful well appointed near to the Midland Hotel and railway station in Derby. Although, only 6pm, on a Saturday night, the Shalimar was nearly full. The Chicken Tikka Masala £8.95 (inc: Pullao Rice) was a large, well flavoured dish and the Mixed Vegetable Roghan Josh £4.95 - was equally generous. Best of all though was the Cheese Naan £2.50. This venue is an equal in service and quality to the nearby Anoki.'* N&JG. Del: £10 min. Secure parking with CCTV. 4.30-12; (to 2am Fri & Sat).

YOU SAY OK :
You may get a discount if you show them this Guide.

DERBY: ABID TANDOORI BYO, 7 Curzon St.   01332 293712. Mohammed Ilyas' 90-seater serves Pakistani and Kashmiri curries. *'Delicious and generous as always. Service always quick and the waiters helpful. BYO, £2.50 a cork.'* NH. Hours: 5.30-3. Branches: Abid, Matlock. (see below) Abid Balti, Causley Rd, Alfreton.
MARSALA ART   6 Midland Rd, DE1 2SN 01332 292629. *'Modern decor and waiters in Indian costumes. Starter: Galoti Seekh Kebab, far from the usual blandness and three rather than the usual two. Main Course: Masala Chooza. well spiced, generous; Sabzi Masala, ditto. Total with pops and a pint: £30, well worth the outlay.'* JP.
MOGUL 43 Green La, Derby. 01332 203303 70-seater. *'Pleasant and friendly. Cracking blend of spices with a real zing!'* RW. Hours 6 -late
SHABUZ BAGAN   80 Osmaston Rd, Derby. 01332 296887. *'Very friendly'* GAM.
RIPLEY: SHEEZAN II PAKISTANI 11 Church St. 01773 747472. 42-seater.Chef N Hussain & mngr M Sharif since 1983.6-12; 1 Fri & Sat.

Glossop

BULL'S HEAD ALE & CURRY HOUSE
102 Church S, Old Glossop SK13 7RN
01457 866957   www.bulls-head.co.uk

There are other curry-serving pubs in this Guide, but this one in this Peak village at the foot of the Penines is in CAMRA's Good Beer Guide and in ours – a marriage made in heaven. The Bull's Head was built in 1604, with stone floors, low beams and open log fire. Paul and Barbara have beeb hosts since 2003. They have opened up the top half of the pub for guests to stay overnight in 4 modern en-suite rooms. Most important they kept curry chef, Fais Ahmed. His full curryhouse menu is served evenings only. No Juke box or gaming machines. Specials board. T/a: 10% disc. Pops.50p; CTM £6.80; Pullao Rice £2, Naan £1.90. 5.30- 10.30 (4-10 Sun).

Matlock Bath

ABID TANDOORI PAKISTANI & KASHMIRI
129 Dale Road, Matlock Bath   01629 57400

Mohammed Bashir's 70-seater is in this delightful Peak District spa town, nestling on the River Derwent, with its many pleasant walks and even a cable car to take you to the top of the cliffs. Just the thing to work up an appetite for Chef Maroof's Pakistani and Kashmiri cooking. *'The Lamb Bhuna was huge and excellent.'* AGR. Del: £20 min, 5m. Hours: 6 - 12 (1am Fri & Sat). Branches: Abid, Derby. (see above) Abid Balti, Alfreton.

DEVON

Area: West Country

Adjacent Counties: Cornwall, Dorset, Somerset

Beer

The SPICE MERCHANT
Fore Street, Beer, EX12 3JF   01297 22203
www.spicemerchantatbeer.co.uk

Beer: a delightful resort with a delightful name and one or two delightful inns and pubs. *'The Spice Merchant is a delightful restaurant'* RL serving all your favourite popular dishes like Butter Chicken, Korma, Tikka Massala etc. All year: 5-11.30 Apr-Oct 12-3.

YOU SAY OK
You may get a discount if you show them this Guide.

BOVEY TRACEY: SPICE BAAZAAR 38 Fore St. 01626 835125. *'I guess it's pretty well bog-standard, but round here it's gold dust'* TR. 6-11.30.
EXETER: DANA PANI 116-117, Sidwell Street, 01392 274787. You say it's the best in town now. So send us reports please.
EXETER: GANDHI   7 New North Rd. ~ 01392 272119. *'Remains reliable; friendly staff, tasty food.'* CS.
ILFRACOMBE: BOMBAY PALACE 36 Green Close Rd. ~ 01271 862010. 60-seater owned by R.Miah and family. Specialities: duck, salmon items and Nargis Kebab, meat, wrapped around hard boiled egg. Del: 2m £15 min. T/a: 10% disc. Hours: 5.30 - 11; 11.30 Sat. Branches: Barnstaple and Exeter.
ILFRACOMBE TANDOORI 14 High St Ilfracombe.   01271 866822. Est 1987. Head Chef: Jamal Miah. Birthday Parties enjoy a comp cake. Min Ch: c£11. 6-11.
NEWTON ABBOT: PASSAGE TO INDIA 137 Queen St. 01626 688543.
EASTERN EYE 120 Queen St ~ 01626 352364. Est 1990. *'When complimented on the food, the waiter replied, "It's Indian!" mimicking Sanjeev Baskar from Goodness Gracious Me! It was a good evening.'* SO. Del:4m £2 . Hours: 12-2 / 5.30 - 11.30; -12 Fri & Sat.
RAJ BELASH 41 Wolborough St. ~ 01626 332057. *'A few Nepalese dishes. The food was good'* JAP. Sun Buffet: 12.30-8, £8 adult, £5 child. 12-2.30, not Fri & Sat / 6-11.30; 12 Fri & Sat.

Ilfracombe

RAJAH   TOP 100
5 Portland St, Ilfracombe, EX34 9NL   01271 863499

Janet Wild's son James is head chef. There isn't a Bangladeshi in sight. And it's this which makes you love it or hate it. Some say whites can't cook Indian food. Apaart from being radist, it is a ridiculous statement. And I should know. The fact is that quality Indian cooking is achievable by all. *'We stumbled across what can only be described as a piece of curry heaven. Welcomed you into atmospheric surroundings via a very comprehensive and reasonably priced menu. Good ambience and helpful waiting staff. Tantalising smell of orders being prepared was almost too much to bear, but in no way prepared for the cuisine placed in front of us, nothing short of perfect. Shame we found this piece of heaven on our last day in Ilfracombe. Wish they could post their curries to Hull.'* M&JR. *'I and my wife, first went there in 1993 and found it a pleasant, friendly restaurant. We have visited it once or twice a year most years between then and now. Meals take a while to be prepared but are worth the wait. I have tried Chicken Dopiaza and Lamb Rogan Josh and both are different to the 'traditional' fare found where we live in Sutton Coldfield. That said these interpretations are nice in their own way, but do not expect lots of tomatoes in the Rogan Josh. The standards have remained high on each visit. Finally I must mention the Peshwari Naan, the best I have had.'* RGC. Mr Chapman (RGC above. and no relation) has put his finger on why some people like this restaurant while a few seem less keen. Put simply it is NOT curryhouse food. For example, there should not be tomatoes or red peppers in the authentic, aromatic Roghan Josh. The dish originated in Moghul Kashmir before such ingredients were 'discovered' in the Americas. 12-3 & 6-11.

Plymouth

JAIPUR PALACE
144 Vauxhall St, Barbican, PL3 ODF   01752 668711

Syed Wahid's a/c 70-eater is in two rooms. Snapshot: Chicken Pakoras £3 - fried with lentils and green chilli; Chicken Laflong £6.10 - barbecued chicken, Satkora (Indian citrus fruit); Egg Bhuna £3.50; Coconut Rice £2.50. T/a: 20% disc. Del: 4m £10 min. Sun - Th: 12-2, & daily: 5.30-12. *Branch: Meghna Ivybridge.*

Sidmouth

CINNAMON TREE
2 Radway Pl, Vicarage Rd, Sidmouth   01395 514190

Opened in 2006. *'Well worthy of inclusion, especially since good curries are hard to find in Devon. It was busy and lively when we visited. Staff seem proud of what they do. All the dishes we tried were excellent. Menu features a lot of duck as well as all the usual dishes. I hope this helps you with the next guide edition, which I find invaluable.'* NC.   12-2 & 6-11.30.

Torquay

MAHA-BHARAT
52 Torwood St, Torquay, TQ1 1DT   01803-215541

'In the three years, that we have lived in the curry-free-zone that is south Devon, we have tried some 25 restaurants from Plymouth to Teignmouth to Paignton to Torquay. Sometimes we have stuck with a particular restaurant for 3 or 4 months, only to find that the chef leaves and it all goes downhill. We have eaten some of the worst curries ever cooked and we've eaten some pretty good (but never great) curries. You have to understand that we moved here from Berkshire and regularly ate at great exponents of Indian food. But now we have found an oasis. It's plain ugly to look at from the outside. I was surprised to find that inside it's great. The staff are wonderful. They remember my name after only 3 visits. But the food - oh the food is wonderful. We went there with a group of 9. The waiter looked after the children (3 x 5 year olds - entertaining them with the HUGE fishtank) while we revelled in dhansaks, vindaloos, jalfrezis and bhunas with wonderful naans & parathas. Then the kids were served a terrific (unspiced) chicken tikka which they all thought was very grown up. All in all a tremendous restaurant with a great chef and staff that recognise what customers are all about. Up there with the best and after trawling through dozens & dozens of restaurants in South Devon I'm pleased to report that there IS somewhere where it is worth eating Indian food in this part of the world.' AR. *'PS: ... just don't be put off by the outside decor! I was ~ BIG mistake!'* Daily: 11am - 11pm.

Seaton

RAJPOOT
41 Harbour Road, Seaton EX12 2LX.   01297 22223

'The lights of the comfortable Rajpoot, shine like a beacon through the mist and rain, in this quiet, little town. Warm welcome from proprietor brothers Mizzen and Azziz. I don't know what we did without them!' JB. 12-2 & 6-11.

Email your opinions to
pat@patchapman.co.uk
from a one-liner to
an essay! All welcome.

DORSET

Area: South West

Adjacent Counties: Devon, Hants, Soms, Wilts

Boscombe

SAJNIZ
487 Christchurch Rd, BH1 4AE   01202 391391

'Situated on a corner premises, Sajniz is elegant and comfortable and spacious with a classy bar. The menu has all your favourites and some new things to try. The following are all worth a try at c£9.50: Sajniz Oriental Express, sliced chicken tikka and egg noodles is medium curry and very acceptable; Their Bonnani Chicken, chicken breast with slices peppers, mushrooms and chillies is hot and racy; Asary Lamb is lamb and pickle curry has oomph and good edge and Taal Chicken mixed masala and buna styles to give a warm but mild curry. From the high street standards their Butter Chicken, Dhansak and Ceylon are worth considering and are nor ferociously hot. Sensible variety of vegetable side dishes including Kala Bajee (kidney beans). Be warned, Nan at Sajniuz comes the size of medium blanket and will easily do for two people. Banquet Nights Tue & Weds and a really fine set meal for two c£22, four £44 and six £56. Very busy at weekends. All told an experience that will make you feel thoroughly spoiled. You feel trouble is taken to please.' RG.

Poole

THE GATE OF INDIA
54 Commercial Rd, Lr Parkstone, Poole 01202 717061

Messrs Choudhurys 80-seater in 2 rooms, est 1993. 'The very posh Poole Yacht Club is not far away and their membership is noticeable here. Poole Hospital medics frequent it. Spacious (free in the evening) parking at the rear. Each visit is a delight. Long may they prosper.' RG. And here is Bob's update: 'It has recently undergone a redec and come up bright and smiling with some fine new additions to their already extensive menu, e.g: Asari Chicken / Lamb, sweet and sour curry, meat is marinated in herbs, yoghurt and delicate spices and cooked mixed with chutney and garnished with coriander; Naga Curried Chicken / Lamb, for the Old Sweats (it's one of the Vindaloo Brigade). The meat is marinated in herbs, yoghurt and various spices and then cooked with tomatoes, garnished with coriander and naga chilli; Shatkora Curry Chicken / Lamb cooked with tomatoes, onions, capsicums, green chillis, spices and the citric vegetable, Shatkora to produce a fairly hot curry; Chom Chom Chicken / Lamb meat is marinated in herbs, yoghurt and spices and cooked with ground almonds, capsicums, honey and fresh cream. At the next table was a convivial group, obvious strangers to the area, all having a splendid time and exclaiming on their good fortune at landing up at such a splendid eatery. I asked how they had lighted at The Gate of India, be told they'd ordered a taxi at their hotel and asked the driver where they should for a really good curry. "He didn't think twice. And here we are...." And you can't say fairer than that.' RG. T/a: 10% disc. Hours: 12-2.30 / 6-12.

PLANET PAPADOM
222 Wimborne Rd, Poole BH15 2EL 01202675978

Located at the rear of Oakdale's New Inn Pub but run by Bangladeshi chefs and managerment independently (with its own license). Set on two levels, spacious and simple. A full formula menu at reasonable prices inc the drinks. 12-2 & 5-11.30.

YOU SAY OK
You may get a discount if you show them this Guide.

BOURNEMOUTH: ANGLO INDIAN 223 Old Christchurch Rd ~ 01202 312132. Owner Runu Miah. T/a: 15% disc. Min Ch: £8. Hours: 6-12.

MUMTAZ 736 Christchurch Rd, Boscombe E   0120 393323

CHRISTCHURCH: STARLIGHT 54 Bargates ~ 01202 484111. Owners Ian Clasper and Abdul Hai. 12-2/6-12.

POOLE: MOONLIGHT   9 Moor Rd, Broadstone ~ 01202 605234. A.Malik's reliable house where might give you a disc if you show him this Guide.

POOLE: TAJ MAHAL 2 38 High St, Poole ~ 01202 677315. 'A large group of us proved no problem to the staff on a busy Sat night. Lots of duck speciality dishes. Well worth the visit.' SO.

SHERBORNE: RAJPOOT   House of Steps, Half Moon St ~ 01935 81245. Shatkora and fish dishes here.

WEYMOUTH: BALTI HOUSE 24 Commercial Rd ~ 01305 766347. 'Always a staff welcome you. Tables laid with fresh flowers. Food always excellent. Recommended.' LD.

SAMMY'S
193 Bournemouth Rd, Lower Parkstone, Poole BH14 9HU 01202-749760

'Sammy's previously trading as the Royal Lahore, offers an enjoyable night out with memorable food. The service, menu and cooking are of a very high standard. But there's much more to it all than that. We visited during the Easter holiday and the place was packed to the ceiling. It was noticeable how many family parties there were; all with children – all having a great old time. This was clearly Sammy's policy, encouraging family visits, parties and children. It pays dividends. The staff are vociferous, jolly, vigourous, helpful, charming and attentive. Lights out for the cake with candles! Enthusiastic choruses of "Happy Birthday to You" with three hearty cheers! This is more than a meal. It is a night out. The menu is very fine and all dishes are cooked to order as you watch them at the grills and ovens with the occasional exciting flare-up (all safely behind glass). Among tasty starters Champ Gosh (marinated lamb chops) £4 Chicken Wings £3.; Liver and Kidney £4.

Sammy's is to be especially commended for having a well appointed disabled toilet and although the high doorstep makes wheelchair access a bit problematic, they'll all lend a hand to get you aboard and spoil you rotten when you're settled in. Sammy himself circulates among his guests and makes you feel so much more than just a paying customer. Free del. Very highly recommended. Not to be missed.' RG. 12-3 & 6-11. Branch: Sammy 's adjacent Ashley Rd, Poole.

Wareham

GURKHA NEPALESE & ORIENTAL
Sandford Rd, Sandford, BH20 7A **TOP 100**
01929 556959   www.thegurkha.co.uk

Opened 2006, it looks remarkably like a tea planter's bungalow in Raj India. It is Nepalese owned (by former Gurka Captain Asbahadur Gurung) and run (by Jennie) and billed as an oriental restaurant with dishes from Thailand, China, Nepal, Malaysia, India and Singapore, as well as a smattering of British cuisine (chips). It has good parking which is nearly always full. Although it does have an a-la -carte menu, the main theme is an e-a-m-a-y-l buffet of 30 or so dishes and takaway at reasonable prices. *'Inside, the décor is simple and no nonsense. It's obvious the money was spent on the outside of the building – which is the reason we stopped by, so it works – but when you can bamboozle customers with such an array of culinary experiences, the wallpaper isn't going to come up in conversation too often. After being escorted to your table, it is then up to you to grab a plate and join the game of musical dishes when you spy a gap at the buffet table.'* Sam Revel, Daily Echo. *'Seats 100+ in pleasant, comfortable surroundings, with modern-style wooden flooring and a bar at one side. More importantly, the buffet counter offered a good selection about 30 items including two soups, three different rice, noodles and popadums. In addition there were various vegetable garnishes, pickles and sauces. What's more, the trays were not full so as to gradually get cold and congealed during the evening, but were regularly topped up by small amounts being continuously cooked by several chefs in the open kitchen behind. As I made a total pig of myself I can't recall everything I managed to sample, but I do recall that it was all very good indeed. I had to rest my stomach on the table in exhaustion. It was all delicious.'* MW. *'Between us we had Gurkha chicken, Gurkha lamb curries together with Gurkha aloo, saag aloo moderately tasty but very pleasant and Chinese sweet and sour pork simply off the peg Chinese and no messing. We were there quite early on a weekday evening and the place was very busy. It was mercifully free from pretentious twerps knitting their way through Oriental food with chopsticks. The staff is charming and helpful and the service faultless. They will prepare dishes not listed on the menu, provided you give them time – useful to know.'* RG. How can you operate a take away system from an e-a-m-a-y-l buffet? Gurka have an ingenious takeaway system ... fill plastic containers (supplied) with your choice then pay per container. Lunch: £7.95 adult £5.95 child. Dinner: £12.95 adult £5.95 child Kids must be under 4'6" to qualify, and they do measure doubters. 12-3 &

DURHAM
Known as County Durham
Area: North East

Adjacent Counties:
Cumbria,
Northumberland,
Tyne & Wear,
N Yorkshire

Barnard Castle

BENGAL MERCHANT
7 The Bank, Barnard Castle, DL12 8PH 01833 630700

Chad and Mufti Choudhury bought Bailie's restaurant. The Grade II-listed property (which dates from the mid-18th century) is close to the landmark Butter Market in the middle of the main street of the village that is renowned for its public school and ruined 12th-century castle. It offers a bar a dining in three interconnecting rooms for 44 guests, and a rear timber-decked patio for alfresco dining. *'Second visit to this restaurant that opened in 2008 (plus numerous takeaways). There is already a good Indian restaurant in the town, Spice Island, but the Merchant is equally as good regarding quality of food – delicious. The staff are even more friendly and attentive, giving occasional free side-dishes and taking care of you. The Merchant wins hands down as regards comfort and décor. In the other restaurant, everyone sits in two table rows like a school canteen all facing wall-length smoked mirrors so it feels like you are hemmed in on top of each other. Not good when they often seem to have children in on an evening. The Bengal Merchant is more comfortable, roomy and relaxed and you can have private conversations as you are not sat on top of other people.'* GD. Hours: 6-12

Darlington

GARDEN OF INDIA
43-44 Bondgate, Darlington DL3 7IJ
01325 467975   www.gardenofindiadarlington.co.uk

Est 1987 and filled with Hindi arches and decor. *'I found myself in Darlington and used the Garden. It was a very acceptable experience-the Tandoori chicken starter was good as was the lamb dish (whose name I forget, but the restaurant claimed it as the "original" Lamb Koorma). I would certainly go back. The only slight gripe, given that there was a maximum of three in the restaurant, was that the service was just a tadge slow. I also looked at the Reema (18 Coniscliffe Road), but as there was no menu displayed I gave it a miss. Also their external publicity was inconsistent in that the window display claimed traditional cuisine, but a hanging display board contemporary cuisine!* JP

Durham

ALISHAAN EXCLUSIVE INDIAN
50-51 North Road, Durham, DH1 4SF
01913 709180   www.alishaandurham.com

'I was in Durham yesterday and came across the Yes, the title of the establishment is slightly pretentious. I'm not sure how long it has been open as last time I was in Durham, the establishment was a Chinese Buffet restaurant. The decor is very clean-lined, traditional but not obsessively so. The menu is extensive. At 1830 on Saturday it was reasonably busy. A starter of mixed kebab (£4,50), a main course of Syhlet-er-Jhinga (baby lobsters) (£13,95) was excellent The total bill including papadoms, pickles, naan and a pint of Kingfisher came to £26,75. If it keeps its standards it is a must for future guides and very possibly a candidate for the top 100. Durham seems well blessed with excellent establishments.' JP.

CAPITAL
69, Claypath, DH1 1QT   0191 386 8803

Opened 2007 by Mohammed S Miah on the premises of an auction house. Chef Syed Islam has spring lamb, duck and fish dishes are on his menu. *'Good quality of food –* delicious. The staff are friendly and attentive. But everyone sits in two table rows like a school canteen all facing wall-length smoked mirrors so it feels like you are hemmed in on top of each other. Not good when they often seem to have children in on an evening.' GD. Hours: 6- 11.30.   Branch: Spice Lounge Durham.

SHAHEENS INDIAN BISTRO,
48 North Bailey, Durham City   0191 386 0960

'Bright and lively restaurant, pleasantly sited in an old post office on one of the side streets leading up towards the cathedral and castle. As you enter you can't miss the large painting of the Taj Mahal along the right hand wall and the backlit plastic vines, which peep through a wooden latticework suspended just below the ceiling. Sounds awful I know but actually it's OK! King Prawn Puri £5.90, had a good balance between the tomato, herbs / spices and the acidity although it seemed a bit light on the prawns for that price! Mutton Tikka Masala Balti £9.20, was perhaps angling for the most number of Indian Dishes in one name, although as it included rice they could probably have got away with chucking a Biriani in the title somewhere! However, it had a good balance between the spices, the tomato and the rich ghee sauce. The Pullau Rice that accompanied this dish was very pleasantly aromatic and flavoursome. Service was OK. Overall opinion – slightly pricey but good, would recommend and return.' SO. Opens 6pm.

SPICE LOUNGE
St Nicholas Cottage, Durham Market Place DH1 3NJ
0191 383 0927   spiceloungedurham.com

Same ownership as Captital. This one opened first in 2005 in the old market hall and it incorporates part of the listed wall. Decorated in slate grey and royal purple. Menu Snapshot: Xenuk £4.45 - mussels; Palak Pakora £3.45; Crab Bhaji on Puri £4.95; Chicken Biryani £8.80; Lamb Tikka Jalfrezi £7.95; Mushroom Pullao £2.95. Set meal for 2: £40. Hours: 6-12.

YOU SAY OK
You may get a discount if you show them this Guide.

BISHOP AUCKLAND: THE KING'S BALTI   187 Newgate St. 01388 604222 Owned by Mohammed Boshir Ali Hussan. Chutneys and Pickles 50p a portion or £3 a jar – brilliant idea! Hours: 5-12; 11.30 Sun.

CHESTER-LE-STREET: GOLDEN GATE TANDOORI   11 South Burns Rd ~ 0191 388 2906. 45-seater est 1993. Ample parking in front. House specials: Kaleeya Beef or Chicken, hot cooked with roast potatoes, marinated in yoghurt. Sylhet Beef or Chicken, strongly spiced, dry with eggs and tomatoes. Takeaway: 10% disc. Del: 6m £10min. Hours: 12-2 / 6-12.

DARLINGTON: GARDEN OF INDIA   43-44 Bondgate, DL3 7JJ ~ 0871 714037. Hours: 12-2.30/6-11.30; 12 Sat.

REEMA   18 Coniscliffe Rd , Darlington. ~ 0871 7141346

SHAPLA 192 Northgate ~ 01325 468920. Established in 1980, SA Khan's 80-seat restaurant is *'Brilliant.'* PJ. *'Excellent.'* DMC. *'Enough to feed a small elephant'* SS. Hours: 12-2 (not Fri) / 6-12.

SPICE GARDEN   112 Parkgate, Darlington. ~0871 7141557

SPLENDIDLY INDIAN, SUPERBLY SMOOTH

Tow Law

MEMSAHIB
Boundary Cottage Farm, Inkerman, Tow Law DL13 4QB
01388 731818   www.memsahibindianrestaurant.co.uk

Fully licensed 60 seater in the wilds of the countryside some 10 miles NW of Bishops Auckland. It has a full formula menu. . You can purchase a whole jar or pickle or chutney at £2.70 each – probably a good idea if you are eating in a large party of perhaps eight or more. T/a: 10% disc. Del: £10 minimum. Happy Nights: six course set meal £11, Mon- Thurs. Hours: 5.30-11, (11.30 Fri & Sat). Branch: *Monju Stanley DH9 7OG.*

ESSEX

Area: Home Counties, (east of London)

Adjacent Counties: Cambs, Herts, Kent, London, Suffolk

'GL' denotes those former Essex suburbs absorbed by Greater London in 1965.

Chelmsford
(includes Great Baddow and Writtle)

ESSENCE INDIAN ON THE GREEN
30 The Green Writtle   01245 422228

You've guessed it, this huge 200-cover restaurant overlooks the village green, furthermore this is nth reincarnation of an Indian restaurant on this site. Essence has a contemporary interior with a soft neutral background enhanced with inviting pictures that reflect the history of Writtle and the essence of India. Pre-dinner drinks are on offer in the Piano Lounge, where diners can sit back and relax in comfortable leather sofas, sipping on a cocktail and view pictures of famous patrons of the restaurant's other branches that decorate the walls. Essence serves an extensive Indian & Bangladesh combined menu, with a large choice of intriguing fish dishes and chef specials that are put together by Head Chef Jahanger Hussain. Essence is the latest venture of the Essence Group, a family run business established in 1998 and owned by Sharife Ali, Tariq Ali, Abi Kabir, Farouk Ullah and Sam Uddin. *They have three other sites - Chadwell Heath, Romford, Essex; Redhill, Surrey and Sedgley, West Midlands.*

SURAYA TAKEAWAY
159, Main Rd, Broomfield, Chelmsford   01245 442014

'This is a humble takeaway, but nothing else has ever come close. Bhajia are flat and to die for with Raitha. Chicken Tikka starter, succulent. Dal, hot and gorgeous. No over use of cardamom. *Always hot and fresh, you can watch the chef and cooks preparing. Never a wrong item. The BEST still after nearly twenty years. Shame they do not have a restaurant.'* JS.
Menu Snapshot: Reshmi Kebab £2.60, minced lamb burger spiced and dressed with fried egg; Chicken Kebab £4, pieces of meat with salad sandwich in freshly made bread; Cheese Naan £1.80; Jal Murgi £6.80, spiced spring chicken cooked with green chillies and tomatoes, served with Pullao Rice; Lamb Achari £4.90, tender slices of lamb cooked in sweet,sour and hot sauce; Lamb Kashmiri £4.10, mild curry prepared with banana and served in rich creamy sauce; Garlic Mushroom Bhajee £2.30, Chana Paneer £2.70. Free Onion Salad with every takeaway. Delivery: £12min, 4m. Hours: 5-11.30.

YOU SAY OK
You may get a discount of you show them this Guide.

BARKING: TASTE OF INDIA SOUTH INDIAN 87, London Bridge Road, IGII 8TB 020 8591 9291 www.restauranttasteofindia.co.uk . Branches at 340 High St North E12 and Kumbakonam 612 001, Tamil Nadu, South India.
BASILDON: ASIA SPICE 2 Adams Busn Square 01268 5253527
BENFLEET: MAHARAJA 358 London Rd. Keith Vaz and Ed Miliband started the Tiffin Cup, where 100 UK curryhouses are entered by their local by MPs into a national curry cooking competition. Siraj Ali's Maharaja was runner up in 2007.
BENFLEET: MUMTAZ MAHAL 10 Essex Way, Benfleet 01268 751707 Abdur Rahid opened his two-floor 90-seater in 1977. His is a typical, friendly, competent curry house.Large car park adjacent. *'It's all done sumptuously'.* IDB. 12-2.30/6-12.
BRAINTREE: CURRY PALACE 28 Fairfield Road, Braintree ~ 01376 320083. 52 seater est 1975 by MA Noor. T/a: 10% disc. Hours: 5.30-11; closed Mon.

> Please let us know which are your favourites. And the one you hate too.
>
> Email to pat@patchapman.co.uk

YOU SAY OK
You may get a discount of you show them this Guide.

BURNHAM-ON-CROUCH: POLASH 169 Station Rd. 01621 782233. Owner Sheik Faruque Ahmed. Hours: 12-3/6-12. Branch: 86 West Rd, Shoeburyness, Essex. 01702 294721
CHELMSFORD: TAJ MAHAL 6 Baddow Rd ~ 01245 259618. Modern, trendy chrome and pale wood. Hours: 12-2.30 /5.30-12.
CLACTON-ON-SEA: EAST INDIA TAKEAWAY 182 Old Rd.~ 01255 427281. Manager: M.A Salam. Hours: 5-11.30; 12 Sat
DUNMOW: JALSA GHAR QUEEN VICTORIA 79 Stortford Rd 01371 873330.www.jalsaghar.co.uk Owner Iqbal Chowdhury opened in a pub (Queen Victoria) in 1998. Menu Snapshot: Crispy Sardines, marinated and shallow fried; Vegetable Roulade , spiced vegetables, rolled in Indian pastry. T/a: 10% disc, min £10. Hours: 12-2.30 &6-11; 12-10.30 Sun
EPPING: RAJ 75 High Street ~ 01992 572193. 40-seater owned by Mumin Ali & Chef Abdul Ali. 12-2.30 & 6-12.

Colchester

KOVALAM   SOUTH INDIAN MEAT & VEG
27 Water Side, Brightlingsea, Colchester, CO7 OAY
01206 305555

The Brightlingsea Kovalam is one of three, also Ipswich and London. *'It is so hard to find a real Indian restaurant. I only found Kovalam by accident. Where can you find rasam Brightlingsea - of all places*.' G.B-P. Av Dinner: £22. House wine a very fair £9.50. Sun - Sat: 12-2.30, Sun - Th: 6-11(Fri-Sat to 12).

SAGARMATHA GURKHA   NEPALESE
2 St Botolphs Circus, Colchester CO2 7EF
01206 579438

Est 1999. eats 42. There are of course many if not all your old favourites on the menu, and done well too, as they are so often by Nepalese chefs. Specialities includtraditional Nepalese 'village' meal c£10, the most unusual dish being Shanjali Kukhura (chicken marinated in ginger, green chilli, herbs and spinach). Two large car parks with CCTV in front and rear. T/a: 10% disc. Del: £15, 5m. Hours: 12-2 & 5.30-11.30.

MIRCHI RASOI
71 North Station Road, Colchester, CO1 1RQ
01206 576496   www.mirchi-rasoi.co.uk

Mirchi Rasoi sits in the very centre of Colchester. With 3 chefs from the northern, southern, and western regions of India, the restaurant offers a unique blend of all three cuisines, offering flavour combinations that no other restaurant can boast. Tuesday to Sunday: 12:30 - 14:30 & 18:30 - 23:30. Have not tried Mirch Rasoi. Looking at the menu, only a few unusual things - like uttapam, Sikindari lamb and Hyderabad veg. However, those alone will get me to try them. I will let you know. G.B-P.

Dagenham GL

CHANDNI CHOWK   PUNJABI CUISINE
756, Green Lane, Dagenham, RM8 1YT
020 3222 2000   www.chandnichowkrestaurant.com

Chandni Chowk (Moonlight Street) is Old Delhi's former Moghul trading zone still known for its unique set of restaurants and halwai's (professional sweet makers). Dagenham's Chandni Chowk does traditional Indian sweets, andt also offers the finest Punjabi Indian cuisine is backed by chef Sukhdev's 30 years in perfecting Indian cuisine. *Branches, B'hm B21 & Southall*.

Gants Hill GL

KANCHANS   PUNJABI   TOP 100
53 Perth Road, Gants Hill IG2 6BX
020 8518 9282   www.kanchansgroup.com

'*Location, location, location*', they say. And it is almost on the roundabout, near the tube, with a huge plate glass window with large ornately carved wooden double door with brass studs. Unmissable. But is Gant's Hill in suburban Essex the right location. Only time will tell. Because this restaurant is a real cut above anything forms around. Inside it's a beautifully decorated restaurant, with creamy walls, crystal mirrors, Indian artefacts, lavish upholstery and place settings. Upstairs is a huge banqueting suit which is ideal for large family-and-friend parties. And does well for smaller Asian weddings. The owners have run a standard curryhouse down the road for years, but they decided to do the job properly. The chefs all Indian, cook authentic Punjabi Indian curries and accompaniments – everything wonderful from the spicy Lamb Knuckle to the Black Urid Dal. Definitely worthy of our top 100. Gants Hill is very lucky indeed. Parking at rear. Cover ch £1.50. Hours: 12-3 & 6-11.30. *Branch: Kanchans Rasoi, 807 Romford, Manor Park, E12 5AN 020 8514 7500*

Ilford (GL)

JALALABAD 2   TOP 100
992 Eastern Av, Newbury Park, Ilford, IG2 7JD
020 8590 0000   www.jcuisine.com

There is no longer a Jalalabd 1. It has closed, H Islam

SPLENDIDLY INDIAN, SUPERBLY SMOOTH

now just manages this one. Has attracted the likes of world embassy champion snooker player Ronnie O'Sullivan. Menu snaoshot: Nargis Kebab Spicy Mince Lamb patties and pan-fried served with an omelette on top £2.80; Chicken Peshwari Charcoal grilled in an exotic sauce, garnished with Indian herbsand spices. £7.95; Chicken Kebull Tender pieces of diced chicken, cooked with chick peas, sweet red peppers and garnished with roasted pistachio nuts. £7.95; Ghosht-E-Lazzez Barbecued Lamb pieces with tomatoes, green chillies and enhanced with thinly sliced potatoes in a thick sauce. £7.95 *'My first impression was pleasant surprise. The décor was of high quality minimalism. I was greeted at the door by the waiter, who showed me to my seat, followed up by the menu. I was intrigued by the variety of the cuisine available. Chef's special sauce tasted exquisite. I was particularly taken in by the Motka Kulfi dessert, £2.50 which came in an exclusive ceramic pot filled with highly luxurious rich saffron and pistachio flavoured ice cream topped with nuts. Bollywood music videos play on a large widescreen television to depict the exotic and carry on the theme of the Indian cuisine.'* FA. Hours: 5.30-11.

MIRCH MASALA   PUNJABI   BYO
13 Goodmayes Road, Goodmayes, Ilford, IG3 9UH
020 8590 2505

One of seven branches with identical meat, fish and veg menu. See SW16 for full details.

MOBEEN   PAKISTANI   NO ALC
80 Ilford Lane, Ilford , IG1 2LA   020 8553 9733

The owners of this chain of Pakistani caffs are strict Muslims, so BYO is not permitted and it's unlicensed. Go for darned good, inexpensive, value-for-money, Punjabi, Kebabs, tandoori items and curries of all sorts, selected from the counter, with specials varying from day to day. No credit cards. No smoking. Can be heaving with local Asians, who know you won't find better food, and which adds to a fab atmosphere. Being Punjabi, it's a bit short of vegetarian fodder. Hours: 11-10. Branches: Mobeen, 229 High Street North, E6; 222 Green St, E7; 725, High Rd, Leyton, E10.

SARAVANAA BHAVAN   SOUTH IND VGTN
115 Cranbrook Rd, Ilford IG1 4PU
020 8911 8718   www.saravanabhavan.com

Third of a new chain of 5 south Indian vegetarian cafés. Capacity 250. See London E12 for menu & details. No licence. Cash pref. 10am to 10:30pm.

SURUCHI
506 High Road, Ilford, IG1 1UE   020 8598 2020

Cuisine is a strange combination of: South Indian and Chinese. Specialists in vegetarian dishes, Indian style, including such favourites as: Bhel Puri £2.95, Masala Dosas £3.25, Onion Utthapam £3.25, Vada (2) with chutney and Sambar £2.50. If you prefer a little Chinese delicacy, try the Mogo Chilli Fry £3.50, Spicy Szechuan Noodles £3.50, Spinach and Bean Sprouts with dry chillies £3.50. All sounds great to me!! Service charg10%. T/a: 10% disc. Lunch Special: three courses £4.99 – good value. Hours: 12-3 & 6- 12.

SRI RATHICA   TAMIL NADU CUISINE
312 High Road, Ilford
020 8478 7272   www.srirathiga.co.uk

65-seater. Raj Mohan Ramadass' restaurant specialises in Tamil Nadu cuisine – fabulous south Indian food – though they do abit of curryhouse too. So our advise is not to ask for the kormas and the CTMs. Try things form this snapshot of what you can expect to eat: Thayir Vada £1.95 - fried doughnut made of black gram batter, ginger, onions, green chilli, curry leaves and cumin, then soaked in seasoned and tempered yoghurt; Cashew nut Pakoda £3.95, nuts dipped in spicy batter and deep-fried; Chicken 65 £4.95; Fried bone chicken marinated and fried, served with cucumber, onions and lemon; Mutton Mysore £6.95, with ginger, garlic, coriander leaves and red chillies; Rasam £1.95, hot pepper soup of tomatoes, tamarind and spices; Ghee Roast Masala Dosa £4.95, crisp pancake, roasted in butter, filled with potato masala, served with sambar (lentil curry) and chutneys; Utthapam £3.50, rice and lentil flour, topped with chopped, onions, green chillies, tomatoes, curry leaves and ginger, served with sambar and chutneys; Nandu Varuval £7.95; Fried crab curry; Vazhakkai Poriyal £3.25, green banana curry. Del: £15 min, 2m radius. T/a: 10% disc. Price Check: Popadum 50p, Chicken Chettinad £5.95, cooked with curry leaves and mustard seed, Pullao Rice £1.95. 12-3 & 6-11 (12 Sat). *Branch: 57 Station Rd, Harrow. 020 8863 8822*

Southend-on-Sea

KERALAM   SOUTH INDIAN
28 Clifftown Rd, Southend, SS1 1AJ   01702 345072

It's easy to find, being opposite Southend railway station.! It is another south Indian restaurant, and with it. Mr Sadique's vibrant fresh food breaks away from the curryhouse mould. Don't think that all South Indian food is vegetarian or fish dishes – not true – chicken and lamb feature very nicely. Menu Snapshot: Kappa and Meen Curry £3.95, cassava, herbs, spices, served with fish curry; Kadkka Porichathu £3.25; Fried mussels; Erachi Olathiyathu £5.95, lamb fried with fresh sliced coconut (one of Pat's favourites); Malabar Meen Biriyani £6.95, marinated Kingfish, onion, cashew nuts, sultanas, curry leaves and rice, served with coconut chutney, raita and salad; Avial £3.25, fresh vegetables cooked with coconut, yoghurt, cumin, curry leaves and spices; Kaipanga Varatiathu £3.25, curry leaves, mustard seeds, cumin, fennel, deep-fried bitter gourd and puréed fresh coconut; Pickle Tray is expensive at £2. I hope it contains some tasty home-made delicacies! 'The food is as good as ever.' JAR. Price Check: Popadum 50p, Cheera Chicken £5.25, Pullao Rice £1.75. Hours: 12-2.30/5.30-11.30; 11 Sun. Reports please.

DESI WAY TAKEAWAY
373, London Rd, Westcliff, SS0 7HT   01702 333414

Owner, Ruhul Shamsuddin says *'my father taught me the industry, but rather than opening a restaurant, I decided to launch a takeaway and opened Desi Way in 2005.'* It boasts leather sofas, a big plasma screen for Bollywood films, posters, flame-lighting, a delivery vehicle parked outside, which is a real rickshaw. The menu has dishes such as Bollywood Bad Boy! The talking point is the bank of five 10 inch LCD screens placed on the counter, which transmit live the cooking process from the kitchen to the customers right up to the point of packaging so that customers can see how the food is prepared. *'I offer a complementary drink or kulfi if they have been waiting long. So the customers never get bored.* The delivery transport fleet includes one of the subcontinent's and Thailand's icons, the tuk-tuk, the motorised three-wheeler taxi which buzzes around like a dodgem. A fun sight in Westcliff. 11am-11pm.

POLASH
84 West Rd, Shoeburyness, Southend SS3 9DS
01702 293989   www.thepolash.com

The Polash and its slightly younger branch have been in our Guide since we began, which makes them old friends to these pages. Manager SA Motin tells us his decor is *'wonderful, air-conditioned, with water fountain'.* But there's a third Polash in the same ownership. Not in Essex, nor even Britain. It's in Sylhet, Bangladesh, the town where so many of our curryhouse workers come from. Polash is the best hotel in town, which doesn't mean much. Their restaurant, the Shapnil, has an item on its 200-dish menu that amazed us when we visited. Item 95 is no less than CTM! It is the only place in the whole of Bangladesh where it is to be found. And, says owner Sheik Faruque Ahmed, *'it sells really well!!!'* His UK partner, M Khalique, agrees. *'The food was beautifully prepared, tasty and the right strength. Service excellent. Atmosphere relaxed and friendly. Despite the fact that the proprietor informed us that they did not give CC disc on a Sat, they gave us a disc of 10%.'* BP-D. min charge £10. Hours: 12-3 & 6-12; Branch: Polash, Burnham on Crouch.

YOU SAY OK
You may get a discount of you show them this Guide.

HALSTEAD: CURRY COTTAGE 73 Head St. ~ 01787 476271. Manager Forhad Hussain. Opened Dec 2006. Branch: Spice Zone Indian, 1c Head St, Halstead. 01787 479701.
HARLOW: ESSENCE OF INDIA 2 Hart Road, Old Harlow ~ 01279 441187. *'My husband has taken a liking to their side dish Aloo Bahar, potatoes and lentils'.* HS.
HEYBRIDGE: HEYBRIDGE TANDOORI 5 Bentalls Centre. ~ 01621 858566. Abdul Rofik, Abdul Hannan and Nazrul Islam's

70-seater. *'Four non-curry eaters have become converted.'* SJ. Del: £10 min, 3m. Hours: 12-2.30 & 6-11.30; 12 Sat.
HORNCHURCH (GL): CINNAMON SPICE 10 Tadworth Pde, Elmpark. ~ 01708 478510. Owner Syed Ahmed. Service ch 10%. Del: £10 min, 3m. Hours: 5-12.
ILFORD (GL): MASALA 910   PUNJABI 910 Eastern Avenue Newbury Park Ilford IG2 7HZ 0845 345 1723. Serves authentic Punjabi Cuisine. 20% off collected orders. Hours: 12-2 & 6-12; Sun: 12:30-4 & 6.30-11.30.
LEIGH-ON-SEA: MUGHAL DYNASTY 1585 London Rd, Leigh 01702 470373. Pretty, upmarket 68-seater from Nazram Uddin.
LEIGH-ON-SEA: TAJ MAHAL 77 Leigh Road, Leigh 01702 711006. 70-seater, est 1973 and owned by manager Shams and chef Noor Uddin. Hours: 12-2.30 & 6-12.
ONGAR: VOJAN Epping Road, Ongar 01277 362293. Proprietor Jamal Uddin. Hours: 12-2.30 & 5.30-11; Fri & Sat 11.30; Sun Buffet: 1-10, £9.95 / £4.95 child.
RAYLEIGH: SPICY TAKEAWAY 159 High Street, Rayleigh 01268 770769. 36 seater. Del: £10 min, 4m. Hours: 5.30-11.30; 12 Sat; 11 Sun.
ROMFORD (GL): ASIA SPICE 62 Victoria Road, Romford 01708 762623. 54-seater owned by Yeabor Ali since 1975. Branch: Rupali, South Woodham Ferrers, Essex.
SEVEN KINGS (GL): DOSA RANI AND ROYAL SWEETS 58 Goodmayes Rd, Seven Kings, IG3 9UR 020 8598 8333 11-11
WESTCLIFF-ON-SEA: SHAGOOR Hamlet Court Rd. 01702 347461. *'Very large and beautifully decorated. Food good to excellent.'* AS. 'Highly commended' SS.

GLOUCESTERSHIRE

Area:
South West

Adjacent Counties:
Bristol, Gwent,
Somerset,
Wilts

Cheltenham

JOY
9, Montpellier Cresc. GL50 1US 01242 522888

'Tidy restaurant, nicely decorated, reasonably spacious. Service a bit hurried as they squeezed us in 10 minutes before closing. Menu interesting with main dishes only being served as lamb and chicken, only four fish dishes on whole menu. Popadoms OK with usual array of chutneys. I ordered Onion Bhajia - three golf balls, moist and nicely spiced. Chicken Tikka, Pullao Rice, plain Madras Sauce - large portion of chicken (ten pieces), small portion of rice, large portion of sauce. So, in all, too much tikka, not enough rice and a gallon of sauce. Despite these portion anomalies, food excellent. As gang of five, ordered far too much food, can't remember what others had, but all said how good the food was. £117 (£15 drinks) for five.' DB.

SPLENDIDLY INDIAN, SUPERBLY SMOOTH

KOLOSHI RESTAURANT & BAR
London Rd, Charlton Kings, Cheltenham, GL54 4HG
01242 516 400   www.koloshi.co.uk   **TOP 100**

It is located a couple of miles SW of Cheltenham on the A40 in the one-time Reservoir Inn adjacent to the Dowsdwell reservoir. Koloshi appropriately means water carrying vessel in Hindi. Chef Owner Azad Hussain opened it in December 2011, to *'provide a culinary experience like no other and a menu taking the diner on a gastronomic journey across India'*. The smartly furnished bar and 70 seat restaurant in muted browns and fawns and white is invitind, and in addition, they are offering a full bed & breakfast service. Menu Snapshot: Lamb Rampuri, Welsh lamb cutlets marinated with raw papaya, garlic ginger paste, paprika, fennel and malt vinegar £7.50; Shan E Kalvebattak, pan-fried scallops with fresh garlic, green chilli, and tamarind sauce £8.95; Battak Tikki Kandari duck breast with green papaya paste & ground spice, Kashmiri chilli and pomegranate, grilled in a charcoal oven £7.95; Aloo Tikki Awadhi, Spiced potato cakes with a filling of chickpeas coriander puree, dry mango and black peppers and drizzled with tamarind chutney £6.95. Mains: Sikandari Badi Lamb, braised lamb shank with whole spices, malt vinegar finished in the tandoor oven with Kashmiri chillies £15; Hyderabadi Murgh Masala, hicken pieces cooked in a sauce of garlic, ginger paste, red and green chillies, lemon juice, saffron, yogurt, curry leaves and ground spices £12. {That's CTM}; Battak Achari, tandoor grilled duck breast, marinated with ginger, chilli, yoghurt and cloves served on bed of seasonal vegetables with tamarind sauce, £16. Mon-Sat: 12- 2.30 & 6-11 (Sun: 12-3 & 6-10).

Gloucester

BABURCHI
42 Bristol Road, Gloucester   01452 300615
www.indianrestaurantgloucester.co.uk

Est 1988. *'Still my favourite in Gloucester.'* CS. *'Better than ever (following a fire). Wide range of meals, service is good and prices reasonable eg: Onion Bhajia , CTM. I enjoy vegetarian meals on occasions and the menu has a Special Vegetarian Dishes section. Particularly like the Vegetable Jeera. Well worth a visit.'* DT. 12-2 & 6-12.

SAFFRON
72, Bristol Road, GL1 5SD   01454 411102

'Welcoming restaurant amongst an enclave of eateries tsouth of the city with a friendly feel and smiling, youthful staff. 52 seatsin a well furnished interior, comfy seats and pleasant decor. Decent menu with all the favourites plus specials. Reshmi Kebab £3, lovely, juicy, tasty meat, well spiced and topped with light and fluffy omelette, served with deep yellow sauce and crisp salad. Superb Begum Bahar £7, rich satisfying dish of quality lamb and juicy tikka in thick sauce, bountiful in onions - very satisfying. Special Naan £2.70, a little odd, being essentially a good Keema Naan, moist and light with a pleasant filling, then with slices of Chicken Tikka draped on top covered with melted (and pongy) grated cheese. The overall effect was OK, but on reflection I wish I'd had a Garlic Naan. Tarka Dal £2.50 - was quite superb, nicely fluid, perfect balance of ingredients correctly assembled. A thoroughly enjoyable dish and unreservedly recommended.' RW. 12-2 & 5-12.

Koloshi's striking exterior and inviting lounge.

Tewkesbury

RAJSHAHI
121 High Street, Tewkesbury GL20 5JU
01684 273727   rajshahirestaurantltd.co.uk

'From strength to strength, that's how the Rajshahi has grown. Reputation with local, business visitors, tourists and boat people (the rivers Severn and Avon join at Tewkesbury) make it necessary to book to ensure a table. Warm, fresh Popadums and tangy pickles. were washed down with draught Cobra, followed by lovely Meat Samosas, Chicken Tikka Roghan Josh, Sag Aloo, Pullao Rice and Nan. The Pistachio Kulfi was beautifully present, delicious and not rock hard as is often the case.' TE. T/a: 10% disc. Hours: 6-12 (12.30 Fri & Sat).

Thornbury

MOGHULS SAMRAT
8 High St, Thornbury , BS35 2AQ   01454 416187

'Converted Inn, wood panelling, low beams. Waiters very smart, food formula curry house. Tasty Sheek Kebab, Ayr-Biran – colleague had to contend with bones. King Prawn Dhansak, niced. Service OK.' MS. 12-2 & 6-11.30.

MUMTAZ INDIAN
7 St Mary's St, Thornbury, BS35 2AB   01454 411764

The Mumtaz is on two levels. The downstairs seating area and small bar are for T/a customers and perusal of the menu. The restaurant is upstairs. 'Menu not too extensive, but food extremely good and large portions. Clean European-style decor and music! Very helpful staff and friendly. Would go back.' WW. KB was less enthusiastic about the decor and other reports talk of standard curries of generous proportions. AE-J found the Phal too hot on one occasion and too mild on another, although his fiancée 'loves the Kormas'. 'Good' G & MP. Evenings only.

Aldershot

JOHNNIE GURKHAS
186 Victoria Rd, Aldershot, GU11 1JZ 01252 328773

One thing you learn in marketing, is never change a unique and successful brand name. Johnny Gurkha's was founded in c1975 by one Mr H.J.Kakhi (aka Johnny) former captain of the Gurkhas. A few years ago, he retired and sold up and the new owners changed the name (to Gurkha Raj Doot). But all its fans, me included, plus half the British army (including generations of actual Gurkhas troops from their now closed barracks at Church Crookham) still call it Johnny Gurka's. Fortunately little else has changed. It's still a cheap and sometimes cheerful canteen-style basement dive. 'Glad to see the restaurant is still as seedy as ever. Mint sauce is excellent. Famous Dil Kusa Nan –

HAMPSHIRE

Area:
South England

Adjacent Counties:
Berks, Dorset, Surrey, Sussex, Wilts

an enormous bread topped with cherries and coconut.' PD. 'Food is very plentiful, beautifully cooked and spiced and nothing was left!' JW. Ignore the formula names and go for the Nepalese dishes (which for the geographically challenged is where our fighting force is recruited from). Gurkha Pork Buhtuwa is fiery hot and Gurkhali Chicken Chilli include s green olives, both £6. Wed & Thur nights banquet night £8.95 curry, popadums, starter, main, rice or naan and side. 12-2.30 & 6-11.30.

Basingstoke

THE AGRA BALTI HOUSE
34 Winchester Street, RG21 7EY   01256 475566

'We were greeted like long lost friends especially my daughter who was attending her first curry club outing. We were a party of 13, a bit of a squeeze in this narrow restaurant but we were well looked after as we tucked into the delicious Popadums and pickles. The highlight as usual was the Tamarind sauce. Some of the food included Methi Kaleia, Chicken Darzaling and Lamb Rogan Josh. Taylor went for the Vegetable Bhoona which she adored and I went for the fiery but delicious Prawn Jalfrezi. All food was of great quality and enjoyed by everyone. I couldn't fault the side dishes either; Mutar Ponir, Chana Masala, Bombay Aloo and Tarka Dahl were fantastic. The rice was superb and, as I always say, the Cheese Naan served here is the best I have ever tasted anywhere! The service throughout was well paced and attentive. Drinks were kept topped up and food came all at once, even with 13 covers to deal with. The staff were warm and friendly and went the extra mile, just like they always used to. Unfortunately this is a tired looking restaurant which is desperately in need of a makeover.That said, this is still one of my favourite restaurants but definitely worth steering clear of at the weekend when the clientele dips to match the look of the place!' IC.

Fareham

CAFE TUSK   CURRY BUFFET
4 West Street Fareham, PO16 0LF
01329 235511   www.cafetusk.co.uk

An interesting formula - the Indian Buffet - seating 176. Several display islands, each containing piping hot

COBRA
SPLENDIDLY INDIAN, SUPERBLY SMOOTH

Indian food: starters, curries from the very mildest Korma through to Vindaloo, and a chill island with dessertys. Generous portions are assured, as you quite simply help yourself from 50 lunch and 60 dinner dishes. Mon-Fri: Lunch: £6.99, Sat, Sun & Bank Hols: £8.50. Dinner: Sun-Thur: £12.99, Fri & Sat : £13.99 - Discounts for children. Obviously no t/a or del. 12-3 (to 4 Sat & Sun) & 5.30-11.30 (to 11 Sun).

Fleet

GURKHA SQUARE   NEPALESE   TOP 100
327 Fleet Rd, Fleet, GU51 3BU
01252 810186   www.gurkhasquare.com

Of the several Nepalese restaurants in the area, reports received place this one at the top. And it is actually patronised by Nepalese. This 67-seater, owned by AB Gurung and managed by Om Gurung, is as good as you'll find. *'Delighted to see the Gurkha Square in the TOP 100. My wife and I can certainly back this up. Perhaps slightly on the pricey side, but superb value for money. We particularly like the Mis-Mas, and the rice and naan are quite excellent.'* DT. *'Comfortable, polite service, excellent food.'* GR. Del: 3m.   12-2.30 & 6-11.30

WE THE RESTAURANT
333 Fleet Road, Fleet, GU51 3BU
01252 628889   www.wetherestaurant.co.uk

Sammi Choudhury opened this curiously-named Indian/Thai restaurant in 2003. 'W' represents the West and 'E' the East. The design is by top Bangladeshi architect Enamul Karim Nirjhar with modern, clean decor, waterfalls and coi-carp pools targeted at the top end of the market, as its prices show. Sammi's claim to fame was the night Prince William booked for 40 army chums from nearby Sandhurst for their pre-passing-out blow-out. Sammi revealed to this publication that Wills ate CTM and ordered seconds, and that he drank Jack Daniels and Coke. Flushed with success Sammi placed an ad in the local rag proclaiming that *you too can eat the same food as heir to the throne at £19.95'*. The menu(s) are comprehensive and here's a Snapshot: Indian starters: Tialioa Bhuna £ 12.95, cooked in a spicy thick sauce; Indian Tantaliser £6.50, including Lamb Tikka, Chicken Tikka, Chithol Kofta and Vegetable Kofta; Mains: King Prawn Roshney £15.95, with garlic, green chilli, tomato, green peppers and Lamb Shank Satkora £5.95, with a citric Bangladesh vegetable. There is an equally diverse Thai menu and you can mis and match. The wine list is remarkable. House whites and reds start at £12.95 but the 1970 Lafite Rothschild sells at £399.95, as does 1997 Louis Roederer Cristal champagne, billed as the *'ultimate'*. Personally I put Krug into that position, but this is a curry Guide and if you can afford it, go for it. 12-2.30 & 6-11.

CINNAMON BAY
4-7 High Street, Hamble, SO31 4JE   023 8045 2285   cinnamonbayhamble.co.uk

Ten minutes drive from east Southampton is the pretty town of Hamble, home to thousands of sailing yachts and motorboats. You can see them from the M27. It is also home to Cinnamon Bay, a rather good Indian restaurant, set back off the High street with car parking in front. It has been newly refurbished and has a new menu which offers all your favourites. And though they do them well, it is their specials which catch our eye: eg: Spicy Tikka Wrap £5.50 (£9.95 large) spicy chicken tikka stir-fried with onions, green peppers. Garnished with sliced tomatoes, red onions and fresh coriander, wrapped in a soft chapatti; Khushboo Patha Meethi £3.95, sliced chicken strips cooked with onions, green peppers and fresh curry leaves; Jalayia Agnipath £9.95 an extremely hot dish and extremely popular dish, it seems, using Bangladeshi Naga chillies; Shathkora Tangi £9.95, features the tart Bangladeshi citrus fruit, Shathkora which is simmered with lamb and Bengali spices; Mashooka Mashooka £9.95, is unique, we think, being diced pepperoni, cooked in a hot and spicy sauce; Bideshi Loggi £9.95, again unique, is sliced sausages cooked with mashed potato and tomatoes, in a thick curry sauce with crushed garlic and ginger. Indian bangers and mash. Original if nothing else. Takeaway 20% discount. 5:30-11:30.

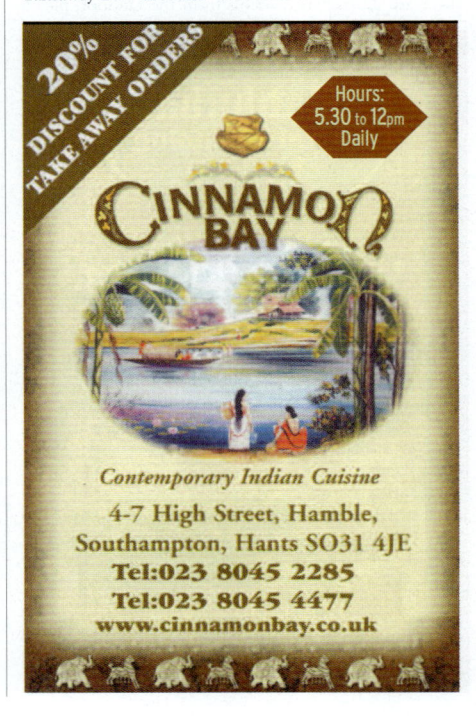

20% DISCOUNT FOR TAKE AWAY ORDERS

Hours: 5.30 to 12pm Daily

CINNAMON BAY
Contemporary Indian Cuisine
4-7 High Street, Hamble,
Southampton, Hants SO31 4JE
Tel: 023 8045 2285
Tel: 023 8045 4477
www.cinnamonbay.co.uk

Liss

MADHUBAN   TOP 100
94 Station Road, Liss, GU33 7AQ
01730 893363   www.madhubanrestaurant.co.uk

There is probably no better success story than the Madhuban's. It opened in 1987 in Liss village population 1300. Under the circumstances this may have been ill-judged. How could an Indian restaurant survive with such a small footfall, with only 30 seats? Furthermore it has been done by self-financing, albeit enhanced by extracting bank loans from pessimistic bank managers. But survive it did, and within years it had expanded first to 70 seats then to 86. Against all the odds the Madhuban was so successful that turned away many customers, particularly at weekends. In 2008 it expanded to 130 seats. A new kitchen was built alongside. The original plate-glass windows reveal an inviting bar and waiting area. Now with help from Lodue's brother Bedar, and some experienced waiters, you will not find better customer care anywhere. Customers names are remembered as old friends. Such is the success that despite doing two sittings and 100 takeaways, it often still cannot fit in all diners at the weekend, so book early. The eight-page menu epitomises the Madhuban's attention to detail. It is illustrated in full colour and fully describes all the dishes. There are 22 starters, 7 items from the tandoor, plus 5 naans. There is an ample choice of old favourites, and they are all done well. *'Given the extensive menu, it took some time to make any choices.'* HC. *'Highly rated – long may it remain.'* J&JM. *'It's is my local; have just got back from there in fact. Hussiani Kebab followed by Dhaba Gosht, Bhindi Bhajee and their superb Pilau'.* RP. One more thing: Prices here are among the cheapest in the area. This helps its appeal, but there is much more to it than that. It is the epitome of a good house. 12-2.30 & 5.30-11.30. *They also own Honey Garden, Madhuban Curry Sauces. www.madhuban.co.uk. See p43.*

Portsmouth

BLUE COBRA
87 London Rd, North End, Portsmouth, PO2 0BN
023 9266 5000   www.bluecobra-restaurant.com

Opened 2006 as a 200 seater on two floors. Menu Snapshot: Chicken Shahee £7.95, lightly spiced, tandoor, mint, garnished with grated cheese, served with salad on sizzler; Kanchi Tandoor Chops £4 / £8, with salad on sizzler; Moglai Poratha £1.50, flaky thick fried Indian bread with a spicy omelette. *'Everything totally excellent. Decor, ambience, food, presentation, service'* CF. T/a: 10% disc. Mon-Sat: 12-2 & 5.30-12 (Sun: 12-12).

STAR OF ASIA
6 Market Way, Portsmouth   023 9283 7906

Opposite the M&S car park, is this great little 40-seater, with a gorgeous sapphire blue, shiny terracotta tiles and blue mosaic front. Est 1992 by Abdul Mothen, who manages while Chef Gian Uddin cooks. *'Far enough away from the circuit drinking area. Hot and crispy Popadums. Excellent Rashmi with large portion of succulent kebab, topped with fluffy and tender omelette. Tandoori Chicken beautifully tender. Lovely Meat Bhuna and tangy Chicken Dhansak. Late generally means 1am, though when I left at 2.30am people were still arriving!'* RW. 12-2.15 (Fri closed) & 6 to late; Sat & Sun 12pm to late.

YOU SAY OK
You may get a discount of you show them this Guide.

ANDOVER: PINK OLIVE: Weyhill Rd, Andover, SP11 0PP 01264 772356. Taj Uddin offers family recipes with modern fusion. Set in a grand old English building its modern interior seats 112 in 3 areas. Head Chef Sufian Khan cooks signature dishes such as Tandoori Sea Bass and Lamb Xacuti.
FARNHAM: BENGAL LOUNGE : 1 The Street, Wrecclesham, 01252 713222. Est in the former Cricketers Pub in 2006. Bangladeshi food eg: Maas Biran starter, fish appetizer and Main: Lamb Mishti khodu, cooked with butternut squash, a traditional Bengali home dish. 12-2/6-11.30. *Branch: Benares, Farnham.*
LYNDHURST: PASSAGE TO INDIA 3 Romsey Road 8028 2099. AA Kaysor offers venison and duck specials. T/a: 20% Hours: 12-2/6-11.30.   www.passagetoindia-lyndhurst.com
WATERLOOVILLE: INDIAN COTTAGE 51 London Rd, Cowplain 01705 269351. At Sheik Shab Uddin's tiny 30-seater Chef AH Khan's *'food is excellent and the staff always attentive'*. D&BR & L&AC. Hours: 12-2.30/5.30-12. Branches: Indian Cottage: Port Solent, Gunwharf Quays & Horndean.

WINCHESTER: TIFFIN CLUB at the Westgate Inn, Romsey Rd, 01962 840804 www.tiffinclub.co.uk. Chef Miff likes Indian fusion eg: Chilli Crab Cake; Stuffed Baby Squid; Whitebait & Cachumbar, Zyava Chicken, dark chocolate with chilli & tamarind. 12-2 & 6-11. *Branch: 1 Oxford St, Southampton, SO14 3DJ.*

Southampton

BADI MIRCHI   TOP 100
190 Leigh Rd, Eastleigh, Southampton SO50 9DX
023 8064 1313   www.badimirchi.co.uk

A couple of miles north of Southampton is entrepreneur Pravin Sood's Badi Mirch (big chilli) located in a fine old English detached ex pub, 'The Leigh' built in the 1930's in the mock Tudor style complete with black beams and white surfaces. Prood grew up in India and came to England in the 1970. He missed the authentic Indian cuisine he had been brought up on and so he opened his own restaurant here in 2011. The refurbishment transformed the venue with a new smart and sophisticated interior. And there is a patio for al fresco dining. Chef Mukesh Sharma, and all the staff have Indian five-star hotel backgrounds. There are 'favourite dishes', but you should try the unusuals, eg: Chicken Tikka Casear salad £3.97; Rasam £2.97, lentil soup with tomatoes, garlic, cumin; Aloo Ki Tikki, pan-fried potato cake served with chick peas, tamarind sauce & yoghurt £3.57; Tawetawetawe Waliwali Machi, pan-fried sea bream marinated with light spices , £5.27; Crab Tikki, shallow-fried white crab meat cake, sautéed in chopped ginger, garlic, green chilli & lemon juice, served with sweet chilli sauce £5.27. Mains include: Adla Gosht, an Awadh region classic, lamb marinated overnight and cooked in a sealed pot or Pahari Gosht, classic from Uttaranchal, lamb cooked in its own stock, Peppery Duck, pot roasted duck breast marinated with salt, lemon juice, turmeric and ground mixed spices, cooked in a black peppercorn, star anise, served with pepper sauce and pilau rice.each £11; Patrani Macchi £12, sea bass fillet marinated with coconut, coriander, green chillies and lemon juice then wrapped in banana leaf and steamed; Tamil Biryani, south India style, chicken on the bone, cooked in basmati rice, flavoured with star anise and served with a choice of veg, £11. Set menus from £15 to £25 (min 8 diners).   12-2 & 5-11.

KUTI'S BRASSERIE   A-LIST
37 Oxford St, Southampton, SO14 3DP
023 8022 1585   www.kutis.co.uk

Named after the owner, Mr Kuti its lavish decor includes hand-painted murals using a theme of lotus flowers contrasted by silver finishing. The reception area is now styled as a lounge with a Bedouin feel again in a myriad of colours, while retaining thepurple as the core shade. Kuti's serves Bangladeshi and Indian cuisine and there is a Head Chef for each region. Romis Miah, who has been at Kuti's for 20 years is in charge of the Bangladeshi cuisine while India-trained Kamal Kishore formerly at Delhi's Hyatt Regency, heads the Indian cooking specialities. Menu Snapshots: good fish dishes, including: ayre, sea bass, sole and trout; also a good selection of popular curry house dishes made with beef; Bonhoor Delight, diced venison, served with a rich orange-flavoured Grand Marnier-based sauce. £8.95, Paneer Shashlik £4.50, cubes of cottage cheese, green chilli, ginger and coriander; Kerala Chicken £7.95, coconut, chilli; Lobia Dhal £5.95, black eyed peas, onions and tomato. We have had a lot of correspondence on this, and here is some of it. 'This upmarket establishment features a doorkeeper in traditional dress, novel presentation of mixed warm and crisp popadums in a basket, and a varied menu that is proud of Bangladeshi / Sylheti cuisine and meats not regularly encountered such as Venison, Duck and Beef. The 'Beef Bangla' is very tender and almost melts in the mouth. Expect to pay £20 per head for popadums, slightly adventurous main course, and a large Cobra.' GR. 'The quality of the food has been excellent. On my most recent visit, very much enjoyed Bonhoor Tikka, tandoor marinated venison, served with a delicious sauce. I like the signature dishes. Tandoori Quail, particularly noteworthy. Unconditionally recommended.' SO. 12-2.30 & 6-12. Branches: Kuti's Noorani - Fair Oak, 465 The Square, Fair Oak, Eastleigh, SO50 7AJ ~ 023 8060 1901; Kuti's Wickham.

P.O.S.H. TOP 100
1 Queensway, City Centre, Southampton, SO14 3AQ
023 8022 6377   www.poshindianrestaurant.co.uk

Upstairs you find inviting armchairs in a comfortable lounge. Go through to a huge nautically-themed restaurant, seating 150 diners, with bar, grand piano, band stand and a dance floor - quite a place. What does P.O.S.H mean? Port-Out Starboard- Home! And what did that mean. In the old days when ships were the main transports to India, experienced travellers chose their cabins to be 'POSH' to avoid the hot sunshine flooding through the porthole. Mr Menoj's Southampton P.O.S.H captures a colonial feeling with its decor and ambience, especially when someone it tinkling on the ivories. The restaurant has a large dance floor (often used for functions & live bands etc – weddings are popular here), and a well stocked, spacious bar. There are private dining rooms. Menu Snapshots: Paneer Tikka £4.95, curd cheese, flavoured with ginger, coriander and lime juice; Honey Glazed Salmon Tikka £7.75; King Prawn Toast £5.95, round of toast, smothered in an olive and anchovy butter, topped with garlic and chilli stir-fried king prawn; Duck Tiika Dhansak, £12.95. Buffets available at lunchtime and evening buffets. Both of these include 3 courses. £7.50, lunch;£15 Evening (£17.50 Fri/Sat). 'It is well decorated and has quite a good ambience. I have eaten there and been very pleased with items like swordfish and salmon tikka starters. The Baked Sea Bass was very delicate and succulent and the Sea Bass in Red Wine was also very pleasant, rich and spicy. Duck Bhuna was tender with a very nice spice balance but was too salty. The Chatt, which was chickpeas in a pleasant, tangy sauce, had a nice heat and clean coriander leaf finish. Overall opinion – OK, would probably give it another try'. SO. One regular who has attended weekly for 6 years says: 'Last week, my girlfriend was away on a dancing weekend, so I ordered a takeaway for one. When I went to collect my order, a member of staff happened to enquire as to the whereabouts of my girlfriend and wished her well on her endeavours. Granted, it doesn't sound like much, but it made me feel valued as a customer. Such touches are rare in the service industry these days.' Del: 3m, £15 min. 12-2 & 6-11.

Southsea

BOMBAY BAY   TOP 100
Fort Cumberland Rd, Southsea Marina, PO4 9RJ
023 9281 6066   www.bombaybay.co.uk

In 2005, Southsea Marina handed the operation of its all-day bar and restaurant to the Pompey Gandhi Group (twelve brothers and cousins, surname Karim) based in Kingston Road and who already operated two other restaurants. Parking is usually sufficient. Up a flight of stairs the restaurant has primrose yellow and burgundy walls with wall mounted seafaring artwork. It has a two-aspect panoramic view of the sea, the 'mainland' and Hayling Island. The window seats, with their views are the most popular, especially in daylight. On a good day, full service is available there on lthe adjoining large outside terrace. Exec chef Lahin Karim oversees the kitchens, and has aimed his menu at healthier food 'with less ghee and crunchy vegetables'. He also presents his food on rather smart white china plates. Menu snapshot: Starters, which come with a splendid salad include Mussels £5.50, stuffed with rice, served with garlic and coriander sauce; Bombay Missali: Chicken tikka, lamb tikka, sheek kebab and squid or Hush Tikka, duck fillets marinated in spices in orange flavoured sauce both £11. Mains include (£14 & £15) Goan Chicken or Lamb Tikka, cooked with red goan chilli, garlic, green peppers, coriander, coconut milk and fine spices, fairly hot. Vegetable dishes (£3.50) include Broccoli Bhajee and Niramish. Set lunch 12pm to 4 is good value at £9.95. Set meal £14. They are usefully open all day (the only venue in the area to do this) mainly to offer a bar and snacks service for the marina boat owners, and anyone else. Mar-Sep: Sun-Th: 12-11; Oct-Feb: Mon-Th: 5-11; Sun: 12-11; All year: Fri: 3-12; Sat: 12-12. Branches: 141 Kingston Rd, Portsmouth, PO2 7EB, T & J Mahal, 39 Elm Grove, Southsea, PO5 1JF.

COBRA — SPLENDIDLY INDIAN, SUPERBLY SMOOTH

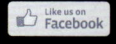

P.O.S.H. spices
Indian cuisine with style

- À la carte
- Lunch Buffet
- Evening Buffet
- Corporate Events
- Entertainment Evenings
- Charity Functions
- Engagement Functions
- Hen Nights
- Wedding Receptions

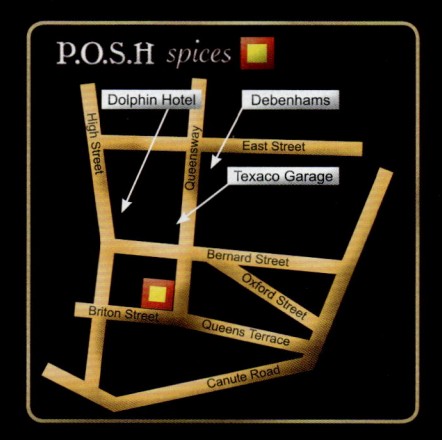

1 Queensway, Southampton, SO14 3AQ
Telephone: 02380 22 63 88

Web: www.poshindianrestaurant.co.uk
email: poshindianrestaurant.co.uk

HAMPSHIRE to HERTFORDSHIRE

GOLDEN CURRY TOP 100
16 Albert Road, Southsea, PO5 2SH 023 9282 0262

The 52-seater has been owned by Salim Hussein (manager) and Razak Ali (head chef) since 1979, and has a justifiably loyal following. I am often sent letters & emails by people bemoaning the loss of taste these days compared with 'the good-old-days' Well here you find it, done as it used to be. One secret is that they cut no corners. At Golden Curry you can taste fresh and finest ingredients. Whole chickens, for example are pot-simmered in light spices, then boned and cooked off in your curry dish, with the resultant great flavour to match. (As opposed to tasteless pre-boned breast). It has a huge local following all of whom know the waiters by name, and vice-versa. It is common to see three generations at table, all of whom have been regulars almost since birth!. This is what a decent curryhouse is all about: a friendly home-from-home, where you get cared for with decent food, decent service and an unpretentious price tag which doesn't require a new mortgage. Average pos & 2 course meal: £16. *'An excellent restaurant which my husband and I go to for a "curry fix". Salim is a wonderful host, greeting his clients with courtesy and friendliness, the waiters follow his lead. Ali runs a wonderfully efficient and clean kitchen.'* C&CH. *'Excellent food and service. Our regular curry restaurant.'* DKM. *'Staff always friendly and attentive. Extremely clean and cosy restaurant. Meals range from very good to superb! Good sized portions which are very filling.'* GB. *'An excellent restaurant. Received a nice welcome. Table, decor – clean and tidy. Meal was as I ordered it – HOT! I have been all over the country but it would be hard to beat this curry house.'* EC. PS: The locations is great if you have a night out at the gorgeous King's Theatre, next door, and they do a quick meal if they know your plans. Del free, 2m over £20 (under that £2.50 charge made). 12-2 & 5.30-12.30. (Sun to 12).

HEREFORDSHIRE

Area:
Welsh Border

Adjacent Counties:
Gwent, Powys,
Shrops,
Staffs,
Worcs

Hereford

KAMAL
82 Widemarsh St, Hereford, HR4 9HG 01432 278005

'A narrow-fronted and impressively named enterprise that fronts a surprisingly long and capacious curry house.

THE GOLDEN CURRY

16 Albert Road
Southsea, Hampshire
PO2 2SH
023 9282 0262
Top 100

Helpful and friendly staff. Menu contains usual suspects, plus specials. Real cloths and hand towels. Jangra Purr – unusual, almost spring roll, delightful chat style curry with salad and sweet sauce, enjoyable. Lamb Tikka Biriani – very good, well cooked, a shade greasy, boiled egg rather than usual omelette topping. Lamb absolutely top quality, mouth watering. Recommended.' RW. 3 course Sun Lunch: £8. Del: £14 min. Hours: 12-2 / 5.30-12.

RAZBARI

156 Eign Street, Hereford HR4 0AP,
01432 265440   www.razbari.co.uk

Modern look of blacks, white and chrome, a space-age chadelier and a balcony area. Highlyrated for food and service. Sun-Thu: Fri-Sat: 5.30-11 (to 12 Sat). *Branch: Jalsagor, 60 St Owens St, Hereford, HR1 2PU 01432 343464.*

Kington

HYDERABAD

57, Bridge St, Kington, HR5 3DJ   01544 231999

'Run by brothers Eklim (very popular with the locals) and Shalim Khan, who experience is over 20 years, (their father ran a restaurant in Stourbridge). The family is originally from Khar Bari, Syhlet' I think virtually every Bangladeshi restaurant owner is from Syhlet, I am surprised their is anyone still left! (only joking! I've been there and can confirm that the population is thriving!). *'Worth the forty minute drive to eat there, service is excellent and so is the vegetarian food. Have tried various dishes including the Baked Bean Balti £5. Lamb Passanda £9 (including rice) is to die for. There can be a bit of a wait when they are full, but this is rural Heref'd – we go with the flow! Fantastic.'* SSL. Takeaway: 10% discount. 5.30-11.

Leominster

JALALABAD

33 Etnam St, Leominster, HR5 3DJ   01568 615656

Well promoted by the ebullient owner-manager Kamal Uddin Owner-chef Abdul Mukith's food menu attracts regular praise from Leominster locals. *'Menu Conventional Quality Excellent Quantity Very generous Decor Obtrusive peacock feathers arranged around the wall - disturbing for some Service On the slow side Comfort Good, not too close seating Comments Starters: Popadums 50p x 2 plus £1.20 chutney; Onion Bhaji £2.25 – taste good, texture fine; Tandoori Mix £3.95; Presentation good, slightly small portions. Main Course: Chicken Keema Mattar £6.95; Garlic Chicken £6.95. Mushroom Pullao Rice £2.15; Peshwari Nan £2.15. Drinks: Tiger x 2. Bill £31.40. Mark 8 / 10.'* G&MP.

YOU SAY OK
You may get a discount of you show them this Guide.

BROMYARD: TASTE OF INDIA 22 High St.   01885 488668. *'Had a good meal in here.'* 12-2.30/5.30-11.30; closed Tues.

HEREFORD: KHAN'S Plough Inn, Canon Pyon, 01432 830577. *'In a pub! Excellent food at very reasonable prices – best in Hereford.'* PJM. No credit cards. Hours: 5.30-12.

ROSS-ON WYE: CAFE ZAM ZAM 24 High St HR9 5BZ – 01989 764030 *'In a different league.'* JC.

ROSS-ON-WYE: OBILASH 19a Gloucester Rd. 01989 567860. Est 1985, Janu Miah's Obilash seats 40. Del: 3m, £25 min. T/a: 10% disc. Hours: 6-12.

BENGAL LOUNGE 1 Copse Cross St, Ross. 01989 562803. *'Sizzler Mix starter, £3.75 enough for two. Signature dishes come in at £10.95.T/a: 10% disc.'* MC.

CAFE ZAM ZAM BYO 23 High St, Ross. 01989 764030 *'Very reasonably priced – house specials all at c£7. The mixed platter for two (starter £6.90, main £13.80) gives a nice variety of tastes to try; those who like a kick to their meals may enjoy the garlic chilli chicken. Staff are very welcoming. BYO allowed'* MC.

Ross-on-Wye

ROADMAKER INN GHURKHA

Gloucester Rd, Gorsley, Ross   HR9 7SW
01989 720352 www.theroadmakerinn.co.uk

'Owned and run by four ex-Ghurkha soldiers; it maintains a pub bar with the restaurant serving Nepalese cuisine in the evenings. We started with the Ghurkha Special (£12) which is was a very nice mixed grill and certainly enough for two. We also had Momo (£6), steamed lamb mince dumplings with a spicy tomato chutney, again very good. The main courses of Himalaya Chicken (£10) and Nepalese Lamb Curry (£910) were delicious and the children voted the Chicken Tikka Masala as the best they had ever tasted. The accompanying Naans were beautifully light.' MC.

HERTFORDSHIRE
Area: Home Counties, (north of London)

Adjacent Counties: Beds, Bucks, Cambs, Essex, London

'GL' denotes those former Herts suburbs absorbed by Greater London in 1965.

Abbots Langley

FOREST OF INDIA

39 High Street, Abbots Langley, WD5 0AA
01923 270077   www.forestofindia.co.uk

Owner AK Chowdhury established this 120-seater in 1996. Menu Snapshot: Tandoori Trout £7; Tandoori Mixed Grill £9, including King Prawn and Naan bread – great!; Ponir Masala, special cheese barbecued in tandoori oven cooked with cream, £6.95; King Prawn Tufan, fresh herbs and garam masala cooked with tandoori spice, £9.95; Duck Nawabi £9.25, marinated duck, mushrooms, onions, tomatoes and brandy – fit the a King or even a Nawab! Del: 2m £12 min. T/a: 10% dis. Banquet Night,£10.85, Tuesday night: 1 each Starter, Main, Side Dish, Rice or Nan. Sunday Buffet: £8.9512–5: e-a-m-a-y-l – min 14 dishes. Children £5. 12-2.30 & 6-11.30. *Branch: Sema, Whitecross St, WC1.*

VICEROY OF INDIA
20 High St, Abbots Langley WD5 0AR
01923 261382   www.viceroybrasserie.co.uk

Est in 1989 by Ronney Rahman. *'Food delicious, always fresh and elegantly presented. Waiters friendly and attentive.'* D&PM. Chef Tarik Hussain's menu is standard with the addition of a number of specials. Viceroy Threvue £6.75, selection of barbequedchicken, lamb & duck, seasoned in ginger, onion, cooked in a special sauce Khatta Chicken £6.75, in lemony flavoured Bangladeshi herbs & spices; Misty Lau Chicken £6.75, with red pumpkin Set menu £30 for 3: Starters - Pops, Chicken Tikka, Murg Bora, Sheek Kebab. Main course - Butter Chicken, Balti Ghust, Mixed vegetables, Shak Aloo, Pillau Rice & Nan Bread) Finishes with Kulfi. Hours: 12-2.30 & 6-11.

Hemel Hempstead:

MOGUL
91 High St, Old Town, Hemel HP1 3AH 01442 255146

'I feel this is the best in Hemel – beautifully decorated and always good food and service. Took two work colleagues and two customers – all agreed the best meal! Chicken Roushini, Chicken Rezala and Mogul Special Masala – all fantastic. Side dishes and breads – all very good.' [and JH returns]: *'Phoned and collected within half an hour, all hot plus free Popadums!'* [and JH keeps returning]: *'Busy Sat night, party of nine. Table booked for 9.30; Sat down at 10pm. Main courses at 10.45, no starters. Food as good as ever – well loaded chicken and mushroom Rizato, thoroughly enjoyed by two. Only let down was Tandoori King Prawn looked great but lacking in flavour. Bill at 12.20am. An enjoyable night but too long!* [and JH keeps returning]: *'Deep fried aubergines on the house to start absolutely gorgeous. Roushini seemed a but rich. Mushroom Rizoti and Chicken Gastoba – as good as ever!'* JH. T/a: 10% disc. 12-2.30 & 5.30-11.30; 12 Fri & Sat.

YOU SAY OK
You may get a discount of you show them this Guide.
BARNET (CL): SHAPLA TANDOORI 37 High St. 020 8449 0046. SI Ahmed's smart 50 est 1981 is 'always very reliable, clean and cosy.' CT. Del: £1.50, 4m. Hours: 12-2.30/6-12.

BERKHAMSTED: CURRY GARDEN 29 High St, Berkhamsted 01442 877867. *'An old converted pub, lovely low beams and cosy booths. Very impressed. Will most definitely be back.'* SW.

BISHOPS STORTFORD: SHADONA High St. 01279 508149. *'Excellent cuisine and sharp service and we were all stuffed! Prices above average.'* AE. Hours: 12-2.30/6-11.

CHESHUNT: RAJ VOGUE 48 High St.   01992 641297. 82-seater est 1991 by Khalek Quazi. GR likes *'the Nawab Nargis, cooked with spicy minced chicken and fresh mint.'* T/a: 10% disc. Del: £15, 3m. 12-2.30; 2 Sun lunch buf £6.95./6-11.30; 11 Sun.

HATFIELD: PRINCE OF INDIA 10 Market Pl. 01707 265977. 48-seater est 1993, managed by SF Ali. *'Romantic and pleasant atmosphere.'* RL. Hours: 5.30-11.30.

HEMEL HEMPSTEAD: CHUTNEYS 79 Waterhouse St, Hemel 01442 243 595. 70-seater owned by Saber Khan. Menu unusuals: Noodles, with spicy minced meat, egg, ; Special Beef, tandooried fillet steak; Chilli and Coriander Naan. Del: 4m £15 min. 2-2 Sat & Sun. Sun lunch buffet £7.95 / 5.30-11.30.

HITCHIN: INDIA BRASSERIE 36 Bancroft Rd, Hitchin 01462 433001. M Chowdhury's restaurant seats 32. *'The best in Hitchin.'* SW. Hours: 12-2.30 Tue-Thur/ 5.30-12; 1-11 Sun, buffet £7.95..

LETCHWORTH: CURRY GARDEN 71 Station Road 01462 682820. Chef owner Afiz Uddin's. Chef owner Afiz Uddin has a *'huge friendly menu.'* MT. Hours: 12-2.30 / 6-12; 12-12 Sun, buffet 12-5.30. Branches (all named Curry Garden) at: Berkhamsted; Rickmansworth; Dunstable Beds; Hornchurch Essex.

TANDOORI NIGHT Knight St, Sawbridgeworth 01279 722341. *'We had our wedding reception in this great restaurant.'* JP. 'Hours: 12-2.30/6-11.30; 12 Fri & Sat.

STEVENAGE: GATE OF INDIA 20 The Glebe, Chells Way. 01438 3176195. Abdul Salam's and Chef Arosh Ali's 57-seater in 4 rooms. Del: £10 min, 4m. Hours: 12-2.30/6-12.

WALTHAM CROSS: CAFÉ SPICE 63 High St. 01992 717546. Rezaul Huq Syed's 48- seater does Chicken Chauk, chicken in batter, breadcrumbs, deep-fried, served with mixed vegetables. Sun Buffet c£7. Del: 3m, £10 min. T/a: 10% disc. Hours:12.30-3.30 / 5.30-11.30; 11.30 Fri & Sat.

TRING: OLIVE LIMES 60 High St, HP23 5AG 01442 828444. Opened in October 2007 on the former Kristal Spice Restaurant. The owners are fast becoming part of Tring community, entering into the spirit of the apple festival, Christmas festival and even handing out tastings during the carols in the car park on Christmas Eve.

Kings Langley

CINNAMON LOUNGE
18, High St, WD4 8BH 01923 263923
www.cinnamon-lounge.co.uk

Situated in a lovely old English building, apparently 500 years old. The front of the building has black beams and lovely herringbone bricks. The interior, which has been still retains its original inglenook fireplace, but not much else. Comfortable, high backed leather chairs, sit around tables which are cleanly laid with white linen, blue or red glass chargers and sleek cutlery. Suka - king prawn or duck, tamarind sauce, herbs and honey; Pitta Paneer Saag - cheese, spinach wrapped in puri; Chot Poti - chick peas, eggs, potatoes, tamarind sauce; Lamb E Kodu - with Bangladeshi green pumpkin; Sharabi - chicken or lamb slices, simmered in a mild buttery, red wine sauce, garnished with nuts. 6-11; 11.30 Fri & Sat. Sunday Buffet: 12-3. *Branch: Cinnamon Lounge, London Colney, AL2 1LP.*

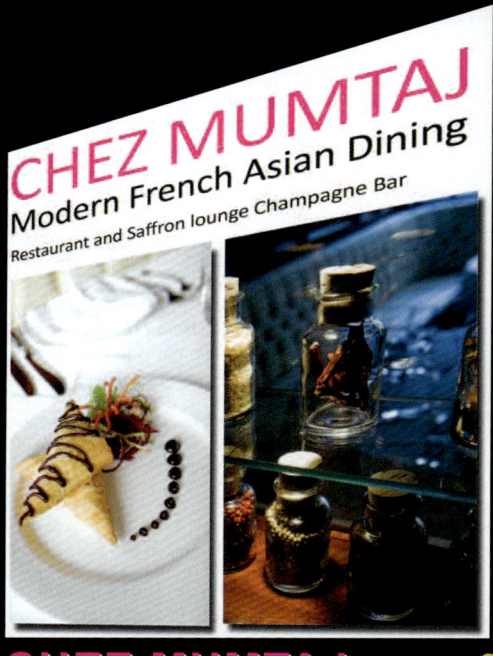

CHEZ MUMTAJ
Modern French Asian Dining
Restaurant and Saffron lounge Champagne Bar

Two A-Listed Indian restaurants in St Albans

- Champagne Lounge
- Canapé Parties
- Private Dining
- Prix Fixe Menus
- Tasting Menu
- Open Theatre Kitchen
- Corporate Dining
- Early Bird Dinner

One Award-winning Chef

" I am a firm advocate of only sourcing the freshest seasonal ingredients and spices which are potent in flavour with nutrition in mind. "

Chef Director Chad Rahman

CHEZ MUMTAJ
136-142 London Road
St Albans, Herts AL1 1PQ
Tel: 01727 800033
www.chezmumtaj.com
Email us
info@chezmumtaj.com

MUMTAJ
115 London Road
St Albans
Herts
AL1 1LR
Tel:
01727 858399

Pictured above: Chez Mumtaj's private dining room, seating 12 in luxury.

innovative, progressive, persistent and passionate

A-Listed in the COBRA GOOD CURRY GUIDE since 2009

St Albans

CHEZ MUMTAJ   A-LIST
136-142 London Rd, St Albans, AL1 1PQ
01727 800033   www.chezmumtaj.com

Chad Radman had a dream. His dad had run a succesful Indian restaurant (see next entry). Chad liked the enviroment (of living over the shop) so much that he decided to get proper training as a chef at the Conrad Hilton Hotel School He then worked at Houston's Hyatt Regency then at the Hilton Group specialising in French, Indian, Malaysian, Thai and Mexican. Chad's dream was to deliver a menu of 'Modern French-Asian cuisine'. Mumtaj was doing just fine, but when a former carpet warehouse just across the road became available in 2008, Chad acquired it and spent a couple of million transforming it into a two part very upmarket venue. Saffron Champagne Lounge (evenings only) and Chez Mumtaj Restaurant (lunch & dinner). The lounge takes up to 50 for cocktails. It has rich mahogany panelled walls, luxurious brown leather banquette and pouf seating, mirror-panelled walls and booths for privacy. The restaurant echos the walls but an identical array of leather banquettes are cream, seating colours. There is a private dining room for up to 16 guests. Chad is a remarkable chef, able to retaoin Indian flavours whilst innovativing. He has chosen a capable brigade with chefs who have worked at Benares, Cinnamon Club and the $1200-a-night Burj Al Arab hotel, Dubai. The menus are remarkable. The lounge has its own Asian 'Tapas' Menu. eg: Squid Salad Tempura, Satay, Chicken Tikka Burrito Wrap, Lollipop Drumstick. A la Carte snapshot: Starters eg: Mixed Meat Platter: green herbed duck breast, lamb chop, achari chicken tikka, trio of homemade fresh fruit preserves; Loch Duart Salmon Tikka, chargrilled salmon fillet marinated in smoked paprika, dill, mustard, honey & fennel, coconut infused beetroot. Seared Foie Gras, pan-seared foie gras glazed in kumquat with vanilla honey compote, schezwan pepper crush, lightly curried confit of cauliflower purée, hazelnut crumb oil and hand baked fenugreek biscuits. A la Carte Starter examples: Menu Snapshot: Starters: Mixed Meat Platter: Green-herbed duck breast, lamb chop, achari and chicken tikka with homemade chutneys; Chez Mumtaj Salad, green seasonal salad with cilantro, shaved mango, fresh pomegranate and papaya tossed with roasted cashew nuts, honey-mustard vinaigrette; Seared Foie Gras, with schezwan pepper-crush with lightly curried confit of cauliflower purée and hazelnut crumb oil; Soft Shell Crab, wild-catch blue-swimmer soft-shell crab in chilli and garlic tempura batter served with homemade ginger, prune, mango and fig marmalade. Mains examples: Seafood Biryani, dum phukt-style mixed seafood, saffron and rose water sealed in clay pot with puff pastry served with roasted cumin and cucumber boondi raita; Risotto, chargrilled freshwater king prawns, Devon crabmeat risotto with braised baby leeks, smoked aubergine caviar, basil and truffle cappuccino foam; Duck, seven-spice-dusted Barbary duck breast in sesame chilli ginger honey glaze with a stir fry of young vegetables, oriental rice, cassia & star anise apple and rhubarb compote; Guinea Fowl, classic homemade Thai mussaman curry, crushed peanuts, baby potatoes, pak-choi greens and wild mushroom rice; Spinach Dumpling, quenelles of spinach & sweet potato stuffed with goat's cheese served with chick pea cake, tomato fenugreek beurre blanc sauce and dill-saffron herbed rice. Oxtail Madras, gently clay-pot-roasted queue de boeuf in robust Franco-Asian spices, jaggery, ginger & turnips sealed in pastry;Guinea Fowl pan roasted supreme in Ras-El Hanout [Moroccan spice mix] stuffed foie gras & truffle mousseline, fricassee "A la Persillade" of braised savoy cabbage, edamame beans and mushrooms & homemade smoked chorizo, tomato rice. Set Meals plus a glass wine: Lunch: 2 course £14.95; Dinner: 6-7.30, Sun, Tues-Thur. Hours: 12-2.30 & 6-11. *Branch Mumtaz, see next entry and previous page.*

MUMTAJ   TOP 100
115 London Rd, St Albans
01727 858399   www.mumtaj.co.uk

The original opened in 1962. Muklasur Rahman Mojumder took over in 1983. His son Chad Rahman now runs the 44 seater which is in two rooms partitioned by an archway. Located next to the Esso petrol station (opposite the cinema) the Mumtaj offers. all the old favourites at reasonable prices, rather than the fusion of Chez Mumtaj. St Albans ex MP Kerry Pollard loves the place. '*Having visited many, many UK curryhouses, as well as in Brussels (ugh), Amsterdam (great), Stockholm (ugh), Riyadh (ummm), and the USA (hmmm), I am always pleased to get home to St Albans, and eat at my local, the Mumtaj.*' PFM. Lunch: 1 main, 1 side dish, rice or nan £6.95. 12-3 & 6-12. *Branch: Chez Mumtaj see previous entry and previous page.*

KENT

Area:
South England

Adjacent Counties:
Essex, London, Surrey, Sussex

'GL' denotes those former Kent suburbs absorbed by Greater London in 1965.

Bromley (GL)

KOSTURI
18 Station Approach, Bromley, BR2 7EH
020 8462 8594   www.kosturi.co.uk

Chef Sarawar Uddin Khan's Kosturi seats 82 and has

SPLENDIDLY INDIAN, SUPERBLY SMOOTH

lavender walls accented by strategically positioned spotlights installed in a hanging wooden beam while long-shaded contemporary lighting hangs over the rest of the restaurant, adding to the natural light that pours in from the large glass window at the entrance. Bangladeshi chef Sarawar Uddin Kan's menu ranges from Goa to Lucknow and Punjab. -Weds Banquet: 5 course £11, Live Piano. E-a-m-a-y-l Sunday buffet: £7.95 12-4.

TAMASHA   A-LIST
131 Widmore Road, Bromley, BR1 3AX
020 8460 3240   www.tamasha.co.uk

Established in 1993. Owner is Shekor Tarat. Attached to a small hotel, great if you need a decent curry followed by a bed for the night. Tamasha means *'something worth seeing'*. And it is! There is ample car parking, and you enter past a smartly saluting beezer, via an awning flanked by tub plants. Inside, there's a well-stocked bar. The dining room seats 120 in seven rooms, and is superbly decorated like a British Raj Club, with polo sticks and hats, black and white photos of polo teams, Maharajas and sumptuous banquets. Cane furniture with palms in copper planters. Head chef Rajinder Kumar cooks food from north and south India, Goa and Kashmir. Curry house formula, it certainly is not. Favourites are there but a little exploring can yield some treasures: Goan Fish Curry, fish cooked in coconut and red chillies and garnished with fresh coriander leaves. Dum Pukht Gosht, marinated sliced baby lamb in a variety of spices and then steam-cooked in sealed earthenware, and Chicken Mirchi Wala, boneless chicken cooked in strongly spiced red chilli curry with potatoes, is popular, and Abrakebabra! so is the table magician who entertains the kids during Sun lunch buffet. *'Prices above average, but not excessive for quality of restaurant and location.'* MW. Service charge 12.5%. Sun lunch buffet with in-house magician. T/a: 10% disc. 12-2.30 & 6-11.

Faversham

INDIA ROYAL
16 East Street, Faversham ME13 8AD   01795 536 033   www.theindiaroyal.co.uk

Est 1991, this ia a favourite curyhouse serving all the favourites at sensible prices. Pops (plain or massalla), 55p; Chicken/Lamb Tikka, £2.95; Royal Aloo Special, £2.95, mashed potato coated with mint, egg and breadcrumbs and deep fried; Chicken Pakora, £2.95, marinated diced pieces of chicken fried in batter. Mains Chicken lamb Muchrani £6.75 cooked with lemon, almond, coconut, cream & mild spices. CTM £6.95. 12-2.30 (Not Fri) & 6-11.30.

Folkestone

GURKHA PALACE   NEPALESE
97 Enbrook Valley, Folkestone, CT20 3NE   01303 257700   www.gurkhapalace.co.uk

Kishore Sapkota owns this 60 seater. Try the specialities:

Kalejo Bhutuwa £4, stir-fried chicken liver; Aloo Choo £3.50, deep-fried cakes of mash potatoes and exotic herbs; Kalejo Bhutuwa, £4. chicken livers stir-fried using a traditional Nepalese recipe; Staff Curry £8; Momo £6.50, chicken dumplings with Nepalese chutney. Del: 3m £12 min. T/a: 10% disc. 11-2.30 & 6-11.

INDIA   INDIAN FINE DINING   TOP 100
1 Old High St, Folkestone, CT20 1RJ   01303 259155

We like the ebullient Mr Ali Ashraf who chose Folkestone to establish his 42 seat India in 1985. Being a French-trained Indian chef (born in Calcutta) and speaking French too, perhaps he felt being close to France would be au fait. In some cases he combines French methods (cream, wine and brandy) with Indian spices to provide an original interpretation of his Indian dishes. Of course this place isn't for bone-head drunks looking for a vindaloo fix. The 'closed' sign goes up well before the pubs close. *'Only subtle clues reveal that this restaurant is special; I can't help feeling they could be overlooked by a casual observer. The building fabric may be faded, but the table presentation and service was impeccable. My main basis for visiting the India was the Guide's recommendation on the basis of food, and I can confirm reports that this was special. I had the Crab in White Wine for Entrée followed by Chicken Jalfrezi and Special Fried Rice. I have never before experienced such exquisite flavours. Every morsel exploded with new surprises and made the experience one that you wished would never* end. Anything you believe you know about curry is turned on its head and it was a truly culinary experience. I shall certainly be visiting again and can whole heartedly agree that this establishment deserves its listing in your top 100.' DTH. 'Six of us ate there last Sat and it was excellent. My favourite Chicken Jalfrezi was superb.' BT. Mr Asraf is getting on a bit now and he has reduced his hours to 6-9.30 Th to Sat.

Halstead

BENGAL MANGROVE
Polhill, London Road, Halstead, TN14 7DR
01959 534688   www.calcuttaclub.co.uk

Of course, they serve CTM etc, but why not try some unusual dishes, eg: Crab Piri Piri £5, fiery red hot chillies, rice vinegar, spring onion and Goan spices; Mysore Bondi £3.50, mashed potato balls, ginger, curry leaves, black mustard seed, deep-fried – all starters are served with salad and homemade chutney. Badami Stuffed Murgh Masala £9, stuffed with vegetables, cream, almonds and pistachio; Sathkari Gosht c£8, lamb, wild lemon, naga chilli, lemon leaf; Vegetable Milijuli £9, baby potatoes, mange tout, stir-fried in garlic oil. 'Food superb. Polite waiter. Manager gave me guided tour of conservatory area (70 seats). I'll be back in the near future.' CO. T/a: 25% disc.

CALCUTTA CLUB TOP 100
London Road, Polhill, Halstead TN14 7BG
01959 534 688   www.calcuttaclub.co.uk

Back in the early 1800s Calcutta's clubs served British officers of the Company and the Raj the very best of Indian cuisine. This smart Club is on the A224 and has a conservatory and bar, the Striped Elephant. Feast your eyes on this menu; it includes some absolute corkers! Snapshot: Pudina tikka £5.50, boneless chicken marinated in freshmint, coriander and cooked on bamboo skewer; Afghani Murgh Malai Tikka £5.50, fresh ginger, green chilli, black cumin, cardamom, cottage cheese; Jhinga Palak Pakora £5.50, deep-fried fritter, baby prawns, fresh spinach, gram flour, onion, spices; Victoria Prawn £12.50, seawater prawns marinated in dark rum, ground black cardamom, black cummin, dry ginger, yoghurt, cream, spring onion and tomato; Murgh Khandhari £9.95, boneless chicken, rich cashew nut, red onion gravy, tomato, fresh coriander and ginger; Kakori Kebab £9.50, finely minced lamb, saffron, rose petals and cardamom; Dum Pukht £10, lamb escalope, half cooked in aromatic spices, flavoured, slow steamed in sealed earthenware pot; Kaju-Kismish Korma £9, tender lamb, ground almonds, raisins, cashew nuts, saffron; Bihar Mirchi Aloo £5, spicy baby potatoes, green chilli, black cummin; Avial £4.95, green vegetables, tamarind, ginger, coconut; Amritsari Masala Kulcha bread stuffed with spicy potatoes, Wonderful Indian desserts are on offer - Gajar ke Halwa £3.95, grated carrot, milk, khoya, sugar, served hot with dry fruits (I like this with vanilla ice-cream); Bengali Rassogulla; Thandi Rasmalai. First floor private room seats 60. 12-2.30 (to 4 Sun) & 6-11.30, (from 7 Sun).

YOU SAY OK
You may get a discount of you show them this Guide.

GILLINGHAM: TWYDALL TANDOORI 50 Twydall Green. ~ 01634 386110. S Rahman's curryhouse 'does some nice things eg Lamb Albadami £6.50, mango, creamy, mild sauce' RL. . T/a: 10% disc. Hours: 12-2.30 not Fri / 5.30-11.30, 10 Sun.
MARDEN: MARDEN TANDOORI Albion Rd.~ 01622 832184. 'Lucky there are two Indian restaurants in such a small village, both providing a good formula curry' MW. Hours: 12 -2.30/6-11.
MARDEN: ROYAL 27 High Street, Marden ~ 01622 833224 . 65-seater in 2 rooms and 'good-weather' garden. 'Service friendly and efficient'. MW. Hours: 12 -2.30 / 6-11.
MINSTER, ISLE OF SHEPPEY: SHERAZ 10 High St.~ 01795 876987. 'Interior looks like a Kebab House. Friendly service. Punjabi cooking surprisingly good. Nappali Chicken – good, hot, chillies. Dhal Samba – tasty.' MW. 11-11.30; 12 Fri & Sat.
MINSTER, THANET: MINSTER TANDOORI 1 High Street, Minster, Thanet   01843 822517 'Kakra Bhuna (minced crab), Tikka Salmon, and spiced Red Mullet and some duck dishes. All a good meal – which is no doubt why they were full.' MW.
ORPINGTON (GL): CURRY HOUSE 24 Station Sq, Petts Wood ~ 01689 820671. Basth (Baz) Wahab runs this 42-seater. 'Food good but atmosphere non-existent. Eventually won the waiters round and managed a laugh and a little conversation. Flavoursome fish tikka. Main dishes were well up to expectation.' CC&GM. Hours: 12-3 (not Mon & Fri) and 6-12; closed Mon.
RAJ OF INDIA 4 Crescent Way, Green St Green, Orpington ~ 01689 852170. 72 seater est 1987 by owner-manager Muzibur Rahman. 12-2.30/6-12. Branches: Raj of India Sheerness, Swanley and Sittingbourne; Raj Bari Sevenoaks; Maharajah Bexley; Juboraj Brentwood, Essex.
RAMSGATE: RAMSGATE TANDOORI 17 Harbour S. ~ 01843 589134. 70-seater, owned by Rezaur Rahman. Cooking by head chef Joyanti Mendas. Del: £10 min. Hours: 12-2.30 / 6-12.
ROCHESTER: SHOZNA 153 Maidstone Rd. ~ 01634 847 847. Owner Jamal Udin. Starters: Chicken Cutlet; Stuffed pepper (meat or vegetable) c£4. Mains: Monchorian Chicken, chicken fillet, mango, cream, c£8. Hours: 12-2, resvn only/5.30-12. Branch: Shozna, 18 High St, Stroud, Kent.

Maidstone

SHAMRAT
36 Lower Stone Street, Maidstone, ME15 6LX
01622 764961   www.shamrat.co.uk

Jamal, Selva and manager Tahmul tell us they offer 'authenticity and a variety of regional dishes chosen with great care to show off the wondrous cooking of India'. Starters include Tandoori Aloo £3.95, Baby potato cooked in tandoori masala; Salmon Dil Tikka £5.95 infused with dil, parsley and light spices; Aloo Pakora £3.75 thin cut potato with coriander and curry leaves; Thali Starter for 2 persons or 4 person £8 or £16, selection of seekh kebab, chicken tikka, onion bhajee, chicken wings. Served with salad and fresh mint raitha. Spicy Crab Cake £5.95 with mashed potatoes with finely chopped onions, ginger & spices; Machli Lal Mirchi £4.75, south Indian Specialty, spicy fish stuffed in a grilled red pepper. Mains: Duck Salon £12.95 cooked with onion, fresh coriander & aromatic spices with Pilau rice; Murgh Malaian £12.95 Chicken marinated & cooked with couscous, pure butter, fresh cream and garam masala with cashew

COBRA

SPLENDIDLY INDIAN, SUPERBLY SMOOTH

Both traditional styles of cooking and creative flair are celebrated within our menu allowing us to offer time-honoured dishes to satisfy and innovative meals to thrill.

Shamrat
INDIAN BRASSERIE

t: 01622 764961
www.shamrat.co.uk

36 Lower Stone Street
Maidstone
Kent, ME15 6LX

nut rice; Vegetable Makhani £8.95, with medium spices, butter, almond, pista, cream sauce. Served with Pilau rice; Asparagus Turwala £4.75 Baby corn with asparagus cooked with aromatic spices; Mon-Sat: 12-2.30 & Mon-Th: 6- 11.30. Fri-Sat to 12. Sun 5.30 -11.30.

Margate

THE AMBRETTE   INDIAN FUSION
44 King Street, Margate, CT9 1QE   A-LIST
01843 231504   www.theambrette.co.uk

I must be a rarity; I love Margate;. I summer holidayed there over many years a child at a sea frontal B&B. There were no Indian restaurants then and even when they opened, they were meritless. The Indian Princess was one.. Then it was sold to new ownership and opened as as The Ambrette (an Indian flower) in 2010. Its USP is Calcutta-born chef Dev Biswal. He worked at Dubai's Sheraton, aged 26 in 2003 cheffed at Eriki, London NW3. Indian fusion is his bag *'avoiding'* what he describes as *'the curry house fast-food mentality'*. So this place isn't for bone-head drunks looking for a vindaloo fix. The 'closed' sign goes up well before the pubs close. The short, daily changing menu features just five protein and three veg starters. eg: Wood pigeon breasts £5.25, char-grilled with spices, served with game-mince-paté served with cucumber raita. Crispy pooris filled with potatoes and crushed chickpeas £4, topped with sweet tamarind chutney and yoghurt [Bhel puri]; Dosai with gently spiced potatoes and onions, £5. All Main courses are served with flavoured Basmati rice and naan. Eg: Tender and juicy loin of Kentish pork £13, spice crusted with cinnamon and fennel then pan-grilled. Served with an aromatic Goan style sauce of malt vinegar and garlic wine. [Goan Vindaloo]; tender brochettes of leg of Kentish lamb £15, slow cooked in gravy of exotic Kashmiri spices. Vegetarian Thali £12.25 a selection of vegetarian dishes. The wine list needs more thought. Of the 3 whites offering Gewurztraminer because it is described as 'spicy' went out a decade ago. 12.5% optional service chargeTue-Sun: 11.30-2.30; Tue-Thu: 6-9.30; Fri-Sun: 5.30-10.

Dev Biswal

SIMLA CUISINE
∞ INDIAN RESTAURANT ∞
2 Church Road
Paddock Wood, Kent
TH12 6EZ
01892 834515
www.simlacuisine.co.uk
out of hours booking text Abdal:
07981 796894

We're opposite Waitrose and we look forward to welcoming you

Paddock Wood

SIMLA CUISINE
2 Church Road, Paddock Wood, TN12 6EZ
01892 834515   simlacuisine.co.uk

Celebrating its 25th year the friendly staff at this well run curryhouse in the small town opposite Waitrose wil make you comfortable. You can use the Waitrose car park when visiting. Aloo Puri - Diced boiled potatoes mixed with green pepper, tomatoes and special 'Chat Massala, £2.80; Chicken Chat with,green pepper & tomatoes mixed with special 'Chat Massala' £3.10, Dal Soup £1.80, Onion Bhaji £2.50. Cuuries: Medium, Madras Fairly Hot, Vindaloo Very Hot £4.95 Korma Very Mild Bhuna, Rogon, Dupiaza Medium, Chopped Onions, Green Peppers, Kashmiri With Fruits, Ceylon Fairly Hot With Coconut and Malaya Medium with Pineapple Chicken all £5.50, Meat from £5. Elvis is in the building on selected and very popuplar nights throughout the year. 10% discount for takeaway.
12-3 & 6-11.

Rochester

BENGAL BRASSERIE
356 High St, Rochester, ME1 1DJ   01634 841930

It's an old friend of this Guide and the many regulars who adore the 46 seater Bengal Brasserie. It opened in 1993. Ashahin Ali is manager, Abdul Roob and Ashamim Ali chefs. *'My favourite Indian restaurant.'* BP-D. Takeaway: 10% discount. Menu extracts: Honey Murghi £7, tender chicken, honey, sultanas, creamy sauce. Anda Bhuna £6, omelette shredded and served in a heavily spiced thick sauce. King Prawn Puri £6, tomotoes, onions, fresh coriander herbs and spices, served on a small pancake. Delivery: 6 miles, £12 minimum 12-2.30 & 5.30-12am.

Tenterden

THE RAJA OF TENTERDEN
Biddenden Rd, St. Michaels   01233 851191

'Opened in 2004 in a former country pub a couple of miles north of Tenterden. A doorman in full traditional Indian costume greeted us as he opened the door to usher us in. Within a minute of arriving we were led through the packed restaurant to our table. Despite seating a generous 90 people, the place was packed. The restaurant is modern with wooden flooring, light coloured walls and low ceiling without being ostentatiously contemporary. The seating is comfortable with cutlery and tablecloths of good quality. The menu was also more exciting than the norm, as although it offered most of the standard dishes, there were very many different and enterprising dishes, including venison, duck, pheasant, scallops and mussel. As for the service, the waiters were all smartly dressed in uniform and busily engaged throughout

-Namästé-
BENGAL Brasserie
World Class Indian Cuisine
Fully licensed and fully air-conditioned
356 HIGH STREET, ROCHESTER, KENT ME1 1DJ
FREE HOME DELIVERY
ON ORDERS OVER £12
DELIVERY HOTLINE
01634 818011 or 404478
FOR RESERVATIONS
01634 841 930
OPEN 7 DAYS A WEEK INCLUDING ALL BANK HOLIDAYS
FROM 12noon to 2.00pm • 5.30pm to 11.45pm
LAST ORDERS TAKEN AT 11.45pm

the evening dealing with the large and full restaurant; efficient and attentive without being overbearing - and the owner, R.K.Raja, was always on hand to lend a hand in serving and have a friendly chat. Prices were surprisingly reasonable, particularly for the type of place it was. In fact, it really wasn't any more expensive that the average high street Indian restaurant, which came as a pleasant surprise. The portions were also quite sufficient. All in all it was an excellent meal, with each dish having a differently distinct flavour. MW. Branch: Mouchak St. Michaels.

Tunbridge Wells

JUNAHKI
63 St Johns Rd, T' Wells   01892 615200   www.junahki.com

Junahki is a firefly, those amazing insects which light up in the dark. For Tun W it's a recent bright light in town with rather plain decor but good Indian food cooked by Indian chefs. Hours: 12-2.30 & 6-11.30. T/a: 20% disc.

West Kingsdown

RAJDANI
17, London Rd, W Kingsdown
01474 853501   www.rajdhani.net

Proprietor Suna Meah runs it with other members of the family, including the chef. Good sized car parking; two ponds; a little decking-style bridge to cross over the ponds. Separate area for T/a. Visited for dinner. Ate plain pops with chutney tray. Onion Bhajia, Chicken Aliza (chicken pakora), Tandoori Prawn, Chicken Chat in puri with plenty of crispy salad main course, huge tandoori king prawns in a cashew nut korma sauce, chicken with cashew nut sauce – delicious chicken tava – spicy but not hot. Plain Nan – light, fluffy – all breads that came out of the kitchen were really good. Red rose on leaving; We were introduced to a couple who dine here six days every week, and on the seventh, they visit other Indian restaurants. There's loyalty. 12-2.30 & 6-11.30.

Westerham

SHAMPAN
The Spinning Wheel, Grays Rd, Westerham, TN16 2HX
01959 572622   www.shampangroup.com

The Shampan was established in 1989 in Bromley by Sufian Miah. In 2002, Shampan 2 was opened, close the original restaurant which is now a Chinese restaurant., the property still belongs to Shampan Group. Abdul Malik joined Shampan to oversee the opening of Shampan 3 in Welling, Kent in 2006. Shampan 4 opened in July 2011 in the former Spinning Wheel pub a rambling building in the sticks with a large car park. It is now the group's flagship , having a massive 350 seats within five separate dining areas, two wine and cocktail bars, a coffee bar, an al-fresco dining area and a lounge, as well as a private dining suite suitable for parties, conferences and weddings.Starters include Roasted Scallops with Raw Mango Chutney served on a bed of roasted garlic and mango or Red Mullet in Goan Spices both £6; Aloo Chop £4.50, spiced potato and mixed vegetable rissoles, deep-fried with breadcrumbs; Chicken Cheese Laffafa £5, spiced chicken & spinach patties with a melted cheese centre. Mains include all the old favourites plus some rather more interesting dishes: Avocado Nawabi Lamb £12, slow cooked and garnished with avocado; Lamb Sali £12, lamb tikka cooked with garlic and chilli, served with fresh spinach and a naga bhuna sauce. Very spicy. Garnished with matchstick fried potatoes; Sagothi £10, Lamb or Chicken cooked with a special creamy mild sauce of roasted coconut, honey, herbs and spices. Manchurian Murgh £9, Chinese-Indian fusion dish of chicken slices in a gravy-style sauce with spring onions and egg; Bemisal £9, a unique smooth dish of spicy chicken tikka pieces, where the smoothness of the buttery tomato sauce is followed by the spicy flavours of brown onions. Tomato Dhingri £8, roasted tomatoes stuffed with dhingri mushrooms and melted cheese, laid on a bed of saag crème. Serv Ch 10%. Mon-Sat: 12-2:30 & Mon-Th: 5:30-10:30 (Fri-Sat to 11). Sun: 12-10. *Branches: Shampan 2 a 150 seater at 38 Chatterton Road, Chatterton Village, Bromley, Kent, BR2 9QN. 020 8460 7169. It is located over two floors, with two bars and two lounge areas. Shampan 3 a 60 seater at 8 Falconwood Pde, The Green, Welling, DA16 2PL 020 8304 956.*

YOU SAY OK
You may get a discount of you show them this Guide.

SANDWICH: INDIA VILLAGE 11 The Butchery01304 611991. *'In former fire station. Duck curries on the very large menu.'* SC.
SEVENOAKS: ASIA CUISINE 107 London Rd. ~ *01732 453153*. *'My local. Does a brilliant CTM and always friendly service.'* KT. *'Nice place, very cosy, love the Indian music. Portions more than ample and prices just right.'* RL.
SPICE CLUB 57 High Street, Sevenoaks, TN13 1JF. 01732 456688. *'Very helpful staff smartly dressed in black. Food outstanding. Sevenoak's best!'* KT. 12-2.30/6-11.30.
SIDCUP (CL): BLACKFEN BALTI 33 Wellington Pde, Blackfen Rd. 020 8303 0013. A friendly, pleasant, 48-seater, owned by Muzammil Ali since 1983.
SIDCUP (CL): OVAL BRASSERIE 49 The Oval, Sidcup 020 8308 0274. Owned since 1988 by Anwar Miah with chef Mohibur Rahman. 12-2.30/6-11.30.
STOCKBURY: LILY SPICE A249 at Detling Hill, Stockbury ~ 01795 844628. Ali and Mukid Choudhury opened in 2006 in a former a Little Chef.Plenty of free parking. Hours: 12-3/6-11. *Branch: Ace of Spice, Watling Street, Chatham, 01634 578400*
SWANLEY: RAJ OF INDIA 23 High St. ~ 01322 613651. *'Excellent meal, just right.'* BP-D. *Branch: Raj Bari, Sevenoaks, Kent and Alishan, Tonbridge, Kent.*
TONBRIDGE: ALISHAN 149 High St. ~ 01732 770 616.
UNBRIDGE WELLS: RAJ PAVILLION 20 Grove Hill Rd TN1 1RZ ~ 01892 533 153. Jewel Zaman Manager.Pictured below.
TUNBRIDGE WELLS: KIRTHON 60 The Pantiles   01892 526633
WEST WICKHAM: BLUE GINGER 101High St. ~ 020 8777 4080. *'Staff, welcoming, knew what they were doing. Aloo Bora, particularly good and flavoursome. Spicy Bindi, hot and crispy. We'll be back.'* G&CM. T/a: 10% disc. Banquet Night: Weds £9.95. Sun lunch buffet £7.95.

Shampan 2

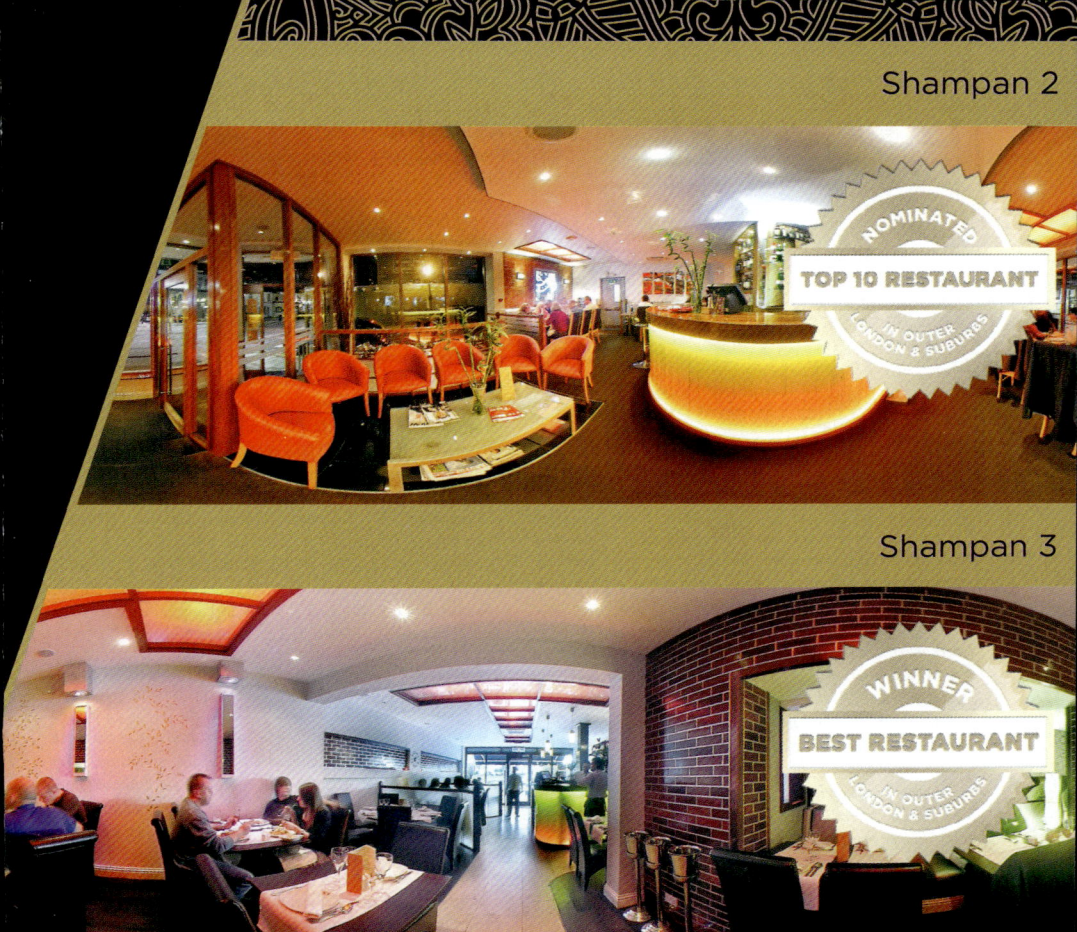

Shampan 3

Shampan at The Spinning Wheel - Now Open!

WWW.SHAMPANGROUP.COM

LANCASHIRE

Area: North West

Adjacent Counties:
Cumbs,
Greater Manchester,
Mers, N Yorks,
W Yorks

Blackpool

AKASH
76, Topping St Blackpool, FY1 3A   01253 626677

'Charmingly unchanged upstairs restaurant. Formulaic decor and menu, but none the worse for it. Compactly arranged with seating for 54 in booths down the walks or central tables in a single room. Friendly staff, in fact despite this being a tourist town, the staff were chatting to all the other diners, who seemed to be locals or regulars. Standard menu with a couple of specials. Popadoms and Chutneys £2.50. Decent starter - Rashmi Kebab £2.90 - two, slightly tough, patties of perfectly seasoned and succulent meat served with a cool Salad and Yoghurt Sauce. Absolutely perfect Tarka Dall £2.50 - thick and satisfying with a perfect balance of lentils, garlic, onion and coriander. Good main course - Lamb Tikka Kharahi £6.75 - rich herby sauce with an almost BBQ sauce note. Slightly gristly lamb but tasty nonetheless. An enjoyable meal, definitely recommended, particularly to curryholics of a certain age with fond memories of the first Tandoori Restaurants.' RW. Popadom 50p, CTM £7.50, Pullao Rice £1.60. 3 Course Lunch £4.90. 1-2 & 6-12.

ALI (CARLTON HOTEL),
282, North Prom, Blackpool, FY1 2EZ   01253 622223

'Innovative 'fine dining' restaurant seating at least 40, in part of the impressive art deco pile that is the Best Western Carlton Hotel, at the north end of the Prom in the seedy seaside town of Blackpool. Nicely decorated. Real tablecloths and napkins. Very smart and efficient staff, the females in saris. Compact menu, but with plenty of interest, especially the 'kiosk' style selection. Pops Chuts £1.50. Beautifully presented Ghost Ke Shammi £4.95 - rectangular plate with four patties, intensely flavoured, well spiced, but very dry and the meat ground into a paste with the lentils and a side salad with a swirl of yoghurt sauce. Pleasant but too much style over flavour. Interesting Pan Flash Bazaar £15.50 - very good quality Chicken Tikka chunks served in a 'kiosk-style' stir-fry sauce, with my choice of vegetables - mushrooms and peas. Very wet sauce, with lots of whole spices but overwhelmed by aggressive use of chillies. Texture added by the vegetables, plus peppers and onion, though there was so much oil leaking out of the dish you'd think Halliburton were project managing the kitchen! Recommended.' RW. 10% service charge. 5-10.

ASHIANA
Fleetwood Road, Greenhalgh, Kirkham, Nr Blackpool
PR4 3HE   01253 836187

'Large roadside restaurant on the outskirts of Blackpool with seating for over 120 diners in two rooms. Nicely decorated and furnished in 'traditional' style (but no flock wallpaper) with comfortable seats and real tablecloths and napkins. Friendly and efficient staff. Comprehensive menu with plenty of specials, mostly Bangladeshi. Good Meat Samosa £2.50 - nicely spiced if a little petite, served with fresh salad and sauce. Enjoyable Lamb Bahari £9.90 - good quality and tasty lamb with just a bit of gristle in a thick and rich sauce. Lots of herbs and spices used and quite hot, with green chillies evident. Nicely accompanied by a very good Garlic Nan £2.60 - thin and light with a crisp base and a great taste. Excellent Tarka Dall £3.50 - very thick but with a spot on blend of garlic and lentils. A great meal and recommended.' RW. Takeaway Tandoori Banquet - Massala Popadoms. Chutney and Pickle, Shik (sic) Kebab, Tandoori Chicken, Lamb Tikka, Chicken Tikka, Tandoori King Prawn, Naan, Pialu Rice, Massala Sauce and a choice of sweet and coffee - £32 for two and a great deal for that special occasion. 12-2 & 6-12. Branch: Newark.

BOMBAY
227 Dickson Rd, Blackpool, FY1 2JH   01253 296144

'Compact traditional 36 seat single room restaurant at the north end of Blackpool, nicely decorated in shades of orange. Very welcoming and homely with friendly staff'. Real tablecloths and napkins. Decent menu with a few specials and all the old favourites. Good Popadoms with Vegetable Pickle included in the Daba. Very nice Macheyr Biran £4.20 - two sizable fillets of tender white fish fried to give a nice golden tinge, topped with caramelized onions and served with a squeeze of lemon and a small salad. Decent Lamb Biryani £8 - very good basmati rice, but a little lacklustre otherwise, pleasantly hot in spicing. Fatty Lamb, but tender and tasty. Poor, thin and uninteresting sauce. Just about worth a recommendation, but don't expect to see critics flocking there!' RW. T/a: £12 min, 10% disc. Del: £12 mini, 2m. 5.30-11.30.

DIYA
12, Market Sq, Lytham, Nr Blackpool   FY8 5LW
01253 731133   www.diyarestaurant.co.uk

'Stylish modern 30 cover restaurant in the heart of this sleepy seaside resort. Beautifully decorated, one of the places where you could have a romantic meal with confidence. Real tablecloths and napkins. Outstanding menu, with a range of unusual dishes. Young and friendly staff who were more than happy to explain the dishes to diners. Popadoms were ordered but never materialised. Well, I've never had rubbery fish before! This I think was due to the light batter more than anything, which was otherwise restrained and commendably light in its spicing. The fish though was bland, not mild or delicate, just bland. Not a great choice. Nice salad though. Impressive Lamb Nihari £8.10 - perfect meat in a delightfully sharp sauce, with caramelised onions on top. Went very well with the Reshmi Naan £2.70, soft and moist with a hot and rich fillings of spiced minced lamb.

Pleasant Tarka Dal £3.10 - smooth and well balanced, but a bit light on the garlic. Overall very enjoyable and recommended.' RW. Menu Snapshot - Shahi Jeera £6.90 - boneless tandoori chicken cooked with cummin seeds medium spice, fresh garlic and coriander, Chicken Tenga £6.90 - cooked with onions, green pepper and tamarind with mango, Tikka Fish £6.90 - Tiger fish marinated in a specila blend of herbs and spices, barbecued in a clay oven, Pea and Cashew Nut Pilau Rice £2.10. 5-11 (Fri-Sat to 11.30).

FAYEZ TANDOORI
82, Victoria Road West, Thornton Cleveleys, Blackpool, FY5 1AG   01253 853562

Est 1982. 'Very traditional restaurant above a row of shops in a Blackpool suburb. Single room partitionsed to seat 90 in comfort. Helpful staff, although language was a bit of a problem. Popas & Chuts £3. Fabulous Shahi Torka Lamb £3.95 - a sizable lamb steak, skewer cooked in the tandoor, fat and gristle free and melt in the mouth. Superb Duck Kapsila Special £9.95 - what must have been a whole tandoories duck breast, filleted and served in a hot and rich sauce of great complexity that was really enjoyable. Served as a plated dish, topped with sauteed peppers and placed inside a ring of top notch Pilau Rice. Perfect Tarka Dhal £2.40. A great meal and highly recommended for really great food in unpretentious surroundings.' RW. 6-12, (to 1 Fri-Sat).

FAR PAVILION,
By Pass Road, Bolton Le Sands, Carnforth, Nr Morecombe   LA5 8JA   01524 823316

'We visited on a very busy Saturday evening. The staff were pleasant and courteous although the service was a little slow. Generous portions.' N&JG. Menu Snapshot: Chicken Tikka Shingara £2.95, Vegetable Shingara (spring roll) £2.95, Lamb Achar (pickled) £7.95, Chicken Jaflong (cream and orange segments) £6.25, Sagh Aloo (spinach and potato) £2.75, Cucumber Raitha £1.60, Buttered Chapatti £1. T/a: 10% disc. 12-2 & 5.30-12. Sun 12-12.

SAGAR PREMIER
Clayton Brook Rd, Clayton Brook, Nr Preston PR5 8HZ 01772 620200   www.sagarpremier.com

'We first visited Sagar Premier in 1992 when it opened at Clayton Brook and my children were little, we have been regular customers there ever since because of the 'consistency of excellent service, fine cuisine and value for money. We attended, with adult children and their spouses, the 17th year anniversary event to view its extensive refurbishment and sample some new menu dishes. The event ran over two evenings and was a great success, thanks to all the 'curryholics' from Lancashire and beyond. The layout of the restaurant, bar area and function room is basically the same but has been radically transformed with modern and tasteful decoration, soft furnishings and lighting, creating a relaxing ambience. The new dishes were innovative, exciting and delicious, they are a fine complement to the existing classic menu. It's also good to see that the management (and most of the staff) at Sagar Premier are still the same people from 1992, resulting in strong customer focus and attentive, cheerful service plus the best Indian cuisine within the North West and one has to venture into either Rusholme (Manchester) or even Bradford to find and equivalent level of quality, service and value for money.' TE. Menu Snapshot: Jhinga Lussi - king prawns in sweet and sour sauce, Vegetable Stuffed Khumbi - deepfried, Hash Ka Modhu - breast of duck marinated in honey and avocado, lightly spiced with orange zest, South Indian Murghi - tandoori chicken, taken off th ebone then coked in mincemeat, coriander and spices, Sondia - very hot spiced dish prepared in green chilli and coriander, Keema with Chilli and Garlic Naan. 'Another visit to this rather good restaurant. Generous portions of both Pialu Rice and Chicken Tikka Massala. The food appeared quickly after the order was placed despite the fact that the visit was on a Friday evening. We will certainly visit again.' N&JG. Mon-Fri: 5-11.15; Sat-Sun: 1-11.15.

RIVAJ OF INDIA
278, Mossy Lea Road, Wrightington, WN6 9RN
01257 426648   www.rivajonline.co.uk

'In December 2009 Badrul Alom opened the doors of the newly created Rivaj of Indian restaurant, in what used to be the historic Hinds Head Inn at leafy Wrightington. Rivaj means 'tradition' or 'custom' in Indian Sanskrit and this was reflected in the tasteful interior decor (a fusion of traditional Indian with modern style), from the sumptuous lounge to the equally spacious and separate areas for the bar, buffet (Sunday to Wednesday), restaurant and takeaway service. We were welcomed in the lounge by cheerful Faz Rahman (manager) whose waiters brought our drinks and took our food order swiftly, efficiently. As Faz walked us to our table we realised how lovely and spacious the Rivaj really is. Fresh Popadoms with a selection of Pickles (all made in-house) were an excellent start, followed by Mixed Kebab (sheek kebab, chicken tikka and lamb samosa), Lamb Samosa and Lamb Tikka all delicious and beautifully presented in elegant long dishes with a side salad. The main courses of Chicken Madras and Chicken Tikka Dupiaza were deliciously spiced and served with fragrant Pilau Rice and Indian Salad (fresh onion, tomatoes, cucumber, coriander leaves, lemon juice, salt, garden milt and olive oil), again in a selection of elegant designer dishes that enhanced their presentation. Everything was so delicious it was quickly consumed leaving no room to choose one of the many desserts on offer. We all agree that the whole dining experience had been absolutely perfect and will revisit again very soon. Definitely recommended to all curryholics!' TE.   Mon-Fri: 5-11; Sat-Sun: 1-11.

LEICESTERSHIRE

Area: East Midlands

Adjacent Counties:
Derbs, Lincs,
Northants,
Notts, Rutland,
Staffs, Warks

Kegworth

JEE JA JEES
1, Market Place, Kegworth, DE74 2EE   01509 6700050

A Building you can not miss as it was red. On arrival was greeted and asked if I wanted takeaway, I asked for a table for one and my heart sank when I realised they were almost full!! Excellent news for them on a Tuesday night. Within a few minutes I was shown to a table (that could seat six). I was seated and offered a drink, the whole place ha a very friendly vibe. It has been recently decorated, there was a nice smell of fresh paint, the ceilings are white with original beams, the walls are cream and all the wood work freshly painted in chocolate glass. The table linen matched the chocolate paint. An extensive menu, with many chef special dishes, and all the regular dishes that we all know and love. My meal was Popadoms 60p with Pickles (mango, tamarind, lime, yoghurt with mint). Starter: Onion Bhajia £2.25, two round flat bhajias, nicely spiced; Main Course: Garlic Chilli Chicken Tikka with Pullao Rice £8.95 and a Plain Paratha £1.90. The food was fantastic, the curry was garnished with two big rings of white onion and coriander. I also had two pints of Cobra. The total cost of my meal was £28.00. I very much enjoyed my meal and would certainly return. Good food, friendly and attentive staff, reasonably prices and only a ten minute walk from my hotel. Credit cards accepted. Cheques not accepted. Del: free. T/a: 10% disc, min £10. 5.30-11.30.

Leicester

AMBALA   SWEET & SNACKS CENTRE
1 Chatsworth St, Leicester, LE2 0FQ   0116 262 0906

A branch of the famous chain. See page 149.

ANJUNA RESTAURANT   GOAN
76 Highcross Street, Leicester, LE1 4NN
0116 2512229   www.anjunarestaurant.com

Next door to the Travel Lodge Anjuna is named after the Goan beach famous for its vast weekly flea market its golden sands. Ajuna bills itself as the first Goan restaurant in the Midlands. We go further to say its only the second Goan in the UK (see London SW15). As such it is precious. Goan flavours are a unique fusion of Portuguese and Indian cuisine which culminates in a distinctive mixture of flavours consisting of coconut, palm vinegar and Goan red chilli which gives a deep red colour to the cooking without the fierce pungency of the normal Indian chilli. With an abundance of fish. All along the Goa coast fishing boats can be seen casting their nets and 'fish curry and rice' is Goa's staple diet. Try Goan Fish Curry £8.25, Kingfish cooked with Goan spices, tomatoes and fresh coriander. Or Shark Fish Ambotik £9, shark fish cooked with Kashmir chillies, tomatoes and tamarind pulp for a sour hot taste. Sorpotel £8.75, is one of Goa's national dishes made with pork belly and liver, fried then cooked in hot spices and vinegar. Chicken Xacuti £8.75, is another Goan national dish. Pronounced 'schar-cout-tee' it contains chicken pieces slowly cooked with Goan 'roasted' spices and coconut to a dark, consistency- Goan Pork Vindaloo, £8, a must for aficionados, it bears no resemblance to the curryhouse pastiche. Pork is slowly cooked with toddy vinegar, galic, chillies an roasted spices. Leave room for Goan Dessert. Bibic (or Bebinca) £4.45, a pudding made from multi-layers of coconut omelette and syrup creating a subtle caramel taste served warm with a scoop of vanilla ice cream. 3 course lunch, £6. Licensed. Tue-Sat: 12- 2.30 & 6-10.30 (Fri & Sat: 6-11.30).

AKASH TANDOORI
159 London Rd, Leicester   0116 255 9030

Bangladeshi formula curryhouse says it's *'Leicester's legendary price-buster'*. So it's packed students for £2.95 lunch, evening £6. *'Décor ia bit rough and ready, but the service friendly and the lamb bhoona is mouth-watering'*. GB.

BOBBY'S   GUJARATI VEGETARIAN
154 Belgrave Rd, Leicester, LE4 5AT 0116 266 2448

For over 35 years Atul Lakhani (aka Bobby) has run this restaurant with two advantages – a license and very reasonably priced food, so it's ever-popular with a cafeteria-type atmosphere. Mostly Gujarati food, which is light and slightly sweet. And sweets and snacks at the glass counter. You pay (credit cards taken) at the till. 11-10.30.

CHENNAIDOSA SOUTH IND/SRI LANKAN
78-80 Belgrave Road Leicester LE4 5AS
0116 251 2121   www.chennaidosa.com

South Indian Meat & Veg. One of a chain of 14. See London E12 for menu & details. No licence. 11am-10:30pm.

CURRY FEVER   PUNJABI   A-LIST
139 Belgrave Road, Leicester, LE4 6AS
0116 266 2941   www.thecurryfever.co.uk

Established in 1978 by Anil Anand (head chef) and Sunil Anand (manager). They are related to the Brilliant and Madhu's Brilliant of Southall, Middlesex. The food is Punjabi, cooked just as they eat it at home. House specialities, which show the owners' Kenyan background, include: Jeera Chicken £15.50/£8.50, one of their signature dishes, a must-eat, fabulous whole chicken briskly fried with cumin seeds and powder; Pili Pili Chicken £15, whole chicken, hot and spicy sauce, another must -eat; Mogo £4, cassavawith a tamarind sauce; Machusi Lamb £8.75, Kenyan style lamb, fenugreek sauce. Previously we gave it our BEST IN THE MIDLANDS Award. Though this time the award has moved elsewhere, it is an award which lasts for ever. *'Curry Fever – still the best in Leicester'* CM. T/a: 10% disc. Service: 10%. Min Ch: £10. Tues to Sat:12-2 & 6-11 (to 11.30 Fri-Sat). Monday closed.

CHUTNEY IVY
41 Halford Street, Leicester, LE1 1TR
0116 251 1889   www.chutneyivy.com/

'Stylish and comfortable with a hint of warehouse about it, with high ceilings and suspended light gantries. We chose the 'Ivy Feast' at £19.95 per head. There are less expensive options available, including a pre-theatre menu. Starters comprised a very generous helping of mixed vegetable bhajias, Aloo Tiki (Indian potato cakes) shish kebabs and chicken Tikka served with poppadoms and various chutneys. The main course was equally diverse offering for example Chicken Tikka Masala, Karahi Gosht (braised lamb), Subzee Milloni (spiced vegetables) and lots of Basmati rice. Price per head: £25-£30 (three courses & drinks). NCP opposite.' Great Food web. Mon-Fri: 12-2.30 & Mon-Sat: 5.30-11.

FLAMINGO BAR & GRILL   PUNJABI
179 - 183 Loughborough Road Leicester LE4 5LR.
0116 261 0109   www.flamingobargrill.co.uk

Established in a run down bar in 1996 by three Kenyan Asian brothers, Dev, Janelle and Jo Matharoo, Flamingo couples a buzzing bar atmosphere with exciting and innovative food. Cooked by Punjabi chefs, the menus are constantly changing and adapting. Dev and his brothers regularly visit Europe, the Far East and East Africa as well as India itself in search of new culinary ideas. Tues- Fri: 5-12 ; Sat: 12-12 (Sun: to 11.30 Mon: Closed

FEAST OF INDIA
411 Melton Road, Leicester, LE4 7PA |
0116 2582590   www.feastindia.co.uk

Take a former supermarket and turn it into a 'lavishly designed' bar (The Pavilion Bar) and restaurant. All around are India artefacts, favourite of which is the three-wheeled tuk-tuk taxi imported from Mumbai, its function: the salad counter. At restaurant's centre is a big open kitchen called Masala 360, because you can walk all around it and watch an army of chefs beavering away six live theatre kitchens, or smilingly explaining their offerings whilst frequently refilling the large copper food bowls in front of each station, known as 'food bazaars'. It is these which are the stars of the show; they are the deliivery points of a gigantic e-a-m-a-y-l buffet, £14 served all day, billed as *'all the flavours of india under one roof'*. At £15 a head it's very good value, but the place is generally packed with noisy families. They serve a big variety of India food, and they serve Chinese, Pizza, etc etc. Only visit if you like this kind of thing. (There is no a la carte) Dinner is £14.95 pp (£11.50 Sun lunch) & £7.95/£6.50 for children). Mon-Fri: 6-11 Sat from 5); Sun: 12.30-3 & 4-10.

INDIGO
432 Melton Road, Leicester, LE4 7SN
0116 261 1000   www.indigos.co.uk

Indigo is really popular with oIndian families. Opened in 1999 at the north end of the road in a large detached ex pub (and yes it is licensed) with white walls and black beams its interior is functional, canteen style tables and chairs, It loves families with kids. They do really a fine south Indian menu but perversely local Indians want international cuisine, so they do Indo-Chinese (Hakka) cuisine plus Pizzas and Pastas. Kids menu from £4.25. E-m-a-y-l buffet luch £6.99 (can be t/w at £7.50. !0% serv ch for dine-in. Paan availabe 85p (see A to Z fo menu). Mon-Fri: 12- 2:30 & 6-10:30 pm); Sat & Sun: 12-10.30

KHYBER
116 Melton Rd, Leicester, LE4 5ED
0116 266 4842   www.khybertandoorirestaurant.co.uk

The 40-seater Khyber opened in 1984 and still under the same ownership of Dinesh (front) and Ashok Raval, (head chef). *'It is cosy and immaculately clean with a substantial following among the affluent end of the Leicester Asian business community. After so much of the plodding, ghee-flooded rubbish pedalled in too many restaurants around the country, the Khyber's food is a delight and an altogether more subtle experience than the food presented in the other establishments you list in the area that supply meat-based dishes. The food is simply outstanding and, many of the loyal clientele would agree, is rightly regarded among the cognoscenti as the best in the city. It is a little more expensive than its rivals, but genuine lovers of good food do not begrudge paying. So please, please honour them with a visit next time you are in town and I would absolutely, 100 per cent, guarantee that you will not be disappointed.'* JR. Specials include: Lamb Chop Curry £9; Chicken Staff Curry £8; Chilli King Prawns £14, mild, sweet and sour, fried in crispy batter and cooked with spring onions, garlic, black pepper, chillies and soy; Special Naan, stuffed with vegetables, coconut & nuts. 12-2 & 6.30-11.30. Sun closed.

NAMASTE
65 Hinkley Rd, Leicester, LE3 0TB, LE3 0TB
0116 254 1778   www.namaste-restaurant.co.uk

Partners, DK Dey (manager) and R Paul opened their 54 seater restaurant in 1994. Show a copy of this Guide to manager Mr Dey and you will receive a free starter. Regulars are treated to a complimentary drink after their meal. Chef Aziz says that his Mossalla and Pasanda dishes are most popular, however please try his Balti Special Menu, all served with choice of either Boiled Rice, Pullao Rice, Naan or Tandoori Roti. How about the Royal Kurzi

Lamb for four c£60, which includes all the business AND a complimentary bottle of wine. T/a: 10% disc. Sun Special Lunch: c£6. Tues-Thur & Sun Special: Starter and selected Main £10. Tues-Thur & Sun 5.30-12 (to 1am Sat & Sun).

KAYAL   KERALAN
153 Granby Street, Leicester, LE1 6FE
0116 255 4667   www.kayalrestaurant.com

By the railway station Kayal, meaning Keralan Backwater gives the clue that it serves authentic South Indian cuisine. Idli, Dosa, Vada and the usual vegetarian items. More unusual are the Keralan fish, poultry and meat dishes such as Cheera Erachi Curry £9.39, chef's signature dish, lamb cooked in spinach, spices, red chillies and onions; Kappa Erachi, £12.89, 'Kallu shaps' (toddy shops) are the popular local pubs in all over Kerala where you will find this dish: lamb cubes cooked together with tapioca and aromatic spices; Kozhi Kurumulagu £10.79, one of the most famous dishes in Travancore area of Kerala. Boneless chicken cooked in black pepper sauce with onion, ginger, garlic, turmeric, and cashew nuts; Ammachi Pidiyum Kozhiyum £10.99, from the Great Malabar coast of Kerala, small rice dumplings steam=cooked then added to a chicken curry made of Keralan spices; Kumarakom Duck Roast £13.49 a festive Keralan dish, boneless duck breast cooked in style with aromatic spices and herb. Originally this recipe uses wild duck which inhabit the beautiful backwater lake Kumarakom. A good selection of desserts includes: Unnakki £4.29, mashed plantain dumplings filled with coconut, raisins, and cashew nuts and served with vanila ice cream;Panchamrutham, £3.79. consists of five 'secret' ingredients and is the divine 'prasadam' made for many 'festive occasions. Weekday Lunch £5.95: three curries, one side dish, rice of the day and dosa with chutneys. Mon-Fri: 12-3 & 6-11, Sat: 12-11; Sun to 10. *Branches Kayal , Nottingham & Leamington Spa, Warks.*

POPADUMS INDIAN
330 Welford Rd, Leicester, LE2 6EH
0116 244 8888   www.poppadomsrestaurant.com

Opened April 2005 by owner/manager Abdul Giash then expanded it into a bright and airy 130 seater a few years back. House Specials include: Mixed Karahi £10, Tandoori Chicken, Chicken and Lamb Tikka, Sheek Kebab cooked in a sauce, served in a 'souk'; Genghis Said £6, barbecued chicken and spiced minced meat cooked with peppers, onions and tomatoes, served in spicy sauce; Aloo Gosht £6, potatoes and lamb; Cheese and Chilli Naan £2. Those who spend £20 or above on their T/a are rewarded with a bottle of wine. Sun Buffet Lunch: £6 adults, £6 children. Del: 5m. min £8. Sat -Thur:12-2 & daily 6-11.

SARAVANAA BHAVAN   SOUTH IND VGTN
2-16, Loughborough Rd, Leicester, LE4 5LD
0116 261 3113   www.saravanabhavan.com

Opened in 2011as the fourth of a new chain of 5 south Indian vegetarian cafés. Capacity 120. See London E12 for menu & details. Cash pref. No licence.10am to 10:30pm

SAYONARA THALI   GUJARATI VEGET'N
49 Belgrave Rd, Leicester, LE4 6AR
0116 266 5888

Not large (c 40 seats) with upstairs room, not plush but neither are the prices in fact a Thali consisting of many different veg dishes, dhals, pickles plus bread and rice starts at a meagre c£7 '*Try the the Gujarati speciality Kudhi (aka Kari) a yoghurt and gram flour based dish.*' PR. Set Dinner: £6.50, 3 course; £12.50, 4 course. Sun-Fri: 12-9.30; Sat: 12-10.

SHARMILEE   VEGETARIAN
71 Belgrave Rd, Leicester LE4 6AS   0116 261 0503

Opened way back in 1973 by Gosai brothers (manager, LK Goswami), this is a two-part venue. The sweet mart serves a rich assortments of Indian sweets, and such delightful items as Vegetable Samosas, Pakoras and Dahi Vadia, from 9.30am-9pm daily, not Mondays. The licensed restaurant is upmarket and vegetarian, decorated with marble pillars in shades of brown and dusky blue marble-effect walls, high-backed black chairs, white table linen. Tasty starters of Pani Puri, crispy puris served with spicy sauce, chickpeas and onion. Chanabateta, chickpeas and potatoes in a tamarind sauce garnished with onions. South Indian specialities: Masala Dosa, thin crispy pancake filled with potato and onion, Idli Sambar, flat pulse buds, both served with Sambar & coconut chutney. T/a 10% disc promised if you show them this Guide. 12-2.30 & 6-9.30; 12-9 Sat. closed Mon.

YOU SAY OK
THE CURRY HOUSE 64 London Road, Leicester LE2 0QD 0116 255 0688 www.thecurryhouse.net What it says on the can, a curryhouse, but popular.
GANIS 295 St Saviours Road Leicester LE5 4HG A few doors from the post office. Excellent karahis- all the food is cooked fresh Run by Indians not Bangladeshis.
The GRAND DURBAR 294 Melton Road, Leicester LE4 7PB 0116 266 6099 It's a Bangladeshi curry house so you don't see any Indians there.
INDIAN QUEEN CLUB 2 Halkin Street Leicester LE4 6JU 0116 266 4090   A hidden gem. The food here is excellent, the pints are great and also serve kingfisher.
RAHAT 1 Suffolk Street, Leicester LE5 4JA 461212 a takeaway with space for eating. Functional tables and chairs, jugs of tap water available and a Bollywood film blasting away behind the counter. Small portions (£4-5), large (£7-8).
TIFFIN 1 De Montfort St, Leicester, LE1 7GE. 0116 247 0420, www.the-tiffin.co.uk. Curry house menu whose fans rate it as the best indian restaurant in Leicester.

**Send us your reports.
We update on our website.
www.patchapman.co.uk**

LINCOLNSHIRE

Area: East Midlands

Adjacent Counties:
Cambs, Leics,
Norfolk, Notts,
E & S Yorks

Cleethorpes

ME2RAJ
47 Market Street, Cleethorpes, DN35 8LY
01472 319 952   www.me2raj-restaurant.co.uk

Mitu Ahmed's Me2Raj opened in 2008 and is usually jam-packed (so book). There is a 'bustling atmosphere. Cheerful staff laugh and joke with customers. The stylish interior combines dramatic deep red walls with minimalist dark wood furniture and comfortable leather chairs.' GT. Some interesting things on the menu, eg: ME2RAJ's Special Karahi, Lamb, chicken, king prawn, peas, mushroom and Chana Dahl in an extremely rich sauce £8.50; Nawabi Khana, The most complex of all great curries. Comprises 21 roasted and ground spices lending a deep rich brown colour to this chicken dishShimla Choice Lamb or chicken in tandoori spices cooked in a butter sauce with a touch of wine, both £7.95. Mitu loves a gag. You'll find the Spice Girls on the menu: Chicken or Lamb dishes eg: Ginger Spice, Scary Spice with naga chilli, scotch bonnet, Posh Spice with fresh cream, egg, mango and coconut. Baby Spice with coconut cream, cocoa powder & malibu. £7.95. Sun-Th: 5-11 (to 12.30 Fri-Sat). *Branch: Mithu's Grimsby.*

Grantham

BINDI
22 London Road, Grantham, NG31 7EJ
01476 570777   www.bindirestaurant.com

This pink, black and silver restaurant is managed by Ella, appropriate since Bindi means femininity. Chef Muhammed Karin does a standard menu and some specials, eg: Ghust Ka Salom, Haandi-cooked lamb in a rich curry. Order in advance for on the bone; Lal Mirchi Borta, Long sweet red peppers grilled and pan fried, stuffed with a lightly spiced shredded chicken or aloo chat for that vegetarian option, served on a bed of cooked spinach. They aslo sell a range of own-label chutneys. Banquet Mon 6-9pm: a mixed starter, 2 mini curries, rice & mini Nan bread, £8.95 adult & £5.95 child under 12. 12-3 & 6-11.

Grimsby

MITU'S
The Square, Laceby, Grimsby   01472 314155

The former Laceby Arms pub has been transformed by Mitu Ahmed into a 120-seater Mitu's with has three rooms; one for relaxed dining, a traditional lounge and a tiered decking space outside for alfresco dining. And therre are 72 car parking spaces. Exec Chef Abbas, ex London's Cinnamon Club presides over the menu, which is identical to the Cleethorpes' menu, plus here they do an English menu as well. Sun-Th: 5-11 (to 12.30 Fri-Sat). Branch: Branch, Me2Raj Cleethorpes .

Lincoln

MACH BAR AND RESTAURANT
Wragby Road East, North Greetwell, Lincoln LN2 4RA
01522 754488   www.machrestaurant.co.uk

It's located just outside the historic city of Lincoln. Says owner Mavinder Gosal 'We chose the first two letters of our names, Mav and Charlotte, to create MaCh' Menu Snapshot: Breaded Khumbi. mushrooms stuffed with spiced vegetables, coated in golden breadcrumbs; Chicken Nambali Tandoori breast chicken, garnished with mozzarella, Salmon Pakora marinated, coated in a spicy batter & deep fried, served with a fresh crispy salad. Punjabi Jhinga, King prawns marinated in yoghurt, fresh coriander and mustard, cooked to perfection in the tandoor. Mains include Shimla Pepper Chicken, cooked with sweet peppers in a spicy tomato based sauce; Sajon Special. shredded tandoori chicken pot-roasted with minced lamb, ginger, garlic & selected herbs & spices; Haash Tikka Sizzler. duck breast marinated and cooked in special spices, garnished with orange zest. Hours: 6-11.

PARADISE INDIAN BUFFET
339 High Street, Lincoln, LN5 7DQ   01522 244407

Indian Buffet from £6.99pp. You either like them or you hate them. It's cheap and cheerful and you can e-a-m-a-y-l. Fully licensed Sun-Thur:12-11 (Fri-Sat to 12).

Sleaford

AGRA AND BOLLYWOOD LOUNGE
1 Pride Parkway, Enterprise Park, Sleaford, NG34 8GL
01529 414162   www.theagra.co.uk

This huge restaurant, seating 110, opened in 1988 and was taken over in 1994 by Enus Karim, who is incidentally the Head Chef. His specials include: Agra Capsicum Noorani, whole green pepper barbecued and then stuffed with tender chicken cooked with 'chat masala', scrumptious!; Akbhari £9.75, filletted pieces of chicken or lamb cooked in the tandoor and mixed with richly spiced minced lamb, mustard seeds, capsicum and topped with fresh coriander; Mango Delight £9.75, barbecued strips of chicken breast, cooked in a creamy, mild, rich sauce topped with ripe mango.Menu Snapshot: Chingri Nisha £4, Bengal Tiger Prawn coated with sweet almond and coconut powder wrapped in a crispy pastry; all Balti dishes are served with Naan bread for that essential sauce scooping; Del: 20m, £10 min. T/a: 10% disc. Mon-Th & Sat: 12-11.30; Fri: from 5.30; Sun: 6-11.30. *Branches: Agra 2, Ruskington, Lincs; Agra 3, Blyth, Notts and Choti, Lincoln.*

LA ROYALE TANDOORI
A17 - Newark Rd, North Rauceby, Sleaford NG34 8ET
01529 488 858   www.laroyaletandoori.co.uk

La Royale is in a one-story flat-roofed, white-washed former diner called Roosters in bleak location whose only neighbour is a Murco gas station. The interior is equally stark, white walls and black chairs. So you and the food provide the colour. RAF Cranwell is literally round the corner, and since the lads and lasses come multi-handed, they provide the noisy chatter, and the friendly staff know how to keep order. Standard curries but it gets 'fab' reviews. Because of passing trade it is open 12-11 (Fri: 5.30-11.)

Stamford

BOMBAY COTTAGE
52 Scotgate, Stamford, PE9 2YQ
01780 480138   www.thebombaycottage.com

Established in 1994 by A Hussain and managed by H. Rahman. Menu Snapshot: Fish Chutneywali £3.50, tasty fish kebab with spicy fresh mint, coriander and green chilli chutney; Royal Quails £55, whole quails marinated in crushed spices, grilled over clay oven; generous Tandoori Mixed Grill £11, tandoori chicken, chicken tikka, sheek kebab, lamb chop, king prawn, salad, BUT, Naan Bread not included. Del: 5 m, £15 min. T/a: 10% disc. Sun Buffet: £9.90 per person. 12-2 (Sun to 3) & 6-11.30.

YOU SAY OK LINCS
You might get a discount if you show them this Guide.
BOSTON: BOMBAY BRASSERIE 53 West St, PE21 8QN *'a good quality meal "out in the sticks. Mark 8/10.'* G&MP.
BOSTON: STAR OF INDIA 110 West St, PE21 8QN 01205 360558   www.starofindia-boston.co.uk
BOURNE: SHALIMAR BALTI HOUSE 8 Abbey Rd. PE10 9EF 01778 393959   www.shalimarbaltihouse.co.uk
GRANTHAM: BOMBAY BRASSERIE 11 London Road, Grantham NG31 6EY   01476 576096
GRANTHAM: GORKHA SQUARE NEPALESE 1 Wharf Rd, NG31 6BA 01476 574477   www.gurkhasquarerestaurant.co.uk Go for the Nepalese items, rather than the formula curries. Price: £13-£19 11-2 & 5-11.
GRIMSBY: SPICE OF LIFE 8 Wellowgate, DN32 0RA 01472 357476
LINCOLN: PASSAGE TO INDIA 435 High St. LN5 8HZ 01522 526166. Chef prop Gulzar Hussain's 75-seater. 12-2 & 5-12.
STAMFORD: RAJ OF INDIA 2 All Saints St PE9 2PA 01780 753556   www.rajofindiastamford.co.uk
SKEGNESS: SAFFRON, 43.Roman Bank, Skegness, PE25 2SN www.saffronskegness.co.uk

MANCHESTER (Greater)
Area: North West

Adjacent Counties:
Cheshire,
Lancashire,
Merseyside,
Yorkshire

Greater Manchester was introduced as a county in 1965, though this was regarded as an imposition by many of its residents, who still refer to the counties that Greater Manchester gobbled up, e.g. parts of Lancashire and Cheshire. We have adhered strictly to the official current Greater Man territory for town locations in this Guide.

Altrincham (inc Hale)

CINNAMON
134, Ashley Road, Hale, Altrincham, WA15 2UN
0161 928 3696

'Attractive, upmarket restaurant, nicely decorated in a modern style. Very comprehensive and interesting menu with a great selection of specials including a full selection on fish. Very efficient and friendly staff with a manager in the best Captain Peacock tradition. 70 seats some on the second floor. Pops & Chuts £1.65. Outstanding Machli Kolivada £4.50, perfectly cooked tasty fish in a light tempura batter with just the right amount of spices to bring out the best in the fish. Nicely presented with a small salad and drizzled with a tamarind sauce. The Hyderabadi Ghost £8.95 more than matched the expectations engendered by starter. Seriously tender high quality Lamb Fillet served in a fabulous sauce rich with a good dose of cardamom, given bite by both chilli and mustard. Brilliantly crafted. Lovely Peshwari Nan £2.50, soft and light with nice fruit pieces and with a swirl of honey on top. An outstanding meal, highly recommended.' RW. Sun-Th: 5.30-11.30 (Fr-Sat-12); Sun: 1-4.

DILLI   FINE INDIAN DINING   TOP 100
60, Stamford New Road, Altrincham, WA14 1EE
0161 929 7484   www.dilli.co.uk

Dilli is the original name of modern India's Capital city, Delhi, India's gourmet capital. The Dilli restaurant delivers classic Indian Cuisine. Chef is Raminder Pal Singh Malhotra. Dilli is owned by Taj-trained chef-restaurateur Kuldeep Singh who brought real Indian food to the north west. He says *'we broke the mould by challenging the curry houses in the area to stop serving make-believe food that just didn't exist in the subcontinent.'* The risk was that customers would hate the genuine article. They needn't have worried, despite difficult parking, the venue has thrived. *'This is not your usual standard curry house, out have gone the Madras, Vindaloos, Dhansaks etc.* DB. Inside is a softly-lit, intimate venue, decorated in neutral tones featuring intricate wooden wall-hangings hand carved by skilled Delhi carpenters. Seats 60 downstairs and 45 upstairs. With chefs from many Indian regions, the weekly changing menu includes dishes from as far apart as Hyderabad, Pondicherry, Mangalore and Lucknow and styles like bhunao, pot-roasting, Parsi dishes, Tak-a-Tak, Kozi Chettinad, Kesari and Elachi Gosht. There is street food from places like Kolkata, Andhra, Konkan, Tamil Nadu, Nizam and Mumbai. Menu Snapshot: Dilli Ki Aloo Tikki £3.25, shallow fried patties of mashed potato and green peas, spiced with ginger and topped with yogurt, tamarind and mint dips. Champ Taazaar £12.95, select cuts of lamb best-end, soaked overnight in beer marinade, spiced with crushed garlic, pounded chillies, cloves, coriander, mustard and yoghurt, cooked over live charcoal. Lobster Pepper Fry £18.95, fresh lobster tossed in a peppery onion and fennel masala with mixed peppers, tempered with curry leaves. Mirch Baingan Ka Salan £5.50, baby aubergine cooked with chillies in peanut flavoured, yoghurt based gravy. *There is a sizable window that looks into the kitchen which is quite entertaining. Efficient if a bit gloomy staff. Bare tables but real napkins. Amazingly good menu with a real assortment of classic, traditional Indian dishes. South Indian vegetarian dishes feature prominently, following ayurvedic practices. Stunning starter, Kebab Platter £5.50, a juicy grilled prawn of impressive dimensions with a piquant sauce, a seriously well-marinated breast of lovely chicken and a hot, juicy and tender lamb chop in an exquisitely hot and spicy coating. This was served with a nice green dip heavy with garlic. The main course was Kadai Chooza Kali Murch £9.25 - delicious melt in the mouth chicken with a rich sauce, (just enough to cover the meat), packed with pepper heat. A fabulous blast of tastes in the mouth! Served with some of the best Basmati rice I have ever tasted - Jeera Pulao £2.35. My dining companion had a superb Peshwari Nan that I could have eaten a plate of on its own served with cream as a dessert. Lovely hot and sweet Gulab Jamans £3, served in tall glass. Unhesitatingly and very highly recommended to all.'* RW. Service Ch: 12.5% discretionary. 12-11 (10 Sun). Branches: Mela and Chowki, London W1 and WC1

HALE BARNS TANDOORI
14, The Square, Hale Barn, Altrincham, WA15 8ST
0161 904 9909

'Attractive restaurant in a small shopping precinct. Nicely decorated with an open feeling created through extensive use of mirrors. Seating only for 30 or so. Friendly staff. Real tablecloths. Unusual starter, Chicken Halim £3.50, best described as Mulligatawny Soup with added lentils and chicken pieces. Thick and pleasantly spicy, but the flavours didn't quite get together. Beautifully presented Meat Thali £13.95 - a large salver with seven small pots and bread in the middle. Excellent portion of hot and spicy lamb and chicken Tikka, great quality meat. Small but succulent Seek Kebab. Fantastic Lamb Bhuna. The Chicken dish was rather plain though and the bread doughy. Great Rice. Couldn't finish the Tarka Dall as it was too tough. Enjoyable overall and recommended.' RW. Menu

Snapshot: Samosa £2.50; Special Sea Bass Masala £13.95 - marinated in herbs and spices, cooked with tomatoes, chillies and garnished with coriander; Indian Chicken Noodle with Egg garnished with tomatoes and coriander £4.95/£6.95. Mon-Sat: 5-12. Sun:3-11.30.

Ashton-under-Lyne

INDIAN OCEAN   A-LIST
83 Stamford St East, Ashton-under-Lyne, OL6 6QH
0161 343 3343   www.indianoceanonline.co.uk

This is one of those rather rare establishments. It's a perfect curryhouse. It is the extraordinary level of care which we're talking about. Chef/Owner Nahim Aslam founded it in 1993. Seats 120. Large lounge with regular entertainment which attracts diners to stay and enjoy after dinner drinks. The kitchens boast a team of twelve first class specialists, with all the experience and skills to produce the traditional authentic tastes of India, Kashmir and the Punjab. to local area diners for to enjoy. Long gone are dishes like Vindaloo and much more subtle flavours have come in such as Chicken Gorkali an Indo-Chinese dish with Chicken red and green peppers and special chilli sauce. He has come up with Lamb Hari Boti, delicately spiced and with a light mint to reflect the British love of mint with roast lamb. Chicken, fish and lamb Tandoor-barbecued platters are very popular. Another feature of the new menu is the daily special – a specially prepared dish, changed each day which Nahim describes as 'food my mother would prepare at home'. In other words it is prepared in a way that many Asian British families will eat when they are at home. The cooking techniques are very time consuming so are not often seen in the modern Indian restaurant. Having tried the idea as both a restaurant dish and T/a item, it proved so popular that it has become a permanent feature of the new menu. And to finish try the traditional Indian desserts such as Sheer korma and Pistachio Kheer. *'We are regulars, where the welcome is always warm and friendly. First impressions are good as it is an attractive, clean and well presented restaurant. Good menu, appetising food, served pleasantly. Recommended.'* PR. *'Have had a few parties here and have really been looked after.'* JW. An outdoor area called the Terrace has just opened. T/a ordering available online. Hours: 5-1; 12 Sat; 1-1 Sun.

LILY'S   VEGETARIAN
75-83 Oldham Road, Ashton under lyne OL6 7DF
0161 339 4774

5 minutes walk from Ashtonstation & opposite IKEA, with an Asian superstore next door (to let you stock up), it serves Gujarati and south indian food vegetarian food. There are several varieties of dosa here and street food like Sev Puri. Mains include tasty Tarka dall and Palak mushroom both were fresh, in plentiful portions and we hear of a really tasty Paneer Butter Curry,, soft creamy paneer in a lightly spiced, buttery sauce full of fresh tomatoes. Beer available. Note early closing: 11am-7 (6 Sun)

Atherton, M46

FAR PAVILION
138, Bolton Rd, Atherton, M46 9LF   01942 875077

'My wife and I have been to a few restaurants in the Guide the staff who are absolutely superb people. have yet to dine in one better, the service appears to be better along with the menu, the personal touch like after dinner mints, Brandy and Bailey's, also there's the oranges and hot towels.' DS.

SYLHET CITY
4-5, Eckersley Precinct, Mealhouse Lane, Atherton. M46 0DR   01942 889516   www.sylhetcity.co.uk

'Open and nicely decorated a/c 68 seater in a small precinct of shops in the centre of the town and incorporating that rare beast, a free municipal car park. Nicely laid out table, with well spaced out tables with real tablecloths. Friendly, young staff with bags of enthusiasm. Good menu, plenty of Bangladeshi specials along side the standard fare. Popadoms and Chutney £1.80. Nice enough starter, a big, greasy and under-spiced Shami Kebab £3.15, but succulent and with great quality mince. Served with a small, crisp salad and sauce. Very good Lamb Tikka Dupiaza £6.95, loads of translucent slices of onion and pepper in a rich medium sauce. The only niggle was the chewy buy very tasty Lamb Tikka. Great soft Pilau Rice £1.80, with a fragrant aroma and no stickiness. Reasonable attempt at Tarka Dal £2.40, great texture and balance, buy just a bit think in taste. Overall a very pleasant meal and recommended.' RW. 5-11.30, (from 4 Sun to 12.30 Fri-Sat).

Bolton

INDIA GATE
876 Bradshaw Rd, Turton, Bolton BL5 3NB 01942 815 900

'Converted pub, seating c150 very comfortably, with excellent views (when it is not raining) of the West Pennines, about 4 m north east of Bolton. Service was excellent, and the selection extensive. Portions generous-and an (unsolicited) digestif on the house at the end finished off nicely. Bill for 4 with quite a few drinks-£95 - one of the best I have been to in the north. Not quite in Aagrah class, but not far below.' SS.

SIZZLING PALATE
20-22, Bradshawgate, Bolton, BL1 1DG   01204 525757   www.sizzlingpalate.co.uk

'Strikingly modern small restaurant on the main street in town with a big picture window looking out on to the passing world. Wooden floors and smart furniture add to the visual impact and are matched by the smartly turned out young staff. The menu is limited, and is a combination of Indian, Thai and Chinese with Noodles and Pasta. It has obviously caught the imagination as on my visit the restaurant was nearly full with Indian couples and families. Quartered Popadoms, served in a basket with a lovely selection of sauces and chutneys - £3.95. Sheekh Kebab £2.95. Pleasant if unspectacular Hot Lamb Balti £7.45. Decent lamb, gristle free and tender, in a rich sauce that wasn't quite right. Not as hot I was expecting or indeed would have liked. Good Nan £1.90 bread, plenty of garlic but a tough doughy. Very nice, slightly sharp Salty Lassi £2.25. I was still unsated so I finished with a portion of industrial Vanilla Ice Cream. A not unpleasant way to pass an hour and a half, in the absence of a DVD.' RW. Younger Asians are more adventurous about eating alternative cuisines than their parents. However, having looked through the menu, I am not sure that I would order a Lamb Sheek Kebab with Oyster Sauce? Mixing two very different food styles simply doesn't work for me. 11.30-2.30 & 5-11.30 (to 12 Sat-Sun).

Dukinfield

CHUTNEY MASSALA TAKEAWAY
1 The Square, Fir Tree Lane, Dukinfield SK16 0161 3030101

'Excellent T/a with multi-award winning chefs (real ones, not the 'pay and display' variety). Open kitchen, comfy chairs, comprehensive menu, good selection of fish dishes. A freshen-up towel and mint provided in your carrier bag.' RW. 4.30-11.20 (to 12 Fri & Sat).

MISTER MO'S
5, Oaktree Drive, Dukinfield, SK16 5ER 0161 338 2211

'Pleasant and clean takeaway in a precinct in a housing estate. Decent menu with a few specials. Pizza, Burgers, Fried Chicken and kebabs also available. Great starter Shami Kebab £1.75 - more authentic than usual Shamis, with a blend of finely minced lamb and lentils, blended with warm and aromatic herbs and spices and bound with egg. Served with a really garlicky Yoghurt Sauce - fabulous. The Nawab Special Biriani £5.95 - was abit greasy and lacking in aroma, but tasted lovely. Really well cooked basmati rice, rich with meats and prawns and topped with a far better than average medium Vegetable Curry Sauce. Plenty of different tastes and textures and very hearty. Good simple food and good value. Recommended.' RW. 3-11.30.

Hyde

ALPANA
32, Market St, SK14 1AH   0161 368 3374

'Unusually, the decorators were aware of masking tape and the expression, 'cutting in,' so the paint work has none of the common curry house traits of being done by primary school children. Great young staff. Shiny vinyl seats and disposable tablecloths detract from overall impression. Reshmi Kebab stunning, very succulent, well spiced patty, presented in a diaphanous bird's nest of egg rather than ubiquitous omelette, a masterpiece, wrapping gave wonderful mouth feel, topping of onion, delicious yoghurt sauce. Kabuli Lamb top notch exquisite curry with al dente Chana, accompanied by cool lettuce salad, mint dressing, sculpted tomato. Flawless. Perfect light, fluffy Garlic Naan, stunning Tarka Dal Fresh melon served afterwards. Very highly recommended.'* 5-11 (12.30 Fri & Sat & 4-11 Sun).

YOU SAY OK
You might get a discount if you show them this Guide.

ASHTON: BLU SPICE 160, Albans Ave, OL6 8TU ~ 0161 330 4900   *www.blu-spice.co.u'Spread across three retail units in a housing estate.'* RW. 5-11.30; to 1.30 Fri / 1-11 Sat & Sun
HYDE: CINNAMON TAKEAWAY 18a Market Street, , SK14 1AY ~ 0161 368 4449   *'On site of burnt-down Megna. Large open plan kitchen, spotless, keen staff. Enjoyable meal.'* RW. 5-11, from 4 Sat, Sun
HYDE: FAIZAH 32, Market St, SK14 1AH   0161 368 3374   *'42-seater. Efficient, friendly staff. Recommended.'* RW. 5-11, 3 Sun.
HYDE: SAFFRON TAKEAWAY 30 Manchester Road, Hyde, SK14 2BD 0161 367 8600. *'Open kitchen with smart, enthusiastic staff. Highly recommended.'* RW. Hours: 5-11.30; 4-12 Fri-Sun
LEIGH: INDIAN GOURMET 239 Church La, Lowton, Leigh WA3 2RZ   01942 727262. Smart modern restaurant, in shopping precinct. Hours: 5-11.

Manchester City
M1 to M45

For the purpose of this Guide, we have included M postcodes (M1-M45) in our Manchester City entries. They are mostly inside the M60 ringroad. There is no geographical logic to our putting postcodes into numerical order. They are frankly a jumble. But it is the system which exists, and to help narrow things down, we have divided the city into Central, East, South, West and North, using major roads as our arbitrary boundaries.

Manchester Central
M1 to M4

AKBARS   BEST GROUP
AUTHENTIC PAKISTANI CUISINE
73-83 Liverpool Road, Deansgate, Manchester, M3 4NQ   0161 834 8444   www.akbars.co.uk

RW, one of our finest correspondents visited this restaurant and found ... *'horrible pakoras - greasy, average food, open windows to kitchen, chatty waiters, Nan Bread stands - still there though Gordon Ramsey told them to get rid, very large very busy restaurant and a bizare auto-booking seating system.'*RW. [pagers that beep when your table's ready.] Branches: This is the fourth branch of ten of the rapidly expanding chain. See Bradford, W. Yorks for menu details.   Mon-Fri: 5-11 (Sat: to 11:30;Sun: 4-11).

ASHOKA
105 – 107 Portland Street, Manchester, M1 6DF
0871 246 5680   www.ashokamanchester.co.uk

The Aslam family run one of the longest established Manchester restaurants. It's just around the corner from the Palace Theatre. They do pre-theatre offers. *'The service can be a little slow, but the standard of food here is well worth the wait. Rashmi Kebab – god what taste, beautiful! £19. for one, but worth every penny.'* mb. *'Lunch time and there's only one other sad git needing a fix. Generous helpings, nicely spiced sauces. Pullao Rice - generous portion, good flavour, light and fluffy.'* DB. Menu extracts: Chilli Chicken , green chillies, ginger, fresh coriander, capsicum and red chilli sauce. Rashmi Kebab, minced chicken, onion, green chillies, fresh mint, coriander, cooked over charcoal. Quail Makhani, butter, tomatoes, cream sauce.12-2.30 & 6-11.30.

BOLLYWOOD MASALA
15-25 Liverpool Road, M3 4NW. 0161 832 1290
www.bollywoodmasalauk.com

The decor is fun and what is says on the can, Bollywood, colourful and extravagant.The place is buzzing and busy. The manager had been at Rusholme's Lal Hawelli. Formula curries. Speciality dishes on the menu are all named after famous Bollywood stars and movies. *'The menu as it was all about bollywood. But that's where it ended. Where were my favourite superstars' pictures?'* ME. All your old are there. There is a section listed as 'Apna-style' meaning 'our own' or home-made home-recipe curries. It seems to be a big thing in Manchester, though very few actually achieve the claim. Luncheon deal: 5 courses, £6.95. If you book in advance for a meal at , they will even pick you up and drop you off for free. Open for lunch and dinner.

EAST Z   PUNJABI
East Ibis   Princess Street, Manchester, M1 7DL 0871 230 5346   www.EastZEast.com

Pron zee (!) it's inside the Ibis Hotel, close to the Palace Theatre. The food is really tasty Punjabi, and quite unlike the formula curryhouse. See Liverpool Merseyside entry for details. Mon-Thu 5-11.30; Fri-Sat: 5-12 (Sun to 11). Branches: East Z East 19 Church Street Preston PR1 3BQ   01772 200084; Unit 2, Kings Dock Liverpool L3 4BX   0151 707 9377 and below.

EAST Z EAST RIVERSIDE   PUNJABI
Blackfriars St, off Deansgate, Manchester, M3 5BQ
0871 231 7768   www.EastZEast.com

Owners Bradford's Raja brothers opened the huge flagship branch of the above Punjabi restaurant next to the 5 star Lowry Hotel, and opposite the Marriott Renaissance at the end of Deansgate, it's just around the corner from the MEN Arena, Royal Exchange Theatre and Manchester's main shopping district. 250 diners, take away service. Valet Parking Concierge Service. Mon-Th: 5-11.30; Fri-Sat: to Mdnt; Sun: 2-11.

IMLI BY LAL QILA
310 Deansgate Manchester M3 4HE
0161 839 6730   www.imlibylalqila.com

Owned by Rusholme's popular Lal Qila, this one opened

2011 as Lal Qila in a fine corner building near the Opera House and Manchester Central. Imli's 200 seat interior is dramatically set on two floors. The ground floor features 'The Gallery', a raised dining area which overlooks the main dining room. Designer Usman Malikis describes his scheme as *'gentle pallets of taupe, oyster white and deep walnut are complemented by dashes of vibrant reds and shimmering glitter'*. The menu is pure curryhouse, glamourised by serving in mall copper Karahis. Indian sweets eg gulab jaman and rasmalai are both £3.20. House wines from £14. Louis Roederer Cristal champagne £250. Bottled Cobra £3. Sun-Thur: 5-12 (Fri-Sat to 2am)

RED HOT WORLD BUFFET
48 Deansgate, Manchester, M3 2EG 0871 231 7799 | www.RedHot-WorldBuffet.com

Huge buffets seem to be highly popular in Manchester. and none are larger than this one. On the corner of Deansgate and Blackfriars Street, it was the biggest in Europe when it opened in April 2011, serving 700 guests at any one time with over 35 chefs churning out some 300 freshly dishes including Indian, Thai, Italian, Chinese, Japanese, Cajun, Med, Tex-Mex, English and more. Sushi is on offer, along with live pasta stations, a noodle bar, pizza, 30 desserts, and even a waffle and crepe counter. The Nottingham-based company spins that it *'gives people a new and fresh dining experience with a 'wow factor'*. That's as maybe and we only enter it and others like it in this Guide because it's there, and because some of you like it, especially young kids . Branches: *Leeds, Liverpool, Nottingham, Northampton and Milton Keynes & Cardiff*. Daily: 12-4 / Sun-Th: 5-10:30; Fri & Sat: to 11pm.

THIS AND THAT   TOP 100
3 Soap Street, Manchester, M4 1EW 0161 832 4971 hisandthatcafe.co.uk

Run by the Mallu family since 1990, it's down a bendy alley with a fun name. In the beginning it was a spartan café, highly popular with the discerning. We've listed it for all that time and it gets more popular than ever, so much so they've opened a branch. but it's far from tatty now. The approach reminds one of Innocent's Smoothie brand: really excellent products delivered with humourous packaging and humourous website. And yes, T & T have all three. Outside the formerly drab exterior is enlivened with a quirky new mural designed by Manchester architects Rina Yunus and Marhami Arifin of Mystreetretro. They have carried their theme inside, but it's still a business with a simple concept: cheap, tasty food delivered by a smiling, no-nonsense team from large food warmers. Diners sit at easy-clean plastic furniture. By complete contrast with the previous entry, the food here cannot be bettered anywhere. And the formula is genius. Each day of the week up to ten curries are on offer. Each day they are different. Rice & 3 Veg is £3.30; Rice & 3 Meat, £4.90.

The menu is identical each week. Breads, Sams and Bhajis, Lhassi and fizzy drinks extra. Unlicensed. Mon-Th: 11.30-4.30; Fri-Sat: to 8pm; Sunto 4pm. *Branch: 5-7 Butter Lane, Deansgate, M3 2PD.*

YADGAR
71 Thomas St, Northern Quarter, M4 1ES. 0161 831 7753

Another 'rice and three' no-frills canteen with an uninviting exterior, and more inviting interior (blonde plastic round tables with matching chairs sitting on a tiled floor). A few prints adorn the walls, amongst them Mona Lisa. The counter at the end displays the canned drinks and food (curries not on show) the prices displayed on an illuminated board. And cheap they are. They do: kebabs 50p (they have a charcoal-grill), doners, samosas, channa masalas, naans, tikkas and curries from £2.50 Rice with three curries is £4.70 though portions are smaller than T&T. Specials include Lamb Karela, £3.50, lamb with bitter squash and potatoes, and Dhai Baray £2.50, lentil balls served in yoghurt with a tamarind chutney. Chapattis 40p. Traditional desserts include kheer, £2).

ZAIKA
Zaika Manchester 2 Watson St, Manchester, M3 4EE 0871 230 3916 www.ZaikaRestaurants.co.uk

Next to the Opera House, it seats 180 on two floors, each having its own bar facility, plus external seating on the front forecourt for 60. Inside dark wood tables contrast with white linen serviettes and fresh flowers. Zaika's owner, Bob, explained that Zaika translates as "Sense of Taste". Lamb Handi on-the-bone £9.95; Murag Silsella, Spicy Chicken on-the-bone £9.95; Lamb Rezalla on-the-bone £10; Khara Masala Lamb, cooked with whole spices, £115. For a taster, order the gut-busting Banquet £40, min 2: Pops, Starters: Chicken Tikka; Sheekh Kebab; Onion Bhaji; and Fish Amritsari served on a long, oval platter followed by a tumbler of nimboo pani, fresh lime juice with mint and iced water. Mains: Chicken Do Piazza; Chooza Makhani; Saag gosht; Karahi Fish; Sabz-e-bahar (Mixed Vegetables); Naan; Pilau rice and 3 desserts again on a long, oval platter. Mon-Fri: 12- 12; Sat: 5-1am; Sun 1:30-11.

ZOUK   PAKISTANI   TOP 100
Unit 5, The Quadrangle, Chester Street, Manchester, M1 5QS 0161 233 1090 www.zoukteabar.co.uk

This £1m venture by Amjad 'Peter' Bashir and sons, Mudassar and Tayub, and daughter, Habiba opened in 2006 opposite the Palace Theatre with 240 seats, a mezzanine, alfresco dining and an open kitchen. Traditional curries, Karahi and Handi dishes are on the menu. Taking influences from Pakistan, India and North Africa, there are Punjabi, Lahori, Delhi and Mughlai specialities. Dishes such as Beggar's Chicken, coated in clay to keep the meat moist, and Full Leg of Lamb, Turkey and Duck, roasted on embers and served on skewers, a traditional dish from Baluchistan known as Sajji. The choice of seafood dishes is, say Zouk, unrivalled. Red Snapper, Halibut, Monk Fish, Sea Bass, Salmon, Black Cod and Lobster are all on the menu. The 'Al Fresco Shisha Lounge' offers Egyptian Shishas (four fabulous flavours of fine authentic Egyptian tobaccos) and the area is fully licenced with heated parasols. *'we visited this restaurant, food better than other places. open kitchen, chatty waiters, very busy.'* RW. Av price: Lunch: £16; Dinner: £25. 12-12. *Branches*: Zouk Tea Bar & Grill, Liverpool city centre and Bradford.

Manchester North
M7, M8, M9 M24 (Middleton), M25 & 45 (Whitefield) M25 (Prestwich), and M26 (Radcliffe)

AL MAIDAH   PAKISTANI BUFFET   NO ALC
Sagar Street, Off Bury New Road, Manchester, M8 8EU 0871 246 2018   www.AlMaidah.co.uk

Yet another lavish buffet. It's a stone's throw from the MEN arena and Victoria Station this huge multi-million pound Indian buffet restaurant and banquet hall (on the first floor), opened in 2011. It took over 2 years to build from scratch, and no expense has been spared in attention to detail. From marble floors to crystal chandeliers, Al Maidah means "table spread with food" or "the banquet" and its Indian & Pakistani cuisine buffet style restaurant has over 60 dishes (£12.95 per head) on offer and counting, including Starters, Curries, Breads and Desserts. There's also a selection of Chinese and pizza dishes. The open kitchen running the length of the restaurant enables you to watch chefs prepare the food, regardless of where you are sitting. Strict No Alcohol policy, instead, mocktails, freshly squeezed juices & non-alcoholic wines are available. Free parking for 100 cars. Daily: 5:30-11.

The LIME TREE
213 Bury Old Road, Heaton Park, Prestwich, M25 1JF   0161 773 3748   www.thelimetree.info

Don't select the wrong Lime tree. Confusingly there's one in W Dids doing *'cutting-edge Modern British'* whatever that is. Lime Tree is a curious name, you'd imagine it's Thai not British never mind Indian, but it's the Indian we're talking about, located not in a leafy lane but opposite a walled park in pink-walled former pub, The Turf, once a bit rough now gentrified with tiled floor, Hindu icons, exposed beams, dark brown leather chairs, pale walls, abstract art on the walls, and the once ubiquitous curryhouse feature, the fish tank. This divides the lounge from the dining area, and the lucky fish lurk in a 1/16 scale plastic Revell kit of the Bismarck, the one time Nazi flagship. Curious. Maybe it's a warning to the rough element. Set meal for 2 Price : £31.95, Pappadums and Chutney Tray, Shami Kebab, Onion Bhaji, Chicken Tikka Massala, Lamb Jalfrezi, Sagg Aloo, Vegetable Fried Rice, Plain Nan Bread. Sunday Buffet Price, 2pm to 6pm. £11.95 Adults/Kids £5.95. Mon-Sat: 5-11; Sun 1-10.30.

RADCLIFFE CHARCOAL TANDOORI
123-125, Blackburn Street, Radcliffe, Manchester, M26 3WQ   0161 723 4870 www.radcliffetandoori.co.uk

Originally opened in 1986. Menu Snapshot: Tray of Pickles and Chutneys £2.45, Popadom 60p, Chicken Tikka Bhajia and Puri £5.05, CTM £8.50, Pullao Rice £1.95, Aloo Methi (fried potato in fenugreek leaves) £2.95. RW. Delivery: £10 min, 3ms. 5 -11.30 (Fri-Sat to 12.30); Sun: 2 to 11.

SECRET SUPPER CLUB
http://spiceclubmanchester.com/upcoming-events/

Sunita and dau Monica run this in their north Manchester house. You book along with 24 strangers and the secret location will be revealed. Seating is at large dining tables of 8 in the lounge Each meal includes a soft drink, appetizer, entrée of 4-5 dishes with Basmati rice and chappati), a dessert and chai. BYO. Donation min £27.

Manchester East
M11 to M13, M18, M34, M35, M40, M43

VERMILION & CINNABAR
Lord North St, Manchester, M40 8AD 0871 978 9600

The owners of this Thai/Indian/Asian fusion restaurant near Man City stadium, claim it is *'the most spectacular out-of-this-world restaurant and bar to have ever opened in Manchester!* It's up to you to agree or not, whether the £4.5 million it is alleged to have cost fulfills the claim. Of interest are the specific Indian set menus. Sun-Fri: 12-3 & 6-1am, Fri & Sat: 5- 2am.

Manchester South
M14 (Wilmslow Road, Rusholme) M15, M16, M19 to M23, M32, M33 and M90

CHENNAIDOSA   SOUTH IND/SRI LANKAN
Unit 119 Chester Rd, Stretford Mall, Stretford, Manchester, M32 9BH   0161 865 7777

ChennaiDosa first opened in London in 2003 and this is its 11th of 14 branches. The two floor 125 seater at the front of the mall serves south Indian/Sri Lankan meat & veg cuisine, rare in to Manchester. South Indian GM/chef is Suresh Baska. See London E12 for full menu & details. No licence. 11am-10:30pm.

ZAM ZAM TANDOORI
452, Wilbraham Road, Chorlton-cum-Hardy, Manchester, M21 0AG   0161 862 0999

*'Small (28 cosy seats) and friendly, effervescent staff at this café in a single long room that's spotlessly clean in the student-laden area of Chorlton. Pleasant Chicken Pakora £1.20 - five strips of tender chicken in a spicy batter and served with yoghurt sauce and chilli sauce. Very good Lamb Kashmiri £6.50, a really sweet dish, rich with coconut yet

balanced with a decent spicy kick. With plenty of decent quality lamb this was a great meal, particularly with the large portion of perfect Basmati Rice, really fragrant. Interesting variation on Tarka Dall £2.90, tender lentils in a spicy tomato sauce, very nice but not what I was expecting. Lovely light and frothy Salty Lassi £1.30 - with a nice sour bite rounded off a great meal. Recommended to all and a great place to show that you can get lovely food in humble surroundings.' RW. Cash only. Halal. Delivery: £15 minimum, 3 miles. 12 to late.

Manchester M14
Wilmslow Road, Rusholme

The six mile Road runs passes through Rusholme, the city's main Asian area, which was always home to dozens of curry cafés. Publicity has entitled this section of the road 'The Curry Mile' transforming the 70 curry eateries, Indian snack and sweet shops from drab and run-down to Vegas-style strip lighting and hype. Some of the cheap and cheerful all-day cafés allow BYO (but always ask – it can offend some Muslims). Some are quite expensive licensed restaurants, the largest of which seats 400! A conservative estimate on curry consumption is 65,000 curries a week here. Most open all day and many until 1am. Don't try reserving, you'll be lucky if they answer the phone. Just turn up, and if one is busy go to another. Popularity may have taken the edge of authenticity. Our regular and prolific correspondent – DB – tells us that, *'my overall experiences of Rusholme have been a little disappointing both culinary and service wise, considering there are so many curry houses vying for your custom.'* Here are some of your favourites:

KING COBRA   INDIAN & SRI LANKAN
IFCO Centre, Wilmslow Road, Rusholme, Manchester M14 5TQ   0161 248 9999

The only restaurant in Rusholme that offers Indian and Sri Lankan cuisine. Mon-Thur: 5-3; Sat: to 4; Sun to 2.

MUGHLI   MUGHLAI-CUISINE
28-32 Wilmslow Road, Manchester, M14 5TQ
0161 248 0900   www.mughli.com

Stylish time-honoured family restaurant & charcoal pit on the Curry Mile that serves authentic Mughlai-cuisine from the northern regions of India and Pakistan. The menu focuses on freshly prepared traditional and contemporary dishes and features an extensive range of vegetarian, meat and sea-food dishes. Mon-Th: 5-1 (to 2 Fri) Sat: 3-1; Sun 12-12.

SPICY HUT   PAKISTANI
35 Wilmslow Road , Rusholme, Manchester, M14 5TB   0871 230 5335   www.spicyhut.co.uk

Popular informal family-friendly curry house at the start of the Curry Mile in Rusholme. Specialising in sizzlers and Pakistani cuisine. Former National Curry Chef Award winner. Takeaway delivery is also available. Mon-Thu: 5-1am; Fri-Sat 5-3am; Sun 3- 12.30.

Elsewhere on Wilmslow Road

AL BILAL 87-91 Wilmslow Rd, M14 5SU ~ 0161 2570006. **AL NAWAZ BYO** 74 Wilmslow Rd, M14 5AL ~ 0161 249 0044. Punjabi cooking. **DARBAR BYO** 67 Wilmslow Rd, M14 5TB ~ 0161 224 4392. **HANAAN BYO** 54, Wilmslow Rd, M14 5AL ~ 0161 256 4786.. **LAL HAWELI BYO** 68 Wilmslow Rd, M14 5AL ~ 0161 248 9700. **PUNJAB TANDOORI BYO** 177 Wilmslow Rd, M14 5AP ~ 0161 225 2960. BYO. **ROYAL NAZ BYO** 18 Wilmslow Road, Ifco Centre, M14 5TQ ~ 0161 256 1060. **SANAM SWEET HOUSE** 145 Wilmslow Rd, M14 5AW 0161 224 8824. Est c1968 by Haji Abdul Ghafoor, it was the second on the road. Now managed by AQ Akhtar and despite being huge (seating 160, plus a further 200-seat function room), it is so popular locally that it's often full, with queues waiting to be seated. No alcolhol allowed. 12-12. Branches: **ABDUL'S**, 121 & 318 Wilmslow Rd, and 298 Oxford Rd. **SANGAM** 9 Wilmslow Rd, M14 5TB ~ 0161 257 3922 www.sangams.co.uk Branches: **SANGAM 3**, 202 Wilmslow Rd, Heald Green, Cheadle, Cheshire, 0161 436 8809. **SANGAM 2**, 762 Wilmslow Rd, Didsbury, M20 ~ 0161 446 1155. **SHEZAN** 119 Wilmslow Rd, M14 ~ 0161 224 3116 **SPICY HUT BYO** 35 Wilmslow Rd ~ 0161 248 6200. MS Mughal's 60-seater. 5-2; 3-1 Sun. **TABAK** 199 Wilmslow Rd, M14 5QU ~ 0161 257 3890. Mohammad Nawab's Tabak seats a MASSIVE 350 diners, on two floors. 12pm-1am. **TANDOORI KITCHEN** 133 Wilmslow Rd, M14 5AW. The Hussein family were the first to open on Wilmslow Rd (in 1967). **ZAIKA** 2 Wilmslow Rd ~ 0161 224 3335.

NAWAAB   BUFFET   NO ALC
1008 Stockport Rd, Manchester M19 3WN
0161 224 6969   www.nawaab.co.uk

It's yet another noisy, busy, non bookable, alcohol-free e-a-m-a-y-l buffet at £12pp, u11 £6. Set in a former cinema, Mahboob Hussain bills this as the UK's biggest curry house (350 seats on the ground floor plus 600 on the first floor) though it also does chips, pizza pasta, etc. It's popular with traditionally dressed well-healed Asians eating anything but curry. Mon-Th: 5.30-11.30; Fri-Sat -12.30; Sun: 4-11. *Branch details: see Bradford.*

SWADESH
810 Wilmslow Road, Didsbury, M20 6UH
0161 445 3993;

Swadesh is a group of six formula up-market curry restaurants, two of which are named Sangham (see below). Marketed as an exclusive alternative to Curry Mile eateries, the decor, ambience and the food lives up to the claim. Prices a bit higher than the regional norm. Best bargain:Early Dinner Menu Adult £9.90, u12 £5.90 Mon-Sat 4-7, Sunday 1.30pm-4.30pm: Papadam, starter, main Boiled Rice or Pilau Rice or Naan or Chapati Ice Cream for Children. Mon-Th:12- 11; Fri-Sat: -11.30; Sun: 1- 10. *Branches: Sangham, 3 Richmond Rd, Bowdon, Altrincham, WA14 2TT 0161 941 5311 Sangam, 762 Wilmslow Rd, Didsbury, M20 2DR 0161 446 1155; Sangam, 202 Wilmslow Rd, Cheadle, SK8 3BH 0161 436 8809; Swadesh Manchester, 98 Portland St, M1 4GX, 0161 236 1313; Swadesh, 28,Green Lane, Wilmslow, Cheshire, SK9 1LD, 01625 525 902.*

Manchester West

M5, M6 (Salford) M17, M27 to M31, M41, M44

Oldham

MITALI
23-25, High St, Uppermill, Saddleworth, OL3 6HS
01457 874 797

A couple of miles east of Oldham is this '*spacious light and airy 52 seater establishment smartly decorated in vibrant colours and. Great menu with plenty of specials, including some Bangladeshi dish dishes. Friendly and enthusiastic staff. Fantastic Reshmi Kebab £3.20 - two juicy and well spiced patties encased in a soft omelette and served with a small fresh salad. Would have benefitted from some yoghurt sauce. Outstanding Mitali Thawa £9.95 - perfectly cooked and really tasty King prawns in a well crafted, quite dry sauce, full of rich spices and with colour and balance added by onions and peppers. Stonking. Great Garlic Nan £2.50 - a touch doughy perhaps, and a bit light on the garlic, but still enjoyable. Very good Tarka Dal £3.20 - a perfect balance of lentil, onion and garlic that combined into a great tasting dish. Excellent food and highly recommended to all.*' RW. Del: £12 min. 5-11.30 (Fri-Sat to 12.30).

Ramsbottom

SANMINI   TAMIL NADU CUISINE   TOP 100
7 Carrbank Lodge, Ramsbottom Lane, Ramsbottom, BL0 9DJ   01706 821831   www.sanminis.

We'd like them to delete their claim to be the '*first authentic purely South Indian restaurant outside London*'. It is not the case as this Guide shows. That said, south Indian food is really scarce in the area and this is a gem of a find. Husband and wife Bolton doctor Padmini (Mini) and Rochdale anaesthetist Dev Sanhkar are both Tamils and had a dream to open a restaurant featuring Tamil Nadu food. Assisted by their two sons and daughter-in-laws, they acquired a gorgeous grey stone cottage, once a gate house, dating from 1857, and converted it into a two-floored restaurant in 2008. Sanmini's derives from their names, and at once filled its 40 seats (and booking is essential). Entering via a side door you arrive in a small bar area to a warm welcome. Next door is the dining room. Portion sizes are generous. Menu explanations are eagerly given. (See also pages 74 &75). Pops are served with home-made chutneys. Starters include Bonda, Vadai, Dosai & Uthappam each with chutney & sambar; Fish Vadai £5.75, crisp tuna and lentil cakes, with a chilli kick, Cashew & Spinach Pakora; Cauliflower/vendiakai florets & sliced okra with coriander & green chilli chutney; Mutton Chukka Varuval, pan-fried lamb pieces. Mains include: Kothu Kari Kozambhu minced lamb dish with potato; Chettinad Chicken a spicy dish with coconut; Nadar Khozhi Kozhambu £8.75, chicken cooked with poppy, fennel & cashewnuts; Sivakasi Eraal Masala £12, king prawns in a mild tomato/chilli sauce. Eral is an inland town in Tamil Nadu's Chidambaranar coastal region; Ennai Kathirikai, aubergines tossed with tomatoes & herbs; Keerai Kootu, Leaf spinach cooked with lentils. Lemon rice £5.75, with lemon zest, turmeric, mustard seed, ginger, chilli and curry leaves and smeared with cooling raita. 10-dish thali is £20 (£10 children) including unlimited refills but excluding service. Served Sundays only. Licensed but the overpriced Indian wine is not worth £19.95. Go instead for their own-label ale, Samini's India Pale Ale. Tu-Fri: 6.30-9.30 (Sat-Sun to 10.30); Sun: Thalis 12.30-3. *Branch: Sanmini's Express, Stand 5, Toulmin Block, Bury Market, 07553 779195 Curry £3.50. Over 60 Indoor Stalls. Mon-Sat:9-5 (Tu to 1)*

Rochdale

COPPER POT
Sandbrook Park, Sandbrook Way, Rochdale, OL11 1RY   01706 651881   www.copperpot.com

'*Large and airy establishment located in a business unit of a modern retail park, yet the decor is very well thought out and you feel you are in a bright, airy, modern restaurant that buzzes around making sure everyone is enjoying themselves and made to feel welcome. Real tablecloths and napkins. Very comprehensive menu with a great selection of specials. Fantastic Chicken Momo £4.25 - nice pulled chicken and paneer with a sweet but spicy sauce wrapped in a puri and lightly shallow fried, a sort of sausage roll effect! served with a nice garnish of red onion. Brilliant Machli Tarkari £10.75 - perfectly cooked chunks of white fish in a tomatoey sauce with a subtle blend of herbs and spices which developed the flavour of the fish. Tamarind and nuts added an extra dimension. Perfect, aromatic Pilau Rice £1.95. Marvelously flaky and buttery Puri 95p and excellent Tarka Dall £3.95 - a faultless balance of garlic, onion and lentils. Complimentary glass of sparkling wine with the meal and a small brandy with the bill. Seriously enjoyable meal and unhesitatingly recommended to all.*' RW. 5-11 (to 12 Fri-Sat); Sunday 3 to 10.

Stockport,

INDIGO RESTAURANT
6-7 The Precinct, Romiley, Stockport, SK6 4EA
0161 430 8000 & 430 8430   www.indigoromiley.com

Joynal Abdin opened his 90 seat Indigo in 2000 offering a wide range of formula curries which they list as '*Old School Favourites*'. Under the capable hands of Head Chef Atikur Rahman their extensive menu ranges far wider than those, and we commend you to adventure into the unusual. For example, Starters such as Spicy Kholizi £3.50, a popular Bangladeshi starter of lambs liver with lentils, spices and herbs, fairly hot served on a puri ; Stuffed Redpepper £3.80, stuffed with herby and spicy minced lamb or morsels of roasted chicken with spices. There are also Scampi, Crab, Mussels and vegetables starters. Notable House Specialities include Rezella £6.90, chicken or lamb tikka cooked with yoghurt and garlic in a creamy, hot and spicy sauce with chillies; Bindhi Gosht £7, lamb cooked with okra in a medium sauce; Naga Cocktail Mix £7.80,

INDIGO

Cheshire's premiere Bangladeshi & Indian dining experience.

Gift Voucher
Indigo gift vouchers from £10 for all occasions.
Friday & Saturday Special
Try our special regional of Bangladeshi dishes.
Tuesday Special
Happy Hours 5-10: 3 course a la carte meal, £9 per person.
Take away offers
Orders over £18 receive onion bhaji or a side dish of chef's choice.

INDIGO RESTAURANT
6-7 The Precinct,
Romiley, Stockport, SK6 4EA
0161 430 8000 & 430 8430
www.indigoromiley.com

Monday to Thursday: 5pm-11pm
Friday & Saturday: 5pm-12.30am
Sunday: 4pm-11pm.

Last sitting 1 hour before closing.
Takeaway served up to closing time.
Terms and conditions apply
Management has right to change offer(s) at any time

---

chicken & lamb tikka & sheek kebab with tomato, potato, fresh herbs, nagaa chilli; Murgh Uree £6.80, bbq chicken with green beans in a garam masala sauce with garlic, ginger and fresh herbs; Shatkora Gosht, £8, Lamb cooked with the Sylhet citrus fruit to create a hot and tangy taste; Haleem, £8, tender lamb slow simmered with aromatic spices, chick peas, 3 types of lentils and wheat to create this ever popular dish. An Ample choice of vegetable main course dishes include: Shobji Kofta, £7.20, herby spinach & potato dumplings on a mint & coriander flavoured chick peas sauce; Mishti Khodu-Chana Puri, £8, roadside fare of melt-in-the-mouth butternut squash, chick peas with chilli, spices and puri bread; Benganburta Ebong Mutter, £9, tandoor-roasted aubergine crushed with green peas, fresh herbs and spice with pilau rice. Other dishes use Duck, Salmon, Lobster and Lamb shank. Price check: Pop,50p; Pullao Rice, £2.50, CTM, £6.90, Naan £1.80. Pint beer: £3; House wine £9.50. See ad for special offers. Mon-Th: 5-11 (Fri & Sat: to 12.30am); Sunday: 4-11.

Wigan

SPICE LOUNGE BYO
19 Bretherton Rd, off Wallgate WN1 1LL 01942 494909 www.thespicelounge.co.uk

It made the headlines when local woman, Louise Thomas, got curry withdrawal symptoms during the late stages of pregnancy. For her fix she chose here, asking the staff which curry would start her labour; they said they had just the recipe. Within minutes of leaving the restaurant that night she went into labour and gave birth to Lucy. *'Since then'*, says owner Giash Uddin, *'pregnant women have flocked in to test the curry for themselves. We get around three or four women a month coming in asking for the special dish.'* All the regular curries plus specials like Handee, £9, lamb on the bone the way it's eaten in Bangladesh. BYO no corkage charge, and they provide free glasses. 3 course: £11. 4-10. *Branch: Taste of Bengal, 11, High Street, Standish, Wigan.*

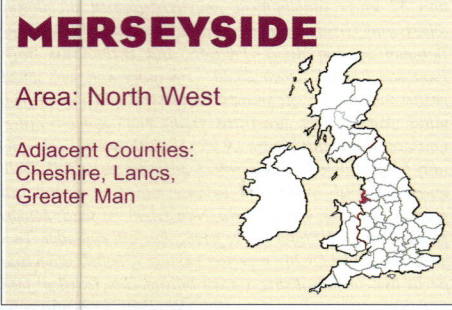

MERSEYSIDE

Area: North West

Adjacent Counties:
Cheshire, Lancs, Greater Man

Liverpool

AKSHAYA   SRI LANKAN
290a Kensington, Liverpool City Centre, L7 2RN
0871 963 8471   www.akshayacuisine.co.uk

ITreasure this one please Merseyside. It specialises in Sri Lankan cuisine. It's modern and spacious and colourful surroundings with contemporary fittings, 60 seats, a/c and free car parking at rear. The Akshayapatra was an inexhaustible bowl, in Hindu mythology, which supplied a never-failing supply of food as daily offerings to the Pandavas (gods) every day. which provided a never-ending supply of food at the temples. But the restaurant's offerings of Sri Lankan dishes (particularly main courses) are in short supply. Perhaps this is because they are so unlike the formula dishes which have to inhabit the menu,for the unadventurous, just as in London, otherwise they' the venue would not survive. Although they cook the formula well, we are adamant that you try the Sri Lankan specials. Space precludes a full description here *(but see page 75 and the A to Z)*. Starters include: Vadai £1.70, Hoppers £1.45, String Hopper (Idiappam) £4,King Fish Fry £5.75, Devilled dishes, eg Chicken, Lamb, Crab etc from £6.45. Nine different Dosai (thin and crispy rice and lentil crepes) from £2.95, Pittu £4, Idli £3.25. Rasam (a spiced soup made with tamarind, pepper, coriander and jeera) is £3. Various main course curries range around £5.45 to £7.45, Biriyanis from £5.25 (egg) to £7 (mixed special). Kothu dishes (chopped paratha mixed with shredded veg £4.50), or chicken £5.75 or Mutton £6. Cheeni Sambol (chutney) £2.25. For dessert miss the ice creams and go for Vattailapam £4, (coconut/caramel pudding) or Vattalappam £4, made from cardamom, coconut milk, palm sugar and eggs. Set meals from £6.45 (veg) to special Thali, £12 available until 6pm. Tue- Sun: 12-3 & 6-11.

COBRA
SPLENDIDLY INDIAN, SUPERBLY SMOOTH

EASTZEAST — PUNJABI
Unit 2, Kings Dock, Aigburth, L3 4BX
0151 707 9377   www.eastzeast.com

Near the Beatles Museum this is a branch of the Manchester EastZ. The food is really tasty Punjabi, and quite unlike the formula curryhouse. Punjabi Traditional Desi Dishes, are on the menu, such as Karahi Sookha Bouhna £12, lamb on the bone cooked with tomatoes, onions, garlic, ginger and spices; Karahi Chicken/Gosht Bhindi £11, cooked with Okra (lady fingers), Karahi Lamb Karela £11, Karahi lamb cooked with fresh bitter gourd. Handi dishes include: Jholay Lal Handi £12, chicken, tiger prawns and chana cooked in a sauce, specially prepared for this dish with onions, tomatoes, garlic, ginger and spices; Raam Lal Handi £11, chicken, aloo and mushrooms cooked in a sauce, with onions, tomatoes, garlic, ginger and spices. Mon-Thu 5-11.30; Fri-Sat: 5-12 (Sun to 11). *Branches, Manchester and Preston.*

GULSHAN — TOP 100
544 Aigburth Rd, Grassendale, Liverpool, L19 3QG
0151 427 2273   www.gulshan-liverpool.co

In 1986 Mustafa and Salina Rahman set up their new Indian restaurant in Grassendale. Gulshan is a Persian girl's name meaning *'paradise or a mystic rose garden'*. A few years ago the couple created an additional fifty covers on a newly-opened first floor and transformed the interior. The original bar downstairs was replaced, a spacious new reception area added and a substantial second drinks area built on the first floor. Says Mustafa: *'My father would be proud. He set up Liverpool's first Indian restaurant in the early 1960s.'* In that case your editor dined there, because it was the city's only Indian. Can't remember its name. In those days I had to tell taxi drivers I was not looking for Curry's Electrical shop! Notable starters include puri dishes with a choice of toppings: aubergine, spinach lentils, mushrooms or buttered prawns, etc. Main Courses include the usual cast-list of Tandoori, Masala, Balti, Biriani and vegetarian dishes. Specials include: Murghi Mossaka, chicken barbecued tandoori style then prepared with keema (minced meat), tomatoes, cream and wine, topped with cheese; Kalla Chicken, chicken kebab cooked with banana and yogurt; Almond Maas Korma, boneless white fish cooked with ground almonds, yogurt, cream, coconut and rose herbs. *'As a birthday treat, I was wined and dined by Jacs, she who now eats curry. Quite busy for a early Tuesday evening. Place a bit scruffy, but this was due to refurbishment work. Service was attentive, very good knowledge. Popadums, lovely, warm, crisp. Chutneys, uninspiring, only mango and onions, no lime. Keema Muttu with Puri, meat samosa filling on bread, tasty, very nice puri but large! '...Tilapia fish was covered in spicy sauce, overpowering it. Nantera, chicken tikka, green peppers, tomatoes, wine, fresh herbs, Jacs was happy. Chicken Tikka Rezalla, spicy, good portion of chicken. Garlic Naan, stuffed with slices of garlic and overpowering, as my work colleagues will testify.'* DB. Useful if you are staying at the Travelodge opposite. Hours: 5-11.

MAHARAJA — SOUTH INDIAN
34 London Rd, City Centre   0151 709 2006
maharajaliverpool.co.uk

Have the Rasam £4, (hot and spicy soup, with floating slivers of garlic, curry leaves and a red chilli! – this is editor DBAC's benchmark, which if she doesn't get hiccups, it's not hot enough for her! Masala Dosa, Sambar and Coconut Chutney are south Indian favourites. fish dishes are the norm in south India. Try Chicken Puffs £4, spicy chicken with masala stuffed in a puff pastryerved with tomato sauce and salad; Kerala Fish Fry (Poricha Meen) £3.95, marinated in spicy paste of ginger, garlic and dried red chillies and fried. Masala Dosa £6, paper thin pancake made of rice and black gram batter filled with spiced potatoes, served with sambar (lentil and seasonal vegetable curry) and coconut chutney. Duck Olathu £9 a Kerala Christian speciality. duck cooked in a thick sauce with onion, ginger, garlic, coriander and other exotic spices; Lamb Mappas £9, traditional curry cooked in a green masala made from green chillies, ginger and garlic. And for pud Payasam £3 traditional Keralan sweet rice pudding with cashew nuts and raisins. or Kesari £3.50 ade of semolina, mango cashew nuts and raisins.. *'I was the only lunchtime diner. Opted for lunch Special Thali, non-veg. Spinach and Dhal Curry, quite bland, but a lot of garlic. Chicken Curry, very reminiscent of a Thai curry, with after taste of aniseed, beautifully spiced, very tasty. Fish Curry, again beautifully spiced with great flavour. Spicy Potato Curry, slightly undercooked. Basmati Rice, nice and fluffy. Chapatti, excellent. Followed by Rice Pudding, again excellent. Lightness of curries surprised me and portions a bit on the small side'* Dave, it is a lunch! *'but found myself completely stuffed when I'd finished very impressed a great dining experience.'* DB. 2-3 & 6-12.

THE RAJ
9-11 Allerton Rd, Woolton Village, Liverpool L25 0NN
0151 421 1264   www.rajfood.com

Opened in 1992 in an attractive white walled, black beamed former chemist then village club. It's a formula house with Baltis to Vindaloos. Vegetarian are well catered for with specials such as Vegetable Makonwalla, and Vegetable Rogan Josh. Sunday buffet 12-7pm. *Branch: Raj Takeaway, 285 Speke Road, Woolton, L25 0NN*

SAFFRON INDIAN — PUNJABI & NEPALI
92 St John's Road, Waterloo, L22 9QQ
0151 920 8398   www.saffronliverpool.co.uk

Messrs Netra, Talwar and Tiwari tell us *'do not think that the menu we offer is limited to what you read on the page, not only will we know your favourite dish, our chef will be able to cook it as well'*. Delhi-trained Head Chef Chhabilal cooks Punjabi dishes, whilst a master chef cooks Nepali. Take Away 20% off a la carte at all times. Quick Lunch £5, Lamb or Chicken plus Vegs, Pilau Rice and Naan. Mon-Fri: 12-2:30 & 5-11; Sun Buffet £5.99, 12.30-5.

YOU SAY OK
You might get a discount if you show them this Guide.

LIVERPOOL: ASHA 79 Bold Street, Liverpool ~ 0151 709 4734
MILLON TANDOORI 189 Allerton Rd, Mossley Hill, L18 6HG 0871 811 4755. One of Liverpool's best curry houses. **MASALA HOT BYO** 447 Ranelagh St, L1 1JR 0871 963 0576. Indian/Chinese buffet £9. (Mon-Thur day) £10 after 5.30.
MASTER CHEF TANDOORI 57a Renshaw St, L1 2SJ 0871 811 475. Est 1990, bright, modern restaurant.
ROYAL TANDOORI 453 Smithdown Road, Wavertree, L15 3JL 0871 963 0637 One of Liverpool's oldest, est 1971.
SHANTII 124a Church Road, Formby, L37 3NH 0871 811 4833 Modern 60-cover Indian. Owner Ali has been in the Formby area for nearly 20. 2 for 1 every Monday.
SULTANS PALACE 77 Victoria St, L1 6DE 01514 382203 Has been providing authentic Indian cuisine since 2002.
NEWTON-LE-WILLOWS: TASTE OF INDIA 56 Market Street, Newton ~ 01925 228458
THINGWALL: RED CHILLI 513 Pensby Rd, Thingwall 0151 648 5949. 65-seater run chef G Miah. 5-11.30; 12 Sat.

Southport

THE KASTURI
40, Eastbank St, Southport, PR8 1ET   01704 533102   www.kasturirestaurant.com

'Fairly large restaurant, in nice 'seasidey' exterior.' RW. *'I visited a friend in Southport. He reckons this is the best in Southport. The food was good, marred only by the serving of cold chicken tikka as a starter (the restaurant were good about it), the service was good (otherwise). It should remain in the Guide.'* JP. Hours: 5.30-12; 1 Fri & Sat.

Wirral
Bromborough, Moreton, Wallasey, West Kirby

The Wirral is neither a town nor a county and, until 1965, was part of Cheshire. Since then the northern part – a small, digit-like, curry-rich peninsula between the rivers Mersey and Dee – has been part of Merseyside. Ellesmere Port (q.v.) remains in south Wirral but is in Cheshire. Your choice of Merseyside Wirral curryhouse towns are in alphabetical order:

BROMBOROUGH: CURRY NIGHTS 5 Coronation Dr, 0151 343 9200. *'Ever-present and ever-reliable, can't beat it.'* JN. *'Food delicious, brilliant menu, staff v friendly.'* JO. Pops free; spend £15, and Onion Bhajia free; spend £20, Veg Bhajee free.
MORETON: SURMA TANDOORI 271 Hoylake Rd, 0151 677 1331. 48-seater opened 1995 by Sharif Ali. *'Impressive upstairs restaurant. A great meal, recommended.'* RW. 5.30-11.30.
UPTON: HALAL BALTI 167 Ford Rd, Upton 0151 604 0166. Shofiul Miah's venture est 1996 is **BYO**, big and relatively cheap. Wed-Sun: 5-11.30. *Branch: Manzil, 73 Grange Rd East.*
WALLASEY: BANGLA VUJON 225 Wallasey Village ~ 0151 637 1371
WALLASEY: BHAJI 135 Wallasey Village, Wallasey ~ 0151 638 9444. *'At last a biriani was some flavour.'* DB. Hours: Daily to 1030; 11 Fri & Sat; 10.30 Sun.
TANDOORI MAHAL 24, King Street, Wallasey 0151 639 5948 This is one of Dave's favourites, and he updates us in each Guide. *'They will never win awards, but they will never be short of custom, hope this doesn't change.'* DB.
MAK SYED 285 Wallasey Village Rd, Wallasey CH45 3HA 0151 639 9889 Weds -Mon: 4:30-12.
WEST KIRBY: ROYAL BENGAL 150 Banks Rd, Kirby ~ 0151 625 9718. Est 1971, taken over in 2000. http://www.royalbengalwirral.co.uk

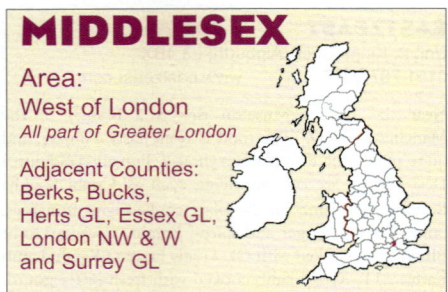

MIDDLESEX

Area:
West of London
All part of Greater London

Adjacent Counties:
Berks, Bucks,
Herts GL, Essex GL,
London NW & W
and Surrey GL

Middlesex once contained most of London, though diminished when central London became autonomous during Victorian times. What was left of the county (located west and north of London) was completely 'abolished' when Greater London was formed in 1965, a move unpopular with Middlesex residents. Confusion exists because the Post Office still use Middlesex as a postal county. Postcodes add to the confusion. Enfield, for example, is EN1, EN2 & EN3 in postal Middlesex but is in (Hertfordshire) GL county. Potters Bar EN6 is the same. Barnet, in postal Herts with EN4 and EN5 codes used to be in Middlesex but is now a GL borough!

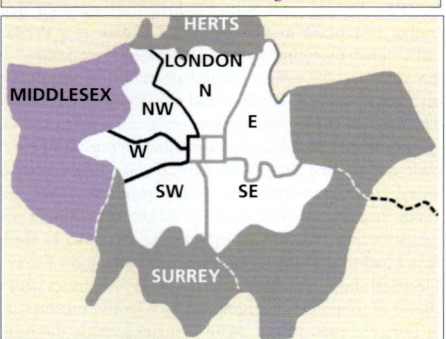

Brentford

PAPPADUMS   FINE DINING   TOP 100
Ferry Quays, Ferry La, Brentford, TW8 0BT   020 8847 1123   www.pappadums.co.u

Smart, modern 150-seater on the bank of the River Thames and Grand Union Canal, alongside luxury apartments overlooking Kew Gardens. Personable Alston Wood from Sri Lankan manages. Park in the underground car park (or you'll get a wheel clamp). Owners Narinda and Satvir Sindhu pulled out all the stops creating its modernistic, double frontage, which looks out onto a large promenade area. Steps then lead you down to the the river. When weather permits, diners are welcome to eat outside, on wooden benches with chairs. The restaurant's weighty wooden doors were shipped over from the subcontinent. Chef Gupta worked in Oberoi hotels . His light lunch menu includes Wraps,

SPLENDIDLY INDIAN, SUPERBLY SMOOTH

PAPPADAMS

Pappadams
1 & 2, Ferry Quays
Brentford, Middlesex
TW8 0BT
Tel: 0208 847 1123
info@pappadums.co.uk
Open: Mon-Fri
12:00 - 14:30 and 17:30 - 23:00
Sat-Sun 12:00 - 23:00

Riverside location
Overlooking Kew Gardens

Kath Rolls and Indianised paneer Spring Rolls. and dishes from China and Thailand. Under the heading *'Exotic Oriental Delicacies'*, you will encounter Nasi Goreng £15, lamb and chicken satay served with spicy fried rice, topped with fried egg and peanut sauce; Honey Spiced Chicken £10; Thai Gaeng Pak 'stir-fried vegetables, tofu, scallions, mushrooms, hot and sour sauce. *'I decided to stick to Indian and chose Machhli Ke Pakode, fried cod strips coated with mild spiced gram flour. A generous portion was presented with a good salad and I enjoyed it very much. Pat had Kashmiri Lamb Seekh Kebab. Again a generous portion of tender, well pounded, spicy meat with salad. The chutney tray was left on the table for us to help ourselves. The menu highlights various dishes with a chilli logo, so we homed in on those choices. Chicken Chettinad, tempered with curry leaves, sun-baked red chillies and peppercorns,(three chillies). I ordered Aloo Udaigiri potatoes braised with coriander, cumin and Bikaneri spiced chillies. The Dal Makhani, slowly simmered black lentils came in a small, highly polished brass bucket, complete with handle, filled to the brim and decorated with a swirl of fresh cream came to the table - quite delicious. A portion of Steamed Rice escorted everything.'* DBAC. 12-2.30 & 5.30-11; Fri-Sat: 12-11.

Eastcote

NAUROZ
219 Field End Road   020 8868 0900

This restaurant means 'new' in the context of new year etc. But owner Raza Ali is an old hand; he specialises in creating new venues, then selling them. (Five Hot Chillies, Mirch Masala, SW16 & 17 and Karahi King, Wembley). All have good pedigrees making them popular venues for the locals who tell us how much they enjoy it. *'Nauroz is a family concern attracting Asian families. All fresh food, including vegetables. This time they seem to have settled. Which is great for Eastcote. Authentic food, beautifully prepared, served in a spartan 'works canteen' kind of setting. Excellent quality and value.'* DT. *'Friends 21st birthday dinner. Open kitchen, which offers you the chance to see how the food is prepared. a little bit of theatre is always a good thing. Delicious food, value for money.'* LS. Another LS visited and agreed. *'I stumbled upon this restaurant during a business trip. I travel a lot and consider myself some what of an expert!. The food I ate was delicious and great value for money, all freshly cooked that day. It was extremely busy and had a great atmosphere.'* LS.

Edgware

HAANDI   PUNJABI   TOP 100
301 – 303 Hale Lane Edgware, HA8 7AX
0208 905 4433   www.haandirestaurant.com

Sister branch to Haandi SW3 (see entry) managed by Ferdinand Muhanand has the same tasty Punjabi cooking with an African twist at a much smaller price point. Everyone likes the Kake di lamb on-the- bone, Asian style (and there are always plenty of local Asians in there.) is juicy aromatically flavour chunks of meat in a garam masala gravy. Also the Sag Paneer was a fine rendition. Service charge: 12.5%. Wed-Sun: 12.30-3 & Mon, Wed Thur: 5.30-11 (to 11.30 Fri & Sat from 6 Sun). Branches: London SW1, Nairobi, Kampala, Dar es Salaam & Sudan.

KABUL CITY   AFGHAN   BYO
34 Station Road, Edgware, HA8 7AB
020 8952 6036   www.kabulcityrestaurant.co.uk

It features traditional Afghan dishes from Mantoo to Qabili, charcoal grilled barbeques as well as side dishes including Bamia and Sabzii. In addition, There are vegetarian meals such as the Vegetarian Asshak and many other Vegetarian Platters. For those unfamiliar Afghan food before, not to worry! The Kabul City Restaurant offers brief descriptions for all menu items so that you can best find what you are looking fThough not related, it has a very similar menu to Ariana 11 (see London NW6) though at considerable lower prices. Av prices: Lunch: £15; Dinner: £26. 12-11.

REGENCY CLUB   PUNJABI KENYAN ASIAN
21 Queensbury Station Pde, Edgware   HA8 5NR
020 8905 6177   www.regencyclub.co.uk

Spot the yellow awnings and floral window boxes announcing the long frontage of Rahul Sharma's Regency Club. Usefully located between Meera's Pan House and Maruthi Asian grocers, it was established in 2002 and

THE Regency CLUB

Impressive, Sophisticated, Distinctive and Award Winning

www.Regencyclub.co.uk

welcomes non-members, to *'enlighten and elevate people's experience with our culinary delights, premium beverages and excellent customer service'* [sic their website]. As for the food: *"If you're looking for a change from your normal curry house then look no further - you have landed on gold. Yes the place is busier than a church, yes the service can be a bit up n down but the food makes up for all of that and then some. Always fresh and bursting with flavours, I'd love to meet the man marinating those wings and give him a high5. The chilli paneer (aka the acid test of an Indian Club) is the best I've ever had in London, the wings are annoyingly addictive as are the lamb chops, the meshkaki which is the Swahili word for Lamb Tikka is honestly even better than the famous ones in Nairobi or Dar es Salaam. If you have room for mains then more power to you but I feel that starters are were the real magic is as BBQ style cooking is part of East African culture. Don't go down for a relaxing meal as you will have to wait for a table and then turn it over quickly, but if your after flavour then welcome home!'* Sidgi. *'The best Indian food outside of India'.* SY, Stanmore. Takeaway available. Tue-Th: 12-2.30 (Fri-Sat: to 3); Mon-Th: 6-10.30 (Fri-Sat:to 11) ; Sun: 12-10.

YOU SAY OK

EDGWARE: TASTE OF RAJ 221 Deansbrook Road, Edgware, HA8 9BX 020 8906 8911
ENFIELD: CHASE SIDE INDIAN 135 Chase Side, Enfield ,EN2 0PN 020 8367 9979 www.chaserestaurant.co.uk Commenced trading in 2002 under Aktar Hussain. has many restaurants to his credit. Duck Tikka £8; Village Style Begoon £7, (okra). 6-12 & 12.30-5 Sun. *Branch: Tikka Cottage, Hot House and Bengal Spice, all Hertford.*

MEHEK 424 Hertford Rd, Enfield EN3 5QS 020 8443 1844 www.mehekcuisine.co.uk Cheerfully modern, curryhouse run by Ashik Miah. Branch: Bombay Spice, 201, Ordnance Rd, Enfield Lock, EN3 6AB. T/a only. 5-11.
FELTHAM: TAJ MAHAL High Street, 8 Cavendish Terrace, Feltham, TW13 4HE 020 8890 2347.
HARROW: JAFLONG 299 Northolt Rd S Harrow HA2 8JA 020 8864 7345 www.jaflongrestaurant.com Est 1991 Curryhouse menu. Mon-Fri: 12-2.30 (Sun -3) / Sun-Fri: 6-11.30.
JAI DURKA MAHAL 64 Station Rd, Harrow, HA2 7SL 020 8863 3593
SHAHI NAN KABAB, 64 Station Road, North Harrow, HA2 7SJ 020 8424 0600

SHREE GANESHA   GUJARATI VEGETARIAN
4 The Promenade, Edgwarebury Lane, Edgware, Middx. Branch Surya

See details on branch: 59 Fortune Green Rd, London, NW6,.

ZANZIBAR   PUNJABI/KENYAN
113 High St, Edgware HA8 7DB   020 8952 2986

Opened 2001 by married couple, Sameer and Sheetal Malik in a converted pub with decent beer in a large, bright dining room serving Punjabi/Kenyan-Asian food. Packed with Asians and filled with Bangra sounds. 'The decor is basic, with plainwooden tables,mostlywhitewalls and some rather odd, glittery wallpaper on one wall. Service was friendly and good. Bhindi, which most Indian restaurants overcook to a mush; was light and still had distinct texture. Garlic naan was well made, as was a paratha. Sweet Lassi was excellent, again a very simple thing but so rarely done to its best. Plain rice was impressive also, the grains distinct, cooked just right. I was impressed by the technique shown by the chef, who learnt his trade in the Taj Group. To be able to cook rice this well, and good bhindi, immediatelymarks himout asway above the norm. Portions are almost absurdly large. The waiter said at the end "oh, we could have done half size portions for you"whichwould have been great but was a bit late by then. I paid £40pp' AH: AndyHayler.com review.Mon-Fri: 12-3 & 5.30-11; Sat; 12-11, Sun. 12-10.

Harrow

BLUE GINGER   PUNJABI
383 Kenton Rd, Brent, HA3 0XS
020 8909 0100   bgrestaurant.com

Blue Ginger Restaurant & Bar Whisky Lounge, to give it its full name, gives the clue that it's a favourite with well-healed Asians, who love their whisky. It's open to all, of course and the *'sports bar with a penchant for all things Bollywood features comfortable, laid back leather seating'* [sic]. The recently expanded Dining Hall, complete with waterfall, has a more formal setting and is usually packed with Asian families. The menu is in two sections: Indian, featuring dishes from the northwest Punjab region to Goa and the south and Hakka Chinese, which is adapted to an Indian palette meaning spiced up. It includes many Thai & Chinese favourites as well as fusion. Food: Tue-Sat: 12- 11.15, (Snacks only 3- 6); Sun; 1-10.30.

CONNOISSEUR CUISINE OF INDIA
FINE DINING TOP 100
37 High St, Harrow-on-the-Hill, HA1 3HT
020 8423 0523   www.theconnoisseur.org.uk

It's near the School, right up on the hill. Once you've found a parking place, admire the views overlooking London. Proprietor Sonny Walia and his team ensure you get a warm and professional welcome. Chef Ramesh Honatha trained at India's Sheraton Group. *'He's attractive and single – girls should try to book a table in the kitchen!'* DBAC. [Last time I go there with my wife, Ed.] *'Piaz Ke Pakode, gram flour coated crisp onion slices, sprinkled with chat masala, a large plate of crisply fried onion Bhajias as most know them arrived with a neat pot of coriander chutney – delicious. Pat loved his soft shelled crab, which came with a small salad of cubed tomato, onion and cucumber. Lachadar paratha was light and buttery. Aubergine, the smallest, plump baby aubergines, smothered in a spicy sauce. Chicken with pepper, lovely and spicy. Portions are generous.'* DBAC. Tu-Fri & Sun: 12-3 Tues-Fri Tu-Sun: 6.-11; closed Mon. Branch: 702 High Rd, N.Finchley, N12 9PY.

EASTERN FIRE SRI LANKAN & S INDIAN
430 Alexandra Av, Rayner's Lane, S Harrow, HA2 9TW
020 8866 8386

Local south Asian families adore its comfy decor, friendly service and accurately cooked, inexpensive vegetarian and meat dishes. Starters include fish cutlets or lamb chops or chilli pakora. Devilled dishes are a specialty with choice of meat, veg or seafood pan-fried in spices and onions . Curries such as kormas and bhuna and biryanis are there, but the S Indian & Sri Lankan dishes are the highlights such as Sri Lankan noodles.plus a few Malaysian dishes. Av meal price: £12.Mon- Thur: 6-11; Fri-Sat: 12- 12 (Sun: to 11).

MAZAR AFGHAN
3 Headstone Drive, Wealdstone, Harrow, HA3 5QH
020 8427 9999   www.afghanirestaurant.co.uk

It has an excellent selection of authentic Afghan food. Though not related, it has a very similar menu to Ariana 11 (see NW6) though at considerable lower prices. Afghan food has roots to Indian though with lighter spicing (see p71), for example Dopiyaza (Dashi) is spiced meat with onions. One way to try it is their set meals, eg: Mazar 1: Qabili Palow (rice with carrots, raisins, almonds and lamb), Mixed Kebab,Montoo (steamed mince-filled pasta), Ashak ditto with leeks, Kofta (meat balls), or Qurma (mild spice meat dish) , Sabzi (veg) or bamia (okra), Naan, Salad & Soft Drink. £25(large portions serving 2-3). Mazar Mix Grill: Lamb Kebab, Chichen Kebab, Shami Kebab, Montoo, Kofta or Qurma , Sabzi or Bomia, Naan, Salad & Soft Drink, £49, serves 3-4. 11am till late.

RAM'S SURTI   GUJARATI VEGETARIAN
203 Kenton Road, Harrow, HA3 OHD **TOP 100**
020 8907 2022   www.ramsrestaurant.co.uk

You would imagine that every regional Indian cooking style now has a home in a restaurant somewhere in London. Yet here is another one – Surti a style of vegetarian cooking from Surat, Gujarat's main seaport city. Surat was where the English first landed in India in 1608, although this has no relevance here, not to say they must have eaten Kadhi (see below and p72) which passed into language as 'curry'. Your editor's first chef-training was fromGujarati chef, Sat Gupta. He was fromBaroda, but his wife was fromSurat. Themost memorable piece of advice she gave me was not to cook green vegetables in iron vessels or they will turn black. Let me set the scene: Gujarat has many vegetarians, and many superb restaurants in Wembley and Leicester. Gujarati cooking is mild and slightly sweet, using yoghurt and gramflour in many guises accompanied by fluffy rice, puffy puris, wonderously-cooked vegetables, sweet pickles and tempting puddings. Some Surti cooking differs in detail, especially with its use of green ingredients: green onion leaves (leela kanda) green garlic leaves, green moong lentils, fresh fenugreek and coriander leaves. The Surti Vaghar is a cooked mix of garam masala, red chilli, ginger and garlic. Favourite dishes include Lachko, a cake made from toovar dhal, turmeric, ghee and water served with sev and green chilli & onion chutney. Pattice, a potato rissole with astuffing of coconut, chilli and sev. Patra a kind of Swiss Roll made from colcasia leaves on which is spread a spicy paste, rolled into cylinders, steamed sliced and fried. Ram's is a plain, white-walled café. The food is typically Gujarati sweet, though Surti chilli hot.Many typical vegetables were on the menu: such as beans, plantain, karela (bitter gourd), okra, purple yam (they turn out a good rissole version of this) and red and yellow, sweet potatoes (sakkarkan). Undhiyu is probably Surat's national dish. It contains all the above and typically has Muthias (deep-fried besan dough and fenugreek leaf). Dahi Kadhi (turmeric-gold yoghurt & gramflour-based curry with ginger, curry leaves, mustard seeds and red chilli, appears with several vegetable options. A good rice dish is the ghee-laden Khichadi (rice and lentils). Prices are more than reasonable, A la carte main courses from £4. The Thali meals offers a good choice of items, £5 lunch, £9 dinner. The ultimate choice is the £22 set meal of unlimited food and soft drinks. Service ch 10%. 12-3 & 6-11. *Branches: Vijay NW6 and Satay, Uxbridge.*

SARAVANAA BHAVAN SOUTH IND VGTN
403, Alexandra Av, Rayners Lane, Harrow HA2 9SG
020 8869 9966 www.saravanabhavan.co.uk   )

2nd (2008) of a new chain of 5 south Indian vegetarian cafés. Capacity 80. See London E12 for menu & details. Cash pref. No licence. Mon-Th: 11am-10.30/Fri-Su: -11.

Hounslow

HEATHROW TANDOORI
482 Great West Road, Hounslow, TW5 0TA
020 8572 1772   www.heathrowtandoori.com

So you need a bog-standard formula British Indian, despite all the gorgeous authentic dives all around. This is the place to find it. *'Another business trip to London and another visit here. The door was opened by a Nepalese waiter, big smile and warm "Good evening Sir". Showed me to a table, brought menu and lager immediately. Managing owner, Meojanur Rahman popped over for a chat. Chicken Tikka Bhuna £7, beautifully served in a white ceramic pot and comprised large thick slices of smoky breast meat in rich, piquant sauce. Mr Rahman says he adds more chilli when the weather is cold! Highly recommended.'* TE. Sun Buffet: £9, children half price. T/a: 10% disc, £10 min. 5.30-11.30.

KARAHI MASTER LAHORE
PAKISTANI (HALAL)   BYO
795 London Rd, Hounslow, TW4 7HT   020 8572 2205 www.karahiexpress.com

40-seater opposite Hounslow Bus Garage run by Mohammad Akmal. Specials include: Roast Lamb Leg £17.50, or, if celebrating with friends, Stuffed Whole Lamb £100 sounds great. Lunchtime specials for £5.95. BYO is allowed, 1 bottle per person. A free drink to Curry Club members from Mr Akmal – cheers! Del: £15 4m. 12-12. *Branches: 746 Uxbridge Rd, Hayes, UB4 0RU 020 8848 9845; 296 Farnham Rd, Slough, SL1 4XL 01753 825649.*

Ruislip

RARA NEPALESE
528-530 Victoria Road, South Ruislip HA4 0HB
020 8845 7094 www.rarafood.co.uk

Rara Lunch buffet pictured below by Noms. £5.50. Sat 12-3pm & 5.30-11. Sun 12-10. Details see London, SW5 branch.

**Entries as chosen by you
Agree? Disagree?
Something missing?
Something wrong?
Tell me: pat@patchapman.com**

RUISLIP TANDOORI   NEPALESE
115 High Street, Ruislip, HA4 8JN 01895 632859

52-seat restaurant in black & white with flowering trees, Nepalese handicraft, pictures and a beautiful golden Buddha, which is, we're told, 'the main attraction apart from the Nepalese food' by owner KB Raichhetri who might give you a disc if you show him this Guide. Sun buffet c£10. Del: £15 min, 2-m. 12-2.30 & 6-12.

YOU SAY OK
HAMPTON: MONAF'S 119 Station Road, Hampton ~ 020 8979 6021. Named after its owner, Mr A Monaf. 10% T/a disc. Hours: 12-2.30 / 5.30-12. Branch: Sheesh Mahal.
HARROW: SAFARI PUNJABI/KENYAN ASIAN 14A Broadwalk, Pinner Rd, Harrow 020 8861 6766. Another pit-stop, this one is a bit daunting from the outside (dark windows – like stretch-limos) but once inside it's all go (if a bit dark) with Asian families having a good time on above average Punjabi Kenyan food (hence its name and decor). 6-12 Mon-Th; 1-12 Fri-Sun
HARROW: SANGEETHA SOUTH INDIAN 196 Kenton Rd, Harrow 020 8907 9299. Part of a south Indian chain. The dosa are light and yet satisfyingly chewy, their stuffing redolent of curry leaves, green chilli, coconut and mustard seeds. Their sambar and rasam had the right degree of tempering, piquancy and flavour. If my wife doesn't get hiccoughs when she sips her rasam, it ain't hot enough. On this occasion she did. Service: an inexplicably weeny 2.5%. 11-10.30.
HARROW: SARAVANAA BHAVAN SOUTH IND VGTN 403, Alexandra Av, Rayners Lane, Harrow HA2 9SG 020 8869 9966 www.saravanabhavan.co.uk 2nd (2008) of a new chain of 5 south Indian vegetarian cafés. Capacity 80. See London E12 for menu & details. Cash pref. No licence. Mon-Th: 11am-10.30/Fri-Su:-11.
HOUNSLOW: MIRCH MASALA. PUNJABI/KENYAN ASIAN 101-105 High St Hounslow, TW31QT 020 8572 2668 www.mirchmasalarestaurant.co.uk One of seven branches with identical meat, fish and veg menu. See SW16 for full details.

SPLENDIDLY INDIAN, SUPERBLY SMOOTH

Southall

From a single acorn (the long-gone Maharaja), there grew an astonishing number of sweet/snack centres, cafés and restaurants on South Road and the Green, but mostly on the the Broadway, the main artery through Southall. Expansion westwards continues, where its unexpected bonus is a pleasing growth of Sri Lankan suppliers. These places cater primarily for their indigenous Asian population, a generally peaceful mix of Indian and Pakistani Sikh and Punjabi carnivores, enhanced by East African Asians and most recently, Somalis. If you are none of these, do not feel inhibited from entering. Everyone is treated equally and all are welcome. Some venues are licensed and modern, aiming at the younger Asians. Others are café-style and unlicensed. At all of them you'll find good, authentic cuisine in straightforward, functional eating-houses, at realistic prices. The food is served from early morning to late night, fast and fresh. Here we examine our (and our correspondents') favourite eating holes:

BOMBAY 177

177 The Broadway, Southall UB1 1NN 020 8560 4646

It is modern and trendy inside and out – all black and white paint and stained wood. There is a bar on which to prop yourself up on (if you can elbow the proprietor's friends out of the way who seem to treat the place like their local pub), a big TV for entertainment, many framed pictures of 'stars' and a party room which always seems to be full of beautifully sari-ed ladies having a roaring time with a booming disco and disappearing trays of steaming food being carried upstairs by some gormless youth. The menu is small but that's OK, with all you really need listed. The waiter noticed me gaping at the TV, turned over to Eastenders and put on English subtitles! Good value wine list. Enjoyable. £10-20 per meal and drinks.

BRILLIANT   AWARD WINNER

72-76, Western Road, Southall, Middlesex. UB2 5DZ
020 8574 1928   www.brilliantrestaurant.com

The Brilliant is owned by Gulu and Kewel Anand and is one of the UK's most popular Indian restaurants Kewel was awarded our Lifetime achievement Award in 2007. The decor is Africal themed in orange, black and white, paying homage to the family's Kenyan background. They escaped the troubles in 1975, having to leave behind their successful Nairobi Brilliant and set up as a 36 seater on part of the current site. Today it has spread into two further shopfronts and now seats 250, with a further space upstairs. While Gulu and Kewel still oversee the running of the Brilliant, the mantle of carrying the restaurant's success into the future is passing to a new (third) generation of the Anand family. Gulu's daughter Dipna, (pictured below) is overseeing the menu. Shankar, her younger brother, is now GM. Both have inherited a passion and understanding of Indian food. If only more sons and daughters got into the lucrative trade of their fathers, instead of playing

doctor and lawyer. On a cold and rainy May evening your editors visited with young neice, Celia and nephew, Harri. We were warmly greeted by Gulu. Our smartly laid table, with starched white cloth and sparkling cutlery, was tempting as it displayed the new and delicious range of, 'Brilliant Chutneys and Pickles and a plate, stacked high with Papadoms. Starters included Chilli Paneer, pan-fried chunks of home made Indian cheese with onions and fresh capsicum. This dish was new to Celia and Harri. However, Harri is a confirmed meat eater and was quite suspicious of the idea. Celia, however, is now a paneer convert! she loved it! Gulu, spotted that we hadn't ordered a portion of their signature dish, Brilliant Butter Chicken, it was very succulent and we all enjoyed it very much then along came another suprise starter - a beautifully decorated plate of, Papri Chat - a crispy snack with chickpeas, low fat yoghurt and tamarind chutney. Our mains were beautifully presented on a custom made stand, holding our individual choices in gleaming brass karahis - a stunning display, and we all experienced a 'wow!' Masala Chicken in a Kenyan-style sauce; Karahi Chicken tossed with fresh red and green capsicums in a thick masala sauce, and side dishes. All were delicious, as was Pilau Rice with fresh green peas, imbued with fresh ginger, garlic and cumin seed, a mixed salad and a home-made yoghurt Raitha with cucumber. Harri chose Coriander Naan bread which was warm and soft. Celia chose Chapatti and after seeing it, worried that hers wasn't going to fulfil her needs, so eyed the Nan Breads. She needn't have worried. We all made a valiant effort to finish our banquet, but failed! Portions at The Brilliant are made for sharing, so are generous. No room for pudding, although we did have a quick look. There is a wonderful choice of authentic Indian desserts and quality ice-creams - perhaps, next time. .The Brilliant is a busy restaurant, so booking is advisable. Tues-Fri:12-3 & 6-11.30 (Fri-Sat-12. Closed Mondays. *See pages 42, 60 & 61.*

CHAUDHRY'S TKC   PAKISTANI   NO ALC
163 The Broadway,   UB1 1LR   020 8571 5738
www.tkcgroup.com   BREAKFASTS SERVED

In 1965 AF Chaudhry opened his Tandoori Kebab Centre (TKC), and has now added his name to it. There have been numerous copiers, not least the ones dead opposite. It is uncompromisingly Asian food style (Halal) and service, though, all are welcome, of course. It's inexpensive, and attracts regular custom several times a week at breakfast, lunch, tea or dinner. Full-length windows ensure that when walking past, you are attracted to the display cabinets containing all sorts of tempting snacks such as Pakora, Bhel Poori, Gol Goppas, Jeera Pani (cumin water), Tikki, Samosa, Indian sweets, etc. Alongside, and equally on show are the chefs, under head chef Farooq, flourishing skewers and breads in the Tandooris, Kebabs. Punjabi Karahis and curries are cooked to order, and are quite delicious. Inside is a clean and tidy, no-frills café-style restaurant, seating 66, with formica tables, and waiter-service. The menu says *'please specify your taste of chillies when ordering'*. Appetisers include: Reshmi Spring Lamb Boti, tender succulent pieces of lamb marinated in double cream roasted in the tandoor £4.50. Paneer Tikka, chunks of vegetarian cheese marinated with spices and baked in tandoor £4. House Specialities: Nehari, lamb shank in a spicy sauce; Chargha, roasted Punjabi spiced chicken, £6.50; Chappal Kebab, beaten mince steaks cooked and served on a sizzler, £4; Unique to TKC: Chinioti Kunnah from Mr Chaudry's home town of Chinoti, a slow-cooked, semi-dry meat dish. Try the Kulfi Faluda, a Pakistani version of the Knickerbocker Glory £1.80. Alcohol is strictly prohibited. It gets very busy with all age groups, from pensioners, mums and babes in the day to the young trendy ebullient fun-loving Asians at night and weekends. Recently they introduced a range of Indo Chinese (Hakka) dishes. Mr C proudly tells you that he caters for the Pakistan cricket team. 9am-Md'nt. *Branch: Jalebi Junction, 93 The Broadway, Southall.*

JALEBI JUNCTION   NO ALC
93 The Broadway, Southall, UB1 1LNI
020 8571 6782

Owner Abdul Chaudhury, manager Mr Shauket, and head chef Rassaq's bright and colourful venue appeals to the local young and trendy population. It is often full of chattering, bright young Asians babbling on in animated Southall cockney accents. A richly painted and decorated rickshaw can be seen outside on the wide pavement which enhances the environment. Also a cook makes Jalebis, those crispy, deep-fried squiggles, immersed in syrup, right there on the pavement. You can't get fresher than that, and if you've not seen it done, here's the only place in Britain we know of that does it on view. Great Pakistani curries and fresh breads are a big pull, along with snacks such as Samosas, Pakoras, etc. There is also a vast sweet counter to pile on the pounds (weight that is, not the bill). Starters include: Club Sandwich, finest chicken and lamb BBQ fillings £3. Shami Kebab, mince meat and lentil burger 50p. Dahi Bhalla, lentil flour doughnuts soaked in yoghurt £1.50. House specials: Masaladaar Raan, whole leg of lamb roasted in the tandoor with all the natural juices and flavours sealed within, a Moghul dish from Lakhshmi Chauk, Lahore, £15. Alcohol is strictly prohibited. 9am-11pm. *Branch: 161 The Broadway.*

KABUL   AFGHAN
1st Floor, Himalaya Shopping Centre, 65, The Broadway, Southall, UB1 1LB
020 8571 6878   www.kabulrestaurant.co.uk

Kabul is capital of Afghanistan so not surprisingly, this place opened in 2000 serving Afghan food. What is surprising and pleasing is that 12 years on it is thriving in an area no known for eating Afghani food. That said it does sell Indian food too. You go upstairs 50 seats to a brightly lit, aqua blue room. Starters include: Dogh £1.99, Afghani drink with cucumber, mints and salt; Mantu Gosht £8, lamb mince wrapped in steamed pastry, served with yoghurt and topped witch chick peas, Ashak £8 Vegetable wrapped in steamed pastry, served with yoghurt and topped with lamb mince or Vegetables; Bulani (2 pieces) £6, potato wrapped in pastry cooked on a tawa; Showr-Na-Khot £3, Chick peas with vinegar sauce and boiled potatoes , Korma Kachalo £4.50 with potato and tomato curry sauce. Gosht Banjan, £6.10, lamb & aubergine. Top of the bill is Do Pyaza £15 lamb with onions served with an Afghani style naan. Credit cards accepted. 12-11.

MADHU'S   BEST IN UK AWARD 2004
39 South Road, Southall. UB1 1SW
020 8574 1897   www.madhusonline.com

Opened 1980. Punjabi cuisine with Kenyan twist. In those days it was a friendly, busy cafe-style restaurant It is as different now as it could be, though it remains busy and

SPLENDIDLY INDIAN, SUPERBLY SMOOTH

extremely friendly. In our 2004 Guide we made it the UK's number one restaurant. We know that when we make a restaurant number one, all the celebrity critics beat a path to the door. We are flattered, but this being Southall, we waited for them to pooh-pooh our decision, but to a man and woman, they all agreed. But more importantly you, our contributors, agree too. Loads of you have visited and written in. But before we quote a few of your views, I must describe one of our own visits. A friend of ours is a top international sales person in a blue-chip computer systems company. We promised to take him and his wife to the UK's number one Indian restaurant. He had not heard of Madhu's before, and as we got closer, you could sense a slight anx in him. We managed to park outside (very rare) and the anx was visible. But once inside, the décor, setting, table lay-up, and service, not to mention the food and drink, literally blew him away. *'Incredible . We get a lot of foreign visitors come to our offices. Often they ask to be taken for a curry. Up till now, no one had been able to guarantee a prestigious local. Now we can',* he confided later. Here are some more comments: *'I need to say that food quality, service and ambience were as excellent as would be expected for a restaurant aiming to keep it's place right there at the top. My notes aren't copious but suffice to say, my visitor from the USA and I were suitably impressed with the magical Buzi Bafu and the other dishes that we ordered. Overall opinion – outstanding, will continue to recommend to lovers of authentic Indian food and will continue to come back as often as I can!'* C & MC. SO. *'We moved to the curry desert of Devon from Berkshire and regularly ate at Madhu's Brilliant, a great exponent of the skills of cooking great Indian food.'* AF. *'We were delighted to be told by Annan that the Iceland car park can now be used again for Madhu's for a visit to savour. Can you get him to disclose the Jeera chicken recipe please'* C & MC. Menu Snapshot: Masala Fish £10, fillet of Tillapia (fish from Kenya's Lake Victoria) cooked with a sauce, flavoured with roasted cumin seed; Makni Chicken £10, chicken pieces simmered in a mild gravy, enriched with butter and cream, aromatically spiced with cardamom and cinnamon; Methi Chicken £10, chicken pieces simmered with fresh and fry fenugreek in a traditional savoury Punjabi sauce; Karela Aloo £7, combination of bitter gourd and potatoes, flavoured with pomegranate; Dall Makhni £6, black urid lentils, stirred over a slow fire for many hours, flavoured with green cardamom; Hara Bhara Kebab £6 for six pieces, finger sized kebabs made from cottage cheese, green peas and fenugreek, flavoured with coriander (another one of my favourites); Aloo Papri Chat £5 for two, crunchy combination of fried wheat crisps (papri), boiled potato cubes, chickpeas, chopped onion in a fresh mint and tangy tamarind sauce, garnished with fresh coriander, served cold (delicious and again, one of my favourites); Mogo Jeera Fried £5 for two, fresh cassava pan-fried with roasted cumin and ground black pepper, or deep-fried and seasoned with spices (do try these really good); Boondi Raitha £3.50, yoghurt flavoured with cumin, ground black pepper and tiny crisp gram flour puff balls. House Special, Boozi Bafu, on the bone £18/£36, spring lamb chops, gently simmered in onion and tomato sauce, with freshly ground spices. 12.30-2.45 & 6-11.30, Tuesday closed.

MOJ MASTI KARACHI PAKISTANI BYO
37 Featherstone Rd, UB2 5JS 020 8893 6502
www.mojmasti.co.uk BREAKFASTS SERVED

Serving authentic Karachi Pakistani food and opened by Natasha Shaikh with husband Anees in 2005. Moj Masti seats 130 people in four modern-imaged rooms managed by Ali Ikram – the Kat-a-Kat food bar, Ju Ju`s jungle with water features, low lighting and greenery, an Oriental-style dining zone (upstairs) inspired by Pakistan`s northern border with China with has some influence on the country`s cooking culture (fried rice and chilli chicken on its menu). The fourth room is available for hire and has a dance floor. Moj Masti opens 8am for buffet breakfast (with such light dishes as lassi, halwa, chana, puri and aloo curries). Children will enjoy Lollipop Chicken with chips and salad. Head chef Asif Ali's starters include Udaan Lajawab £3.50, chicken wings BBQd in special sauce. Specials include Goan Fish £7.20, coley or kingfish grilled or steamed with Goan spices; Nihari Lamb £5.90, Haleem, £5.90, lentils, wheat and lamb puree; Lahori Fried Fish and Chicken Peer Bhai. The most remarkable dish is Kat-a-Kat (Tak-a-tan) a Karachi speciality dish, rarely-found in the UK, named after the clattering noise the chef's special tools make as he simultaneously chops and cooks the ingredients on a tawa (flat pan). This is Pakistani's version of Tepinyaki in that it is performed in front of its customers. Diners select their own chicken (murgh), minced lamb (keema) brains (magaaz), liver (kalegi) , kidneys (gurda) or lamb testes (kapooray) and vegetables. Then they watch as it is cooked in front of them. All Kat-a-Kat dishes cost £6. This is one dish you must try. No alcohol served but BYO OK no corkage charge. Del 3m, but no T/a. 8-12, main menu 12-12.

NARCIS KAPURI PAN
25 The Green, Southall 020 8574 5041

In the subcontinent, Paan, pronounced 'parn', is a massive industry, involving an army of 'paan-wallahs', traders, who prepare 'paan masalas' or mixtures, dispensing their wares in smart restaurants, at home door-to-door, or at street kiosks. Paan is best defined as a collection of edible ingredients, ranging from very bitter to very sweet folded, samosa-fashion in the paan leaf. Paan (Betel) leaf eaten in one mouthful, as a digestive after a meal. The darkish green, heart-shaped leaf is bitter, the mouth-feel coarse and the taste acquired. The ingredients include certain aromatic spices, for example aniseed, green cardamom, cloves and fennel, cucumber, marrow, watermelon and pumpkin seeds. To counter the bitter tastes, sugar crystals or sugar balls are used. The exact choice of ingredients is left to the customer. For a small price you can experience a major taste aspect of real India in Southall. And the Indophile can buy tablas and sitars at Bina Musicals, a few doors down the street.

SOUTHALL MIDDLESEX

NEW ASIAN TANDOORI CENTRE
BREAKFASTS SERVED   BYO   TOP 100
114 The Green, Southall, UB2 4BQ   020 8574 2597

There is nothing new about this venue, so why the name? It began trading in 1959 and is still known as The Roxy, although its English transport caff namesake closed over five decades ago. In its place came an Asian version of the same. There may be a queue, even outside the door, but it won't take long before it's your turn. Long glass counters display tempting Indian sweets and savoury snacks (Bhajias, Kebabs, Samosas, Aloo Tikki, Dahi Vasa, etc.), curries (Murgh Masala, on the bone, Bombay Potato, Sag Paneer, Sag Gosht and more, all cold but will be reheated in the microwave on request), Chana Dal, Rice (Plain, Pullao and Biriyani) and breads. *'Pick up a tray and tell the chap behind the counter what you want and whether you are eating in or taking out. Portions are generous and I have to restrain myself from over-ordering. When you have paid (cash or cheques only), take your tray to the other room and seat yourself.'* DBAC. *'The absolute curry experience, should be compulsory to visit! Sample the vast range of dishes on offer, all authentic and served up in a no-nonsense style. We ate vast quantities of food. Service with a smile, staff friendly. Highly recommended.'* DB. They also serve a wonderful chutney, sticks of carrot, slices of onion, embalmed in a tamarind and yoghurt sauce, delicious. You can BYO (but please ask) though they do sell Cobra. Fresh fruit juice and Lassi are available. They don't take credit cards, hardly surprising as your meal will be under a tenner. You can get an early Punjabi breakfast: try Mango Lhassi (as good as any smoothie) with a lentil dish eg (Kabli Chana) and bhatura, large deep-fried bread like a large puri, on which you sprinkle sugar, all washed down with Indian tea. Ask before BYO. Also does Punjabi breakfast. 8am-11.30 (to 12 Fri-Sun).

OMIS RESTAURANT   TOP 100
1-3 Beaconsfield Rd   UB1 1BA 020 8571 4831
www.omisrestaurant.co.uk

Established way back in 1976 as a tiny caff, by Mukesh Kharbanda and partners. Mukesh himself cooks north Indian and Kenyan Asian curries. Smart plastic tables and chairs and tiled floor make for a clean and tidy restaurant, but it's the freshly-cooked food you go for. Omi's seats 80, and you rarely need to spend more than a tenner for a fill-up. The front stands slightly back from the pavement, making room for parking for 6-8 vehicles. A short menu above the counter describes what is on offer, along with the Specials of the Day. Typical dishes are Karahi Lamb, boneless £5; Saag Lamb, on the bone £4.75 boneless £5.50; Chicken Tikka Masala, boneless £5; Amritsari Fish £4; Specials: Maki Di Roti & Saag, available Thursday to Sunday, £4.25; Lamb or Chicken Biryani £6; Satya's Special Lamb or Chicken £6. Aloo or Gobi Naan £1.75; Mooli (white raddish) Paratha £1.50; Bhatura 50p. Gulab Jaman or Rasmalai 75p. Since we

were taken here years ago by Indian journalist KN Malik (*'I want to show you Indian food at its best'*), we can safely say this is the Indians' Indian restaurant. We love Mukesh's food and adore his idiosyncrasies. Licensed. Del: small charge. Omis is high in our TOP 100. 11-10.30pm; to 11 Sat; to 9.30 Sun.

PALM PALACE   SRI LANK / S.IND TOP 100
80 South Road, Southall, UB1 1RD   020 8574 9209

Sri Lankan/south Indian, a scarce resource in the UK, Managed by Ruban and Paul brothers who opened it in 2000, the look is polished wooden floor, biscuit coloured wallpaper and smart high backed wood, metal and maroon suide chairs and peach tables with waitresses in black uniform as friendly as ever. Their service, though a tad slow is always with a flourish. It is marginally busier than before, but I said it before and I'll say it again: Southall's Asians are a conservative lot – but the if-it-ain't-Punjabi-it-ain't-edible view is slowly changing. Even Sanjay from Madhu's is a convert to Palm Palace. And, as we say every time, so it should. My bench mark crab curry from an early ownership has never matched, but it's still an exciting dish, especially fired up to incendiary level for those of us who cannot do without chilli. There's nothing like picking and sucking out crab meat from legs and shell and dousing it in rich Sri Lankan gravy. Messy shirt-sprinkling stuff, yes, but a slow, pleasurable experience, which is a contender for my desert island luxury. 12-3 daily; 6-11 Mon-Thur; 6-11.30 Fri-Sun.

YOU SAY OK

CHANDNI CHOWK   SNACKS & SWEETS
106 The Broadway UB1 1QF   020 8867 7200 www.chandnichowkrestaurant.com 12-2.3 & 6-11.30 daily. *Branches: West Dulwich, SE2 branch for details. Dagenham Essex.* **CHHAPPAN BHOG   SNACKS & SWEETS** 1 The Broadway, UB1 1JR 020 8574 760 www.chhappanbhog.co.uk An Asian sweet shop, (Mithai), est 1992 in Lucknow by Ravinder Gupta and now here. 'Chhappan Bhog' was an ancient Hindu royal get-together at which the attendees would enjoy Indian sweets such as Burfi (fudge) and Halva. They sell 56 sweetmeats and snacks. *Branch 145 Ballards Lane, Finchley, N3. 020 8371 8677, Pinner and Hounslow.*

DELHI WALA   PUNJABI VEGETARIAN 11 King St, Southall, UB2 4DG   020 8574 0873 UK Punjabis are largely carniverous. In fact 40% of the Punjabi population are vegetarian, as is Deli Wala, serving robust curries like Methi Aloo, Aloo Ghobi Methi, Sag Paneer and Mattar Valor – Pea and Bean Curry. The food is very savoury and fenugreek leaf (methi) and mustard leaf (rai) are virtually staples. 10-10.

GIFTO'S LAHORE KARAHI   PAKISTANI BYO 164 The Broadway, UB1 1NN 020 8813 8669 www.gifto.com *'The Lahori leg of lamb was pre-ordered and so special. How they get the flavour so deep into the meat I know not, but the dressing and marinade were excellent and tasty right through. Pretty upmarket after its revamp, though still soft drinks only. (the Cobra came from the "cousin's" shop next door)'.* C & MC. Open all day. *Branch Gifto Express, 147, The Broadway Southall. 020 8843 0101.*

MEHFIL   PUNJABI 45 The Green, UB2 4AR   020 8606 8811 www.MehfilHotel.com   Near Southall station. It has 31 rooms and a bar and a 24 hour porter. The licensed restaurant serves above-average Punjabi food and Tandoori items, is friendly and has parking facilities, useful in Southall. Avg pp: Lunch: £16, Dinner: £25. Hours: 12-3 & 6-10:45; 11.45 Fri & Sat

PUNJABI KARAHI 175 The Broadway, Southall   020 8574 1112 Once you get towards the Hayes end of Southall's

COBRA — SPLENDIDLY INDIAN, SUPERBLY SMOOTH

Omi's

Restaurant and Caterers Est 1976.

TOP 100 Rated in this Guide since 1992.

1-3 Beaconsfield Road,
Southall,
Middlesex UB1 1BA

info@omisrestaurant.co.uk
www.omisrestaurant.co.uk

020 8571 4831
or
020 8571 7669

Upstairs private dining room seats 75

PAT CHAPMAN'S CURRY CLUB TOP 100

Broadway you are spoilt for choice of Karahi Kebab houses. The menu and concept, prices and hours is identical to the others on the block and is just as worthy of your visit.

SHAHANSHAH VEGETARIAN & SWEETS 60 North Rd, Southall UB1 2JL 020 8574 1593 Since 1984 Gill Baljinder (manager) and Johl Sarbjit have specialised in north and south India vegetarian cuisine in their tiny 30 seater. Samosas and sweets are made on the premises, so you can be sure they are fresh. Set dinner £5. Sun lunch £4. *Branch: Shahanshah Vegetarian, 17 South Rd,.*

SUDBURY: FIVE HOT CHILLIS PUNJABI BYO
875 Harrow Road, Sudbury 020 8908 5900 A cheap and cheerful caff. The clientele is largely Asian, and the atmosphere is intensely friendly. Meat and Chicken on-the-bone burst with flavour. They take credit cards. Unlicensed. BYO corkage no charge. 11-11.

TWICKENHAM: ATITHI 27 York St, TW1 3JZ 020 8744 3868 www.atithi-indiancuisine.com *'Pretty food and pretty tasty too'* RCF. 12-2:30 & 6-11. Sun: Closed

Sunbury-on-Thames

INDIAN ZEST BEST BOUTIQUE RESTAURANT
21 Thames St, Sunbury, TW16 5QF 01932 765000
www.indianzest.co.uk

When their Indian Zing (W6) took off into profitability during 2005, chef Manoj Vasikar and his manager partner Bhanu Pratap opened this venture. See their story and ethos in the London W6 entry. Set over two floors, it's divided into a number of dining rooms. The 70-seat main area is the Colonial room, which opens on to a private patio (with seating for 35 on warm days). Upstairs, the 35-seat Polo Suite is decorated with historical photos from archives of Indian libraries depicting the sport. The Regal Room is available for parties of up to 15 and also benefits from an open-fireplace and dedicated butler. The décor is designed to revive the Old World charm of the Raj clubs, with opulent fabrics, antique furniture and exposed wood. Manoj likes to blend Indian ingredients with modern techniques and flavours and all his tried and tested favourites are here. Starters include Vegetable Bhanavla – Manoj's version of an onion bhaji, a dish from his native Maharashtra, unusual in that it is first steamed and then griddled; Vegetable Bhanavla and Mussel Rasam. Main courses include dishes such as Monkfish Tikka; Tropical Vegetable Kofta and Lotus Leaf Curry; Nawabi Lamb Sali; Karawari Fish Curry,from India's west coast with an unusual flavour of the spice (trifala) only native to that area; Tandoori Artichoke and Paneer with a rich spicy gravy of cashew nut and roasted vegetable sauce; and Jumbo Prawns marinated in yoghurt, pomegranate seeds and dill griddled and served with onion, green & tomato relish. Amongst the desserts, which fuse British and Indian influences, are Tandoori Figs; organic Apple Muesli Crumble; and Mango, roasted coconut and saffron Kulfi. The food is complemented by an enticing wine list created by sommelier Vincent Gasnier designed to match Manoj's light and contemporary cuisine, including an Indian Sauvignon Blanc from the renowned Sula Vineyards in the Nashik Highlands, near Mumbai. Av price: 3 courses: £20 exc wine. Service: 10%. Parking: 30 cars. 11–3 & 5.30-12. *Branch: Indian Zing, London W6.*

Twickenham

TANGAWIZI TOP 100
406 Richmond Rd, Richmond Bridge, E. Twickenham, TW1 2EB 020 8891 3737

Mr and Mrs Meghji opened in 2004, its name giving no clue re cuisine. In fact Tangwizi is Swahili for 'ginger', (the couple are Kenyan Asians). 'The dining room is narrow and long, with upmarket furnishings: black wooden tables with inlaid fabric, clever lighting, walls in purple and orange with backlit panels. Waiters are in smart uniforms and the service is efficient and friendly. The chef is from the ill-fated W1 Yatra went and he is joined by a tandoor chef from the famous Bhukara in Delhi. My Chicken Tikka was six very tender, large pieces, which had taken on the marinade spices, served with a few smears of mint sauce. Tandoori Prawns were also very delicate, in this case the marinade being coconut-based. A little glass of Mango Lassi followed. Prawn Biriani did not have the traditional pastry top, nonetheless had superbly fragrant rice, cooked beautifully. There were not too many prawns, but other than that the dish was most impressive. Bhindi, a great test of a kitchen, was very good indeed, dry and retaining its texture with no hint of greasiness. Makhni Dhal superb, made with kidney beans as well as lentils, and is just the same as at Bhukara in Delhi, with great texture and vibrant flavour. Both naan bread and paratha were very good indeed. This is Indian cooking at a very high level indeed (not the bought in desserts). £45 pp for meal and house wine'. AH: Andy Hayler.com Review. 6-11, Sun.

TASTE OF MOGHUL TOP 100
47, York Street, Twickenham, Middlesex. TW1 3LP
020 8892 9841 www.tasteofmoghul.com

The 70 seater is brightly decorated with, large pieces of art on salmon pink walls, velvety blue seating, and white table linen with blue napkins. The entire frontage is plate glass doors which open to allow for alfresco dining on the pavement. 'We started with a good selection of Popadoms 50p, with the, 'Five Pot Chutney Tray £2, Cachumber, Imli, Mint Raitha, Mango Chutney, and a rather good, Mixed Pickle, with cubes of red carrot. Manager Abdul Rokib, passed us menus, which were bound in deep tan leather - very nice. After much discussion, we all decided to share everything and so chose different dishes. For our starters, Abdul brought us Onion Bhaji £2.55 two large flat and crispy discs arrived with side salad and lemon wedges. Hash (Duck) Tikka £4.50, tender pieces marinated in yoghurt with Indian spices and barbecued in a clay oven – just wonderful! top quality, with not a scrap of unwanted matter, perfectly marinated, barbecued and melted in the mouth - delicious! 'Reshmi Kebab £3.25, minced lamb with herbs and spices, wrapped in a lightly spiced omelette in a very attractive square. We all enjoyed this dish very much. Paneer

COBRA — SPLENDIDLY INDIAN, SUPERBLY SMOOTH

TASTE OF MOGHUL

Taste of Mogul
45-47 York Street
Twickenham
London
TW1 3LP

020 8892 9841
020 8892 3610

We at *Taste of Mogul* invite you to experience a kaleidoscope of fragrances and flavours unique to our establishment.

Special Sunday Buffet
Eat as much as you like
Adults: £7.95   Children £4.95
Between 12.00pm till 3.00pm

Monday to Wednesday Offer!
Buy One Main Dish
Get A Second For Free
*Eat In Only
(cheapest dish free (excluding King Prawn Dishes))

Thursday Night Banquet!
5 COURSE MEAL Only £11.95
FOR RESERVATION PLEASE CALL
020 893 9841/3610
*Eat In Only

Open seven days a week including bank holidays.

Mon - Sun:
12:00pm - 2:30pm
5:30pm - 12:00pm

Tikka £6.50 was four huge pieces on a sizzling plate! It was amazingly good, a must try dish. Our main courses were Almond and Coconut Butter Chicken £6.95, chicken tikka cooked with almond, coconut milk, yoghurt, butter and special aromatic spices, garnished with almond flakes and cashew nuts.' A rich and creamy dish, reminiscent of a classic Moghul White Korma. Emperor Akbar, when living at Fatehpur Sikri, (the city of Victory), had a chef who could cook a different Korma for every day of the year. This dish would not have been out of place. Chicken Dhansak £7, sweet, sour and hot flavour I immediately got hiccups, so had to resort to the glass of water trick! Thoroughly enjoyable. Panggas Beguni £8 - marinated fish fillets lightly fried in butter, then cooked in medium spices with baby aubergine. I was a little unsure that I would like this dish. However Abdul insisted that is was very good and that we would enjoy it - he was right! The baby aubs had been sliced longways, with their skins and stalks on, so the flesh was firm. The fish had been cut into individual fillets and cooked very carefully, so they too, retained their shape. The sauce was thick, as described in the menu, but delicate, so not to overpower the aubergine and fish, and lastly, Dham Dham Chicken £8, cooked with onions, tomatoes, green chillies, mixed peppers and yoghurt, which was lovely but not as chilli hot as we were expecting. Other dishes sincluded, Saag Prawn £6.25; Vegetable Curry £3, a good combination of vegetables including mushrooms and chickpeas. I can say, without a doubt my Kulcha Naan £2.50, stuffed with mixed vegetables was the best stuffed bread that I have ever tasted, it was soft, light and fluffy with a thrilling spiced vegetable filling, just delightful! Sunday Buffet 12-3pm, adults £7.95 kids £4.95. Thursday Banquet: 5 courses £11.95. T/a: 10% discount, £10 min. Delivery: £12 min. 12-2.30 & 5.30-12·

Wembley

For Asian produce, cafés, restaurants and atmosphere Wembley is in our view as good as Southall. Unlike Southall, its large Gujarati/East African population gives Wembley food a different (predominantly vegetarian) taste from Southall. We observe that the Gujaratis are spreading further afield (to places like Harrow for example) and as with Southall, their places are being taken by south Indian, Sri Lankan and Somalis. There are still many good sweet/snack shops/cafés and restaurants crammed with Indian goodies, but now there is more choice. Here are your favourites:

FOCUS ON EALING ROAD, WEMBLEY
Going north from nearby Alperton tube station.

CHANNAI DOSA SOUTH INDIAN & SRI LANKAN VGTN 3 Ealing Rd, Wembley, HA0 2AA 020 8782 8822 Corner site: pure veg. No credit cards. No licence. 10:30am-11pm. See London E12 for details.

TULSI IND VEG 22 Ealing Rd, HA0 4TL 020 8900 8526 tulsirestaurant.co.uk

GANA S.INDIAN/SRI LANKAN 24 Ealing Rd HA0 4TL 020 8903 7004 Authentic Sri Lankan food including the celebrated Kotthu Roti (strips of chupatti interspersed usually with a spicy minced meat (keema) curry. Here it is more akin the Brum's Tropical Balti, in that the kitchen sink goes in: '*very special sir*', said the waiter – lamb, beef, chicken fish and prawns. And it was too. No credit cards. Set lunch £4.50 House wine £7. 10-11.

KEBABISH NORTH INDIAN 40 Ealing Rd, Wembley, HA0 4TL 020 8795 2656

PAAKWAN SOUTH INDIAN V & NV 44 Ealing Road Wembley, HA0 4TL 020 8902 0660

SURAJ SWEET MART 44A Ealing Road Wembley HA0 4TL 020 8900 1339

NAKLANK SWEET MART 50b Ealing Road, Wembley, HA0 4TQ 020 8902 8008

LAHORE GRILL PAKISTANI 58 Ealing Rd, HA0 4TQ 0871 075 5536

SAGAR SWEET MART 99 Ealing Road Wembley Middlesex HA0 4BP 020 87951734

SAKONIS JUICE BAR & VGTN NO ALC 129 Ealing Road, Wembley, Middlesex 020 8903 1058 www.sakonis.com. Alcohol not allowed which seems not to deter from its popularity as its longer hours (breakfast!) and expansion proves. This founder branch is now enormous, with its conservatory extension. It's family-run by Gujaratis Kenyans who offer dishes such as Chinese vegetarian noodles and Bombay Sandwich, white sliced bread with spicy spreading as well as Sakoni's authentic Indian items (Dosai, Vadai, Utthapam et al), in a pleasant and informal atmosphere. 9am-11 & 12-10. *Branches: 116 Station Rd, Edgware; 6 Dominion Pde, Station Rd, Harrow; 180 Upper Tooting Rd, SW17.* **DADIMA XPRESS** GUJERATI AHMEDABAD PURE VEG 228 Ealing Rd, Wembley 020 8902 1072 www.dadimaxpress.co.uk Gujarati owner Montey Patel is from Ahmedabad (Mahatma Gandhi's birth place). Dadima (granny in Gujarati) is family run, and I wouldn't be surprised if Granny herself was in charge of the kitchen. Gujarati food is sweet and mild. Those like it 'hot', will find the food of Ahmedabad, and of Dadima, quite robust and spiky. '*We cook it with Lal Masala (mixture of red spices')* including chilli, turmeric & coriander. Try Gran's Thali for a filling selection of Dadima-style cooking. Vegcurries, rice, dhal, yoghurt, pickles and puris from £4. 12-3 & 5-10 Mon, Wed-Fri; 12-10 Sat & Sun.

MARU'S BHAJIA HOUSE VGTN KENYAN ASIAN NO ALC 230 Ealing Road, Wembley 020 8903 6771. Maru's was opened by yes, Maru in 1984, and it was one of the road's first, and as

Dadimas Thali

they say the first is often the best. Their Bhajias are the real thing, and they are even spelt correctly, rather than the formula Bhaji. Try Potato Bhajias, served with tamarind (imli) chutney as a real treat to die for. Strictly no alcohol allowed. 12-9.30pm.

CHOWPATTY KUTCHI GUJARATI 234 Ealing Road Wembley Middlesex HA0 4QL 020 8795 0077. The owners come from northern Gujarat, in the desert area which borders Rajasthan, where the cuisine is called Kutchi. Try Kadhi, Gujarat's national soup-like dish of turmeric, gram flour and yoghurt, or Bajra Roti, Rajasthan's millet bread, or Kutchi specialities like oBaingan Oro (aka Baigan Burtha, the smokey grilled, mashed aubergine dish). Other Gujarati breads (not usually encountered in the UK) include Missi Roti maize flour bread with red chilli and Methi Thepla a wheatbread with fresh fenugreek leaf. Veg Kebabs are masterly, as are the Pakoras. On offer are Thalis £4-£9 are great as is the satisfying set buffet (11-4 Sun) at just £4.50. 'Chinese' items too, but there is enough original choice on the menu to leave that for another time. Service: 10%. Del 5m over £12. Mon-Fri: 11-3 & 5.30-10; 11-11.30 Sat; to 10 Sun.

PANACHAND PAN HOUSE & SWEET MART 238 Ealing Road Wembley Middlesex HA0 4QL 020 8902 9962

MARUTI BHEL PURI VEGETARIAN 238a Ealing Rd, Wembley

SPLENDIDLY INDIAN, SUPERBLY SMOOTH

020 8903 6743 Serving inexpensive melt-in-the-mouth delights, such as Dosas with Sambar and, of course, the namesake Bhel Puri. Try their Karahi Corn-on-the-Cob. *'When there is something on at the Stadium, a set dinner buffet is provided. Dishes were full of spices and excellent. Service was very friendly.'* AN. 12-10; closed Tues.

ASIAN KARAHI PAKISTANI 272 Ealing Road, Wembley 020 8903 7524. Small venue (25 seats) with the usual range of Karahi /Haandi style cooking. At the weekend, they offer some really authentic stuff, not for the faint-hearted: Nihari – marinated leg piece (shank) of lamb served with a spicy gravy, Paya – lamb trotters with thick gravy, Brain curry, Haleem – an almost gruel-like mash of crushed wheat and lamb and dishes all of very high quality.

ROYAL SWEETS SWEET & SNACKS 280 Ealing Road, Alperton, Wembley, Middlesex, HA0 4L 020 8903 9359. Branch of the operation run by Lord Noon.

JASHAN VEGETARIAN 1-2 Coronet Parade, Ealing Road, Wembley, Middlesex, HA0 4AY 020 8900 9800

MOMO HOUSE NEPALESE 2 Glenmore Parade, Ealing Road, Wembley, HA0 1PJ 020 8902 2307 www.momohouse.co.uk

FOCUS ON WEMBLEY HIGH ROAD
And if this is not enough at the T-junc at the north end of Ealing Rd, turn left onto Wembley High Road for:

SARASAS INDIAN SEAFOOD 545 High Road Wembley, HA0 2DJ 020 8900 0998

SARASHWATHY BAVANS PURE VEG S.IND 549 High Road, Wembley, HA0 2DJ 020 8902 1515 www.sarashwathy.com Branch: 70 Tooting High Street, SW17 0RN 0208 682 4242

MASTI 576-582 High Road, HA0 2AA 020 8782 2252 www.masti-wembley.com. Specialises in seasonal fish and vege dishes. Live bangra bands, popular DJ's, karaoke nights.

POOJA COTTAGE NEPALESE 305 Harrow Rd, Wembley 020 8902 4039 Est '85 by T Moniz, as 45-seater is Nepalese. Baban in the kitchen cooks up unusual delights which include Mariz (pepper) Chicken £5.95, Nepalese Chicken Bhutuwa, highly spiced £6.25. Chicken Chowla, tandoor-cooked with ginger/garlic £5.95. 'Not terribly impressed with the food.' rm. 'Very impressed with the food.' ct. Hours: 12-2.30/ 6-11.30.

At the T-junc at the north end of Ealing Road, turn right onto Wembley High Road (heading east) for:

SARAVANAA BHAVAN PUNJABI VEG NO ALC 531 High Rd, Wembley 020 8795 3777 No-nonsense, no-alcohol, no-haut-décor caff which serves substantially good Punjabi and Chinese veg food at non-nonsense prices.11-10. Branch: Manor Park, E12.

CHANNAI DOSA SOUTH INDIAN MEAT & VEG 529 High Road, Wembley, HA0 2DH 020 8782 2222 www.chennaidosa.com One of a chain of 14. See London E12 for menu & details.

CHETNA'S BHEL PURI 420 High Road, Wembley 020 8903 5989 A large, very popular vegetarian licensed restaurant with vegan dishes. *'You often have to queue here. We waited on the pavement until they called out our number, but it is well worth it. They do deluxe Masala Dosas, and a great Vegetarian Thali main course. Their Bhel Puri is gorgeous, with its crispy, crunchy textures, and its tart, hot and savoury tastes, and there is a variant called Aloo Papdi Chaat'.* JM. Gujarat and S Indian dishes plus pizzas reflecting the craze, not only amongst Wembley Asians, but in Delhi and Bombay! 12-3 & 6-10.30.

HANDI RESTAURANT AFGHAN, BRAZILIAN, ASIAN 414 High Road, Wembley.

TASTE OF LAHORE PAKISTANI 417 High Road, Wembley

JEEVAN'S 381 High Rd, Wembley, HA9 6AA 020 8900 0510

KARAHI QUEEN PUNJABI 332 High Rd, Wembley, HA9 6AZ 020 8900 1312

Elsewhere in Wembley

GURKHA VALLEY NEPALESE 305 Harrow Road, Wembley, HA9 6BD 020 8902 4039.

KARAHI RAJA PAKISTANI BYO 195 East Lane, Wembley, HA0 3NG 020 8904 5553 Established in 1993 by Mushtaq Ahmed. Restaurant seats 150 in two rooms. Pakistani curries are cooked by B Hussain. House specials include: Haandi Chicken – chicken on the bone cooked with herbs, tomatoes and spicy thick sauce. Paya – lamb trotters Lahori style. Vegetarian dishes: Karahi Egg, scrambled egg, tomatoes, coriander & green chillies. BYO allowed, no corkage charge. 12-12.

KARAHI KING PUNJABI BYO 213 East Lane, Wembley 020 8904 2760 Fabulous food, Kenyan Asian curries, kebabs and Tandoor items being showily prepared by the on-view chefs in their open kitchen. Try Mogo Bhajia a pakora of sweet potato complete with a super imli (tamarind) chutney, or the fabulous tandoori (including the breads) and note the love-it-or hate-it taste of Kala Namak (black salt). If you do get past the starters, try the curries for meat-eaters and vegetarians. Methi Murgh divine. No credit cards. No corkage, BYO. 12-12.

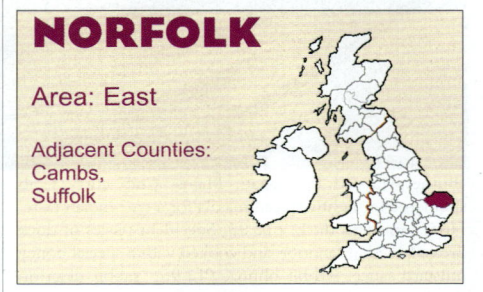

NORFOLK

Area: East

Adjacent Counties:
Cambs,
Suffolk

Great Yarmouth

PLANET PAPADUM
5 Marine Parade, NR30 3AH
01493 330777   www.planet-papadum.co.uk

'With its seafront location, modern décor and colourful paintings of Bollywood dancers, PP has quickly become by far the best around. Manager Naz runs the front, while Head Chef Khan works his magic in the kitchen, producing food to suit all palates – a subtle, fragrant Lemon Grass Chicken for those who like things flavoursome but not too spicy; a zingy, tangy Balti Chicken Peshwari for those in the mid-range; and a fiery, explosive chilli chicken for those who prefer things sizzling hot. Vegetable sides are particularly good, making this a popular place for vegetarians, and if you're lucky enough to visit on a quiet night, Khan might have time to cook you one of his many 'off menu' specials – just let him know how hot you like it and let him do the rest! Khan, has should stick far more of his own dishes on the menu, but I guess like lots of otherss, he feels obliged to serve the chicken tikka masalas, kormas, etc, rather than presenting people with a menu where they might not recognise anything.' SA. 12.30-3 & 5.30-11.30.

Norwich

MERCHANTS OF SPICE
32 Colegate, Norwich NR3 1BG
01603 660128   www.merchantsofspice.co.uk

The attractive, detached former Merchants of Colegate, a 1760 coaching inn pub has reopened (2012) as a smart curry house. Affsor and Juned Ali have invested £80,000. glass side of the kitchen so you can see the chefs at work Chicken Kathi Rolls, £4.50, Succulent pieces of chicken tikka, a tangle of onions, tomatoes and herb

Spice Paradise's enormous 2 foot Masala Dosa with Coconut Chutneys, Sambar in the tumbler and Rasam in the steel pot.

chutney, wrapped in chapati. Mains: Crab curry Crab simmered in slightly spiced masala for a true indian taste. Honey mustard duck, £12.95, Succulent pieces of duck breast baked in tandoori and cooked with a special honey mustard sauce. Rabbit bhuna, £12.95, rabbit tikka on the bone cooked with garlic, ginger, tomatoes green peppers and nicely spiced. Price check: Pop 70p, PR £2.60, CTM £8.95, Naan £2.30. Sun-Th: 5.30-11 & Fri-Sa: to 12.

SPICE PARADISE SOUTH INDIAN
41 Magdalen Street, NR3 1LQ
01603 66601   www.spiceparadise.co.uk

Two menus: North Indian with favourite curries, Balti, Tandoori etc. They bill themselves as the only South Indian in East Anglia and this menu has a good selection such as Rasam, £2.95, consomée laced with garlic, tamarind and tomatoes. Starters: Mysore Bonda or Vada both £2.75. Dosa from £5.75; Travancore Fish Fry £5 king fish marinated then fried and served with salad; Crab Varuthathu £9, chef's signature dish cooked shell-on, with ginger, curry leaves, chillies & mushroom. Kappa & Fish Curry £9 spiced tapioca served with kerala fish curry; Nadan Lamb Curry, £6.75, a most popular Keralan dish, cooked with roasted coconut, great with Malabar parathas. *'I went for the south Indian and wasn't disappointed with a starter of Crab Thora (£4,95) and a main dish of Spicy Lamb Fry (£6,45). It appeared to be popular with local Indian community – a good recommendation.'* JP. Tues-Sun 5:30-11:30.

ZIN ZEERA
Boundary Road, Hellasdon, Norwich, NR6 5LA,
01603 408888   www.zinzeera.co.uk

A 200-seater opened in 2011 in the refurbished U-shaped building at the centre of a busy roundabout. Says owner Motin Uddin *'You can see in when you drive past. It looks spectacular from outside at night.'* And it's pretty zany from the inside looking out of the curved frontage onto endless traffic. Chef Anwar Khan cooks the familiar and the unusual eg: 'Aubergine Pittas, batter-dipped, deep-fried and served with

sweet lime chutney. Mains: Bengal Fish Platter, Pangaas, fish pan-fried and served with Indian-roast veg; King Prawn Biriani is finger-licking good, and Chicken Palok with spinach, garlic & onion & fenugreek was mopped up with a naan. We left impressed. The food didn't reinvent the wheel but it was well done and presented and the service made it an enjoyable experience.' Simon Parkin, Norfolk News 12-2.30 & 5.30-11.30.

YOU SAY OK
You might get a discount if you show them this Guide.

DISS TANDOORI 1 Shelfhanger Rd Diss ~ 01379 651685 Owned by Jahal Khan and M Ruhel in 1986.
DOWNHAM: DOWNHAM TANDOORI 56 High St, Downham 01366 386110. 40-seater opened 1996 by Abdul Ali. T/a: 10% disc. 12-2.30/6-11.30.
GREAT YARMOUTH: BOMBAY NITE 25a King St ~ 01493 331383. *'Rhongpuri chicken is a must for mint lovers, since it positively bursts with the stuff! Manager Naz ensures a friendly welcome. No one in your party need go home hungry'*. SA
KING'S LYNN: INDIA GATE 41 St James Street ~ 01553 776489
NORWICH: SPICE LOUNGE 8-10 Wensum Street, NR3 1HR 01603 766602 *'Deceptively large. The food was good.'* JP

NORTHAMPTONSHIRE

Area: Central East Midlands

Adjacent Counties: Beds, Cambs, Leics, Oxon

Brackley

DHAN SHIRI
10 Banbury Road, Brackley, NN13 6AU
01280 841846   www.dhanshiri.co.uk

'A splendid local' according to BB *'and located in a splendid detached house with a relaxed and friendly*

COBRA
SPLENDIDLY INDIAN, SUPERBLY SMOOTH

Dhan Shiri — INDIAN & BANGLADESHI CUISINE

A Truly Exotic Treat for your Tastebuds!

An opportunity to savor the true delights of South East Asian Cuisine!

- Bangladeshi Delicacies
- Special Banquets
- Sunday Lunches
- Licensed Bars
- Fully Air-conditioned
- Two Exotic Floors
- Great Atmosphere

OPEN MON - THURS 5.30 - 11.00pm FRI - SAT 5.30pm - Midnight
SUN 12 noon - 2.00pm / 5.30 - 11.00pm

10 BANBURY ROAD, BRACKLEY
Telephone 01280 841846 and 841830
www.dhanshiri.co.uk

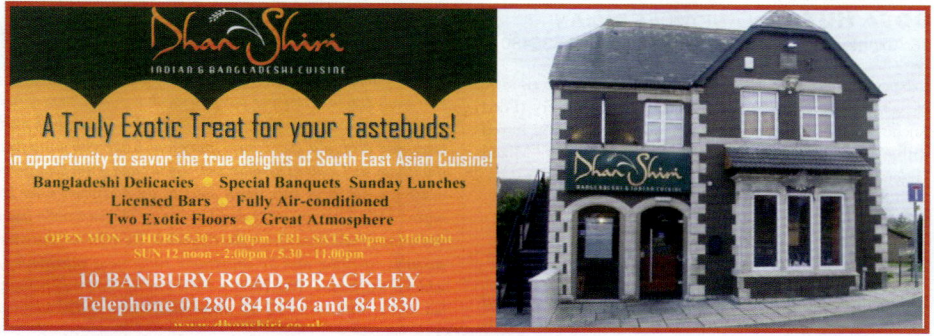

---

atmosphere'. The owners tell us they are passionate about their food. Their extensive menu carries all your favourite dishes plus some unusuals made with the very best ingredients and seasoned with authentic flavours. Starters include Onion Bhajee £2.50, Chicken or Lamb Sheek Kebab £3.25, Paneer Tikka Pakora £3.50, Lamb Sheek Chat, £3.95, King Prawn Butterfly £4.95, Thandoori [sic] Salmon £4.95, Garlic Crab £5.25 and Amli Duck, £5.25. Mains include Chicken Nehari £7.50, Gaust Laziz £7.50, Haryali Chicken Masala £7.95, Duck Kati Adrak, £7.95, King Prawn Delight £9.95, Chicken or Lamb Rezala £7.95, Kofta Special Handi £7.95, Murgh Ahm, £7.95 and Salmon Tindora £7.95. *'Pat, I'd love you to try their 'Lamb Misti Kurdu' it is consistently outstanding I always have it.'* SP. Steven Poole. The full range of favourites are on the menu. Dhan Shiri's experienced team is on hand to explain each dish. Sunday Special Buffet: 12 noon -2:30pm. Minimum order of £15 within a 5 mile radius, for delivery. Takeaway service. Min del order £15–5m rad. Sun Buffet -12-2:30/Mon-Th: 5:30-11 (Fri- Sat: 12).

Corby

CARDAMON   NEPALESE & IND TAKEAWAY
182 Gainsborough Rd, Corby, Northants. NN18 0RQ

Owned by Prince Sadik Chaudhury and Tipu Rahman (See Tamarind below), best seler dish is Tipu's Chicken Hariyo Kursani, a Nepalese dish, of chicken first marinated in green chillies and then cooked in a spicy sauce with fried chillies and yogurt. It is just one of a dazzling selection of specials. Sun - Th: 5-10.30pm (to 11 Fri-Sat).

Kettering

MAZZA
2, Kettering Bs Pk, Pegasus Ct, NN15 6XS
01536 524888   www.mazza-restaurant.co.uk

'On arrival despite the venue being very busy we were shown straight to our table and offered drinks, Pops etc were delivered promptly and were excellent. Waiter took our orders using a PDA which beams the orders to the kitchen. Overall a pleasant venue with excellent service and delightful ambience, offering something very different. Will visit again soon.' DL.

THE RAJ
46-50 Rockingham Road, Kettering NN16 8JT
01536 513606   www.therajrestaurant.net

Est 1992 in a two storied corner terrace building identified by its black marble fronatage. *'Smart waiters greet you. The 110 seat restaurant is downstairs and the Piano Bar is upstairs with white and black armchairs, a full bar and a tinkling piano. which seems to need attention at present but menu same as branch (see below)'* PM Largely formula menu with Specials eg: Jhinga Mossalada £14, marinated king prawns, tandoored then served with fresh onion, tomato, garlic and coriander; Sherabi Jalsha, chicken or lamb Tikka stir fried with onions, green peppers and spices blended in a rich, brandy sauce; Swordfish Maach, in a sauce with fresh herbs and spices; Lobster £25, whole lobster stir-fried with black bean, mango and chilli sauce, button mushrooms and steamed spinach, served with Raj spicy red onion fried rice. *Branch: Maharaja Northampton.*

Northampton

BOMBAY PALACE
9 Welford Rd, Kingsthorpe, NN2 8DE
01604 713899   www.bombaypalacerestaurant.co.uk

A full menu with specials such as Akbari Cham Cham, £11, large pieces of chicken tikka in a spicy sauce, served with pilau rice, vegetable bhajee, fried onion rings and salad. Meat Thali £11, chicken tikka, sheek kebab, chicken tikka mossalla, mutton bhuna, chicken dhansak, pilau rice, nan bread and salad. *'very generous portions, beautifully cooked, I couldn't finish it all . First class service. Will not leave it so long to return!'* DL. 5.30-1.30; 12 Fri & Sat

DANGS   VIETNAMESE CUISINE
205 Wellingborough Rd, NN1 4ED   01604 607060

Vietnamese curries are way different from Indian but it's on the Curry Mile and the delightful owner-chef Hao Dang is dubbed the city's "Curry Queen" *'She cooks spicy aromatic dishes including Vietnamese fish and chicken curries at her ground floor open kitchen with a 40 seater on the floor below. The Menu is refreshing and makes a nice spicy change from formula curry stuff.'* Paul Motley

DOSA HUT SRI LANKAN / S.INDIAN
18 Abington Square, NN1 4AA   01604 636480

Inexpensive vegetarian, meat and fish dishes. Rasam, consomée of ginger, black pepper & garlic, £3.50; Nethali Fry (Fried Anchovies) £3.50; Vegetable Kothu Roti hopped roti mixed with vegetable, onions & chilli, £5; Chettinadu Mixed Vegetable Curry, £4 .See page 75 for cuisine details. 5-12.

LAZEEZ   BYO
39 Barrack Road,Northampton, NN1 3RJ,
01604 622178   www.lazeez-restaurant.co.uk

Lazeez meaning 'delicious' has moderately priced food and service. Starters are from £1.75 av u£3. Mains include Jholokia Gosht £8, a highly spiced and extremely hot lamb speciality the hottest chillies in the world, Bhoot Jholokia Naga chilli, providing a fantastic fiery and tangy aroma. (They warn you it's extremely hot; or Bangla Egg Curry £8, strips of chicken in sauce enhanced withdried red chillies, diced potato, fresh tomato and aboiled egg. Baingan Kasthuri £7, includes fresh flash fried aubergine, lentils, chana lentils, coconut milk and curry leaves. BYO wine/beer no corkage charge but they charge £1.25 if you BYO soft drinks. That's only fair. 5.30-11.

The MAHA-RAJ-A
140-150 Wellingborough Road Northampton NN1 4DT
01604 637149   www.maha-raj-a.co.uk

It was purchased by 'larger-than-life' Raj Miah in 2009, hence the play on words. Its black marble exterior is adorned with golden graphics such as "Moet & Chandon". Inside is light, airy and modern with light wood tables and matching blue upholstered chairs and tan leather wall banquettes. *'My elderly Mother used to teach Raj and when we took her there he did her proud and made her feel really special. The menu has a good choice of favourites, and house specials. When we arrived Raj asked us to leave it them to choose which was just as well because they must have spent many hours in advance preparing our meal. After popadoms we had starters of various kebabs, potato pakoras, and onion bhajis. Mains were Raan, whole baked masala chicken, a fish dish, Dhal, Palak Paneer and veg dishes. Then came a large platter of fresh exotic fruits and ice cream; a superb finish to a more than excellent meal;they really did make a tremendous effort. We arrived about 7.30 and left at 1.30am'.* Paul Motley.

MEM SAAB   PUNJABI
357 Wellingborough Rd, Northampton, NN1 4EU
01604 630214   www.mem-saab.com

'The Memsahib opened in 2001 in the old Mansfield shoe factory and is owned and managed by Glaswegian Punjabis. It's spacious, light and airy with minimalist decor. The lounge boasts very comfy cream leather sofas. All the staff are smartly unpretentiously presented. It is very quirky to hear the Asian owners speak in a very broad Scottish accents like Billy Connelly. I went on Sunday for a buffet with the added bonus of Live Jazz. I have never been impressed with the e-a-m-a-y-l buffets as they tend to be very unimaginative. However, the Mem Saab however surpassed itself on every course. The starters consisted of a salmon and red snapper dish, seekh & shaslik kebabs, bhajis, garlic mushrooms, vegetable pakoras, chilled shrimps and pops with fresh homemade pickles and chutneys. The main course offered a mildly spiced garlic chicken, a rich lamb dish in a clinging spicy gravy with very large cubes of good quality lamb, a mixed aubergine and potato dish, ma-ki dhal, whole black urid dhal in a spicy buttery gravy and Kudi with gram flour dumplings, the Gujarati speciality with yoghurt and gram flour gravy, which I would never have dared order as the description never has appealed to me but I'm really glad I did try it. The sweet trolley had a vast array of fresh seasonal fruits plus Rasgullah. The afternoon was a very enjoyable experience and the unobtrusive background entertainment added to the pleasure.* Paul Motley. Meal average: £19 - £25 Mon-Sat: 6-11; Sun Buffet 12-4.   Branches: *Bedford & Leamington.*

SAFFRON
21 Castilian St, Northampton, NN1 1JS 01604 630800

Naz Islam owns the 60 seater Saffron. They do good Bangladeshi and Nepalese dishes such as Mitho Swadillo, chicken cooked with coconut milk, almonds, honey aadn saffron or Chicken Hariyo Khursani, with green chillies in a spicy yoghurt & chilli sauce. and Price range: £5 - £20. Weds 4 course £9.95. Th seafood spiecial £17. Sun-Th: 5.30-11.15 (to 12 Fri & Sat). Branches: *Tamarind and Taj Mahal.*

The Cobra Good Curry Guide is compiled using information supplied by you.
Agree?
Disgree?

Let us know your views, which ever they are. Only that way do we get it right.
email:
pat@patchapman.co.uk

COBRA
SPLENDIDLY INDIAN, SUPERBLY SMOOTH

Tamarind ★★★★★

**151-153 Wellingborough Road,
Northampton
NN1 4DX
01604 231 194
08448 000 170
www.tamarind-restaurant.com**

★ ★ ★ ★ ★ Tamarind ~ five star service ~ five star food ★ ★ ★ ★ ★

★ Tamarind offers you a gastromonic banquet of flavours with a unique menu highlighting new and exotic dishes from Bangladesh, India and Nepal.

★ Tamarind only uses freshly ground spices and finest herbs, the best cuts of meat and the freshest vegetables, all sourced locally where possible.

★ Tamarind is proud to advise that all dishes are cooked with the healthy option of minimal oil and ghee.

★ Tamarind also boasts a vast choice of vegetarian and vegan options.

★ Tamarind Chef-Patron, Tipu Rahman is one of the most highly awarded UK chefs.

TAMARIND CELEBRITY CHEF
153 Wellingborough Road, Norhtampton, NN1 4DX,
01604 231194 www.tamarind-restaurant.com

We went as guests of the house on a Monday night and we were amazed to find the place absolutely full. Who knows if it was papered; it created a buzzing atmosphere, and if Tamarind does this sort of business every night, it deserves a pat on the back. All sorts of N'thmptn VIPs dropped in to meet and greet us, Prince Chaudury and the delightful Hao Dang see above. A beaming Tipu Rahman emerged from the kitchen clad in chef's reds, and burst into flamboyant flow. Tipu is a curry industry character, and there is nothing he loves more than chatting about food, and the contribution he himself has made to it. *'Tamarind boasts too many awards to list'* says the website, *'you will learn about my developed skills and talents'* it continues *'and will also you on how I managed to achieve the title of 'the curry king'* [along with Lord Noon and yours truly. Ed}. Tipu has cooked for the Bangladesh PM, Ed Milliband and the Bangladeshi cricket team. Tonight it was for us and his full house. On the menu you'll find a long list of unusuals: Chicken Banjar, £3.25, with yoghurt, garlic, ginger, peanut, cheese and lemon juice with a touch cardamom; Chicken Karai £6, tikka pieces in herbs & spices; Cinnamon Duck, £7.45, Bangla Macher Malai, £8.45 tandoori grilled then finished in a special coconut sauce; Chicken Rai, £7.45, cooked with mushroom and mustard seed. Mon-Thur: 5-11.30; Fri-Sat: to12 (last orders 1 hr prior); Sun: Closed.

NORTHUMBERLAND

Area: North East

Adjacent Counties:
Borders, Cumbria,
Durham,
Tyne & Wear

Berwick-upon-Tweed

MAGNA   **TOP 100**
39 Bridge Street, Berwick, TD15 1ES
01289 302736   /www.magnatandooriberwick.co.uk

Jahangir Alamgir and Oliul Khan own this 80-seater family business. It has been in our Guide since we started it in 1984. *'And no wonder'* says Guide-reader Michael Fabricant, MP. Free car park 100 yards away. The building is impressive, made pretty by flower boxes. Inside is cosy, with inviting green sofas in the bar and the Magna's certificates, many of them ours, line the walls. *'A pretty restaurant with smartly dressed black-tie waiters.'* MF. Specials include: Murghi Mossalla, Ash de Bash and Chandee Dishes, very mild with fresh cream and mango. Shim Dishes, cooked with green beans.

'Once again I felt I had to put pen to paper. I feel my local, The Magna, still comes out on top for taste, quality, service, cleanliness, value and very polite friendly staff.' BA. 'My husband and I have been coming to this restaurant for many years. We never book a table, we just turn up. Always greeted pleasantly and politely and given excellent service while we are there. We feel fortunate to have the Magna here.' SS. 'Having spent the day visiting the many attractions, it is always important to have a good meal, in pleasant surroundings with good quality service and value for money - all is provided at the Magna. Staff always courteous, taking your coat and carrying drinks through to the table.' KR. 12-2 not Sun & 5.30-12.

Corbridge

THE VALLEY   A-LIST
The Old Station Hs, Corbridge, NE45 5AY
01434 633434   www.valleyrestaurants.co.uk

Corbridge station building in the beautiful Tyne valley, was built in 1835 for Stephenson's railway. It is no longer used as a station although it is on the important Newcastle-to-Carlisle railway line. Trains stop at Corbridge station throughout each day, but passengers do not use the old building any more. That is until Daraz (Syed Nadir Aziz) turned it into a stylish, upmarket Indian restaurant in 1991. Seats 80, car parking for 20 directly outside. A feature of which is a unique service, for parties of 10 to 80 from £32.50 a head, including return travel. Uniformed restaurant staff welcome you at Newcastle Central Station and escort you by train to The Valley. En route, choose four courses from the à la carte menu. The order is rung through on a mobile. Your starter is awaiting your arrival. 'It beats ordering a taxi.' GM. Of course, individuals can make their own way here and back by scheduled train – but beware a fairly early last train. Or, there is parking for 12 cars. Why not book your T/a by phone en-route, collect, pay and eat it, without leaving the train As for the restaurant, there is a reception room and 80 seats in four connecting rooms (one of which opens onto the eastbound platform). Decor is lush and Indian. And Chef Pervez Ahmed's menu contains all the CC (currinarily correct) favourites plus some good specials. 'Arriving at this impressive we studied the menu in the bar, complete with a photograph of Daraz, the owner and Pat Chapman. Were shown to a window table, we watched a train pull into the station, just outside the restaurant. Entertainment as well! Very impressive menu, had quite a problem deciding on main dishes. A memorable meal.' T&MH. Chef's Choice: seven course surprise (the only surprise being that the chef chooses your meal) dinner - £65 for two and £120 for four. T/a: 20% disc. Hours: 6-10; closed Sun. *Branch: Valley Junction 397, The Old Station, Archibold Terrace, Jesmond, Newcastle. and Valley Connection 301, Hexham (see below).*

VALLEY CONNECTION 3 Market Place, Hexham 01434 601234. Prime location in the centre of the market place, next to Hexham Abbey. Very smart inside. For details see www.valleyrestaurants.co.uk.

Hexham

DIWAN-E-AM
4- Country Mills, Priestpopple, NE46 1PH
01434 606575

Diwan-e-am was the exclusive meeting room in the Indian's Moghul palaces. So Mr Choudury's 86 seat venue, est in 1983 is aptly named. *'Pleasant decor and environment, friendly and helpful staff. Menu extensive, but no curry house inventions such as vindaloo here. Starters include the excellent Diwan Khata Mita Soup (garlic and lentils) and Mathu Vortha (grapefruit with chilli and coriander). Main course selection includes a wide range of duck and fish dishes. More expensive than the 'usual' curry house, but good value given the high standard of the meals.'* CF. House-style cuisine (staff curry) on demand for regular customers. You might get a discount if you show them this Guide. Takeaway: 20% discount. 5.30-11pm (Sun. 6.30-10.30).

YOU SAY OK
You might get a discount if you show them this Guide.
BEDLINGTON: FRONTIER KARAHI HOUSE 46 Front St, West Bedlington ~ 01670 820222. Hours: 5.30-1; closed Mon.
CORBRIDGE: CORBRIDGE TANDOORI 8 Market Square, Corbridge   01434 633676 SM Shahjahan's small restaurant est. 89 is above a bookshop. Hours: 12-2.30/6-11.30.

Morpeth

MANZIL TANDOORI
2b Oldgate, Morpeth, NE61 1LX   01670
515405   www.manzils.com

What would they do without this Guide, the restaurants, I mean. Their website fails to tell you where they are or when they open, let alone who they are. But that's why we are here for you. The opened in 1982 by the Clock Tower, in an attractive stone building, the inside of which is quietly elegant. Their menu is formula, with no surprises. Average two course meal price £12. They are open 12-2 (not Sun) & 6-12.

TANDOORI MAHAL
17 Bridge Street, Morpeth   01670 512420
www.tandoor-mahal.co.uk

Running neck and neck in the Morpeth popularity stakes, Suroth Miah opened his doors in 1980. The interior is white walls and red carpet, large red ceiling lamp. Food is served on large white oval platters, which shows off the vibrant colours of the food beautifully. Starters include: Milijuli Sabzi or Khumb Paneer mixed veg or mushroom cooked with cottage cheese, onionsand spices £3.50; Tikka lamb or Tikka Chicken Masala cooked with exotic spices, cream desiccated coconut and ground nutsVery mild and sweet. £7.95; King Prawn Sag, cooked with onions and spinach £9.95. Mon-Sat: 12-2.30 & 6-12; to 11.30 Sun.

COBRA
SPLENDIDLY INDIAN, SUPERBLY SMOOTH

NOTTINGHAMSHIRE

Area: East Midlands

Adjacent Counties:
Derbs, Leics,
Lincs, Yorks

the mint
Restaurant - Food - Takeaway

Clerkson Hall
Clerkson Street
Mansfield, Notts
NG18 1BQ

01623 659 911

Mansfield

The MINT TOP 100
Clerkson Hall, Clerkson Street, Mansfield, NG18 1BQ 01623 659911 www.themintindian.co.uk

Foysal Choudhry's Mint is behind the Railway Inn in an attractive black-beamed building. There is ample free parking alongside, and disabled access. The menu includes formula and signature dishes (the latter only available for dining in). Menu snapshot: Onion Bhaji £2.50; Lentil Soup £2.50; Aloo Tikka £2.80; Paneer Tikka, spicy & hot £3; Chicken Makhani £7.50 diced chicken with yoghurt cream, almond powder in a mild sauce, served with mango cream; Mixed Biryani £10.50, with chicken tikka, lamb tikka & mushroom, served with a plain omelette, cucumber & tomatoes and a vegetable curry; The Mint Karahi Chicken Tikka, Lamb Tikka & Tandoori King Prawns cooked with fresh garlic, onion & green peppers. Served with rice or naan Naan.£10.50; Rice £10.50; Poppadom £0.60; Plain Naan £1.90; Pilau Rice £2.00. 4 course meal: £11.95. and a wide range of exclusive Indian beers and wine (house red 750 ml £7.95, a very fair price). Free delivery service above £12; 15% discount for collect. Sun-Th:6-11.30; Fri-Sat to 12.

Nottingham
(includes Basford, Beeston, Mapperley, Radford, Sherwood, and West Bridgford.)

4500 MILES FROM DELHI
41 Mount Street , Nottingham, NG1 6HE.
0115 947 5111   /www.milesfromdelhi.com

Danny Punia owns this 4000 sq m former public house named after his family city, which is literally 4550 m from Delhi. The inside has been transformed internally and externally to include a ten metre high glazed atrium in which the bar is located. A halved motorised-rickshaw (tuk-tuk) gives a new meaning to wall-hanging. Suspended cylindrical stainless steel lights over the bar, a bronze staircase and solid oak and recycled slate flooring on which sit 130 Italian made chairs with bronze inlay work in the dining area overlooking an open kitchen. Chef Mahaneshwar Pal, previously with Delhi's Taj Palace Hotel has developed a North Indian menu that also includes a choice of set meals priced at c£20 per person. Popular dishes include Tikkas, and Seekhs, Aloo Tikkis and a selection of simmered curries cooked by the Dum Pukht pot method. (see p76). An open 'theatre' kitchen enables you to watch the chefs from Delhi as they work. 'Can you mention that restaurant is closed on a Sun, we made a trip there last weekend only to be disappointed.' JB. It is now open on Suns, but always ring first. Punia hopes to open further branches, naming each after its distance from Delhi and has plans to open Bristol, BS1 4ST 0117 929 2224

ANOKI TOP 100
Barker Gate, Nottingham NG1 1JU 0115 948 3888.
www.anoki.co.uk

Located in the heart of the historic Lace Market district, Anoki is very smart indeed with beautiful interior and artwork, the scene is set of by smart staff in Indian costumes, including the doorman. The food is well reported and menu details are the same as the Burton Derby branch (see pages208/9). Special Offer or diners arriving before 6:00pm and vacating by 7:30pm. Mon-Sat 5.30-11; Sun: 3:30-9:30.Branches Burton & Derby.

CHENNAI   SOUTH INDIAN
70 Long Row, Nottingham, NG1 6JE 0115 994 0769
www.thechennai.co.uk

Named after the South eastern capital city of Tamil Nadu, the ormer 'Madras', this smart upmarket, licensed

NOTTINGHAMSHIRE

60 seater opened in May 2010. The interior has carved booths, tiled floors, whitewashed walls and interesting photographs of south Indian architecture and women in beautiful saris. It serves a wide range of. south Indian meat and veg dishes. Let's hope it can keep afloat without resorting to CTMs and Vindaloos and dunderheads who don't realise what they're eating. Signs are good. It is frequently full with newly gained aficionados (so booking advisable). Because their food is 'something we have never tried before and it's wonderful'. HEG. Menu snapshot: Methu Vada, doughnut-shape made with urid dha; Idli, rice & lentil patties, steamed; Mysoor Bonda, potato masala mixed with mild spices, coated in besan flour batter and deep-fried; Gobi Munjurian, cauliflower coated in a batter and fried with onion and soya sauce. The above average £3 each and are served with sambar (lentils) and chutneys.Mains include Mutton Roll, cumin-flavoured snack-sized rolls made up of tender pieces of mutton & potato seasoned with spices; Chennai Special Fish, is boneless, marinated in a Chennai spice combination and deep-fried; Kozhi Chettinad, a south Indian speciality, chicken cooked with 23 different authentic ingredients; Nilgri chicken, marinated and cooked with turmeric, mint & spinach; Chettinad Crab Curry, fresh crab in shell (but cracked open for service), cooked in a chettinad sauce and flavored with authentic spices. Veg dishes include Paruppu Kuzhambu, Seasoned lentils cooked with turmeric, red chilies and coriander leaves and Palak Paneer, fried cottage cheese cooked in spinach gravy along with tomato and onion paste. Various Dosa. Mon-Th: 12-3:30 & 5:30-11; Fri-Sat: 12-11:30; Sun: 12-10:30. Last orders 15 mins prior.

The CUMIN   TOP 100
62-64 Maid Marian Way, Nottingham, NG1 6BJ
0115 941 9941   www.thecumin.co.uk

Sunny Anand and Exec Chef Shelley own the Cumin. Situated just a moment's walk from Market Square, on Maid Marion Way, the remarkable success story of the Anand family, originating from Nairobi, Kenya is told on page 259 see Brilliant and Curry Fever in Leicester page 240. Cumin is the new boy on the block. The dining rooms are on two floors, with 20 seats on the ground floor and 54 on the first. The overall look is sophisticated with polished oak floors, claret coloured chairs and banquettes and dark wood tables, smartly laid up with square charger plates, linen napkins in silver rings and stemmed glassware. Windows let in ample daylight. It's very inviting and usually busy, so booking is advisable. Although the menu carries many of the favourite dishes, *'these are cooked with those unique Punjabi flavours putting curry houses to one side'* RL. With his East African background Chef Shelley has incorporated some African tastes and ingredients – Starters such as Jeera Mogo pan-fried cassava battons with roasted cumin and black pepper or Masala FriedTilapia £7, freshwater fish found in Lake Victoria. Typical main dishes include Murg Mulabari £9.50, a delicately spiced chicken curry flavoured with coconut, curry leaves and mustard seeds,

Broccoli Baby Corn Tawa Masala; broccilli florets and baby corn tempered with garlic and chilli flakes tossed in an onion and tomato masala, and Goan King Prawn Curry £12.50 cooked with roasted coconut, coriander a& paprika. Drinks include East African Tusker Beer. Early Diner £13.95.Wed-Fri: 12-2.30; Mon-Thur: 5 to 11 (Fri-Sat to 11.30; Sun to 10.30). Last orders min 1 hr prior.

DESI DOWN TOWN
7 Hockley, Nottingham NG1 1FH   0115 950 2666
www.desidowntown.co.uk

Following on from the successes of Simla and Desi Express, Inti and his brother Jack have now opened the chic and stylish desi down town. it's laid back, with soft lighting and the chefs work in an open theatre kitchen. Menu snapshot: Veg Spring Roll £2.25, carrot, onion and sweet corn garnished with a touch of spices & wrapped in a crispy pastry; Chicken Pakora £2.95, chicken spiced and coated with gram flour & deep-fried; Malia Chicken, starter £3 main £6 marinated in ground almond, cream and white pepper, char-grilled; Lamb Bihari, starter £3.50 main £6.50, char grilled pieces of lamb fillet, marinated in spices and papaya; Nali Nihari Gosh, lamb shank on the bone, with a thick curry sauce topped with fresh ginger, coriander and fresh chilli. Krahi Gosht pieces of chicken cooked in a rich tomato sauce, with a blend of desi spices; Sagg Gosht, mustard leaf, spinach, dill and fenugreek, cooked with spices; Saffiad Korma Gosht onion and cream based sauce with butter and mild spices. All £4.95; Imly Cod, marinated pieces of cod fillet, deep-fried and drizzled with tamarind sauce. £9.95; Bindi Desi Okra cooked in a rich tomato sauce and garnished with coriander starter £2.95 main £4.25. 5.30-11.30. Branches: Desi Express, 11Radford Road, Hyson Grn, Not'm, NG7 5DU 0115 978 7872. www.desi-express.co.uk & Simla, 5 James St Kimberly, Not'm, NG16 2LP. 0115 945 9350   www.simla.me.uk;

EVEREST BHANSAGHAR GURKHA
NEPALESE   www.everestbhansaghar.co.uk
384 Carlton Hill, Carlton, Not'm NG4 1JA   0115 961 8355

Rana's aptly named Everest is located on the west side of the city.Krishna Kharel cheffed in Dubai's Five Stars. His menu offers formula curries but the Nepalese items are worthy of a try. For example: Chhoyla (Lamb/Chicken), £4.95; Sekuwa(Chicken/ Lamb/Duck, £4.95; Grukhali Chilli ChickenAll £4.95. Mains: All £8.30: Lasun Kukhura (Garlic Chicken); Palungo Chicken/ Lamb; Chicken/Lamb Bhutuwa; Hans Bhutuwa (Duck); Aloo Tama Karai, Potato & Bamboo shoot curry. Mon-Th:5.30-11.30; Fri-Sat:-12; Sun: 6- 11.

GURKHA KITCHEN   NEPALESE
Glaisdale Drive West, Nottingham NG8 4GY, England
0115 929 0194   www.gurkhakitchen.org

Over on the east side of the city is the highly rated Gurkha. Chef Andeep and his team cook regular formula curries and real Nepalese cuisine. Stareters include: Sano Macha £3.25, prawns in a light crispy batter served with salad & sweet chilli dip; Gurkha's Geda £2.95, mildly spiced meatball mixed with egg & coriander, pan-fried and served with yoghurt, dip and salad; Sekuwa £2.95, diced spicy chicken with crisp green papers and onion in sweet and sour coriander sauce with salad; Bhutwa £2.85 chicken coated in a spicy sauce; Chouwlya £2.95, chicken breast or lamb cooked in a spicy sauce; Kathmandu Chicken £6.65, festival dish of marinated chicken cooked with masala spices & cream; Lekali Chicken, £6.25 highly spiced dish with roasted coconut, mustard seeds & topped with red chillies!; Thulo Macha, king prawns and prawns cooked in a mildly spiced garlic & creamy massala sauce. Veg St Meal for 2, £18. Special Lunch £5.50: starter and played main of. Veg curry, rice or naan. Free deliveyr £15, rad 3 miles Mon-Sat: 12-2 & 5-11; Sunday buffet (Adult £9, Children £6, u5 Free) 1-10.

HAVELI
10 Attenborough Lane, Chilwell, Nottingham NG9 5JW   +0115 922 7778   www.havelifinedining.co.uk

The front is fairly average, but inside, the first thing that strikes you is the stunning outfits the smiling waiters wear. Bright red long kurtas with dupta scarf and turban, sparkling white 'pyjama' trousers and matching pointy-toed Alibaba shoes. The lounge has black leather sofas and beyond the restaurant -draped tables. The short menu is on the pricey side. Starters (10) include chilli fish £7.50, fresh cod tossed in a piquant chilli sauce; Onion Bhaji / Vegetable Pakora £7; Tandoori King Prawns £8.95. Mains (13) include Kasturi Murgh £12, chicken breast with mild and smooth ground cashew nuts and cream; Goan Sea Bass curry £16, fillet tossed in a blend of green chillies, cumin, ginger paste, tamarind and coconut milk; CTM £12; Veg dishes (9) £12 main, £7 side. Naan £3.50; Plau Rice £4. Mon-Sat: 5-10.30; Sun: 12.30-5.

KAYAL   KERALAN
8 Broad Street, Nottingham, NG1 3AL
0115 941 4733   www.kayalrestaurant.com

Kayal meaning a Kerala backwater, opened in late 2007 and has been very popular from the outset. is licensed and has extended its original dining room to a large 1st floor area on the street behind. Keralan snacks are displayed in glass cupboards. Starters include Kizhangu Kathrika porichathu £3 deep-fried, battered potato or aubergine slices, served with chutneys, Banana Boli £4.29, banana slices dipped in a batter of rice and chickpea flour with black sesame seeds, crispy fried andserved with peanut and ginger chutney. Vada £4; Masala Dosa £6, rice and lentil pancake with a traditional filling of seasoned potatoes, onions and peas. Mains include Cheera Erachi Curry, £9.39 chef's signature dish of lamb cooked in fresh spinach, aromatic spices, turmeric, red chillies and onions; Kappa Erachi £12.89, lamb cubes cooked with tapioca and aromatic spices; Thalasserry Mutton Biriyani £9.49 Keralan Muslim speciality of rice and mutton cubes baked in rich gravy to produce a highly aromatic spicy preparation. Desserts: Unnakkai £4.29, mashed plantain dumplings filled with coconut, raisins, and cashew nuts and served with Vanila ice cream; Semiya Payasam £3.39, vermicelli, milk, ghee and garnished with cashew nuts and sultanas. Lunch £6 weekdays includes 3 curries a side dish, rice and dosa with chutneys. Mon- Fri: 12-3 & 6-11. (Sat:12-11; Sun to 10). *Branches: Kayal Leicester & Leamington Spa*

LIME   BYO NO BAR   PUNJABI
4 Upminster Drive | Nuthall, Nottingham NG16 1PT
0115 975 0005 www.lime-restaurant.co.uk

Lime is a family-run 64 seater, with a Lahori flavour coming through. It is less than three minutes' drive from the M1/J26 and has amplefree parking, and a large open kitchen where diners can watch the Chefs, cooking the likes of Murgh Masala, slow-cooked chicken in a rich sauce of caramelised onions, garlic and ginger; or Mussalam, leg of lamb that serves 4, marinated for 24 hours then tandooried, as well as all the favourites and rice dishes. Finish off with either a traditional Indian dessert. Lime only serve low and non-alcoholic beers and wines so BYO with no corkage fee. Av price: £15- £20. Tues: 2 for 1. 5.30-11.

LALON RESTAURANT
A52 Radcliffe Road, Holme Pierrepont, Nottingham, NG12 2LF. 0115 994 0732

This 100 seater opened in July 2009 with a luxurious interior adecorated in deep rich colours It also boasts beautiful views over the lake, with large windows opening out towards the water. Recommended dishes include the Bemisal, £11, char-grilled Scottish salmon in a coconut, buttery tomato and lemon-grass sauce complemented by sautéed brown onions; and the Lamb Hyderabadi, £12.50, a very rich dish packed with stir-fried spices, coriander, yoghurt, tomatoes, garlic and ginger purée in juices of bay leaves, cloves and cardamom. There is also a wide vegetarian selection with Paneer dishes or Sweet Gobi £7.50 main £4.50 side, stir-fried butternut squash and cauliflower tossed with chilli and coriander; or Khumb Aloo, stir-fried wild mushrooms and potatoes in herbs and spices with puréed tomato. Mon-Sat: 5:30 to last orders 10; Sun: 1-8.

MEMSAAB
12-14 Maid Marian Way, Nottingham, NG1 6HS 0115 957 0009   www.mem-saab.co.uk

Naj Aziz sold his long-standing 150 seater to Deepak and Amita Sawheney, and Sanjeev Sachdevay. The menu is evolving to Punjabi flavours and exotic ingredients rather than curryhouse, so we hear. Starter examples: Tandoori Ostrich £8.50, locally farmed free range ostrich fillet infused with garlic and red chilli, unique to MemSaab; Aloo and Paneer Bhaji £4.25, lightly fried potato filled with paneer and sweetcorn, seasoned with coriander; Murgh Malai Boti £6.25, boneless, diced chicken leg marinated in cream, soft cheese and chilli, flavoured with garam masala;,Pan Fried Mussels, £8.50, Marinated in lemon juice, olive oil and garlic, served with fenugreek and saffron sauce. Mains include: Lamb Shank £17, slow-roasted with masala mashed potato, spinach and cardamon jus; Fillet of Beef Stack £17.50, charcoal-grilled beef tenderloin with masala gratin potatoes, lemongrass, coconut and chilli sauce; Baigan Bhartha Side £4.50, smoked aubergine cooked with tomato and garam masala Main £7.50; CTM £10; Dumpukht Lamb Loin (served with masala semolina tikki and saffron sauce) £16.50, slow-roasted lamb fillet stuffed with spiced spinach and paneer. Early Evening Menu created by Michelin Chef Atul Kochhar. Veg £13.50, NV £19. Sun- Fri to 6.30pm max 6. Mon-Th 5.30-10.30; Fri-Sat: to 11; Sun: 5-10. Last orders 1 hr prior.

MOGAL-E-AZAM   TOP 100
9 Goldsmith St, Royal Centre, Nottingham, NG1 5JS
0115 994 0856   http://mogal-e-azam.com

The 295 seat family-run Mogal-E-Azam opened in 1977 and is located behind the Theatre Royal and you may find many a star of stage and screen patronising the venue. It is theatre in its own right, with different decor themes in different dining areas, authentic decorated with Indian ornaments and rich colour schemes featuring deep reds, blues and luxurious gold. Classical Indian music adds to the atmosphere along with the friendly waiters dressed in traditional costume. The owner prides himself on the use of his mother's authentic recipes. Popular curries such as Biryani, Rogan Josh, Dopiaza and Korma, are available as are vegetarian dishes. The real stars are the specialities which feature dishes such as mackerel, monk fish, salmon, cod and either halibut or fresh tuna fried with green chillies, onion, garlic and coriander; or Akbari lamb tikka cooked with lean lamb with mushrooms and mango. 12-3 & 6-12.

SAAGAR TANDOORI
473 Mansfield Road Sherwood Nottingham NG5 2DR
0115 962 2014   www.saagarrestaurant.co.uk

Front of house is managed by Imtiaz Ahmed, leaving owner Mohammed Khizer to do his thing in the kitchen, assisted by Amjaid Parvaiz at his Victorian-style 98-seater on two floors est 1984. *'Been a regular eating at above since 1984 ! Was there last night - still SUPERB - nead I say more !! Prawn poori, lamb tandoori et al.'* HW. Menu Snapshot: Kashmiri Chicken Tikka £5, topped with Kashmiri sauce; Chicken Anguri £11, mild and fruity, cooked with pineapple, banana, prunes, grape juice and fresh cream; Nizami Masala Chicken £10, cooked with nuts, coconut, yoghurt and sesame seeds; Butter Chuppati £1. Spinach and Yoghurt Bhajee £4.50. T/a: 10% disc. Discount for Guide readers at lunch times. 12-2.15 & 5.30-12.

SPICE TAKEAWAY   TOP 100
459 Westdale Lane, Mapperley, Nottingham, NG3 6DH
0115 962 3555   www.spicetakeaway.com

Farooq Younis is the proud owner of this takeaway to the north of the city, and is the nephew of the Saagar's Mr Khizer (see previous entry). He opened it in 2000 and has built up a loyal customer base. They deliver within a 10 mile radius of Mapperley, NG3 with an average delivery time under 45 minutes. Farooq promises it *'always piping hot. It saves you time and there are no pots to wash up afterwards! You are most welcome to call to place your order or pop in to the shop and we will prepare your meal while you wait.'* Most-ordered dishes are Chicken Korai, £5.95 and Spice Special BMG, £6.45, and Tandoori dishes. Delivery: Min order £10. Order and pay on line or via the website or phone in. The average delivery time is under 45 minutes. Look out for discounts and if you mention this Guide, Mr Younis will give you a generous 10% discount. Hot Meal Deal for Two (Poppadums and Chutney for 2, any 2 Starters, any 2 Mains, 2 Pilau Rice andany Naan Bread, £17.95 collection £19.95 delivered. Valid on every Monday, Tuesday and Wednesday. *'Excellent food, was so nice to have a Takeaway curry that wasn't swimming in fat, enjoyed it immensley we're looking forward to our next Takeaway'.* 5-11.30.

Sutton-In-Ashfield

NILA   KERALAN
18 Brook Street, Sutton-in-Ashfield NG17 1AL
01623 55 1010   www.nilarestaurant.co.uk

Starters Vegetarian Uzuhunnu Vada, fried crunchy doughnut made of lentil, green chilli, onion and ginger served with sambar and chutney; Parippu Vada, fried crunchy patties made of lentils, ginger, onion and curry leaves, served with coconut chutney. Idli, rice and lentils battered and steamed; Koonu Fry, mushrooms dipped in a special batter and fried. Aubergine Pori, finely sliced aubergine dipped in asafoetida-flavoured thick batter made from chick peas flour and deep-fried and comes with fresh red onion chutney, each £2.95. Mains: Amb Uluva Kootu, Lamb prepared with onion, tomato, capsicum and fenugreek leaves; Lamb Cheera Curry, lamb with spinach; Lamb Malabar, speciality of North Kerala – cooked in a roasted coconut sauce with tomato, spices and curry leaves, each £6.95. Mon-Sat: 12-2.30 & 5.30-11; Sun: 5.30-10.30. *Branch Kovalam, London, NW6.*

NYOU SAY OK NOTTS
You might get a discount if you show them this Guide.
BEESTON: BEESTON TANDOORI 150 High Rd, Beeston ~ 0115 922 3330.
STAPLEFORD: MOUSHUMI 124 Derby Rd. ~ 0115 939 4929.
NOT'M: KASTURI 3332 Mansfield Road, Nottingham NG5 2EF 0115 960 3500   www.nottinghamkasturi.co.uk Housed in an attractive period building, opposite Lidl with free parking facility. All the favourites from £8. Special Lamb Nehari, £8, fillet of lamb cooked with a thick sauce, yoghurt, mild to medium spices finished with golden brown onions, fresh ginger and lemon; Rupakote Lamb Chops £8.   **N**
EWARK: ASHIANA Bathly Lane, North Road, North Muskham, Newark, NG23 6HN. 0115 994 0653 A trendy 110 seat Bangladesh. 5-11(last orders 10.30)

Spice

a modern taste of India

Pat Chapmans Curry Club TOP 100

Spice Takeaway

Collect ~ 459 Westdale Lane, Mapperley, Nottingham, NG3 6DH

Collect or Delivery ~ Order by Phone ~ 0115 962 3555

Hours ~ 5pm to 11.30, every day

Order Online ~ spicetakeaway.com

OXFORDSHIRE

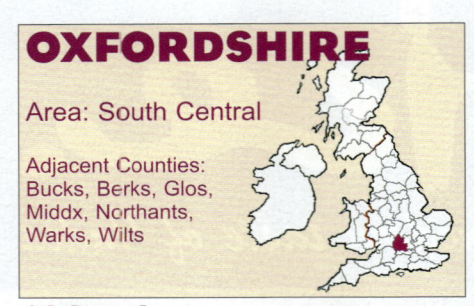

Area: South Central

Adjacent Counties:
Bucks, Berks, Glos,
Middx, Northants,
Warks, Wilts

Abingdon

THE VINE
High St, Long Wittenham, Abingdon OX14 4QH
01865 407832

This pub was sold by Greene King to Angur Miah who provides standard cuisine. Lunch £10; 2 course Dinner £20. 12-2.30 & 5-11.

Bicester

ARZOO
15 Market Square, Bicester OX26 6AD
01869 242434

'For starters we had Tandoori Duck and Sheek Kebab, both of which were beautifully cooked and well presented. We chose Boal Dopiaza and Roshini Lamb for our main course together with lime jeera rice and a garlic nan bread. Both main courses were excellent. A very rare event for us was that we ate everything put before us. The restaurant is nicely decorated and the staff were all very pleasant and attentive. We shall certainly be making the long journey back to Oxford again to sample more of this restaurant's fare.' LH.

Cholsey

MEMORIES OF BENGAL
12 Wallingford Rd, OX10 9LQ   01491 652777

'Thank God this place is only 200 yards from my house! I visit weekly. It's in the former the village pub and was restored at considerable expense by Angur Miah some years ago You may even see Tim Henman dining if you're lucky!' CI. 12-2 & 6-11. Branches Dil Raj, Ock Street, Abingdon, The Vine Abingdon.

Henley-on-Thames

SPICE MERCHANT
25 Thameside, RG9 2LJ   01491 636118
www.spicemerchantgroup.com

Its USP is a small launch, moored at the restaurant, on which you can dine Indian and enjoy your drinks while cruising the Thames. Menu and details, see Beaconsfield. Avg Price: £45. 12-2.30 & 6-11. Branches: Beaconsfield, Cookham, Dost, Uxbridge.

Kidlington

OVISHER TANDOORI
11-13 Oxford Road, Kidlington, Oxford, OX5 2BP
01865 372827

The ten Hindi arches make Ovisher stand out in an otherwise plain building on the Oxford road. And it i extremely popular, not only getting the most votes for Indian cuisine in the area, but for all restaurants in Oxford. It is a standard menu but the food is subtle, yet spiced correctly and served with quiet panache. 12-2 & 6-11.

Oxford

4500 MILES FROM DELHI
41 Park End Street   Oxford   OX1 1JD
01865 244922   www.milesfromdelhi.com/oxford

Fun places. See Nottingham branch for details. Mon-Fri: 12- 2.30 & 5.30-11. Sat to 11.30; Sun: 5-10.30.

AZIZ
228 Cowley Road, Oxford OX4 1UH
01865 794945   www.azizuk.com

Azizur (Aziz) Rahman is an extremely personable man, and a successful restaurateur. From a start-up in 1990, he now has four Aziz restaurants in Oxon. This smart 90-seater has always cooked real Bangladeshi food, and not in the manner of so many Bangladeshi-owned curryhouses. His ace in the hole is Master Chef Nurul Amin, a veteran chef with decades of top hotel experince in Dhaka. Because the menu is using Bengali words, dishes may seem unfamiliar, but it is an encyclopaedia of Bangladeshi food, and many of the old favourites are there too. Starters include Maach Bora £6, a fish cake; and Chott Pottie £4.50, chickpeas, egg and potatoes spiced with coriander. Mains include Hush Bhuna £10, duck with onion and tomatoes; Razalla £10 lamb or chicken with yoghurt, cream, butter and chilli; Murgh Kaliya £8.50, chicken with black pepper in a creamy sauce. Bangladesh being big fish on curries, there is a good selection: Bhuna Aiyr £9 with onion & tomatoes; Sak Buaal £9 with spinach; Galda Chineri Kodu £11 is large king prawns with pumpkin. Vegetable dishes (from £6.25) include the delightfully named Dimm Dall, egg and lentil curry; Sarso Baigun, aubergine fried with mustard seed; Sobzi Korma £6 mild and creamy; Sobzi Razalla, vegetables with butter, cream & chillies. 'The ambience, service and food are all top quality. All the dishes that we tried were beautifully served, expertly cooked and well crafted, with a number of dishes (including a good range of vegetarian dishes) that I have not seen before. Will definitely return.' SO. 'A splendid meal.' WC. 'Mid-week the place was packed. Decor is upmarket and smart, the food well prepared and served in generous quantities. This is where the middle class, the academics and well-off students of Oxford eat and entertain. Service was slow but the place was very busy.

SPLENDIDLY INDIAN, SUPERBLY SMOOTH

Parking can be a problem.' PAW. T/a: 15% disc. 12-2.15 (not Fri); & 6-11.30 (12-4.30 Sun). *Branches & same details at Aziz, High St, Burford, Oxon; 01993 823340; Aziz, High St, Witney, Oxon, 01993 774100. Aziz Pandesia, serves Indian, Bangladeshi and Thai cuisine at 1 Folly Bridge, Oxford, 01865 247775.*

CHUTNEYS   PUNJABI
36 St. Michael Street, Oxford, OX1 2EB
www.chutneysoxford.co.uk

Good Punjabi food at this smart licensed modern café . *'I had Boti Kebab £4 Lamb Tikka pieces cooked in the Tandoori Charcoal Oven which was nicely cooked. For main course I went for Masala Dosa £8, Keralan style Potato Curry served in a rolled rice and lentil pancake with a small portion of Sambar (Mild Vegetable Curry) and Mint Raita served in small side dishes. Pancake was good as was the potato curry but I felt that it could do with a bit more curry leaf/mustard seed flavour for that truly authentic South Indian flavour. The Sambar was also a bit on the mild side and I didn't think the Raita added very much to the eating experience. Criticisms aside though, overall it was good and would have represented a pretty decent balanced meal on its own.'* Steve Osborne.

THE STANDARD
117 Walton Street, Oxford OX2 6AJ   01865 553557

Opened in 1972 and is opposite the Phoenix Cinema in the heart of the Jericho area of Oxford. The food on offer consists of familiar classics, house specialities and an extensive vegetarian menu. Satarters av £4, Mains av: £8. 12-2:30; Sun-Th: 5:30-11; Fr- Sat to -11.30

YETI   NEPALESE
237 Cowley Road, Oxford OX4 3QT
01865 295959   www.yetinepalese.co.uk

This small family run licensed business was opened in 2011 by its lady owner who cooks as does head chef Mr Govind Sapkota. The menu contains Indian standards (ignore these) and Nepalese items. Vegetable Momo £3 steam dumplings, with homemade achar (chutney); Timur Chicken £7.25, cooked typical Nepali style with mustard; Naspati Chicken £7.75, cooked with pears, tomatoes, coriander & spices; Sherpali Bhans a£7.25, lamb cooked with potatoes & mooli, seasoned with brandy; Sherpa Patan Masu £8, chicken or lamb cooked with green chillies, peppers & tomatoes. 5:30-7:30 10% off Home Deli Min £12 – 5m rad. Hrs:- 12-2.30 & 5.30-11.

YOU SAY OK OXFORD
BANBURY: SHEESH MAHAL 43 Oxford Rd, Banbury OX16 9AB 01295 266489 http://www.sheeshmahalbanbury.co.uk/ Mohammed Khalid is owner and manager. 6-12 (from 4.30 Fr-Sat)
CHINNOR: CHINNOR INDIAN 59 Lower Rd. ~ 01844 354843 www.chinnorindiancuisine.co.uk Owner Saidur Rahman. Hours: 5.30-11.30; 12am Sat.
CHIPPING NORTON: ANARKALI 6 West St, Chipping Norton OX7 5AA 01608 642785. Owner A.Uddin. 12-2.30/6-11.30.

DIDCOT: SUNKOSHI TANDOORI NEPALESE: 226a Broadway, Didcot OX11 8RS 01235 812796.Roshan Aryal owner. Set meal: Dal Bhat Tarkari, Chicken or Meat Curry, Rice, Dal, Veg Curry, Roti & Dahi;,Lasun Aloo (Garlic) Sungur/Poleko Roast Pork - Nepalese Style 12-2.30/6-11, 11.30 Fri & Sat.
FARINGDON: AZAD 14 Coxwell Street, Faringdon SN7 7HA 01367 244977. Rabia Khanom Ali's venue. 5-11.30; 12-11.30 Sun.
HENLEY-ON-THAMES: GAZAL 53 Reading Rd, Henley RG9 1AB 01491 574659. Hours: 12-2 / 6-11.
Raju's 21 Reading Rd Henley RG9 1AB 01491 572218 http://www.rajus.co.uk.'Traditional food and decor.' MS. 'Best in Henley'. RP. Oxford:
OXFORD: AZIZ EXPRESS Ozone Leisure Park, Oxford OX4 4XP 01865 395870   www.azizexpress.co.uk Buffet & A la carte menu. Rashel Rahman GM says 'We don't offer fine dining What we do offer is quick and exquisite cuisine.. The 'Aziz' way!' Lunch £7; Dinner £13. Kids half price.12-2.15 (to 3 Sat-Sun) & 5.30-10.30.
OXFORD: EVEREST   NEPALESE 151 Howard St, Oxford ox4 3az, 01865 251555 Good Nepalese selction.Y
OXFORD: PUNJABI KITCHEN 84 Cowley Rd Oxford OX4 1HR   01865 243390.. Cheap and cheerful Punjabi grub.

RUTLAND
Britain's smallest county
Area: East Midlands

Adjacent Counties:
Cambs, Leics, Lincs

It's geographically smaller than Birmingham city.

Oakham

VOUJON BALTI HUT
t4 Burley Corner, High Street, Oakham LE15 6DU
01572 723043   www.voujonrestaurant.co.uk

Anwar Hussein established his flagship Voujon in 1995. It is on the first floor in a corner building with floor to ceiling windows overlooking the High Street. You need to book those tables with a view, or there is a conservatory and an al fresco area. *'It's much more fashionable than most local Indians. Service is extremely impressive with friendly waiting staff If you need to wait for a table they seat you with a menu in the very comfortable bar area. The Voujon is equally as good with takeaways. The food itself is perfect – well presented, fresh and extremely tasty!'* RB *'A chance to galivant off in our caravan to somewhere exotic - well Oakham and the Voujon, a modern looking restaurant with large mirrors making it seem larger than it actually is. We decided to forego starters as many restaurants seem to be very generous with their main courses. Service was quick and friendly. It was Tawa Murgh Tikka Jalfrezi for me and Balti Tikka Gosht for M, plus our usual Naan & Mushroom Jalfrezi. The food arrived promptly, mine on a sizzling tawa. They looked similar in colour but tasted different. My Jalfrezi was marked as hot but I found it less than hot – !M calls me 'asbestos gob' We thought the price was quite high at £40 inc a tip, though Voujon was certainly popular. We'd eat again if we were in this neck of the woods.'* T & MH.12-2.30 & 6-11. *Voujon Branches: Stamford, Oxford, Cannock.*

SHROPSHIRE

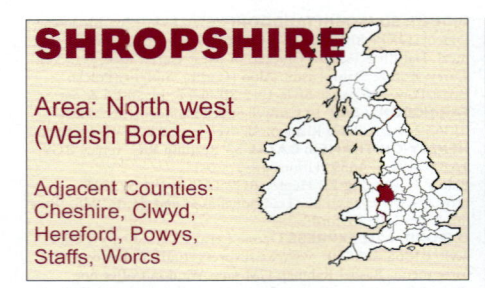

Area: North west
(Welsh Border)

Adjacent Counties:
Cheshire, Clwyd,
Hereford, Powys,
Staffs, Worcs

Ironbridge

PONDICHERRY
The Old Police Station, Waterloo Street, Ironbridge, TF8 7AA 01952 433055 www.pondicherry-ironbridge.co.uk

A remarkable late grey brick building with round arch windows in a pretty town full of remarkable buildings. Afon Azam's former the cop shop retains the magistrates bench, high ceilings, oak floors, cells and a gallows in the courtyard. Pondocherry is the east Indian French city. But the food doesn't reflect that, being mostly 'old favourites' £11 and Specials av £12 by Chef M.Kahil. 5-11.

Shifnall

SHIFNAL BALTI TOP 100   BYO
20 Broadway, Shifnall, TF11 8AZ
01952 460142   www.shifnalbalti.co.uk

Shifnal Balti Faz Ali's 90-seater, est 1992 is divided into two dining sections and a takeaway area. The decor is quite 'space-age' with trendy colour-changing lighting panels on the wall. Indian music plays quietly. Staff are friendly and attentive. Typical Menu Snapshot: Starters: Sheek kebab £3.35; Bahar tandoori £3.50. Mains: Tandoori Murghi Massala £12.95; Balti lamb tikka £8.25; Meat Shatkora £7.95, cooked with a Bangladesh citrus fruit which gives a unique sour flavour; Bangladeshi Fish Fries £4; Machli Diya Bhojan £9 - fresh water Bangladeshi fish, garlic, coriander, lemon juice, green chilli; Chicken Tikka Coriander £9, served with salad; Apna Pachando £10, whole trout, fresh coriander, garlic, green chilli, lemon, turmeric, cumin, cinnamon and cardamom; Garlic and Mushroom or Peshwari and Coriander Naan c£3.50; Chutneys and Pickles are FREE. 'Celebration' meals include lobster from £45 and whole leg of lamb from £50 - wonderful for a special occasion, like a big birthday. Hot towels are served before desserts. Desserts include: Kulfi £1.95; Gulab Jamon £3.5); Selection of teas and coffees. The bill comes with chocolates and a rose for the lady. Decadent but nice. Sun-Th:5.30- 11.30; Fri- Sat to 12.30.

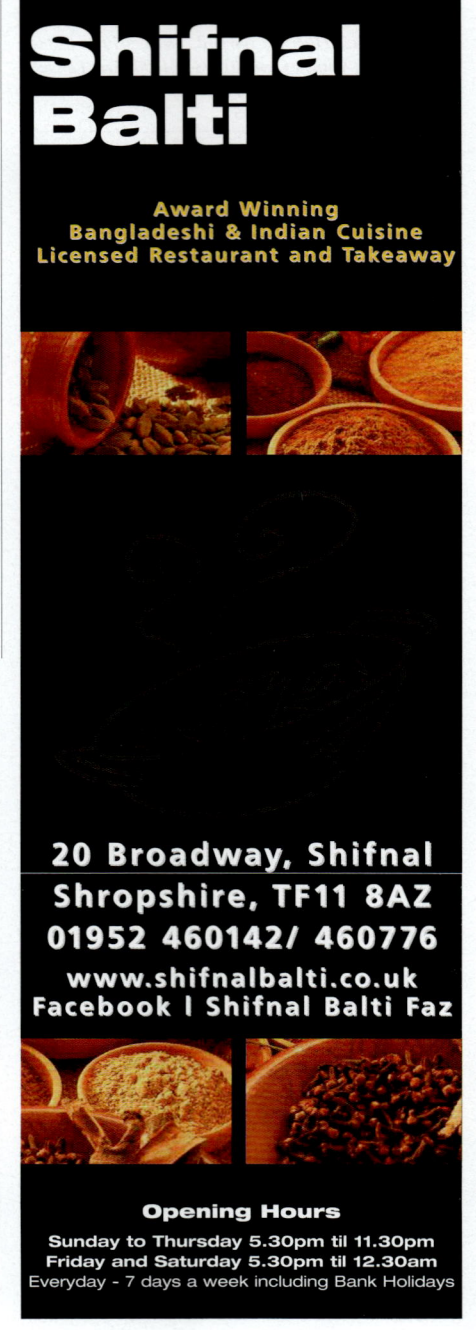

Shifnal Balti

**Award Winning
Bangladeshi & Indian Cuisine
Licensed Restaurant and Takeaway**

**20 Broadway, Shifnal
Shropshire, TF11 8AZ
01952 460142/ 460776
www.shifnalbalti.co.uk
Facebook I Shifnal Balti Faz**

Opening Hours
Sunday to Thursday 5.30pm til 11.30pm
Friday and Saturday 5.30pm til 12.30am
Everyday - 7 days a week including Bank Holidays

SPLENDIDLY INDIAN, SUPERBLY SMOOTH

Shrewsbury

CAFE SAFFRON
25 Hill's Lane, Shrewsbury SY1 1QU
01743 246753   www.cafesaffron.co.uk

Abdul & Azad.established their 110 seater in 2001. The menu contains all the standard items with interesting specials such as Black Peppercorn Chicken or Lamb Tiika £4 cooked with crushed black pepper, with peppers, onions & tomatoes; Jeera Murghi £8.25 flavoured .with cumin and fresh coriander; Luhari Karahi £9 marinated chicken or lamb tikka, cooked in a karahi dish with grilled onions, fresh peppers & tomatoes with ground spices & fresh herbs; Roshuni Baghar £8.25, marinated lamb or chicken tikka cooked with onions, green peppers with fried a garlic topping. The restaurant promotes a USP of rare meat curries, when available and not all at the same time. How about Kangaroo Jalfrezi; Ostrich Maslam; Venison Rogan; British Buffalo Sagwala; Bison Labra; Crocodile snap masala; and Bison Madrasall at £11 and Pheasant royalty; £13 Wild Rabbit Karah & Shark Takari at £13and Wagyu Kobe Beef £15. Reports please. 5 course indian Gourmet dinner on Sundays £9.95 per head   6-late. *Branch Saros, Bridgnorth.*

YOU SAY OK SHROPSHIRE

BRIDGNORTH: SAROS 1-2 Moat Street | Bridgnorth, Bridgnorth, 01746 762848 www.sarostwist.co.uk Chicken Tikka Mango chilli Massala, Salmon Pakora; Machli Buna; Banana Fritters. 10% Off Sun & Wed sonly Hrs: 6-11;, Closed Tues.

BRIDGNORTH: EURASIA 21 West Castle Street, Bridgnorth WV16 4AB   01746 764895   http://www.eurasiatandoori.co.uk   Standard menu. Av main course £9. Mon-Sat: 6-12.; 22 dish Sun Buffet e-m-a-y-l, £9.95, u10 £4.95: 4-10.30. Mon-Sat: 6-12; Sun -10.30

CHURCH STRETTON JAIPUR Sandford Avenue, Church Stretton SY6 6BW   01694 724667   Rated OK by T&MH.   5.30-11.30.
LUDLOW: GOLDEN MOMENTS Broad Street, Ludlow SY8 1NH
MARKET DRAYTON ORUNA Shropshire Street, Market Drayton,
OSWESTRY SIMLA 42 Beatrice St, Oswestry, SY11 1QG 01691 659880 Est 1982. A well liked local. Chicken Tikka, £3.95; Pasanda lamb with rice, £8.95; Bengal Fish, £9.95;
SHREWSBURY SHERAZ 79 Wylecop, Shrewsbury SY1 1UT 01743 242321

SOMERSET

Area: North west (Welsh Border)

Adjacent Counties:
Cheshire, Clwyd, Hereford, Powys, Staffs, Worcs

Bath

EASTERN EYE   A-LIST
8a Quiet Street, Bath, BA1 2JN   01225 422323

140-seater, owned by Suhan Choudhury, pink and blue with most impressive Georgian interior, in one large room with three domes. *'Average high-street curry house it is not! It's a spectacular, huge and most impressive first-floor restaurant. Soft lighting, pink and blue colours, restful atmosphere. Tablecloths and cutlery are of good quality, even the hot towels are so thick they could almost have been squares of carpet! Stuffed pepper, whole green stuffed with spicy diced chicken, barbecued, nicely blackened, delicately spiced, interesting but filling starter. Onion Bhajia, two round bhajias, the best we have tasted for a long while, light, crispy and spicy. Prawn Puree – excellent, large succulent prawns, tangy sauce. Good, fresh and varied salad garnishes. Chicken Tikka Masala – most ordinary, standard offering. Chicken Mon Pasanda, excellent, different, mild, yoghurt based sauce, very herby. Lamb Jalfrezi, large tender chunks of lamb, thick dark sauce, hotness hits you after first couple of mouthfuls. Vegetable Bhajee, good variety of diced vegetables, nicely spiced and enjoyable. Peshwari Nan and Pullao Rice were both good, nan not sickly and rice contained smattering of diced vegetables to make it interesting. Prices slightly above average, but for decor and type of restaurant, very reasonable. Service efficient and friendly. An excellent meal in an elegant restaurant.'* MW. *'Incredibly wide menu Quality Excellent Quantity Copious Decor Out of this world Service Prompt and polite Comfort Excellent Comments We went for the non vegetarian set meal which came to £38 for the two of us. It included: Kebab; Chicken Jalfrezi; Sultan Puri Pullau; Mixed Vegetables; Naan; Popadums; Chutney; Sweet; Coffee. Also bottle of Bangla (£4) Mineral water £1.70. The kebabs were mightily impressive and highly spiced. Mark 9/10.'* G&MP. *'Unbooked visit. To their credit they accommodated us very well indeed, including bringing over a highchair for our 2 year old daughter, Lily, something I wish more Indian restaurants would do. The food was absolutely faultless. Lily has a liking for lentils so we tried her with a thin Dhal soup; she absolutely loved it! I had a Vegetable Dhansak and I asked them to make it a little hotter than usual; suffice to say it was absolutely beautiful, full of fresh vegetables (not just potato!) and just a little sweet as well as hot. Jackie's Vegetable Jalfrezi was equally impressive, including some chilli's with serious attitude! The accompanying Garlic Nan was light and was not overpowering in terms of garlic content. Our single side dish of Saag Ponir was soft and creamy yet still retained sizeable chunks of Ponir that sometimes disappear when the dish is cooked in this style. Overall, really excellent food and at about £40 in total, not bad value for money either. I must do start navigating by something other than your Guide as it continually points me to good restaurants and I end up writing positive reviews .'* AG. And the Guide be the pooorer without them Andy. Serv: 10%. Specials include: Mon Pasanda – slightly hot, enlivened with herbs and yoghurt, Shah Jahani – chicken breast, slightly spiced, shallow fried in ghee, blended with homemade cheese and cream, Sultan Puri Pilau – from Uttar Pradesh, spiced rice with lamb and cashew nuts, served with a gravy. Bangladeshi food nights, seafood buffet. Service 10%. min charge: £10. T/a: 10% disc. 10% discount if you show them this Guide. Hours: 12-2.30/6-11.30. Awarded best in the west. See ad on page

THE MINT ROOM
Indian Dining

The Mint Room, Longmead Gospel Hall, Lower Bristol Road, Bath, BA2 3EB 01225 446656
www.themintroom.co.uk info@themintroom.co.uk

Some of Our Other Restaurants in the South West

THE VICEROY
INDIAN RESTAURANT

100 Middle Street,
Yeovil, Somerset,
BA20 1NE
01935 421758

Cinnamons
INDIAN RESTAURANT

10 South Street,
Axminster, Devon,
EX13 5AD
01297 631185

Signature **VICEROY**

98 Middle Street,
Yeovil, Somerset,
BA20 1NE
01935 426210

COBRA
SPLENDIDLY INDIAN, SUPERBLY SMOOTH

JAMUNA
9 High St. Bath, BA1 5AQ www.jammunabath.co.uk 01225 464631

Find the tardis-like door in this gorgeuos front, golden stone building in this gorgeous town. Go up to the first floor. Get a window seat if you can which overlooks the abbey. Then settle down to you meal at Ahmed Choudury's 64 seater. Menu Snapshot: Tandoori Platter £12.50, tandoori chicken, chicken tikka, sheek kebab, lamb tikka, Naan and Pullao Rice - what a feast!; Sultan Puri Pulao £13, spiced rice with lamb and cashew nuts, served with lamb curry; Vegetarian Platter £9.25, potato and cauliflower curry, mushroom bhajia, lentils, yoghurt, bread and rice; Garlic Naan £2.30. *The menu offers the usual dishes, with perhaps one or two less common items (for example Xacutti), but basically it is a standard list. The Onion Bhaji starters were very good indeed. The Chicken Tikka starter was less remarkable, having a few pieces of only very lightly tandooried lumps of chicken, which were not particularly flavoursome. My main dish of Lamb Pathia was cooked in a rich, dark sauce it was certainly hot and pleasantly spiced, but the lamb was rather chewy. The service was quick and efficient, and the prices (perhaps predictable in Bath) were above average, plus they add 10% for service (although to their credit they do not leave an empty space for a further tip). Portions were just about adequate and the meal, while OK, was nothing more than a reasonable standard high street formula curry. It's nowhere near as good as the Eastern Eye.* MW. T/a: 10% disc. 12-2.30 & 6-11.30; 12.30 Sat. Branch: Rajdoot and group.

THE MINT ROOM TOP 100
Longmead Gospel Hall | Lower Bristol Road, Bath, BA2 3EB 01225-446656 www.themintroom.co.uk

The Mint Room, formerly Bombay Nights, is the flagship of a number of Luthfur Rahman's restaurants in the south-west, the Mint Room being the flagship where Indian tradition and modernity go hand in hand. It has a relaxing ambience, first-rate service, fine wines and cocktails. Head chef Mamrej Khan heads a talented kitchen team whose food is well above average. 24 starters include: Aloo Tikki, batter fried mashed potato cakes stuffed with Brie and flavoured with ginger and cashew nuts accompanied by tamarind sauce or Roti Sag whole chickpeas and sautéed spinach in an onion and tomato stack served on a mini chapatti bread, both £4.50. There's Rabbit Varuval, chunks of rabbit meat tossed with onion, chilli, curry leaves and ground spices or Crab Cake mashed with with potato and fresh herbs, served with sweet chilli sauce and garnished with baby cress leaves, both £5.95. Fish-lovers can indulge in Punjabi Sword Fish, char roasted Caribbean sword fish steaks flavoured with honey and mustard, served with smoked beetroot raitha £5.50. All the favourites are there from £8. Signature dishes include Masala Dosa (see p74) stuffed with spiced mashed potatoes tempered with turmeric and mustard seeds served with sambar and tomato chutney£9.95; Lal Maas Rajasthan's favourite: lamb chops cooked in a smoked spicy tomato curry served with spiced rustic mashed potato £12.95;

Keralan Duck, oven roasted seared Barbary duck breast served with mixed bell peppers, in a curry leaf and coconut milk sauce £10.95; Mango Mach, a traditional Bengali style preparation of pan-fried red mullet, simmered in coconut milk, five-spice and a sweet and sour sauce of green mangoes served with spiced potato tempered with mustard £13.95; and Goa's favourite sweet, hot and sour dish: King Prawn Balchao in a flavoursome sauce infused with red chilli, Goan jaggery, coconut and palm vinegar £14.95. Wines from £13.94 to £145 (Chateau Pichon Longueville Baron). Champagne from £53 (Moët) to £390 (Louis Roederer). A very good house. 12-2:30; Sun-Thur: 6-11 (Fri & Sat: to 11:30). Branches: Viceroy Dunkswell and Viceroy Yeovil.

RAJPOOT
4 Argyle Street, Bath BA2 4BA www.rajpoot.com 01225 466833

Rajpoot was established in 1980 and is owned by Ahmed Choudhury (Mngr Mr Ali) The name means legendary warrior. You are greeted outside by one such with a turban. The inside is a wealth of nooks and crannies crammed with Indian art and specially commissioned Mughal style carved murals and mosaics in seven dining areas. Chef's Specialities: Rajpoot Feast £24 pp: Starters: Chicken Tikka, Shish Kebab, Machlee Bora (Fish Ball), Salad; Main Course: Rogan Josh, Bhona Chicken, Chana Massala, Lemon Rice, Nan, Dessert: selected Sweets, Tea or Coffee. Vegetarian Delight £21.50 pp: Starters: Vege Shingara, Spiced New Potatoes, Onion Bhajhee, Salad; Main Course: Rajpoot Vegetables, Sag Paneer, Gobi Bhajhee, Rice, Chapati, Raita, Dessert: selected sweets, Tea or Coffee. 12-2.30 & 6-11 (11:30 Fri-Sat).

YAK & YETI NEPALESE
12 Pierrepont Street, Bath, BA1 1LA www.yakyetiyak.co.uk 01225 442299

The've moved to here since our last edition, but the menu's the same with accurate Nepalese items including pork and beef dishes. Starter examples: Momos Pork £5.50 Vegetable £5.20 steamed fragrantly spiced dumplings, served with fresh hemp seed chutney. Hemp eh?; Polayko Masu £5.50 grilled boneless strips of lamb marinated in traditional spices; Malekhu Macha £5.90, salmon pieces marinated in traditional spices and deep fried until crispy; Cauli Pakora £4.70, florets dipped batter and deep-fried. Main course examples: Muglingko Kukhura £7.80, chicken stir-fried on the bone with spices, tomato, onion, garlic and ginger. Pork Sag Aloo £7.80 slow-cooked in its own juices with potato then finished with spinach and coriander; Pork Bhutuwa £7.90, pieces of pork marinated in our own mix of freshly ground spices and stir-fried with tomato and spring onion; Lamb Tamar £7.90, slow-cooked with bamboo shoots, black-eye peas and potato finished with tomato and coriander; Yak Yeti Yak Beef £8.90, marinated then stir-fried with peppers, onion and tomato. Vegetable dishes: Aloo Tamar, fermented bamboo shoots stir-fried with new potatoes and black-eye peas; Hario Simi ra Aloo, green beans and new potatoes stir-fried in our own blend of spices; Bakula Banda all £5.60, broad beans and white cabbage stir-fried with ground spices; Chamsur Sag, spinach and watercress stir-fried with a classic blend of fresh herbs and spices,£5.90 Hario Cauli ra Kurilo £6.10 Delicately spiced broccoli and asparagus stir-fried with peppers (subject to availability; Bhuteko Bhat £3.30, Fried rice Nepalese style with turmeric, mustard seeds and mixed vegetables. An how about this pud? Freak Street Apples £4.30,spiced apple tart, the hippies most lasting contribution to Nepal with cream or ice-cream. Nepalese Set meal NV £17, V £14. Mon-Sun:12 -2; Mon-Thur: 6-10:30; Fri-Sat: 5-10:30; Sun: 6-10.

Kensham

MEHEK at the GRANGE HOTEL.
42 Bath Road, Keynsham, Bristol, BS31 1SN
0117 986 7091   www.mehak-bristol.co.uk

Book one of the 12 rooms at the Grange, located between Bath and Bristol and be sure to use Mehek, meaning a fine aroma, their new Indian restaurant which opened in Feb 2012. Amit Lakhani of Bristol's Myristica, is the mastermind. . Front of House management is led by Anuj Jaiswal, formerly of The Bristol Hotel.Head Chef Silva Pitchai has worked at London's Mint Leaf, Cinnamon Club and Tamarind and cooks pan Indian cuisine. Yes, they turn out dishes like Bhuna, Korma, CTM and Vindaloo from £8.45. But Pitchai's more adventurous dishes include starters such as Baby Squid £4.95, squid rings deep fried and tossed with bell peppers, chilli flakes and honey; Mussel Fry £5.45, stir fried iwith mustard seeds in a spicy tomato masala. Served on a mini naan bread; Rabbit Varuval £5.45, south Indian specialty of rabbit meat tossed with onions, chillies, curry leaves & ground spices, served with strips of naan bread. Mains: Prawn Moilee £10.95, Peeled tiger prawns curried in the classic south Indian sauce of coconut, lime leaves and ground mustard seeds; Tawa Ki Lamb £9.95 Pot roasted lamb neck fillet cooked with fresh onion, tomato ginger and garlic. Dessert: chocolate soufflé served with chilli custard £3.95. Mon-Sat:12-2.30 & 5:30-11. *Branch Mysterica, Bristol.*

Taunton

MINT AND MUSTARD   TOP 100
10 Station Road, Taunton, TA1 1NH
01823 619208   www.mintandmustard.com

Following successful trading at his Cardiff Mint and Mustard restaurant, Ajit Kandoran, a senior surgeon at Taunton's Musgrove Park Hospital opened this branch in 2012, bringing authentic Indian cooking to Taunton. The main chefs are both from Kerela so expect some truly correct south Indian food. Exec Chef Pramod Nair worked at Coromandel South India and Taj Sri Lanka, while Jaipuri-born Chef Siddartha "Sid" worked at the Oberoi Vanyavilas. Starters include: Scallops Thengapal, £7.50, simmered in lemon zest flavoured coconut milk, Anchovy Fritters £5.50, in a garlic sauce, King Fish Steak Vattichathu Masala tossed in shallots & tomatoes served with salad and potato cake. Mains include: Nadan Kozhi Curry £10.50, Kerala-style chicken curry with coconut milk, tomatoes and spices; Syrian Beef Curry £11.50, a spicy preparation of the Keralan Syrian Christians; Cheera Parippu Kootu £7.50, spinach and bengal gram with coconut and cumin; Olan £4.50, butternut squash and cow peas simmered in spiced coconut milk; Goan Porc 'Vindalu' £11.50, from the Portuguese 'vin d'alho' meaning 'wine and garlic', pork cooked with home ground red chillies and spices, intensely flavoured with garlic and wine vinegar, reduced for a unique taste.   Sun-Fri: 12-2; Sun-Th: 6-11, Fri-Sat: 5-11. *Branch Cardiff.*

Yeovil

SIGNATURE VICEROY   TOP 100
98 Middle Street, Yeovil, BA20 1NE
01935 426210   www.signatureviceroy.com

THE VICEROY   TOP 100
100 Middle Street, Yeovil BA20 1NE
01935 421758   www.viceroyindianrestaurant.co.uk

We list these two together because they are both highly regarded locally being owned by perfectionist Luthfur Rahman. Chef Mamrej Khan has all the familiar favourites are on his menu, but more interesting are the Bangladeshi fish specialities like Roop Chanda, a whole fish on the bone

THE VICEROY
INDIAN RESTAURANT
100 Middle Street
Yeovil,
BA20 1NE
01935 421 758
or
01935 421 4000
www.viceroyindianrestaurant.co.uk
BRITISH Curry Awards
Regional Finalists ...
Every year since 2005
innovative cuisine
inspired

SPLENDIDLY INDIAN, SUPERBLY SMOOTH

fried with spices and coriander, traditional Bengali style or Ayre Korahi cooked with mixed pepper, ginger, tomatoes and coriander. Then there is Sylheti Bengal (Shatkora) Chicken cooked with Bengali citrus fruit and our own blend of spices or Rum Joy Puri Grilled lamb cooked with white rum and served in a specially blended sauce all £12.95; Jeera Chicken, cooked with cumin seeds and peppers in a special sauce with fairly hot spices to produce an aromatic flavour £8.95. 3 course special between 5.30-6.30 Sun-Thur £10pp min 2. 12-2 & Sun-Thur: 5.30-11 (Fri & Sat to 12). *Branches: The Mint Room Bath and Viceroy Dukenswell, Devon.*

YOU SAY OK, SOMERSET

BATH: MOUCHUCK TAKEAWAY 136 Wells Road, Bath BA2 3AH 01225 333449 www.mouchuck.co.uk
BATH: PANAHAR BYO 8 Moorland Road, Bath BA2 3PL 01225 471999 http://www.panaharbath.co.uk Regular menu. BYO- No corkage charge. 12-2 & 5.30-11.
BRIDGWATER: THE SPICE GALLERY 44 Fore St, N Petherton, Bridgwater TA6 6PZ 01278 663800 www.spicegallery.co.uk Est 2006 by a group of friends and is now part of the Viceroy group Somerset and Devon with identical menu. See Yeovil, Som.
CHEDDAR: CHEDDAR COTTAGE Union street, Cheddar, bs27 3nb 01934-742331 www.cheddarcottage.com Anwar Hussain's and Russal Alis Cheddar opened in1994's is near the Gorge and offers the formula menu. Banquet night Weds £9.95. 12-2 & 5:30-11.
CLEVEDON: MONSOON 5 Old Church Road, Clevedon BS21 6NN 01275 87828. Siraj Islam who ran Guide entry Moghuls at 33 on this road has reopened at no 5 as Monsoon with brothers Ralph, Shof and Naz, his wife Shima and her bro Shimon. Tue-Sun: 12-2pm & 5.30-11pm; Fri-Sat: to11:30.
MINEHEAD: ALCOMBE TANDOORI 67 Alcombe Road, Minehead, Exmoor National Park. 01643 706591
WESTON-SUPER-MARE ZEERA 38-40 Orchard Street, Weston-sSuper-Mare BS23 1RH 01934 642266
WILLITON: THE BENGAL SPICE 7 Fore Street, Williton TA4 4PX,

STAFFORDSHIRE

Area: Northwest Midlands

Adjacent Counties:
Cheshire, Derbs,
Shrops,
W Mids, Worcs

Alton

THORNBURY HALL RASOI TOP 100
FINE PAKISTANI CUISINE
Lockwood Road. Kingsley Holt, Nr Alton, ST10 2DH
01538 750503   www.thornburyhall.co.uk

Situated approximately 10 miles east of Hanley (off the A52) and just 3 miles from the renowned tourist attraction, this delightful Georgian Grade II listed building with Tudor origins was converted from near ruin in 1990 by Mohammed and Parveen Siddique. They brought style and fine Pakistani food to this beautiful location. It has three public areas in which there is now a mix of *'Bollywood glitz and Mogul exoticism'*, with a dance floor with mirror ball, starlight effect and sound system countered by relics, artefacts, a huge Chinese urn and crystal chandeliers. The restaurant leads from the bar and is decorated in gold and terracotta, ceramic floor and open fire for winter evenings. The Shalimar room, named after gardens in Pakistan, is decorated in green and gold, large windows and doors leading to garden. The Lahore dining room is large, elegant, and richly decorated with Georgian plaster ceiling, swagged curtains and a brass teapot, it nearly reached the ceiling! Rasoi appropriately means 'kitchen' and from it emanates a vast 90-dish menu with house specialities such as Karhai Murgh Pasanda, chicken fillets marinated in spices and yoghurt or the sizzling hot Karhai Lahori Chaska. *'The in-laws live close by. It is very grand, elegant and comfortable. Service good, including some staff from the village in Pakistani dress. Excellent flavours and quality.'* DRHM. *'Fantastic restaurant. Magnificent settings. Karahi Murgh Jalfrezi, the best my husband has ever tasted.'* Mr&Mrs C. The Sun Lunch buffet is a real family occasion, Booking advisable. c£10, kids c£6, u5 free. Sun-Th: 6-9.30 (Fri-Sat: to 11). *Branches: Riverside Restaurant in Trentham Gardens: Traditional English and Indian dishes from the a la carte menu. Eastern Express in Alton Towers. Serves a range of curries and daal, kebabs, salad stuffed wraps and jacket potatoes with an eastern twist.* 10-6.

Chadsmoor, Cannock

SANAM BALTI HOUSE BYO
193 Cannock Rd, Cannock, WS11 5DD 01543 513565

A huge restaurant seating 160 in three rooms on two floors. First original balti house established 1992, Waheed Nazir took over in July 2000. Unlicensed so BYO. Head chef, Mohammed Zabair's, Mixed Grill at £12 is very popular and includes: Chicken Tikka, Sheek Kebab, King Prawns, Tandoori Chicken, Curry Sauce and Naan. Menu Snapshot: Fish Masala c£3.50 - marinated haddock, deep-fried; Balti Chilli Masala c£8 - finely chopped onions, capsicum, tomatoes, hot green chilli sauce; Aloo, Mushroom, Peshwari or Vegetable Paratha £1.75; Mushroom Fried, Egg Fried, Garlic or Peas Pullao £2.65, Pickle Tray £2.50. Del: 10m. do not accept credit cards. Sun-Thur: 5.30-12. (Fri-Sat: to 1).

Eccleshall

LONDON HOUSE
28, High St, ST21 6BZ   01785 850055

'Food is of a very high standard. My wife particularly enjoys the Chicken Rezala, I go for the Chicken Lamb Vegetable Mirchi. Presentation is excellent and the whole restaurant is light and attractive on a principal side street in this small town. Prices c£6 - £7 per dish.' DF. 6-11.

Keele

PRACHEE
Keele Golf Centte, Keele ST5 5AB   01782 636060

'An interesting setting for a curry house. The Prachee occupies the first floor of Keele Golf Club, and is clean and well decorated. Ali runs it. Service was good, staff were polite. I had a Prawn Rogan Josh, naan, plain rice, a beer, and a liqueur coffee for dessert. The curry was very well made, not overpowering but certainly well spiced. The Prachee caters very well for larger groups, and the dishes were served promptly. Recommended.' DW.

Lichfield

THE LODGE   BYO
24 Birmingham Rd, Shenstone Wood End, Lichfield WS14 0LQ   01543 401187   www.thelodgerestaurant.co.uk

Family owned and run since July 1996 and specialising in all the favourites with the favourite ingredients plus duck, trout and salmon. 'We had Paneer Chilli, strips of Indian Cheese, cooked with a blend of herbs and spices and sweet Mango sauce, followed by Main Course, Red Murgh Curry, tandoori chicken cooked in extra juicy tomatoes with chopped green chillies, black pepper corns and a hint of yoghurt. For Dessert we had Iced Hazelnut & Honey Parfait, and yes it was all parfait'. HEG.

Leek

BOLAKA SPICE   TOP 100
41 Stockwell Street, Leek   ST13 6DH
01538 373734   www.bolakaspiceleek.co.uk

Proprietor. Abdul Choudhury established his Bolaka in 1998. 'Primarily a formula curryhouse, but two features make it stand out - the Haandis menu and a small specials board. Keema Motor is an outstanding and rich mix of lamb, chick peas and spices. At Christmas, a divine Turkey Tikka Masala with vegetables. Aubergines in a Sweet Sauce is Wow! Service polite and efficient.' PK. 'Friendly and cosy, good welcome. Tables clean and ready with candles and flowers. Quality unbelievably good every time.' JA. 'Have dined here many times, food always very fresh and tasty.' RM. 'The best we have been too. Very friendly staff, clean tables, relaxing atmosphere and the best food - absolutely fabulous. Our favourite.' SS. You might get a discount if you show Abdul this Guide. 5.30-12 (to 1am Fri-Sat).

PABNA
16 Ashbourne Rd, ST13 5AS   01538 381156

Mohammed Shuyab is the owner. 'Pleasant clean decor and highly attentive staff. Well spiced Chicken Tikka for starter. Excellent CTM and delicately flavoured Pullao Rice. I have visited on previous occasions with my father and look forward to the next visit!' NG. Menu Snapshot: Gilafi Sheek Kebab £3, spicy; Melon with Cointreau £3, not curry at all, but sounds delicious, very pallet cleansing!; Tandoori Duck £8; Butter Chicken £6, tikka in creamy sauce; Amere Chicken £8.75, mango, wine, cream and almonds served with Pullao Rice; Naga Fall £7.50, yes, it's the famous Bangladeshi chilli - very hot!!!; Zeera Aloo £2.50; Banana in Ghee £2.50. Hours: 5-12.

Lichfield

EASTERN EYE   TOP 100
19b Bird St, Lichfield, WS13 6PW   01543 254399

Abdul Salam's venue represents a Swat valley house, right up in Pakistan's northern mountain ranges (just a nan nudge from Baltistan). It is famous for its forests and ornate wooden carved furniture, showing Buddhist influences going back 2,000 years. The beams, pillars and window are from Swat. The bar front is from neighbouring Afghanistan, the chairs are Rajasthani and the table tops are from 150-year-old elm. 'Count the rings,' enthuses Mr Salam. The toilets are a 'must-see' on your list. The theme is Agra's Red Fort - probably India's best example of a Moghul residence. The food is well spoken of. Specials include Murgh with Apricot, marinated chicken with apricot yoghurt sauce, cream and fresh coriander. Rajasthani Paro Breast - pigeon. Michael Fabricant, MP, MCC continues regularly to take his seat at the Eye as a loyal local, rating it highly, as do so many other reports we get, e.g. 'From entering you know it'll be good. I had Murgh Special with apricot which was delicious. My friend loved his Eastern Eye Mixed Massala (king prawn, lamb and chicken).' RL. 'Still my favourite. Mr Salam still very much in charge, evolving the menu and new dishes. Cooking excellent - far superior to average curry fare. All excellent. Amazingly light Naans. Wine list still consists of an armful of bottles placed on your table to take your pick from - a tradition I hope will remain.' PJ. 'The food was unusual and beautifully presented on huge oval china plates.' K&ST. Discount promised on Sundays if you show them this Guide. Hours: 12-2.30 Sat only / 5-12.

Stafford

CURRY KUTEER
31, Greengate St ST16 2HX   01785 2536279

Established: 1968. 'This traditional curry house has been refurbished, since we last visited in 2007. the service was prompt, attentive and although the visit was very early on a Friday evening, the restaurant was busy with diners and takeaway customers. The Chicken Tikka £3.30 - was pleasant, creamy, serving generous. Curry Kuteer, remains a value for money venue, run by a family who undeniably, love their customers.' NG. Menu Snapshot: Adraki Kofte £3.50 - spicy tuna, ginger kebab, shallow fried, served with salad; lamb Biriani £7.95, served with vegetable curry; Chana Masala £5.75, chicken peas, coconut cream sauce' Kulcha Nan £1.95, vegetable filled. 6-11.

Newcastle-under-Lyme

KAVI   HOTEL
Ramada Hotel, Clayton Rd, Newcastle, SST5 4AF
01782 613093   ramadanewcastleunderlyme.co.uk

The former 50 room Clayton Lodge Hotel is now a Ramada (from £44 per nt). It is about 2 minutes from J15 / M6 and has a major attraction for readers of this Guide – its Indian restaurant Kavi. It is split level and bursting with design features such as the furnishings imported from India, the soft silk-tented ceiling and stunning marble floors. But the pièce de resistance has to be the imposing black granite wall of water, crossed by a glass bridge with koi carp swimming below. On the lower level a plasma screen with Bollywood movies vies for attention with the open-plan kitchen. This is the preserve of chef Avinash Kumar, ex Baylis, Slough, Berks (see entry) and Claridges Delhi. Starters include Panjabi Jhinga, Shakarkandi Chaat, and Kalmi Kebab. Favourite dishes include Amiritsari Talli Macchi, pan seared fillets of sea bass on a bed of sautéed red cabbage with a korma sauce, and Lamb Shank, a leg of baby lamb simmered in Kashmiri masala sauce served with steamed basmati rice Quail Hara Masala £10, Whole fresh quail simmered in a mint and coriander chutney. Veg dishes include Palak ke Kofte £8, spinach dumplings stuffed with prunes and served with a korma sauce. Desserts include: Gajar ka Halwa £4.25, carrot pudding wrapped in a French crepe; Rasmalai £3.75, milk pudding dumplings dipped in sweetened reduced milk. Open from 6pm, Mon-Sat. *Branches Kavi at Ramada Hotels: Birmingham, Warwick and Wolverhampton.*

Stoke-on-Trent

ALESSI
50-54 Church Street, Audley, Stoke, ST7 8DA
01782 720845   www.alessidining.co.uk

This family-run business opened in Mar 2011. All the favourites plus specials are on the menu, though their claim that some are unique to Alessi is pure spin. That said you like the freshness of the food, the staff and the service. '*Lamb Handi on the bone is authentic £12.95*'. There is an outside courtyard for alfresco dining. Starter & main special, Sun-Th 5-8 £12.50 pp. Tu-Sun: 12-2 & 5-11.30.

BOMBAY CLUB   www.bombayclub.co.uk
325 Hartshill Road, Hartshill   01782 719191

Mafazzul Meah (Faz)'s thoroughly modern restaurant, minimalist chic, wooden floors, plain walls. Chef Jabi Lal-Kharel's menu snapshot: Banjarra Chohila, chicken strips cooked in tandoor with spring onion & Himalayan spices; Mulai Lamb Chops marinated in rich herbs & spices and garlic £5; Surkh Uran Pari , sliced duck breast sauted with cumin seeds & onion served in an aromatic spicy sauce £13; Nilgirii Koorma, cubes of mutton sautéed with onion & cooked in a green massala sauce; Kabbuli Gosht, lamb & chich peas flavoured with fennel garlic & ginger, both £11. '*Most of the curry houses I have visited serve curries which are surrounded by a pool of oil but not this one. I have yet to find a place like it. The chef cooks the most delicious curries I have ever tasted. I have tried many times to get the recipes for two of my favourites but, not being adept at making curries I have ben unable to recreate it.*' MM.

YOU SAY OK
You might get a discount if you show them this Guide

HANLEY, STOKE: MANGO TREE Ivy House, Bucknall New Rd, 01782 207470 '*Bringing remarkably good dishes to the area*'. DW. www.the-mango-tree.co.uk
HEDNESFORD: BENGAL BRASSERIE 44 Market St, Hednesford ~ 01543 424769
RUGELEY: BILASH 7 Horsefair, Rugeley ~ 01889 584234
STOKE-ON-TRENT: BLUE TIFFIN 1003 Uttoxeter Road, Meir, Stoke-on-Trent ST3 6HE 01782 595978 www.blue-tiffin.com Popular venue serving good fromula food. Sunday buffet two servings, 12-4pm and 5-10pm.
STOKE-ON-TRENT: KISMET 1A Queen Street, Stoke-on-Trent 01782 818 278 www.kismetstoke.com
UTTOXETER: KOHI NOOR 11 Queen St. 01889 562153

SUFFOLK

Area: East

Adjacent Counties: Cambs, Essex, Norfolk

Bury-St-Edmonds

THE LAST DAY OF RAJ
Station Hill, Bury St Edmonds   01284 725727

'*If I could name on fault in The Last Day of Raj, it is its location, in one of the less fancy areas of my home town Bury, it being near the railway station. The bright green lighting in the windows may also put some people off, if they were averse to such illumination. However, the food is of a very good standard, and the menu is extensive. A group of us dined there, and the service was not slow, but not too quick. I had a Lamb Ceylon, and it was rich, with a definite hint of fresh coriander, and a generous coconut influence in the sauce. The Kulcha Naan was quite sweet and fresh, accompanied with some clean plain rice. My friends enjoyed a Chicken Vindaloo, a Chicken Madras, bhajis and a special rice dish, which had liberal helpings of fresh saffron on the side. The pricing for the meals was good; main courses between £4.50 and £8. However, Serv came to £10.80, which was rather high considering two of my friends were not eating main courses, but were enjoying some lighter dishes. I am very pleased with the level of service, the music, and the cleanliness. Recommended. Five cost £44.80*'. DW.

VALLEY CONNECTION
42 Churchgate St, Bury IP33 1RG   01284 753161

'White painted walls. black and white throughout. comfortable leather chairs. service all waiters dressed in black, extremely attentive, prompt and polite. Some exciting dishes I've never seen before. Quality excellent. quantity copious. a couple of outstanding lamb dishes. very busy for amonday night. overall a most enjoyable experience. Bill £42.20 for one. A top notch restaurant with mark, 8.7/10.' G&MP.

Felixstowe

BLUE NAAN
7, Hamilton Rd,   IP11 7AX   01394 671779

A stunning 130-seater owned by Anwar Hussain. His sons, Humayun and Tahir manage. It's beautifully decorated in a minimalist style, featuring rich blue and burgundy walls, with complimentary modern furnishings. Chef Motin offers Korai dishes, Balti Specials, Jalfrezi dishes, Biriani, plus English, Persian and many other dishes. Private dining lounge for 25.

Ipswich

GULSHAN TAKEAWAY
9 Stoke Street, Ipswich   01473 692929
www.gulshantakeaway.co.uk

Originally opened in 1996, taken over in 2003 by Mohibur Rahman. Menu Snapshot: Vegetable Chat £2.40; Butter Lamb £6.75 - lightly spiced, butter, fresh cream and almond; Balti dishes from Jalfrezi to Tikka Masala, all c£8 regardless of whether you choose chicken, lamb or prawn, served with Pullao Rice or Naan ; Mushroom or Onion Fried Rice all £2.25; Stuffed, Peshwari, Keema, Garlic with Coriander or Onion Naan all £2. Del: 6m £12 min. 5-12 daily.

YOU SAY OK
You might get a discount if you show them this Guide.

BRANDON: BRANDON TANDOORI 17 London Road, Brandon 01842 81587
BURY ST EDMUNDS: ORISSA INDIAN 108 Risbygate Street, Bury St Edmunds, IP33 3AA 01284 719116 www.orissa.com Serving standard Bangladeshi curryhouse menu at medium prices. 12-2:30 & 5:30-10:30.
FELIXSTOWE: BLUE NAAN 7 Hamilton Road, Felixstowe IP11 7QS 01394 671779 www.bluenaan.co.uk Serving standard Bangladeshi curryhouse menu at medium prices.
IPSWICH: DOSA EXPRESS Indian and Srilankan BYO 25-27 Upper Orwell Street, Ipswich IP4 1HN 01473 515349 www.dosaexpressipswich.co.uk Don't go for the formula curries, it is not a curryhouse. Try their Indian and SriLankan dishes. See page 74. There is a full range at affordable prices and the staff are very helpful with expanations.
IPSWICH: MY KERALAM 24 St. Helens Street, Ipswich IP4 1HJ 01473 288 599 As with Dosa Express above go for their South Indian food. It's at affordable prices. See page 74. 6-10.30.
IPSWICH: PASSAGE TO INDIA 327 Fore St 01473 286220. www.apassagetoindiaipswich.com 140-seater in 3 rooms est 1991

by R Uddin. Brother Nassir chefs. 44 starters! T/a: 10% disc. Del: 3m £30min. 12-2.30 & 5.30-12.
LOWESTOFT: AHMED 150 Bridge Rd, Oulton Broad ~ 01502 501725 Boshor Ali's tiny 28 -seater is *'brilliant.'* PJ. Hours: 12-2.30 & 6-11.30. Branch: *Jorna Takeaway, 33 Wherstead Rd, Ipswich.*
IPSWICH: ZAIKA St. Nicholas Street, Ipswich, IP1 1TW 01473 210110 http://www.zaikaipswich.co.uk Husband and wife Kashwi and Mohammed Abid pened I 2005 and provide the standard menu. 5.30-11.30.
LOWESTOFT LABONE INDIAN Station Building Bridge Rd.,Oulton Broad (North Station), Lowestoft, NR32 3LP 01502 515617 www.labone-indiancuisine-norfolk.co.uk 5-11.
LOWESTOFT: SEETA 176 High St, Lowestoft ~ 01502 574132
NEWMARKET: ARIF INDIAN 30 Old Station Rd ~ 01638 665888. *'An excellent, well served meal.'* JP.**NORTH WALSHAM LABONE INDIAN** 13A Mundesley Road; North Walsham; NR28 0AD 01693 500062 12-2pm & 5-10.30.
SHERINGHAM;LABONE INDIAN 40 Cromer Road; Sheringham; NR26 8RR 01263 821120 12-2pm & 5-10.30.

SURREY

Area: Home Counties (south of London)

Adjacent Counties: Berks, Hants, Kent, London, Sussex

Addlestone

NILIS
198 Station Road, Addlestone, KT 15 2PD
01932 830424   www.nilisrestaurant.com

Mohammed Rob's Nilis serves the full standard menu in generous portions. Intriguing specials include unusual use of the option of flambéing with liqueur (extra £1) eg: Khushbu Bilash £9, chicken with a sauce including wine, rose water & saffron; Shorabi Pasanda £7, Chicken/Lamb tikka with rum, almond, sultanas & coconut, mild & sweet; Scallop Paneer Pasanda £8, scallop & soft cube cheese ditto; Chana Chicken/ Lamb TikkaPalok £8, Bed of spinach with chick peas,Indian ghee, very dry; the following East Bengali Sylhetti specials are fairly hot with a fragrance of citrus (shatkora). 'A Nili secret – beware of Vampire's teeth [sic menu]: Rupchanda Bhujon £9 special fish dish normally served for aspecial guest in Bangladesh. 'Be aware, this fish comes with bone[[sic]; Osmani Bhujon £11, king prawn with butter beans and a seasonal Bangladeshi vegetable, thick sauce, little sour & hot; Shurovi Shurma £9, a mixture of seafood with dark rum, spinach with chickpeas. Fri-Sun: 12-2 Tu-Sun: 5-11.

Ashtead

The MOGUL DYNASTY
1 Craddocks Parade, Ashtead KT21 1QL 01372 274810   www.moguldynasty.co.uk

A well-loved fully licensed a/c restaurant run by

experienced, friendly staff, offering all the favourites. As they say, many of their dishes are 'cooked in tandoor'. Cheques accepted supported by a bankers card. Minimum charge pp £14.

Cheam Village

SAMSARA
23-25 High Street, Cheam, SM3 8RE
020 8642 4488   www.samsararestaurant.com

The favourites are available plus starter specials such as: Crab Cake £6.25, marinated with ginger, coriander red chilli, fresh cream and cheese served with tamarind sauce; Tandoori Smoked duck £6, served with a salad of red cabbage, apple and orange chutney; Bagan-E-Bahar £4.25, baked aubergine steak, mixed with cheese and sesame seeds and a yoghurt sauce; Mains include: Salmon Shah £12, home smoked tandoori salmon flavoured with mustard oil and dill, served with a cold salad; Adraki Champen £8, lamb chop marinated with fresh ginger and tandoori spices; Spiced Monkfish £12, marinated with crushed roasted spices, pan fried and served with coconut and tomato sauce; Railway lamb £12, with baby potatoes cooked with coconut, curry leaves and fresh herbs, served with spinach, an Anglo Indian speciality, developed when the British were laying railway tracks in India; Tawa Duck £12, marinated in garlic, ginger, mustard, coriander and honey, served with stir fried noodles and a sauce. Mon-Fri: 12-2.30; Mon - Sat 5.30-11. (Sun to 10).

Cobham

MASSALA   FINE INDIAN DINING   A-LIST
19 Anyards Road, Cobham KT11 2LW
01932 865005   www.massalacobham.com

Cobham is a prosperous commuter village just 20 miles south-west of central London. It is home to under 11,000 people and Chelsea football training ground, many of whose players and staff live in the vicinity. The Daily Mail has proclaimed it as the UK's best place to be. Even so, Cobham is an unlikely location to pioneer authentic fine Indian dining. Few had attempted it outside central London. Nor was its location going to help its haute-cuisine image. No: 19, is at one end of an ordinary terrace of five shop units. At the other end is one of the two bog-standard curryhouses in the village; in the middle is a fish and chip shop. However there is nothing ordinary about Massala. The owner's dream was to serve real authentic Indian cuisine, not the curryhouse pastiche. Cobham is his home town and he owned owned no 19. He decorated it simply with white washed brickwork and a hard floor, making it a bright and clean looking restaurant. The bar at the back is not ideal, as you are relying on the staff to be eagle-eyed when entering and greeting you without delay. Colourful artwork of Rajasthani puppets hang on the walls together with quality gold leaf silk paintings. To realise his dream he recruited exceptional Indian chefs. Heading the brigade is Chef Sunil Kumar Sinha. He has cooked for British royalty and is Taj-trained and that means he is hands-on. But he likes to welcome his guests, old and new and he will be found in the restaurant, making dish suggestions and taking initial orders. He really cares that you order the right dish, one that suites your palate. Sunil is assisted by Chef Ravi Deulkar, ex Oberoi and Rasoi Vineet *(see p132)*. A great introduction is the Five Course Taster Menu, £29.95pp (min 2) exceptionally good value considering the dishes served, which pops & home-made chutneys. Starters include Methi Machchi Tikka, fenugreek-flavoured fish; Zafarini Malai Tikka, saffron & cream chicken; and Gillafiseek Lamb; Mains: Murg Tikka Lababdar; Lamb Rogan Josh; Aloo Hara Dhania Massala, potato with green herbs; Tadka Dal; Pilau Rice and an assortment of Naan and Paratha. Followed by (if you have the room), a choice of dessert: Chocolate Chili Brownies, (they're hot, using habañero chillies, but also wonderfully chocolatey); Exotic Ice Cream or Gulab Jamun. Vegetarians are not left out, as they have their own special menu. The test of a great chef is Dal Makhani, black lentils cooked over charcoal with cream and butter for 30 hours. It is exquisite at Massala and is their signature dish. A-la-carte starters include Zafarini Malai Tikka £5, chicken marinated in cream, cheese, cardamom & coriander, tandoor-cooked; Delhi Aloo Tikki £5, potato patties filled with a combination of spiced dates, ginger and cashews topped with a tamarind and mint sauce; Punjabi Gilafiseek £6, minced lamb tandoor-cooked in and wrapped in fresh aromatic vegetables flavoured with ginger and hot spices. *'Celia, having recently discovered Indian cheese, decided that Tandoori Paneer Khaas - Punjab Region £5.50 - Indian Cottage Cheese filled with piquant chutney and pickles and marinated and grilled with vegetables in a clay oven, would be her choice and beamingly reported that it was amazing.'* DBAC. Starters are stylishly presented on white plates. Mains' take the diner on a Pan-Indian voyage, for example: Lucknowi Safroni Chicken Korma £10, is infused with saffron & cardamom and cooked with cashew nuts, onions and topped with almond flakes. *'It's unlike any other Korma that you may have tried, it is a deliciously rich dish. It is the best Korma I've ever tasted! I don't think I'll ever order a Curry House Korma again!'* HB. Delhi Murg Tikka Lababdar £11 is Chicken Tikka cooked with fenugreek-flavoured onion & tomato sauce with coriander and cream. Saffron Pilau Rice £3.75, Naan Bread £3. The wine list is very impressive too. Massala has a team to be proud of. Everything is stunning and I don't say that very often. Cobham is very lucky indeed to have such a fine restaurant in their town. Such cooking and service outclasses many of the so-called top Indian restaurants in the West End, but at Massala it's under half the West End price. Takeaway and delivery services available. Booking advisable. 12-2.30 & 5-11.30. *See page 1*

"A jewel in the crown of Cranleigh"

Curry Inn
fine indian dining ■84■

Est 1984

Open Every Day
12-2.30pm
& 5.30-11.30pm

**214-216, High Street,
Cranleigh, Surrey, GU6 8RL**

01483 273992 - 271785

info@curryinn84.co.uk
www.curryinn84.co.uk

Voted The Best Indian & Bangladeshi
Restaurant in the South East
Awards 2010 and 2011

Cranleigh

CURRY INN
214-216, High Street, Cranleigh, GU6 8RL
01483 273992   www.curryinn84.co.uk

A smart jet black frontage picked out with blue neon signage denotes the presence of the Curry Inn facing the smart green in this tidy village. You'll see the numbers 84. It denotes the start-up year of this family business; headed by Jubair Zaman. Something to be proud of – we should know – this Guide started in the same year. Selim Ahmed manages and all your favourites are competently cooked. There are some unusuals too, eg: Crab Claws £3.09, lightly spiced white crab meat ball with claws-crispy fried; Pepe Calamari £3.59, spiced battered squid-crispy ring; Murgh Malabar £8.99, spring chicken marinated and infused with spices, char grilled and then slowly cooked in a rich velvety sauce truly authentic and highly recommended, Monkfish in Masala £9.99, with mild spices and lime leaves, fresh herbs-coconut milk curry; Chasnidargh £8.99, chicken breast cooked with honey, balsamic vinegar & slices of lemon zest in a sweet & sour flavour sauce, recommended with lemon rice; Sobz-E-Kazana £6.99, fresh vegetables and roasted peppers tossed in hot spicy sauce finished with crushed melon seeds. Sunday e-a-m-a-y-l buffet: £8.99 pp, £6.49 kids. Daily: 12-2.30 & 5.30–11.30.

Croydon

BANANA LEAF
7 Lower Addiscombe Road · Croydon CR0 6PQ
020 8688 02977   www.thebananaleaf.com

Opened in 1988 by Rajkumar Rengaraj, who will greet you on your visit, as he is also the manager. Nearest Tramlink / Rail Station East Croydon and Bus Route 289 and 410. Seats seventy in two dining rooms. Menu Snapshot: of course the menu lists all the usual North Indian favourites, but let's forget those and go straight to Chef Thirumugam Sundaram's well cooked South Indian dishes: Chicken 65 £3.80, chicken marinated with a paste of green chilli ginger, garlic & coriander; Mini Masala Dosai stuffed with spiced potato and onion; Masala Vadai £2.75, savoury spiced snack made with chana daal, ginger and fennel seeds; Curd Vadai £2.75, plain vadai in fresh yoghurt with coriander and tomato; Malaba Fish Curry £7.50, 2 pieces of Indian Ocean Kingfish in a sauce made from fresh coconut milk & a mixture of fresh spices; Khozi Chettinadu £7, chicken cooked in a rich, dark sauce of cinnamon, cardamom & onions, is chef Sundaram's signature dish; Ginger Chicken £7, with lots of fresh ginger paste; Spicy South Indian Fried Meat £7, lamb marinated with ginger, garlic, almond & coriander.   12-2.30 & 6-11.30; 11 Sun.

COBRA — SPLENDIDLY INDIAN, SUPERBLY SMOOTH

CHENNAIDOSA SOUTH INDIAN/SRI LANKAN
239 - 241 London Road CR0 2RL 020 8665 9192 www.chennaidosa.com

Located in the former Deans premises. Now part of the growing chain. See page 100 for details. Hrs: 9am - 11pm.

CHILLI CHUTNEY PAKISTANI
Allders Mall, Croydon, CR9 1SB
020 8726 0780 www.chillichutney.com

Owner Neelofar Khan's mission is *'to make authentic, contemporary Lahori food accessible to all,in a thoroughly modern and vibrant ambience'* [sic]. Following, he says, frequent visits to India and Pakistan to develop the concept and source qualified Lahori chefs, the 130-seat restaurant opened in late 2003. It very soon became the official caterer for the UK Pakistan High Commission. Hours: 12-11 daily. *Branch: Chilli Chutney, 20 The High Parade, Streatham High Road, SW16 & Chilli Chutney, 47 York Road · Waterloo, SE1 7NJ 020 7021 0202*

KERALA BHAVAN SOUTH INDIAN
16, London Road, West Croydon, CR0 2TA 020 8668 6216 www.keralagroup.co.uk

Conveniently next to West Croydon Railway Station. *'The usual Indian background music was playing as we entered this pleasant restaurant. There are about 50 seats, set in alcoves, which gave a more intimate feel and was very nice. The waiter was very friendly and attentive. For a starter Ray had Parippu Vada, two spicy fried lentil cakes. I tried a bit and said it tasted like a dry spicy bun. Ray said I was a Philistine, smothered his with onions, lime pickle and raitha and said I did not know what I was missing. For his main course,he had Kerala Meat Chilli. This consisted of quite hot cubes of very lean and tender lamb, which had been marinated in a sweet & sour marinade, then cooked with green chillies and capsicums. It was a dry dish, but very spicy. Ray enjoyed it and said he would recommend it. He also had a Kerela Veesu Paratha, a sort of bread in strands. This was most unusual but a good accompaniment to the chilli meat. He also had a dall, which was very runny & bland'.* R&RE. 10% Serv. 12-3 & 6-11. *Branches and menu details, see p150, Rhada Krishna Bhavan, London SW17.*

MIRCH MASALA PUNJABI/KENYAN BYO
40-42 Southend Road, Croydon CR0 1DP
0208 680 3322 www.mirchmasalarestaurant.co.uk

One of seven branches with identical meat, fish and veg menu. BYO. No corkage. 12-12. *See p 146, SW16 for full details.*

PLANET SPICE A-LIST
88 Selsdon Park, Addington, Croydon CR2 8JT
020 8651 3300 www.planet-spice.com

Opened in 1999 by the very talented Emdad Rahman of Babur SE23 fame. This fantastic restaurant is well decorated in a modern and colourful style. Raj Pandey, ex Taj Madras is head chef and he delights his regulars with such starters as Scallops Pondicherry £6.95, French inspired recipe cooked in southern spices; Pathia Puree £5.75, Spicy prawns cooked with garlic and onion served on a moghlai pancake; Murg Kofti £4.95, fillo pastry filled with potatoes, carrots, beans and cashew nuts; Ragda Pattice £4.95, potato cakes topped with dried chick pea curry; Bombay Qutabshai £5.25, chunks of tasty saithi fish trapped in a light batter and garnished with tangy coriander sauce. Mains include: Masala Roast Lamb Shank £9.75, braised with spices and ground sesame seeds, then marinated in a strained yogurt and slow pot roasted to melt in the mouth; Beef Xacuti £9.50, a goan speciality of beef in a spicy sauce; Chicken Peri Peri £8.95, a classic Portuguese dish with a touch of aromatic Indian spices; Karai Duck Tikka £9.95, marinated charcoal grilled duck cooked in thick medium spicy sauce with fresh garlic, ginger, green pepper and tomato; Chilli Paneer £7.50, fried fresh cottage cheese with onions, peppers, tamarind and chillies. Papadoms and chutneys £1.25 pp. Serv: 10%. Sun Buf:£10.95 pp, £6.95, 7-12, u7's free. Del: 3m £10 min. 12.30-2.30 & 6.30-11.30. *Branch: Babur, 119, Brockley Rise, Forest Hill. SE23.*

YOU SAY OK
You might get a discount if you show them this Guide.
BYFLEET: RED ROSE 148 High Rd, 01932 355559.
CAMBERLEY: DIWAN EE KHAS 413 London Rd, Camberley 01276 23500.
CAMBERLEY: RAJPUR 57d Mytchett Road, Mytchett, Camberley 01252 542063.
CARSHALTON GL: ROSE HILL TANDOORI 320 Wrythe Lane, Rose Hill 020 8644 9793.
CHIPSTEAD: CHIPSTEAD TANDOORI 32 Chipstead Station Parade 01737 551219. Seats fifty diners in two rooms. Sun Buffet: c£8 adult, c£6 children. Banquet Night: every Tuesday, £9.95 each. T/a: 20% disc, £10 min - cash only. Del: £12 min. 12-2 / 5.30-11; 11.30 Fri & Sat. Monday closed.
CROYDON: BHARAT BHAVAN INDIAN 10 Lower Addiscombe Road, Croydon, CR0 6AA 020 8680 5553 www.bharatbhavan.net Formula dishes such as Butter chicken, kormas, Baltis and many other Indian specialties. Over £10 for free del, or £2 for orders below. Daily 6-11.

Dorking

RED CHILLI
A24 Horsham Rd, Mid Holmwood, Dorking 01306 644816 www.redchillidorking.com

Wasimul Choudhury opened his 100-seater in 2005 in this stand-alone detached house on the A24. It's on the northbound carriageway, about a mile south of Dorking. Locals love its ample parking and good food. Newcomers spot the large roadside red chilli sign *'Decor, really attractive and modern. Water feature in entrance. Lovely quality china and cutlery, waiters all in blue shirts and ties. Menu large but very conventional, shame, had hoped for a more adventurous choice. Wine opened incorrectly, plates handed across the table to the diner. But the food was excellent and attractively presented in plain white dishes. Overall a very pleasant evening.'* HC. Menu Snapshot: Paneer Pakora £3.75; Batak Raja Naga Shahi £8, duck with the famous chilli; Dhal Makhni £5, black lentils with ginger, garlic, cream & butter. Weds Banquet Night: astarter, main course, side dish rice dish or naan & coffee: £15. 12-2.30 & 5.30-11; 11.30 Fri & Sat.

Epsom

BLUE MINT
21 Waterloo Road, Epsom, KT19 8EX
01372 724167   www.blue-mint.co.uk

Owner Moin Uddin and manager Parvez have all the favourite items on their menu plus special starters eg: Baby Squid with garlic, ginger, green chillies & curry leaves; Spicy Crab Cake, a fried rissole with mashed potato & fresh coconut; Cashew Nut Roll, spicy mashed potato coated with cashew nuts and deep-fried until golden. Mains include: Doi Mass, seabass curry; Chilli Chat chicken or lamb, with green herbs & chillies, coriander & spinach purée; Khodu, hot and spicy lamb or chicken cooked with sweet pumpkin. 12-30; Sun-Th: 6-11.30; Fri-Sat: 6-12.

LE RAJ   FINE INDIAN DINING   A-LIST
211 Fir Tree Rd, Epsom Downs ,Epsom, KT17 3LB
01737 371371   www.lerajrestaurant.co.uk

Le Raj began quietly in 1989 in an outpost of well-healed Epsom. Its owner Enam Ali was more in the kitchens than out front, and one of his ventures was as offering an airborne curry called 'Raj Avion', a one hour flight out of City airport aboard chartered a Dash 7 with chef Enam serving his curries to diners paying £99. Great fun but short-lasting. Enam searched about for more things to do and he set up the Guild of Bangladeshi Restaurateurs in an attempt to unify the industry. He is publisher of the industry's ***Spice Business*** magazine. In 2005 he produced his first ***British Curry Awards***. Meanwhile Le Raj was growing in stature. Recently Enam undertook a redec with the oak-panelled dining room straight out of Downton Abbey. The food is as far removed from curryhouse as can be. Starter examples include : Xenuk Lahar £4, mussels in shell cooked with garlic, roasted spices & fresh organic lime juice; Malai Maach £6, cod fillet marinated in cardamom; Chuto Chingri £5.60, tiger prawns marinated and tandoored. Main courses include: Murg-e-Morchana £10.95, marinated lean chicken cooked with hand-ground roasted spices, green chillies, fresh coriander; Kata gosht £9.95, lamb cooked with lentils, chillies &d curry leaves; Lamb Haleem, meat cooked with chickpeas, barley, crushed wheat, lentils & spices in a slow process. Side dishes include: Peaz Pilaw £3.95, basmati rice with eggs, spring onion a& parsley; Khumbi Bhaat £3.95, plain rice with & green herbs; Shak Aloo £4.20, spinach and potatoes; Paneer Nan £3.50, with chillies, mint, cheese & garlic. When he's there get Enam talking about food, someting he likes doing. And get him to explain his innovation 'involving a complex process so unlike common taste of nan acclaimed by food critic as E-nan'. [sic]. 12-2.30; 6-11.

Esher

SHERPA KITCHEN   TOP 100
132 High Street, Esher, KT10 9QJ   01372 470777   www.sherpakitchen.co.uk

A branch of our Award-Winning Gurkha Kitchen, Oxted. See Oxted, Surrey entry for details .

Ewell

SRI KRISHNA INN   SOUTH INDIAN
332 Kingston Rd, Ewell. KT19 0DT   020 8393 0445

M Krishna Das took over this 70-seater in 2001. Masala Dosa is their most popular dish. See p74 for cuisine descriptions. Del: 3m £20 min. Set lunch/dinner £24 for 2. Min charge: £15. 12-3 & 6-11.

SRI GANESH   SOUTH INDIAN
397 Kingston Rd, Ewell KT19 0DT   020 8393 3511

In the block of shops on the opposite side of the road this Sri also serves an identical southern Indian menu (see p74 for cuisine descriptions) and formula items too. 12-3 & 6-11.

Farnham

FARNHAM TANDOORI
47 West St, Farnham, GU9 7DX
01252 711860   www.the-farnham-tandoori.co.uk

This 50 seater opened in 1983 and offers all your favourites at reasonable prices. Chicken, lamb, duck, fish, prawns, and vegetables are all on offer. Set meal £36.50 for 2: Starters, Surma Chicken, Garlic Chilli Lamb, Sag Aloo, Naan & Pilaw Rice. Veg ditto £27.50: Onion Bhaji & veg Samosa then Veg Rogon, Karahi Veg, Sag Aloo, Rice & Naan. Weds Nt 4 Course £10.95. Sunday Buffet : e-a-m-a y-l £11.95 (£7.50 u12). T/a 10% off over £15. 12-2 & 6-11.30 (to 12 Fri-Sat)

The Farnham Tandoori Restaurant

Fully Licensed
Est 1983

We will provide you the best Tandoori and Curry dishes

Take away service available
**47 West Street, Farnham
Surrey, GU9 7DX**
Opening hours: 12:00 – 2:00pm and 6:00 – 11:30pm

01252 711860 / 716853
www.the-farnham-tandoori.co.uk

COBRA — SPLENDIDLY INDIAN, SUPERBLY SMOOTH

Fetcham

FETCHAM TANDOORI
248 Cobham Rd, Fetcham, KT22 9JF
01372 374927   www.fetchamtandoori.co.uk

'Made very welcome. Extensive menu, nothing unusual. Relishes good, with exceptionally delicious mango chutney.'Onion Bhajee £3.95, flat disc style, very good. Chicken Makhone £9,excellent, lovely thick almondy sauce with very good Mushroom Rice. Excellent and generous Fish Boal Masala, I was encouraged by one waiter to have the fish as, 'it only has one bone in the middle'. It was good. Sag Bhajee, one of the best I have had. Brinjal Bhajee also excellent. We were really pleased, all the food was well above average. Service, friendly, attentive and efficient with a very pleasant atmosphere - we shall return very soon.' HC. New Specials all £9.05 include: Jairpuri Murog , half roast chicken with Garam & Kashmiri Mussala & fresh coriander; Katmondi Gurkha, Half Tandoori Chicken, cooked with mincemeat & different herbs & spices, Sylhety Lamb, with coconut in home made yoghurt- medium spiced & Madras Hot); Labra Veg £4.50, potato, peas, carrot cubes, onion, garlic & fresh green chilli. 12-2; (to 3 Sun) & 6-11 (to 12 Fri-Sat).

Guildford

PURBANI
98 Stoke Rd, Guildford, GU1 4JN
01483 579393   www.purbanitakeaway.com

'We've used this takeaway for several years when we want a Indian meal delivered to the house. We have always been very happy with the quality, variety and service provided which certainly match those of high quality restaurants. There is a full selection of the usual items plus a list of about 20 specialities. Oneis Swadi Chicken which is well worth a try. The Chicken Tikka Dhansak is also great and can be ordered 'Vindaloo-hot' which is my favourite. Other of my favourites are Chicken or Lamb Xacuti medium spiced Goan dishes flavoured with roasted fennel seeds, garlic ginger and coriander. My favourite side dish is Vegetable Samba, a selection of vegetables in a spicy lentil- based sauce. Some free paps are usually included. There is a 10% discount on collections. Chicken Madras £5.10 and CTM £7.20 to give an idea of prices.' EB. Free del over £12. 5.30-11.30.

YOU SAY OK

EAST MOLESEY: SHAHEE MAHAL 101 Walton Rd, East Molesey ~ 020 8979 0011. Owned by Shiraz since 1974. *'It really is first class – we had our wedding reception there.'* FE.
ESHER: PANAHAR TANDOORI 124, High Street, Esher ~ 01372 463081. *'Easily the best in the area, no mistake.'* D&DP. 12-2.30 & 6-11.30; 12 Sat.
HAMPTON WICK: ORCHID 5 High St, Hampton Wick, KT1 4DA 020 8977 9111. Est 2006. *'Food is some of the best we've ever tasted, and the service superb.'* S&NB.
HAMPTON COURT: COCUM: 20, Bridge Road, Hampton Court, KT8 9HA 020 8979 1531 See head branch Rhada Krishna Bhavan, London SW17, p130. www.keralagroup.co.uk
HERSHAM: RESHMI 90 Molesey Rd.~ 01932 219291. *'My mum, born and brought up in India, loves it!'* A&UK.

HINCHLEY WOOD: PANSHI 7 Station Approach, Hinchley Wood, Esher, KT10 0SP   020 8398 8585 www.thepanshi.co.uk Chef proprietor S.Rahman opened his Panshi (a traditional Bangladeshi boat) in 2011. The menu is formula stuff. Reports please. Sat-Th: 12-2.30 & 6-11.

Horley   2 miles north of Gatwick

JAI HOI
The Coppingham Arms, 263 Balcombe Road, Horley, RH6 9EF   01293 782283   www.jaihorestaurants.com

Suresh Mehra who is also the GM and Sam Ahluwalia took over the former Coppingham Arms pub, a rather cute roadside Swiss Cottage-like building with ample parking. It has been refurbished throughout, revealing a light, contemporary and spacious interior. It has a separate bar and diners can also enjoy drinks on the terrace in good weather. Jai Ho means "Victory to you". It is also a song from the hit film *Slum Dog Millionaire*. Indian Chefs Samwal and Natra Singh are in charge of cooking. Starters include: Chicken Lollipop £4.95, drumsticks coated in Chinese style batter and deep fried; Mari Chicken £5.25, marinated in crushed black pepper and herbs cooked in a clay oven; £4.25 Fish Kholiwada £5.50, fillets marinated with dry spices and herbs and deep fried. Mains include: Lamb Chop Massala £10.95, Lamb on the bone, cooked in spices and herbs, Murg Bhagum Bahar £10.95, boneless chicken dumpling with minced cottage cheese, green chutney and pan fried finished in a rich cashew gravy; Goan Prawn Curry £11.95, King prawns prepared in Goan home made spices; Samunder Bahar £12.95, chef's special seafood curry. To prove the chefs are Indian they do the wonderfully thin Romali Roti £2.50, Indian thin flat bread folded to give a handkerchief like appearance. It's beyond curryhouse skills. Ask to see them make it. The Dhum Pukht Biryani from £9 is a dish dating back to 1784 and was a royal delight among the Nawabs. It's cooked in a slow simmering pot with hot coals placed on top and sealed with dough to retain the food's natural aromas and flavours. Mon to Fri Lunch £4.95 to £6.95. 10% off collected takeaways of min £20. Mon-Sun: 12-3 & 6 - 11.

Kingston-on-Thames GL

MONTYS TANDOORI   NEPALESE
53 Fife Road, Kingston KT1 1SF   020 8546 1724

70-seater owned by Kishor Shrestha. Indian face-masks decorate the white walls and hang from cream drapes. Hand-painted silk pictures of Indian scenes cover the walls, the floor is tiled. Top notch Nepalese food. *'Service is excellent, unobtrusive, polite.*12-2.3 & 6-12. Branch: See Ealing, W5, for details.

SRI KRISHNA INN   KERALAN
332 Kingston Rd, Kingston, KT19 0DT
020 8393 0445

It's their south Indian Keralan food which you should

go for, rather than the curryhouse favourites. No one does better vegetarian food than Kerala. The bench mark is the dosa, sambar lentils and rasam soup. *'I tried these for the first time since returning from Cochin. Lovely'.* RC. *'Lentils, gourds and light spicing means inexpensive ingredients and the cost here is minimal. Two of us filled up for £28 inc Cobra'* RL. Set thali Sun £10. Sun-Th: 12-3 & 6-11 (Fri-Sat to 11.30 *Branch: Sree Krishna Inn, Ewell, Surrey.*

ROZ ANA   PAN INDIAN FINE DINING TOP 100
4-8 Kingston Hill, Kingston, KT2 7NH, 020 8546 6388

Meaning "return daily" it delivers a casual, comfortable and buzzy ambiance to modern Indian dining. It is in three parts: the ground floor, the lounge bar and the 'brasserie'. They have an innovative childrens' menu with real Indian food the way kids under 10 like it. On the first floor is the more formal 40 seat restaurant managed by Igor Hotez.. It focuses on regional cuisine prepared by the Roz Ana Indian chefs. Starters include Jungli Soor £8, piccata of wild boar marinated with vinegar and robust spices, roasted over charcoal served with mint chutney and Punjabi pickled beetroot & onion; Chaat in a Box £6, is vegetable cutlet in a crisp semolina box, topped with pomegranate, smooth yoghurt, tamarind chutney, mint chutney and chopped red onion; Seared Scallops £9, seared with garlic, pepper, coriander and served with lotus root crisps; Coconut Soft Shell Crab £9, coated with toasted coconut, accompanied with pickled tomato & shrimp dip; Bhalla Papadi Chaat, £5.00, soft lentil dumplings with crisp semolina chips; topped with cool silky yoghurt, and tamarind chutney; Punjabi style Asparagus and Corn Samosa £6, Golden homemade samosas served as traditional with channa and chutney. Mains include the "wonderful" VC Chicken Tikka Laphroaig Masala £10, the nation's favourite dish flambéed with smokey single malt Laphroaig whisky; Chicken Chettinad £9.50, south Indian curry cooked with aromatic spices, curry leaves, tamarind an coconut; Patiala Shahi Lamb Shank £13 from the Royal House of Patiala, pot roasted shank in a spicy ginger, cardamom and clove sauce. Pork Belly Vinha d'alhos £13, commonly known as 'Vindaloo', [but not curry house style, Ed]. This uses slow-cooked pork belly in a tangy, piquant Goan spicy sauce; Mooplah Beef Curry £12, from a small south Indian community made with roasted ground spices and curry leaves. Desserts include Gulab Jamun, £4 and Rasmalai £5 (there for Hilary C) but try the Earl Grey Crème Brûlée £5, infused with Earl Grey tea served with homemade mandarin and white chocolate cookies. Mon-Sat:12-2:30 (Sun to 4pm) & 5:30-10:30 Fri-Sat to 11; Sun to 9pm.

Mitcham

CHAK 89   PUNJABI
Bond Road, Mitcham, CR4 3HG
020 8646 2177   www.chak89.com

Opened in 2005 by Fukhera Khalid. Seats a huge 140 diners and serves Punjabi food: Tawa Chicken dishes, Garlic and Chilli Fish and Grilled Tilapia being house specials. Fukhera also has an adjoining banqueting room. Weddings and parties can be catered for in this elegant room, up to 600 people: Free pops. Hours: 6-12; 1am Fri & Sat. Monday closed.

Morden

BLUE JUNCTION
2 Crown Parade, Morden, SM4 5DA
020 8540 2583   www.bluejunction.co.uk

Opened summer 2005, primarily as a contemporary bar. Its outdoor seating enhances its popularity as a stop for afterwork drinks and weekend parties. At lunchtimes there is a mixture of European and Indian dishes eg. Lamb Kofte Burger c£5, served with a yoghurt sauce, salads and sandwiches. Gourmet Wrap £4, Roti, or Naan with Spicy Lamb, Chicken or Paneer & Pea fillings served with lime pickle & yoghurt. Or there is the Balti Bowl c£5. In the evenings they serve a classical Indian menu. An old friend of this Guide and now restaurant critic on The Guardian, Humayun Hussain has even commented on the *'excellent vegetable dishes'* and he likes the chef: *'There's much to like about Chef Sebastian Fernandes menu'.* HH. Here are some of the evening dishes: Lollipop Chicken £3.50, a starter of chicken drumsticks dipped in lightly spiced gramflour batter and fried. Lamb Dum Biriani £10, lamb sautéed in herbs & spices, cooked with basmati rice and mint leaves. Raarha Chicken £8, a Punjabi delicacy made with chicken, minced lamb, ginger, garlic & fresh chillies; Paneer Tikka Shashlik £8.50, cubes of paneer marinated in a yoghurt masala, with peppers, onions & tomatoes; Kerelan King Prawn Moilee £10, sautéed with curry leaves, cooked in coconut milk. Mon-Th: 11-11 (to 12 Fri) Sat: 2-12; Sun: 4-11.

Newdigate   nr Dorking

ALI RAJ
Parkgate Road, Newdigate, RH5 5DZ   01306 631057

It was established in 1994 on a quiet country road near Gatwick directly opposite an excellent pub, the Surrey Oaks, which serves real ale, though Ali Raj is fully licensed. We occasionally turn up on the way back from Gatwick after a week in Spain. On our last visit, it was nearing midnight and as we approached the lights were still on. We stopped right outside the door. Was the chef still there? We were in luck! No problem.. So, Chicken Dhansak £7 including Pullao Rice and King Prawn Jalfrezi £9 was ordered to take. While we stood at the bar, eagerly waiting for the brown paper bag containing our feast to emerge from the kitchen. I must keep a plastic fork and spoon with napkins in the glove compartment for our next visit! During the summer the owner grows tomatoes in the back garden. Large plants line the perimeter, heavy with ripening fruit. I don't think you can eat in the garden which is a shame as it has a very sunny aspect. Sun Buffet: 12-2.30, adults c£9, children c£6. Min charge: £10. Hours: 12-2.30 & 6-12.

New Malden

SESAME RESTAURANT TOP 100
216, Kingston Road, New Malden, Surrey. KT3 3RJ
020 8949 2211   www.sesamerestaurant.co.uk

It opened in 2009 and is one of the small but growing band of restaurants which serve both Thai and Indian cuisine. The kitchen is blessed with Bangladeshi chefs who have worked in top Thai restaurants. As for choice, there are no rules you can mix and match as much you like. 'The tables were laid up with deep red and white table linen, sparkling glasses and polished cutlery. We started with warm and very crisp Plain Papadums 50p and the Chutney Tray 50p. We still had to make our choice. My companion was seriously tempted by the Thai Chicken Cashewnut £5.95, stir-fried with cashew nuts, pineapples, potato, ginger, onion, peppers and mushrooms. Then he saw Jaipuri Maas Tikki £4.25 tender minced lamb patties flavoured with cardamom and cloves, griddle-fried and served with fresh mint sauce. They are indeed scrumptious. I chose Aloo Tikki £3.25, mashed potato cakes, deep-fried, served with mint sauce. Then our mains arrived. Chicken Passanda £6.50, cooked with almonds, nuts, cream, yoghurt and a touch of wine and served in a well-polished detchi. The that arrived contained all of the dishes description. I chose Chicken Dhaniya Adhraki £6.50, the sauce enhanced with fine particulates of onion and tomato, flavoured with delicate juliennes of fresh ginger, which melted in the mouth - delicious. For sides we chose Badal Jam £3.25, a colourful aubergine delicacy topped with coriander and yoghurt, Pullao Rice £2.50 and Plain Nan £1.90. Other new mains include Seek-e-Macchi £9.95, marinated seabass flavoured with ajwain and cooked in tandoor, and,Chicken Rezala £6.50, flavoured with yoghurt and green chilli – a classic Bangladeshi dish.Needless to say, we didn't have a dessert, but the coffee is filter and nicely strong.' DBAC. Log on to to view all Special Offers, Live Music Events and Food Festival Menus. 12-2.30 & 5.30-11 (Fri-Sat to 11.30).

Oxted

GURKHA KITCHEN NEPALESE A-LIST
111 Station Rd, East Oxted   RH8 0AX
01883 722621   www.gurkhakitchen.co.uk

The floor is boarded, which makes it slightly noisy, but the whole look is very elegant. Beautiful hand-forged black steel chairs, the seat and back were wickered, the seat then covered in a small patterned carpet with a fringe on two sides. White linen tablecloths and napkins, large, fragile wine glasses, drinking receptacles for the connoisseur, their slender stems making a lovely bottle of Argentinean Norton red wine the more enjoyable. I asked our waiter if a lot get broken. 'Yes,' he said proudly, 'and I break the most.' The food is accurately cooked Nepalese. But it isn't earthy village food; it's slightly evolved and modern, yet indisputably Nepalese. Palungo Sag, steamed spinach sautéed with fenugreek seeds; the spinach was fresh. Gurkha Aloo, diced delicately, prepared in turmeric and cumin seeds, mild potato cubes fried a little brown on the sides. Rashilo Bhat, rice cooked with bay leaf, cardamom, garnished with brown onion £2, fluffy and flavoursome. Joano Patre, bread with carom seed £2, like a Naan, very good. Golbeda Ko Achar, fresh tomato pickle, spicy, a good accompaniment. Everything was delivered in separate white china dishes, the plates hot. 'Yes, it's spot on. Extremely interesting menu with not one dish that appears on a standard curry house menu. We had first class starters: Bhutuwa, excellent melt-in-the-mouth chicken livers stir-fried in a delicately spiced light sauce served in a small wafer basket, Vegetable Khaja' filo pastry wrapped up like spring roll, but not so thick with vegetable filling and mint and mustard dressing. They were cut in half, diagonally, a small green salad with the dressing decorating the centre of the plate, the Khaja in four corners. Extremely mild, but tasty. Main dishes Mooli Chicken, Piro Lamb and Hariyo Machha, monkfish wrapped in spinach prepared in a mild, dry fruit sauce were all superb, with the flavouring of each being totally different and distinct from the others. Portions not large, but sufficient. Prices marginally higher than average.' MW. 'A mystery into the unknown as nothing whatsoever on the menu was familiar. Fortified by large bottles of Kathmandu beer, we chose dishes that sounded good. All were, nicely spiced and tasty. Well worth a visit, helpful, friendly waiters. Only £60 for three – worth every penny!' CS. 12-2.30 & 6-11 (to 11.30 Fri-Sat. Sun buffet 1-10pm.

YOU SAY OK
You might get a discount if you show them this Guide.
PURLEY: RAJ of PURLEY Russell Hill Rd, CR8 2LE 020 8660 6601
REDHILL: EXOTICA TANDOORI 18 Cromwell Rd 01737 778624
REIGATE: VILLAGE BRASSERIE 10 West St 01737 245695
RICHMOND: SWAGAT 86, Hill Rise, TW10 6UB ~ 020 8940 7557. Modern, light and airy, cafe-styled eatery, with a wooden floor, pale wooden open backed chairs, white-washed walls and white tablecloths. Looks out for specials, such as Kadai Gosht, Kurkuri Bhindi and Murgh Lamai Tikka.

Richmond-on-Thames GL

ORIGIN ASIA   TOP 100
100 Kew Road, Richmond, TW9 2PQ
0208 9480509   www.originasia.co.uk

This uniquely named venue opened in 2002 as a 90-seater on two levels, the lower level extending past the semi-open glazed kitchen, which allows you to see the chefs at work. There is also a very pleasant alfresco dining *area at the front on the restaurant.. 'What a gem this is. The quality of the food is superb having a number of innovative and authentic tasting dishes on offer. The Bater Khada Masala marinated quails pot roasted in onion and tomato masala with crushed dried mango was truly outstanding, as were the Lehsooni Whitebait whitebait marinated in crushed garlic and caraway and then gram flour batter fried, Bhutta Kebab kebab of fresh baby corn wrapped in a spiced mash of corn and potatoes and the Gilafi Seekh Kebabs char grilled minced lamb kebabs wrapped in fresh aromatic vegetables for starters. For main courses, the Lamb Shank Xacuti cooked in a hot and spicy Xacuti masala was sensational along with the Tawaki Bathak duck breast pot roasted with coconut, cumin, mint and coriander to name but a few. The service was excellent as well, with the staff coping admirably with our group of 12 raucous friends enjoying a stag night together. In fact we enjoyed it so much that two of us slipped in the day afterwards for a 'light' lunch! Obviously our behaviour couldn't have been too bad the night before, as we were not banished on sight! Overall opinion – truly excellent and innovative. I would not hesitate to recommend this establishment or to return here.'* SO. 12-2.30 & 5.30-11; 10.30 Sun.

RARA   NEPALESE
279 Sandycombe Road, Richmond, TW9 3LU
020 8332 1020.   www.rara-kew.co.uk

Named after a Nepal's biggest lake and run by Baz and Prakash, from Bangladesh and Nepal respectively. A lovely stylish restaurant, decorated with silver wallpaper, beige high-backed suede chairs, mushroom-coloured banquet seating and classic white linen laid on square tables. In fact, the only colourful thing on the tables, are the crushed raspberry menu cards – very attractive. Pradip is the chef and Idira runs the front. In fact most dishes are not Nepalese but formula curries. These are most of the Nepalese items: Starters: Chilli Chicken £4.50, a Nepalese village dish consisting of sliced chicken breast marinated in spices and sautéed with capsicum, onion, spicy tomatoes and fresh green chillies. Kebab Rasilo £3.95, skewered minced lamb with freshly ground spices, tandoor-cooked; Pahar Peero Lamb £4.75, pieces of lamb tandoor-cooked, sautéed with green chillies, onions, green peppers, mustard seeds and curry leaves. Mains: Royal Rara, £13 a whole chicken breast opened out and wrapped around a huge king prawn, slowly cooked in a masala sauce with cream, butter, methi, green herbs and newly-ground spices – their signature dish! Shahazadi Masala, £11, chicken breast cooked in dry French white wine and a blend of Nepalese spices, popular in the luxurious palaces of Kathmandu; Masu Maslals £8.75, spring lamb initially tandoor-cooked, finally slow-cooked in Nepalese herbs and spices. 6-11.

YOU SAY OK
You might get a discount if you show them this Guide.
STAINES: ANCIENT RAJ 157 High St   01784 457099
SURBITON:THE RAJ: 163 Ewell Rd, Surbiton, KT6 6AW   020 8390 0251   www.theraj-surbiton.co.uk
SUTTON: THE RAJ 25 Church Hill Rd, SM3 8LJ   020 8641 8996
TANDAV 260 High St, Sutton SM1 1PG   020 8642 1833   www.keralagroup.co.uk   See Rhada Krishna Bhavan, London SW17.
THORNTON HEATH, GARAM MASALA: 842 Road, Thornton Heath, CR7 7PA   020 8683 2234   www.garam-masala.biz
VIRGINIA WATER: VICEROY OF INDIA 4 Station Apr   01344 843157 *'A great exponent of the skills of cooking great Indian food'* AF.
WALTON-on-THAMES: ORIENTAL CURRY CENTRE 13 Church St, Walton ~ 01932 222317

Tolworth GL

JAIPUR
90 The Broadway, Tolworth KT6 7HT   020 8399 3619

The external decor makes this venue unmissable. Its huge pink stone pillars make it stand out, a fact not unnoticed by the local council, who in the early days spent a considerable amount of time, and presumably money, trying to force owner Mr S.U. Ali to remove them. Fortunately bullying bureaucracy lost, and the pillars remain; indeed, they continue inside, giving a very Indian feel to the interior. India's Jaipur is the pink city, where every building is made from pink sandstone. Naturally the Jaipur's theme is pink too, with *'an amazing sugar-pink decor, with friezes of dancing ladies seemingly sculpted out of the wall.'* DD. It's a thoroughly conventional formula menu, which is cooked well. *'Thoroughly enjoyable.'* DRC. *'One of my regular haunts.'* PD. Mr A Khan manages. The food is above average formula. 12-2.30 & 6-11.30.

Wallington

AKASH TANDOORI
145 Stafford Road, SM6 9BN
020 8647 5592   www.akashtandoori.co.uk

The energetic owner Mr S.U..Khan, runs the Federation of Bangadeshi Caterers and organises their annual Awards show. His restaurant is an old hand, being established in 1989. It is located in a long row of terraced shop units selling typical suburban goods, and is identified by its chocolate brown conservatory frontage with five triangular peaks. The menu describes the cuisine as *'serving the traditional foods of India'* And that's what you get – a perfect suburban curryhouse

Established 1979

AKASH
Tandoori Restaurant

145 Stafford Road Wallington
Surrey SM6 9BN
www.akashtandoori.co.uk

Tel: 020
8647 5592
8647 4200
8647 8036

VOTED INTO THE TOP
100 CURRY RESTAURANTS
IN BRITAIN 2006, 2007 & 2008
BRITISH
Curry Awards

Free Home Delivery

on orders under £12.50 an additional charge of £2.00

Delivery Time 45 mins approx
Areas Beddington, Wallington, Purley, Carshalton

INDIA DINING
www.indiadining.co.uk

"Flavours are well balanced and ingredients fresh and vibrant, hardly any surprise to learn then that the kitchen team has been recruited from the likes of India's distinguished Taj and Oberoi hotel groups."
theguardian

EXPERIENCE EXCELLENCE ★ ASAD KHAN

T: 01883 625905
6 The Green, Warlingham, Surrey CR6 9NA

serving its local area establishment serving a satisfied local curry-loving band of regulars. That's what you tell us. *'We go at least once a week, my wife and I. We always order the saqme – we almost don't have to tell the waiters they know us of old.'* AJK. Pops 50p, Starters from £2 to £10. Mains av: £7. Veg sides av £2.50.Pullao Rice £1.85. Naan £1.65. Mid-week specials. No cheques. Free Home Delivery over £12.50). 12-3 & 6-11.30. (Sun 12.30-5.30 buffet).

Warlingham

INDIA DINING TOP 100
6 The Green, Warlingham. CR6 9NA
01883 625905   www.indiadining.co.uk

Ex Cinnamon Club Asad Khan opened his own restaurant in 2003 with the aim to provide consistently high standards of food and service in a unique environment. He decorated in a modern style, with a deep brown wooden floor, white linen, cream walls, deep brown chairs. Art work on the walls is for sale if you can afford it. Khan recruited a core team with high credentials. From Dubai's Burj-Al-Arab came Golam Morshed as the GM and chef Naresh Chand came direct from the Oberoi's first-ever hotel, the 5 star Cecil Hotel in Simla. Starters include Red Deer Tandoori Chops with crushed fennel and cumin seed, £12; Chilli-fried Squid tossed in hot, sweet and sour spices, c£8 ; South Indian stir-fry lamb on mini naan bread, £8. Mains include Rack of Lamb with sweetcorn sauce, £16.95 ; Pan Seared Duck breast with dill sauce £14 and Grilled King Prawns with seasonal vegetables £27. All mains come with masala mashed potato. Sun Lunch: two courses £9.95, 12.30-3. Early Dining: two courses and coffee £10.95, 5.30-7 Sun to Thurs. Del: 4m £15 min. Serv: 10% of parties of six or more. 12-2.30 & 5.30-11.

Woking

JAIPUR TOP 100
49 Chertsey Road, Woking, GU21 5AJ
01483 772626   www.jaipurrestaurant.co.uk

Jaipur is the pink city of India. This elegant 60-seater, established in 1993, is owned by Nizam Ali and his two delightful sisters, Reggi and Sophi, all of whom I met in their gorgeous Sylhet home, during a monsoon storm a few years ago. Menu Snapshot: Raj Badak Shaslik c£5, duck with capsicum, onion, ground cumin; Lal Masley Tava £10, red salmon with tomato, onions and aromatic spices, served sizzling; Lal Pari £15, Lobster and King Prawns cooked with crispy vegetables in a garlic sauce; Raj Badak £19, cooked with crispy vegetables in a mild creamy sauce; Dumpuk Chicken £8.95, slow cooked in a special sealed pot to retain its full flavour. Chutney Tray £2.50 includes mango chutney, coconut chutney, lime pickle, mint sauce, tamarind sauce & onion salad. T/a: 10% discount. Del: £12 min. 12-2.30 & 6-11.30.

Worcester Park

MUNAL NEPALESE
76 Central Rd, Worcester Park, KT4 8HX
020 8330 3511   www.munalrestaurant.co.uk

Amrit Thapa established his 74-seat Nepalese restaurant in 1998. Mahesh Rana cooks, for example: Momo, meat dumplings lightly spiced Nepalese style, served with salad; Squid, marinated in herbs and deep-fried; Bhuteko Prawns, fried prawns, highly spiced all £3.50. Min Charge: £12. Del: 3m. T/à: 10% Disc, min £10. Sat-Sun: 12-2:30; Tu-Th: 5-11, Fri-Sat: to 12; Sun to 10:30.

THE SHALIMAR
372 Malden Road, Worcester Park, KT4 7NL
0208 330 7990   www.theshalimar.com

Raj and Sara opened the Shalimar in a corner building with parking behind, in 1989. Before that it was a sweet shop. Years ago Gary Bushel (remember him?) named it as The Sun's best curry house with the heading 'Windaloo'. Luckily it survived this and it has a really strong loyal local following of folk who have been going weekly and more for all those years. Raja and Sara make excellent hosts and they provide decent Indian food. The menu looks curryhouse with all the favourites but the dishes are top notch an inexpensive. Open daily.

SUSSEX
EAST & WEST
Area: South of England

Adjacent Counties:
Hants, Kent, Surrey

Brighton

400 restaurants in this town and most including the Indians are overpriced for tourists. Here are the best of a mostly poor bunch (see also Hove)

DELI INDIA
81 Trafalgar St, Brighton BN1 4EB 01273 699985

An Indian deli /teashop owned by Jamie Keen and Farida Pathan, a cook since the age of 13 provides Indian meals and snacks with a regularly changing menu which always includes at least two meat curries such as Chicken Kalya, and Minced lamb curry, both c£5 and two vegetarian curries, eg Gujarati vegetables and Kidney bean and pepper, £5 and at least one dhal all served with either basmati rice or two chapattis in the price. Also available are savoury snacks, dips and soups and Indian sweets such as halwa, gulab Jamun and naan khataay (Indian shortbread).

'I've eaten here several times and thoroughly enjoy the delicious food, the good portions and reasonable prices.' PL. 'The vegetable thali lunch was excellent and good value at £6 and a great way to taste different dishes. It all tasted fresh, healthy and home-cooked. It's great to have good quality Indian food in such nice, bright surroundings. I'm a big fan of Indian food and definitely recommend Deli India.' JP. 11-7.30; 6.30 Sat.

EASTERN EYE   SOUTH INDIAN
58 London Road, Brighton, BN1 4JE   01273 685151
www.easterneyerestaurant.co.uk

Chef Murrali Dharan hails from Madras and has cooked in luxury hotels across the world. There is a mix of north and south Indian and both are good. Here is a menu snapshot: Starters: Masala Panner Fingers £3.50, cottage cheese dipped in flour batter-fried; Aloo Mutter Tikki £3.35, rushed red potatoes and peas shallow-fried; Dahi Samosa Chat £2.95, chick peas and samosa with yoghurt and chutneys; Ragada Patties £3.50, potato tikkies with chick peas and chutney; Tomato Rasam £2.95, roasted plum tomato soup with cumin and garlic; Machi Amritsari £3.95, thilapia fillet coated with spices flavoured with aiwain and shallow fried; Main Courses: Malabar Chicken £6.75, with coconut, cinnamon & curry leaves; Chettinad Chicken Curry £6.50, cooked with twelve ground spices. 12-9.30.

PLANET INDIA   GUGARATI VEG
5 Richmond Pde, BN2 9PH, Brighton   01273 81814

The Gujarati. husband and wife owners used to run a corner shop and sell frozen curries in Preston Street. They moved in 2009. The double frontage is in bright magenta pink so you can't miss it. Their head-board announces 'Authentic home-made Indian food, made by Authentic home-made Indians'. Humour continues apace on the menu, with spelling mistakes and deliberated quirks. The eccentric owner frequently walks around barefoot, jigging about to Bob Marley Reggae tracks. But the food is seriously good. It all has Indian home-cooking tastes, (like it says on the headboard) and we hear that from the Indian clientelle who love the place. It is NOT curryhouse, so the vindaloo bufoons can stay away. Begin by nibbling on Bombay Mix (free) and Papads, plus homemade pickles and chutneys, each £1.The menu impishly advises that the mango chut isn't Pataks. Starters include Kechoris £2.90, 2 pastries stuffed with coconut, served with yoghurt and tamarind sauces. Veg Samosas with potato and peas £2.40, and Dahi Bhell Puri £4.80.The curries have two-tier pricing, £3.50 for a half portion (220g says the menu) or £4.77 double (360g). Mombai [sic] potato curry, or Masoor Dall Curry, Mixed Veg or Veg Korma, and Spinich [sic] and paneer curry and more. The chickpea with a little bit of potato curry in a light tomato masala sauce is delicious as is the curried spinach and paneer dish'. AN. Try their Thelpa Bread £2.40 which is like a chupatti with fenugreek leaves and sesame seeds. Spicy Cumin Rice is £1.75. They are licensed and sell organic, vegan wines and beers and lhassis.. Tu-Sat: 6pm-9,45 and 'some Sundays'.

COBRA
SPLENDIDLY INDIAN, SUPERBLY SMOOTH

INDIAN SUMMER FINE DINING TOP 100
69 East Street, Brighton BN1 1HQ, 01273 711001
http://www.indian-summer.org.uk

Indian Summer was founded in 2001 by Minesh Agnihotri & Byron Swales who wanted to bring real Indian food to Brighton. To achieve it Minesh gave up a career in medicine and searched out a brigade of highly qualified real Indian chefs. Rajasthani Head Chef Maharaj Jaswant Singh had worked in the celebrated 'Bukhara' Delhi and Karavalli, Bangalore (see pp 127 & 8). Keralan Biju Joseph specialises in southern Indian cuisine and had worked in 'Azure' restaurant at Surya Palace Hotel, Barodar. Gujarati' Chef Parth worked in the Dumpukht restaurant at Sayaji Hotel, Indore. Between them and the rest of the brigade, they cook pan-Indian fine cuisine. Starter examples: Paruppu Adai, a medley of dal soaked and then stone-ground into a batter, then mixed with green chilli & ginger, & served with sambhar & ingi (ginger) salad; Laal Maas, Rajhastani favourite, meaning 'red meat': tandooried lamb chop, served with an earthy tomato, clove, chilli, bayleaf sauce; Tawa Paneer, cubes of paneer stir fried in a tomato & onion based sauce, served with fried roti. Main courses: Veg Sundri, field mushroom & baby aubergines stuffed with a cashew nut & kalonji mint marinade. Served with a roasted green garlic sauce & beetroot upma (a thick savoury semolina 'cake' seasoned with fried ginger, mustard seeds and curry leaves); Subz Miloni , parsnips, sweet potato, broad beans and peas in a whole-spice sauce, served with papaya and mango kachumber, roti and basmati rice; Lamb Kolhapuri, slow-cookeddiced lamb cooked to an original Mahastrian recipe using toasted peanut, red chillies & coconut, served with masala rice & mint raita; Adraki Murgh, roasted melon seed & ginger-spiced chicken breast with a rich black urid dal & masala rice; Swordfish Nariyali, in a coconut and mint marinade, served with masala rice and a coriander & curry leaf sauce; Patra Ni Macchi, Cape hake in a fresh coriander, garlic, mint & cumin marinade-paste, wrapped in a banana leaf and steamed, served with basmati rice, raita & carrot spring onion salad. Meal price pp: £21 - £43. Tu-Sun: 12-3; Mon-Sat:6-10.30 (to 10 Sun).

MEMORIES OF INDIA
9B The Board Walk, Waterfront, Brighton Marina, Brighton BN2 5WA   01273 600088
www.memoriesofindiabrighton.co.uk

A first floor curryhouse with two assets, free parking in the marina (difficult in Brighton) and good food by executive chef Razzak. *'An unusual place to find an excellent Indian restaurant. A large well decorated emporium with plenty of good ambience, the staff helpful, friendly and attentive. We only had main courses, the Chana, Chicken Bhuna, and CTM were all good. The Chicken Dhansak was exceptional. Side dishes of Bombay Potato and Pakoras were also up to standard. If there is any slight criticism then it is that the prices were slightly high, but in view of the location, décor and quality it is a minor point.'* 'AG. 12-11.30.

Chichester

KOHINOOR [ROYAL BENGAL]
11 Adelaide Rd, Chichester, PO19 7NB, 01243 778605

A neat, clean 30 seater with white table linen and matching red napkins. The cheerful waiters are, without fail very pleased to see you, however, the service is rather laid back. This is not a complaint, just an observation, so be sure that you order your drinks and Pops promptly. The menu is as expecte. Pat ordered Phal,' which the chefs do, very competently. It is very chilli hot without being harsh, He also ordered a, 'arka Dal,' and a Paratha, lightly fried and flakey, and a portion of, Dahi - plain yoghurt.'I decided to order a dish that I haven't had for a very long time, a sizzling platter of Chicken Tikka. Our meal for the evening, came to £32.74 – excellent value, since it included a bottle of red wine (£8.95). Del min £12. T/a: 10% discount. 12-2.30 & 5.30-12. Branch: Magna Tandoori , Bognor Regis.

MEMORIES OF INDIA   [OLD BRID GE RD]
Main Road, (A259) | Bosham Roundabout, Nr Chichester, PO18 8PG   01243 572234
www.memoriesofindiabosham.co.uk

This former pub set alone in its own grounds has the advantage of a car park for 30 cars. Formula curries at sensible prices. Mon-Th: 12-2 & 5.30-12; Fri-Sun: 12-12. (Sunday Buffet from 12 - 4:30pm)

OLD COTTAGE INDIAN RESTAURANT "TERRIBLE LTJ"
37 West Street Chichester PO19 1RP
01243 780859   www.indiancottagechichester.co.uk

It is just that, located in a former old cottage at a prominent position by a ring road roundabout. The small venue is licensed and air conditioned and despite difficult parking it gets busy at times. Menu snapshot: Meat Thali £16 pp: Lamb Bhuna, Chicken Tikka Mossalla, Pieces of Tandoori Chicken, Pillau Rice, Raita and Naan. Veg Thali £14 pp: Bombay Aloo, Mushroom Bhajee, Sambar, Pillau Rice, Raita and Naan. 12-2.30 & 6-12.

Crawley (2 miles south of Gatwick)

BLUE INDIA TOP 100
47 High Street Crawley, RH10 1BQ
01293 446655   www.blueindia.co.uk

We ate here before a flight from Gatwick. The portions were so big, (and delicious) we had the overs packed up and took them on the flight with us to be enjoyed next day on the terrace accompanied by a bottle of Rioja – lovely! The menu includes a good choice of Chef Kirti Rewart's Specials: Appetisers: Crab Malabar cookedin white wine and mango, topped with cheese, c£6; Salmon Shah, flavoured with mustard, dill, coriander and fresh lime, c£5; Bollywood Shank: lamb cooked in a rich tomato and coriander sauce, cooked with spicy mince lamb, £14; Chicken Kama-Sutra. Lovers beware this is an aphrodisiac. (*'didn't work the time we had it!'* RCF).Chettinad, a dish comprising 18 different spices, chicken or lamb - in a hot sauce of ginger, garlic & coconut; Akhni biriani, cooked in a sealed pot, flavoured with cardamom, cinnamon, cloves and rose water served with a medium bhuna sauce. Wide choice of choice of vegetable dishes and breads. Some Indian desserts on the menu but we liked the Menage a Trois: a mix of white and black chocolate mousse topped with dark chocolate. 'Restaurant is bright and spacious and is aimed more upmarket than average.. We all thought the food excellent and very tasty. Service was friendly and efficient.' MPK. Hours: 12-2.30 & 6-11. *Branch Haywards Heath.*

TAJ MAHAL
2 High Street, Crawley RH10 1BJ
01293 529755   www.tajmahalcrawley.co.uk

Crawley's oldest Indian eatery opened in 1969. Owner Belayat Hussain's 150-seater is divided over two levels. The large glass entrance windows let in a bright natural ambience. It is anaged by Rajpal Singh with Chef, Gurudath Panapil, who trained at New Delhi's Taj Hotel. His speciality is Mangalorean cuisine, from Karnataka, with a dish like Kori Gassi alongside better known options like Saag Gosht and Chicken Shaslik. Good dessert choice inc Gulab Jamun Prices a wee bit above average, but *'worth every penny'* RCF. 12-2.30 & 6-11.

ZARI A-LIST
214 Ifield Drive, Ifield, Crawley, RH11 0DQ
01293 525107   www.zarirestaurant.co.uk

Zari is fine gold or silver wire thread used in traditional Indian and Pakistani garments. Samples of Zari, as unique pieces of art, decorate the walls of this lovely restaurant. Proprietors Mr and Mrs Miah and their highly trained chefs serve authentic cuisine far removed from the curryhouse formula. There is a small, tempting bar menu, with treats like Mini Samosas and Kebabs. In the first dining room, bright and beautiful silk cushions snuggle around you on the banquette seats. Through to the main dining room, tables are well spaced, and you are treated to exciting views of the theatre kitchen, where the chefs will thrill you with their Roomali Roti throwing and impressive skewers of tandoori, tikka and kebabs. The third dining room is for parties and leads out to the al fresco Zari Pavillion, where an Indian BBQ can be enjoyed. *'There is a wonderful selection of starters, that make is quite impossible to choose, so Pat and I decided that we would order all dishes to share. We kicked off with, Poppadums & fresh made-in-house chutneys, £2pp. We then moved on to the Kebab Tasting Sampler - trio of king prawn, meat and chicken kebab grill £7. They were attractively plated, subtly spiced and very succulent. Other interesting starters include, Fresh mint & coriander basted tandoori chicken morsels, apple & orange salad £5.25; Pan-griddled lamb marinated in garlic and red chilli, with Pomegranate Raita £5.50; Char grilled seasonal fruit skewers flavoured with mango & rock salt £4.95; 'Vegetarian Dosa,*

---

zarî stunning cocktails
zarî Innovative food
zarî Immaculate service

ZARI Bar & Restaurant
212-214 Ifield Drive,
Ifield, Crawley,
West Sussex,
RH11 0DQ

01293 525107
& 01293 562308

Reservations:
01293 560606

Fax: 01293 553009

www.zarirestaurant.co.uk

HOURS:
Lunch:
Mon to Sat:
12 - 2.30pm
Lunch Sun:
12 - 3pm
Dinner:
Sun to Fri
5.30 - 11pm
Dinner Sat:
5.30 - 11.30

Eastbourne

IMLI
42-44 Seaside Road, Eastbourne, BN21 3PB
01323 645877   www.imlirestaurant.co.uk

The former Zara is now replaced by Imli (tamarind) in this impressive double fronted unit. The menu has all the favourites plus specials such as: Medley Chilli crab cake, spiced seabass & prawns in tomato sauce £6; Stuffed Poneer Stuffed with potato mash, spinach & nuts served with green chutney £5. Mains: Keralan Fish Curry, seared seabass cooked with coconut milk and served with tomato rice £15;; King Prawn Mango Curry cooked in coconut oil, fennel seeds, garlic, ginger & coconut milk £13;; Masala Dosa Indian crêpe stuffed with spiced vegetable, served with coconut chutney & sambar curry, £12; Duck Chettinad Spiced duck breast slow cooked in tandoor, served with aromatic sauce £12. 5.30-11.

Findon

TAJDAR
Tower Lodge, The Square, Findon, BN14 0TE
01903 872225   www.tajdar.com

Abdul Monnan opened this 80-seater in 2006 in this pretty village a few miles north of Worthing, just off the A24, having sold Worthing's Mahaan. Chef's Specialities: Chicken Chilli Masala - spicy hot dish, fried in a mixture of chillies, capsicum, coriander and tomatoes, served with Pullao Rice; Salmon Chutney - small flakes of red wild salmon, cooked in ghee with garlic, red chilli, coriander and served with boiled rice; Lamb Rezala - slightly hot and sweet, cooked in a tangy sauce, served with Pullao Rice - all £10.45. Chauffeur Service: a pick-up and drop-off service, for customers within 5 miles of the restaurant and are in a party of four or six, the cost for this is £5 each way - sounds like a good deal! And if you don't feel like the traditional stuffed and roasted turkey with all the trimmings, but do feel like a curry, then you are in luck, 'cos Abdul opens for lunch on Christmas Day. Del: 5m £10 min. T/a: 10% disc. Hours: 12-2 & 5-11.30. *Branch: Millan, 274, Upper Shoreham Road, Shoreham , West Sussex*

Hove

CURRY MAHAL
169 Portland Road, Hove, BN3 6 QJ   01273 779125

The Curry Mahal seats 100 in three a/c rooms. Est 1971 and taken over in 1999 by Shykul and brother Shane Malique. Menu Snapshot: Chatga Prawns £13.95, king prawns, marinated in a mixture of spices and cooked in a clay oven, curried in medium hot sauce with onions, green peppers, tomatoes and coriander; Komlapuriya Chicken or Lamb £11 flavoured with Grande Marnier and mandarins; Lamb Satkora £12 cooked with tender slices of lamb, satkora, tomatoes, onions, garlic and garnished with chillies and coriander, fairly hot. T/a: 10% disc. Del: £15 min. 12-2.30 Sat-Thurs & 5.30-11.30.

---

paper thin pancake £6, made with rice, urad dal, with spicy potato filling and coconut chutney and sambar, traditional south Indian lentil & vegetable curry, tempered with mustard and curry leaf,. The dosa was small by some standards, but perfect for sharing. Our main courses were Chicken Lababdar- white chicken tikka in white gravy of pumpkin seeds, cashew nut and mixed peppers £11. It was amazingly delicate with a smooth, silky and nutty sauce. Pat's main Jungle Venison Curry £14, was a spicy affair and he enjoyed it very much. Also on the menu was Vegetable Chettinad in roasted spices and fresh coconut £7.50; Pea & Mint Dal £3.75; Lemon and Mustard Seed Rice £3.25; Rose Petal Masala Chicken £11; Alleppey Fish Curry £10, white boneless fresh water fish in coconut milk, fresh ginger, raw mango and curry leaf; Tandooried Paneer Flakes £8, in cumin, red chillies and wok-tossed green peppers. If you can, leave room for dessert, made by the Zari's pastry chef such as Selection of Freshly Made Ice Creams £4, or Selection of Freshly Made Sorbets £5 or Peshwari Nan Pudding with caramelised oranges £5.25, or the Chocolate Pear, pictured below £7. Superb food. Lucky us, lucky Crawley!' DBAC. Tasting Menu £24.95. Banquet Night Tu: £11.95. Sunday Brunch £10.95. Hours: 12-2.30 & 6-11.30.

Lewes

CHAULA'S   GUJARATI
Eastgate House, 6 Eastgate Street, Lewes, BN7 2LP
01273 476707   www.chaulas.co.uk

Chaula and Janak's menu contains some well known curries plus traditional Gujarati vegetarian, meat & fish dishes. There are four areas. Downstairs is the fully licensed bar with snacks including samosas and bhajis. To the right there is the shop, selling herbs, spices and frozen meals. There are two dining areas, one with a colourful mural depicting Indian village life and the other offering more formal dining. Outside is wooden decked seating area for alfresco dining. Starters include: Kachori £2.50, 2 balls of spiced lentils coated with batter and fried; Petis £2.50, 2 cakes of mashed potato spiced peas & hint of onions; Patra £3.25, colocasia plant leaves coated with spicy batter, rolled up, and steamed to make delicious spiral snacks; Chatpata Mogo £3.25, cassava chips, marinated and fried. Mains include: Chicken Sarjahani £15 (serves 2) breast fillet stuffed with lamb kheema and served with mild creamy and kadai sauces garnished with almonds; Fish Malvani £10.50, salmon delicately cooked with coconut, tomatoes & spices; Bhindi kadhi £5.7), a savoury Gujarati curry of okra gramflour and yogurt. Sun-Th: 10- 3 & 5-11; Fri -Sat: 11-11. *Branch: Chaula's, 2-3 Little East St, Brighton, BN1 1HT 01273 771661.*

Newhaven

VICEROY
4 Bridge Street, Newhaven, BN9 9PJ
01273 513308   www.viceroynewhaven.co.uk

Owner: A.Ahmed (Mngr Zahid Islam) AS Ahmed's fifty-seater opened way back in 1986. There are two menus, one with Korma to Vindaloo for the diehards, and the other with more useful dishes such as: Goat Cheese Samosa £5, pastry parcels stuffed with spinach and delicately spiced goat's cheese; Jalapeño Delight c£5, stuffed with cream and cheese, fried with coated breadcrumbs; Chicken Lazeez c£8, fillets in a silky smooth almond and tamarind honey sauce; Mahi Monk Fish £10, prepared in a rich lentil sauce; Lamb Shank £10, garnished with curry leaves, coconut milk, mustard and black cumin seeds; Shan e Pumpkin £4, cubes spiced with fresh curry leaves. Del: £15 min. Daily: 5.30-11; Sat-Sun:12-2.

Peacehaven

SPICE & FLAVOUR   INDIAN & NEPALESE
314 South Coast Road BN10 7EJ 01273 585808

Faizur and Ayesha Choudhury opened in 2002. Bright and airy restaurant decorated in citrus colours with a wooden floor and polished wood tables. Menu Snapshot: Chicken Bahar c£6, with sliced mango; Lamb Korai c£6, with peppers, tomatoes, and dry thick sauce; Dhal Samba £3, sour & hot lentils; Nepali Dishes: Prawn Duck Salad c£3.50; Napali Beef £6.50, with garlic, peppers and tomatoes; Roast Chow Chow £6.50, noodles stir-fried with roast tikka chicken and lamb, medium hot or spicy; King Prawn tawa £7.50, shallow fried (in shell) with spices served with salad. 5-11.

Rye

THE AMBRETTE at RYE   A-LIST
24 High Street, Rye, TN31 7JF
01797 222043   www.theambrette.co.uk

Following his success in Margate, Kent, Dev Biswal has opened his second venture in Rye's 5 AA starred White Vine House. The original building was destroyed during one of the many French raids on the town during the 100 Years War. The Elizabethan Dining Room named for its exquisite and unique French oak panelling, which probably cost more than the original building, with each panel individually formed to fit the timber frame. The room is "signed" with a carpenter's mark visible just above the fireplace. There's a second Georgian Dining Room, which dates back to when the building was extended the C19th. Outside the Magnolia Garden offers al fresco dinings et under a magnificent magnolia tree. The menu changes frequently and is described in our Margate entry. *'The toilets were spotless, On arrival we were shown into a reception room with an open fire and comfy sofas, where we studied the short, but unique menu and offered a drink. The décor is smart and stylish, with soft classical music playing and the service not only attentive, but highly knowledgeable re the food's provenance and cooking methods. The light, deftly spiced dishes were interspersed with little titbits from the kitchen. Presentation of the the food is a work of art and the flavours exquisite. This is the best food I've eaten in an Indian restaurant. We can't wait to go back and I can't recommend it too highly. Food: £42, Drink: £18, Service: £5, Total: £55'.* GM.. Tue-Sun: 11.30-2.30; Tue-Th: 6-9.30; Fri-Sun: 5.30-10.

Shoreham-by-Sea

MILAN
274 Upper Shoreham Road, Shoreham BN43 6BF
01273 440699   www.millantandoori.co.uk

It opened in 1992 and has built up a loyal customer base who enjoy the affordably priced formula menu and some interesting specials such as Duck Narangi, £9.95 sliced breast cooked in a tomato based sauce, served with coconut rice; Khakra Jhool, £8.95,crab meat in a thick medium sauce, garnished with coriander, served with pilau rice; Tawa £8.95, Grilled and poignantly spiced chicken or lamb, cooked with onions, tomato, and peppers. Served with pilau rice. Del: Min £10 (£1 u£10). 12-2.30 & 5-11.

SPLENDIDLY INDIAN, SUPERBLY SMOOTH

Uckfield

RAJDUTT
Eastbourne Rd, Uckfield TN22 5QL   01825 890234

Owner, Amol Sil's restaurant seats 70 in three rooms and there is a car park. Menu Snapshot: Amere Chicken c£8 - mild sauce with mango, fresh cream and almonds; Lamb Nashille c£8, fillets of lamb in green chilli, ginger, spicy hot sauce; Tandoori Chef Specials £10, chicken and lamb, skewered with tomatoes, capsicum and onion cooked in a brandy sauce; Murgh Noorani c£8, breast of chicken, stuffed with minced prawn in light herbs, finished in sweet, sour and hot sauce, served sizzling; Akbari Murgh c£8, tender chicken medallions smothered with pineapple, almonds, raisins, finished in a delicately ginger sauce. Interesting fish specialities: all £8, Kalamari Vojon - squid in delicately spiced, fairly hot sauce with thinly sliced capsicum, onions, crushed chillies and crushed mustard seeds; Roop Chanda Biran, pomphret fried with light spices onions and potatoes; Boal Dopiaza, fried chunks of boal in medium sauce. T/a: 10% disc. 12-2 & 6-11; 5.30-11.30 Sat. *Branches: Maloncho, Staplehurst, Kent; Malonco, Peacehaven, East Sussex and Raj, Calpe & Jeava, Spain.*

Worthing

ALISHAAN
West Street, Sompting, Nr Worthing, BN15 0AP
01903 204466   www.alishaanweb.co.uk

Opened in 2008 by the Ahmed brothers in a 400 year old building known as the "The Smuggler's Restaurant". History says contraband was hidden there. Following a rebuild it now seats 106 in 4 rooms. The lobby has a long leather sofa, one room is the bar behind which is a party room for 12. The main dining room seats 64. Shahin Ahmed is head chef. Menu Snapshot: Chicken or Lamb Tikka Almashriqi, a mild dish topped with spinach; Chicken or Lamb Tikka Flaming, cooked with Sambuca , cream and cashews; Garlic Chicken Tuk-Tuk, marinated in garlic sauce, then grilled served with salad and mint Sauce, all £6.95. *'In our daily hectic schedules, it is a pleasure to be able to enter this oasis of calm and tranquillity, where the general ambience is of a high quality and attention to detail is of paramount importance. As frequent diners, we have always been impressed by the courtesy and friendliness of the staff and the high quality of the food. For example, our two course meal last week included a starter of pops and chuts. My main course was a Vegetable Shahi Kurma topped by a boiled egg, while my husband chose a Chicken Tikka Noorjahan, accompanied by exotic coconut fried rice. Revd EKH. 'The best Indian food we have ever had anywhere (UK, USA, Australia and Asia). The curries are complex, warm, delicious and chef is always willing to indulge me with extra chillies and spices. My advice is always order something you have not tried before.'* VW. 12-2 (not Fri) & 5.30-11.30.

INDIAN OCEAN TAKEAWAY   TOP 100
66 Teville Road, Worthing BN11 1UY
01903 528888   www.indianoceantakeaway.co.uk

Located near Worthing main railway station. Established in 1998 by Yusuf Khan, who has clearly built up a loyal following, by *'giving them just what they want!'* These are just some of their comments: *'Indian Ocean was recommended by a friend. Food is very tasty and always cooked to perfection. Service is extremely polite and friendly.'* D. *'Not only is it across the road from where I live, the proprietor, his family and staff are always very polite and friendly. Very nice food, very tasty and plenty of it.'* SB. *'Tasty, well priced food and good polite service.'* JN. *'Del service is very quick.'* BF. *'THE BEST PRAWN BHUNA - C£5.'* HE. Menu Snapshot: Mixed Starters £3.45 for two - Onion Bhajia, Lamb Tikka and Chicken Tikka, served with salad and mint yoghurt sauce; Chicken and Mushroom Curry £5.45; Keema and Peas Bhuna £5.45; Prawn and Mushroom Korma £5.45; Keema, Peshwari, Garlic, Panir, Spicy (chilli, garlic, coriander) and Kulcha (vegetable) Naan all £1.75. Desserts also available, from Chocolate Mousse to Raspberry Parfait - all £2.95 - just the way to finish off a spicy meal! Credit card accepted and over the phone, so no fiddling change with the Del driver at the door. Del: 5m £8 min. Hours: 12-2 & 5 to late!

MAHARAJA   NEPALESE
67 Rowlands Rd, Worthing, BN11 3JN
01903 233300   www.themaharajofworthing.co.uk

Roj K Lama is the owner and Head Chef. Decor is simple & soothing with several original hand-carved traditional peacock windows, thangkas (buddhist paintings) and water colours of Nepal. Typical dishes include: Momo, Nepalese minced chicken or lamb dumpling, steam cooked then served with a tomato pickle; Khasi Taang, lamb shank cooked on a low heat and prepared with marrow in a medium sauce; Khasi ko Choila, grilled lamb mixed with spices, tomato, onion with a touch of chilli. Sun Buf: £9 adult, £5.50 under 12. Mon: e-a-m-a-y-l, £10. 12-2.30 & 6-10.30.

YOU SAY OK
WORTHING: AKASH TANDOORI 62 South Street, Tarring, Worthing, BN14 7LS ~ 01903 210597. 'Their Phal is the hottest in Worthing.'. ND

WORTHING: OM   NEPALESE 67 Rowlands Road, Worthing, BN11 3JN   01903 233300 www.omrestaurant.co.uk   Rajkumar is in charge. Best to enjoy their accurately cooked Nepalese dishes rather than normal Indian. 12-2.30 & 6-11.30..

SHAFIQUE'S 42 Goring Road, Worthing ~ 01903 504035. At Shafique Uddin's 48-seater, est 1986, the Thali's are good value: Del: 5 miles. Sun Lunch: buffet c£8. Hours: 12-2.30/5.30-11; 12 Fri & Sat. www.shafiques.com

TASTE OF BENGAL TAKEAWAY 203 Heene Road, Worthing ~01903 238400. Est 1984; Managing owner AM Kalam; Chef, Faruk Kalam. Hours: 5.30-11.

TYNE & WEAR

Area: North East

Adjacent Counties: Durham, Northumberland

Gateshead

THE LAST DAYS OF THE RAJ **A-LIST**
168 Kells Lane, Low Fell   0191 482 6494
www.thelastdaysoftheraj.co.uk

LAthair Khan's upmarket 100-seater has stylish decor – pure 30's Art Deco, complete with grand piano. Live music Thursdays. Crisp linen tablecloths laid on beautifully presented tables, brass light-fittings, ceiling-fans, trellis-climbing plants, and fresh flowers. Luxurious surroundings, with friendly and efficient waiters. The bar is spacious and well stocked. This restaurant must have one of the biggest and most comprehensive menus in the country; it is quite a delight. You will find all the regular formula curries with some regional and authentic dishes including recipes from the British Raj, Country Captain, a dry dish cooked with chicken breast, onion, ghee, chillies, ginger, garlic, turmeric and salt. Raj Lamb and Cabbage is cooked with yoghurt, poppy seeds, lemon juice, green coriander, garlic, onion, fresh coconut, green chillies, ground coriander, ginger, cinnamon and cumin with ghee. You will also find on the menu a few dishes with an oriental flavour, such as Dim Sum, Oriental King Prawn Rolls and Butterfly Breaded Prawn, and there is a Pizza or two – quite fabulous, definitely a TOP 100 restaurant. Hours: 12-2 (closed Sun) & 6-11. *Branch: Last Days of the Raj, Durham Road, Low Fell, Gateshead.*

RAVAL
Kent House, Church St, Tyne Bridge, Gateshead, NE8 2AT 0191 477 1700   www.ravalrestaurant.com

In 2007 IT entrepreneur Sumanta Khan commissioned local architects TTH to transform the derelict building opened this rather splendid restaurant in 2007 in a former department store once known as the "Harrods of the North", a hop and a jump from Newcastle's Tyne bridges. The long frontage is distinguished by several claret-coloured awnings at the centre of which is the inviting front door. Inside is an 80 seat formal dining area managed by Avi Malik, and separate 40 person bar and lounge space. The first floor private dining room overlooks the Tyne Bridge with views of the River. Daylight floods in from the many windows. The food attractively presented on variously-shaped attractive white crockery dishes. The menu carries familiiar dishes plus some fusion of local produce with traditional Indian cooking methods and special spices. Starters include Spicy Cream of Lobster Soup; Crab Cake; Monkfish Tikka, marinated in yogurt, mustard oil and special spices. Main course examples: Achari Chicken, breast meat with mixed pickle and whole spices, Lamb Pasanda, in a rich cashew nut, cardamom and saffron sauce, or Sea bass Dakshini, cooked with coconut cream, cinnamon and curry leaf, south Indian style; Lamb shank,marinated in yoghurt and aromatic spices and slow-cooked; Eggplant Lababdar is baby aubergine stuffed with cottage cheese in mustard seed and tomato sauce. Desserts include Carrot-pistachio (halva) with mango ice-cream or honey-glazed Gulab Jamun with pistachio ice cream The Magpie's Alan Shearer is a regular and Sir Cliff and Hank Marvin and other stars visit after their shows at the Newcastle Arena. A la Carte dinner av £30 pp. Fixed Dinner: £9.95 (2 course), £12.95 (3 course) Mon-Fri: 5.30-7. Mon-Sat: 5.30-11.

YOU SAY OK
You might get a discount if you show them this Guide.
GATESHEAD: BILL QUAY TAKEAWAY 78 Station Rd, Bill Quay 0191 495 0270. Owner Syed Amir Ali.
GATESHEAD: CURRY GARDEN TAKEAWAY 53 Coatsworth Rd, Bensham 0191 478 3614. Owner Abdul Malik Choudhury.
GATESHEAD: JASHN Whickham Bank, Swalwell, Gateshead NE16 3BP, 0191 4888 505 Jashn opened in 2010 in the former Gamekeeper pub. The decor is highly ornate and Indian.
GATESHEAD: LAST DAYS OF THE RAJ TAKEAWAY 218 Durham Rd, Shipcote 0191 477 2888.
GATESHEAD: LAST DAYS OF THE MOGUL RAJ 565 Durham Rd, Low Fell, Gateshead 0191 487 6282. Run by Ali and Ali. Special: Raj Lamb and Cabbage. 12-2 Mon-Sat/6-12.

Award Winning Indian Cuisine

Best Restaurant in the North East - Asian Curry Awards 2011
Best Restaurant in the UK- Spice Times Awards 2010
North East Caterer of the Year 2010 - BCA Awards 2010

We pride ourselves in providing mouth watering cuisine with exemplary service in elegant surroundings which has made us into one of the best restaurants in the country.

168 Kells Lane, Low Fell, Gateshead, NE9 5HY
www.thelastdaysoftheraj.co.uk   01914826494

COBRA
SPLENDIDLY INDIAN, SUPERBLY SMOOTH

GOSFORTH: THE DAYS OF THE RAJ Harewood House, 49 Great North Rd, Gosforth NE3 2HH 0191 284 9555 www.thedaysoftheraj.co.uk *'Situated above a golf shop.'* DMck. Hours: 12-2 Mon-Sat/6-11.

NEWCASTLE: KOMAL BALTI 14 Brentwood Avenue, West Jesmond, Newcastle, NE2 3DH 0191 281 4878

Newcastle-upon-Tyne

AKBARS   AUTHENTIC PAKISTANI CUISINE

Unit 1, City Quadrant, Westmorland Rd, Newcastle, NE1 4DP   0191 232 3234   www.akbars.co.uk

10th (2011) of 10 Akbar branches. See Bradford, W.Yorks for menu & details. Mon-Th: 5-11/30/Fri-Sat:- 12/Sun: 4-11.

BINDI CAFE

261 Whickham View, Denton Burn, NE15 7HP
0191 274 5505

'It is, as it says, a cafe-style curry house with ceramic tiled floor and wrought iron chairs and tables. Greeted at the door by a well dressed waiter. Starter with Fried Paneer - looked a little lonesome on the plate by itself, but tasted great. Chutney Mary.' [is that your wife?] *'had King Prawn Bhajia £3.50 - got the thumbs up. My main course was delicious - Chilli Chingri Masala c£8, while Chutney Mary opted for King Prawn Uree, which she enjoyed, especially the fresh green beans. We shared Pullao Rice and Egg Naan - of a good standard. Staff very pleasant and attentive and facilities very clean - lilac toilet seats - cool! All very reasonably priced.'* DMcK. Del: £8 min. Hours: 5.30-12.

DABBAWAL   STREET FOOD   TOP 100

69-75 High Bridge, Newcastle, NE1 6BX
0191 232 5133   www.dabbawal.com

Following London trends, Indian Street Food and 'Tapas' aka snacks, came to Newcastle in mid 2011. Managed by Jo Nassa it is located in the former Flatbread Café on the narrow cobbled High Bridge street. The name is derived from the legendary Mumbai Dabbawalas who home-collect and office-deliver city workers' lunch tiffin boxes, returning them after lunch. The chefs are Indian and there is an open kitchen complete with Tandoor. You know they are Indian because they have the skill to make Roomali Roti,'handkerchief' bread which is spun into the air to achieve the thinnest texture. It is used to, wrap spicy potato, seekh kebab or spicy chicken. 'Tapas' includes: Lamb Samosa Parcels or Jaffrani Salmon, marinated in honey, dill and saffron; or Punjabi Chilli Chicken Tikka in a chilli, cumin, garlic and ginger marinade; or Kukuri Lentil Battered Okra and their signature Sweet Potato Chaat is served with yoghurt, tamarind and coconut chutney. Av price for these is £5. Mains include a full range of curries and specials like Seafood Makalia, pan-fried fillet in a mustard and yoghurt sauce with baked potatoes or Duck Nilgiri, slow-cooked in a peppery sauce. Licensed. Lunch £15; Dinner £24; Mon-Sat: 12-2.30; Daily: 5-10.30.

SINGHS   PUNJABI

20, Stanhope Street, Newcastle, NE4 6BH 0191 272 2992 www.singhsrestaurant.co.uk

The menu looks pure curryhouse, the food isn't Bangladeshi formula; it has those puchy, savoury tastes that Punjabi chefs achieve. Starteres include Punjabi Gol Guppa, Punjabi cocktail size fried bread stuffed with vegetables in a tangy dressing; Fish Pakora Punjabi £3.50, marinated with spiced batter golden fried over small salad and mint sauce. Mains incude: Punjabi Lamb Curry £7.50, cooked in a ginger, garlic fresh tomatoes and roasted spices with fresh coriander; Lamb Keema Mattar £6.50, minced lamb infused with aromatic herbs and spices with Fresh pan fried garden peas; Fish Tawa Masala £7.50, marinated and served with seared peppers, onion, Tomatoes with roasted spices. Deserts each £2.50 include: Kheer , traditional Panjabi rice pudding; Gulab Jamun with ice cream, sweet dumpling with vanilla ice cream or Gajrela, sweet grated carrot. Daily: 5-11.

KHANS   PUNJABI   BYO

178 Heaton Road, Newcastle, NE6 5HP   0191 276 0400   www.khans-restaurant.com

This family run business was established in 1999. Indian artwork on the walls, chandeliers, and Indian-style high-back chairs make for a great atmosphere. The menu carries all the old favourites and some rather fine Apna (home-cooked Punjabi dishes, all at reasonable prices. BYO with corkage and glasses provided free. E-a-m-a-y-l buffet £9.95 Mon-Weds. Del Sun-Th. Hours: Daily: 5-11.

LUIGIKHAN'S

358 Westgate Road, Newcastle, NE4 6NU
0191 272 4937   www.luigikhans.com

LuigiKhan's opened in 2011 as the Best Western Ryokan Hotel's only restaurant. It operates in the evening, is licensed and serves reasonably priced traditional Punjabi Indian food (though European food menu is available for the wimps). Non residents are welcome. . Chicken Karahi, cooked in tomato and yoghurt sauce with special Punjabi style Asian spice & garnished with fresh coriander, bullet chilli & ginger.£8.25; Chicken Liver & Spinach Massala is cooked in a tomato & onion sauce with whole chilli & fresh coriander.£7.95; Luigikhan's Special HaleemLamb and chef's choice of various lentils freshly cooked on low heat for a minimum of 6hrs. Served with sliced chillies, fried onions, sliced lemon & freshly cut ginger and coriander. Paya Lamb Trotters Soup with sautéed onions, tomatoes and garlic to which chefs secret spices are added. Garnished with freshly chopped coriander.£7.25; Nehari Lamb Shank slow-cooked on-the-bone in a sauce, served with chillies, lemon, ginger

RASA SOUTH INDIAN TOP 100
27, Queen Street, Newcastle Quay, NE1 3UG
0191 232 7799   www.rasanewcastle.co.uk

This Rasa branch is the only one that is outside London and is situated on the glamourous quayside overlooking the Tyne. Menu Snapshot: Seafood Karu Muru £5 - crunchy stir-fried king fish, telopia fish and prawns tempered with shallots, curry leaves, green chillies and zest of lemon juice; Rasa Utthapam £5.50 - the Indian pizza made of rice and lentil batter, topped with tomatoes, curry leaves, chillies and onions, served with Sambar and Coconut Chutney; Tharavu Roast £8.75 - duck in a thick sauce of ginger, garlic, onion and coriander; Crab Varatiathu £10.95 - fresh crabs cooked in turmeric and chilli water, stir-fried with shallots, black pepper and curry leaves (try this dish was a bread, eg: Paratha £2.50. Service: 12.5%. 12-3 & 6-11. *Branches London N16, W1, WC1 (see these for more menu details).*

SACHINS PUNJABI A-LIST
Old Hawthorn Inn, Forth Banks, Central Newcastle NE1 3SG   0191 261 9035   www.sachins.co.uk

It originally opened in a gorgeous corner building in 1984 as the only Punjabi restaurant in town. Regular patrons, Kulmeet ('Bob') and Neeta Arora loved it so much that they bought it in 2000. No longer the only Punjabi, but by your vote, the best. 'There is nothing artificial about our food,' says Executive Chef Dinesh Rawlley 'we don't use crazy-hot spices or extra colouring in our dishes and all our spices are roasted and ground right here on the premises. Our reds come from chillies, our yellows from turmeric and so on'. His starters include: Papri Chaat, crisp pastry topped with chickpeas, yoghurt, tamarind sauce and mint chutney, the original Mumbai snack; Gol Goppa, hollow crisp baby puris filled with chickpeas and potato with spiced tamarind water; Lucknowi Tikka, spiced chickpeas, paneer and baby spinach cakes, pan-fried and served with tamarind sauce, each £6. Mains: Machhi Tandoori £10, pieces of monk fish marinated and barbecued in the tandoor and served on a mint and coriander dressing; Nali Nihari £13, lamb shank served on-the -bone in a smooth onion sauce; a classic dish from; Nilgiri Goshat, diced lamb cooked in south indian spices including mustard seeds and fresh curry leaf with fresh coconut milk; Khundan Murgh, £12, chicken breast cooked in a delicate onion and cashew nut sauce with cream and yoghurt, from Lucknow; Chingri Malabar £14, king prawns cooked in a rich sauce with curry leaves and mustard seeds, south indian spices and coconut milk. Daal Makhani, black lentils simmered overnight tempered with garlic, ginger, fresh tomato and a touch of fresh cream a traditional punjabi dish £8.95, the ultimate chef test, and never found at the Bangladeshi curry house. Hours: Wed-Mon: 12-13.30; Daily: 6-11.

and coriander £7.25. Hours: 5.30-11.

SPICE CUBE PUNJABI
Gate Complex, Newgate St, NE1 5TG
0191 222 1181   www.thespicecube.co.uk

Located on the top floor of The Gate leisure complex, is Jalf Ali's Indian bar, cafe & restaurant. This Punjabi venue has a glassy, stainless-steel modern look with hard floors, and Punjabi Zee Music pounding out on on a large wall-mounted plasma screen in the lounge area. A huge, glass-sided staircase dominates the interior and you can coose to eat on the balcony which overlooks downstairs.The service is professional and discreet, Cheffing is now by Raj Kumar. Lunch food includes wraps £5 or curries £8. A la carte starters include: Kurkuri Bhindi £3.95, mustard seed and gram flour coated okra, crisp fried; Chicken Chilli Fry £4.25, with chillies, coconut and turmeric dressing. Chef Kumar's main courses are an ducation. I wish I had space to list them all. Meanwhile, how about: Steamed Roller Chicken £11.50: Legend has it this dish was created after a man witnessed a chicken flattened by a steam roller. This version, roller-free, kids please note, uses chicken-on-the-bone, marinated in a red onion, chilli and coriander masala, finished with vegetables. Chicken Tikka Shashlik £10, with mixed pepper and onions. Served with rice and a Makhani Masala sauce. Indian Railway Lamb Curry £10, served in only to first class passengers in the days of the Raj; lamb gently cooked with potatoes in a curry leaf, onion and mustard seed gravy with coriander; Karawali Fish Curry £11.50, is eaten daily come *'hell-or-high-water'* [sic] in Kerala. Marinated salmon fillets are simmered in coconut, coriander and mustard flavoured spicy sauce. *'All cooked to a high standard at reasonable prices'*. L.C. Regional special menus run throughout the year. Gourmet Buffet: starters, salads, chutneys, main courses, side dishes, rice, breads and desserts. Thur from 5pm £11.50;Sat Lunch £7.95. 12-5; Sunday Lunch £7.95 12-5pm. 50% disc u10. Hours: 12-2.30 &5.30-11.30; 12-11.30 Sat & Sun.

SOLOMON'S DHABA
3-4 Studley Terrace, Fenham Newcastle NE4 5AH
0191 272 4426

In India the Dhaba is the roadside caff (greasy spoon in our parlance). There are millions of them, mostly shacks, mostly frequented by truckies and always with delicious food for pennies. Solomon's is none of those things. It overlooks a pretty park; it is smart and simple with wooden flooring, red walls and iron chairs and smart table settings. except delicious food. Above all it is inexpensive Pops & picks £1. Starters such as Onion Bhaji £1.50. Curries clock in at a mere £2.95, pilau rice or naan £1 each. *'One in my group described the fare as "a bit basic" but the popadoms and breads were fresh and the starter and main dishes full of the appropriate flavours.The wine selection is limited but at £5 a bottle you can't really complain.I think Marcel Hubert's table wine is the only brand on offer, and we chose a dry white which arrived nicely chilled and did the job. Because of the cheap menu and almost cafe-like feel Solomon's is popular with students. On the Friday*

SPLENDIDLY INDIAN, SUPERBLY SMOOTH

night I went, the crowd was mixed. My table was probably the loudest of the lot once the wine-fuelled discussions broke out. It is the kind of place you can have a heated debate without feeling self-conscious. Service is unpretentious, lively and friendly and the staff obviously enjoy their work. I reckon this is a great mid-week, cheap weekend or pre-pub venue - our total bill was £26.35 - but perhaps the real treat about Solomon's Dhaba is that it is less than 100m from my door. Wonder if they deliver?' 4.30-11.

SOLOMONS   PUNJABI / KASHMIRI
Thorntree Farm, West road, Denton Burn, Newcastle upon Tyne. NE15 7EX   0191-2742323

Solomon's was established in 1992 in a grade-two-listed farmhouse and it was their first branch. The food is Punjabi / Kashmiri which is quite definitely not curryhouse. Starters include: Spiced Battak, duck cooked with onion, green peppers and tomatoes bhuna style, served in a puri with mint sauce; Doyi Bengan, tandoori-baked aubergine, filled with fresh vegetables, spiced with chatt mossalla & yoghurt and Shahi Machli, chunks of cod coated with spices, deep-fried to a rich golden colour & garnished with fried onions. Main courses include King Prawn Punjabi Masaledar made with butter-battered deep-ried king prawns, sliced onions, peppers, fresh garlic & tomatoes; Palak Gosht, lamb & spinach cooked in fresh garlic with chopped tomatoes, ginger, herbs, spices & garnished with garam masala. 5-11.30. *Branch: Solomon's Lounge 404 Chillingham Rd, Newcastle, NE6 5QX*

THE SPICERY
Denton Bank, 4 Denton Rd, NE15 7BD   0191 274 9464

Bangladeshi restaurateur Martin Rohman, whose chain of restaurants the largest in the North East, entirely revamped Denton Bank's previously neglected Sporting Arms pub in 2006, pulling it away from its former notorious reputation. It holds 100 covers in the main dining area and 20 in the bar. The contemporary minimalist and elegant decor is defined by its dark wooden floors, aubergine walls and discreet lighting establishing an intimate and stylish ambience. Head chef Moklis Rahman creates the regular menu withspecialities including Machli Tomato and Murgh Handi Lazeez. *Branch: Cinnamon, North Rd, Durham.*

VALLEY JUNCTION 397   A-LIST
397 The Old Station, Jesmond, Newcastle North NE2 1DH   0191 281 6397

Daraz and his brother Locku are correct when they claim to have 'the most original Indian Restaurant in Great Britain where you can dine in style in an old signal box and railway carriage'. They sure do have a penchant for purchasing old railway things and making money from them. Style is the word, First they spend a great deal to achieve it. This venture was formerly the 'Carriage Pub'. The carriage in question was built for the Great Northern Railway at Doncaster in 1912. Numbered 397, it was a saloon for 'wealthy families to hire for their journeys'. Says Daraz: 'we bought it in the third month of 97. It was numbered 397, and the coincidence couldn't be ignored, hence the name 'The Valley Junction 397'. Now incorporated into the restaurant, it is decked out in greens and golds, and still earns its keep for the well-heeled. Like its sister restaurant, it has quickly earned a reputation for good food, indeed the menus are identical. Says RL: '*A delightful dining experience. (For those not familiar with the area, it is next to Jesmond Metro station, down a subway. Our table was in the old railway carriage – a tight squeeze, so a lot of 'scuse me's. Chringri Moslai delicious, Chicken Kebab great too. One minor quibble would be the phone ringing, and the waiters calling through to the bar.*' RL. Chingri Varkee, grilled green pepper stuffed with spicy prawns. Tandoori Dhakna, chicken wings marinated in fresh herbs and spices, served with minty yoghurt sauce. Murgh e Khazana, breast of chicken cooked mainly with mild spices and honey, in a creamy sauce. Mangsho Pesta Ke Shadi, top side of beef cooked with a blend of mild spices and pistachio nuts. *Branch: The Valley, The Old Station House, Station Road, Corbridge, and Valley Connection, 301, Market Place, Hexham, both Northum.*

VUJON   A-LIST
29 Queen St, Quayside, Newcastle, NE1 3UG
0191 221 0601   www.vujon.com

Established in 1990 on Newcastle's quayside, by the elegant Mr Matab Miah, it translates as 'gourmet food and it is a stylish restaurant, seating 90 on two floors, with a party room for 40, Matab invested £250K in a refurbishment to mark the restaurant's 20th anniversary. The waiting area at the front of the restaurant is bright and cheerful. The dining room's high windows now have chocolate brown, cream and gold curtains. The chandeliers and other features remain as before, comfortable, well-lit and very clean. Like its owner, Vujon exudes class, care and style. From the uniform to the decor, it's all just perfect. '*The waiters seem to smile all the time.*' RL. ' *No standard curries, but starter and main courses proved interesting and a good choice.*' kdf. '*Most luxurious surroundings in Newcastle. Excellent tandoori starter.*' T&KM. The food is somewhat stylised and can disappoint those expecting the regular curryhouse experience. But stick with it and be open-minded. But be prepared for a high-end price tag. Starters include Kathi Kebab £5.90, lamb with onion and tomatoes served in a butter chapatti and Boro Chinghri Bhoona £6.90, king prawns with garlic, ginger and onion. Main Courses include the ever-popular Murgh Tikka Makhani £11.90, CTM with butter, ground almond and cream) and Goshtaba £10.90, a Kashmiri dish of lamb cooked with fresh spices, green chilli and coriander. Rice is £2.50 and naan £2.90. Dehli-style monkfish, marinated rainbow trout and salmon kalia cooked with tomatoes and coriander; Horin Mangsho is beef to-pside with pistachios, and Hash au Bassh is from the Chittagong hills cooked with bamboo shoots and ginger. For those with an inexhaustible appetite, try the Vhandaris Surprise, a ten course banquet. *'We had it and enjoyed it, but we dieted for a day per course – 10 days!'* HEG. Vujon received our best in the north East 2004 Award. Remains in our A-list. Av Lunch: £20; Dinner: £34. Set Dinner: £30 (3 courses + coffee). Mon-Sat: 12-2.30; Daily: 6.30-11.30.

Sunderland

CAFÉ SPICE
7 Douro Terrace, Sunderland, SR2 7DX
0191 510 2002   www.cafespice2000.co.uk

Café by name but not by building. It is set in a leafy conservation area of Sunderland, this magnificent Victorian building was converted from Cafe Spice Indian Restaurant in the year 2000. It took several months of intensive repair and refurbishment to turn it into one of the most luxurious Indian Restaurants in the North of England. Starters include: Xenuk £4.45, mussels-in-shell cooked with spices; Kakra £4.45, lightly spiced crab meat Dosa, £3.45, wafer thin rice flour pancake with spiced vegetable filling. served with coconut chutney; Palak Pakora £3.45, spinach and onion savoury and Dahi Begoon £4, vegetables in a boat of aubergines, garnished with yoghurt. Mains include: Jal-Jhool-Hansh £8, duck breast cooked in a spicy sauce, a very hot traditional Bengal curry; Jal-Jhool-Ha Makhoni Tikka chicken in a rich creamy sauce - preparation of the sauce consists of butter, fresh cream, ground almond, ground coconut etc. and a mixture of usual mild spices 7.95nshBreast cooked in a spicy sauce, very hot - a traditional Bengal curry £7.95.

YOU SAY OK
You might get a discount if you show them this Guide.

NEWCASTLE: RAJ 31 Pudding Chare. 0191 232 1450. *'A cosy little restaurant with a friendly atmosphere and pleasant decor'* DMcK.
NEWCASTLE: RANI 2 Queen Street, Quayside, Newcastle, NE1 3UG, England 0191 221 2202.
SOUTH SHIELDS: PASSAGE TO INDIA 4 Burrow St. 0191 427 5202. *'The food is nice, the staff very obliging. Food reasonably priced.'* DRK. Hours: 12-2/6-12, 1am Fri & Sat.
SOUTH SHIELDS: STAR OF INDIA 194 Ocean Rd ~ 0191 456 2210. First in South Shields, it opened in 1960, owned by M Faruque since 1972. Seats 60.
SUNDERLAND: CHESTER TAKEAWAY 69 Chester Rd High Barnes ~ 0191 510 8835. Owner- Chef, Syed Moynul. Credit cards accepted. Hours: 5-12, 1am Sat.
WHICKHAM: JAMDANI 3 The Square, Front St. ~ 0191 496 0820. Owner A Miah. Hours: 12-2/6-11.30.
WHICKHAM: MOTI JHEEL TAKEAWAY 9 Front St. ~ 0191 488 0851. Owner Mr MM Rahman. Hours: 12-2/6-11.30
WHITLEY BAY: SHAHENSHAH 187 Whitley Rd 0191 297 0503. Owner Abu Taher. *'Food first-class.'* MB. *'My local for a year.'* SN. *'Busy in a quiet and efficient way.'* PP. Hours: 12-2.30/6-12.
WHITLEY BAY: TAKDIR 11 East Pde ~ 0191 253 0236. Owner Majibur Rahman. 5.30-12. *Branches: Akash, 3 Tangier Street, Whitehaven, Cumbria; Al Mamun T/a, 5 John Street, Cullercoats T&W.*
WINLATON: BALTI HOUSE 18a The Garth, Front St. ~ 0191 414 2223. Est 1996. Seats 42. Specials include: King Prawn Peli Peli, King A 34-seater. Owner F.I. Khan continues to promises a T/a disc of 20% if you show them this Guide. You can't get fairer than that! Hours: 6-12. Branch: Balti House, Newcastle.

WARWICKSHIRE

Area: Midlands

Adjacent counties:
Derbs, Shrops,
Staffs, W.Mids,
Worcs

Coleshill B46

POLASH BALTI CUISINE
85 High St, Coleshill, B46 3AP   01675 462868
www.polashcoleshill.co.uk

A chapatti throw from the NEC, [we said it first, not the rival on the same street] and just inside the Warwickshire/W Mids border, is Coleshill. And much, it seems to the delight of the locals, is this 32 seater cosy curry house, opened in 1997 and run since 98 by Adbul Mannan. It is decorated in cream, blue velvet chairs and carpet, with engraved glass screens dividing the seating. Parking for 30 to rear of restaurant. Chef Taj Ullah cooks up the curries. Special: Bengal Fish Masala, Bangladeshi fish on the bone, cooked with herbs, coriander, served with rice. 'What an experience! Such attention, such luxury, such choice and such cooking! Our congratulations and thanks to the Polash'. hfc. 5.30-12.

Leamington Spa

BALTI VHUJON TAKEAWAY
50a Queen Street, Cubbington, Leamington Spa
CV32 7NA   01926 423 828

MJ Hussain is the proprietor of this Bangladeshi takeaway and he has provided ten large whicker chairs (with cushions), so you can sit back and wait for your takeaway in comfort. Snapshot Menu: Tikka Roll £4, chicken tikka wrapped in a Naan, served with salad and mint sauce; Akbori Murghi Keema £6.50, chicken tikka cooked with lamb mince meat and boiled egg, medium spiced; Delivery: 3 miles, £10 minimum. Credit cards accepted. Price Check: Popadom 45p, CTM £5.60, Pullao Rice £1.80. 5.30 - 11 (Fri-Sat to 11.30. Sunday closed).

BOMBAY TANDOORI
38 Regent St, Leamington CV32 5RG   01926 420521

Established 1980, and managed by MK Ahmed. Seats 58=. Delivery: 3 miles, £9.95 minimum. Minimum Charge: £9.95. Takeaway: 20% discount, 10% on Saturday. Menu Snapshot: Fish Kufta £3.95, spicy fish balls; Prawn or Chicken Fried Rice £3.95; Tandoori Mixed Grill £10.95, served with salad and Naan; Lassi Sweet or Salty £1.50. You might get a discount if you show Mr Ahmed this Guide. : 6 - 1, (Fri & Sat to 2).

KAYAL SOUTH INDIAN
2, Leamington Spa, CV32 5EG   01926 314410
www.kayalrestaurant.com

Branches See Leicester & Nottinghamfor menu details

Nuneaton

THE BULL AND SPICE
Bull Street, Attleborough, Nuneaton, CV11 4JX   0247 632 8089   www.thebullandspice.co.uk

A pub managed by Mich and Noah, its USP is Head Chef Shahab Uddin who cooks the standard curryhouse menu at affordable prices I(starter av £3.50, Mains, £6. Pops 50p, Chut £1.50, Pullao Rice £2.25. Naan from £1.70. Open normal pub hours.

CROSSED KHUKRIS GURKHA
Abby Street, Nuneaton CV11 5BX,   024 7634 4488
www.omsrestaurant.com   **NEPALESE**

It opened in 1998 and its owner OM Gurung is a former British Army Gurkha, and of course the Kukri is the iconic knife carried by all Gurkhas. Menu snapshot: Veg momo £2.80, steamed, gently spiced dumplings served with special momo chutney. Aludam £2.70, spicy potato with sesame, fresh chillies, coriander and spring onions. Spring roll £2.70, mixed potato, turnip, onions, carrot and sesame.. Chyau ko suruwa £2.90, mushroom soup with fresh chilli. Sun-Th: 5.30- 11. Fri-Sat: to 11.30.

Kenilworth

COCONUT LAGOON PAN INDIAN A-LIST
149 Warwick Rd, Kenilworth CV8 1HY
01926 851156   www.coconutlagoon.com

Opened in 1999 within the Peacock Hotel, Kenilworth. It is an astonishingly good restaurant, as good as any in London and big surprise for the provinces, where genuinely "Indian" establishments are so few. Since our last Guide, more Coconut Lagoons have been opened, see branches. Decorated in the vibrant spicy colours of southern India. Seats 60. *'Bright, clean, very pleasant surroundings. Very knowledgeable staff gave clear explanation of food, origin, preparation etc. So good we went back the next night!'* AD. *'Our first visit, recommended by friends. Warm, courteous welcome. Excellent guidance to menu, food beautifully presented.'* JK. Menu Snapshot. Masalai Paniyaram, spongy and savoury crumpets served with tomato chutney. Karaikudi Cutlet, minced lamb cutlets with almonds and sultanas on a spicy sauce. Paneer Roti, pan fried crispy soft cheese with onions and tomatoes in a light and fluffy roti. Shakoothi, Goan style chicken roasted with mild chilli, tamarind, mustard seeds and fenugreek in a thick sauce, served with mango rice and Avial. Goanese Vindaloo, cooked with garlic, red wine and flavoured with cider vinegar and dried chillies, served with tamarind rice and lentils with snakegourd. Konkani Porial, crisp mangetout parcels of minced pork cooked in sherry and lightly steamed - mild and flavoursome. Accompanied with mango rice and stir-fried vegetables. Malabar Omelette, strips of Malabar coast omelette in a thick curry with lemon rice - a complete meal!. Avial, poached aubergines, french beans, carrots, potatoes and green banana in a thick coconut sauce. *'Starters innovative, main courses small but well presented, excellent quality.'* GS. *'Different from any other we have visited, from internal decor to the ambience one experiences and most importantly the cuisine. Choice and quality of food that really is a world of difference. Well done!'* JEC. We can verify the above as we have visited several times and have stayed the night, which is a must - lovely colonial suite with everything you could possible want - recommended. Feast dinner c£26, four courses. BYO allowed - corkage c£8. T/a: 10% disc. 12-2.30 & 6-11.

RAFFLES   MALAYSIAN   A-LIST
95-97 Warwick Rd, Kenilworth, CV8 1HP
01926 864300   www.rafflesmalaysian.com

Under the same ownership as Coconut Lagoon, Raffles has moved up the road into the Grand Hotel. *'The menu is made up of Malaysian Malay, Malaysian Indian and Malaysian Chinese. Very different range of dishes from each culture, from starters to main courses. Style of restaurant redolent of old Empire and evokes a real feeling of being in Raffles Hotel in Singapore. Lighting and atmosphere good. Make the best Gin Slings I have ever tasted - including Singapore.'* [That, Clynt, wouldn't be difficult; the Singapore Slings at Raffles, Singapore are very poor indeed, however, I am pleased to say that the cocktails served here are fantastic. DBAC] *'Caution: take great care if you go beyond three. Food is truly out of this world. Menu changes with new dishes being introduced every few months or so, but favourites have been retained. Claypot and Pandri Perratal are simply a must. Absolutely delighted.'* CRS. *'Our favourite restaurant. Unusual and imaginative menu, food superb, beautifully cooked and presented. Service impeccable. Toilet immaculate.'* IS. *'Group of 60, prearranged banquet Malaysian menu. Greeted with a Singapore Sling , good start to evening, food served on platters, more than ample. Everyone has an enjoyable evening. Highly recommended.'* RD. *'Superb Colonial decor, fine crystal glasses and crisp well laundered linen. Ikan Goreng - delicious, Udang Bakar Kerinc - sensational, Hianese Chicken - unforgettable - I could go on!! Exceptionally consistent - can't wait to return!'* BW. Murtuabale - savoury Indian bread layered with minced beef, lightly toasted in a griddle, a light and crisp texture; Mysore Anda, slow cooked lamb served with Roti and Malaysian Coleslaw.; Pandri Perratal, pan fried spicy pork in a uniquely blended rich sauce served with yoghurt rice, beetroot, a bundle of long green beans, coleslaw and Appatam, an exquisite dish given the contrasting spicy pork together with cool yoghurt rice. A superb experience, but at a price! 2 course dinner £19.50, 4 course dinner £27.50. Hours: 12-2.30 & 6.-12.30. *Georgetown branches: Stratford-on-Avon, Leeds & Not'm.*

Rugby

TITASH INTERNATIONAL BALTI
65 Church Street, Rugby, CV21 3PT
01788 574433   www.titashcuisine.co.uk

'First visit to this impressive establishment. Furnished in a contemporary style. The food did not disappoint with a large and tasty Garlic Naan to accompany the Vegetable Rogan Josh. Equally generous from a portion perspective was the delicately flavoured Chicken Tikka Masala. Service attentive but not pushy. Not the cheapest meal we have experienced but it certainly represented good value for money.' N&JG. Menu Snapshot: Popadom 80p - thin wafer of pea flour [well, actually, no! - popadoms are made from a white lentil - dall moth]; Fish Tikka £4.90 starter / £9.70 main, cod pieces, delicately spiced and grilled in a charcoal clay oven; Chicken 65 £11.20, pieces of chicken cooked in Chef's ingredients – hot! 5.30 - 12.

Stratford-upon-Avon

COCONUT LAGOON   AWARD WINNER
21 Sheep Street, Stratford   CV37 6EF   01789 293546

This is the second-to-open branch of Coconut Lagooon, Kenilworth, where you will find menu and other details. The restaurant is on two floors, with an interesting balcony overlooking the ground floor.

GEORGETOWN   AWARD WINNER
23 Sheep Street, Stratford CV37 6EF   01789 204445

Malaysian restaurant and a branch of Raffles, Kenilworth Warks, where you'll find menu details.

THESPIAN'S
26 Sheep St, Stratford   CV37 6EF
01789 267187   www.thespiansltd.com

Fully licensed and air-conditioned. Menu Snapshot: Aam Chicken £3.50, cooked in spicy hot mango sauce; Grilled Quail £4.95, marinated in honey, tamarind and chilli, then roasted; Shami Kebab £3.50, minced lamb spiced with fresh garlic, coriander, chick peas and fried; Chicken Naga £7.50, hot and spicy, marinated chicken with Bangladeshi chilli (Pat's favourite, however, he prefers lamb!). 'Provided me with a very enjoyable curry at sensible prices. Portions very generous and very pleasant management!' CC. Mrs Chapchal - have a look at the 'fishy' meals - great choice: Roshni Delight £7.25 , mildly spiced Tiger Prawns, cooked with egg yolk, cinnamon, cardamom and garnished with cheese; Saffron Fish £10.95, salmon soaked in egg yolk, pepper and garlic. Shallow fried in olive oil, served with salad and Saffron Rice; Meen Kakri £8.95, Silver hake in a spicy sauce, turmeric, chillies, coriander, onions and garlic; Lobster Beruda £11.95, medium spiced with aubergine, served with Pullao Rice; Boal Bhuna £8.95, Boal from the rivers of Bengal cooked with green chillies; Kamal E £9.50, lightly spiced halibut fillets in medium sauce. Delivery: 3 miles, £15 minimum. Takeaway: 10% discount. Price Check: Popadom 50p, CTM £7.50, Pullao Rice £1.95. 5.30 - 12.

USHA
28 Meer Street, Stratford   CV37 6QB
01789 297348   www.usha-indian.co.uk

Opened way back in 1966, then it was called the Kashmir. Nazrul Islam took the restaurant over in 1995 and renamed it Usha. Menu Snapshot: Tandoori Mixed Grill with Naan £10.95; Lemon Chicken £7.95, with onions, tomatoes and fresh lemon; Achar Lamb,£7.95, lamb with onions, tomatoes, and pickle; Murgh Akbari £7.95, very mild and creamy, almonds, sultanas, coconut, fresh eggs. Takeaway: 15% discount. Cobra, £3 a bottle, glass house wine £1.90. Price Check: Popadom 50p, CTM £7.95, Pullao Rice £1.90. Th-Sun: 12-2 (seasonal). Sun-Th: 5.30 - 12, Fri-Sat to 12.30.

Warwick

WARWICK SPICE
24 Smith Street, Warwick, CV34 4HS
01926 491736   www.warwickspice.co.uk

Proprietor, Hussain, took over this 60-seater in 2000, when it was called Veranda. Menu Snapshot: The full range of curryhouse favourites plus specials such as Jingha Masalla £9, king prawns tandooried with classic masalla tomato-based, medium spicy sauce, garlic, coriander, garam masala, fenugreek, cream and butter, sharpened with lemon juice; King Prawn Pasanda £9, cooked in a mildly spiced, nutty sauce with almond, pistachio and yoghurt, to give a fresh taste; Fish Bhuna; £8.50, chunks of Bangladeshi fish (Boal) cooked in a medium spiced, thick sauce flavoured with fenugreek, coriander and chillies. One of the most popular dishes in many Bangladeshi homes; Chicken Sorisha £6.75, a popular Bangladeshi dish, marinated in garam masalla and mustard. Fairly hot & strong tasting. 5.30 - 11.30 (Sat to 12).

YOU SAY OK

HENLEY-IN-ARDEN: NAYA 148 High Street , Henley, B95 5BS 01564 793089   www.nayarestaurant.co.uk   Opened in 2009. Standard menu and prices. 5.30 11.
NUNEATON: INDIA RED Upper Abbey Street, Nuneaton, CV11 5BT, 024 7634 2090.
RAJDHANI 9 Horeston Grange, Nuneaton, CV11 6GU   01203 352254   Good curryhouse where you might get a discount if you show them this Guide.
STRATFORD-: AVON SPICE   7 Greenhill Street, Stratford, CV37 6LF, 01789 267067   www.avonspice.co.uk   Standard menu. Standard prices. Sun-Th: 5.30-11.30 Fri & Sat: to 12.30
STRATFORD: THE BALTI KITCHEN Greenhill Street, Stratford upon Avon, Stratford   01789 415800.
WARWICK: THE RIVERCROSS   204 Emscote Road, Warwick CV34 5QT   01926 734086

WEST MIDLANDS

Area: Midlandst

Adjacent Counties: Staffs, Warks, Worcs

West Midlands has been a metropolitain county since 1974 and contains the conurbations from the Black country at its west, through to Coventry in the east. At its hub is Birmingham

Birmingham Central
Postcodes B1 to B5 and Broad Street part of B15

ASHA'S — PUNJABI
Edmund House,12-22 Newhall Street, Birmingham, B3 3LX   0121 200 2767   www.ashasuk.co.uk

Asha is a Bollywood superstar singing diva and a self-proclaimed cook. *'As a little girl,'* she says Asha, *'I used to wander around in the huge kitchens of my father's traveling theatre company of more than 500, their food being cooked by his chefs in huge cauldrons. This is where my interest in cooking began.'* Her boast is that in 2013 Asha's will be the: *'largest dining indian restaurant 'chain in the world!'* [sic]. It's as much news to us as it may be to you. True they have branches in Abu Dhabi, Dubai, Kuwait, Qatar, and Bahrain. Here in Brum the bar overlooks the dining area some of which is contained within attractive circular railings. Staff wear smart uniforms, the women, black or cerise-pink saris. Background music is modern, mixed by a DJ with some of Asha's tracks. The venue serves quite specialised Indian cuisine under the mantle of Delhi's Chef Modh Saleem Quereshi (son of the legendary Lucknow dum pukt. Menu Snapshot: Chandni Chowk Ka Keema £15.45, minced lamb cooked with fresh onions; Nally Gosht £15.95, lamb shank cooked in thick onion gravy with saffron and roasted garlic essence; Bharwaan Baigan £11.45, slitted and marinated baby aubergines tossed with fresh onion- tomato masala and ginger juliennes; Hare Baingan Ka Bartha £11.45, mashed eggplant cooked with green chillies, garlic and fresh coriander; Amritsari Chole £10.95 a tangy, spicy preparation of chickpeas and baby potatoes topped with with onion & chutney. For dessert, if you have room, try another restaurant rarity, Agra Ka Shahi Tukra. It's a kind of bread and butter pudding, where fried bread is soaked in a sweetened saffron milk reduction, garnished with nuts. It's much nicer than it sounds! The dishes are far-removed from curryhouse fare, and may get criticised for their unfamiliarity. But the cooking and the reports we get are good. Mon-Fri: 12-2.30; Mon-Wed: 5.30-10.30; Th-Fri to 11.00pm Sat 5-11; Sun to 10.

BARAJEE
265, Broad St, 1st Floor, B1 2DS
0121 643 6700   www.restaurantbarajee.com

98 seater owned by successful restaurateur Moula Miah, of Rajnagar International Restaurant Group, (see Solihul, West Midlands). Barajee overlooks Brum's exciting canal system. Dishes on the menu include monkfish cooked in olive oil, garlic and bay leaves and simmered in spiced tomato sauce. Chefs: Abdul Rouf and Abdul Khalique have also developed set menus where prices start at c£16 per head for a veg meal and c£20 or a meaty version. Open 5 to late.

BLUE MANGO — PAN INDIAN
Regency Wharf, Broad Street, Birmingham, B1 2DS
0121 633 4422   www.bluemangobirmingham.co.uk

If their name conjours up an image of blue strip lights and Vegas vulgarity, forget it; the interior this 120 seater is hugely elegant, with dark leather wall, chairs and floorings. The food is fine Pan Indian, under the guidance of chef Nitin Bhatnager. Items such as Kori Gassi £9, a chicken dish from the coastal Karnataka (southern India) region, flavoured with roasted coriander seeds and fresh grated coconut; Lamb Rogan Josh £9, gets its name from the rich red of tomatoes, paprika and ground red chilli; Goan Fish Curry £10, Cubes of monkfish cooked in a gravy spiked with use of kokum, ideally served with steamed basmati rice; Hydrabadi Nalli Gosht £11, slow-cooked lamb shanks cooked with mild smooth nutty gravy; Paneer Tak-a-Tak £12, cheese cooked with capsicum, ginger and green chilli in a tangy onion and tomatoe gravy; Butter, Pepper and Garlic Lobster £22, the Mangalorean Christian delicacy of fresh lobster chunks stir fried in a tamarind and butter sauce finished with freshly ground black peppers. Classical Indian desserts include Rasmalai or Gulab Jamun each £4. *'Good food, great surroundings and excellent service.'* PF. *'Very modern decor with lots of crazy huge flower arrangements on the tables. Only visit if you are very hungry - the enormous Onion Bhajia starter is a meal in itself. They should make a separate dish out of the delectable chickpea curry with accompanies the Samosas - excellent food.'* JG.

BOMBAY MIX
218 Broad St, Birmingham, B15 1AY   0121 643 3557

Bombay Mix offers all the favourites. Specials include Rezela Garlic Chilli £6.45,steam-cooked in hot chilli garlic sauce and garnished with coriander, available in chicken, meat, prawn, king prawn and vegetable or Fish Tikka Makhani, £6.45, salmon steak simmered in delicate sweet and sour butter sauce with fresh coriander and fenugreek, delicious to taste. Dinner for 2: £26.50, Chicken Tikka Puri and Tandoori King Prawns, Paps and Chuts, CTM, Lamb Keshri, Vegetable Makhani, Pullao Ricel, Batura Bread. 25% off for Students and for girlie groups on Ladies' Night. 12-3 & 6-11.

CELEBRITY INDIAN RESTAURANT
44 Broad Street, Birmingham, B1 2HP
0121 643 8969   www.celebrityrestaurant.co.uk

Set on the first floor in a Grade II listed building, family-run Celebrity also overlooks the regenerated canals. Chefs Zakaria Ibrahims and Kamal Hussain's star dishes include Roshun Mussels cooked in a creamy garlic and white wine sauce served with naan; Chicken Tikka marinated with yoghurt and cumin; and Sheekh Kebab made with freshly minced lamb, coriander, tomatoes, mint and spring onions. 3 course meal£13. Mon-Th &, Sun: 5.30-12; Fri-Sat: to 1am.

CHOOLO   NEPALESE
27 Warstone Lane, Birmingham, B18 6JQ
0121 236 0818   www.choolo.co.uk

This 40 seater is located in a listed converted Mill. Access is via an alleyway adjacent Paul Green Jewellers off Warstone Lane. Starters include: Momo £4.50, bite sized steamed, spicy dumplings stuffed with minced chicken/lamb, served with tomato and coriander chutney; Chowela £4.50, chicken/lamb marinated with nepalese spices, tandoor-baked and served on a bed of salad. Mains include Masu Tarkari, Dal & Achar £10.50, a typical Nepalese meal combining tender mutton curry (tarkari), black lentils, and chutney; Rashilo Masu £8.50, lamb cooked with spring onion, shallots and capsicum; Lasoon Kukhura £8.50, medium hot tender chicken, infused with garlic and cooked in Nepalese spices); Hanss £10.50, duck breast curry made with ginger, garlic, shallots and capsicum. Mon-Sat 12-2 & 6-11. Sun closed.

ITIHAAS BRASSERIE at SELFRIDGES   TOP 100
Upper Mall, East Bullring, Birmingham, B5 4BP

It offers Itihaas's original renowned Indian cuisine (see next entry) in a casual setting. India's most loved Mumbai Street food and South Indian cuisine favourites, including Chicken Samosa and Gol Guppa. The menu is inspired by rich and aromatic North-western Indian flavours, giving customers the chance to taste award winning Indian food in the heart of the city.

ITIHAAS   BEST IN UK AWARD, 2007/8
18 Fleet St, B'ham B3
0121 212 3383   www.itihass.co.uk

Raj Rana is the driving force behind Itihaas. His previous background was jewellery and property management. At 28 in 2005, and with no catering experience he opened a restaurant. But he didn't want just another Birmingham curry house, of which there are hundreds. He wanted to bring to Birmingham the type of upmarket Indian establishment till then only seen in London. Birmingham until then had nothing like it before. Raj says *'Itihaas is a pure labour of love for me and is simply one man's interpretation of royal cuisine and royal service, yet still having a relaxed and informal atmosphere.'* His property background led him to a 5,500 sq ft site on the corner of Fleet Street and Newhall Street, rather aptly in the Jewellery Quarter and the edge of Brum's Business Sector, and he bought its 125 year lease. *'What I got was, a concrete shell.'* It was below seven storeys of luxury apartments, requiring a massive odour filtration system which pumps smells to the roof, where they are cleansed. Next Raj set about furnishing and decorating it with literally no expense spared. It cost Raj some £2m to achieved this goal, but you need more than money. Very early on he recruited Satpal Gill (Saif) to take charge of the culinary side. Until then Saif had been a senior chef at Madhu's Southall Middlesex, the Top UK restaurant in our 2004 Guide. Itihaas is a unique name in the trade; it means history, and apart from its own recent history, the menu, which is one of the best we've seen, carries a fascinating history of India, and more of that later. Next Raj employed a manager: Ajay Bhatia, who glides around supervising front of house. On arrival, pretty hostesses wearing traditional silk saris will receive you and will seat you in one of their three dining rooms. The 'Colonial Dining Room,' seats seventy diners, has plate glass windows which are shuttered in traditional colonial style, with dark polished wood. The windows overlook the canal, and a terrace, which can be accessed through double doors ... a great spot to enjoy a cocktail and canapé party or for a more formal seated occasion and enjoy the waterway. Inside, the luxurious look is completed with white table linen, sparkling crystal, and chandeliers. Perhaps you could say it is decorated a little like a Gentleman's club, it's definitely very smooth. Downstairs the 'Maharajah Dining Room' which seats sixty, is decorated with Indian artefacts, paintings and carved stone elephants. The third dining room, the 'Tiffin Room' is accessed from the Maharajah Room, through two large, 300 year old Indian wooden doors. The 'Tiffin Room' seats an exclusive twelve, and to add to the experience, the room possesses it's own bar and you will be assigned your very own butler, wow! Under Saif is head chef, Sheraton Delhi Hotel trained, Amardeep Saka, who heads the, twenty-strong, kitchen brigade. The food is Punjabi with a Kenyan Asian twist, with a little fusion and a soupcon of Chinese. Menu Snapshot: Mirchi Murgh c£8, tender baby chicken, tossed in fresh ginger and garlic, pan fried with fresh chilli, dressed with coriander and tomato juliennes; Chingari Jingah £9.95, king prawns, with chillies, roasted garlic and lemon; Chotte Kofta c£9, lamb balls spiced with cardamom and clove, with tangy sauce; Nana-sa-Dosa c£7, crispy pancake, filled with spiced potato and vegetables, served with coconut chutney and lentil soup; Maari Aloo c£7, dry roasted potato wedges, ground black pepper, drizzled with tangy soy sauce; Pilli Pilli Bhogah c£6, assorted fresh vegetables lightly fried in spiced crispy batter; Masala Champay c£10, juicy lamb chops barbecued in the clay oven

COBRA
SPLENDIDLY INDIAN, SUPERBLY SMOOTH

drizzled in a chutney made from paprika and lemon, VERY good!; Padhina Keema c£10, minced lamb, tossed with ginger, garlic, cumin, coriander and mint leaves, Pat really likes Punjabi-style Keema; Paneer ka Tukrah c£9, homemade cheese, marinated in garam masala, yoghurt, ginger, chilli and coriander leaf; Koila Murgh c£13, whole chicken marinated in yoghurt and herb paste, seared over hot charcoal; Bhangan Aur Tamatar ka Bhartah c£7, smoked aubergine with sun dried tomatoes, peas, red onions and thick masala sauce; Hara Bara Kofta c£7.50, pan fried mixed vegetable dumplings, think dry tangy sauce, garnished with ginger and chilli; Pyaz aur Lassan ka Kulcha £2.50, garlic and onion stuffed bread; Gosht Basmati c£11, spring lamb, cooked on the bone, basmati rice, saffron and herbs, we both fight over this one!; Bhundi Raita £2.50, deep-fried gram flour pearls, homemade yoghurt, roasted cumin and coriander. Now to the puddings!!, Garam Gazarh Hallwa Naraam Kulfi £3.25, hot carrot cake with almonds and pistachio, served with kulfi, I know this is good, 'cos I've tried it. Coconut Kheer £3.75, Punjabi rice pudding, grated coconut, cardamom; Mithai Chawal aur Hallwa £3.75, sweet basmati rice, raisins, cashew, almond, a semolina cake, lovely! 12-3, Mon-Fri only and 6-11.30 daily, 10.30 Sun.

JIMMY SPICE'S
5a, Regency Wharf, Broad St, B1
0121 643 2111   www.jimmyspices.co.uk

Over the past 15 years, Amrik Singh Uppal and Kuldip Singh have been involved with such Guide entrants as Killermont Polo Club, Poppadum Express, Shimla Pinks, Blue Mango, 4550m from Delhi and Pickle Johns, not to mention the pan-Asian Yellow River Cafe chain. Now under the trading name East & West Restaurants Group, Jimmy Spice's Buffetworks opened in 2004 in an old glassworks in the prestigious Regency Wharf development and seats 180. The concept was novel then and much copied now: it offers authentic cuisine from the Far East, India, Middle East, Europe and the Americas- all for one price, served as an e-a-m-a-y-l buffet. Each cuisine has its own chef who will cook in front of you. Uppal and Singh have a strong management team. To run their Indian culinary activities, they hired Gopal Singh, who had been with India's Hyatt, Oberoi and Taj hotels. Lunch: Mon-Fri: £7. 99 12- 4, Sat-Sun to 5: £10. 99. Dinner: Sun-Wed £12. 99, 5-10. 30; Th-Sat £14. 99. Kids u10 half price, u3 free. *Branches: The Piazza, NEC B'ham, B40; The Parade, Sutton Coldfield, B72; 66 Station Rd, Solihull B91; Windsor St, Stratford-upon-Avon, Warks, ; 8 Dorchester St, Southgate Shopping Centre, Bath, Som, ; Derby Square, Waterloo Rd, Epsom, Surrey; Thames Edge, 18 Clarence St, Staines, Surrey,*

LASAN   A-LIST
3-4 Dakota Buildings, James Street, St Paul's Square, B3 1SD   0121 212 2664   www. lasan. co. uk

It is not easy to find nor to park at the 64-seater Lasan, located near St Paul's Square. Indeed its is an unlikely venue for a restaurant with such high aspirations. Aktar Islam is chef-owner assisted by Chef Khalid Sami Khan. Jabbar Khan is the FOH Director Islam and Khan have created quite a stir with their lashing opinions, of which more later. As for their menu, it is at the haute end of high in both achievement and price, and this is not to everyone's liking, and certainly if it's cheap and cheerful Balti/curryhouse you want, you won't find it at Lasan. Isam's menu changes frequently, and these examples are typical: Starters: Afghani Lamb £11. 50, tandooried cutlet with a lentil pattie spiced with cinnamon and black cardamom, accompanied by lightly pickled red onion and green chutney; Theen tharah ka murgh £11, spicy shredded chicken & corn samosa, spiced minced sheek with a hint of mint, fresh curry leaf and star anise scented tikka with honey mustard and green chutney; Konkan kekada £13, soft shell crab dipped in a crispy ajwain and Kashmiri chilli batter with Devonshire crab, green pea and potato cake with cucumber raitha and sour raw mango chutney. Mains: Thengapal Duck £20, on lightly spiced carrot and courgette served with Keralan style caramelised onion and bell pepper sauce scented with ground fennel seeds; Chukkandar Gosht £17, bhuna of mutton spiced with ground chilli and coriander; simmered in reduced gravy with shredded beetroot and caramelised shallots; Dum ki biryani £18, Goat and basmati rice cooked together in a sealed pot with yoghurt and mint. Scented with cardamom, mace and dum masala served with dhal and raitha;; Murgh jalfrezi £17, Free range Cotswold white chicken simmered in hot spicy onion, tomato and bell pepper sauce spiced with sun dried chilli, green cardamom and cassia leaf; Kukkar makhani £17, Punjabi-style chicken tikka marinated with hung yoghurt and tandoori masala. Roasted in tandoor then simmered in light tangy tomato, honey and cashew nut makhani sauce; Dhaniwal beef £21, Marinated rump of naturally reared Stokes Marsh Farm beef alongside slow braised blade and peas, spiced potato bartha, confit tomatoes with reduced caramelised shallot and bone marrow dhaniwal gravy. Desserts include: Gajar Halva Somosa £7, sweet carrot and ground pistachio pudding in traditional samosa pastry flavoured with cassia leaf and cinnamon, served with kulfi and mixed berry coulis; Gulab Jamun aur Rabri £7, warm khoya roundels with chilled North Indian cardamom scented custard. That's what they sell. Sun-Fri:12-2:30 / Sun-Sat: 6-11. *Branch Lasan Eatery, 1355 Stratford Road, Hall Green, Birmingham B28 9HW 0121 777 9090* . This is what they have to say: Mr Khan accused Lasan's imitators of having inadequate education or practical experience to run a high-end restaurant. He said: *'The wave of "fine dining" Indian restaurants opening in Birmingham has been sparked by saturation of a mid-market sector serving poor quality food little better than basic chilled food from supermarkets. This is often a vanity exercise and, sadly, many of these are not up to the task. Their food suggests that they often have bad palates and poor ingredients knowledge, that they rarely eat out to test their performance against the wider market, and that they* haven't even been to India'. Aktar Islam has previously criticised *'bog-standard Indian restaurants for serving formulaic, poorly prepared curry and bastardised Indian food'* [sic]. He describes the Balti Triangle as being *'a sort of alcoholic's paradise with the same old, same old' baltihouse décor'.* B'hm Post's Richard McComb joined the debate with *'The problem ... is that we have got used to the warped idea that food should be cheap. This is why nasty Indian restaurants serving slop survive but it is also why nasty £4. 99-a-go pub carveries flourish, serving catering pack gravy, tasteless mass-produced meat and death-by-vegetables. It is also why half-wits query the price of dishes at Lasan.'* Balti King Andy Munro was outraged. *'The recent unprovoked attack on Balti by Lasan's head chef, Aktar, gave me an attack of gross indigestion as well as indignation but I've now recovered in order to set the record straight. First of all, Lasan is a great restaurant doing mainly 'authentic' South Asian cuisine with an innovative twist . . . therein lies the key because for 'innovation' read 'invention', the very thing that Aktar criticises. Yes, Balti is a Brummie invention yet isn't that the same with all styles of food at some stage? The fact that when I spoke to Aktar a few months ago, he didn't even know what Balti was, to me, speaks volumes. To remind him, it is a simple but effective style of preparing food and perhaps it could be said to be Brummie equivalent of tasty, inexpensive compared to Lasan's platinum prices, street food – the latter concept being one that Lasan have proudly featured at various times.'* Munro continues: *'As for baltihouse décor, Indian' flock wallpaper is as rare in the Balti triangle as the proverbial rocking horse droppings'.* Andy Munro has contributed the Balti Section below:

MANZIL
112 Digbeth, Birmingham, B5 6DT
0121 643 4051   www. manzils. co. uk

The 100 seat family run, licensed Manzils was established in1966 just below the Bull Ring It offers Tandoori dishes, Mixed grills, Balti and Curry selections, and also some contemporary and interesting Indian dishes. Typical starters include Tandoori Fish £3. 80; CTM £7. 20; Lamb Tikka Pasanda £7. 40. It has the latest openings in Brum: Sun-Th: 6-2am; Fri-Sat to 4am.

MAHARAJAH   A-LIST
23 Hurst St, Birmingham, B5 4 4AS   0121 622 2641

Nat Bhatt's Maharajah is a small place 62 seats on two floors, which opened in 1972. Its recent refurbishment includes a modern-design carpeting, new light walls, and contemporary artwork Booking is recommended. Service is mature and careful, and the place is often full to bursting. Waiting bookers are deftly dispatched to the downstairs bar. Such competence is rare and welcome. The food is Indian, cooked by Gurmaj Kumar and Jaskarn Dhillon. The menu looks a little ordinary, but the food is still always spot on. Menu snapshot: *'The popadums were exemplary in their crispness; the mint sauce, mango chutney and chopped onions were also fabulous.'* PM. Starters include Pudina Paneer Tikka £5, tandooried mint paste-coated paneer tikkas; Murgh Patiala £9. 25, chicken marinated with spices, fresh Indian herbs and fruits. Mains: Murgh Musallam £9. 55, rich and creamy chicken flavoured with fresh herbs and egg; Maharaja's Classic Gosht Rogan Josh £9. 55, an aromatic and colourful dish originating from Kashmir where lamb pieces are marinated in yoghurt, cooked with spices and nuts; Saag Gosht £9. 25, lamb cooked with fresh spinach and spices; Bangaarey Baingan £7, a special aubergine dish; Maharaja-Di- Daal £7, black lentils overnight-cooked in a rich creamy and buttery sauce, one of the best chef tests there are curryhouses don't do it, and always perfect at Maharajah. 12-2 & 6-11; closed Sun & bank hols.

MILAN INDIAN CUISINE   PUNJABI
93 Newhall Street, Birmingham B3 1 LH
0121 236 0671   www. milanindiancuisine. co. uk

Dhirendra Patel's 120-seater, est 1989, is decorated in pastel shades, giving it a light and airy feel. The bar area is typically Indian with beaten copper drinks tables and large coffee pots. Chef Parvinder Singh Multani is ex India's Oberoi hotels and menu reads like curryhouse but the food is Punjabi in taste, so has the edge. Snapshot: Paneer Shalik £5, spicy paneer cooked in the tandoor; Stuffed peppers, £4. 25 filled with coconut, potatoes and coriander. You might get a discount if you show Mr Patel this Guide. 12-2. 30 & 6-11. 30; Sun closed. *Milan Sweet Centre Branches: 238 Soho Road, Birmingham, B21 9LR 0121 551 5239 and Stoney Lane, Balsall Heath B12 8HB 0121 449 1617 and 296 Abel St, Milpitas, nr San José, CA, US.*

PUSHKAR   FINE PUNJABI DINING
245 Broad Street, B1 2HQ
0121 643 7978   www.pushkardining.com

Cambridge economics graduate Raj Singh had a dream to open a restaurant called Pushkar. 'I love the name', he says. 'It means born to a flower'. The dream came into being in late 2009. Singh wanted an elegance, not often associated with Punjabi venues. As you stroll down restaurant-laden Broad Street, you cannot but notice the gorgeous decor inside Pushkar through its wall to ceiling plate glass window. As to the electronic fish tank in the floor, you'll just have to visit to see it. The venue has 'striking artwork, a specially commissioned chandelier, stylish furnishings, gorgeous table settings and the beautiful dresses worn by the waitresses.' Paul Fulford, B'hm Mail. All this costly decor is fruitless without a competent chef. As luck would have it, Bishal Rasaily was available. He trained with Taj then went to Delhi's Maurya Sheraton Dum Pukt restaurant where he worked under India's legendary top chef Imtiaz Qureshi. Bishal was head-hunted to join London's Chutney Mary as sous chef. He moved to Lancashire's Victoria's India for a while before Singh chose him to set up Pushkar's new kitchen in 2009. Bishals menu is pan Indian with a nod to Punjabi favourites and delivers superbly executed food. Starters include: Dahi Puri Chaat £4.25, crisp pastry shells filled with a tangy mix of potatoes and chickpeas topped with sweet yoghurt, fruity tamarind and gram flour vermicelli; Spinach and Prune cakes £4.75, chopped prune with a piquant hint of balsamic vinegar encased in a mildly spiced spinach cake, golden fried; Punjabi Tokri Chaat £4.95, crisp potato-lattice-basket filled with street food favourites, strained sweet yoghurt and chutneys. Mains include Qasoori Methi Murgh £10, chicken breast dish with fresh fenugreek and a hint of garlic; Tariwala Murgh £10, a house speciality, breast of chicken slow simmered with onions and tomato; Punjabi Nalli Gosht £11, a traditional preparation of lamb shanks. Rarha Gosht £11, a traditional Punjabi bhuna of lamb and Keema mince, slow-cooked in a rich sauce with selected spices; Salmon Dildar £14, Scottish pink salmon steak marinated with fresh dill leaves, char grilled in tandoor, served with salad. Side dish portions £4.45 each, eg: Dal Makhani, black lentils, the ultimate chef test, and perfect here, Bhindi Singara Do, spicy okra with water chestnuts and Pyaza Baingan Masala, baby aubergines in a tangy sauce. Desserts are not neglected: Garam Masala Brullée £5, is Raj's pride and joy or there's Chocomosa £5, golden fried parcels of filo pastry stuffed with a roast almond and chocolate filling, served with vanilla ice cream. Gajar ka Halwa £4.45, is finely grated carrots cooked on slow heat with cardamom and nuts, served with ice cream. Lunch: £7 (1 course), £10 (2 course), £13 (3 course). Dinner: £25 to £35 (3 courses). Mon-Fri: 12.-2.30 & Daily: 5.30-11.

RAJDOOT   FINE INDIAN DINING   TOP 100
78-79 George Street, Burmingham, B3 1PY
0121 236 1116   www. rajdoot. co. uk

Rajdoot was the first up market Indian restaurant in B'hm, opening in 1965. It was the height of Indian elegance in its day and though it is out glamourised by the numerous younger fledglings in the area, it still holds its own, for service, decor and food. 'Rajdoot is one of my favourites' RCF. Muraliraj Narashimaraj, is now chef in charge.. Menu snapshot: Starters: Malai Tikka Kali Mirch £6.50, Succulent morsels of chicken breast marinated with cheese, cream and cracked peppers, glazed golden in the tandoor. Mildly spiced; Murg Gilafi £6. 50, Minced chicken rolled on skewers with a mixture of bell peppers and fresh coriander cooked over charcoal; Duck Tikka £8, marinated overnight in mild spices, touch of garlic, honey, red wine and orange juice, gently chargrilled; Paneer Tikka £5. 50, marinated in aromatic spices and chargrilled; Aloo Tikki £5, golden-fried mini cakes of mashed potatoes and selected spices. Mains include: Methi Murg £11. 50, diced chicken breast cooked with fresh fenugreek and a hint of garlic and coriander; Chicken Tikka Biryani £15. 50, basmati rice cooked together with chicken and flavoured with cardamom and garnished with nuts and caramelised onions. Served with vegetable curry; Rogan Josh £12, lamb sautéed and simmered in its own juice with tomatoes and freshly ground spices, garnished with cashew nuts, Kashmiri-style; Keema Mutter £12, minced lamb with a touch of ginger ,

garlic and green peas flavoured with cumin; Lobster Rajdoot £27, whole lobster expertly prepared to chef's authentic recipe with special Himalayan herbs. 6-11.30. *Branches: Manchester Carlton House, 18 Albert Square, Manchester M2 5WD 0161 834 7092; 26-28 Clarendon St, Westbury Centre, Dublin 2 00 35 31 679 4280; Cutnall Green, Droitwich. Worcestershire WR9 0PW –01299 851000 and Lama de Espinosa, Fuengirola, Malaga, Costa del Sol, Spain 00 34 95 246 29 10.*

SAFFRON
126 Colmore Row, Birmingham, B3 3AP
0121 212 0599   www. saffronbirmingham. co. uk

Situated in Colmore Row, in a former Caffè Uno, the 60-cover Saffron is the third in a small group run by Aklasul Momin who says his food uses 'modern Western-style presentation which is not "just another curry house." Taj-trained Chef Shankar Saha Sudha describes his food as *'a fusion of seasonal produce with global influences to give diners the most sensational food they have ever tasted'*, which means it is not to everyone's liking. Pops & chuts £3. Typical starters include Subzi Brie Tikke £5, spiced potato and vegetable cake stuffed with Somerset brie, mixed fruit salsa and micro herbs; Papdi & Channa Chaat £4. 50, spiced chick peas, cubed potato and wheat crisp on baby gem, topped with green chutney and tamarind fool. Mains include Tikhi Kargosh £6. 50, spiced wild rabbit and spring onion pie, cumin flavour organic vegetable pickle, & assorted micro herbs; Gosht Roganjosh £10. 95 the traditional lamb curry from the North West frontier of India, flavoured with fennel powder; Sorso Maach £13 fish cooked in an east Indian-style marinade of mustard, chilli and coconut. Mon-Fri: 12-2. 30 & 5. 30-11; Sat-Sun 12-11. *Branches: Saffron Red 78 Leadenhall St, EC3; Saffron Quarter 19 The Foregate, Worcester; Multi Cuisine Buffet; Saffron, 909 Wolverhampton Road, Oldbury, B69.*

SHIMLA PINKS
Five Ways Leisure Complex, 214 Broad Street,
Birmingham, B15 1AY   0121 633 0366

Starters include Kastoori Machli Tikka £10, tilapia marinated in fresh yoghurt, ground fenugreek seeds, green chili and a ginger and garlic paste, seared in the tandoor; Jhingha Kaali Mirch £10, king prawns marinated in fresh yoghurt, cream cheese, crushed black peppercorns, garam masala and a ginger and garlic paste, cooked in the tandoor. Subz Kakori Seekh Keebab £10, finely chopped carrots, green peas, cauliflower, broccoli and onion spiced with green chillies, garam masala, fresh ginger and garlic, cooked on a skewer in the tandoor. £6. Mains are from £14 eg Dhaba Murgh, chicken cooked in a thick sauce with spring onions, fresh coriander & Punjabi spices. Lunch: 2 course £13; 3 course £16; Dinner: £31. Beer £3, Wine £16 per bottle. Mon-Th: 12-3 & 15-12; Fri-Sat 12-12; Sun 12:-11.

Birmingham Balti Zone

Consits of B10 to B13   **ANDY'S TOP.** Genuine Balti as opposed to a good curry!
Brum's Balti King, Andy Munro makes his choice of the best Baltis:

The balti phenomenom started in the late seventies/early eighties in Birmingham when a Pakistani restaurateur decided to 'fuse' the North Pakistani/Kashmiri slow one-pot cooking method with the Western custom of having curry served up without delay to the hungry diner. A special flat-bottomed karahi the Balti, made of thin pressed steel was designed and commissioned from a Birmingham manufacturer. This heated up quickly using vegetable oil rather than ghee as the cooking medium. Ingredients including a selection of herbs and spices were thrown in during the fast-cooking process over a high flame with no generic curry powders or pastes being used. This process gave a clean and unadulterated taste, preserving the individual integrity of the spices used and was served sizzling at the table in the karahi for the traditional naan-dipping/ no-cutlery routine ... the balti was born! Andy Munro.

SHAHI NAN KABAB   353 Stratford Rd, Sparkhill, B11, 4JQ

ANDY'S TOP. The Shahi Nan Kebab remains an outpost of the 'old' traditional baltihouse order. Although recently refurbished, it has retained its front of house chill cabinet and grilling paraphernalia and is very popular with the local Pakistani community. Free pops were accompanied by dips including a testingly hot tamarind and chilli one. My Sheekh Kebabs £1-60 for two, were top notch as are all the grilled and tandooried offerings. My companion's Balti Chicken Korma £6-50, was both coconutty and spicy whilst my Balti Chicken and Mushroom £6-90, passed muster as it should do with a restaurant chef who used to be in the Pakistani Navy. The accompanying Peshwari Naan £2-20, was also moist and tasty. Incidentally it's worth asking for your balti 'western style' if you prefer it with more sauce as the Shahi caters for the local populace who like a drier dish. Service couldn't have been more friendly at this small but perfectly formed restaurant. 5% Credit card charge. 12 to late.

ADIL BYO   353 Ladypool Rd, Balsall Heath, Bham B12, 8LA   0121 449 0335

At the time of writing, they are displaced from their ancestral home in nearby Stoney Lane which is undergoing a problematical refurbishment, Adil probably has the most legitimate claim of producing the first ever balti and Rafique and the staff are rightly proud of that fact. On my visit, I opted to start with Tandoori Lamb Chops £3-80, which was a quartet of tasty but not overspiced pieces of lamb. One of the other starter options is the Green Chilli Bhaji £1-50, which are not normally deseeded so only for the brave! Main course was a Balti Chicken and Paneer £6-80, plenty of chicken and paneer complemented by a rich and plentiful sauce. Naan dipping was courtesy of, in my experience, a ginger variety £2-10, chosen from a wide selection of over a dozen varieties. No room left for the selection of Asian sweets on offer. Plastic payment OK. 4-12.

AL FAISAL   BYO   136-140 Stoney Lane, Sparkbrook, B12, 8AQ 0121 449 5695

Al Faisal, for so long a stalwart of the balti scene and allegedly the inventors of the Karak family, Naan, has had the sort of facelift that would make even Anne Robinson envious. With tinted glass windows, a giant cinematic TV screen and sheeshas, it is obviously a favourite with locals on a night out with its glitzy feel. You can even purchase bottles of Bateel which is a sparkling date juice drink for that champagne moment for abstainers from the demon drink. As might be expected, prices are a bit higher but, in fairness, only fractionally so. I started with Chicken Boti £3-90, but I'm pleased to say that the chargrilled pieces were from the breast. The portions were generous, subtly spiced and all round it was an excellent starter accompanied by a well stocked chutney tray. Next up was the main course and I opted for a Ginger Chicken Tak Tak Talwa £7-50, - try saying that quickly even if you've only drunk date champagne!. Its combination of minced chicken and ginger was tasty if slightly dry in presentation. The accompanying Garlic and Coriander Naan was faultless. Al Faisal certainly care about their food and are undoubtedly an asset to the Balti Triangle. Plastic payment OK. 12-12.

COBRA

SPLENDIDLY INDIAN, SUPERBLY SMOOTH

AL FRASH BYO 186 Ladypool Rd, Sparkbrook, B12, 8JS 0121 753 3120

ANDY'S TOP. The restaurant has been established for quite a long time but in recent years Al the butterfly, has become a little bit Al Flash decorwise but the food still makes a genuine claim to being one of the best baltis in Brum. Things started off well with some excellent poppadoms and a trio of dips ranging from a mild mint yoghourt to a chilli variety of flame thrower strength. . a real culinary ying and yang. All served up on Al Frash logoed plates although lepidopteramists amongst you can decide whether it's a genuine butterfly or just a balti butterfly. My starter of Aubergine Pakora £1-90, was thinly sliced aubergine in a succulent lightly spiced batter. The Chicken Tikka £3-50, though not a massive portion was also tender and nicely spiced. Main courses were served up sizzling in the authentic black balti bowls and my Balti MeethaGosht £7-95, was a wonderful combination of spiciness and sweetness superbly balanced. The Balti Chicken White Rose £7-50, was an unusual cashew nut and cardamom take on a Korma, creamy without being cloying. Accompanying Garlic and Coriander Naans £2-30, were doughy , fresh and a delight to dip. This is definitely a butterfly worth catching! Plastic payment OK. 5 to late.

GRAMEEN KHANA BYO 310-312 Ladypool Rd, Sparkbrook, B12, 8JY 0121 449 9994 www. grameenkhana. com

'It's a Bangladeshi curryhouse in the balti triangle but is not budget stuff. That said it'll not break the bank. 'My brother recommended it having eaten there himself after seeing it praised in The Independent. The food there was wonderful. Truly wonderful. I'll certainly be going back there again. Bangladeshi-born spice master Mohammed Abdul Basid's 100-year-old family recipe won him Best Balti chef award. "If the balti was 'invented' in Brum in the 70s, how can this recipe be a century-old? Ian Halstead. Pops and a more than decent dip selection £1-50. I had a deliciously spiced Garlic Mushroom and Potato starter £2-60, whilst my companion had an excellent Monk Fish Kebab £3-75, . Choosing a main course was difficult and for fish aficionados, there is a wide selection including a Sardine Saag Bhuna £6-25. My companion ordered a good sized Chicken Dhansak £6-75, which came with a thick tasty sauce and the obligatory pineapple, unfortunately the work of the man from Del Monte rather than a fresh slice. I had Lamb Shatkora £7-50, but it was extremely tasty with the tasty citrusy vegetable which the waiter helpfully advised me to mash up to infuse the distinctive flavour. The accompanying Peshwari Naan £1-90, was honeyed and coconutty and one of the best that I've ever tasted. The bill was served up with the traditional After Eights which rounded off an excellent meal. Plastic payment OK. 5.30-2am.

IMRANS BYO 262 Ladypool Rd, Sparkbrook, B12 8JU 0121 449 1370

Usman Butt's Imrans has always been one of the Balti Triangle heavyweights and on a busy evening we were shown to one of the few spare tables. Paid for Poppadoms 80p, were accompanied by a quite bewildering array of chutneys and dips. From the usual yoghourt and mint smoothie to one which I'm sure would be better than a torch in the dark. Imrans are well known for their Tandoori Lamb Chops £4-50, and these were superb. Others in my party went for the Sheeshk Kebab £2-50, and they were similarly excellent with a decent kick. For mains I had the Balti Chicken Bhuna £6-50, served up in a rich tomato based sauce but still with that hint of dryness expected of a Bhuna. The accompanying Garlic Naan £2-50, was slightly dry but was offset by a minefield of garlic cloves. I was too full for a dessert which was a pity as Imrans now have their own in house Sweet Centre. Plastic payment OK. 12-12.

POPULAR BALTI BYO 139 Ladypool Rd, Sparkbrook, B12, 8LH 0121 440 0014

ANDY'S TOP. A compact, well used haunt for late night taxi drivers – in itself usually a good recommendation. With complimentary pops, I rashly asked for their 'under the counter' crushed green chilli dip which left my mouth feeling like it had been attacked by a flam thrower, tasty though it might have been. I sat opposite a wall mounted TV which was featuring somebody with a bad case of eczema on 'Embarassing Bodies' just as I was flaking up my poppadom. The waiter sensing my slight discomfort – now that's what I call customer care! Our starter was a shared Mixed Grill £6-80, which had tikkas and kebabs served up sizzling but the star of this culinary show was some excellently flavoured, tender tandoori chicken. Mains were Balti Chicken and Mushroom £6-80, substantial portions nestling in a delicious sauce. A fresh, doughy Cheese and Tomato Naan £2-50, was a perfect foil for the mains. The restaurant also serves up Pakistani specialities such as Paya, Batera Quail, and a scrumptious Chicken Mince and Karela, a starter at £6-80. Popular by name and by its level of custom. Plastic payment OK. 5% surcharge on credit cards. 5 to late.

SHABAB BYO   163 Ladypool Road, Sparkbrook, B12 8LQ   0121 440 2893

ANDY'S TOP. Zaf's recently refurbished Shabab has still kept its baltihouse 'street cred' with its glass topped tables and menus underneath to read at leisure. It is however nice, bright and airy with its unusual henna patterned wallpaper and panoramic window views of the Ladypool Rd. Free poppadoms and some great dips including a spicy red variety accompanied a couple of fabulously tender and spicy Sheeshk Kebabs £2-40, . My companion's Chicken Pakora £2-80, was encased in a tasty feather light batter. Both the Balti Chicken Rogan Josh £6-50, for me and the Balti Chicken Korma £6-50, for her were a savoury and spicy delight with that perfect consistency which is neither too liquidy or too dry which ensures the meat or veg is embued with all the flavours. Shabab may have had a makeover but the food remains at its original best with their vintage balti bowls now polished by a thousand naans being dipped by balti buffs. On the topic of naans, the moist and rich Cheese variety £1-75, was a perfect consistency neither with the flakiness of an athlete's foot or the dry stodginess of a piece of stale Madeira cake. Shabab's legendary late hours means balti aficionados can get their fix at almost anytime. Plastic payment OK. . Unbelievable opening Hours; Sun-Th: 5-3am; Fri-Sat 5pm-5am.

SHEREEN KADAH BYO   543 Moseley Road , Balsall Heath, B12 9BU   0121 440 4641

The Shereen Kadah has been around in the Balti Triangle for sometime outlasting its long term rival opposite, Nirala, which has now unfortunately metamorphosed into a 'Dixie Chix' fast food emporium. However, Shereen Kadah has kept true to its balti roots with its glass topped tables and a display of long skewers in its display cabinet which wouldn't have disgraced the Zulu armoury before Rorke's Drift. Known for its charcoaled starters, to order anything else would have been culinary treason. My bargain priced Sheekh Kebab £1-40, didn't disappoint having a strong charcoaled taste without being overdone. My companion had Chicken Tikka £3-50, which was tender and distinctively flavoured. Main courses were Balti Chicken Korma and Mushroom £6-50, chosen on the basis that the restaurant has a reputation for being a bit hot on the balti front…luckily it was pronounced as being thoroughly enjoyable, thick and creamy. My Balti Chicken Masala £6-50, was quite superb. . rich , well spiced and tomatoey with the latter almost sundried in its delightful richness. Both dishes were served up in silver bowls with the accompaniment of a wonderfully fluffy Mushroom Naan £2, . No After Eights, no frills but plenty of thrills on the culinary front. No plastic payments.

KABABISH   LICENSED NO BYO   29 Woodbridge Rd, Moseley, B13, 8EH   0121 449 7556   www. kababish. co. uk

Khawaja Shaffique's first restaurant was the 'Lazy K' in Small Heath, where in 1972 a three-course curry diner cost 50 pence. He set up his friendly, long-established Kababish in 1983. It is now run by sons Saj and Sydd and cousin Farooq, assisted by family member chefs. True to form you are welcome to dip your naans into your bowls of curry rather than use cutlery. It is popular with local Pakistanis and the Sahffiques want you to know celebrity guests have included Michael Atherton, Ian Botham Muhammad Ali, Imran Khan, and locals UB40. Poppadoms 70p, were light and crispy served with a trio of dips including a dusky coloured one with a hidden but not unpleasant kick. My starter of Buckrawta Parcels £4, contained goat's cheese, spinach, minced lamb and herbs parcelled up in filo pastry. Even if filo can be a bit 'British party buffet', they were absolutely delicious. My main course was Lamb Pinee £9-50, described as succulent pieces of lamb shank cooked in aromatic spices with fresh coriander, mint, chillies, herbs and masoor lentils. It was as tasty as it sounds and the accompanying Peshwari Naan £3-10, was just the right consistency if a little dry. The bill came with organic mints and hot flannels and whilst more expensive than a standard Balti Triangle meal, it was by no means extortionate. Service throughout was fast, efficient but friendly. Plastic payment OK. Mon-Th: 5. 30-11. 30 Fri-Sat-12; Sun-11. *Branch: Kababish, 266 Jockey Road, Boldmere Sutton Coldfield B73 5XP 0121 355 5062*

YOU SAY OK BALTI TRIANGLE

MUSHTAQ SWEET CENTRE Food & Agribusiness [sic] 451-453 Stratford Road, Sparkhill, B11 4LD   Good samosas.
PIQUANT 18 St. Marys Row, B13 8JG ~ 0121 249 1216 very good venue. Full on Bangladeshi curryhouse formula menu.
ROTI & CURRY JUNCTION 80-82 Stoney Lane, Sparkbrook, B12 8AF ~ 0121 771 2777. probably more a take out place 2 formica tables at the last count.
SWEET CHILLIES 836 Yardley Wood Road, Yardley Wood, B13 0JE ~ 0871 2070926 www.sweetchillies. co. uk Full on Bangladeshi curryhouse formula menu in their case wrapped up in fancy Indian names with one section described as 'The Usual Suspects'.

Birmingham B13

DEOLALI BAR RESTAURANT
23a St Mary's Row, Moseley, B13 8HW
0121 442 2222   www.godeolali.co.uk

Better known for its Pakistani Balti houses, Moseley, is now unexpectedly home to a new Indian fine-dining experience, Deolali. Even its name is unexpected. Deolali is a town 100m north-east of Bombay. In the 19th century the British Raj army had a transit camp there. Soldiers who had finished their tours of duty were posted there to await their return home on troop ships. But these only left India between November and March, and at worst a soldier might have to wait for eight months in the raging Indian summer, with literally nothing to do. Sheer boredom caused some to behave eccentrically, and the word 'doolally' entered the dictionary meaning "mad" or "eccentric". Co-owner Tariq Zaman smiles if you know this (so tell him!), but he is serious about his restaurant and has dug deep into his bank of ideas and his pocket to ensure the restaurant stands out from the crowd. Taking his extensive restaurateur knowledge, Tariq knew he wanted a design concept completely unconventional that wouldn't necessarily depict a standard Indian restaurant. The building was an old coach-house for the next door pub that dates back to the 18th century, where he fashioned a minimalist interior, which he describes as a barn conversion because of its high ceilings and solid oak beams. Split across three levels, the first floor leads into the entrance and stepping up to the second level is the 50-cover bar and a private dining area that seats around 15, with views of the 130-seat restaurant. The dark brown leather seats and oak flooring and tables are each placed to complement the beams, which are the highlight of the interiors. Head Chef Salim Sukha picked up his trade at Goa's fabulous seven-star Leela Beech Hotel and Delhi's luxury Hyatt, before joining Tariq at Spice Avenue and The Spice Exchange (Guide entrants) which Tariq owned. Sukha takes a modern approach to traditional cooking. The menu, which is brimming with fresh dishes includes such specials as Goan Green Masala Salmon and Deolali Monkfish as well as sweet desserts like Lemon Mousse served with Mango Sorbet and Gulab Jamun with Honey and Ginger Ice Cream.

K2
107 Alcester Rd, Moseley, B13 8DD   0121 449 3883

N Pasha and M Niam's 58-seater is named after the highest mountain in Pakistan, shown on the biggest map of Baltistan (to prove it exists to the doubters) on one wall. Peppered Chicken £3.50, is Chino-Tibetan (a Baltistan influence) with its sweet and sour chicken prepared with a mixture of black and green pepper, ginger, soya sauce, sugar and lime. 6-11.

SPICE AVENUE
562-4 Moseley Road, B13   0121 442 4936

In a corner-site on the fringe of the Zone, it's a smart licensed restaurant with rear car park *'which is handy. Attentive and friendly staff. Food OK. A bit overpriced [compared with the rest of the Zone].'* RE. *'The Balti Ginger Chicken is a straightforward but excellent combination. However, the lamb Shahan is an excellent exotic alternative with tender lamb cutlets stuffed with garlic mushrooms. Accompanying onion kulcha will make your eyes and mouth water.'* AM. 'Menu Conventional Quality Outstanding Quantity Adequate Decor Pale walls Service Superb Comfort Acceptable Comments Starters Popadums x 12 Prawn Puree £3.95 Tandoori Mixed Grill c£5 x 5 Main Course Balti Mix c£8 x 3 Balti Chicken Tikka £6.25 x 2 Hara Gosht c£7 Naans Keema Naan £2.25 x 2 Peshwari Naan £1.95 x 2 Garlic Naan £1.75 Plain Naan £1.25 Mark 9/10 Extremely impressive meal all round.' G&MP.

SWEET CHILLIES CUISINE   A-LIST

836 Yardleywood Rd, B13 0EJ
0121 443 2737   www.sweetchillies.co.uk

Iqbal Hussain's impressive building, houses this stylish restaurant. A very grand porch welcomes you, complete with colonial palms and a red carpet! Inside, a modern, contemporary feel, including wooden floors, deep brown leather high back chairs or booths (they look really comfortable!), white linen and spot ceiling lights - lovely. Menu Snapshot: Bombay Duck 80p, dry roasted fish; Sweet Chillies Spice Wings £2.90, marinated in sweet, hot and tangy paste, stuffed with ground herbs, barbecued in the clay oven, served with fried onions, peppers, tomatoes and coriander leaves; Baigan Maza Dhai £3.50, aubergine deep-fried and filled with spiced minced chicken and vegetables, garnished with home-made, low fat Raitha; Shobzi Celery £2.80, chopped and fried celery in butter sauce, cook with citrus flavour vegetable and topped with poppy seeds; Pigeon Musaka c£7, layers of pigeon breast, stuffed with spicy mushrooms, served with a spicy game sauce and Paratha; Lamb Shank Tara c£8, lamb shank braised, medium hot, served with spicy mint and curry sauce, served with herb noodles; Deewana Naga Gosht / Murgh c£7, marinated lamb or chicken, cooked with Sylheti chilli and onions, in a very hot and spicy sauce; Shahi Chocolate Korma c£7, chicken, lamb or vegetable braised in a chocolate gravy, enriched with cream, almonds and coconut, Neramisha £2.75,red kidney beans, Bengali runner beans, medium gravy with onion, capsicum and coriander; Bengal Spice Naan £2.40 – garlic and coriander filled unleavened bread with cheese topping, chillies can be added. 5.30-11.30; to 12 Sat; to 11 Sun. *Branches: Sylhet Spice, Kings Heath, Birmingham; Shahi Palace, Foleshill, Coventry; Bengal Delight, Holbrooks, Coventry.*

Birmingham North
B6, B7, B19 to B24, B32, B42 to B44

MILAN SWEET CENTRE
238 Soho Rd, Handsworth, B21   0121 551 5239

A branch of the Milan restaurant in 93 Newhall Street, Birmingham B3 (see entry). This is a takeaway venue for Indian sweets, and savoury snacks. The selection is huge and satisfying, at prices too cheap to ignore. Sister t/a branch at 191 Stoney Lane, Sparkbrook, B11.

NOORAANI BALTI HOUSE
248 Slade Rd, Erdington, B23   0121 373 2527

Proprietor, M Jahangir, opened his forty seater Balti House in 1994 and Chicken Balti at £4.50, a plate full (or should that be a Balti full,) just rushes out of the door. The modern kitchen is open, so diners can see the chefs cooking and all meat and poultry is Halal. Menu Snapshot: Chicken or Lamb Balti with a choice of mushroom, spinach, okra, channa, aubergine, aloo, vegetable, kidney beans or egg - all £4.50; Prawn Balti with a choice from the above - all £4.95; King Prawn Balti with a choice from the above - all £5.50. Traditionally eaten with Naan 85p, or Family Naan £2.75, that's big enough to share! However, there is a large selection of stuffed Naans, choose from keema (minced meat), garlic, vegetable, cheese, peshwari (fruit and nuts), coriander - all £1.60. Delivery: 3 miles, £7 minimum, telephone your order through and pay by credit card. You might get a discount if you show Mr Ahmed this Guide. Price Check: Popadom 40p, CTM £5.75, Pullao Rice £1.75. Students Discount: 10% on all takeaway. 5 - 2.

SAMRAT TANDOORI
710 Chester Road, B23   0121 384 5900

Established 1983 by Iqbal Raza Chowdhury. Seats forty eight diners. Licensed: stocks Cobra and Kingfisher, £3 a bottle, house wine £7.95 a bottle. Delivery: 6 miles, £10 minimum. You might get a discount if you show Mr Raza this Guide. Price Check: Popadom 50p, CTM £6.15, Pullao Rice £1.75. Hours: 5 - 1, Saturday to 2.

Birmingham East
B8, B9, B25, B26, B33, B34, B36, B37, B40 (NEC)

YEW TREE COTTAGE
43 Stoney La, Yardley, B25 8RE
0121 786 1814   yewtree-cottage.co.uk

Established 1979 by Jamal Chowdhury. The unassuming exterior hides a huge restaurant, seating 180 diners on two floors. Inside it is nicely decorated with wooden flooring, large green plants, white linen and comfortable upholstered chairs - all very bright and tidy. Restaurant Theme Nights: Sun: Buffet, c£7 children/c£5 children – booking advisable; Monday: Gourmet Dinner £9.95 adult/c£7 children – four courses from the a la carte

menu; Tuesday: Balti Night - £6.50, choice of any Balti with a Naan; Wednesday: Chef's Choice c£8, tasty treats the from the head chef, starter and main course; Thursday: Ladies Night c£9: Bhajia, choice from a la carte menu and a glass of wine - sounds great! Menu Snapshot: Could be the biggest menu I have ever seen, there are an incredible 223 dishes to choose from - Tikka Sandwich £3.50, Tikka in a Naan with salad dressing; North Bengali Fruity Murch c£7.50, creamy, mild, fruity dish with barbecued chicken pieces; Masala Kulcha £1.50, leavened bread stuffed with capsicum, onions, spices then cooked in the charcoal oven. Del: 3m, £15 min. T/a: 10% disc, £10 min. You might get a disc if you show Mr Chowdhury this Guide. Sun-Th: 5.30-12.30; Fri-Sat: 5-1.30.

YOU SAY OK
B9 SMALL HEATH, IIB NE GHANI 264 Green La, B9 ~ 0121 772 8138. Est 1981, taken over by Nazrul Hussain in 1998 with Bilal Miah manager. Chef Abdul Ahad' in open kitchen. BYO. T/a: 10% disc. Del: £8 min 3m. Hours: 4.30-12; 1 Sat..
B26: SHELDON, SHABAR TANDOORI 4 Arden Oak Rd, B26 ~ 0121 742 0636.
B26: TITASH INTERNATIONAL 2278 Coventry Rd, B26 ~ 0121 722 2080. Decent alternative to the ghastly offerings at the NEC and hotels of varying pretensions.
B26: VARSHA 2250 Coventry Rd, B26 ~ 0121 743 6572. *'Achari and Handi dishes have not been bettered elsewhere.'* JP.

Birmingham South
B14, B27 to B31, B45, B47, B48, B60

B14, KING'S HEATH: KINGS BALTI 13 York Rd, B14 ~ 0121 443 1114. 62-seater est 1994 by Salim Miah. Licensed to sell beer, not spirits or wine, so BYO (no corkage charge). T/a: 10% disc, £5.50 min. 5-11.
B14, KINGS HEATH: MILLENNIUM BALTI 796 Alcester Rd S, B14 ~ 0121 430 6155. Seats 44. Unlicensed, BYO OK. T/a: 10% disc. Del: 3m £8 min. Hours: 5.30-12.30.
B27 ACOCKS GREEN: MOGHUL 1184 Warwick Road, B27 ~ 0121 707 6777.
B28, HALL GREEN: MIZAN 1347 Stratford Road, B28 ~ 0121 777 3185. KA Rahman's 66-seater. T/a: 10% disc. Min charge: £5. Special: Saag Kamal Kakri, spinach and lotus roots. Hours: 12-2 / 5.30-12; 12.30 Fri & Sat.
B29, SELLY OAK: DILSHAD INTERNATIONAL 618 Bristol Rd, B29 ~ 0121 472 5016. Est 1978. Seats 80. Specials: Achar Gosht, Champa Koli Bahar, Fish Bengal. T/a: 10% disc. Hours: 5.30-late.
B30, COTTERIDGE: RAJPOOT 1831 Pershore Rd, B30 ~ 0121 458 5604. Watir Ali's 94-seater is *'A glitzy, friendly little place. All the family use it regularly.'* JAD. Hours: 6-2.   **B30, STIRCHLEY: YASSER TANDOORI** 1268 Pershore Rd, B30 0121 433 3023. 80-seater est 1987 by A Hussain and Sarwar Khan. Unlicensed BYO OK. Balti Chef's Special Tropical £7, prawn, chicken, lamb and mushroom. Parking for 12 cars. 4.30-12; 1 Sat.

Birmingham West
B15 to B18 & B32. *See also B1 for Broad St part of B15*

AKBARS   AUTHENTIC PAKISTANI CUISINE
184 Hagley Road, Birmingham, B16 9NY
0121 452 1862   www.akbars.co.uk

300 seater + 200 func rm   Mon-Sat: 5-Mdnt / Sun: - 11:30. Branches: Ninth branch (2009) of ten of the rapidly expanding chain. See Bradford, W.Yorks for menu & details. Mon-Sat: 5-Mdnt / Sun: -11:30.

CHENNAIDOSA SOUTH IND/SRI LANKAN
169 Hagley Road, Edgbaston, Birmingham, B16 8UQ
0121 454 1111   www.chennaidosa.co.uk

South Indian. Meat & Veg. The large international chain of south Indian restaurants has its 10th (of 14) UK branch and its only one in Brum. See page 100 (E12) for menu details. Nsz licence. 10:30am-11pm.

YOU SAY OK - BIRMINGHAM WEST

B16, EDGBASTON: J JAYS 2 Edgbaston Shopping Centre, Five Ways, B16 ~ 0121 455 6871
B32, QUINTON: SOHO INDIA 417 Hagley Rd West, B32 ~ 0121 421 3242

Smethwick B66

HAWELI   TOP 100
509 Hagley Rd, Bearwood B66 4AX   0121 434 5717

A small shop unitin a terraced row. It's been around a long time, and it's always busy from early on till late. Some websites carry unsubstantiated comments telling of rudeness and unsmiling waiters. Your reports to us say none of this, so read this Guide not rubbishy websties. What we do hear of is a buzzing atrmosphere with groups and couples and singles and laughter and fun. Asians use it. More than that: every one loves the food. No surprises, really, but oodles (large portions) of tandoori / tikka / kebab and deep-fried starters, and all your favourite curries, including a big vegetable selection. All the items you expect of a competent curryhouse are there and above all they are at a good price. It lacks flock wall paper, but is this the nation's best curryhouse? Booking essential. We're making it a TOP 100. Reports please. Sun-Th: 6-11.45 (Fri-Sat: 12.45).

Coventry

THE FARMHOUSE
215 Beechwood Avenue · Coventry, CV5 6HB
024 7671 4332   thefarmhouserestaurant.co.uk

It's a former pub in the industrial Canley area, west of Coventry rather than a farm. So a car park in place of fields and a typical pub beer garden/kids' play area. They serve English and Indian food all day. In fact it's a full on balti menu with some 28 staters averaging £4 Most are as expected though Chicken Tikka Yorkshire Pudding £5 is indeed *'something different, a starter unique to the farmhouse, home baked yorkshire pudding stuffed with chicken tikka topped with grilled mozzarella.'* There are upwards of 80 different balti curries. Mon Buffet from 5pm, £8.95pp. Mon-Th: 2 for £10,12-5. Takeaways All Day 15% off; Deliveries from 5 inc a free bottle of wine for orders over £20. 12-12. *Branch: The Farmhouse, 51 Cordy Lane, Brinsley, Nottingham, NG16 5BY* .

MONSOON
20 Far Gosford St, Coventry, CV1 5DT
024 7622 9651

'We visited Monsoon as two work colleagues because it was listed in the Good Curry Guide 2008 as Top 100. Monsoon is clean inside though is very basic in its furnishings and decoration. We were the only diners for the time we were there. We had tandoori chicken starter which was fine. For main course we shared chicken jalfrezi and chicken tikka dhansak. Both were served in the wok style pot they were cooked in and were quite tasty. The sauces were well liquidised in a more of a balti style. Tarka dhal and channa massaia were really good. We had garlic nan and a paratha aloo which were both really good, especially the paratha. Service was very good. Bill was £40 including drinks. Very enjoyable but not top 100 anymore.' EB. 6-12 (to 1am Fri-Sat).

THE OCEAN
46 Jubilee Cres, Radford, CV6 6AS   024 7659 9455

'Old style Indian, kitsch flock wallpaper, service outrageously over the top. We were greeted with "you're late!" as we arrived. Nothing is too much trouble and we exchanged witty badinage throughout the meal. Quantity copious. Four outstanding starters. Main courses almost as good with the chicken dansak which was thickened with lentils to give a sweet/ sour contrast. Lamb Bhazaa, Chicken BegumBahr well marinated, tingly and spicy without being overspiced and Chicken Jaipuri all superb. £60 for 4.' Marks visit 1: 88.3%. Visit 2: 89.4%. *Rated no 2 in Coventry.'* G&MP.

ROJONI
477 Beake Av, Coventry, CV6 2HT   024 7633 2211

'Menu Fairly wide with some unusual special dishes. Quality Very Good. Quantity: Copious. Décor: Strikingly colourful. Vibrant. Service: Exemplary. Comfort: Excellent. Starters: Popadums x6 Dhal Soup £2.50 Very comforting with slices of garlic and lemon. Tandoori Chicken £2.85 Absolutely gorgeous- marinade spot on. Chicken Chat c£3 Very spicy. King Prawn Puri Not very special. Main Course Tandoori Mixed Grill £8.50 Very good. Lamb Mirch Masala c£6 Sauce excellent but lamb chewy c£6. Chicken Jhallosi c£7 x2 Very well done ˆ chicken very spicy. Accompaniments Peshwari Nan £1.85 Pilau Rice £1.85 x 2. Side Dishes: Cauliflower Bhajee c£3 Mattar Paneer c£3 Total cost £80.20 + £8 tip. Mark 87%. We were very impressed!' G&MP. So are we and the media are always asking us for the wherabouts of a red-flock venue. It should be Grade 1 listed!

TURMERIC GOLD   TOP 100
166 Medieval Spon St. CV1 3BB
024 7622 6603   www.turmericgold.co.uk

Opposite Bonds at Skydome. Jay Alam's restaurant seats ninety diners in six rooms, on two floors (the waiters must be fit!). The exterior of the building has been painted royal blue, and is alive with a gorgeous forest of flowers. For real twosome pampering you can dine in one of the luscious booths. Menu Snapshot: Crab Spring Rolls £5.25, beansprouts, carrot, celery, crab meat, wrapped in a roll, served with spicy sauce; Goa Tiger Prawns £6.50, grilled tiger prawns, spinach, with coconut and cream sauce; Rawlpindi Curry Puff £5.25, highly spiced lamb, dried red chillies, sweet vinegar sauce, puffed bread, served with chat masala dressed, crispy salad; Emperors Chicken Chilli £12, stir-fried with fresh green chillies, carrots, mushroom, capsicum, pineapple, and coriander leaf, served sizzling. *'Menu Extremely extensive Quality: Good Quantity: Adequate Decor: Garish with pictures of bare breasted ladies on the wall Service: Faultless Comfort: Fine. Bill; £100 (including £15 drinks and £6.70 tip) – the most we have ever spent as a group of 4. Mark 8/10 Excellent meal'* G&MP. 12-2 & 5.30-11.15; 12.15 Sat.

G&MP'S SAY OK: COVENTRY

Coventry residents Graham & Melissa Payne's curry roundup:

AKBAR'S 7 The Butts, Earlsdon, Coventry 024 7622 8899. *'Seats very difficult to get into – the sunken areas didn't help. Pale painted walls with lights everywhere. menu fairly wide if rather unimaginative. Quality good. quantity generous. Service outstanding. We were all extremely impressed with every aspect of the meal. £74.60 for 4.'* Mark: 87.1%. Rated no3 in Coventry.' G&MP.
ALLY'S BALTI HOUSE 48 Earlsdon Street Earlsdon Coventry CV5 6EL ~ 024 7671 5709. *'Quality very good. Quantity moderate. Décor rustic and old-fashioned. Service reasonable and prompt. Comfort draughty. Reasonably priced, unprepossessing and unfashionable but nonetheless good value. Starters were uniformly excellent with the stuffed chicken pepper and chicken pakora best. Of the main courses ally's special balti was the highlight. some of the food was too spicy but generally this was a good effort. £50 for 4.'* Mark: 81%. G&MP.
BENGAL DELIGHT 168 Holbrook Lane, Holbrooks, CV6 4BY ~ 024 7668 6789 Rated no 5in Coventry. G&MP.
BLUE MANGO 76 Albany Road Earlsdon, CV5 3JU. 44-seater. *'The roop chanda and aloo chat both outstanding.'* G&MP.
DESI DISH Far Gosford Street. CV1 5DZ *'Menu Extensive and unusual Quality, quantity, decor ,service and comfort OK. Pops 80p x 3, Peshwari Naan £2.50, Metha Maaz £9.95, Chicken Korma £8.50, Aloo Murgh Masala £8.50, Side Dish Aloo Chole £4.50, Pullau Rice £1.95, Peshwari Naan £2.50, Onion Kulcha Naan £2.50. Lager x2, Coke x 2, Jug of Lassi £5.'* Mark. 80%. G&MP.
THE MINT 13, The Butts, Earlsdon 024 7622 6111. *Menu: very extensive with many unusual choices Quality: Excellent Quantity: Copious and how! Decor: pale pastel painted walls in one long room in ultra modern style Service: Faultless Comfort: Deep leather chairs, beautiful wooden tables widely spaced with no infringement on others Starters: Paneer Tikka, beautifully marinated; Reshmi Kebab , good; Tetul Mix, extremely generous portions, beautifully presented; Chicken Tikka Chat v g and generous. Main course: Chicken Pasala, wonderful marinade in beautifully creamy sauce c£7; Lamb Afghan Chana, lamb slightly chewy but otherwise excellent c£7; Chicken Gurkha Masala very nicely spiced with a kick to it c£8. We have visited several times since it opened in 2006. byo and a very welcoming ambience to boot. All in all a most welcome addition to the ranks'.* G&MP.
NASHAA 154 Longford Road CV6 6DR 024 7636 6344. *'Quality no problem, quantity generous, décor pale yellow walls, service exemplary, comfort pleasant welcoming atmosphere. Starters were better than main courses. tandoori chicken was beautifully tasty and well marinated. Of the main courses the chicken dansak was much too spicy, the tandoori mix grill was fairly average apart from the chicken tikka which was excellent. the chicken korai and chicken rezalla were both exceptionally fine. £76.20 for 4.'* Mark 83.2%. G&MP.
SHAPLA TANDOORI 171 Daventry Rd Cheylesmore 024 7650 6306. *'40-seater with creamy regency with chandeliers and fans décor. Extremely conventional menu, quality excellent, quantity copious, service very good. Generally vg quality meal with few weaknesses. £71.20 for 4'* Mark 80.6%. G&MP.
SONARGAON 153 Daventry Rd., CV3 5HD 024 7650 1120. *'Good'.* G&MP.
VARSITY SPICE 118 Gosford Street, CV1 5DL 024 7652 0799. *'Very dark décor with extensive use of mirrors, service fairly slow but everything was freshly cooked. Menu quite extensive, quality very good,quantity copious. comfort partitioned tables with alcoves which makes it much more comfortable. a couple of minor weaknesses but* overall an excellent effort for this comparative newcomer. good use of marination but one meal was a trifle overspiced, the mutton in the lamb rezella was gorgeous.' Bill £73.05 for 4. Mark 82.5%. G&MP.

Meriden

TURMERIC GOLD at MERIDEN   TOP 100
155 Main Road, CV7 7NH   01676 521055

Located in a Georgian building in the affluent village of Meriden, said to be the centre of England, Jal Alam's new venture combines traditional cooking with a modern, healthy twist, using, he says *'minimum oil at the same time as making sure food colouring and salt are minute'*. Rooms for private parties and gatherings. 12-2 & 5:30-11; 10:30pm Sun. Menu details Turmeric, Coventry.

YOU SAY OK
You might get a discount if you show them this Guide.
DUDLEY: BALTI 4 U TAKEAWAY 63 Halesowen Rd, Netherton, Dudley 01384 240230. Afruz Ali opened it in 2000, Azom Ali is head chef. Del: 4m. Hours: 5-12.30; 1.20 Sat.
HALESOWEN, HASBURY, B63: AMEENA 192 Hagley Rd, B63 0121 550 4317. Hiron Miah's 78-seater (est. 1974) *'Waiters cheerful and attentive.'* MS. Del: 3m £10 min. 5.30-12; 1 Fri & Sat.
HALESOWEN, B63: RED PEPPERS 8 Hagley St, B63 ~ 0121 550 8588. Owner chef, Mr Islam iopened in 1989. Del: 3.5, £10 min. T/a: 10% disc. Hours: 5.30-12; 1 Fri & Sat.
KNOWLE, B93: BILASH 1608 High St, B93 ~ 01564 773030. Mashud Uddin and Nowab Ali's venue seats 64. *'Very good quality.'* J&MCL. T/a: 10% off. 5.30-12am. Branches: Bilash, 90 Priory Rd, Kenilworth. Bejoy T/a, 763 Old Lode Lane, Solihull.
KNOWLE, B93: KNOWLE INDIAN BRASSERIE 1690 High St, B93 ~ 01564 776453. 45-seater est 1995 by Hossain Miah. *'Cheap, quality excellent, quantity huge.'* G&MP. 5.30-11.30; 10.30 Sun.
LYE: HARRYS OF LYE 179 High St, Lye, Stourbridge DY9 8LH *'Food isuperb, but very slow service.'* AHJ: Andy Herrin: yellowfingers.co.uk

Oldbury

KAVI   HOTEL
6 Wolverhampton Rd, B68 0LH   0121 429 3757

Rishi Sharma operates branches of his Kavi Indian Fusion Restaurant at Ramada Hotels. Starters include Punjabi Jhinga, (King prawns in a Greek yoghurt with aromatic spices, grilled over charcoal), Shakarkandi Chaat (Sweet potato chaat and pomegranate seeds) and Kalmi Kebab (on bone chicken thigh in cream cheese and cashew nuts). Favourite dishes include the Amiritsari Talli Macchi, (pan seared fillets of sea bass on a bed of sautéed red cabbage with a korma sauce) and Lamb Shank (leg of baby lamb simmered in Kashmiri masala sauce served with steamed basmati rice), and for dessert; Gulab Jamun, (an irresistible warm treacle pudding with vanilla ice cream). 6-10.30. *See branch: Ramada Newcastle, Staffs for details, also at Ramada Warwick.*

SAFFRON
909 Wolverhampton Rd. B69 4RR   0121 552 1752

This Saffron branch is *'just off the M6, on the way back north from the NEC, and as everyone who has visited the NEC, knows, that the food is awful and expensive, so, no excuse,* off to the Saffron for a lovely meal! It's a modern, well lit and nicely decorated establishment. The service was prompt and unfussy, although I gave up trying to get a plain Madras sauce with Biriani.'[It's not a curryhouse Dave]. 'Pops, crisp and light, Chutneys, onion, mango and yoghurt, very acceptable. Murgh Biriani, seemed like a small portion when it arrived with the rice plated and moulded, but when attacked it was surprisingly a lot of food.' It was garnished with fried onions and coriander (no omelette), the rice had a good flavour, in fact was very spicy, chicken well cooked and tender. Vegetable curry sauce containing peas, green beans, tinned carrots and a hint of cauliflower was quite mild but very tasty. Overall, I would love to try this restaurant in the evening as I feel it has great potential.' I object to a 10% service charge and then having the credit card bill left open.' DB. T/a 10% disc. 12-2.30 & 5.30-11.30. See Birmingham B3 Saffron for details.

Solihull
B90 to B93

JIMMY SPICE'S
64 Station Rd,- Solihull, B91   0121 709 2111

The group's second unit opened here in 2006 in the former Wates Wine Lodge as a 300-seater with a 100-seat bar called NYC. Serves Indian, Chinese, Thai & Italian cooking in a live theatre-style cooking display. 12-2.30 & 5-11. *More comment: Broad St, Birmingham, B1.*

THE LLOYDS   BYO
7 Station Rd, Knowle, Solihull, B93 0HL   01546 477577   www.thelloydsindian.com

Nanu Miah opened his air-conditioned 140 seat restaurant in 2003. Menu Snapshot: Boal Biran (cat fish) £4.95, fried with a touch of butter, herbs and garlic; Tandoori Mixed Grill from 5.95, served with mint sauce and fresh salad. Mains: Jafrani Kurma £8 a very mild Mughul chicken dish with saffron, almond, butter and cream; Chand Rooposhi £11 pomfret fish Bengali style; Chicken Lazam £8, with a variety of herbs & spices, garnished with sautéed tomatoes, green peppers, fresh coriander, garlic & chilli; Chicken Jale Jale with green peppers, onions & green chillies; Boal Bahar Bengali catfish cooked in a slightly hot potato sauce, garnished with coriander. Licensed but BYO allowed. House Wine £9.75. Credit cards not accepted. T/a: 10% disc. Del: £2 min. min Ch: £10. You might get a discount if you show them this Guide. 5.30-11.

RAJNAGAR   TOP 100
256 Lyndon Road, Olton, Solihull, B92 7QW
0121 742 8140   www.rajnagar.com

Dr Moula Miah established it in 1987. He has taken the Bangladeshi curryhouse formula to its heights at his three venues (see branches). It is a useful 10 minutes from the NEC and airport. Modern décor, clean lines, great unfussy food and care from the Doc himself and his staff. *'It really is exceptionally good.'* MM. *'Interior decor, pale pink and cream walls, cream carpet – optimistic re spillages!, stylish tables and chairs with monogrammed linen exudes quality and class. Attentive service, swiftly delivered Popadums, chunky pickles and cold lager. I chose Meat Samosas (spring roll style), Chicken Tikka Dupiaza, Pullao Rice and Nan – ALL SUPERB!'* TE. 5 till late. *Branches: Shades of Raj, 52, Station Road, Solihull, Barajee, Broad Street, B'hm.*

Sutton Coldfield

DELHI 6 RESTAURANT   TOP 100
12a Burnett Rd, Little Aston, Sutton Coldfield, B74 3EJ
0121 353 0682   www.delhi6restaurant.co.uk

Delhi 6 was a Bollywood blockbuster from 2009 starring all the big names of that industry. It has spawned a few restaurants of the same name including this one. M Rahman is chef director. *'We are a fine dining Indian Restaurant.'* he told this Guide. This smart newcomer is no curryhouse. Its menu is short and well constructed, and it is priced to attract well-healed, discerning clients. Starters include: Salmon Dil Tikka £6, fillet marinated with hung yoghurt, chaat masala, and ginger/garlic paste; served with mixed baby leaves and honey, mustard and yoghurt sauce; Scallops In Saffron Sauce £7, in a delicately spiced saffron sauce. *'They can so easily be overcooked, but not here ... they were just perfect and the sauce complemented it superbly'* HEG. Murgh Malai Kabab £5, isc breast of chicken marinated with garlic, ginger paste, cream and a blend of fine spices cooked in the tandoor served with baby leaves and sweet pepper sauce. Mains include: Saag Hiran £17, venison strip loin, marinated in ginger garlic and malt vinegar, pot roasted, served with sautéed spinach and masallam sauce; Kadhu Gosht £1, strip loin of beef with ginger, garlic, ground cumin, cooked in lucknowi marrow, cardamom and mace gravy, served with pumpkin masala; Chicken Chettinad £1 a south Indian speciality of chicken in a spicy sauce of coconut, fennel seeds and star anise; Delhi Ki Duck £1, pot-roasted on a slow fire and cooked with medium spiced gravy, served with sautéed fresh green vegetables. 6-10.30.

YOU SAY OK
You might get a discount if you show them this Guide.

STOURBRIDGE: CELLARS 187, Lower High St, DY8 1TT. *'Opened 2002 and remains as good as when it opened.'* JP.
KARMA 2F High Street, Wollaston, Stourbridge ~ 01384 375919. Former Neel Akash, Chef Mujibur Rahman's 60-seater. *'Good food but we felt didn't somehow feel welcomed.'* AH: Andy Herrin: www.yellowfingers.co.uk 5-12.
SUTTON COLDFIELD B73: ASIAN GRILL 91 Park Rd, Sutton C'fld, B73 ~ 0121 354 7491. Opened way back in 1968. Hours: 5.30-12; 1 Fri & Sat.
SUTTON COLDFIELD, B74: RICKSHAW TAKEAWAY 1 Stockland Ct, 121, Chester Rd, Streetly, ~ 0121 580 9400. Est by Mr Rahman in 1996. Del: 5m £10 min. Hours: 5-11; 10.30 Sun.

WALSALL: EAST END 9 Hawes Close, Walsall ~ 01922 614800. Muhibur Rahman is proud of his veteran 1967 curry house. Hours: 5.30-12.
WALSALL: GOLDEN MOMENTS 3 Ablewell St, Walsall ~ 01992 640363. 100- seater est 1993. *'Having eaten Indian food for 25 years this establishment must rate as the one of the best. Staff, service, surroundings and food are excellent.'* BD. T/a: 15% disc. Hours: 6-12. **WALSALL: KING BALTI** 89 Ablewell Street, Walsall ~ 01922 620376. Good BYO curryhouse owned by Dudu Miah. Hours: 6-1. **WARLEY B66: AL MOUCHAL** 622 Bearwood Rd, Warley, B66 ~ 0121 420 3987. Pakistani-style 100-seater BYO managed by Mumtaz. *'Clean, downmarket, cheap and cheerful.'* PAW. Hours: 6-12.

Wolverhampton

KAVI   HOTEL   www.ramadaparkhall.co.uk
Ramada Park Hall Hotel, Park Drive, Goldthorn Park, Wolverhampton, WV4 5AJ   01902 331121

Park Hall Hotel is set in five acres of grounds and is an 18th century listed building, once the ancestral home of the Dudley family, then a school. In 1947 Grigg and Brettell Brewery bought the building and Park Hall has continued to run as a hotel since that date. It has plenty of rooms and a huge car park, but its real gem is its restaurant. Enter the foyer and the bar and as you come to Kavi Indian note the waterfall and glass floored pool complete with large goldfish. The restaurant itself is on two levels., the upper running along the whole area, looks down onto the main room. A plasma screen playing Bollywood movies is set amongst Indian decor. Menu snapshot: Starters, include Tikkas and Tandoori items with such ingredients as Tiger Prawns, Rabbit, Salmon and Paneer. Prices average £6.50. Main courses include also offers a good mix, 17 dishes, which include Guinea Fowl, Lamb Shank and Duck; Amritsari Talli Machi, pan seared fillets of fresh seabass on a bed of sautéed red cabbage with mild pasanda sauce; Jhinga Kali Mirch both c£10, jumbo prawns in masala sauce. 6-10.

NEELAKASH
31 School St, Wolverhampton   01902 716975

Simply decorated in soft yellow and pale blue, with wooden chairs and white plastic tables, giving an informal cafe style at Mr Ahmed's pit-stop. Menu Snapshot: (with T/a prices) Tandoori Fish £3.95; Lamb Tikka £5.50, served with salad; Methi Gusta £5.50, beef, onion, coriander leaves; Karahi Chinghri and Murgh c£7, king prawns cooked with chicken, fresh coriander, green pepper, garam masala, cinnamon, served in sizzling iron karahi; Cucumber Raitha 90p; Kulcha Naan £1.50, stuffed with vegetables. Del: 3m, £10 min. T/a 10% disc. Price Check: Popadum 50p, CTM £6.25, Pullao Rice £1.95. Branch: Basmati, 230, Birmingham Road, B43.

CAFE RICKSHAW,
20 Chapel Ash, Wolverhampton, WV3 0TN
01902 425353   www.rickshawbalti.co.uk

Its pillar box red frontage makes this venue stand out in its terraced row opposite a leafy green suburban church garden. Inside the red theme continues with tablecloths and drapes. Mirror tiles decorate the wall and a funky chilli-shaped chandelier punctuates the ceiling. The name Cafe Rickshaw might imply it's a casual snack bar, but this is no curryhouse. Chef Owner Sam Hussain and Manager S.Ahmed have produced a lively, fun-packed friendly venue which is an asset to Wolverhampton. Starters include: Crab Cakes £3.75, claw meat tossed with ginger & fresh green chillies bonded with rice and bread crumbs, sautéed on a skillet; Kathi Rolls £3.75, a popular Mumbai snack of crushed spicy chicken breast, scented with finely chopped coriander, wrapped in fluffy bread; Chicken Chaat £3.75, a tangy massala of tamarind with a hint of sweet, served in a crispy rice flour basket. Mains include: Pudina with Bengali Green Bean Seeds £11, julienne strips of corn-fed chicken breast coated with corn flour, panch phoran spice mix, seared & oven-baked served with pomegranate, fresh mint in an aromatic pungent sauce; Asparagus Roulade £6.75, butterfly chicken breast stuffed with sautéed fresh baby asparagus, diced capsicum, sliced wild mushrooms & oven-baked, served with an am chur (mango powder) sauce. Sun-Th: 5.30-11.30; Fri-Sat to 1.30am.

WILTSHIRE

Area: South West England

Adjacent Counties: Berks, Dorset, Hants, Oxon.

YOU SAY OK
You may get a discount if you show them this Guide.

CALNE: SPICE OF BENGAL WOOD, Street, Calne, SN11 0BZ 01249 811833.
CHIPPENHAM: AKASH   SN15 1HA no web
DEVIZES: DEEDAR 6 Sidmouth Parade, Devizes, Wiltshire SN10 1LG 01380 720009 Standard menu. Av price Starters: £2.75. Main: Chicken/lamb curries £7. 12-2 & 5.30-11.30.
DEVIZES: JAL KHABAR   9-10 Maryport Street, Devizes, Wiltshire SN10 1AH 01380 723600

Calne

SPICE OF BENGAL
Wood Street, Calne, SN11 0BZ
01249 811833 www.spiceofbengal.com

'Slightly out of the town centre and doesn't look very impressive from the outside. Two or three tables were occupied, when we arrived. A fairly big restaurant, steady stream of diners and T/as while we ate. Impressive decor, not sumptuous or posh, just very smart and cosy. Prompt service, efficient, slightly friendly, which is the way I prefer it. Sheek Kebab c£3, came on a bed of shredded cabbage, a bit of tomato, cucumber and sweet Raitha, excellent, slightly hot, very moist. A slight delay before our mains were served (four couples came in), Chicken Tikka Patiala (served with mint chutney) and Chicken Korai c£7, perfection. Broad strips of tender chicken tikka, not the usual chunks, with creamy sauce and garnished with strips of boiled egg. Monica's Korai, cooked very well with chunks of onion and capsicum. We shared Mushroom Rice, chopped mushroom a bit chewy, but enjoyed and a Naan. Also, Aloo Gobi as a side dish, his was awful. A very satisfactory £25.30 with linen napkins and microwaved hand towels. All in all, very impressive.' T&MH. 12-2 & 5.30-11.30; to 12 Fri & Sat.

Chippenham

AKASH TANDOORI & BALTI
19 The Bridge, Chippenham, SN15 1HA 01249 653358

Established in 1979 by Nurul Huda Islam, an old friend of this Guide, having been in since our first edition and who might give you a disc if you show him this Guide. His cheerfully decorated restaurant, in lemon with royal blue, seats forty-six diners in three rooms. Lamb Shank c£13, lamb on the bone in a medium sauce is Chef Nazrul's most popular dish. Menu Snapshot: Duck Tikka or Tandoori Chops, each £5mand served with salad; Shahjani Chicken £7.50, with garlic and minced lamb; Chicken Choti Poti £7, with eggs and chick peas.12-2 & 6-12; 12.30 Fri & Sat.

Everleigh

GOA BALTI HOUSE
Everleigh Manor, Devizes Road, Everleigh, SN8 3EY
01264 850850 www.thegoabalti.co.uk

Founded by '*the brilliant and charming Hasan*' says RG on the site of a garage and filing station. Anything less Goan, I cannot imagine. The owner, Haan, the menu, pretty standard curryhouse) and the venue: it's in a whitewashed English cottage-like house in a prety whitewashed English village miles from anywhere. '*Delightful ambience, spacious, obviously well appointed, but somehow homely too, in this very quiet little Wiltshire village. The premises used to be a garage, so has inherited splendid, copious parking. Enterprising menu with old high street favourites are well represented which would satisfy the most hardened old 'blimp.*' Recommended starters Chicken Liver on Puri; Stuffed Mushroom; Prawn Patia; Chicken Stick Masala and the Mixed Kebab is a prize winner. Main courses we have sampled and found delightful are Chicken Shashlick; Karahi Gosht; Kashmiri Chicken; Cucupaka, Tandoori baked chicken with minced meat in metal pot; Goa Special, tandoori baked chicken laced with almonds, sultanas, cashew nut etc in a spicy yoghurt sauce and their fabulous Chilli Chicken Masala. There is also a fine list of vegetable Balti dishes and they have a very good hand in Parsee dishes, sweet, sour and pretty hot, very much my thing at the moment.' Chicken Dhansak is one of my favourites! ' RG. T/a 15% disc. 12-2.30 & 6-11.30.

Marlborough

THE PALM   TOP 100
A4 Bath Rd, Froxfield, Marlborough, SN8 3HT
01672 871818 www.thepalmindian.com

It's out in the sticks between Hungerford and Since then the A one story building has been expended to include 'the Atrium' one side of which is wall-to-celing plate glass windows. large carpark. There's even a staff accommodation block on site. '*Wiltshire boasts a grand, really classy Indian restaurant; and I mean grand. It is a very welcome addition to the curry landscape. It was initiated by Hasan, the founding force behind the brilliant Goa restaurant, Everleigh. and the equally renowned Gandhi, Winchester. Hasan has opened this really spacious and well appointed premises at a former run down steak house. The Palm looks splendid as you pull in and you'll notice the very large parking area at the rear. The entrance is wide and has splendid access and is easily negotiated by wheelchair. Seating is designed comfortably to accommodate groups of diners and there's room for about 140. The menu is is not curryhouse, rather it is real home-style Indian cooking. Menu Snapshot: Palms Machli (sea bass marinated in lemon and garlic, with tamarind and pineapple sauce). There's an enticing range of Kebabs that includes a particularly fine mince lamb Seekh Kanjara and all the usual Tandoori and Tandoori Masala dishes. Mains: listed under 'Authentic Indian Dishes' you will find several utter gems, including Karahj Gosht/Murgh (a Punjabi country dish of braised lamb/chicken with a sauce that includes ginger, onion, tomatoes, red chillies and fresh coriander) and Fish Ameritoshori (salmon fried in chunks with cashew nuts and tomato). The Dhansak is highly recommended and among Chef's Specials you will find a beautifully warm and creamy Kashmiri Chicken; magnificent Green Fish (Halibut) Curry; Garlic Chicken; Lamb/Chicken Jalfrezi and a superb stir fried Chicken Peshwari beautifully seasoned with cumin seeds. The Vegetable side dishes are delicate and well varied and you must try Aloo Baigan – potato and aubergine curry. Have no fears – for the traditionalists there is a fine selection chicken/lamb old friends – Dupiaza, Rogon Josh, Madras (and be warned, this is fiery) and Bhuna. But my advice is go up country and explore new territory. As for prices, well, considering the comforts of the place, the cheerful service and the exciting bill of fare a main dish for more or less £10 plus the odds and ends is very well* worth it indeed. The Palm has the lot.' RG. Hours: 12-2.30 & 5.30-11.30.*Branches: Ghandi 163 High St Winchester, Hants; Goa Balti House Everleigh Manor, Everleigh.2*

Salisbury

ANOKAA   TOP 100
60 Fisherton St, Salisbury, SP2 7RB
01722 424142   www.anokaa.com

Set in the heart of Salisbury, Anokaa is smart and popular. The decor is captures all the colours of India and the chic table settings enhance the venue's understated elegance. Owner Solman Farsi and the waiters in traditional outfits warmly welcome you in true Indian style; their service is efficient and subtle. Chefs Puban Kumar Bhaniya and Asad Rahman have produced a fine menu. 'Hand-picked' Crab Cake has been there from the start. We love those words 'hand-picked' ... what else; feet?' Still priced at £6, it's now spiced with roasted coconut, chilli and dill flavourings. Other starters include: Paneer Cakes £5.10, seasoned with a blend of spices and cilantro, then coated with roasted sesame seeds, apricot chutney and mango dressing; crispy fried Lentil Dumplings £5.10, (shole-madras-ka), with pepper and thyme flavouring dressed with tamarind. Mains include the old favourites but the specials are much more interesting, eg: Duck Jaalsha £15.10, crisped over charcoal then mixed with apricot, ginger and white wine, simmered in a fairly strong spiced sauce with cream of coconut, bayleaf and cardamon, served with lemon rice. Modu Murg £15.10, is strips of chicken breast cooked with honey and coconut in a creamy sauce with shavings of crisp parsnips. Spice-crusted french black chicken breast £19.10, with tomato and fennel sauce served on a bed of risotto style vegetable rice; Char-grilled guinea fowl breasts £12.25, with tomato and fenugreek sauce served with mossala mashed potato and rocket salad. Florets of vegetables and paneer brochettes cubes of cottage cheese, florets of cauliflower, broccoli and with a spiced coating and chargrilled with peppers then drizzled with a cashew nut and basil sauce, served with grilled portabello mushroom and dressed salad. Kasuri aloo £12.10, is scooped out local baby potatoes filled with red kidney beans and plantain (african green bananas) drizzled with a makhani sauce of fenugreek and cream of coconut, served with rice filled baby peppers and parsnip crisps. Top of the price bracket is Mauritius-style fresh Lobster £32, lobster meat in shell, matured with dill, sweet chilli and grand-marnier liqueur, served with herbed pullao rice in a kashmiri fruity sauce. ' Pre and post theatre menu has a two course meal with wine for £15pp available from 5.30- 7 and 9-10.30. Lunch buffet £8.95. Thursday: enjoy the table magician. Hours: 12-2 & 5.30-10.30.

HOX BRASSERIE   TOP 100
155 Fisherton Street, Salisbury, SP2 7RP
01722 341600   www.hoxbrasserie.co.uk

Run by Mr Hoque whose website tells us head chef Rajeev Kumar, worked Chalky's [sic] in Piccadilly. That would be Chowki. He also worked at India's Oberoi Hotel Group, Cinnamon Club and Chutney Mary's. The website also tells us they focus on Southern Indian food, however Rajeev's menu is full-on north Indian. That said, it has a finesse which is only to be found when the cooking is by a highly trained India chef, as opposed to Bangladeshi curryhouse cooks. Starters include: Potato Cakes (Aloo Tikki) £4.25, pan-fried with ginger, fennel and served on a bed of chick peas, tamarind and sweet yoghurt, a street snack in Gujarat ,western India; Goat Cheese Salad £4.45, with lamb's lettuce, rocket leaves, red salad, cherry tomatoes, beetroot, fresh mangoes and smoked cashew nuts; Fish Cake £4.90, fresh cod and swordfish risoole, flavoured with mustard and curry leaves, served with seafood raita; Duck Tikka £7, in a marinade of ginger, garlic, coriander then each c£13); Laal Maans, lamb slow-cooked Rajasthani-style, in a hot curry of kashmiri spices and tomatoes, served with pilau rice; Meen Moilee, monk fish char-grilled with dry spices, served with a smooth sauce of coconut and garlic flavoured spinach, served with steamed rice; Duck Orange Sauce, breast marinated with black pepper and red wine then pan grilled, in a sauce of fresh orange, fennel and cinnamon, served on a bed of garlic with creamed potato and rice. Lamb Shankmarinated with extracts of ginger, garlic, cumin and fresh green chilli, medium spiced dish. Char-Grilled Pheasant, choice of Old Delhi sauce, a close derivative of 'makhni' used to make butter chicken. . Wines from £13.95 to £495 Chat Lat 95. 12-2 & 6-11.

Swindon

PICKLE JOHNS
25, Wood St, Swindon, SN1 4AN   01793 509921

Atul Sarpal's Pickle Johns Pub & Restaurant (named after Indian gentlemen from the early part of the twentieth century, who was sent to this fair land to be educated in some of England's finest public schools (Eton, Harrow, Winchester). On their return to India they had adopted English manners. and the English in turn perceived them as jovial and eccentric characters. In India, they were named "PickleJohns". Most of the dishes are Indian cuisine but some are English and fusion. 12-2 & 6-11:30. *Branch: Popadum Express, Southampton Hants.*

RAFU'S TANDOORI
30 High St, Highworth, Swindon, SN1 3DQ
01793 765320   www.rafus.co.uk

Opened in 1982 by Mr Rafu as the Biplob; renamed to prevent confusion. It remains popular. 'Very *good*' G&MP. *'Menu large and varied choice. Complete*

SPLENDIDLY INDIAN, SUPERBLY SMOOTH

satisfaction. Best Jalfrezi in the West. Good service, pleasant atmosphere, superb location. Everything nice except the prantha (too greasy).' ZI. 'Menu had wide variety and choice. Quantity more than adequate. Service very courteous and polite. Atmosphere very convivial. Very good quality meal and good value.' KS 'We visit weekly. Extensive and varied menu. Generous quantities. High quality. Outstanding service. Excellent Bangra. Hasina Chicken – best in Europe!' IG&JN. 'The wine list is very good for an Indian restaurant. Whenever we go to Rafu's we know we are going to have a top-class meal, with friendly people, in pleasant surroundings.' JS. Hours: 12-3 & 6pm-12am Fri-Sat: 5 to late.

WORCESTERSHIRE

Area: Midlands

Adjacent Counties:
Glos, Hereford,
Shrops, Warks,
W Mids

Bromsgrove

CHENNAI
Kidderminster Road, Dodford, Bromsgrove, B61 9DX
01527 872639   www.chennaiindiancuisine.co.uk

It opened in 2011 and is a mile or so west of Bromsgrove on the A448. Although it's in the middle of nowhere, its advantage is a large car park. Inside it has a light, contemporary feel. Despite the name it's Bangladeshi curries (not south Indian) including standard items plus some specials eg: Barbecued Garlic Quail £3.80, marinated in crushed garlic, lemon juice, crushed red chilli, cane sugar and other spices; Bangladeshi Rolls £2.80, crushed chicken marinated with spices and herbs, deep fried and coated in egg; Crab Tikka £4.50, white crab meat, slow-cooked with fried onions, chopped garlic and delicate blends of aromatic spices and herbs. Mains: Green Herb Lamb £7, made with diced lamb using assorted green herbs, including spring onions; King Feast £9, finely chopped chicken, mince meat, tandoori chicken and egg, cooked in a medium blend of aromatic herbs and spices in a thick sauce with chopped onions, tomatoes and a touch of coriander; Chittagong Fish Supreme £78, a favourite Bangladeshi fish, the Gual, marinated with spices and mustard, shallow-fried and presented on a beautiful sauce, comprising of coconut cream and lime. Av price: £30.00 5.30-11.30

Evesham

MAHEEN'S
68 Bridge St, Evesham, WR11 4RY   01386 49704

'Excellent outlook, over-viewing the River Avon. in bottom storey of a large building. On first impressions, the entrance was not favourable, however once inside we were greeted by a Sanjeev Bhaskar lookalike, Mukit Miah. The restaurant is modern and minimal, in fact it looks more like a wine bar. The tables had black tablecloths with white trim, artificial black lillies were also black, I liked it. Service was prompt, only draught Carlsberg and Tetley bitter. Starters were predictable, but prices were as cheap as we've seen for a long time. My spiced Popadum arrived with burnt edges and Monika's plain looked like it came from a packet. Any misgivings were quashed when our mains arrived, delicious Lamb Zeera c£6, in a rich tomato sauce. Chicken Chilli Bahaar c£6, tender slices of chicken in a bright red sauce with a couple of sliced chillies which despite these was not too hot. A large plate of Mushroom Pullao £2.25 and a Naan £1.50 was more than enough. I really meant it when I said to the waiter that we really enjoyed it.' T&MH. Hours: 6-11.30; 12.30 Fri & Sa.

Redditch

HOTEL MONTVILLE & INDIAN REST'NT
101 Mount Pleasant, Southcrest, Redditch, B97 4JE
01527 544411   www.montvillehotel.co.uk

This small 2-star hotel with restaurant was opened in 2005 by Mukid Rahman. The MD is Mr. Chowdhury and has been recently refurbished with straightforward ensuite rooms and a new-look 86 seat Indian restaurant, now renamed The Montville Palace. The menu covers European and Indian dishes, all of which will be very familiar to curryhouse fans and you can watch them being created by the Bangladeshi chefs. Starters average £3.50 and curries £8, Specials from £8.45 (Shahi Paneer) to £30 (lobster), av £14. Booking essential with priority to residents, though Mr Choudhury says *'we like our customers to make a night of it and to take their time to enjoy our service, relaxed and un-pressured.'* Min Charge: £10. T/a service available. 6-11. Branches: Rilys of Evesham and Waterside, Evesham, both in Worcs.

RILY'S   www.rilys.com/evesham
2-3 Waterside, Evesham, WR11 1BS   01527 60544

Rily's Bar and Restaurant is in a row of pretty low Georgian buildings and alongside the River Avon, Menu snapshot: Monkfish Grilled £6, marinated in a coriander & ginger yoghurt sauce, then flame grilled in the tandoori; Salmon Tikka £4.75, smeared in light spice and roasted in the tandoor; .Tetul Mix £4.50, chunks of chicken & lamb tikka cooked with crunchy green peppers & onions in tangy tamarind and served with a puri bread. Mains include: Lasani Ghust £10, lamb, cooked with pickled garlic, onions and fresh chillies; Bombay Style Naga £9, a very hot dish using Naga chilies with strips of Chicken or Lamb in fresh garlic, herbs and spices. Av price: £28. Mon-Tue: e-a-m-a-y-l buffet. Mon-Th:: 5.30-11.30; Fri - Sat: 5.30-12; Sun: to 11. Branches: See previous entry.

Malvern

ANUPAM www.anupam.co.uk
85 Church St, Malvern WR14 2AE, 01684 573814

Safed Neem Korma £10.50, a korma with a hot taste, based on classical Mughal cuisine. Chicken pieces are marinated in an assortment of spices, and cooked in a cream sauce. With chillies and cashew nuts; Shenaz Chicken £10.40, cooked in a yogurt and ground spice sauce, flavoured with fenugreek leaves; Murgh-e-Chameli £10.40 chicken cooked with a mix of onion, crushed red chillies, and cranberries.This Chettinad-style curry is hot and spicy in the Parsi style, with fruits [sic]. Wqhich we wonder? Neither Chetinad nor Parseeactually, but you tell us you like it, Ed. Sunday course £11, u12 £7, from 12.30-5.

Tenbury Wells

NAZ'S www.nazsindianrestaurant.co.uk
14 Market St, Tenbury W WR15 8BQ 01584 819364

Naz's Wine Bar & Indian does tandooried items such as: Lamb Chops £5, marinated with yoghurt, black pepper, garlic, ginger paste; Sizzling Chicken £4, strips fried then cooked in a sweet & sour hot sauce; White Chicken Tikka £4, marinated in yoghurt, ginger, white pepper, cheese and a generous amount of garlic, skewered, Tandoori Monkfish £4.50, lightly spiced and flame-grilled in the sigri. Mains include: Nawabi Shaslik Duck £10, with onions, green peppers, tomatoes all roasted in a clay oven then prepared in a thick sauce, served on a sizzler; Sylheti Naga Tawa Chicken or Lamb £7.95, prepared with the hottest chilli & spices from Sylhet, garnished with fresh herbs; Shatkora Duck £10, prepared with highly flavoured spices and shatkora citric fruit (only grown in tropical areas of Bangladesh) giving a sharp tangy taste. Desserts include Lemon Cheesecake £4.50. Mon-Sat: 6-11:00; Sun Buffet 5-10.

Upton-on-Severn

PUNDITS www.pundits-upton.co.uk
9 Old Street, Upton, WE8 0HH 01684 591119

'We booked the previous night, a good job, the place was very popular, despite being the most expensive in the area. A memorable place because the maitre'd [Sultan] greeted, my wife with a kiss on the cheek and shook my hand even though it was our first visit. Enjoyed my Morche Roshin (garlic and chilli) Chicken Tikka, billed as hot, however, I may have been suffering from mouth numbness caused by my Chicken Vindaloo in Ilfracombe a few days previously. Good service.' T&MH. Est 1996. Bangladeshi standard menu at resonable prices; Open Kitchen, 2 dining rooms plus a Patio garden in good weather. Takeaway 20% discount. 5.30-10.45.

Worcester

MONSOON TOP 100 www.monsoonindian.co.uk
35 Foregate Rd, Worcester, WR1 1EE 01905 726333

White painted angled pillars and wooden stained concertina doors make this 120 seater restaurant stand out on Foregate Road. Established in 1999 by Rahman (manager), Choudhury and Choudhury. Reception has been painted in a creamy colour with comfortable sofa's upholstered in paprika. The restaurant has a light and airy feel, with bleached wooden flooring, paprika and cinnamon painted walls, original art hangs sparingly on the walls with matching chairs in paprika, cinnamon, turmeric and indigo. Natural wooden tables are economically laid with crisp white linen napkins and generous wine glasses. Specials: Tangri Kebab, drumstick marinated in cashew nuts, spices and served with tamarind chutney. Achar Wali Machi, salmon steak pickled in spices, served cold with salad. Parsi Jhinga, tiger prawns in mint, turmeric, garlic and tamarind juice. Lamb Shikampuri, mince lamb balls stuffed with coriander, ginger, onion, raisins in curry gravy. Daal Panchmela, a mix of five varieties of lentils. T/a: 10% disc. Hours: 4-11.30; Sun: 12-11.30 (buffet-10). *Branch: Cheltenham Tandoori, 2 Great Norwood Street Cheltenham, Gloucs. Tel: 01242 227772.*

PASHA www.pasha-online.co.uk
56 St Johns, Worcester, WR2 5AJ 01905 426327

Manager, N Haque's restaurant, seats 68 diners. Opened in 1987 as Pasha Indian Cuisine and has remained under the same management. Menu Snapshot: Nargi's Kofta £2.50, spicy minced lamb deep-fried in butter, served with a light omelette and fresh salad; Mushroom Delight £2.50, stuffed with spicy vegetables and deep-fried; Methi Gosht c£6, with fenugreek, medium hot; Chicken Hasina £5.50, mildly spiced, dried fruit and nuts with fresh cream; Garlic Potato £2.75, rich sauce; Mushroom Pullao Rice £2.75, selection of Chutneys 45p. Sun Buffet: c£7 adult, £4.50 under 12's, 12.30 - 2. Cobra £3.10 a pint. House wine is a good value c£8 a bottle. You might get a disc if you show them this Guide. Del: £1 charge. 12-2 & 5.30-12.

PETE'S INDIAN
55 London Rd, Worcester, WR5 2DJ 01905 360909

Located in the former 'little sauce factory' (a former English restaurant and not the home of Lea & Perrins, Pete's tell us the menu is *'based on traditional Kashmiri recipes, many of which have been adapted to suit Western palates while retaining flavour and richness.'* In fact it is the formula curry menu wih not a Kashmiri dish in sight. But it seems you like it anyway. Av price: £25.00. Sun-Th: 5.30- 10.30; Fri-Sa to11.30; Closed Tues.

RAJKOT
27 The Tything, Worcester, WR1 1JL 01905 27402

'A good experiences to share. Excellent restaurant, stylish and

very unlike a traditional curry house. They do have the normal standard curries buried in the menu but it's mainly an extensive menu of regional specialities and unusual dishes so lots of new experiences. Particularly strong on fish, seafood and also offer venison, duck and others – we're completely vegetarian so didn't sample them!. The vegetarian Thali is excellent and presentation is superb on all dishes. The service is first class with friendly staff who laugh and joke with the customers. A great experience, not cheap, but worth every penny for a smart night out and one of my all-time favourite restaurants – shame we live 250m away! I believe it's owned by the same people who have the Cafe Mela also in Worcester.' GC. 6-12 (to 1am Fri-Sat)

SPICE CUISINE TOP 100 BYO
39 Bromyard Terrace, Worcester, WR2 5BW
01905 429786   www.spicecuisine.co.uk

Hidden away behind Birmingham Midshires Building Society, just over the river bridge from Worcester Town, it has been owned by the same family for years, Muslims from Pakistan, so this means gutsy savoury tastes, Lahori Kofta, deep-fried meat meat balls, for example and a full menu of good-as -they-get Baltis (which originated in Mirpur Pakistan). 'Plain, simple and clean decor. Friendly and efficient service. Staff Curry - lamb on the bone in a thick, tasty, spicy sauce, cooked for hours with a thin rolled and crispy Nan. Manager - Iffty Shah (cousin of Masteen who manages the Kashmir in Birmingham).Toilets always clean with hot water, soap and dryer. Chicken on the bone and Aloo for me - excellent as usual. Lamb Chops, on the bone, which was the staff curry for the night. About six chops which had been cooking for hours so that the meat was falling off, served with a rich, quite hot sauce - superb. Roti to go with it, what else would you want for a Sun dinner. Washer-upper has been promoted to Tandoori Chef and made a very good start with Seekh Kebabs. Unlicensed: BYO - they will chill and open it for you.' RE. T/a: 10% disc. Del: 3m, £10 min. Small car park at rear. 5.30 -11.30.

YOU SAY OK
You might get a discount if you show them this Guide.

BEWDLEY: THE RAJAH OF BEWDLEY 8 Load St. ~ 01299 400368. Anwar Uddin's 34-seater in a grade 2 listed cottage. 'Food excellent, extremely friendly service.' SH. 'Good' G&MP. Special: Tandoori Lobster. T/a: 10% off. Min ch: £5. Hours: 5-11.30.
BROMSGROVE: SPICES RESTAURANT 151 Golden Cross Lane | Catshill, Bromsgrove 01527 878522 Av price £20. Mon-Sun: 5- 11.30.
GREAT MALVERN: BENGAL BRASSERIE 5 Worcester Rd ~ 01684 575744. Masum Choudhury took over in 2000 . Hours: 5-12.
KIDDERMINSTER: EURASIA TAKEAWAY Unit 1, 19, Stourbridge Rd ~ 01562 825861. Owner Syed Hussain. Del: 4m £10 min. Hours: 5-12.
KIDDERMINSTER: NEW SHER E PUNJAB 48 George St ~ 01562 740061. Puran Singh cooks Punjabi food (est 1971). Eves only .
REDDITCH: REDOLENCE SPICE: 17-21 Unicorn Hill, Redditch, Redditch B97 4QR   01527 65970 www.redolencespice.com 5.30-11.30; Fri-Sat: to 12.
STOURPORT-ON-SEVERN: NAMASTE INDIAN EATERY www.namasteindianeatery.co.uk 1 Lichfield St, Stourport 01299 877 448   3 Course Meal £10 Sun-Th.
WORCESTER: DELHI 6 5a St Johns, WR2 5AE 01905 422228.
WORCESTER: SPICES TAKEAWAY 9 Barbourne Rd. ~ 01905 729101. Del: 3m, £1 Del. Hours: 5.30-12, Sat to 1, Tuesday closed. Branch: Shunarga, 44, High Street, Pershore.

NORTH YORKSHIRE
North of England
Adjacent Counties:
Cumbria, Durham, Lancs, East & West Yorkshire

1997 county changes returned 'Cleveland' south of the Tees, to North Yorks. At the same time, the changes created a 'new' Yorkshire county by transferring territory and towns from 'North Humbs' into East Yorkshire. This restored Yorkshire as Britain's biggest county. Because the area is so large, we deal with these four counties in their current administrative formats and in compass order, N, E, S, W.

Beadlam (Hemsley)

DESI SPICE CLUB
Main Road, Beadlam, Nawton, Nr. Helmsley,
YO62 7SA   01439 772400

It has had a name change to Desi (from Hemsley Spice Club) The venue was once the White Horse Inn, now completely refurbished it is the latest in the Jinnah group. It is situated on the busy A170, midway between Helmsley and Kirbymoorside, off road parking is available in their private car park. It's a modern and contemporary restaurant with 65 covers plus a separate bar where customers are welcome to have a drink whilst waiting for a takeaway or just to enjoy the ambience. Sun-Th: 5.3-11; Fri & Sat: to 11.30pm.

Bedale

TASTE OF INDIA T
32 Market Place, Bedale, DL8 1EQ   01677 423373

Bedale is an old Yorkshire market town with a large cobbled square, plenty of free parking surrounded by interesting shops. Est 1989, this smallish restaurant has undergone extensive refurbishment. 'A group of us decided to try it last Wednesday evening and had a mixed, but enjoyable overall, experience. Popadums with pickles, Mixed Kebab, Meat Samosas £2.10, Onion Bhajia £2.00, Chicken Tikka Curries, Rice, Saag Aloo £2.45 and Naan £1.50 were all fresh, superb quality, nicely spiced an thoroughly delicious. The portions were generous and with drinks and coffee, the bill came to £15 per head, which proved excellent value for money. The service (from a sullen lad with a silly haircut) was second rate and only repeated prompting ensured that our needs were met.' TE. Tony, I can hear myself saying 'the youth of today' just like my parents! T/a 10% disc. Hours: 6-11.30; 12 Fri & Sat.

Harrogate

JINNAH
34 Cheltenham Parade Harrogate HG1 1DB
01423 563333   www.jinnahrestaurants.com

Est 2003 and seats 110 in a converted stone chapel, which was part of a Wesleyan school and is now a listed building. *'The interior is pleasantly different, being cavernous with its high ceilings and two large hanging lights. Seating is either in the main well or along the slightly raised area around the edge. Decorated in terracotta and green colours with brown and beige chairs, and green imitation marble easy-wipe table tops, wall lights, plates and cutlery (yes, even the knives and forks) with the name of the restaurant. Smartly dressed waiters impart the look of quality. It was Sat night and packed. The menu was almost too clever by half with too many dishes described as 'amazing.' Onion Bhajias £2.35, were two large flat patties like hamburgers in shape (they could have been put in a bun and called bhajia burger) and were OK, pleasantly spiced, edges nicely crisp but the middle was stodgy. The service was friendly and efficient.'* MW. Hours: 5.30-11; 12 Sat; 12- 11 Sun . Branches Flaxton Headoffice A64, Malton Road Flaxton York YO60 7SQ 01904 468202

MUJIB
32 Devonshire Place, Harrogate, HG1 4AD 01423 875522

Chef Nazrul Ali specialises in 'Indian fusion' drawing on his experience of Indian, French Provençal, Italian, Oriental and Thai cuisine to create the menu. The dish Joi Yorkshire, for example, mixes traditional English roast lamb and light spices with Yorkshire pudding and Bhuna sauce. *Branch: Mujib Whitby Rd, Ellesmere Port, CH65 8DN ~ 0151 357 1676.*

Middlesborough

AKBARS
192-194 Linthorpe Road, Middlesbrough, TS1 3RF
01642 244566   www.akbars.co.uk

Sun-Thur: 5-11 / Sun: to Mdnt. Branches: Eighth (2009) branch of ten of the rapidly expanding chain. See Bradford, W.Yorks for details.

Richmond

TANDOORI NIGHT
3 Castle Hill, Richmond DL10 4QP
01748 826677   www.tandoorinight-restaurant.co.uk

Popular curryhouse serving all the favourite curries at favourable prices.   E-a-m-a-y-l buffetey every Sun & Weds 6-9,£7.95 u8 £5.95.   Must book in advance. Mon-Th: 5.30-11; Fri-Sat: 4.30-12; Sun: 5.30-12.t

Riccall

THE SPICE MILL   TOP 100
Landing Lane. Riccall, YO19 6TJ
01757 249707   www.thespice-mill.com

Just off A19 between Selby and York, a mill has existed on this site since 1290. It has 8 inch thick walls had four sails and three corn grinding millstones and was converted into a private residence in 1911 and then to a restaurant in 1989. Set in one acre of land it makes the most of its attractive garden views. It most recent lease of life sees it as an Indian restaurant. The main tower is surrounded by a well-windowed, circular dining area. The food is steps better than average curryhouse. Starters include: Malai Murgh Bunda £3.45, strips of chicken tikka stir with pieces of sweet red pepper, spring onions and a light selection of herbs and spices then sprinkled with cheese and served in a plain flour wrap; Morich Bahar £3.45, a fresh pepper stuffed with exotic vegetables cooked with a medium blend of herbs and spices; Mach Biran £3.45, a Bangladeshi river fish lightly spiced with turmeric, salt and black pepper seared in olive with cooked green pepper and onion, garnished with coriander and a slice of lemon; Kakra Puri £4, minced crab and diced potatoes cooked in a coastal-style sauce including spring onions, methi and mustard seeds served with a lighly fried puri bread. Speciality Mains include: Golda Janna £11, tandooried king prawns in shell with green beans and lime in a sauce made from garlic infused olive oil, ginger, fresh green chillies, tomato and a special blend of spices; Hydrabadi Ghosht £9, tandooried lamb with Okra in a sauce made from garlic, oil, spring onions, fresh tomato, herbs and spices garnished with lime and coriander; Nizam-E-Kofta £10, lamb meat balls are cooked with diced baby potatoes in a thick medium sauce.Mon-Sat: 5-11.30. Sun: 2-10.

Ripon

MOTI RAJ
18 High Skellgate, Ripon   01765 690348

'A busy road with many buses passing, the owner was washing the windows when we arrived (using an old ghee bucket for the water!). We sat at the bar and were given ice-cold Cobras and the menus, containing a 'priced matrix' format of meat/fish against the variety of curry sauces, so simple and logical, other restaurants take note. Recently refurbished in soft pastel shades with double layer of linen on the tables. Toilets were immaculate. Warm Pops, fresh pickles, seven delicious curries, four blends of rices, three different breads and a lovely Sag Aloo, were delivered, and demolished by us all, wash down with even more Cobra, nothing was left! A mature favourite of locals and visitors to Ripon. It offers excellent service, high quality cuisine and good TE. *value for money, highly recommended.'* The menu is pretty much standard curryhouse, but probe a bit deeper and you;ll find Ostrich curry £12. You might get a discount if you show them this Guide. Del: 3m, £8 min. 5.30-12.

COBRA — SPLENDIDLY INDIAN, SUPERBLY SMOOTH

Skipton

AAGRAH   A-LIST
Waterside Court, Coach Street, SKIPTON, BD23 1LH
01756 790807

'This was one of the earliest branches of the celebrated Yorkshire chain of 14 restaurants. In fact it has moved to this larger more glamorous venu amidst the canals which seats 100. 3 course buffet Weds to Sat, 6-10.30 & Sun 4.30-9.30pm £12.95, u10 £7. Mon-Fri: 12-2.30; Mon-Sat: 5.30- 11.30; Sun: 4.30- 10.30. Menu details and list of branches see Shipley. W. Yorks.

Tadcaster

AAGRAH   A-LIST
York Road, Steeton, Tadcaster   01937 530888

The 6th Aagrah. 120-seater, opened 1996 on the A64 near York, with easy parking. 6-12; 11 Sun. See above.

Thirsk

RAJ OF INDIA   www.rajofindia.net
42 Long Street, Thirsk, YO7 1AU   01845 526917

Opened in 1990 by Hassan Ahamed and named after his son who now works in the restaurant. *'I was working at the North Yorks Police HQ and they recommended it. Balti dishes with deliciously spiced sauces, served on proper hot plates, swiftly by smart, cheerful waiters who are focused on attentive customer service. Very busy with locals, business people, tourists and race-goers.'* [and cops?] *'I especially liked the smart, elderly (70's) gent with a military bearing who marched in and said to the waiter, "I'll have a large Beef Madras and a litre of house red!"* TE. Free Pickle Tray with every T/a. Menu Snapshot: Aloo Chat £2.30; Raj Special Biriani £6, Tandoori meat, chicken and prawn with saffron rice cooked together in almond and sultanas, served with Vegetable Curry; Sirloin Steak Masala £7, best English steak marinated and served with mushrooms and Pullao Rice; Kulcha Nan £1.90, stuffed with onion and cheese. Sun-Th: 6-11.30; Fri-Sat: to 12 Sun buffet: 12-2, £6.95.

York

AKBARS
6-8 George Hudson Street, York, YO1 6LP 01904 679 888 www.akbars.co.uk

Fifth (2006) branch of ten of the rapidly expanding chain. Mon-Sat: 5-12; Sun-11:30. *Branches: See Bradford, W.Yorks for details.*

BENGAL BRASSIERE
York Busn Park, Ings Lane, Poppleton, York, YO26 6RA
01904 788808   www.bengal-brasserie.com

Owner, Dobir Malik opened his lovely restaurant in 1999. It's a new, brick-built, building with clean lines, and inside, decorated brightly with cream walls, fuschia upholstery, wrought iron light fittings and seats 100 diners. The menu is not your ordinary curry house, with Bengal Special Chicken Patil c£9 being the most ordered dish! Menu Snapshot: Morich Bahar £3.95, fried whole green pepper filled with aloo, chana, begun herbs and spices; Murgh E Dilruba £3.95, fillet of chicken breast wrapped in cheese; Liver Tikka £3.95, chicken livers marinated and served with green salad; Paneer Pakora c£3, cubes of cottage cheese, battered and deep-fried; Duck Tikka Masala c£9; Korma Murgh Tikka c£7, mild and creamy chicken tikka with coconut and almonds; Chicken Tikka Chom Chom c£8, barbecued chicken, potato, chickpeas in medium sauce, garnished with coriander and spring onion; Chilli Begun c£6, aubergine, spicy sauce, green chilli and capsicum, Chilli & Coriander Naan £2. Mon-Sat: 5.30-11.30; Sun: 4-11. *Branches: 1 Goodramgate, York; 65 Haddon Rd, Leeds; Victoria Street, Wetherby.*

JINNAH AT FLAXTON   TOP 100
Malton Road, Flaxton, York, YO60 7SQ
01904 468202   www.jinnah-restaurants.com

Large and imposing purpose built restaurant on the A64 mid way between York and Malton. Seats 150 people in two lounges, two bars and an extensive dining area. *'Cleverly constructed so that the interior is split into cosy areas around a central pavilion. Manned by uniformed staff who glide around in a manner probably not seen since Lyons dispensed with the Nippies.'* Blimey Ralph, that's showing your age. – we're talking the 1940's (and for those who haven't a clue what us wrinklies are on about, educate yourselves on the web!) *'Pleasant starter, Chaat Patta Chicken £3.25, a dish I last tasted in Brick Lane. Plenty of thin slices of breast meat, marinated in an incredibly rich and sticky sauce with a delicious bite. Slices of onion and red pepper added bite, superb. Main course kept up the high standard, Hasina Lamb £9.95, top quality meat without a trace of fat or gristle, mouthwatering sauce, piquant blend of herbs and spices fused in sweated down spinach. Fantastic pungent aroma, with star anise and cardamom and chillies added zing. Good Chuppatis £1.50 for two. Real tablecloths and hand folded napkins. Beaming manager, knew most customers by name. Very enjoyable.'* RW. *'Our Guide has proved invaluable; we have particularly enjoyed our visits here.'* N&G. *'As they do a "Grand Kashmiri Buffet" I decided to try it one Monday evening. There was plenty of choice, although on the evening I was there trade was a bit slack and the dishes although basically well flavoured had been standing a little too long and were a bit tired. I intend to try it again.'* JP. Buffet: Mon & Weds, 5.30-10, adults £10, kids c£6. Hours: 5.30-11; 12-11 Sat & Sun. Sun Buffet, 12-10. *Branches: 2 Cumberland St & Viceroy Monkgate York, Beadlham, Harrogate and Park Street, Selby.*

YOU SAY OK – N. YORKS

SETTLE: SETTLE TANDOORI 9 Commercial Courtyard, Duke St. 01729 823393. 50-seater est 1998 by Abdul Rob. 5.30-11.30.
YORK: TAJ MAHAL RE-ENTRANT 7 Kings Staith, YO1 1SN ~ 01904 653944. Stand on the bridge over the river Ouse and it's easy to see with a great river frontage though only two tables in the window give a view. T/a 10% disc. Hours: 12-2:30/5:30-12.

EAST YORKSHIRE

Area: North of England

Adjacent Counties:
Lincs, N S & W Yorks

1997 county changes created this 'new' Yorkshire county by transferring territory and towns here from 'North Humbs'.

Beverley

Akash 3a Toll Gavel, Beverley HU17 9AA   01482 882090

'*Very popular restaurant, situated upstairs in a pedestrianised centre of this busy market town. Very experienced and efficient staff. Large open room, simply decorated and nicely furnished. Overall an excellent meal.*' RW. Menu Snapshot. Aubergine Bhaji and Puri £2.20; Tandoori Mixed Korahi c£7, chicken and lamb tikka, sheek kebab, tandoori chicken and king prawn, medium hot sauce; Special Nan £1.75, stuffed with cheese, garlic and coriander leaves. Sun-Th: 5.30-11.30 (to 12 Fri-Sat).

DINE BANGLA   BYO
9-10 Wednesday Market Place, Beverley   01482 861110   www.dinebanglaindianrestaurant.co.uk

Standard menu, starter av: £3. Full range of mains with some originally named specials such as Phangasher saalom £14, filleted phangash fish from Sylhet in Bangladesh sautéed in light spices and a moist garnished with onions, green pepper, green chillies and tomato; Endaa-di-torkari £11, diced meat or chicken cooked with boiled egg, lemon juice, green chilli and coriander; Jaflongi (Chicken £10.50 Salmon £14) from the Jaflong district of Sylhet, strips of marinated chicken or salmon steak, cooked in a hot spicy tangy thick sauce, with fresh green chillies and coriander. The above are each served with boiled rice, small nan bread and special dip. Meal for 2: £30: 3 Pops, pickle tray, 1 Samosa, 1 Shish Kebab, 1 Karahi Murgh, 1 Meat Bhoona, 1 Bhindi Bhaji, 1 Mushroom Bhaji, 2 Special Fried Rice, 1 Nan and 2 Coffee. Fri-Sun: 12-10. Mon-Th: 5.30-11.30.

Bridlington

MASALA
10-11 Marlborough Terrace, Bridlington YO15 2PA
01262 671736   www.masalabridlington.co.uk

Masala was established in 2007. Starter av £2.75, Mains av £7. Set Meal For Two £20, (KP add £2), Choice of 2 Starters, 2 Mains, 1 side, 1 Nan & 1 Rice. Daily: 12.30-2.30; Sun-Th: 5-11 (Fri-Sat to 12).

Kingston-upon-Hull

ALACHI   BYO
191 Wold Road, Hull, HU5 5PH   01482 575255

Sited on Wold Road inbetween a row of shops. This unassuming Indian restaurant is '*quite nice inside, has a great menu, pleasant staff and great value for money.*' Bring your own alcohol (it does not have a licence, by choice).

CINNAMON
17 Anlaby Road, Hull, HU1 2PJ   01482 323113
www.cinnamonhull.co.uk

Mr Koyesh's popular Cinnamon serves the full range of curryhouse dishes plus some unusuals. Menu Snapshot: Aloo chat potato with hotspices served on a puri bread £2.95; Kolizisauteed Chicken Liver lightly spiced Mains include Butter Chicken £6.45, cooked with fresh cream, almond powder and spices. marinated in butter sauce; Seafood Bhunaan infusion of king scallops, squid, cuttle fish and tiger prawns cooked in out indian chef's speciality stock. a medium blend of "bhuna" spices and herbs £7.95; Green Chicken Curry £9.95, with brocolli, baby aubergine, fresh beans, coconut milk and spices; cox's bazaar crab £6.25; Soft Shell Crabs fried to become crunchy and served over a bed of aromatic sauce; shahi masala £6.25; Tandoored chicken cooked with almond, coconut, mixed spice, yoghurt and tia maria liqueur. Sat-Wed: 12-2:30 & 5:30-12 (Th-Fri to 1am)

RAJ PAVILION
56a-58 Beverley Rd, Hull HU3 1YE
01482 581939   www.rajpavilion.co.uk

Full range of starters (18 meat and 13 veg av price £3.50) as expected at a good and popular curryhouse. And an equally full range of mains and sides with some interesting specials Raj Pavillion's USP is a chef who uses alcohol to achieve elusive flavours, a rare attribute at the curryhouse. For example: Nawabi Tandoori Masala £9.20, chicken marinated in yoghurt, fresh ginger and coriander over night. Barbecued in the tandoor then cooked in a sauce with fresh cream, cashew nuts, almonds and pistachios, served in a Korai with a dash of Galliano Liqueur; Sizzling Chicken or Lamb £9.20, marinated, grilled and then cooked with Martel Brandy and double cream with various herbs and spices;, Rezella Chicken or Lamb £9.20 is a very smooth, creamy and hot dish, cooked with red wine. Other specials include Duck Goan Shank £11.90, f spiced with onions, garlic coriander and Indian archar; Duck Xacuti £11.90, (pron Shakooti) breast of Barbary Duck in full flavoured masala, roasted seed aniseed, mace, fenugreek, bullet chillies and lentils; Amlee Chicken or Lamb £8.50, a mild exotic dish cooked with almonds, coconut, pistachios, mango slices, honey and fresh cream and dil; Pasand Gaggot £11.90, Bangladesh sweet water fish, marinated in herbs and spices, glazed in honey served in a medium sauce; Shatkora Chicken or Lamb £8.50, from Sylhet region of Bangladesh

SPLENDIDLY INDIAN, SUPERBLY SMOOTH

with the citrusy fragrance of Shatkora. Raj Table is a full meal of whole chicken £70 or whole Lamb Leg £80, includes Starters, Main Dishes, Special Rice Sweets and Coffee.(24 hour notice & 25% deposit required. Set meal: £19: starter; pops, pickles, main course, side dishes, rice, naan bread and coffee. Sun-Th: 6-11.30 (Fri-Sat to 12).

SWADH HOTEL SOUTH INDIAN
Trinity Hotel 309 - 323 Hedon Road, Hull, HU9 1NU
01482 222600   www.trinityhull.co.uk

A32 bedroom hotel (£55 double en-suite inc b&b), in the former Platform 1 hotel, a chupatti throw from the docks. Trinity's USP is restaurant, Swadh, which indeed offers chupattis, but no naans or Bangla formula stuff because it is not a curryhouse. It is a rarity for this part of the country, a real south Indian restaurant, light and airy with a very interesting authentically home-cooked cuisine. Menu snapshot: Rasam Soup £3, made of black pepper, tomato, tamarind juice, ginger, asafoetida, garlic and turmeric, tempered with mustard seeds, curry leaves and dried chilli. Medium but ask and they will spice it up to the correct (hot) level. Four types of vada (lentil rissole including Parippu Vada £3, gramflour mashed with red chilli, curry leaves, ginger, and onions made into crispy patties, served with chutneys;, Mini Masala Dosa £4(£5.50 as main course,) traditional (huge) south Indian pancake filled with potato masala and served with sambar and chutneys;,Mutton Chilli Fry £7.50, marinated in chilli, turmeric, ginger, garlic then deep-fried. Mains include Nadan Kozhi Curry Masala £7, fried chicken breast cooked with spices, ginger, garlic, tomatoes, coconut milk, fried onions and curry leaves; Mutton Olathiyathu, £8, cooked and dry-fried with onion, tomato, chilli, black pepper and coconut pieces; Parippu Curry £4, mixed split lentils (Yellow Pigeon Peas, Mung bean, Red Lentils) cooked with spices, garlic and fresh coconut, tempered with mustard seeds and dried chillies; Kaalan £4.50, green banana cooked in a yoghurt based gravy with ginger, garlic, turmeric powder, black pepper, fenugreek and tempered with ghee, mustard seeds, fenugreek, dried chillies and curry leaves; Coconut Rice. £3.50; Idiyappam (String Hoppers) 4 Pcs £4 made from rice flour and shredded coconut and steamed. There are a couple of non south Indian dishes for those who don't dare try something new: eg Butter Chicken [aka CTM] £6.50, chicken breast marinated in butter, paprika, spices, tomato, sugar and garnished with cream. But we recommend you ignore this and go full-on south Indian. Booking advised. Licensed. 12-3 & 6-11

TAMAN RIA TROPICANA MALAY
45-47 Princes Avenue, Hull, HU5 3RX,
01482 345640   www.tropicana-hull.co.uk

Owner/Chef Vince Lee', his wife Jayne and daughter, Juvina run Taman Ria Tropicana is Hull's only Malayan and Indonesian and the cuisine is actually known as "masakan melayu" or "Malay cuisine". Taman Ria seats 45 and has a modern interior with a touch of the Eastern Orient and an open kitchen with a buffet range,and bar.

The licensed restaurant has seating for up to 45 people. As a matter of interest they do a small range of four Indian curries each £10.50 with rice and salad: (Madras, Vindaloo, Korma, Chicken, Beef ,Vegetarian, Seafood and CTM), and there are Thai curries. But you really should go for the Malay food. If you are unfamiliar with it they offer pelnty of friendly advice. You could of course try the filling set meal £10, or venture into a la carte with starters such as Chicken, Lamb or Beef Satay £4.50, grilled on skewers served with a spicy peanut sauce or Mee Soto (Chicken or Veg) £4.50, Malayan noodle soup with bean sprouts or Mee Laksa (Chicken or Veg) £4.50, a light curry with creamy coconut soup and bean sprouts. Mains include: Nasi Goreng Telor (Meat/Veg) £11.50 fried rice with fresh spices topped with a spicy omelette; Mee Goreng/MeeHun £10.50, Malayan Fried Noodles); Grilled Fish (Ikan Pangang) £12, grilled Haddock Fillet /Salmon Steak/Tuna Steak) as available served with mushrooms & onions.and sambal or fresh garlic/chilli sauce. Special Lamb Curry £10.50, Kampong-style curry prepared with selected curry spices served with rice and salad. Nasi Lemak £10.50, coconut rice with sambal fried egg, crispy anchovies and nuts, chicken curry and cucumber salad. Tu-Sat: 6– 11.

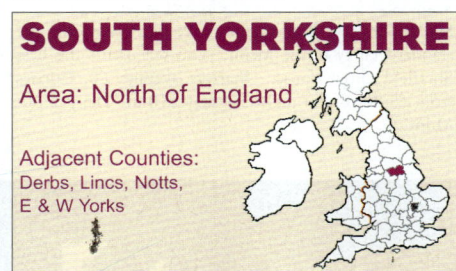

SOUTH YORKSHIRE
Area: North of England

Adjacent Counties:
Derbs, Lincs, Notts,
E & W Yorks

Doncaster

AAGRAH TOP 100
Great North Road, Woodlands, Doncaster, DN6 7RA
01302 728888   www.aagrah.com

The Aagrah group now has 14 restaurants. This one, the 5th opened in 1995 and has a capacity of 100. Buffet Sun/Mon. Mon-Th: 6-11:30; Fr-Sa: to Mdnt; Sun: 4:30-10.30. See Shipley, N. Yorks for menu details.

DOWER HOUSE
5 Market Pl, Bawtry, Doncaster, DN10 6JL
01302 719696   www.dower-house.com

Bawtry has been a market town since 1247 as its wide main street indicates. A dower house is was built to be available for use by the widow of a local estate-owner, in Bawtry's case, the wool merchant who built the local Manor in early Georgian times. It now houses a Bangladeshi curryhouse. The menu contains many familiar dishes and sopme specials. Starters include Zeera Chicken £5, marinated in ground coriander and cumin, and cooked in cooked in Garam masala; Halka

Squid Masala £11, is flame-fried in light spice. Mains: .Murgh Jolpai £11, Chicken cooked with fresh olives in a medium sauce; Chicken Chana Baja £10.90 chicken tikka frtied with chick peas; Chat Masala garnished with fresh onion,peppers, tomatoes & coriander; Shahi Chingriwala Desi £14, fresh water King prawns, cooked with a Jalfrezie stir fry taste; Shahi Chicken Rejala £11, chicken tikka with fried green chilliess & onions; King Prawn Bhuna Desi £12.90 in a thick sauce. 6-11.

Rotherham

AKBARS
Meadowbank Road, Rotherham, S61 2NF
01709 555500   www.akbars.co.uk-

Sixth (2007) of ten branches of the rapidly expanding chain. Sun-Thur: 5-11; Sun: -11.30. See Bradford, W.Yorks for details.

Sheffield

AKHTARS
193B Sheffield Road, Killamarsh, Sheffield, S21 1DX
0114 247 7666   www.akhtars-restaurant.co.uk

Since 1997 the Akhtar family have been providing the standard curry house menu. You tell us it's the best Sheffield curry house. Starters average £3, Curries from £5.80. Buffet night Tuesday £10.50 Daily: 5:30-Mdnt.

ARIF'S VEGETARIAN TAKEAWAY
396 South Road, Sheffield S6 3TF

All-vegetarian curryhouse menu. See Veggie Masala, below. They are not connected but the menus and prices are virtually identical. Slightly longer hours: Sun-Th: 5.30-12 (to 1am Fri-Sat).

ASHOKA   A-LIST
307 Ecclesall Rd, Sheffield, S11 8NX
0114 268 3029   www.ashoka1967.com

Sheffield according to Sheffield folk has never been noted for good Indian cuisine. Of the 60 plus curry vendors, most don't hack it. Even once top-rated Nirmal's doesn't for us.; the sit-in meal we had there was so awful, we asked for it to be packed and we dumped it in a nearby skip. Luckily for Sheffield the Ashoka bucks the trend and serves *'utterly divine food'* JGS. It always has since it was established in 1967 by Mrs M and Kamal Ahmed. This makes it the oldest Indian restaurant in Sheffield if not the oldest restaurant left in the city. We'll go further: the Ashoka is by far the best Indian restaurant in the city. The newer entrants to the city are big chain venues, and good though they are, they cannot better a tiny (they would say unviable with just 38 seats) venue whose owners have had a passion for 44 years and will do ad infinitum. Its tiny size means total dedication to its discerning clientele who appreciate the genuine article, of whom they have many (so booking is advisable). When viewing the menu, you'd be forgiven for thinking it is just another curryhouse. Wrong! The Ashoka has always served really authentic Indian food. Of course, they all say that, the curryhouses up and down the land, not caring how whether cheaply-made pastiche food is respected or not. So what makes the Ashoka different? That four letter word – care. Rahul Amin took over ownership in 2004. he carries the vsion forward: *'In my eyes, says Rahul, a restaurant is a little like a living entity. Its heart beats constantly. Our head chef oversees every dish, salad and bread right down to the last poppadom - we roast ours at the eleventh second to order. Our tandoori chef is also a trained butcher — invaluable as he inspects all meat produce and controls all inhouse butchery. Our starter chef used to be in the army — he's responsible for hand-kneading all our breads. - hopefully you can taste the difference!'* And you can, the annonymous web-site whingers can't, so let them eat the pastiche available elsewhere in the city. Starters include Tandoori Lamb Chops £5.75 marinated with crushed peppers and bengal mustard, tandoored and served with mixed pulses; Dall Puri £4.25a featherlight crisp shell of bread filled with light spiced lentils; Liver (Chicken) Puri £4.25, lightly spiced chicken livers. Mains include:Chicken Tikka Makhni £8, tandoori-baked pieces of marinated chicken in a light cream sauce with toasted cashew nuts; Bangalore Pal Lamb £8, cooked with fresh tomato, green pepper and rich spices; Rajasthani Railway Lamb £8, a classic as served on Indian Rail (Rahul will explain), succulent lamb with baby new potatoes in a rich sauce. The daily specials are always good, eg: Saturday, King Prawn Sag £10; Sunday, Chana Gosht £9, etc. *'The best Indian restaurant we have been to, including many in the London area and Birmingham. We went back to it every night of the week [while attending a scientific meeting in Sheffield]. We cannot praise its delicate and distinct flavours too highly, and the friendly, efficient service.' j&af. 'One of the finest Indian restaurant in South Yorkshire. Diners are assured of excellent service, an amenable atmosphere and outstanding service. Comprehensive and high quality wine list. Book early to avoid disappointment.'* D&CS. *'Just wanted to send you a glowing report. Not only was the vegetarian curry superb, but the waiters were friendly'* KH. The Ashoka would not be out of place in London's west end. Sun-Th: 6 -11 (Fri-Sat: to 12.

AZAAD'S   KASHMIRI
Woodbourn Rd, Attercliffe, Sh'fld, S9 3LQ   0114 243 4406

Kashmiri owner-chef Mohammad Azaad has been in business for over 40 years. His latest venture (June 2011) is in an old schoolhouse next door to the Attercliffe Pakistani Muslim Centre. Pops 50p pickles £1.75. Satrters include Fish Masala starter (£3.75) Mains: Ginger Lamb £6.50, Chicken Tikka Biryani £7.25, Masala Daal £3.15, three different types of lentil and red beans, Pilau rice and a plain naan each £1.70. It is unlicensed and you can BYO no corkage. They do Lassi and non alcoholic brews of fruit, herbs and vegetable extracts such as Rooh e Afza,

and Anari Sharbat, pomegranate syrup with ice and water. £3 a jug.   Wed-Sun: Buffet nights £9.90. Booking Advisable on Fri, Sat. Avg Food Spend u£10.Hrs: 5-11.

DHANISTHA   SOUTH INDIAN /SRI LANKAN
74 Abbeydale Road, Sharrow, Sheffield, S7 1FD
0114 2550779

Sri Lankan Dharmazeelan Periyasamy (Dharma for short), opened this, his first restaurant, in mid 2010. Previously he ran a petrol station in Rotherham. Kerelan head chef Vijayan Narayanan is assisted by Chef Manikam, who amongst other things, makes the Dosas those lacey lentil-flour pankcakes, eg Masala Dosa £5, over a foot long, filled with potato curry and served with pots of sambar (a stew of vegetables and spices), coconut chutney and a mint and coriander dip. Uppuma (the Asian version of couscous, Pakoras, Rolls and Soups. Idly £3.50, comes with coconut, tomato and chill ichutneys. Rasam Soup £2.50 the Kerelan soup made from tomatoes, tamarind , ginger, garlic and chilli. Mains include Konju Manga (prawn and mango) Curry £7.50, Mutton Malabar £6 Cochin Prawn Curry £6.50), each in a coconut sauce. Desserts: Gulab Jamun, syrup drenched balls, Payasam vermicelli, milk, sultanas, cashew nuts, jaggery and sago, and Vattilappam a Sri Lankan dessert made from eggs, jaggery and coconut milk). *'Dhanistha's is a proper sit down restaurant, whereas East and West (next entry) is a small takeaway with a few tables and chairs. I enjoy the laid-back cafe vibe of East and West as much as I enjoy more comfort at Dhanistha's.'*   www.virtualtourist.com No takeaway or delivery option. Lunch Buffet, 12-3. Mon-Sat: 11-3.30 & 5.30-11; Sun: 12-11.

EAST & WEST   SOUTH IND/SRI LANKAN   BYO
227 Abbeydale Road, Sharrow, Sheffield, S7 1FJ
0114 258 8066   www.eastnwest.net

The first S Indian /Sri Lankan restaurant in South Yorks is called East and West. But whatever the cardinal point, if such fare is new to you, try it and become hooked. It is tiny and busy and the cook seems to serve as well. The food is superb and inexpensive and is what you would expect to eat in a traditional South Indian or Sri Lankan home. They offer a very similar menu to Dhanistha (above). Starters include Vadai £2.50, a crispy deep-fried savoury 'doughnut' of urid dal served with chutney.Masala Vadai £2.25,)a ditto with channa dal, onion and chilli. Served with chutney. £2.25; Mutton Rolls £3.25, filled with mixture of mutton, onion and spices; Fish CutletsTuna £3.25, fish and mashed potato with onion, green chilli, curry leaves and spices Amongst other things, the menu has a remarkable 14 Dosa (pancakes made of urid dal,white lentil) & rice with fillings such as potato, chicken, mutton, paneer etc. Served with sambar & chutney. Vegetable Kotthu £5 is chopped parata roti mixed with vegetable, tomato, onions and chilli. 15 curries range from £3 (dal curry) to KP £7. Licensed. BYO. Mon -Fri: 5-11; Sat-Sun: 12-11.

EVEREST TANDOORI
59-61 Chesterfield Road, Heeley, Sheffield, S8 0RL
0114 258 2975   www.everest-restaurant.co.uk

Est 1978 Despipte its name, it doesn't serve Nepalese food. It's curry house with a very long menu. Tues night e-a-m-a-y-l buffet £9. Mon-Th: 6-12:45; Fri-Sat 6-2:45; Sun 6-12:30.

TAMARIND
Old Baths, 223 Glossop Road, Sheffield, S10 2GW
0114 276 6150   tamarindrestaurant.weebly.com'

A notIce from our Sheffield curryholics: *'We are sad to report that the Saffron Club in Sheffield has closed. One of the best there was. RIP.'* Its gourmet menu was upmarket, a bit fusion and didn't come cheap, which might have been the trouble. Saffron Club's ex-owner Naz Islam thinks so. *'Sheffield likes Indian cuisine simple and standard,'* he sighed after selling up. Be that as it may, Tamarind now occupies the same corner-site venue in part of the former Glossop Road Baths, with no changes to the chic-simple design with warm spicy colours mixed with elements of natural dark wood, polished stainless steel and glass. Lighting is bright and modern including the use of fibre optic starlights and artwork, including commissioned paintings by Luca using real gold leaf. Taqmarind is one of a group of restaurants in business since 1985. They offer the curryhouse menu at affordable prices and employ three specialist chefs, one for Mughlai dishes, one for balti and biryani dishes, and one for tandoori and fish dishes. 3 course meal for 2, £10; for 4 £19. Daily: 6-11:30 Mon- Th: 12-2:30 (buffet lunch available at £6. *Branches: Dower House Bawtry; Almas Indian Brasserie, Sheffield; Bay of Bengal, Gleadless, S12.*

VEGGIE MASALA
379 South Road, Sheffield S6 3TD

Veggie Masala is what it says on the tin: like Arif's above, it's an all-vegetarian curryhouse. 15 starters, 4 salads, a range of sauces at £3.50 eg Balti, Bhuna via Madras to Vindaloo. Or there are 40 veg curries at £3.80 plus 15 specials all at £4.95 eg: Vegetable Jalfrezi, grilled onions, peppers & fresh green chillies; Vegetable Tikka Masala potato, carrot, aubergine & cauliflower in creamy sauce. Next are 17 Baltis at £4.75, 11 dishes with Paneer £4, 10 Birianis, 10 rice dishes and 5 breads … Total items 194. Sun-Th: 5-11.30 (to 12.30 Fri-Sat).

YOU SAY OK, SHEFFIELD
BUTLERS BALTI HOUSE, 46 Broad Lane, Sheffield S1 4BT Tel: 0114 276 8141   Accurately cooked Baltis
DILSHAD TANDOORI 96 The Dale, Woodseats, Sheffield S8 0PS   0114 255 5008
ZARA'S 216a Crookes, Sheffield S10 1TH 0114 266 0097. New and good reports. 5.30 to late.   Branch: Ayesha's on Ecclesal Road

WEST YORKSHIRE

Area: North of England

Adjacent Counties:
Derbyshire,
Gtr Manchester,
Lancs, N & S Yorks

Batley

SAFFRON
367 Bradford Rd, Batley, WF17 5PH   01924 441222

120-seater, opened 2006 managed by F.Singh. 'Celebrated my birthday here. It is very tastefully decorated and has friendly staff in black shirts. For starters we had mixed kebabs (one sheek kebab, one chicken kebab and one shami kebab) and also chicken kebabs. Our main courses were Lamb and Lentil Handi (a House Special) and Aloo Chana served with Pilau Rice. They were well cooked and nicely presented, tasty and very enjoyable. It seems to get quite busy, not surprising as the quality of the food is very high.' LH. Del: 5m, £10 min. Branches Ilkeley and Guiseley

Bradford

Bradford has a high pedigree curry background, with its very well-established, largely-Pakistani-Kashmiri population. This means Halal meat and few veg at the many unlicensed cheap n' cheerful spit n' sawdust caffs. Since many are strict Moslems, not all welcome alcohol. In such establishments, please check with the staff that you may BYO, and even if 'yes', always drink discretely and in moderation. The restaurants, sweet shops and cafés are no so concentrated as say, Southall.

AAKASH
Providence Pl, Bradford Rd, Cleckheaton, BD19 3PN
01274 878866   www.aakashrestaurant.co.uk

Cleckheaton, the gritty mill town in the heart of industrial Yorkshire, has been the butt of music-hall jokes for ever', says Maggie Hall in www.virtualtourist.com. Just two miles SE of Bradford city (down the M606/A638) and you're there. The venue, built in 1857 as the English Congregational Chapel, is truly imposing with its Greaco-Gothic frontage, complete with Doric pillars. Even its huge car park has an attendant. In 2001.Mohammad Iqbal Tabassum invested £1.7m transforming the redundant chapel into an 860-seat Indian restaurant describing it as *"the Largest Indian Restaurant in the World".* Maggie Hall again: *'it's praise be to God, not Allah, that the unique eating experience exists! It's housed in a handsome edifice that was until 20 years ago a Chapel. With it's vast seating capacity, it's destined for the*

Guiness Book of Records.' Stunning though it was, could Curry City Bradford support a venture so vast? Answer, no. In 2006 it went bust and was repossessed by the Bank of India. It reopened in 2007 under new management following a further £500K spend on refurbishment. This time and maybe praise be to Allah it seems to be surviving. The interior is amazing as the website shows. Bradford city name it as a tourist attraction and people, treck for miles to see inside. This is why it is in this Guide, for its decor. As for the food it is competent, as to be expected for such nightly volumes. All the traditional curries and sides appear on the menu. Buffet £11, kids half price. On the a la carte, there is tandoored salmon marinated in coriander seeds, lamb chops , samosas and kebabs. Highlight on Thursday nights: they cook a whole lamb on a bed of fragrant rice (when its gone it's gone!). They also have a café offering Starbucks coffee, Haagen Dazs ice cream, fruit smoothies, English desserts and Panini's. Tue-Sun: Aakash Café : 4-11; Restaurant: 6-10.45.

AKBARS TOP 100
1276 Leeds Road, Bradford, BD3 8LF
01274 773311   www.akbars.co.uk

In 1988, Shabir Hussain, then 18, decided he wanted to open his own restaurant. In 1995 the dream was realised with the opening of a small restaurant, seating 28, on this site. Now it's grown to five shopfronts and 150 seats.there are ten other Alkbars and counting. One of the reasons for Akbar's success is the absolute authenticity of Pakistani food. There are Lahori Style Dishes, original baltis, Handi of the day, traditional Desi-Apna Style, accompaniments and Desserts. There are few restaurants that can match Akbar's in London (and we hear of plans to open there. So please bring it on). Liver Tikka, £3.45, Chicken liver mixed with special spices including ginger, garlic and fresh coriander cooked slowly grilled. Chicken or Fish Nambali, £3.90, pieces marinated, grilled and garnished with melting cheese, served with fried onions, peppers, tomatoes and potatoes; Akbar's Special Veg Pakora, £3.75, onion, potatoes, mushroom, bhindi and paneer served with warm salad. Mains specials: Roshan Lal, £9, a spicy lamb dish cooked with onions, tomatoes and peppers in a rich sauce, garnished with onions and coriander; Chef's Challenge, £12, chicken, lamb keema and potatoes cooked in the famous Akbar's balti sauce served with naan and pilau rice. If one can finish this challenge alone you will qualify for a free dessert. If you are new to Akbars, the set menu at £18 is a start. If you're Pakistani or adventurous there are Desi Apni dishes, means "native" (or "authentic") food. And really authentic Lahori dishes on offer, all £8, which attracts custom, and it's great for any adventurous palet. Magaz (brain); Paya (trotters); Gurda Kapoora (kidneys and testicles); Ojri (tripe); Nihari (shanks on the bone); Haleem (a gruel of mutton, wheat, barley, lentils and spices). There is a full range of Indian and other desserts at £2.60, Ras Malai, Gulab Jamon, Kulfi, Gajar Halva, and £2.90: Chocolate Chip Brownie and Sticky Toffee Pudding with ice cream. 'All portions were over generous, so were could not manage a sweet, despite the excellent choices.' I see on the menu, Gajar Halwa (carrot cake), which I love! An upmarket restaurant with excellent cuisine, efficient service, providing a highly enjoyable experience.' TE. House wine from £11.95. CTM £9.45, Pilau Rice or Naan £1.95, pops not served. 'Akbars on Leeds Rd is excellent, always heaving with a good atmos.' AD. Mon-Fri: 5-12; Sat: from; Sun: 2-11:30. Branches: Café below and Birmingham, Glasgow, Manchester, Leeds (2), Middlesbrough, Newcastle, Rotherham and York.

AKBARS BRADFORD CAFE
524 Leeds Road, Bradford, BD3 9SB
01274 737458   www.akbars.co.uk

Seventh branch (2008) of ten of the rapidly expanding chain. Mon-Sat: Noon-Mdnt; Sun: 2-10. See previous entry for Akbar for details.

ANAMS   KASHMIRI   BYO
211 Great Horton Road, Bradford, BD7 1RP
01274 522626   www.anams.co.uk

Anams is another large venue (seating 450) with an extavagant interior. It is in a former Methodist church which has been augmented with a modern two-storey conservatory-style frontage. A huge welcoming bar/lounge leads into the dining room, complete with floor-sited coi carp fish pool, surrounded by brass handrails and a bridge. Seating surrounds the pool and is continued in a gallery above. A huge stained-glass feature is suspended from the ceiling. The menu has all the usual favourites on offer together with some chefs speciality dishes. Why not start your meal with Anams Lamb Chops which is spring lamb chops marinated overnight and then grilled on charcoal. For mains why not try the Nihari which is large pieces of lamb served in a rich aromatic sauce served with green chillies, onions and coriander. Please note the restaurant does not serve alcohol. 11am-1am.

AWADH   PAN INDIAN
1060 Manchester Road, Bradford, BD5 8NN
01274 725565   www.awadhrestaurant.co.uk

Awadh specialise in regional Indian food as they poetically put it *'from the icy mountains of Kashmir in the North, to the back waters of Kerala in the South and from the deep deserts of Rajasthan in the West to lush green fields of West Bengal in the East. Awadh covers gourmet delicacies from all four major regions of India.'* Their claim to be *'the first restaurant in the UK bringing you regional Indian food'* falls short of the poetry. Actual first was the Bombay Brasserie, London SW7. Nonetheless Awadh's food is well-spoken of under chef, Zahir Khan ex Sheraton Hotels, India. And if you wish to enjoy your old school favourites, they will be there too! .They have a lounge bar and ample secured free parking. 12-12.

CARDAMON
102 Main Street, Bingley, Bradford, BD16 2JH
01274 561811   www.cardamonbingley.co.uk

Cardamon opened in 2011. Extensive menu of standard items plus some unconventionals: Bingley Locks £9.95, a unique name which is *'Chef's own creation'* of spring Chicken with rhubarb, garlic, spring onions, roasted ground cinnamon, shallots and methi, served with pilau rice; Hash Special £10.95, grilled shredded comfit of duck with fresh garlic, tamarind and flakes of red chillies, finished in a lingering piquant sauce, served with spinach rice; Ostrich £10.95, known for its lower fat and cholesterol is cooked with tamarind, cloves, garlic, spring onions, shallot and fresh bullet chillies, served with mushroom rice. Cod Rashom £7.95, chunks of fish cooked with onions, garlic, and ginger and crushed hot Mexican chillies in a orange jalfrezi sauce. 5-11.30 (Fri-Sat to 1am).   *Branch: Elachi Barnsley.*

DIAL A ROTI TAKEAWAY
66 Browning St, Bradford, BD3 9DT   01274 742030

582 t Horton Rd, Bradford, BD7 3EU   01274 522722

20 Heaton Road, Bradford, BD8 8RA   01274 490099

308 Keighley Rd, Bradford, BD9 4EY   01274 495199

Four branches selling incredibly cheap naans and rotis (chupattis) £1 with fillings such as Paya,,chicken Keema and mutton currise £3, Dhal £2.   11-10.30

INTERNATIONAL TANDOORI
KASHMIRI   BYO   01274 721449
40-42 Mannville Tce, Morley St, Bradford, BD7 1BE

Inside are basic tables and armless black leather seats. No alcohol served, but you can BYO. The cooking is Kashmiri which means saavoury and gutsy, and familiar items are there. Starters include Prawn Puri £3.90, fried king prawns served with a variety of herbs and spices. Mains include tha favourites £6 each, with biryani & jalfrezi dishes approx £1 more, and balti and tandoori chef specials at around £8 each. Meat or veg set meal £13/£16 each. The Saleem Special is chicken or lamb, cooked on the bone with tomatoes, onions, garlic, ginger & coriander.   £14. *'The food, while not being particularly sophisticated, is excellent.'* MB. Mon-Sat: 12 -2am Sunday: 5-2am.

JALDI-JALDI
Foster Square, Bradford, BD1 4RN
01274 370153   www.jaldijaldi.com

Jaldi Jaldi means "Quickly Quickly" and it is a chain of 14 fast-food outlets in Yorkshire with plans to expand jaldi jaldi nationwide. It is part of the Mumtaz brand (see below) and the menu includes snacks, sandwiches, paninis and a small range of curries.   *Branches: Bingley, Bradford (2), Bramhope, Guiseley, Harrogate, Leeds (5), Manchester (2) & Preston.* All 11-11.

KARACHI
15-17 Neal Street, Bradford BD5 0BX
01274 732015

The Karachi is one of Bradford's several carry caff institutions. Established in 1965 after the Kashmir (see next entry) 1958 and the Sweet Centre 1964. No alcohol served and the menu is limited *'but others dishes can be asked for, provided no long preparation is required. Proudly home-run with friendly and unflappable staff. Cheap, cheerful and excellent food. To round off a cracking meal I had a homemade Pistachio Kulfi, frozen solidly, but melting into a sweet and spicy mush.'* RW. *'Food is good quality, service is friendly. Decor reminded us of a school canteen, and the Guide is correct – the toilets are dreadful. Goes without saying that in Bradford it came with three chapatis. However, this was its undoing, as they were too thick meaning that you left feeling bloated.'* HR. 11am-1am; 2am Fri & Sat.

KASHMIR   BYO
27 Morley Street, Bradford, BD7 1AG   01274 726513

It opened in 1958 and seats a 200 on two floors, in simple caff-style (formica tables etc), and it's usually busy, has night-owl hours and you can't book; aficionados like the scruffier basement. *'Very popular with its local clientele.'* AT. *'Seekh Kebabs 60p very good flavour, Meat Roghan Josh £ 3.90 – not as spicy as other dishes but still good. Good service, pleasant staff.'* L&CH. *'Great basic place with a simple menu, very authentic.'* AD. *'When we asked the manager of our local Aagrah where he liked to go for a curry. he said "Kashmir,"describing the food as "really authentic',* says www.yorkshire.com. [You can't make it up! Ed.] 11am to 3am.   *Branch: Kashmir, 858 Leeds Rd, Bradford Centre. 01274 664357 (near the hospital).*

KEBABEESH   PAKISTANI
165 New Line, Greengates, BD10 0BN   01274 617188

Chef, teacher and entrepreneur Amjad Bashir opened his first restaurant on Whetley Lane in 1979. It moved to Greengates in 1987. Sons Tayab abd Jay run it now, serving Pakistani-style curries with interesting wines usch as Red Bell Black Shiraz from Australia and Cutler Creek Zinfindel from California are (both reasonably priced.) A modern, open plan and strikingly stylish restaurant seats 75. Creamy walls, earthy coloured, large slate tiles cover the floor and absolutely lovely, handmade wrought iron chairs surround marble topped tables. Cubed glass walls, green plants and ceiling spot lighting add to the calming look. 'We all had a fabulous night on Sat, but it was the food that made it!'. ls. Menu Snapshot: Jalapenos c£4, green peppers, filled with creamy sauce and coated in crispy breadcrumbs; Fish and Spinach £9.50, chunks of Haddock, spinach leaves, fenugreek, rich sauce; ls. Menu Snapshot: Jalapenos c£4, green peppers, filled with creamy sauce and coated in crispy breadcrumbs; Chicken or lamb Nahari c£10, cooked Lahori-style; Lamb Peshwari c£9, tender lamb, cooked in a delicious rich sauce, using whole and nectar of almond, garnished with fresh green coriander and medium spices; Spicy and Potato Nan £1.95. Del: 5m £5 min. Hours: 5-12; 1 Sat. *Branch: Zouk, Bradford.*

LAHORE CAFE BAR
52 Great Horton Road, Bradford BD7 1AL
01274 308508   www.mylahore.co.uk

Lahore opened in 2003 and recently refurbished its cafe bar seating 130 in four dining spaces set over four floors. Specialities include burgers and various chargrilled meat dishes, authentic curries, milkshakes, smoothies and especially our range of homemade desserts - from cakes to apple crumble and jam roly poly! Sun-Th: 11am-1am (Fri-Sat to 3am.

MUMTAZ   A-LIST   NO ALC
386-410 Great Horton Road, Bradford, BD7 3HS
01274 571861 · mumtaz.co.uk

Founder / owner Mumtaz Khan Akbar was born in Mirpur, Azad Kashmir, Pakistan and is one of the richest men in Yorkshire, with a personal wealth of £25m made largely from his Mumtaz brand of food and lifestyle products. Stone pillars, a rotating metal sign and a first-floor bow-fronted conservatory make the huge frontage stand out. You enter into via the store selling those own-label products. The restaurant has glass-topped tables and high-backed black leather chairs, cream walls, downlighters and stainless-steel conical plant pots. The Queen dined here in 2007 and described the food as *'beautiful'*. It is always busy and Asian families love it. Starters include Pani Puri, a crisp mini puri shell filledwith chickpeas and tart tamarind sauce or Chicken Boti, which is marinated, chargrilled skewers of chicken each £3.65. Mains include Kahari Murgh Keema £6.85 or £13 depending on portion size, minced chicken curry or Kahari Lamb Sookha Boohna £14.50 a dry curry or Chilli Paneer £9 with garlic, ginger, black pepper, tomatoes and coriander. There are Indian desserts and other Indian sweets, eg Falooda, Gulab Jaman, Kulfi and Rasmalai. Mumtaz permits no-alcohol, but the lassis or freshly squeezed juices £3.75 each are legion. *'Friday lunch time in Bradford means one of two things Mumtaz or International. Mumtaz won this time., and as was usual quite busy.I ordered the Karahai Chicken, as it was so good last time, with plain rice and a tandoori roti and was not disappointed. I also ordered a Coke (expensive) and a bottle of water which arrived in its own Mumtaz bottle at no charge. Meal arrived quickly, with a small bowl of salad, dressing superb. Again the only word I can use to describe the quality is 'OUTSTANDING'. Any curry lover visiting Bradford MUST visit this restaurant. Only let down (for some) is no alcohol) but for this quality even I can forego a beer! Billing is a totally confusing as they only tick what you've had and it is then added up at the counter. This does cause a great deal of confusion on large tables who all paying separately!'* D, J &HB. And another visit: *'Parking is still a nightmare even at lunch time. Busy for a Friday lunch time. Service excellent as a jug of water,) pops and chutney arrived as soon as I was seated. Water cold, Pops warm and fresh, standard Chutney tray. Standard menu with no surprises. Ordered the Chicken Achari with pillau rice which arrived at the table quite quickly. Plenty of chicken in a well spiced sauce with a lovely pickle kick. The rice was nice and fluffy and had a good flavour but was a little on the sparse side. This time they did not charge for the poppadom and chutney and the meal was excellent quality and excellent value at just just £7.95. Glad I'm not in Bradford too often as I would be split between here and the Mumtaz.* Dave Bridge Wallasey. Sun-Th: 11am-12 (to 1am Fri-Sat). *Branch: Mumtaj Leeds.*

NAWAAB
32 Manor Row, Bradford,. BD1 4QE
01274 720371   www.nawaabbradford.co.uk

'Nawaab' literally means 'viceroy, the representative of Royalty'. In 1947, the Indian subcontinent had 528 principalities each of which had its own ruler, The Nawaab who enjoyed a lavish lifestyle. Bradford's Nawaab was a bank until 1988 and now has seating for 200 plus a separate dining area for private functions and a bar. The a la carte menu includes all the regular dishes and some new specials. Nawaab Tandoori Mix £5.45, combination of chicken tikka, lamb chops, king prawn tikka, seekh kebab and chicken livers served on a hot sizzler plate; Garlic Mushrooms £2.50, marinated in a spicy garlic sauce, then dipped in egg yolk and breadcrumbs, then deep-fried; Nirali Special, £9, dchicken marinated with yoghurt and special masala sauce with selected herbs, cooked with fresh tomatoes, ginger, onions and a blend of spices with fresh double cream, garnished with cashew nuts and fried onions; Machli Pakora £2.95, strips of haddock marinated with herbs and spices coated with gram flour then deep-fried. Mains include: Aloo Bukhara Lamb £7.50, marinated in spiced yoghurt, then cooked with plums, ginger, garlic, tomatoes and bayleaf, garnished with fresh ginger & coriander; Mili Juli Sabzi Makhani, £6.95, fresh seasonal vegetables cooked with mild herbs, fresh cream and a delicately spiced sauce. Mon-Th: 5.30-11.30; Fri-Sat -12.30; Sun: 4-11.

NAWAAB
74 Westgate, Hill Street, Bradford, BD4 0YD
01274 681545

The latest 2008 Nawaab venture is a £200K convertion of the former Lapwater Hall in Tong, Bradford into a 120 seat restaurant, banqueting suite for 150 and conference centre. The venue was opened in 2011. Parking for around 90 cars. Menu as above. Mon-Th: 6-11; Fri-Sat -12.; Sun: 4-10. *Branches: Branches: Huddersfield, Leeds, Manchester M19.*

OMAR KHAN'S
30 Little Horton Lane, Bradford, BD5 0AL
01274 390777   www.omarkhans.co.uk

It was established in 1990 and known then as the Shah Jehan. The owner is one Omar Khan and his clients suggested he used is own name for his venue. OK, regulars call it OK's, right? That said it seats 150 over

Its 3 stylish and luxuriously decorated rooms with pretty red chairs for your tables and with lovely leather sofas to relax on, while waiting for a T/a. OK's three branches have identical menus. Good comments on all three branches, usually: *'An extremely smart restaurant with friendly service throughout. We had the whole leg of lamb ordered 24 hours in advance. Superb. Highly recommended.'* CT. *'Very, very, very good.'* LH.t's the regular menu with starters av £3 and mains £7. Non-Veg Meal for 2, £24.50: Pops & Picks. Mix Sizzler – an assortment of grilled starters followed by Chicken Rogalli, Lamb Achaari, Sag Aloo, Pilau Rice & Peshwaari Nan. *'Omar Khans is good, very fresh tasting'*. AD. Tu-Fri: 12-2; Mon-Th: 5-11.30 (Fri to 12.30); Sat: 12-12.30 (Sun to 11.30). Branches: 6 North Gate, Baildon, Bfd N; 726 Manchester Rd, Chapel Green, Bradford S. New: *£1m spent to convert and extend the Snaygill Arms pub to a 100 seat OK branch. Its USP that it is alongside the lovely Leeds Liverpool canal so there's a patio plus an integral stone fireplace midships inside.*

PAZEEKAH
1362 Leeds Rd, Thornbury, Bradford   01274 664943

Ex bus driver Mazhar-ul-Haq's tells us he likes to change the decor and the menu regularly, *'because that's what customers want to see.'* SBYO 130-seater Pakistani venue. Chef/manager is son Mohammed Jamil. 4-12.30; 1.30 Sat. *They also own an 18,000 sq ft Asian Superstore, selling Asian food, and utensils at 91 Edderthorpe St, off Leeds Road, Bradford.*

PRASHAD   INDIAN VEGETARIAN   NO ALC
86 Horton Grange Road, Bradford, BD7 2DW
01274 575893   www.prashad.co.uk   **TOP 100**

Prashad, meaning 'blessed food' was established as far back as 1992 by Mohan and Kaushy Patel, selling traditional Indian snacks and sweets, and by 2004 a restaurant offering traditional Gujarati and Punjabi vegetarian cuisine, at which time eldest son Bobby Patel and his wife Minal joined the team. Minal and Kaushy cook while Bobby and Mohan are 'front of house'. It came to national prominnence when it reached the final of Channel 4's Ramsay's *'Best Restaurant'*. Gujarati cuisine is quite mild and sweet and is represented by Pattra, colocasia leaf rolled Swiaa-roll style with a besan flour filling then steamed and garnished with mustard seed oil; Pea Kachori mashed spiced pea and garlic balls in chapatti casing then deep-fried; Chef's Thali (available until 3pm and all day Weds) £14, a traditional Gujarati meal all in one: Starter, two curries, 3 rotlis, rice, papodom, dhal / khadi, and a dessert. Punjabi cuisine is richer and more robust, eg Chole £9 cooked in a rich spicy onion and tomato base. South Indian cuisine is rice-based, and the best known dish is Massala Dosa, £8.45 rice flour thin pancake served with spicy lentil soup (Sambar), and cool coconut & yoghurt chutney. Monster version (for 2 and the 'WOW' factor) £16.50; Uttapam £8, served with soup and cool coconut & yoghurt chutney. Prashad iis unlicenced and alcohol is not permitted. Lassi Jug (for 4) mango, massala or sweet. Tu-Fri: 11-3 & 6-10.30; Sat-Sunday: 11-10.30. Mon closed.

PUNJAB SWEET HOUSE   UN LIC
126 Listerhills Rd, Bradford, BD7 1JR   01274 720308

The sweet/snack shop was established in 1977 and the restaurant in 2000. Everything is prepared on site in the open kitchen.The restaurant specialises in grilled meats and fish but also serves the popular curries we all know. There are also a number of vegetarian specialities also on offer. You can also get Iranian Kebabs with a choice of grilled meats or fish. Try the Falooda dessert, an Indian Knickerbocker glory or the Rasmalai, a creamy Indian sweet. The restaurant is not licensed but offers soft drinks and Lassi together, teas and coffees. 12-12.

RAWAL   PAKISTANI   BYO
3 Wilton St, off Morley St, B'fd   01274 720030

Owner-Chef Abdul P Butt cooks Pakistani curries in his open kitchen, Mobin Iqbal manages the 50-seater and promises a 10% disc to Guide readers. Special: Grand Slam, mixture of meat, chicken, keema and fresh vegetables, with Pullao Rice £5.70. Zam-Zam Special, meat, chicken, king prawns, and chick peas, served with Pullao Rice £5.70. Rawal claims *'Once tried never forgotten'.* DC agrees: *'Great price, great food'.* T/a: student 10% disc. BYO. 5-2; 3 Fri & Sat; closed Mon.

SAFFRON DESI   www.saffrondesi.com
1362 Leeds Rd, Bradford, BD3 8ND   01274 663999

'If you want to do curry business in an Asian area, you got to be brilliant', says Head Chef Parvez Akhtar. *'We have seating for 230 guests'* he continues, *'and we have a glass-surround VIP suite.'* Starters include: Chappal Kebab.. £2.40, minced lamb mixed with gram flour, spices, green chillies and herbs then deep-fried. Signature Dishes: Chicken Masti £6.90, cooked with chef's special sauce and garnished with fresh ginger & coriander; Gujar Khan Special £7.50, lamb on the bone cooked with fresh green chillies, tomatoes, spring onions, spices and a hint of cheese, garnished with ginger, coriander and fried onions; Saffron Ka Khana £6.90, Chicken or lamb: a complex dish with many ingredients and roasted spices creating a rich colour; Vensi £7.25, cooked with fresh cream=with herbs, spices, tomatoes & peppers; Liver Special £6.50, chicken liver cooked with a hint of cheese, green chillies, tomatoes, special herbs and spices, garnished with a hint of butter and & coriander. Sun- Th: 5-11.30 (Fri-Sat to 12.30).

SHABAB   www.shabab.co.uk
1099 Thornton Rd, Bradford   01274 815760

A modern detached building, with lots of Indian artefacts. Glass covered tables, low Indian-style chairs, nice carpet. *Thoroughly recommended.'* T&MH. Branch: *Shabab, 2 Eastgate, Leeds, 0113 246 8988*

SWEET CENTRE RESTAURANT
110 - 114 Lumb Lane, Bradford, BD8 7RS   01274 731735   www.sweetcentrerestaurant.com

Opened in 1964, and was Bradford's second curry venue. At the counter you order savouries and sweets by the pound weight. In 1983 they acquired next door and expansion began. This sufficed until 1999 when a refurb took place. The 100-seater sit-down restaurant is top-notch too: ' *Excellent. Srvice good and the food very tasty.*' SL. *'I am told the Sweet Centre is fantastic but have never tried it.'* Well, Alastair, you must try it. The massive 280-seater banquet room alongside at 110/4 Lumb Lane shares the phone, the kitchens and the same wonderful food and service. 11.30-11.30 (to 1am Fri-Sat).

THE THREE SINGHS
254 Sticker Lane, Culter Heights Bradford BD4 8RN
01274 688799:   www.3singhs.com

Jaj and Gibby's Restaurant and Bar is on the eastern ring road in a detatched building painted cream with red outlining. It has an enormous car park and two dining floors with modern minimalistic decor including tall black plastic chairs seemingly standing stiffly to attention. *'You're always only a short walk from the bar!'* says Gibby. The menu reads like the conventional formula (starter av: £3, tandoori £4, mains £7. Mon-Fri: 12-11; Sat: 3-11 (Sun to 10:30). *Branch: Three Singhs Takeaway at Bolton Rd, BD2.*

ZOUK   PAKISTANI   TOP 100
1312 Leeds Road, Bradford, BD3 8LF
01274 258025   www.zoukteabar.co.uk

Just 100 metres downwind of Akbars, Mudassar and Tayub Bashir opened Zouk Tea Bar and Grill in October 2006 claiming to be the first Yorkshire restaurant with a theatre-style kitchen. Their father, Amjad Bashir, already 30 years experience in the industry. Daughter Habiba launched the Zouk cooking school.   Zoouk delivers authentic Lahore style Pakistani street cuisine, grills cooked over charcoal or sigri (water) grills and curries. Their seafood menu includes dishes with Red Snapper and Sea Bass to Scallops, King Prawns and Lobster. The chef's specials board changes every fortnight and has unusual regional dishes: Junglee Chicken £4.Char-grilled quarter baby chicken marinated in coriander, chillies and mint leaf; Pahari Tikka, £4 a Kashmir speciality of lamb fillet pieces marinated in mashed papaya and garam masala. Punjabi Lollipop, £3.25, chicken marinated in pomegranite wrapped around a chicken wing then gently cooked over hot charcoal. Mains: Lamb Nahari (knuckle) is so popular; Chicken Haleem, £78, a Delhi speciality: slivers of chicken breast cooked with four different types of lentils and cracked wheat; Sindhi Biriyani, £8.50, chicken fillet with potatoes & plums cooked in basmati rice then tossed with whole garam masalas. Served with raita or curry sauce; Gurda Keema £10, traditional Pakistani dish of minced lamb and kidneys cooked in ginger, garlic and a blend of spices Paya, £7, traditional dish of sheeps trotters cooked slowly until the meat is tender with a rich & spicy broth; Magaz, £7, Pakistani speciality of sheep's brain pan-ried with onions, tomatoes, green chillies & garam masala. More details on Manchester branch, page 248. 10am-12 mdnt.

Huddersfield

AAGRAH   A-LIST
250 Wakefield Road, Denbydale, Huddersfield,
HD8 8SU   01484 866266

'Occupies a former pub on the main road through Denby Dale, a town more famous for its pies! The layout makes for a surprisingly intimate 60 seater restaurant, being spread across two floors. Well executed decoration, in keeping with the former role of the building, think smart pub with a subcontinental theme. Highly enjoyable and equally recommended.' RW. Evening Buffet, First floor Sun/Mon to 9pm. Mon-Th: 6-11:30 / Fr-Sa: to Mdnt / Sun: 4:30-10.30. See Shipley, W.Yorks for details and branch list.

CHILLI LOUNGE-
70 John William Street, Huddersfield, HD1 1EH
01484 517 566   www.chillyloungehuddersfield.co.uk

It has everything you'd expect from a Bangladeshi curryhouse, with some plusses eg: Ostrich, venison curries £9.50 eg Jalfrezi cooked with green chillies; Jaflongee with capsicum & onions, delicately spiced, served on a sizzler; Silsila, sliced onions & peppers cooked in medium strength sauce with fresh coriander; Machli Sallom £7.25, diced fish cooked in a medium sauce with fresh garlic and finely chopped onions, green peppers and green masala. *'Chilli Lounge is back up on form, and contrary to my last e-mail, it still has Staff curries on the menu'* JP. Bangladesh Staff Curry £7.25, chicken or lamb on-the-bone, a traditional home-style curry. Mon- Th: 6-11.30 (Fri-Sat to 12); Sun: 5.30-11.

NAWAAB
35 Westgate, Huddersfield, WestYorks. HD1 1NY
01484 422775

The restaurant is situated in a former bank, built in 1900's in the Georgian style. Its decor complements the original features with seating for around 100 diners. The bar area includes seating where you are able to relax with a drink before your meal.See Nawab Bradford for menu details. Mon-Th: 5.30-11; Fri-Sat from 5; Sun: 1-11. *Branches: Bradford, Leeds, Manchester M19 and six in Mallorca & Benidorm.*

Keighley

SHIMLA SPICE
14 South Street, Keighley, BD21 1NR
01535 602040   www.shimlaspice.co.uk

Three brothers in 1998, Basharat, Mo and Mahmood had jobs in London 'from sink to head chefs and restaurant managers then came "home" to Keighley to set up their first eatery, Shimla Spice in 1998. It is managed by Faisal Hussain. The 75 seater is on a corner site and is decorated beautifully, with ornate plasterwork on ceiling and walls, colonial fans, large chandelier, 'Tiffany' lamps and cane furniture. The menu is huge and contains everyhing you could want and more eg: Chicken or Lamb Pakora £3.10, diced boneless chicken or lamb with special herbs and spices, coated with gram flour and deep-fried, served with mint sauce and salad; Liver Tikka £3.10, chicken liver marinated in spices and herbs, cooked over charcoal on skewers. Desi Dishes are cooked traditional Punjabi style, giving an authentic taste, Mild, Medium or Hot eg: Desi Chicken Handi £6.95, cooked with yoghurt. Sun & Tu-Th : 5.- 11; Fri-Sat: to 12.30. (Mon closed). *Branch: Shipley, see below.*

ZOLSHA

Dalesway Skipton Road, Keighley, BD20 7SA
01535 630339 / 636999   www.zolsha.com

Within six months of working as a porter in his initial job young Tufail Miah decided, that he wanted to open his own restaurant. In 2007, he launched Zolsha as his dream accomplished! The name 'Zolsha' is a word widely known as a 'place of gathering' in Bengali language and thus he thought what better name for a restaurant! The menu is large formula with all the favourites plus ostrich and venison at regular prices. 5:30- 11:00 (Fri-Sat:to 11:30).

Leeds

AAGRAH   www.aagrah.com   A-LIST
See Shipley, for details and branch list.

AAGRAH LEEDS CITY, St Peter's Square, Quarry Hill, Leeds, LS9 8AH   0113 2455 667

165 cap. Under BBC Yorkshire. Mon-Sat: 5:30-12 (Sun to 11).

AAGRAH, Aberford Road, Garforth, Leeds, LS25 2HF   0113 287 6606

Nephew Wasim Aslam manages this 150-seater, opened 1993. Fourth of the very popular Aagrahs, refurbished 2006. Select your favourite fish from the "fruits of the sea" display then have it cooked and served at the table with a range of delicate sauces and marinades. Mon-Sat:5:30-11:30 / Sun: 4:30-10:30.

AAGRAH, 33-39 Harrogate Rd, Chapel Allerton, Leeds, LS7 3PD   0113 262 4722

Cap 100. Buffet Sun/Mon. To 9.30. Mon-Sat:5:30-11:30; Sun: 4:30-10:30. Akbars

AKBARS   A-LIST
15 Eastgate, Leeds, LS2 7LY
0113 245 6566   www.akbars.co.uk

'*After a business meeting our leader invited five of us to Akbars for dinner. Centrally situated on Eastgate (near the famous Playhouse) we were swiftly met at the door by a smiling waiter and seated with a Cobra beer. Akbars is a large Victorian building, converted to be an 'theme' restaurant with lots of black marble and the upstairs bar fronted by an Egyptian Tutenkhamun display. The ceiling was filled with a myriad of star lights (or was that the effect of the drink) The overall effect was an exotic ambience that set the scene for a relaxing meal'* TE. Mon-Sat: 5-Mdnt / Sun: -11:30. *Branches: Second (2003) branch of ten of the rapidly expanding chain.*

AKBARS   TOP 100
Minerva House, 16 Greek Street, Leeds, LS1 5RU
0113 242 5426   www.akbars.co.uk

Third (2004) branch of ten of the rapidly expanding chain. *(see above).* Akbar the Grand was the epithet given to the greatest Moghul emperor. '*A wonderful restaurant, leather chairs, glass tables, pin spot lighting. Certainly lives up to its name with highly modern decor across a spacious split-level restaurant with ceiling, wall and floor lighting creating a luxurious ambience. On entering we were swiftly greeted and shown to our table by a smartly dressed waiter who placed fresh linen napkins on our laps and took our order. The massive 'Family Garlic Nan' arrived hanging on a tall pedestal, we tore into it and found it had a beautifully light texture. Definitely recommended.*' TE. Mon-Sat: 5-12 (Sun: to 11:30) *Branches: See previous entry.*

AZRAM'S SHEESH MAHAL   TOP 100
348 Kirkstall Rd, Leeds, LS4 2DS
0113 230 4161   www.sheeshmahal.co.uk

Opened in 1987, and taken over by head chef Azram Chaudhry in 1999. It seats 76 with a further room for 38. Azram's as the locals know it is easy to find on its prominent corner site. And of those regulars, Azram says '*many eat there every week. I know them on a personal level, and they treat it as a second home. They come from all over, and include personalities from Yorkshire TV just up the road. Even The Australian cricket team have enjoyed the food at the Sheesh Mahal.*' Howzat! Pakistani Specials include: Kofta Special, Balti Murgh, Murgh Punchabi Masala; Chicken Laziz £6, with garlic, lemon, tomatoes and black pepper; Gosht Palak Paneer £7, Indian cheese, lamb and spinach; Keema Chana £6.50, minced lamb with chickpeas. '*Highly recommend the food, service and ambience. All dishes reasonably priced. Azram is a first rate host, well liked by clients. Welcomes children and family groups.*' EP. You might get a disc if you show them this Guide. 5-12. *Branch: Sheesh Mahal, 48, Harrowgate Road, Chapel Allerton, Leeds.*

THE BIRD BY VINEET   A-LIST
Clarence Dock, 4 The Boulevard, Leeds, LS10 1PZ
0113 341 3244   www.leeds.aleacasinos.com/restaurant

This is Michelin-starred Vineet Bhatia's first venture outside London (see page 133). And at first sight it is a venture with curious location and with a curious name. The 90 seater Bird (British Indian Design Restaurant) complete with theatre kitchen and a 16 seat private dining room. It is one

COBRA
SPLENDIDLY INDIAN, SUPERBLY SMOOTH

Azram's Sheesh Mahal
Fully Licensed Restaurant

- Top 30 British Curry Awards
- Yep-Olivier Awarded 18 out of 20
- 4 stars in National Guide of Cuisine
- Best in North of England Tiffin Cup 2011
- Winner Best Indian Leeds Restaurant Awards 2007

346-348 Kirkstall Rd
Leeds LS4 2DS
0113 230 4161
0113 230 7799
5pm to Midnight, daily

48 Harrogate Road
Leeds LS7 4LA
0113 237 4035
0113 237 4036
6pm to Midnight, daily

www.sheeshmahal.co.uk

---

of two restaurants in the Alea casino building. (The other is fronted by James Martin). The casino building is one element of the dock development which includes apartments, shops and restaurants including the 100 cover Café Aagrah and Mumtaz. The nearby car park has a direct link from the 4th floor to the casino. The reception area leads to the ground floor gaming area gaming area which has slot machines and roulette stations. An escalator leads up to the first floor and the large main gaming room. You have to pass this room to access Bird, where the menu is the same as Vineet's London Rasoi but the prices are less than half. Casinos in general have clients with money to spend and their gambling is enhanced buy good food. Alea obliged by head-hunting Vineet and Martin to design menus and endorse the restaurants. Part of the remit is their appearances from time to time. Casinos want their clients' money mainly spent in the Casinos, so Alea subsidise the restaurants prices to make them even more appealing. There is no admission to the building (including Bird) for anyone under 21 (gambling rules) so you are assured of a mature adult-only dining experience. A further escalator leads to the mezzanine floor where the poker room is located along with a viewing gallery which overlooks the main gaming floor and bar. The casino is pure bling, but Bird has an elegance expected of Vineet. Daytime is bright thanks windows surrounding a high ceiling giving cathedral gravitas. Tables are square as are the chairs, and no linen or carpets prevail. The night atmosphere is quite different with hanging lamps and red neon strips making their play. Head Chef Vivek Kashiwale has worked at Rasoi and executes Vineet's recipes faithfully. Starters include Kebabs & Grills £5.25 each, Pan-Grilled Keralan-Style Crab & Corn Cake; Mustard & Curry Leaf Flavoured Chicken Tikka. Indian Street Food £5.25 each: Mumbai-Style Battered Fish Pakodas; Spiced Sesame-Crusted Chicken Lollipops; Crisp Cauliflower Fritters with Bird's Chilli Ketchup. Main Course examples: priced as half or full portions: Konkani Fish Masala £5.50/9.25, with Tomatoes & Peanuts; Fishermen's Poached Scallops £5.50/9.25, Tempered with Curry Leaves Chicken Tikka £5.50/8.25, Tossed with Dill Leaves & Tomatoes; Deccan Lamb £5.50/8.95, with Sorrel & Spinach Leaves, Mumbai's Favourite Pav-Bhaji £3.50/6.50, Rajma-Red Kidney Beans £3.50/6.50, cooked North Indian style. Desserts eg: Fresh Rose Petal - Vanilla Bean Kulfi with Baby Gulab Jamuns; Orange Rice Kheer Dark Chocolate Rabdi, malted teezer ice cream. Early Bird Menu: 2 courses £15, 3 courses £20 (available from 6-8pm). Mon-Weds: 6-12 (last orders 11); Th-Sat: 6pm-1am (last orders 11pm)Sun: 6-12 (last orders 10pm).

DARBAR **TOP 100**
16 Kirkgate, Leeds Centre, LS1 6BY 0113 246 0381 www.darbar.co.uk

Darbar's front door is next to House of Fraser. A turbaned doorman welcomes you at *'a very ordinary street-level door, but upstairs the decor is a revelation.'*

HJC. *'It's exotic, with traditional Moghul paintings and an antique Haweli (palace) door, specially brought from India. Has a very impressive interior. Room is large and the decor promotes the Indian Palace feeling – spacious yet warm and elegant'.* AG *'Excellent restaurant, especially at lunchtime, self service buffet. Probably deserves TOP 100, although I am always slightly suspicious of Indians with grandiose decor.'* RC. [You'd be suspicious of India then, Robert! -Ed]. *'Very good service and cooking. And, the decor is marvellous.'* SL. *'Overall this restaurant is superb.* HJC. Special: Murgh Lahori, bone-off spring chicken, tangy spices, green coriander, cream, yoghurt, tomatoes and ginger. Daal Mash, white lentils cooked in butter with ginger, garlic and fried onion. Strawberry Lassi (large jug). min charge: £18 evenings. Lunch e-a-m-a-y-l c£6. Hours: 11.30-2.30 & 6-11.30; Sun closed.

GEORGETOWN   A-LIST
Dysons Clock Building, 24, Briggate, Leeds, LS1 6EP 0870 755 7753

Opened in Leeds in the historic Dyson's Clock Building attached to the Leeds Marriott Hotel, Colonial Malaysian Restaurant, It is a very elegant restaurant indeed, with all the original shop fittings, perfectly restored. You can eat curries from Malaysia, Indian and China. I have eaten here and it is all fabulous. Singapore Slings are the BEST! Full details see Kenilworth Warks

HANSA'S   GUJARATI VEGETARIAN   A-LIST
72 North Street, Leeds, LS2 7PN
0113 244 4408   www.hansasrestaurant.com

This is a rarity, even in the London area: a Gujarati vegetarian restaurant, but here in Leeds it is a northern treasure owned by Mr Kishor, front of house and Mrs Hansa Dabhi, chef, whose pure Indian vegetarian food proves once again that a good curry need not always contain meat. Hansa has been serving her brand of home-cooking with influences from her East African and Gujarati background since 1987, making it *'Leeds' best kept secret!'* But it is not this Guide's best kept secret. We awarded Hansa's UK Best Vegetarian in 1992 which keeps them in our A-LIST. Hansa does all things perfectly: Starters include: Patra £4.25, tropical colocasia leaves pasted with a curried batter, rolled, steamed and stir-fried with onions, sweetcorn, mustard and sesame seeds; Khasta Kachori £4, a Gujarati snack with a difference! Spicy maag-daal, puri, stuffed with a chickpeas and potato mixture, served with a tangy tamarind and onion chutney garnish; Tirangi Dhokhra £4, a steamed rice-cake, made with red and green-chillic hutneys layered within the savoury cake, served with a spicy mustard and sesame seed garnishing and coconut chutney. Mains include: Ringan na Ravaiya £7, Kenyan aubergines, stuffed with a spice masala with onions and coarsely ground peanuts; Gheloda-ne-Marcha £7, Hansa's creation, a dry curry made with tender mini cucumber (Gheloda), potato and peppers (Marcha); Channa Daal-ne-Doothi (bottle gourd) £6.50, cooked with Channa Daal, black-eyed beans (Chora) and mushroom cooked in a curry sauce. Four desserts include Boondi £4, miniature gram-flour droplets, deep-fried then soaked in mouth-watering syrup and garnished with sultanas and almonds, served hot with cream. Hansa's Special Thali (£11.50, 2 curries, rotli or puri, plain or pilau rice, daal or kadhi, farsan, shrikhand or mango pulp, papad and a glass of lassi – sweet or salty. *'I particularly enjoyed the crunchy, spicy flavour of the Shrikand.'* DM. *'As a non-veg I went with an open mind. Food was fine but portions small.'* DB. *'Exquisite Lassi, portions small.'* DO'R. Mon-Th: 5-10; Sat to 11 Fri 6-11 Sun: 12-2 Sun.

NAWAAB
1 Wellesley Hotel, Wellington St, Leeds, LS1 4WG
0113 244 2979   www.nawaabsheffield.co.uk

'Nawab is a busy, upmarket restaurant. We were swiftly met at the door by a smiling waiter and seated with a Cobra. Part of the ground floor of a large Victorian hotel is converted into a modern 'brasserie' theme. Warm, crisp Popadums and a tangy selection of pickles were washed down with more Cobra's followed by Chicken Tikka Dupiaza, King Prawn Madras and Chicken Madras with fragrant Pullao Rice and Nan Bread. Excellent cuisine, efficient service and provides a highly enjoyed experience with good value for money.' TE. Branches: Nawaab, 35, Westgate, Huddersfield and more info on Nawaab, 32, Manor Row, Bradford. Tu-Fri Buffet 12-2. Mon-Th: 5.30-11.30 Fri-Sat to 12.30. Sun closed.

Shipley

AAGRAH   A-LIST

Aagrah House, 4 Saltaire Road, Shipley, BD18 3HN
01274 530880   www.aagrah.com

In 1977 in Westgate Shipley a 50-seater restaurant was opened by Mohammed Sabir. He called it Aagrah, presumably spelling it with the double 'aa' to get first listing in the phone book. His son Mohammed Aslam was a London bus driver at the time, but he recognised the potential and started to expand, assisted later by brother Zafar Iqbal. The family is Pakistani Kashmiris and they were selling their food style. Decor was also Kashmiri-style with attractive block-print table linen and those fabulous handmade, hand-painted colourful lacquered chairs with the cute tinkly bells, especially commissioned in Pakistan (£60 each). Gradually Aslam encouraged his extended family to join the enterprise as managers, staff and cooks. With increasing impetus the other branches have been brought on-stream, as stylish and upmarket restaurants. Today Aslam is chairman of an expanding empire of 14 restaurants with 400 staff serving 18,000 diners a week. Self-taught cook Aslam has insisted that all family members also learn, training in both the kitchens and out front to NVQ level. This way the service

SPLENDIDLY INDIAN, SUPERBLY SMOOTH

and food in all the Aagrah restaurants is of equal standard. The menus at all the branches is identical. Starters include Yahknee, spicy chicken soup, £2.50, and Chicken Liver Tikka £3.20, marinated and cooked over charcoal, served with salad; Paneer Tikka £4.20, cubed cheese, marinated and tandoored. Main courses include many meat, chicken and fish dishes. Aslam's specials include Murgh Hyderabadi £8.50, spring chicken, tangy spices, coriander, cream, yoghurt, tomatoes, ginger; Nihari £9, lamb shank; Safed Mas £9, the Rajasthani 'white' lamb curry; Monkfish appears in several dishes £12; Vegetable Ginger £7, is cauliflower, courgette, aubergine, carrot, peas, turnip, and capsicum with a substantial amount of ginger, garlic, tomatoes, coriander leaves, aniseed, green chillies and black cardamom. Cheese and Onion Nan, £2.50.Set meals from £18 pp min 4, 4 starters, 4 curries, 4 sides, 2 nan & coffee. The ultimate menu item (advance order and pay) is the Whole Stuffed Lamd, £270. It is marinated in vinegar, yoghurt, garam masala, garkic and spices and stuffed with curried eggs, potaotes, and mushrooms then its tandoored. It comes with 4 veg curries, 7 nan and salad and will serve 15 or more.

The original Shipley Aagrah has long since closed and a huge Shipley premises now houses Aagrah's head office as well as the current Shipley Aagrah, called the 'A La Carte Restaurant', hours: 5.30-11.30. There is a further restaurant next door called 'the Grill & Carvery'. There you can get a 3 Course evening buffet, Sun -Wed £12.95 pp u10 £6.95. Th-Sat £13.95 pp u10 £7.95. Hours: Mon-Fri: 12-2.30; Mon-Th: 5.30-11.30; Fri-Sat: to 12, Sun: to 11. The third Saltaire Road outlet is the Aagrah Food Court 48 Saltaire Road, Shipley, Bradford BD18 3HN 01274 530880 Next door to the Aagrah Shipley restaurant, it does the takeaways plus chilled raw pre-marinaded and prepared food for home cooking. Tu-Sun: 4:30-10.30. *Branches: Bristol; N.Yorks: Skipton, Tadcaster; S.Yorks: Doncaster, Sheffield; W.Yorks: Bradford, Huddersfield, Leeds (3), Pudsey, Shipley (3), Wakefield.*

KERALA CAFÉ SOUTH INDIAN
139-141, Bradford Road Shipley, BD18 3TB
01274 595367   www.kerala-cafe.co.uk

An iceberg in the desert; a south Indian restaurant amongst all those Kashmiri/Punjabi meat-eaters. So it must be relished. The food is. It is totally accurate and the menu wide-ranging. Soups include: Cheera Soup £4, made with spinach leaves, garlic and white pepper; Rasam £2.50, made with tomatoes, onions, ginger, garlic, tamarind, asafoetida and other herbs; Sambharam £2.50, spicy soup made with yoghurt, green chillies, ginger and curry leaves; Uzhunnu Vada (Medhu Vadai) (2 Pcs.) £2.99, Soft crispy doughnuts made of lentils, ginger, crushed black pepper, onions and curry leaves served with green salad and coconut chutney; Kathrikka Fry £2.99, Aubergine, coated in batter made of gram flour, black pepper powder, turmeric powder and cumin seed, deep-fried, served with green salad and mango chutney; Fish Pollichathu £7, Kingfish marinated with special masala and steam cooked inside a folded banana leaf and served with greensalad; Masala Dosa £5, the Keralan signature dish; crispy pancake filled with a potato-based curry rolled into a cylindrical shape served with sambar (lentils) and coconut chutney. Mains include:Aviyal £5, vegetables such as carrots, cucumber, green plantain etc. cooked with coconut, turmeric powder, cumin, garlic and other herbs and spices; Chicken Chettinadu £6.50, breast pieces cooked in a sauce made of roasted coconut paste, turmeric powder and other herbs and spices; Kerala Special Fish Mollie £7, fresh fish cooked in coconut milk sauce with fresh herbs and spices. 12-3 & 5.30-10.30.

SHIMLA SPICE
69 Otley Road, Shipley, BD18 2BJ   01274 599800

This second Shimla Spice brach opened in 2006 and seats over 200 in oppulent settings. Sun- Th : 5.- 11; Fri-Sat: to 12.30. See Keighley above for menu details.

Wakefield

AAGRAH   A-LIST
Barnsley Road, Sandal, Wakefield, WF1 5NX,
01924 242222   www.aagrah.com

The 100 seat Aagrah Restaurant is in a Sandal Court Hotel, which has 19 en-suite bedrooms (£30 per night). The white detached building stands out amongst the red brick homes on Barnsley Road, and it has a generous car park. Good stuff if you're looking for a decent priced bed and a decent dinner. The dining room is typical English hotel style, cream walls with gilt plaster features, and an ornate ceiling and chandelier, claret carpets, brown tables and chairs. The dinner menu is full-on Aagrah (see Shipley above for menu details). 3 course buffet, Sun-Mon, £12.95 to 9pm. No Indian breakfasts though. Mon-Th: 6-11:30; Fr-Sa: 5:30-11.30; Sun: 5:30-11. See above (Shipley) for details and branch list.

YOU SAY OK, WAKEFIELD

JINNAH BALTI 67, Westgate, Wakefield, WF1 1BW 01924 335557   www.jinnahrestaurants.com
'Have tried the Jinnah Balti in Wakefield a little while back. It is definitely good (as is the one in Harrogate)'. JP.

LALA'S 17 George Street, Wakefield, WF1 1NE 01924 445522 www.lalasrestaurant.co.uk
Comprehensive menu.Sun-Th: 5-11:30 (Fri-Sat to12:30). *Branches: Batley, Bradford and Huddersfield*

RED CHILLI 2 148 Doncaster Road, Wakefield, WF1 1TU 01924 384433   www.redchilli2.co.uk
Trendy decor with red leather high-backed chairs, modern spot lighting and abstract art prints. It serves the old favourites like Chicken Tikka Masala and lamb Rogan Josh plus specials such as Chingri Sagwala (made with King Prawns and spinach) and Ostrich Silsila (a personal favourite). 6-12.

ISLES and ISLANDS

When he failed to capture the British Isles, Napoleon dismissed us as a nation of shopkeepers. Were he around today, he might observe that we are now a nation of curry house keepers. Some isles, including Lundy, the Isles of Scilly, Uist, Mull, etc., have no curry houses but, for neatness, we group those that do together. For those who delight in collecting useless information, Lerwick, capital of the Shetland Isles, contains the nation's most northerly curry house (and still probably that of the whole globe). It is 600m from London and 800m from our most southerly curry house in St Helier, capital of Jersey.

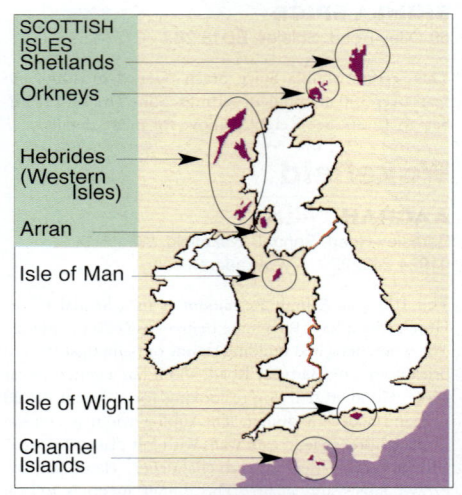

SCOTTISH ISLES
Shetlands
Orkneys
Hebrides (Western Isles)
Arran
Isle of Man
Isle of Wight
Channel Islands

SCOTTISH ISLES

SHETLANDS

Britain's most northerly outpost consists of 100 islands, the main one being called Mainland, principal town, Lerwick

Lerwick

GHURKA KITCHEN NEPALESE
33 North Road, Lerwick, ZE1 0NT   01595 690400

It and Raba are Britain's most northerly curryhouses, and both serve Nepalese dishes as well. 12-3 & 6-11.

RABA INDIAN RESTAURANT
26 Commercial Rd, Lerwick, ZE1 0LX   01595 695554

It and Gurkha Kitchen are Britain's most northerly curryhouses, and both serve Nepalese dishes. 12-3 & 6-11.

ORKNEY ISLES

These are 70 islands, 10 miles south of the Shetlands.

Kirkwall

DIL SE
7 Bridge Street, Kirkwall, Orkneys, KW15 1HR
01856 875242   www.dilserestaurant.co.uk

Opened 2005 by Moina Miah who cooks curryhouse standard dishes. The exterior is in raspberry-yoghurt cloured shocking pink. Rasa of London N16 would love it. Starter, main rice or Naan £16. The biggest surprise is in the desserts menu. Warm waffles accompanied by a scoop of Orkney ice cream & drizzled with chocolate sauce or Orkney Jamun delicious warm Gulabs with a scoop of Orkney ice cream. HRC would love that, each £6. 4-10.30.

INDIAN GARDEN
39 Junction Road, Kirkwall, Orkneys, KW15 1AG
01856 875575

This cream one-storey building with lime green lining-out has a separate t/a entrance selling pizzas & kebabs. 5-12.

HEBRIDES

These are dozens of islands, off the west coast of Scotland, hence they ar also known as the Western Isles.

ISLE OF BARRA
Barra

CAFÉ KISIMUL
Main Street, Catlebay, Barra, HS9 5XD
01871 810645   www.cafekismul.co.uk

Overlooking Kisimul bay and the Castle, this tiny venue is run by Rohal and Pauline Bari who specialize in Indian and Italian food. During the day it's a cafe with home baking.and breakfasts. In the evening, it's a 20 seat restaurant, licensed to sell wines, local beers and ales.All produce is local fish, organic veg and chicken or Barra lamb. Rohal is the main Indian cook. All Indian dishes include pilau rice or naan bread. Starters include Vegetable or Chicken Pakora or Kisimul's signature Scallop Pakora (hand-dived scallops) served with raita and salad. Mains include Monkfish and Cod in a tuna based masala; Prawn Jaipuri, fresh prawns from the Minch in a medium tomato sauce with peppers, fenugreek and cream. Bhoona, Rogan Josh, a rich dish with extra tomatoes; Dansak, Dopiaza with extra onions for a crunchy texture; Korma – mild and delicate with a blend of cream, coconut, and almond or Achari Balti with added pickle and garam masala. It's far from formula, being home-cooked to Rohal's family recipes. Daily early to late. See page 28. .

COBRA — SPLENDIDLY INDIAN, SUPERBLY SMOOTH

ISLE OF ISLAY
Bowmore

TAJ MAHAL
Shore Street, Bowmore, Isle of Islay, PA43 7LB,
01496 810033

Shore Street aka the A846 consists of rows of two-storey whitewashed terraced housing amidst which it the Taj. It's opposite the Lochside hotel and Duffie's whiskey bar, so book in, knock down a wee dram, stagger over the road for your fav curry and slàinte mhath and oidhche mhath! [cheers and goodnight].

Port Ellen

MAHARANI RESTAURANT
57 Frederick Crescent, Port Ellen, Islay, PA42 7BD

On the shorefront near the wee harbour, Standard menu.

ISLE OF SKYE
Kyleakin

TASTE OF INDIA
Alit An Avaig, A 87, Kyleakin, Skye, IV41 8PQ
01599 534134 www.thetasteofindia.co.uk

It's something of a novelty in this Highland village of Kyleakin -Formerly the Crofter's Kitchen selling Scottish fare, it is in a stand-alone building with ample parking on the A87, to the east of the wee village

Portree

PRINCE OF INDIA
Bayfield Road, Portree Skye IV51 9EW
01478 612681 www.princeofindia.me.uk

In a whitwashed corner house in the pretty harbour town and serves standard curries in a beamed room. Winter: 12-2 & 5-11:30. Summer 12-11.30.

ISLE OF LEWIS
Stornoway

BANGLA SPICE
33 Church St, Stornoway, Isle of Lewis, HS1 2JD
01851 700418

Main course £12.50. Three courses £25. 12:-2 & 5-10.45

STORNOWAY BALTI HOUSE
24 South Beach, Stornoway HS1 2BJ, Isle of Lewis
01851 706116

When the Balti House first opened its doors in 1990, it was simply a takeaway – then it was modified to become a 20 seat restaurant as demand for head chef Moksod Ali's meals grew far faster than Mohammeds's father Aborak Ali had expected. It expanded again in 1996 to seat 48. 12-2. & 5-11.

ISLE OF MULL
Tobermory

SAGAR
Main Street, Tobermory, PA75 6NU, Isle of Mull
01688 302422

Standard curries at normal prices.

ISLE OF MAN
Douglas

TASTE OF INDIA www.tasteofindiaiom.com
1 Clarence Terrace, Central Promande, Douglas,
Isle of Man, IM2 4LS 01624 613 909

Standard menu. Sun-Th: 5-11 (to 12 Fri-Sat).

Port St Mary

RASOI UN LIC
1 Bay View Rd, Port St Mary, Isle of Man, IM9 5AH
01624 833366 www.rasoiindiancuisineiom.com

Rasoi an unlicensed standard curryhouse on a corner site. Ask them whether you can BYO. 5-11.

ISLE OF WIGHT
YOU SAY OK

COWES: BAHAR TANDOORI BYO 44, High Street, Cowes PO31 7RR,01983 200378 Let's hope the photos of Sir Richard Branson dotting the walls of this two room venue don't put you off your food. Seems he's eaten there years ago. The menu carries formula items plus some Bangladeshi specials such as Sylet lamb cooked with shatkora citrus fruit with its tang taste.. Not licensed, BYO no corkage.
FRESHWATER: FATIMAS Freshwater Bay Road, Freshwater, PO40 9AS 01983 755121.
NEWPORT: BENGAL PALACE 57 Shide Road, Newport PO30 1HS 01983 822911 www.bengalpalace.webs.com Every Weds Night is Thali Night (Non Veg £10.95, Veg £9.95 Sunday Buffet 12 - 5:30, £9.95; U12 £4.95. After 5:30 Adult £11.95/£5.95. Monday To Sat12-2:30; 5:30-12.
RYDE: CINNAMON 4 Union Street, Ryde PO33 2DU 01983 810944 12-3 & 6-11.
SANDOWN: SWAD 18 High Street, Sandown PO36 8DE 01983 400800
SHANKLIN: SPICE LOUNGE 34 High Street, Shanklin PO37 6JJ 01983 867083 www. spiceloungeiow.wordpress.com The former Maharaja, est 1983 was relaunched in 2010. £11 five course meal, 6-7 nightly. Hrs: 12-3 & 5.30-11.

Email or Facebook your
reports to Pat Chapman.
pat@patchapman.co.uk

CHANNEL ISLES
ALDERNEY

NELLIE GRAYS
Victoria St, Alderney, Guernsey, GY9 3TA 01481 823333

Matin Miah runs Alderney's only curry house. It has provided the island with its curry fix for years now . and a small choice of English dishes. Fully licenced.

GUERNSEY
L'Eree

TASTE OF INDIA
Sunset Cottage, St Pierre Du L'Eree, Guernsey, s, GY7 9LN   01481 264516

Owned and managed by Tony Fernandes, who is from Goa, since 1989. Pink stone wall design with maroon seating for 60 diners. Chef Paltu Bhattachajee holds court in the kitchen serving specialities such as Sardines on Puri, Tandoori Lobster and Bhuna – market price and subject to availability. T/a: 10% disc. Set lunch: c£12 and £26 (for two). 6-11; closed Mon. Branch: *Taste of India, St Peter Port.*

YOU SAY OK GUERNSEY
44 INDIAN RESTAURANT The Pollet, Guernsey, GY1 1WF 01481 722318
TANDOORI KITCHEN Les Grandes Rocques, Castel, Guernsey, GY5 7FW 01481 251815
TASTE OF INDIA Mill Street, St Peter Port, Guernsey, GY1 1HQ 01481 723730

St Peter Port

KING BALTI
44 The Pollet, St Peter Port, Guernsey, GY1 1WF 01481-723246 www.kingbaltionline.co.uk

The say their dishes *'are predominantly of south Indian origin'*. In fact they are standard formula curries. 12-2; 6-12.

TAJ MAHAL
North Esplanade, St Peter Port, Guernsey, GY1 2LJ 01481 724008

Mujibul Hussain's 60-seater has been located in the heart of on the seafront of town opposite the Weighbridge since 1990. Standard menu. *'Charming and attentive staff. Interesting menu – imaginative main courses and unusual vegetable side-dishes (Uri Besi, mangetout and butter beans; Balar Aloo, mashed potatoes with garlic; Baygoon (aubergine, spinach and chickpeas) which was sampled by non-veggies with some envy! Delicious Chicken Sholay arrived fled in brandy. All food was fragrantly spicy with subtle differences between each dish.'* 12-2 and 6-11.

JERSEY
St Aubin

SHAPLA
Victoria Road, St Aubin   01534 746495

'Hasna Kebabs, lamb marinated in yoghurt, tandooried with onions, peppers and tomatoes, really tasty. Chicken Jalfrezi, aroma terrific. Simply perfect Lamb Rogan Gosht. Polite and helpful waiter.' MB. 12-2 & 6-12am. Branch: Shapla, La Rue Voisin, St. Brelade, Jersey, JE3 8AT 01534 746495

St Brelade

BENGAL BRASSERIE
11 La Pulente, St Brelade   01534 490279

'Favourite dish is the Chef's Balti – like no other – chicken, lamb, prawns, egg, kidney beans, mange tout, you name it. Portions more than adequate. Service best on the island, staff very friendly. Al fresco in the summer. Only 30 yards from St Ouens beach. Best place to see the sunset.' GL. 12-2 & 6-11.30.

St Helier

NEW RAJ
8 Burlington Parade, St Saviours Road, St Helier 01534 874131

Owned and managed by Kass Malik since 1984. Seats 60 in two dining rooms. *'Onion Bhaji was good, Chicken Chat not so good, being insipid and needing some salt. Chicken Dhansak was well spiced, my wife's CTM was rated the best she has had for some time..* MW. Hours: 12-2 & 6-12.

SHEZAN
53 Kensington Pl, St Helier 01534 22960

A small restaurant seating 40. *'Meal very good. A bit expensive, but worth it.'* SC. *'Owner, Shani Gill, is always the gentleman. His endeavours to satisfy all his customers have made him many friends.'* GDM.

YOU SAY OK JERSEY
Popular venues serving standard curries.
SHAPLA Jardin Du Crocquet La Rue Du Crocquet St. Brelade, Jersey, JE3 8BR   01534 490638
ST HELIER: CAFE SPICE 53 Kensington Place St. Helier, Jersey, JE2 3PA   01534 73737
INDIAN OCEAN TANDOORI 37 La Motte Street St. Helier, Jersey JE2 4SZ 01534 766118
TAJ MAHAL CENTRAL La Motte Street, St Helier   01534 20147 *Classy and luxurious restaurant. You are surrounded by running water and tropical fish. Had best ever Tarka Dal.'*

Email or Facebook your reports to Pat Chapman.
pat@patchapman.co.uk

SPLENDIDLY INDIAN, SUPERBLY SMOOTH

SCOTLAND

In 1965, much to the Scots' disgust, the age-old mainland Scottish shires and counties were amalgamated into nine large counties (or regions). In 1996 new changes resulted in only three staying totally unchanged (D&G, Fife and Highland). Two others have the same boundaries but new names: Borders became Scottish Borders, while Central once again became Stirling. Tayside is no more, being split into two (Angus and Perth & Kinross). Part of Grampian has been retained, with its western part returning to Moray. Northern Strathclyde has become Argyll & Bute, while the rest of Strathclyde, and the whole of Lothian have been split into sixteen Unitary Authorities, administering the larger cities and surrounds. For the time being, and until Scotland itself takes all these changes for granted, we retain in this Guide, the nine former counties (listing their ancient shires and/or new names within them, as relevant). Scotland's population of just over 5 million (less than half that of central London yet it occupies a land mass of more than half of England. Most of its curryhouses are in the big cities.

DUMFRIES & GALLOWAY

Area: Southwest Scotland

Contains Kirkcudbrightshire (centre) and Dumfriesshire (east), referred to as Galloway and Wigtownshire (west).

Adjacent Counties: Cumbria, Scottish Borders & Strathclyde

Dumfries

DAKSH
55-57 Queen Street, Dumfries DG1 2JW
01387 253876 www.dakshindian.co.uk

Standard menu with all the favourites at normal prices. Some Inidan desserts. Lunch 2 dishes £6.50 3 dishes £8.50 12-2 & 5-10 (Tuesday Closed)

JEWEL IN THE CROWN
48 St Michael Street, Dumfries, DG1 2QF
01387 264183

Good curryhouse where you might get a discount if you show them this Guide. Hours: 12-2.30 & 6-11.

FIFE

Area: East Scotland

Adjacent Counties: Lothian, Tayside

Cupar

ARMAAN OF CUPAR
102-104 Bonny Gate, Cupar, KY15 4LF
01334 650600 www.armaanrestaurant.com

Habib Chowdhury's 80 seater opened in 2004 in the centre of historic Cupar and is only minutes drive away from the most famous golf course in the world, the Old Course (St Andrews). You might get a discount if you show Mr Chowdhury this Guide. Specials: Chicken and Lamb Parsi £8. 12-2 & 5-11.

Glenrothes

NURJAHAN
Coslane, Woodside Road 01592 630649

Manirul Islam's 110-seater is decorated to a very high standard. Roomy carver-chairs at all tables. *'Truly magnificent meal. Spotless. More than generous quantities. The best quality we have ever tasted. A superior restaurant in every aspect.'* MAJF. Waiters very polite and helpful. You might get a discount if you show them this Guide. 12-2 & 5-11. (Fri. & Sat. to 12am); Sun. 4-11.

St Andrews

BALAKA BANGLADESHI
AWARD WINNER A-LIST
3 Alexander Pl, Market St, St Andrews, KY16 9XD
01334 474825 www.balaka.com

The Balaka was established by Abdur Rouf in 1982 and is now run by his son Michael with G.M. Lawrence D' Costa and Head Chef - Abdul Monem, who has been there since it opened. Even before you enter this up-market and sophisticated 52-seater, note the frontage floral display. He has won awards for it. The unique feature is the huge kitchen garden at the rear, in which Mr Rouf grows all his own herbs and many vegetables. More foliage inside with palms dividing tables and hand stitched Bangladeshi tapestries on the walls. Balaka's unusual name means a 'swan'. Unusual dishes on the menu include Mas Bangla – salmon marinated in lime, turmeric and chilli, fried in mustard oil, garlic, onion, tomato and aubergine. I had the privilege of being trained to cook this dish by chef Monem which I reproduced at a lecture at St Andrews University for the Chemical Soc and all of Mr Rouf's friends. I hope they enjoyed it as much as I did. We then moved on to the restaurant for a fabulous meal. And you can mix and match if you so wish. Mr Rouf's team continues to provide outstanding food in superb surroundings. We have lots of contented customer reports. All show a friendly, caring patron, and here's proof: *'Is still excellent.'* M. *'We dined here with a large party of friends from the Netherlands and around the world. The evening was a tremendous success – wonderful food and service.'* TGM. *'Nice decor, good service. Good portion of wonderful Afghani Gosht.'* anon. *'Not bad curries.'* T&KM. William and Catherine were regulars whilst at the uni and if you are really lucky you might just see Sean Connery on the nearby golf course. Advisable to book at peak times. Sun- Th: 12-11.30 (to 12.30am Fri-Sat).

MAISHA
5 College Street, St Andrews, KY16 9AA
01334 476666   www.maisharestaurant.co.uk

Mahfuza Mohi owns this Bangladeshi venue. Maisha meaning 'working with pride' offers a wide range of favourites. More notably they specialise in fish and seafood. The Bay of Bengal provides sweet water delicious fish and seafood such as Bengal Rupchanda - a silvery white pomphet and Tilipia. Some examples of their extensive menu: Jhal Kakra Bhuna £12.95, Hot Crab Curry, is a recipe developed by Mahfuza's wife; Scottish Mas Bhuna £11, Scottish fresh salmon marinated with fresh garlic, ginger, turmeric green chilli and lime juice cooked in a frying pan on a slow heat and then fried quickly in mustard oil with garlic, onion, tomato and aubergine; Jhal Kakra Bhuna £13, crab meat, marinated with garlic and ginger, green chilli paste, coriander and then cooked bhuna-style; Tilapia Dupiaza £11, Bangladesh fish filleted, marinated and cooked in a very thin slice of onion dupiaza sauce; Bengal Rupchanda Bhuna £11, whole white Promphet, marinated with turmeric, fresh garlic and ginger, green chilli paste and baked. 12-2.30 & 6-11.

YOU SAY OK
DUNFERMLINE KHUSHI'S Restaurant   1 Canmore St, Dunfermline, KY12 7NU   01383 737 577   www.khushis.com
BOMBAY BRASSERIE   1, Turnstone Road, Duloch, Dunfermline, KY11 8JZ   01383 623323
www.bombaybrasserieduloch.co.uk

Kirkcaldy

ANNAPURNA   NEPALESE
312 High St Kirkcaldy, Fife KY1 1LB   01592 269460

Nepalese starters: Daram Ko Maccha £3.99, fried fish served with salad and lemon dressing ; Piro Kukhura, £3.99, wok-fried spicy chicken cooked with onion, capsicum and Nepalese style yoghurt; Galkote Kebabd £3.50, diced lamb with Nepalese spices cooked in tandoor , Aloo Tareko tawa-fried potato cake served with home made tomato chutney. Some Mains: Bhuteko Khasi £8.25, tender pieces of lamb cooked with green chilli garlic and spring onion; Poleko Bhale Kukhura £8.25, marinated chicken cooked in thick sauce; Achari chicken or lamb made with homemade pickle. Bhuteko Bhat £3; Nepalese rice with cumin seed, peas and spring onions. Mon-Fri:12-2:30 & 4.30-11. (Sat: 12.-11.00; Sun: 2-11.

GRAMPIAN

Area:
North East Scotland

Contains Aberdeenshire, Banff, Kincardine and Morayshire, all formerly known as Grampian.

Adjacent Counties:
Highland, Tayside

Aberdeen

CINNAMON   TOP 100
476 Union Street, Aberdeen, AB10 1TS
01224 633328   www.lovecinnamon.co.uk

Opened in 2005 by Khalia Miah. His restaurant is stylis. A fairly small frontage is never the less, impressive. Two gun metal grey planters, planted with cacti stand either side of the entrance door. Inside, beige brick walls, round mirrors engravedwith the restaurant's logo, wooden black slatted screens provide privacy for diners and a striking paprika red, metal staircase, takes customers upstairs to the gallery dining area. Presentation and cooking is outstanding, and it's not cheap here. Menu Snapshot: Starters include Scallops Three Ways £12.45, garlic & chilli marinated with Greek olive oil, tandooried with lemongrass, sea salt & coriander then char-grilled and served with their home-made five fruit chutney. Chokki Tikki £7, curried potatoes & spinach crisp bakes with ginger, garlic, sultanas and flakes of roasted almonds dressed with a sauce; Garlic and Chilli Tiger Prawns £9, locally caught, marinated in garlic, chilli & ginger, then roasted in the tandoori and served with a dip; Bataada Wada £7, batter-coated curried potatoes, shallow-fried and served with tamarind chutney. Mains include Hyderabad Ghosht Kali Mirch £12, lamb cooked in browned garlic, ginger paste, black pepper & cream; Rajasthani lamb shank £17, (Raan) is *'rubbed with aphrodisiac spices'* [sic] plus ginger, garlic, chilli & yoghurt & served with chick pea masala, diced onions & capsicums. Lunch: £15 Dinner: £29; Fixed Lunch: £8 (3 courses) Fixed Dinner: £9.95 (4 courses). 12-12. *Branch: Cumin, 25, Victoria Terrace, Kemnay, Aberdeenshire.*

Elgin

QISMAT
202 High Street, Elgin, IV30 1BA   01343 541461

Established in 1987 by Liaquat Ali. Seats 100 diners in a modern and brightly decorated restaurant with wooden polished floor, palms, coloured seat pads and air-conditioning. Delivery: £10 min, in Elgin only. 12-2 & 6-11; Sun: eve only. *Branch: Qismat, Millburn Rd, Inverness.*

Ellon

NOSHEEN
5 Bridge Street, Ellon, AB41 9AA
01358 724309   www.nosheentandoori.com

Established in 1989 by Khalid Ahmed and now under new management, the. 92 seats restaurant has aull standard menu at competitive prices. Set meal £17 for 2. You might get a discount if you show them this Guide. Takeaway: 10% discount. 5-10. (Sat. to 12am).

HIGHLAND
Area: North Scotland

Contains Caithness, Inverness, Nairn, Ross & Cromarty and Sutherland and small parts of Argyll and Moray.

Adjacent Counties:
Grampian, Strathclyde, Tayside

Inverness

CINNAMON
1b, Millburn Rd, Inverness, IV2 3PX
01463 716020   www.cinnamoninverness.co.uk

Opened in 2003 its menu includes all the favourites such as Starters: Mixed Hors D'oeuvres for 4 £15.80, Chicken Pakora, Onion Bhaji, Tandoori chicken, King prawn butterfly or r for two £7.95. All the fav mains at: Chicken £ 8.25, Lamb .£9 and KP £13 Takeaway: 10% discount. 12-11.

Nairn

AL-RAJ
25 Harbour Street, Nairn, IV12 4NX   01667 455370

Sahukat and Najma Ali's 70-seater has helpful waiters who might give you a discount if you show them this Guide. Hours: 12-2 & 5-11.30.

LOTHIAN

Area: Mid Eastern Scotland

Adjacent Counties:
Central, Fife,
Scottish Stirling, Strathclyde

The region of Lothian has been disbanded, the larger cities and surrounds split into a number of Unitary Authorities. For the time being, we are sticking to the old Lothian in this Guide.

Dalkeith

BOMBAY LOUNGE
202 High Street, Dalkeith, EH22 1AZ
0131 660 4141   www.bombaylounge.net

Edinburgh-born Michael and Si Singh, own and run the Bombay Lounge. It's in a 120 year old stone building typical of those on the long street. It used to be Sam's Bar, and now it has been transformed into spacious, vibrant Indian restaurant. One USP is the ex beer garden now called the Grill Bar which has al fresco seating for 36 people and includes a flame-grill barbeque! The other USP is a range of Haggis items, and no ordinary haggis too, it's top brand Macsweens. Haggis Pakora £3.50, is coated with flavoured gram flour deep-fried and served with salad and mint sauce; Karahi Murghi Haggis Massalla £8.25, diced barbecued chicken cooked with macsween haggis, coriander, and green & red pepper; Bombay Spiced Haggis £2.95, haggis and potato with green chillies, very hot; Bombay Haggis Nan £2.50, spiced haggis and potato stuffing in the nan. There is a full range of 'normal' curries. Starters av £3 and mains £4.65, 2 course lunch Mon-Sat only, £6.95 Vegetarian; £7.50 Non-Veg. Hours: Mon-Sat: 12-2 Mon-Th: 5-11 (to 11.30 Fri-Sat); Sun: 12.30-11.

Edinburgh

10 to 10 IN DELHI   NO ALC
67 Nicolson Street, Edinburgh, EH8 9
0131 667 6744   www.indelhi.co.uk

Chef and owner Alieu Badjan opened 10 to 10 In Delhi (sometimes called Delhi Café) on this busy street in 2010. He, says *'I offer our patrons excellent service in an elegant, yet comfortable atmosphere, in which to dine, meet friends, and savour selections from our food, snack, tea and coffee menus'* Bollywood movies blare out. Bollywood posters and pics cover the walls, Indian artefacts fill nooks and crannies while the ceiling is covered with brightly coloured, sari material, chiffons and sequinned drapes. In Delhi sells takeout snacks (sweetmeats, samosas and pakoras), from a glass counter. These and and curries come at really cheap prices. For those who want to dine in, take your seat on an equally colourful bean-bag cushion, faced by low tables are the right height for the seats of which there are only 25. You can't reserve and it gets busy. The kitchen is all open-plan and it's fun to watch the endless work in progress. Spicy Roti Wraps (using chupattis) include chicken, or 3 veg types £4.50, and are served with home-made salads, pickles and chutneys. Curries average £5. They are served on plates with several compartments at the centre of which is rice. Their home-made mango cheesecake. Is a daily offering. No alcohol is allowed, but there is a big rangs of different coffees, teas and exotic fruit juices. Hours and hence the name: 10am-10 pm.

ANN PURNA   GUJARATI VEG
44-45 St Patrick's Square, Edinburgh, EH8 9ET
0131 662 1807   www.annpurna-edinburgh.co.uk

Ann(a) Purna, means 'Food Provider'. Curries (av £4) include:Bhindi Bhaji, Okra, Ghiye ke Kofte rissole veg balls, Sindhi kadhi, gramflour / yoghurt curry, Stuffed tomato, Rajma Rasmisa, red bean curry; kumbi masala, mushroom curry; and saag paneer. Fixed Lunch: £5 (3 courses)   3 course dinner £11, house wine at £8.95.. Mon-Fri: 12- 2 & Daily:5.30-11.

BRITANNIA SPICE   AWARD WINNER
150 Commercial Street, Britannia Way, Leigh, Edinburgh, EH6 6LB   0131 555 2255
www.britanniaspice.co.uk

Where Wali Tasar Udin leads, others follow. Once it was known that the ex Royal Yacht Britannia was to be retired in derelict Leith docks, he decided to open a restaurant to assist the regeneration of the area, now called Ocean Terminal. Now there are a good many rivals but then it was high risk, stand-alone. He chose the former Glenmorangie Whisky warehouse at the dock entrance. He hired Arshad Alam to design the venue to reflect the 'gracious lady of the seas', which had taken up residence within sight of the new premises. It opened in 1999. This gorgeous nautically-themed restaurant, seating 130 diners, (served by frequent buses from the city centre) has blue chairs, polished wooden tables and floors, brass railings and blinds that look like sails and is is perfect stop-off after you have visited the the Yacht or the other people-magnet, the Scottish Executive building. Wali also pioneered joint menu. It is divided by countries - Bangladeshi, Thai, Nepalese, North Indian and Europe - mix and match, if you like! Menu Snapshot: Tom Kha Gai £4.55, (Thai) chicken in a rich coconut soup, flavoured with fresh galangal, lemon grass, kaffir lime leaves and mushrooms; Maccher Bhorta £4.95, (Bangladesh) baked fish, minced with onions, green chillies, mushrooms and fresh coriander leaves, tempered with mushroom seeds; Shatkora Gosht £11.95, (Bangladesh) tender pieces of lamb cooked in a medium hot sauce with rinds of a the Shatkora citric fruit, lemon leaves and Bengali chillies; Special Chicken £14.95, (Bangladesh) diced king prawns, wrapped in thin filleted chicken and cooked in a rich and mild sauce; Pad Ho Ra Pa Kub Nua £10.95 - (Thai) thinly sliced pieces of beef, stir-fried with a selection of traditional Thai spices and basil - hot; Chicken Panaeng £11.95, (Thai) medium to hot, with lime leaves, red pepper, coconut milk and red chilli paste; Himalayan Momo £12.95, (Nepal) minced meat mixed with spices, enclosed in pastry and traditionally steamed;   Palok Gajor Cashew Nut £8.95 - spinach, carrot, cashew nuts, medium hot. *'What a great restaurant, lovely surroundings, great courteous service and the food is just up with the very best. We had Chicken Tikka Chasni Masala bit more spicy than your average CTM and Methi Murgh. The Aloo Jeera was simply divine, the Okra tasty, if a bit oily. TOP 100 stuff no doubt, elegant.'* T&KM. *'Very, very tiny helpings - beautifully plated. Very, very expensive.'* NKC. *'Whilst on business, my colleague and I found ourselves staying at the Holiday Inn Express (adjacent to the restaurant). We walked past the restaurant at 7pm - it was empty, deciding on a beer first. Returned at 8.30pm - it was packed, despite this we got a table! Excellent starters of Assorted Kebabs. Main courses: Northern Indian Garlic Chicken with hot sauce, Harrey*

SPLENDIDLY INDIAN, SUPERBLY SMOOTH

Masaley Ka Gosht, cubes lamb in green masala or coriander, mint, green chilli, curry leaves and spices, a superb, best ever tarka Dal. Very impressive, worthy of its guide entry. Will visit again!' DL. For the totally unadventurous there is a small choice of English dishes – steak, roast chicken etc. Takeaway: 15% discount. Delivery: £50 minimum, 5-mile radius. Hours: 12-2, Sunday closed /5-11.45. See page 11.

THE FAR PAVILIONS   TOP 100
10–12 Craigleith Road, Comely Bank, Edinburgh, EH4 2DP   0131 332 3266   www.thefarpavilions.co.uk

Located at the beginning of an attractive tree-lined residential road, this 125 seat restaurant has since 1987 been delivering an interesting menu to a regular clientelle which includes staff from the nearby hospital and police headquarters. Mr Chaudry runs it with Chef Abdul Aziz. The presentaion is carefully thought out using stylish crockery. Starters include Chatpattae Channae, spicy chickpeas with tamarind dressing; Prawn Balchao, a Goan specialitiy so it comes in a sour and slightly sweet hot sauce, served on Garlic Bread. Mains include: Green Chicken Curry made with fresh puréed coriander, tamarind, mint, green chilli and other herbs; Malika E Dariya, sea bream marinated with mango powder and black pepper; Murgh Butter Masala Chicken Tikka gently simmered in a garlic butter sauce, with almond powder, flavoured with fresh cream. Indian desserts are there:Galub Jamun, hot panieer cheese dumplings served with vanilla ice cream or Gajar Ka Halawa, Carrot Fudge. Gabby Soutar, The Scotsman says *'the walls bore dimpled panels of buttoned velvet. Even the staff were upholstered.'* Guide-readers discount eases the bill as does the e-a-m-a-y-l. Tuesday 6.30-10, £11.95. Takeaway: 10% off. 12-2.30 & 5.30-11.

IGNITE
272 Morrison Street, Edinburgh, EH3 8DT
0131 228 5666   www.igniterestaurant.co.uk

This stylish 60 seater decorated with both Indian and African artefacts, opened in 2004 and we have received good reports all along. Owner Mr Khan says the menu ignites the senses. Starters include Murgh Chaat £4.75 small juicy pieces of chicken cooked in a medium hot flavoured sauce with fresh herbs and spices, served with puri and fresh salad. Bhari Combi £4.75,mushrooms stuffed with spiced minced lamb, coated with spiced batter; baby aubergine pakora, and Sheek kebabs of tender minced lamb served with fresh mint and yoghurt sauce. Mains include Punjab Methi Gust lamb in a savoury sauce of fenugreek and coriander. Tandoori Trout is marinated in yoghurt and spices and served whole. The Main Course menu uniquely suggests a side dish for each choice. Murgh Sarisha £12.05, is sliced marinated chicken, cooked with potato, garlic, tomato, mustard and fresh coriander, recommended side dish: Cauliflower Bhajee; Punjab Methi Gust £12.50, lamb cooked with herbs, fresh methi (fenugreek), fragrant spices and coriander. Medium hot to taste, recommended side dish: Mushroom Bhajee. Ignite also offers veal in several dishes, a rare ingredient at a Bangladeshi venue, but which curries as well as chicken. Try Veal Jhalfrezie £16.95, Veal cooked with fresh green chillies, capsicum, onions and fresh coriander. Fairly spicy and hot to taste. Recommended side dish: Panchrangi Dall. Average price: £8.50 (set lunch) £19 (evening meal). House wine: £14.25 per bottle Min evening charge pp £12. 12-2 & 5.30-11.30.

KEBAB MAHAL
7 Nicholson Square, Edinburgh, EH8 9BH
0131 667 5214

Opened in 1979 serving tandoori, curries, shish kebabs, chicken tikkas and biryanis at affordable prices. *'Very good place. Have eaten in and had takeaway.'* NKC. 'Recommended. Not upmarket or designer, but the food is extremely good and consistent and also quite cheap.' dr dd. 12-12, Fri-Sat to 2am

KHUKURI   NEPALESE
W Maitland Street, Edinburgh, EH12 5DS   0131 228 2085   www.thekhukuri.co.uk

The waiters create the atmosphere in this simply decorated but smart venue by wearing Nepalese caps waistcoats white leggings Nepalese specials include starters: Bhenda Momo £3.45, Succulent steamed lamb mince meat with traditional spices, served with a Nepali dip; Bhenda Choyla £2.85, diced lamb tikka with fresh garlic, ginger, tomato and spices served with a small chapati; Bara, thick lentil pancake, garlic, ginger, spices, both served with Nepali dip. Trusili Poleko Machha, marinated baby fish, cooked in tandoor, served with green salad. Kukhura Hariyali, spicy yoghurt sauce, mint, coriander, green chillies. Mains include: Kukhura Khorsani Masala £7.65, chicken cooked with fresh green chillies and spices; Kukhura Tansen Chicken Tikka £8.55, in a curry sauce with spring onions, tomatoes and chopped green chillies; Himalaya Kukhura Gorkhali Korma £7.75, marinated lamb (or chicken) cooked in fresh cream and honey. Aloo Tama Bodi, potato, bamboo shoots, black-eye beans. Mon-Sat: 12-2 & 5.30-11.30 (Fri-Sat to 12). Sun: 5- 11.

KHUSHIS   BYO
10 Antigua Street, Edinburgh, EH1 3NH
0131 558 1947   www.khushis.com

Khushi's is one of the newest restaurant in Edinburgh; it is also one of the oldest. Punjabi Indian Khushi Mohammed opened his first restaurant, Khushis next to the Edinburgh university in 1947. It was also Edinburgh's first Indian. Throughout the 60's and 70's, the restaurant's popularity grew. Khushi died in 1977 and his wife then took over the business. Down the years it has moved premises several times. In 2008, a controversial fire destroyed the then current luxurious Khushi's on Victoria Street. Their sons now run the latest Kushi reincarnation. The menu is conventional. Starter prices av £4; Chicken curries av £8.50; Meat curries av £9. You can BYO your own wines with no corkage charge but not beers or spirits. Mon-Sat: 12-11pm (to 10 Sun). *Branches: Kushis 1 Canmore Street, Dunfermline, Fife KY12 7NU, Mithas, Edinburgh*

LANCERS BRASSERIE   TOP 100
5 Hamilton Place, Edinburgh, EH3 5BA
0131 332 3444   www.lancersbrasserie.co.uk

70-seater Lancers was opened in 1985 by Wali Udin JP (see Britannia Spice). It is managed by Alok Saha. Head chef is Badrul Hussain. It has recently been refurbished. The main dining room, Lancers Mess, has designer fabrics including a Dixon Turner designed bespoke print covering one entire wall and the chairs are made of the softest Bridge of Weir leather. The flooring was been sourced from Amtico and the bar area has also underwent a full re-design, complete with Staron counter tops and a full-height upper gantry with back light facility. *'It's worth going just to see all that ... but add in superb food and it's a night to remember.'* RCF. *'The life-size mural depicting a mounted Punjabi cavalry regiment, complet with brown mounts, is glorious'* HEG. Try the Non-Veg Thali for One as a taster £235. This complete dinner provides a range of smaller portions from specially selected items on the menu, viz: Lancers' Assorted Kebab, selection of lamb, chicken, fish and vegetable kebabs prepared in the clay oven; Chicken Tikka Massallam cooked in a mild flavoured sauce with fresh herbs and spices; Lamb Passanda marinated ihen cooked in an almond sauce; Sag Paneer, spinach with home-made cottage cheese; Sabzi Pilau, Nan, Kulfi or Coffee. Dinner for 2 £44. Vegetarian Thali £18; Vegetarian Dinner for Two £34. 12-2.30 & 5-11.30.

MITHAS   INDIAN FINE DINING   BYO
7 Dock Place, Leith, Edinburgh, EH6 6LU
0131 554 0008   www.mithas.co.uk

Khushi Mohammed's story is told above (Kushi's Edinburgh). His son Islam Mohammed has recently opened Mithas (meaning sweet tasting) as a decidedly up-market venue. He and his family visited London, so the spin goes, and dined at the likes of Benares, the Cinammon Club and Café Spice and decided it was time to bring *'that sort of imaginative and adventurous Indian cooking to our home city and so Mithas was born'.* [sic]. They recruited a top-notch kitchen team including chefs from the Cinnamon Club and splashed out on the venue. It is located in the revitalised docks/port area, area already bestowed with good restaurants, Indian and otherwise. It is in one of those gorgeous stone buildings, its ground floor picked out in grey paint. Inside the 100 seater is elegant, its tables spaced well apart, surrounded by Indian fretwork and art, private booths, dome-like copper lights, minimalist furniture, and facilities to die for. *'Even the toilets are clad with more marble than all six of The Three Graces' buttocks.'* Gabby Soutar, The Scotsman. There is an open kitchen with two tandoors, one for bread and vegetables and the other for meat and fish. Unsurprisingly, such aspirations come at a price, so expect to pay accordingly. One way to explore is to try the Mithas tasting menu (min. 2, £35pp, but substantial), consisting of Venison Kebab, Grilled Scallops, Monkfish Tikka ~ Sorbet ~ Spinach & Fig Tikka, Murgh Kali, Mirch Tikka, Tawa Lobster or Rané Mithas (Leg of Lamb,) Red Mullet Masala, Raita, rice and breads. There is a vegetarian tasting menu as well. A la carte will cost much the same. They start with an amuse bouche. Usually soup in a coffee cup. of tomato soup. Served in dollhouse crockery-sized teacups, this had an adenoid warming hit of black pepper, cinnamon and a sour tinge of tamarind. Starters av £6 and mains £11 for meat curries, to £19,for duck. Pullao Rice is £2.95 as is Naan and Raita (albeit pomegranate). As at Khushis they do not sell alcohol and you can BYO your own wines with no corkage charge (but not beers or spirits). And for such an upmarket feast, a very good wine would be appropriate, and a rare opportunity to do so at a sensible cost. Alternatively there are a number of fruit-based beverages and lassis on offer. Service is equally high quality. Local whispers is that Mithas is seeking Scotland's first Michelin star for an Indian restaurant. It seems to tick all the boxes and would be another first for this distinguished family. Tu-Sun: 12-2.30 & 5.30-10. Mon: Closed.

MOSQUE KITCHEN   NO ALC
31 Nicholson Square, Edinburgh, EH8 9BX
0131 667 4035   www.mosquekitchen.com

If this were in the subcontinent it would be junremarkable, being ust one such venue amongst millions, outside mosques and temples and on streets upaand down the nation. They are called dabbas. Finding just one in the whole of the UK is remarkable. Alongside Edinburgh Uni on Potterrow is the huge City Mosque. Nearby a curry outlet was opened a few years back. Called the Mosque Kitchen, it had no infra-structure, being set up in some unused space with long formica shared tables under a plastic/canvas roof. It served what must be the cheapest UK curry. This dabbahas nothing to do with the mosque; being a commercial venture. Before long the operators fell out big time and Mosque Kitchen moved round the corner. A further move has seen it locate into a 'proper' shop unit at the above address, with the sub-title *'Tasty Curry in a Hurry'.* It is run by the canny Akbar and Majads whose clients are hungry locals, mosque worshipers and loads of brassic students, boosted by curious tourists at Festival time. All are welcome. Despite the move to conventional premises, and a website (which announces amongst other things, that they do *'weddings, baptism, wakes dicorces or any other celebration'*) it remains a caff with, no frills, no waiters and no nonsense serving cheap and authentic homemade Pakistani food. You go to the counter for service. There is a menu is on the wall but it rarely reflects what's on. There are starters such as samosa (£1) and there are at least three curries. Just choose what is available. Prices starting at £3 for Tarka Dhal with rice to £4 for a veg curry and £4.50 for chicken curry and rice. Nans are £1.50. Portions are huge. Costs are kept down by using disposable plates etc. Strictly Halal. Cash only, no credit cards, No alcohol but lassi or mango juice etc is. Tap water available. Hours: Mon–Sun 11.30am–10pm (Fri closed 12.50–1.50pm).

MYA   THAI AND INDIAN   TOP 100
92 Commercial Street, Leith, Edinburgh, EH6 6LX
0131 554 4000   www.myarestaurant.co.uk

Mya is situated in the fashionable commercial quay in Leith, opposite Scottish Executive. And in easy walking distance of Ocean Terminal and Royal Yacht Britannia. The area is now a bustling, fun place with good restaurants a-plenty. Mya has been around for years and offers both Thai and Indian cuisines, both with a good choice of vegetarian dishes. Sarters include: Pakura £3.85, Somosa £3.95, served with green salad and two different dips, Chana Puri £4.95 chick peas topped with a combination of mild spices and wrapped in puffed fried bread; Seabass Tenga £6.90, crispy seabass salad topped with lime, ginger, chilli and sweet and sour dressing (pathia style). Tandoori Mixed £13.90 consists of tandoori chicken, lamb kebab, chicken kebab and sheek kebab. Served on a sizzling platter with salad and sauce. Tandoori Zingh £16.90 king prawn in a shell marinated in spice and barbecued in tandoori skewers, served on a sizzling platter with a salad sauce. Mains include all the old favourites at £8.95 and Specials such as North Indian Chilli Garlic Chicken £9.60 prepared in green chillies with freshly chopped garlic, capsicum and garnished with fresh coriander. Shat Kora Gosth £10.95 tender pieces of lamb in a calamansi juice, with rinds, lemon leaves and bengali chillies; Gosth Papani £9.95 marinated lamb with peas, chilli, garlic, ginger, tomato and cinnamon; Baguni King Prawn £12.90 cooked with aubergine, cherry tomatoes and selected herbs and spices; Bhindi Bhuna £8.45 okra garnished with onions, green herbs, tomatoes and selected spices; Kerela Chilli Salmon £12.90 spiced with fresh chillies and ground kalimirch, with a hint of coconut, for the slightly hotter palate. The Thai menu is equally accomplished. Mixed Starters £6.90 give a good all round opening: (min 2) mixed seafood in filo pastry, prawn wanton, hoison duck, spring rolls, tod mun and seafood wrapped in rice flour skin. Tom Yum soup from £5. Five Thai curries are each £9.60, eg Gaeng Massamam, chicken cooked slowly in a mildly spiced curry with potatoes, peanuts and coconut cream. Other mains include Pad Nuer Prik Thai Oon £9.85 beef stir-fried with chilli and imported fresh green peppers and spring onions. Presentation and service is smart and efficient. *'Wonderful food, the best Indian food I have ever had. I have been coming here for the past 10 years'.* AG. *'I have been coming to Mya once a week for the past several years, with my family and at times with business colleagues. Love the food and the atmosphere is great.'* GR. *'I enjoy the food, both Indian and Thai. Would recommend this place, either sit in the restaurant for that special day or take-away.'* IL. 12- 2 & 6-11.

MEZBAAN   SOUTH INDIAN
14 Brougham Street, Tollcross, Edinburgh EH3 9JH
0131 229 5578

Once home to Shamiana and since 2005 that of Mezbaan which has the distinction of specialising in that rarity, south Indian cuisine. Cooking is in the experienced hands of specialists Aji Kumara who has worked in the UAE and Cyprus and Shabu Natarajna, ex Radisson, Dubai. And they offer a very full choice on the menu. Here's just a tiny snapshot: Starters: Rasam £3.75 tangy tamarind & tomato based hot soup; Prawn or Fish Pollichathu £5.65 cooked & served in a banana leaf; Mysore-E-Gilafi £3.95 minced lamb kebab cooked with gilaf of chopped onions, coriander and cheese, Fish Vada £4.55 a fish cake where fresh fish is boiled, shredded, mixed with spices as a rissole and deep-fried; Mixed Pakora & Bonda £3.85 Bonda is picy potato, dipped in gram flour batter and deep fried. Served with coconut chutney or sauce.; Medu Vada (V) £3.65 Ground urad lentil and spices, shaped into a doughnut and deep fried. Then served with sambar and coconut chutney. Masala Dosa (£5.45 south Indian pancake, made of rice and lentil flour, with a potato curry filling accompanied with sambar and coconut chutney. Mains include: Kumarakam Konju Kadai £10.75, king prawns prepared with mixed peppers, onion, tomato, green chilli, ginger and garlic plus spices aserved in a kadai; Goan Fish Curry £10.15 sea bass iprepared in coconut milk, tamarind juice, tomato, ginger, garlic, green chilli's, curry leaves and spices; Coorg £8.25 Chicken in a nutty cashew based sauce flavoured with desiccated coconut and cumin. Wajid Ali £7.50 This dish is dedicated to Maharaja's of south India. Tender pieces of chicken breast cooked with Kashmiri deghi mirch, poppy seeds, fenugreek, aromatic spices and garnished with desiccated coconut and curry leaves. 12- 3; 5-11.

OMAR KHAYYAM   PUNJABI
1 Grosvenor St, Edinburgh, EH12 5ED
031 220 0024   www.omar-khayyam.co.uk

A modern Punjabi restaurant with attentive, waistcoated waiters, stylish modern decor and an unusual water feature trickling away in the middle of the dining room. Being Punjabi, the food is very savoury and delicious,, ranging from old favourites such as Kormas & CTM to more unusual dishes like Kabul Chicken (with chick peas, cumin and coriander). 10% Discount on Take-Away, Mon-Fri: 12-2 & 5-12; Sat:12-12; Sun: 4.30-12

THE RADHUNI
93 Clerk Street, Loanhead, Edinburgh EH20 9RE
0131 440 3566   www.theradhuni.co.uk

Radhuni means 'passionate cook' in Bengali. The comprehensive menu offers all the favourites. Starters average £3 and curries £8. Lunch special £4.95 with over 7 Starters and 14 Mains to choose from. 12:-2 Mon-Sat to 4.230 Sun. The Radhuni also offers outside dining in their slabbed garden area. Mon-Sat 12-2 & 5-10; Sun: 12-10.

VERANDAH   AWARD WINNER
17 Dalry Rd, Edinburgh, EH11 2BQ
0131 337 5828   www.verandah.co.uk

It's a tiny 44-seater, and the first opened (in 1981) by Wali Tasar Uddin, MBE, JP. It is now run by his nephew, Foysol Choudhury, who describes it as 'reassuringly low-key' serving northern Indian and Bangladeshi cuisine. DBAC says: '*I first ate there, well, let me see, a very long time ago, the decorations were unfussy, in fact simple but never-the-less effective and the food served in generous portions.*' The menu contains all the favourite dishes and some Bangladeshi specials such as: Chasni Masallam Chicken £7.25, King Prawn £12, lamb £7.25, kebabs in a fairly hot sauce with a touch of mango achar pickle; Shatkora a regional dish cooked with Bangladeshi citrus fruit giving a strong distinctive flavour, Chicken £7, King Prawn £11.55 lamb £7. Mussoorie Dall (Kathmandu) Chicken, King Prawn or lamb (same prices) is barbecued in a cinnamon, onion, ginger, ground roasted cumin and lentil sauce. Kashmiri Kata Masala, ditto steam-cooked with tomato purée, red pepper, garlic, ginger, coriander and Kashmiri spices, finished with fresh tomato & coriander leaves. Good value 'tasters' are: Vegetarian Thali for One £13: Vegetable massalam, tarka dal, palak bhaji, aloo gobi, chapati, pilau rice & chutney.Non Veg Thali for One £16: Keema motor, lamb pasanda, chicken rogan, mixed vegetable bhaji, tandoori roti, pilau rice & chutney. We continue to get many appreciative reports: *'First class restaurant by any standards. The welcome at and the ambience of this establishment is all that one could wish for, when sitting down to dine. The welcome is friendly, the staff attentive and the food is flavoursome and well prepared. We have been before and do recommended it. We are fortunate in having restaurant so this calibre in Edinburgh.*' ANON. *'The staff were very polite and welcoming with an excellent neat table. The candle was a beautiful touch. Been before but only for a takeaway, even better sitting in. Would definitely return. Thank you staff, you were all fabby!'* LH. *'coming here for two years, and always recommend it.'* FC. *'We have been coming here for twenty five years, you may think us biased. However, although visiting once a year, we have never had a poor meal. The extremely high standard of food are a bench mark, which other restaurants can only hope to approach. Even after a years absence, the warm family welcome sets the mood for an excellent experience. Portions generous, menu extensive and meals very reasonably priced.'* CKL. ps. You have to visit their website to see the array of stars who have visited here; to name just two: Clint Eastwood and Cliff Richard. 12-2.30 & 5-12am.

SCOTTISH BORDERS
Formerly called Borders
Contains four burghs Peeblesshire, Roxburghshire, Selkirkshire & Berwickshire.

Area: Southeast Scotland
Adjacent Counties: D & G, Lothian, Northumberland, Strathclyde

YOU SAY OK, SCOTTISH BORDERS
You might get a discount if you show them this Guide.

EYEMOUTH: NABA 36 Market Street, Galashiels 01890 75007 Formerly the Jamuna. New owners but you might get a discount if you show them this Guide.

GALASHIELS: THE SHISH 86 High Street, TD1 1SQ 01896 75873

GALASHIELS: SWAGG 36 Market Street, Galashiels 01896 750100 Ditto. *'Well lit, comfortable little place. Service is good. Very tasty Jalfry.'* GMCG. Hours: 12-2 & 5-11.

HAWICK: SHUGONDA BALTI HOUSE 4 Station Building, Dove Mount Place 01450 373313 Ditto at BM Talukder's 50-seater Bangladeshi curry house. Hours: 12-2 & 6-11.30.

INNERLEITHEN: SAFFRON 68 High Street, EH44 6HF 01896 833466

STIRLING
Formerly called Central

Area: Mid Scotland

Adjacent Counties:
Lothian, Strathclyde, Tayside

Includes most of the county of Stirlingshire (except Falkirk) and the south-western portion of the former county of Perthshire.

Stirling

EAST INDIA COMPANY   BYO
7 Viewfield Place, Stirling, FK8 1NQ
0845 8334258   www.eastindiastirling.co.uk/

It re-opened in March 2012 after renovations to restaurant and kitchen. Go down the narrow staircase into a candle-lit basement 72 seat dark wood room with portraits of Raj tea moghuls evoking the heigh day of the celebrated tea clippers. The menu is formula curryhouse. Buffet available Mon-Th: £9. Indian dessert favourites mango kulfi or gulab jaman. BYO £3 corkage.   5- 11.

MR SINGH'S   PUNJABI   www.mr-singh.co.uk
MR SINGH'S INDIAN BRASSERIE
16-18 Barnton St FK8 1NA   01786 472137

MR SINGH'S INDIAN COTTAGE
11 Dunbarton Rd, Stirling FK8 2LQ   01786 478889

MR SINGH'S INDIA GATE
Fourways Roundabout, Dunblane. FK15 OEY
0786 822098

Mr Singh, with sons Raj & Jackson were the first restaurateurs to introduce Punjabi cuisine to Stirling in 1996. The dining room has an informal atmosphere with casual dining.is bright and cheerful wall colours offset by dark wood chairs. Thea la carte menu has all the familiar names but given the Punjabi treatment you can expect really tasty food. Buffet lunch, £6; 4course buffet dinner £12 on Sun, Tu & Thur nights.

Helensburgh

CAFE LAHORE
33 West Clyde Street, Helensburgh, G84 8AW
01436 674971

Stunning sea views across Gare Loch at this well established venue opposite the wee port from where you can take The Calmac car ferry (four sailings per day) to nearby Kilcreggan and Gourock on the opposite banks. '*Light, clean and simple decor. Helpful, cheerful and friendly service. Very varied menu, one of the biggest I've seen. I opted for the buffet, came with enormous starter of Mixed Pakora, eight main dishes, two rices and bread. However, if you order fresh naan, you are in for a treat – small is the size of a moderate coffee table! Quite fantastic Lassi and Chai or beer. Recommended.*' RT. Menu Extracts: Fish or Paneer Pakora, Garlic Okra, Chicken lyallpuri, green chilli and coriander; Hasina, tender lamb, marinated, onions, capsicums, tomato, baked in tandoor, sauce, served on sizzler; Mix Hot Rice, fried rice, chicken, lamb, prawns, fresh green chillies, served on hot sizzler. Buffet Nights: 6-11, £9.95, u12 half price. T/a: 10% disc. Delivery: £15 min. 12-2.

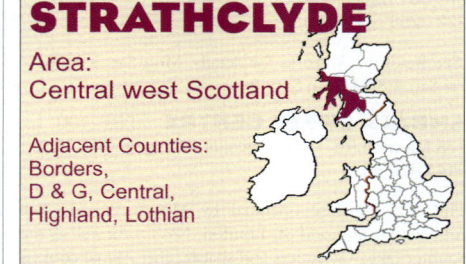

STRATHCLYDE

**Area:
Central west Scotland**

Adjacent Counties:
Borders,
D & G, Central,
Highland, Lothian

Strathclyde (meaning "valley of the River Clyde") currently contains the former counties of Argyle, Ayrshire, Dunbartonshire, Lanarkshire and Renfrewshire It is an historic subdivision of Scotland, and was one of the regional council areas of Scotland from 1975 to 1996.Note: For this edition we are continuing to use the old region of Strathclyde here, but we point out that Northern Strathclyde has become Argyll & Bute, while the rest of Strathclyde is divided into a number of Unitary Authorities, administering the larger cities and surrounds.

Coatbridge

ALISHAN
250 Battlefield Road, Battlefield, Glasgow, G42 9HU
0141 632 5294   www.alishantandoori.co.uk

Proprietor, M Ayub Quereshi, has owned this 48 seater restaurant since 1987. Menu Snapshot: Chef's Platter £9.50, chicken, lamb, vegetable, mushroom, fish pakora; chicken chat; chicken and lamb tikka; shiekh kebab; spiced onions and popadoms. Janter Manter £10, chicken tikka cooked in a sauce with green peppers. Del: 5 miles, £10 min Lunch £7.95, 12-2; 5-12.

ASHOKA SHAK
Showcase Leisure Park, Baillieston, Coatbridge, G69 7TZ
www.ashokarestaurants.com/

The first Ashoka Shak opened 2001 as a fast food outlet. All the favourites. Lunch Thali at £7. Mon-Sat. Hours: Daily 12 - 11. See Glasgow.

PUNJAB EXPRESS
22 West Canal St, Coatbridge, ML5 1PR   01236 422522

Opened in 1993 by the Dhanda brothers, Kally and Tari. The Punjab Express is part of the former Coatbridge Central Station House. Built in 1899, the building still has many of the period features. The station was closed by Lord Beeching in 1963 and the restaurant is situated upstairs in what used to be the station master's accommodation. Downstairs, in the former ticket office, is the Pullman Bar and Lounge. 11am-Mdnt.

Glasgow

AKBARS   TOP 100
573-581 Sauchiehall Street, Glasgow, G3 7PQ   0141 222 2258

See Bradford, W.Yorks for details. Mon-Sat: 5-Mdnt / Fri-Sat: 4:30-12:30; Sun: 2-11

AMBALA SWEET CENTRE   TOP 100
178 Maxwell Rd, Pollockshields, Glasgow G41 1SS   0141 429 5620

This is a franchise operated by Mrs S Ahmad. (See Ambala, Drummond St, London, NW1.) As well as the counter takeaway sweets and snacks, chef Akmal cooks a small range of curries for the 26-seat restaurant. *'Lamb Bhoona is amazing!'* DF. Alcohol not allowed. No credit cards. Hours: 10am-10pm.

ASHOKA   www.harlequinrestaurants.com
Head office, 23 Crow Rd, G11   0141 342 5200

There have been Ashoka restaurants in Glasgow since 1968. Balbur Singh Sumal grew the number to six during the 1980s (including the original at Elderslie Street). They became part of Charan Gill's Harlequin Group. Mr Gill sold the group to Sanjay Majhu who claims it is Europe's largest chain of Indian restaurants, (turnover £12m). The service and food is at a very high standard, high enough for us to give one of their restaurants the BEST IN SCOTLAND award in 2004. The group has shed a couple of venues since 2009 and 's portfolio at the time of writing is 12 restaurants in Glasgow, Renfrewshire, Lanarkshire, Livingston and Dundee. They operate a central reservations, take-away and freephone delivery 'hotline': 0800 195 3195. There's also a cookbook (one recipe of which requires you to use lychees to make their Lamb Rogan Josh!!!) We list the Ashoka Glasgow restaurants here:

ASHOKA ASHTON LANE
19 Ashton La, Hillhead, G12 8SJ   0141 337 1115

Absorbing Indian market scene mural. Manager Vijay. Thali Lunch £4.95 or 2-course Lunch Menu £75, Mon-Sat 12-5. Pre-Theatre Menu £12 served 5-6:30. Mon-Thurs: 12-12. Fri-Sat:to 1am Sun: 5-12.

ASHOKA BEARSDEN
9 Kirk Road, Bearsden, G61 3RG   0800 195 3195

Opened in 1997. It's a franchise, the owner Imtiaz Aslam with manager Vivek. Decor, rich creams and deep browns and a range of colonial artifacts and traditional Indian antiques and bric-a-brac - from sitars and tablas to swords and even bullets - adorn the walls, with subtle traditional Indian lighting giving the restaurant a warm and intimate ambiance. Party room: Harlequin Suite. Kids free Sun when accompanied by an adult. Pre-Theatre Menu £8.95 served 5-6:30. Hours: 5-11.

ASHOKA AT THE QUAY
Unit D2 Springfield Quay, Glasgow, G5 8NP
0141 429 4492

Manager Balraj. 12-11

ASHOKA SHAK
Phoenix Leisure Park, Linwood, PA1 2AB
0800 195 3195

In 2001, the first Ashoka Shak rose from the ashes of the former Harry Ramsden's at the Phoenix Park, close to Glasgow Airport. Manager is Subabish. Thali menu – the ultimate fast Indian dining experience Thali lunch at £4.95 available Mon-Sat. Daily 12-11.

ASHOKA SOUTHSIDE
268 Clarkston Rd, Glasgow, G44 3EA   0800 195 3195

Manager Shalabh. Raj and colonial décor with period pictures, photographs, artifacts and memorabilia adorning the walls. Pre-Theatre Menu £8.95, daily from 5-6:30. Hours Sun-Thurs: 5-11.30; Fri-Sat: 5-12.

ASHOKA WEST END
1284 Argyle Street, Glasgow, G3   0800 195 3195

Opened 1982 near Kelvingrove Art Gallery and Museum on the corner of the longest street and shortest road in the city. Managers Chetan and Manu. Pre Theatre Menu £8.95: 5-7. 25 seats upstairs, 35 downstairs Kids eat free on Sundays when accompanied by an adult. Sun-Th: 4-12.30; Fri & Sat: 5-1am.

ASSAM'S
57 West Regent St Glasgow, G2 2AE
0141 331 1980   www.indianglasgow.com

Assam's opened in 2009 in an elegant red sandstone building which had previously been home to Miso Japanese restaurant. Inside the elegance continues with huge windows, the top parts have attractive stained-glass lights. The friendly, helpful staff in colourful uniforms add to the ambiance. The menu has all the favourites on offer. Av prices: Fixed Lunch: £6.50 (buffet), £7 (tapas), a la carte. £10. Fixed Dinner: £8.45 (tapas). A la carte Dinner: £23. Mon-Th: 12-3 & 5-11; Fri-Sat:12-12; Sun 2-11.

COBRA SPLENDIDLY INDIAN, SUPERBLY SMOOTH

CAFÉ INDIA   www.cafeindia-glasgow.com
171 North St, Charing Cross   0141 248 4074

North street can be found at Charing Cross and runs parallel to the M8 motorway and is accessed from St Vincent Street or Kent Road. It sits across the road from the Mitchell Library. Described (by its owner Abdul Sattar) as *'Britain's first-ever designer buffet restaurant'*. It certainly has changed since it opened in 1979, its seating by 1999 having reached a monumental 560 seats. The ground floor is open-plan and bright. The seats are expensive high-backed pale wood with pink or blue upholstery, depending which zone you are in, and there are some alcove tables. The area called 'the galleries' in the lower floor is moody, with darker reds and wrought iron. Both floors have eye-catching artwork and light fittings. There is provision for self-service via a smart counter for the Fri-Sat e-a-m-a-y-ls (at £12.50). Sattar it seems is proud of the fact that he served 1160 diners in a single day. Takeaway: 10%. Hours: 12-12; Sun. 3-12.

CAFÉ SALMA   NO ALC
523 Sauchiehall Street, Glasgow, G3 7PQ
0141 221 7636   www.cafesalma.com

A unique dual menu opened in 2007 at Café Salma. The spin requests that you *'prepare yourself for a warm welcome as the friendliness of the staff is second only to the gregarious proprietor, Hassan Melloul'*. They wear red fez hats and black salwas and leggings. Not quite Indian, then you place it … north African. And they do indeed have a Morrocan restaurant in the basement with a full menu of starters, mains such as Tajines (c £11) and Couscous dishes and those delightful Arab desserts. On the ground floor the 90 seater Indian is equally homely and informal complete with busy open kitchen and burned orange and red décor. Starters include 7 types of pakoras, crispy samosas and garlic cripsy okra, av £3.50. Punjabi Karahi £8, prepared with fresh meat, garlic, ginger, onions, tomatoes, capsicums and fresh coriander; Lahori Karahi..£8 similar with ginger; Pallak £8, with spinach. Hassan extols the virtues of Salma's four Kofta Specials all £9, meatballs in a sauce of garlic, ginger, coriander, tomato and spices. Kofta Pallak, with spinach; Kofta Anda, with boiled egg; Kofta Paneer with Iindian cheese and Kofta Bhuna with lots of coriander and methi. Whichever restaurant you are in, you can mix and match the two menus. Strictly no alcohol, but a refreshing Moroccan real mint tea is a delight. Delivery: £1 .50. Mon–Sat 12-12; Sun 2-12.

CHARCOALS
26a Renfield Street, Glasgow, G2 1LU
0141 221 9251   www.charcoals.co.uk

A small one-unit shop front doesn't detract from its popularity. Under new management since 2011 we get numerous ticks for this one. The menu is straight forward and includes all the favourites. But it's not what it says, it's how it's done. You like it. Set Lunch £6.95. The pre theatre from 3-6.30 £9.95. Starters include Chicken, Veg or Lahore Fish Pakora, Soup of the Day. Main courses Chicken, Lamb, Prawn or Vegetables. £1 extra for Tikka & Tikka £10, Served with choice of fried rice, boiled rice, nan bread or chapatis eg: Chasni Sweet 'n' sour 'n' creamy; Achari Balti; Chicken or Lamb Saag cooked with spinach and green herbs, Punjabi farmer's favourite; Chilli Fry Jhatpat cooked with green herbs, black pepper & cheese; Paneer Makhni Cottage grilled in the tandoor cooked in special butter sauce; Keema Aloo £9, mince and tatties curry. 11-11.

CHAPATI 1
2017 Dumbarton Rd, Glasgow, G14 0HY   0141 576 0118

Chain of 11 takeaways serving curries, kebabs and pPizza. , est. 1983 by Iqbal S Gill and overseen by Deepa Gill (service) and Harnak Singh (chef). Menu sample: Onion Bhajia £2.50, Potato and Cauliflower Curry £4. Most ordered dishes: Karahi Chicken £5 nd Chicken Jullander £5.80, hot, rich & spicy - tender pieces of chicken cooked in Punjabi masala. This dish is a popular favourite with the staff!. Hours: Sun.-Thurs. 4-12.30; Fri-Sat. 4pm-1.30am. *Branches: (All Glasgow area) Chapati 2, 1576 Dumbarton Rd,G14 9DB 0141 954 3154; Chapati 3, 339 Dumbarton Rd, Partick, G11 6AL 0141 337 1059; Chapati 4, 20 Byres Rd,G11 5JY 0141 334 4089; Chapati 5, 354 Paisley Rd W, G51 1BG 0141 427 6925; Chapati 6, 468 Dumbarton Rd, Dalmuir, 0141 952 9210; Chapati 7, 182 Paisley Rd W, Renfrew, 0141 885 2313; Chapati 8, 5 Lennox Dr, Faifley, 01389 879914; Chapati 9, 3 Greenock Rd, Bishopton, 01505 862 222; Chapati 10 39 Main St, Busby, 0141 644 1971; Sajjan, 2372 Dumbarton Rd, Yoker, 0141 951 1839. Neelim, 1590 Dumbarton Rd, Glasgow, 0141 959 6265.*

GREEN CHILLI CAFÉ
293 Argyle Street Glasgow G3 8TL
0141 337 6378   www.greenchillicafe.com

Green Chilli Café is an Indian Tapas Restaurant in the heart of Glasgow's West End. Owner Sanjay Majhus is following London's newish trend to take old traditional India recipes, mainly snacks and street foods , rebranding them 'Tapas' and serving them in small portions at affordable prices.Masala Dosa, the south indian pancake made from lentils and served with Udi Daal and a double coconut chutney is only £1.50 on Tuesday and Wednesdays. The Trio of Samosa is a popular snack along with curry favourites. Curries are prices as Tapas (small) and normal eg: Chicken Korma is £4.15 or £7.95. Daal Makhani £2.95/ £6.95, black lentils. Wines are picked to achieve the best balance with Green Chilli food. Monday closed; Tu-Sun 5-10.30.

DAKHIN   SOUTH INDIAN
1st Floor, 89 Candelriggs, Glasgow, G1 1NP
0141 553 2585   www.dakhin.com

Established in 2004, Dakhin was the first authentic south

Indian restaurant in Scotland. Set in Glasgow's Merchant city district, the dining room is light and airy with huge windows and light Bentwood chairs and tables and a an open plan kitchen. Starters include Rasam £4, a clear lentil soup flavoured with tomatoes, pepper, garlic, cumin and garnished with chopped green coriander; Meen Porichathu, £6.45, pieces of haddock marinated in ginger & garlic paste, lemon juice, garam masala, malagapudi chutney and gram flour; Chemmen Varuthathu £6.45 King prawn sautéed with assorted peppers in a spicy tomato and garlic sauce; Mamsam Pepper Fry, £6, boneless cubes of lamb stir fried with crushed black peppercorn; Masala Dosa £12, thin rice-based crêpe rapped around a mixture of potatoes, onions, tomatoes and green peas, tempered with spices and mustard leaves. Pathram £6.25 is an assortment of ground rice and lentil pancakes. Chinna Dosa, Sanna Uttapam and Appam. 9, monkfish pieces simmered in a spicy tamarind sauce from 2, a Keralan lamb dish cooked with fried coconut and south Indian spices in a thick sauce; Kodi Koora £11, chicken garnished with fried onions; Avial £8.25 is a medley of vegetables cooked in a paste of coconut, yogurt, and green chillies; Ennai Kathrikai £8.25 is aubergine cooked in a white sesame & peanut based sauce tempered with mustard then flavoured with a tamarind sauce. 12-2 & 5-11.

KAMA SUTRA   PAN INDIAN   TOP 100
331 Sauchiehall Street , Glasgow, G2 3HW
0141 332 0055   www.kamasutrarestaurants.com

In 1996, it opened (opposite the Dental Hospital) to widespread curiosity, with the locals speculating about what might happen behind the stylish frontage. The venue's PR machine added to the mystery: *'the legend comes alive over a candlelit cornucopia of exotic eastern cuisine. You can indulge in the food of love, every which way you want.'* The sultry and sassy design innovation caused a sensation, and the sniggering soon stopped. The minimalist elements of wood, iron, slate and stone are guaranteed to appeal to your most basic instincts. The PR may have eased down a bit, but the website still extols the virtures of the name: *'Kama Sutra: literally means aphorisms of love, the science of love and pleasure. It is not just limited to erotic pleasures but encompasses all sensory pleasures. Thus, aromatic foods, seductive music, sensuous aromas and sultry surroundings all come within the kama sphere.'* Something must be working ... since we last reviewed Kama Sutra they have been breeding; they have new branches in Stirling and Edinburgh (see below). Joking aside, this is a seriously good restaurant. They specialise in pan Indian cuisine. Starters include Pakora choice of: Vegetable £4, Haggis £4.50, Chicken £4.75 Onion Bhaji £4 or Mixed Pakora £4.75; Fish Lahori £5 is white fish marinated in crushed chillies, coriander seeds, fresh garlic, whole spice and deep-fried; Achari Bathak Tikka £5, duck marinated in Indian pickle spices, coriander seeds, cumin and carom seed. Mains include Himalyan Hot Pot £11, lamb or chicken cooked in a spicy sauce with garlic, ginger, mushrooms, peppers, spring onions and carrots; Nalli Wala Gosht £13, a traditional Lucknowi dish of lamb on the bone, in a rich condensed sauce, delicately infused with aromatic spices, kewra and saffron; Dum Ghost Biryani £12, the Hyderabad traditional dish of lamb simmered in basmati rice with a host of aromatic spices, cardamom, saffron and fenugreek, garnished with coriander. Pre-Theatre Menu (2 course £10) 3.30-6.30 daily and Sunday 5-6.30. 12-11. *Branches: Kama Sutra, 109 Lothian Road, Edinburgh, EH3 9AN   0131 229 7747; Kama Sutra, 50 Upper Craigs, Stirling, FK8 2DS 01786 448 460.*

KOH I NOOR   TOP 100
235 North St, Charing Cross, Glasgow, G3 7DL
0141 204 1444   www.koh-i-noor-glasgow.co.uk

Glasgow's earliest Indo-Pak opened in 1961, and boasts to be the originator of the famous e-a-m-a-y-l buffet nights (Mon.-Fri. 7-9pm). Owner and the founder's son Rasul and his son Waseem run it now. Indian and Pakistani decor, with hanging rugs, arches etc. *'Fabulous decor.'* DBAC. Northern Indian formula curries. Its 150 seating is now small in comparison with other Glasgow venues, but is still big considering the national average of 50, and it's still very busy. *'Not only was the service friendly and helpful but the food arrived very promptly, considering the number of people there. The Chicken Dansak was excellent and the naan breads terrific'*. RA. *'Excellent. Samosas so filling, had to leave most of my main course!'* SF. *'Starters very impressive, quantities large. Garlic Nan not for the faint-hearted: beautiful. Chicken Tikka Chasini and Chicken Nentara memorable.'* HB. *'Absolutely superb. In a class of its own.'* BS. Chicken Chatt Patt £9.95, with peppers, onion, green chillies and fresh tomatoes; Chicken Tikka Lalperi £11, tandoori chicken cooked with onions, peppers & red wine. Lamb - £1 extra, Prawn - £1 extra, King Prawn £5, Mince £1 extra, Vegetable £1 less, Lamb Tikka £2 extra, Beef £1 – novel formula. 3 course lunch Mon-Sat 12-3 £7.95. 12-12. (Fri. & Sat. to 1am).

KOOLBA
109-113 Candleriggs, Glasgow, G1 1NP
0141 552 2777   www.koolba.com

KoolBa have tapas-style menu running from lunch time to early evening. Items include: Homemade Vegetable Pakora £5.20; Fish Pakora £3.80; A way to try them all is Combo Platter (for 3 or 4) a selection of pakoras plus chicken chaat. Favourite curries are £9, Specials include Special Lamb Dopiaza £12, with onions and mushroom; Lyllpuri Chicken Tikka £14, cooked in garlic ginger, red capsicums fried mushrooms, onions and touch of honey; Nantara Chicken Tikka & Prawns £14, cooked gently with herbs, onion and fresh chili, garnished with fresh coriander leaves. Tu-Sun: 12-11. Monday closed.

MADRAS PALACE
15 – 17 Kent Rd, Charing Cross, Glasgow, G3 7EH,
0141 248 8333   www.madraspalace.co.uk

Madras Palace, formally known as Panjea and PJ's, is home to Chef PJ. In 1983 he was head chef at Ashoka

COBRA — SPLENDIDLY INDIAN, SUPERBLY SMOOTH

West and Café India with Charan Gill and his partner Gramil. *'PJ apparently has 'mad visions' of curries in his dreams. This could explain some of the more 'inspired' dishes on the menu, such as almond-honey curry, tandoori trout and banana pakora. But it's not just the adventurous who are catered for — safety can be found in all the usual favourites, alongside a wide variety of otherfantastic creations eg: Magic Mushrooms deep-fried mushrooms with five spice.'* Capacity: 350. Buffet 7 Days a week £12.95. House wine: £10 per bottle BYO £3 corkage. Mon-Tu: 12-11; Wed-Th to 12; Fri-Sat to 12.30; Sun 2-12.

MASALA JAK'S
The Quay, Springfield Quay, Glasgow, G5 8NP
0800 195 3195

'Back in the Great American Gold Rush of 1849,' says the venue's spin, *'thousands of prospectors headed to the USA to panhandle for gold. Many found fortunes, thousands died, a few found fame, but perhaps the most famous of all was Jagir Singh, known as 'Masala Jak', who left the Punjab for the USA. Jak found no gold, but did find fortune when he introduced the cowboys of the Wild West to the delights of Indian Cuisine. His fame travelled across America, a legend was born. Old tales tell that the words 'Masala Jak' derived from Mister Jagir Singh, maybe true...maybe not'.* Decidedly not! But the food at the Quay is good at this 100 seater. 12 - 11. (See Ashoka group)

MOTHER INDIA TOP 100
28 Westminster Tce, Glasgow, G3 7R   0141 221 1663

A well-known Glasgow landmark, Mother India opened its doors for business in 1992, and is run by Monir Mohammed. *'The jewel of Glasgow. Small unpretentious restaurant, Top 100 no doubt about it!'* T&KM. *'I've been an avid user of your Curry Guide since 1995 an have travelled the length and breath of the UK always with a copy under my arm! I have eaten curry in most cities and cook my own meal at home ... the best in Glasgow, in my opinion is Mother India. The service, atmosphere and quality of food are second to none in the city. Really fresh ingredients with excellent use of spices cooked to perfection.'* JT. Some starters: Ginger Crab & Prawn Dosa £5.20, cooked with ginger pickle stuffed in a lentil rice pancake; Spiced Haddock & Roasted Tomatoes £5.40, oven-baked with a variety of punjabi spices & roasted tomatoes; Chana Mushroom On A Green Herb Flat Bread £4.80, chick peas & whole mushrooms made with a sweet tamarind sauce. Mains Include Smeena's Slow Chicken Curry £9.20, green chilli, tomatoes & onions cooked for hours with a touch of olive oil, simmered with whole spices; Raan For 2 People £28, leg of lamb, slowly cooked with whole spices then finished off with a sweet almond sauce served with basmati rice, raita and breads. Mon-Th: 5.30-10.30, Fri to 11; Sat: 12-11; Sun to 10. *Branches: Mother India's Cafe, 1355 Argyle Street, Glasgow, G3 8AD 0141 339 9145; Mother India's Cafe, 3-5 Infirmary Street, Edinburgh, EH1 1LT 0131 524 9801, Dining In7 New Kirk Road, Glasgow, G3 7RU 0141 942 3643; Dining In, 1347 Argyle Street, Glasgow, G3 8ADT 0141 334 3815.*

MISTER SINGH'S INDIA TOP 100
149 Elderslie Street, Glasgow, G3 7JR
0141 204 0186

Satty Singh owns this 90-seater restaurant, as its eponymous title suggests, and like other Glasgow restaurants, as part of the Harlequin Group (see Ashoka above) it benefits from group marketing and purchasing muscle. Decor combines ethnic and traditional Scottish with stark white walls and dramatic bursts of cobalt blue creating a magical Mediterranean milieu, and hand-carved wooden balustrades and mirrors. Manager Jamil Ahmed, and the waiters wear kilts and the girls wear salwars; Younis Ahraf (who wears chef's whites, by the way) does curried Haggis! And we hear that there's a French influence at work in the kitchens too. *'Without question the best I have visited! Vast menu. Fantastic food, good portions. Booking essential, even mid-week. For me, it is a 'must' when I am travelling to Glasgow! The food is so good and tasty, particularly the Chilli Garlic Chicken.'* RA. *'We must have been the second couple to enter the restaurant but within 30 minutes the whole place was packed and we took this to be a very good sign indeed. We were impressed by the amount of food on the plate. When the main course arrived I can only say it was the best curry I have ever tasted and that includes my own, spicy hot but very tasty. One of the finest curries in the country'.* GC. For a fusion starter try the Haggis, Neeps and Tatties Samosa, £5. By contrast try the tradional Punjabi Lamb Palak £14, succulent lamb cooked on-the-bone with spinach, sautéed with onion and flavoured with coriander or Chicken Tandoori Masala £14, cooked c on-the-bone with capsicums, onions and tomatoes simmered in a marinade of exotic spices. Lunch Mon-Fri: 12-5, £6.95 Pre-Theatre Daily from 5-6.30, £8.95. Weekend Brunch (Sat: 12-5, Sun 2.30-5) £6.95 (one child u12 eats free for every adult dining a la carte). Mon-Sat: 12- 12; Sun: 3-12.

MODERN PUNJABI
560 Paisley Road West, Glasgow, G51 1RF
0141 427 0521

Established in 1981, it has been the darling of its locals for over three decades. The Singh family who run it proudly announce that it is real Punjabi food from real Punjabis! They produce quality Indian food to authentic recipes which have been handed down by family members. See next entry for more details.

PUNJABI CHARING CROSS
157–159 North Street, Glasgow, G3 7DA
0141 221 3626   www.punjabicharingcross.co.uk

You might be forgiven for thinking that the bright red frontage of this terraced town building heralded a fire station. You'd be wrong. It's the latest 50 seat incarnation from the Punjabi, see above, who after 30 years busy trading south of the river, they opened a new venue north side in 2011. Punjabi food is very flavourful and tasty and the menu delivers all you want. Starters include pakoras, samosas, and specialities not seen on most Indian restaurant menus e.g Haggis pakora, Keema Padora, and Noori dishes (ingredients in a thick north Indian Punjabi sauce with green pepper, onion & special spices with a special tangy taste. It's the staff favourite). There is a full range of starters includes Shahi Kebab £7, steak pieces basted in batter prepared from spiced gram flour, served with rice, salad & curry sauce; Mixed Grill £10, quarter of tandoori chicken, chicken tikka & lamb tikka with mushrooms, onions, herbs & Punjabi spices. House Specials include Chef's Special Curry £6, chicken, lamb & prawn cooked with fruit & Punjabi spices & herbs then garnished with pineapple.Th-Sat: 12-2.30; Daily 4.30-12.

RAWALPINDI TANDOORI
321, Sauchiehall Street, Glasgow, G2 3HW
0141 332 4180   www.rawalpindi-tandoori.co.uk

This 80 seater has there since 1979. *'My friends and I go to regularly to this restaurant. Good prices and quality, unlike others nearby that are overpriced. Would recommend it a good basic Indian.'* JK. Menu Snapshot: Chicken Chat £4.50 - drumsticks marinated in spicy yoghurt and lemon juice just barbecued in the clay oven and cooked in a tangy sauce served with salad; Onion Bhajia £4 - original or rings (rings sound good! I wonder if they are like the fried onions rings, the ones you get in a Pub - hope so!) served with sauce and salad; Tandoori Salmon £7; Scampi Ceylonese £12, Beef Biryani £13. Lunch: 3 courses £8, Pre Theatre Dinner: 4pm - 7, 3 courses £10. Buffet Mon- Sat 12 - 3.30. Hours: Mon–Th: 12-12 (Fri-Sat to 1am; Sun 1pm–12).

SHISH MAHAL   TOP 100
60-68 Park Road, Glasgow, G4 9JF
0141 334 7899   www.shishmahal.co.uk

The Shish Mahal is a Glasgow institution. It goes back to 1959 when one Noor Mohammed founded a café called Green Gates Asian Restaurant on Bank Street. It was frequented by Punjabis and students. Noor decided a move up market was the way forward. It was a risk and Noor's son, the then young Ali Ahmed Aslam now aka "Mr Ali" opened in 1964 on Gibson Street. He chose the name Shish Mahal which means 'mirror or crystal-glass Palace'. The original was built in Agra in 1540 by Mughal emperor Shah Jahan for his bride Nur. Glasgow's Shish Mahal was, at the time a pioneer of elegant dining with raj-style service (dinner-jacketed waiters, crisp white table cloths and King's cutlery) and authentic Pakistani food. Nothing had been seen like it before in Glasgow. It was a USP All Noor's wife Sahra did the cooking. Before long it was packed out. There has always been the urban legend that CTM was invented in Glasgow. Mr Ali claims to have created the dish in the mid-70s using a tin of tomato soup to make a spicy gravy when a customer complained that his Chicken Tikka was dry. Although the dish was in reality a development of the erstwhile Mughal dish, Murgh Makhni (butter chicken) CTM was a further USP for the Shish. So much so that, in 2009, a local MP planned to table a motion in the House calling for CTM to have the same legal protection as other regionally designated foods such as Arbroath smokies, Cumberland sausage and Melton Mowbray pork pies. Basmaii rice want it, and they have a case, but it isn't of European origin, so they won't get it. Neither will CTM. The MP referred to is Mohammed Sarwar, Glasgow Labour MP from 1997 to 2010. Say no more! The Shish was forced to move premises in 2000 when subsidence caused structural damage. Mr Ali's son Raishaid Ali is the current CEO, assisted by his young son Eysha Noor Ali who is the 4th generation to run Shish, another USP in the curry industry. Inside it is attractively 'Indian' with pillars and arches, drapes and artwork, trinkets and light fittings *'and shiny brass inserts stud the glossy dark wood floor, emblazoned with the restaurant's 'S' motif.'* The menu is Pan-subcontinent of which Raishaid says *'it is a Glaswegian embassy for the finest Asian cuisine.'* Menu Snapshot: Chicken Tikka & Mince Samosas, Chicken Chaat Patty, bright red barbecued wings with a spicy sweet and sour sauce; Garam Macher, spicy seafood soup; lamb amrat mirchi Punjabi Khoya (lamb simmered in cream with spices; Lamb Handi Pakistani Kalichain, marinated egg and lamb, with garlic, onion, tomato and diced chunks of whole lemon; Lamb Tikka Garam Masala is deep red, rich and thick, with onions, fresh ginger and garlic butter with an aromatic spice mix. Any main course dish goes well with Chawal e Khas (rice fried in saffron rice. Indian desserts include Kulfi and Gulab Jamun. *'On hearing it was my birthday, four of the staff came to our table with a candle in the dessert and they all sang Happy Birthday. It was brilliant! Then everyone started clapping. I was overwhelmed to say the least, the only downfall was that I had forgotten to bring my camera so no funny pictures'* glasgoweating.co.uk. Four Course Lunch £9.45. 12-2. Beer from £3.35 per bottle, Wine from £13. Booking essential. Shish Mahal Cookbook. Excellent Facebook and S. Mon–Th: 12-2 & 5-11; Fri-Sat: 12-11.30 (Lunch to 2) Sun: 5-10. *Also Shish Mahal, First floor, 1348 Maryhill Road, Lanarkshire, G20 9DG.*

SOUTHERN SPICE   SOUTH INDIAN
325 Sauchiehall Street, Glasgow, G2 3HW
0141 333 9977   www.thesouthernspice.co.uk

Southern Spice opened in 2010 as Glasgow's second south Indian restaurant. The 63 seater has to compete with the 100 or so city curry venues which have acclimatised Glasgow to savoury, meaty Punjabi Pakistani curries with a sprinkling of Bangladeshi curryhouses. South Indian food, is equally spicy, but it's so very dfferent. Mind you, there are ample meat dishes on the menu to satisfy the beefiest, most voracious carniverous Glaswegian. If you must you can order the 'old favourites'. Try the Rasam £2, the traditional south Indian soup made with tamarind, black pepper andspices. Starters include: Thairu Vada (Dahi Vada) Medu £3.75, a savoury doughnut, made with urid dal flour, onion, green chilli and pepper, deep-fried, chilled and immersed in yogurt and spices or Aloo Bonda £3.45, an Indian rissole made with spicy mashed potato balls, gram flour and spices and fried. And there is nothing more fulfilling than Dosas , the south Indian pancake made with fermented ground rice and urid dal flour, served with coconut chutney and sambar (lentils and tender vegetables cooked with jaggery, tamarind and ground roasted spices) served plain of wrpped around a filling. There are a remarkable 14 fillings, from potato curry £7.25, to lamb or fish, £9.75. Mains include: Pappu (Dal Curry) £4 prepared with cooked lentils, green chillies garlic and onions or Dal Spinach, £4. Vorugallu Kodi Koora £8.75 is chicken cubes cooked with cloves, cardamom, ginger garlic paste and fried red chillies and garnished with fried onions; Nellore Chicken Curry £8.75, is chicken cubes cooked traditional Andhra style with ginger garlic paste, chilli powder, yogurt, cinnamon seeds, cloves, cardamom and garnished with fried onions; Swadesi Ghost £11, is lamb with yogurt, lemon juice, ginger, garlic, chilli, and other Indian spices; Chepala Pulusu £11.25 is fish in a gravy prepared with ginger-garlic, tamarind, turmeric, green chillies and onions. Av price: £4.75 (set lunch); £14 (evening meal). Pre-theatre: £9.75. House wine: £12 per bottle. 12–12.30am.

WEE CURRY SHOP BYO
7 Buccleuch St, Glasgow, G3 6SJ
0141 353 0177 www.theweecurryshopglasgow.com

Everything about this eatery is small, including the capacity (40 seats) and the menu – smaller than a paperback book, so is its selection. But the portions are large! *'Really good. Very wee indeed. One chef in the open kitchen and one waiter. Vegetable side dishes seem to have low priority. My pal has been eating here for years.'* GG. *'It's wise to book – it's a snug place with a big reputation'*. HEG. The menu has also probably the smallest selection we have ever seen. However, as the saying goes, better to cook one dish well than ten badly. There are only four starters to choose from: Vegetable or Chicken Pakoras, Aubergine Fritters and Mutter Paneer Puri. There are a few more mains to choose: six Chicken dishes, prices from c£6-£8; one Lamb, a Karahi dish; four Vegetables eg: Aloo Sag, Black Eye Beans and Broccoli and one Dal. To accompany your curries, there is Basmati Rice , Garlic Potatoes, Chappati 60p, Paratha and Raitha £1.20. We agree: you don't need anything more! Av price: £5.75 (thali), £16 (evening meal). Wine: £11.50 per bottle; BYO: £2.50 corkage wine only. Mon-Sat: 12-2.30; Mon-Th: 5.30-10; Sun & Fri to 10.30; Sat: 12-11. Branches: 29 Ashton Lane, Glasgow, G12 8SJ 0141 357 5280 &41 Byres Road, Glasgow, G11 6RG 0141 339 1339.

TAYSIDE
(Inc Angus, Kinross and Perthshire)

Area: East Scotland

Adjacent Counties: Central, Fife, Grampian, Highland, Strathclyde

Dundee

ASHOKA SHAK
Camperdown Leisure Park, Dundee, DD2 3SQ
01382 858169 www.ashokarestaurants.com

Manager: Roytel. See Ashoka Glasgow for details. Daily 12 noon till 11 pm :

CHATNI
15 Main Street, Methven, Perthshire, PH1 3PU
01738 840 505

A wee village pop 1,100 8km west of Perth, has a Chinese takeaway/chippie, a garage and a post office/general store and the village restaurant in an 18th century detached cottage had a change of ownership in Nov 2009, and is now an Indian Restaurant. It is run by Chefs, Edris and his brother, Omar, from Chitagong, south Bangladesh who offer the full curryhouse standard menu. Wed-Mon: 5-11 (closed Tues)

DIL SE AWARD WINNER
99 Perth Road, Dundee, DD1 4HZ 01382 221501

Abdour Rouf's 150-seat Dil Se restaurant (pron dill see and means, 'from the heart.') was presented with the Dundee Civic Trust Award for its outstanding contribution to the improvement of the city when it opened in 2003. It specialises in Bangladeshi, Indian and Thai cuisine Clients dress up to eat here, as the modern and stylish air of this restaurant requires it. The fresh, organic ingredients, herbs and vegetables, are grown in the garden behind its sister establishment, The Balaka, St Andrews. Locally produced salmon is also a speciality, served marinated in chilli, coriander and cumin - delicious and healthy! Dil Se decor is modern and minimalist and the toilets are like a fake leopard skin coat - absolutely spotless. The Dil Se menu is a carbon copy of The Balaka's and every last morsel of food is cooked to order. *'We kicked off with chilli pickle - careful, friends, this red hot stuff will seriously blow your tights off - and a pile of popadoms that were so fresh I'm surprised they didn't try to slip the haun. Then came the real starters - Chicken Tikka and a Shami Kebab. Simple Chicken Tikka is always a smart option if you want to* judge any Indian - or, in this case, Bangladeshi restaurant. The Tikka at Dil Se was perfect. Every mouthful burst with flavour - particularly when smeared thickly with the awesome chilli pickle - and I loved the tasty little burnt bits. From the list of fifteen or so chef specials, I tried the Mas Bangla, salmon fillet, marinated in lime juice, turmeric, green chilli and several other spices then fried in mustard oil with garlic, onion, tomato and aubergine. Believe it or not, it tasted even better than it sounds, and special doesn't even begin to describe it. I said it before and I'll say it again, why can't more curry houses start using salmon? It always works well'. Tam Cowan, Dundee Record. This is an outstanding, caring restaurant, and following the tradition of its sister, the Balaka in St Andrews, Fife, we took great pleasure in giving it our Best in Scotland award 2004/5 award. Delivery: 20 m, £2 min. Sun-Th: 5-1am; Fri-Sat.: 12-1am. Open Christmas Day. *Branch: Balaka, St Andrews.*

WALES

For Wales as with England, the Guide runs alphabetically in county and town order. In 1996 a large number of Unitary Authorities replaced the six Welsh counties (regions) which had themselves replaced the age-old shires and smaller counties in 1965. To provide a convenient geographical division of Wales in this Guide, we retain the six former counties (listing their shires within them).

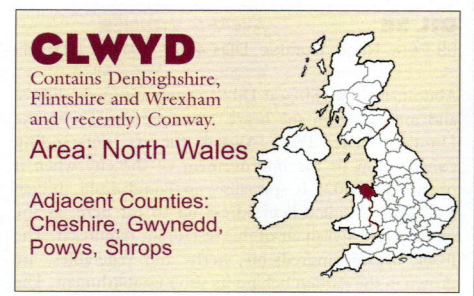

CLWYD
Contains Denbighshire, Flintshire and Wrexham and (recently) Conway.

Area: North Wales

Adjacent Counties:
Cheshire, Gwynedd, Powys, Shrops

Deeside

BENGAL DYNASTY   AWARD WINNER
106 Chester Road East, Shotton, Deeside, CH5 1QD
01244 830455 www.thebengaldynasty.com

Monchab Ali bought a former guest house in 1991 and converted it into a stylish, spacious restaurant. In 2001, the restaurant re-opened after having had a complete face-lift at a cost of over £200,000. A stunning new entrance, bigger windows, change of interior colour, new floor. It is air-conditioned, purpose-built, airy and elegant, luxury and a fabulous Demonstration Kitchen allows diners to see the technical wizardry of the Corporate Chef Partha Mitra and his brigade preparing and cooking their food. The smartly-furnished seats 92 seater, managed by Rico is fully-licensed, with a roomy lounge bar seating 40. It has disabled access. Chef Mitra's north Indian and Bangladeshi include such specials as Bagda Chingri with Nairkol £11, Bay of Bengal Tiger Prawn cooked with freshly ground black mustard, coconut, fresh green chilli, coriander and; Mazedar Duck £12, duck breasts in a sweet & tangy sauce of orange, honey, basil, and other carefully selected ingredients cooked to perfections, Paneer Khurchan, £8, cottage cheese batons combined with pimentos, onions; Mah Ki Dal £8, black lentil and kidney beans boiled overnight and prepared with tomatoes, garlic, butter and cream. *'Truly exceptional place. The food was just the business. This restaurant is well worthy of its Best in North Wales rating.'* MW. *'Outstanding.'* WAJ. Takeaway: 15% disc. Del: £12 min, 5-12-2.30 & 5.30-11.30; Sun. 12.30-11. *Branches: Bengal Dynasty Northwich Cheshire and Llandudno Gwynedd and Hollywood, California.*

AMANTOLA
Welsh Rd, Sealand, Deeside, CH5 2HX
01244 811383   www.amantola.co.uk

Amantoal opened in 1997 in a large and imposing free-standing building by the main North Wales Coast Road (A55) and right opposite RAF Sealand. Large car park complete with fountain and elephant statues leads to an elegantly decorated interior decorated in reds and greens . It has soft, comfortable sofas to relax on while taking coffee and liqueurs after a satisfying spicy meal. It seats 200 in two rooms. *'Incredibly impressive looking restaurant. Very friendly and knowledgeable staff, some of whom are noticeably local! Extensive menu, though the special dishes have made up names, (such as Indian Summer, Asian Love, Beauty of Assam) which I found detracted from the cuisine. Very nice Chicken Chat Puri £4, very light and remarkably grease-free Puri with a pleasant and delicate taste of its own, topped with lovely combination of small pieces of tender chicken in a mouth watering sauce topped with a generous sprinkle of Chat Masala. Lamb Rogan Josh £10, just as good, excellent pieces of lamb, free of fat and gristle, served in a tasty, tangy sauce rich in herbs and spices. This was served with a light and fluffy, mould of al-dente Pullao Rice £2.75, well perfumed and lump free. A smashing meal.'* RW. *'Overall an excellent lunch.'* DB. Takeaway: 10% discount. Delivery: 5-mile radius, minimum charge £15. 12-2.30 & 5-12. Sat-Sun 12-12.

Flint

VERANDA
11-15 Chester Street, Flint 01352 732504

Chef owner, Adbul and his staff are *'friendly and welcoming. Place buzzing and if you get a table at the back, you can catch a glimpse of the cooking in the kitchen. They also make a*

SPLENDIDLY INDIAN, SUPERBLY SMOOTH

chicken Tikka flambée, where they pour Sambuca onto the sizzling platter and flames shoot two feet in the air.' DV-W. Menu Snapshot: Ostrich Tikka £5, served with salad; Mussels £10 - fresh mussels steamed with a lively broth of chillies and curry leaves; King Prawn Gratin £12, barbecued with butter sauce, topped with cheese. 5-10.30.

Llangollen

SAMIRAH TANDOORI
36 Regent Street, Llangollen LL20 8HS
01978 861887   www.samirahtandoori.co.uk

Abul Hussain runs the Samirah (formerly Spice Lounge), in a distinctive red-brick corner building in the tourist town set below the hills in the Dee Valley. Thousands of visitors come in July when it hosts the Llangollen International Musical Eisteddfod. Full regular menu. Banquet Nights, Sun-Wed: 5.30-12, Any choice from menu, Starter, Main course, Side dish, Rice or Nan £9.95, u12 £4.95, Duck & King Prawn extra £2. Hrs: Mon-Sat: 5.30-12; Sun 1-12.

Wrexham

TAVA
Castle Street, Holt, Wrexham, LL13 9YL
01829 270491   www.tava-indian.co.uk

In a white detached former pub, Tava (meaning griddle pan) has been dispensing formula curries for some years. Specials snapshot: Satkora SpeciaL £8-£11, a Bangladeshi vegetable often people put with chicken or lamb to give a very unique tangy taste; Mossomon (Chicken, lamb or prawn) £7.95 Bangladeshi vegetable called Uri seeds combined with local beans cooked in thick medium sauce; Khushboo mild creamy thick sauce with coconut, almonds & roasted cashew nuts, green peppers & light spices. 5-11 (Fri-Sat to 12); Sun: 3-10.

DYFED
Contains Cardigan, Carmarthenshire & Pembrokeshire

Area: West Wales

Adjacent Counties:
Glam, Powys, Gwynedd

Carmarthen

TAJ BALTI
119 Priory St, Carmarthen, SA31 1NB   01267 221995

Opened in 1995 by Lias Miah who might give you a discount if you show him this Guide. *My husband and I always enjoy their fare. Elegant decor, service excellent and friendly, with superb food. Muted traditional music, intimacy of individual booths, a special atmosphere. Tandoori Mixed Grill declared the best ever.'* JF. 6-12.

Llanelli

BENGAL LANCER
43 Murray St, Llanelli, SA15 1BQ   01554 749199

78-seater opened by Ahmed Ali in 1986 who might give you a discount if you show him this Guide. It has recently had an interior refurb, attradting popular praise. Muzaffar heads the cooking. 12-2.30 & 6-12. Branch: *Anarkali , Swansea.*

YOU SAY OK
You may get a discount if you show him this Guide
LLANELLI: SHEESH MAHAL 53 Stepney St, www.restaurantsllanelli.co.uk Llanelli   **SHER KHAN** 20 Market Street, Llanelli SA1 5YD 01554 756316 www.sherkhans.co.uk   Young brothers Sam. Salem and Kalam run this 40 seater with enthusiasm and passion. Formula menu and a popular venue.
LLANELLI VERANDAH 20 Market Street, Llanelli   01554 75956164 seater opened in 1985 by Mr A Khalique. Special: Charga Mossalla (half spring-chicken, with tomatoes, green peppers & red wine). 6-12. (Sat 12.30).
TENBY: BAY OF BENGAL 1 Crackenwell Street Tenby, SA70 7HA   01834 843331   *Very good meal at The Bay of Bengal. Beautifully furnished, restaurant looks out to the sea, food matched the view. Chicken and Chickpea for Linda and King Prawn Bhuna for me - so many prawns!'* MG.

GLAMORGAN
Contains West, Mid & South Glamorgan.

Area: South Wales

Adjacent Counties:
Dyfed, Gwent, Powys

In 1996, the counties of West, Mid and South Glamorganshire were disbanded in favour of 11 Unitary Authorities to administrate the 11 large towns (incl Newport) in the area. For Guide convenience we have retained the former Glamorgan geography. For Newport see Gwent.

Bridgend

ASHOKA
68 Nolton Street, Bridgend, CF31 3BP
01656 650678   www.ashoka-bridgend.co.uk

Mispak Miah established it in 1987, the Ashoka Tandoori is the longest running Indian Restaurant in Bridgend and is not connected to the Glasgow group. Menu snapshot: Special Royal Thali (2 People) £30, kebab platter, spiced papadums, CTM, lamb dansak, mushroom masala, cauliflower masala, special fried rice & nan; Lamb or Chicken Shirazi, £11 thinly sliced then marinated in spices with garlic & green chillies; Honey Chicken £11, cooked in honey, capsicum, onions, mushroom, tomatoes & asparagus. Boal Fish Mazala £13 pan-fried spiced Bangladeshi fish. Mon-Th & Sat: 12-2; Sun-Fri: 5.30-12 (Sat to 1am).

BOKHARA BRASSERIE TOP 100
Court Colman Manor Hotel, Pen-y-Fai, Bridgend, CF31 4NG   01656 720212
www.bokhararestaurant.com   HOTEL

This is a gem hidden away in a maze of country roads, isolated in six acres of landscaped grounds including a waterfall, rose walk and even a dogs cemetery, but just 2 miles from junction 36 of the M4. Court Colman Manor was built in 1776 and bought by retired naval surgeon William Llewellyn and it passed down to family members into the 20th century. In 1981, it was bought by the late Vijay Bhagotra, who converted it into a gorgeous 3 star hotel with 30 en-suite bedrooms (double £60 per night), ten of which are themed rooms (£70), Moroccan, Mediterranean, Venetian, Japanese etc. The interior is unashamedly opulent, with a sweeping staircase and majestic ballroom. Sanj Bhagotra, Vijays son is the current owner. and the restaurant is decidedly Indian, though it serves both Indian and Mediterranean food (and Welsh breakfasts). It is decked out in warm colours – orange, sandy yellow, terracotta and red – to reflect the Indian and Mediterranean food it serves. Starters include: .Kalongi Paneer Tikka £5, kebabs of fresh cottage cheese marinated in a batter of yoghurt, ginger garlic and exotic spices with "Kalongi" (nigella seeds) and tandoored; Bharwan Shimla Mirch £4.50, capsicum stuffed with potatoes, cottage cheese, cashew nuts & sultanas, spiced with cumin, aniseed and roasted in skewer; Barrah Kebab £5, chunks from the leg of lamb & chops, marinated in the mixture of yoghurt and vinegar with melange of spices and char-grilled over red hot amber; Chicken Khati Roll £3.75, tandooried chicken juliennes blended with sautéed onions, coriander and chat masala rolled in whole wheat flat pancakes served with mint chutney and tamarind chutney. Mains include: Rara Gosht Punjabi £10, chunks of lamb with lamb mince mixed with ginger-garlic, green chillies, cinnamon, cumin, coriander and braised in marinade;, Raan–e–Khandar £40 serves 6, 24 hrs notice; whole leg of lamb marinated overnight, and grilled in the Tandoori and finished in fresh a aromatic Masala. Dal Makhani £4, black lentils, ginger-garlic paste and tomato, simmered overnight over slow fire, garnished with cream & dollops of homemade butter; Baingan Ka Bharta £5, roasted aubergine sautéed with tomatoes, onions, garam masala, red chillies & coriander and garnished with fresh green coriander. Desserts include: Gajar Ka Halwa £3. Matka Kulfi £3.50, nutty and creamy cardamom-flavoured India Ice cream made and served in traditional earthenware pots. Non residents welcome. Booking inc residents advisable. 12–2.30 & 6-10.

SPLENDIDLY INDIAN, SUPERBLY SMOOTH

LE RAJ
Porthcawl Rd, South Cornelly, Bridgend, CF33 4RE
01656 741174   www.le-raj.com

Off at J17 M4, a couple of miles west of Bridgend. Follow your nav into South Cornelly near the quarries. Arriving at the whitewashed /red brick low building you wouldn't expect to find such a decadent interior. *'Its a bit like a Victorian drawing room full of trinkets'* says HEG. Friendly staff. They also have a "drive thru" facility to speed up your food collection. Lunch & dinner daily.

Cardiff

JUBORAJ   A-LIST
10 Mill La, Hayes, Cardiff, CF1   029 2037 7668
www.juborajgroup.com

Cardiff's Juboraj Group consists of six quality restaurants, four in Cardiff, one in Newport and the other in Swansea. Menu snapshot: Starters include Bhajees, Samosas, Pakoras, kebabs and Tandoori items. Main courses: Karahi Duck, tender pieces of duck barbecued and tossed in medium spices with onions, tomatoes and green peppers; Chicken Shashlick, cooked in the clay oven with green peppers, onions and tomatoes, served with a mild sauce; Machli Biran, salmon steak delicately spiced & gently fried Sag Paneer, spicy spinach and cottage cheese; Paneer Chilli Massala, with fresh green chillies and Special Fried Rice, with eggs, peas, onions, almond and spices. Desserts include Sticky Toffee Pud, Apple and Blackberry Crumble. This branch is *'Fairly large, comfortable restaurant, good reputation, very popular. Visited by Tom Jones' [wow!] 'In my opinion, one of Cardiff's best. Another visit, and the food once again was excellent.'* JB. *'We took the Guide's advice and headed for this restaurant. Popadoms and Kebabs (Shami and Sheek) both excellent. Main courses, Chicken Madras, Chicken Sagwalla accompanied by Pullao Rice, Nan and Tarka Dal, excellent! Food a little more expensive, guess that was a result of its town centre location! Will visit again.'* DL. 12-2 & 6-12am. Branches 11 Heol Y Deri, Cardiff 029 2062 8894, also 84 Commercial St, Newport 01633 262646 and 20 Wind St, Swansea. 01792 649944. See page 50.

YOU SAY OK
LAHORE KEBABISH PAKISTANI 160 Penarth Road, Cardiff, South Glamorgan CF11 6NJ 029 2022 1354 Sayed Shazad, manages this popular takeaway.
THE MANGO HOUSE 5-7 Westgate Street, Riverside, Cardiff 029 2023 2299 www.mangohouse.co.uk
Mirchi, 89 City Road, Roath, Cardiff Glam 02920 492344
ROYALS INDIAN TAKEAWAY & FISH BAR 31 Broadway Cardiff, CF24 1GE   029 2045 0182. Very popular cheap takeaway in a rundown area. Problem solved if some of the family are normal like Indian and some are abnormal wimps don't. 5pm-1am.
SPICE MERCHANT Stuart Street, Cardiff, CF10 5BU 029 2049 8984 www.spicemerchantcardiff.com Dinner set menu £10. 11.30-11.30.
SPICE QUARTER 8b, The Old Brewery Quarter, Cardiff, CF10 1FG 029 2022 0075. www.spicequarter.co.uk 12.30-2.30 5.30 -11.30 (mdnt Fri Sat 10 Sun)
SPICE ROUTE 6 Red Dragon Centre, Atlantic Wharf, Cardiff 029 2048 8320.

MINT & MUSTARD   INDIAN FINE DINING
134 ,Whitchurch Rd, Cardiff CF14 3LZ
029 2062 0333   www.mintandmustard.com

Ajit Kandoran, a senior surgeon at Taunton's Musgrove Park Hospital opened this restaurant with the spin *'that it is Wales most talked about Indian restaurant'*. He boasts of redefining the whole country's cuisin , aided by local personality chef Anand George (see p33). Don't expect CTM (Chicken Tikka Masala!) or table-sized naans; this is highly refined, deftly spiced cooking, although none the less tasty for it. The menu changes regularly, but getting rave reviews at the moment are Goan Pork Vindaloo and the restaurant's signature dish, Allepey Fish Curry. Executive Chef Pramod Nair is ex Taj Coromandel Hotels in south India and Sri Lanka . Raised in Jaipur, India, Chef Siddartha "Sid" worked at the Oberoi Vanyavilas. Starters include: Scallops Thengapal, £7.50, hand-dived Scottish Scallops simmered in lemon zest flavoured coconut milk; Anchovy Fritters, £5.50, southern Indian spiced anchovies served with a garlic sauce; King Fish Steak Vattichathu, masala-fried steaks of King fish tossed in shallots & tomatoes served with salad and potato cake. Main course examples: Syrian Beef Curry £11.50, a spicy preparation from the Syrian Christians of Kerala; Goan Porc Vindalu £11.50, from the Portuguese vin dalho meaning wine and garlic, pork cooked with home ground red chillies and spices, intensely flavoured with garlic and wine vinegar, reduced for a unique taste; Nadan Kozhi Curry, £10.50, kerala- style chicken curry with coconut milk, tomatoes and spices; Cheera Parippu Kootu, £7.50, spinach and bengal gram with coconut and cumin; Olan £4.50, butternut squash and cow peas simmered in a sauce of spiced coconut milk. 12-2 & 6-10.30. *Branch: Mint & Mustard Taunton.*

MOKSH   BEST IN WALES
Ocean Building, Bute Crescent, Cardiff CF10 5AY
029 2049 8120   www.moksh.co.uk

MMoksh, meaning 'spiritual liberation', has a unique restaurant name and a unique chef-patron in Steven Gomes. It is in the north end of Mermaid Quay, the former Cardiff Bay coal export docks and now regenerated as an attractive waterfront location, less than a kilometre from the city centre. Sadly the Quay is infested with the usual soulless chains of restaurants bars and coffee shops. Indian cuisine was represented, until the demise of Café Naz (coincidentally Chef Gomes former employer). And this makes Moksh all the more attractive and worth seeking out, just round the corner from the main Quay. The restaurant is intriguingly decorated with graffiti art on the walls and ceiling in bright and deep colours, including brown, orange and cream with dark and polished natural wood. The original Pajoda and Buddha masterpieces are on a wall in the private dining room. There is also a huge sleeping Buddha painted onto the ceiling of the main dining room -

very dramatic. Stephen, already a winner of the Cobra Good Curry Guide BEST CHEF AWARD, 2009-2012, regularly produces new menus. This is current at the time of writing: Starters contained four choices, and within each choice there were several different dishes. For example Moksh Delight £6, consists of Chocolate and Orange Chicken Tikka, a generous and moist chunk of chicken breast, with a wonderful hint of plain chocolate and citrus orange; Hyderbadi Mince and Potato with Chilli Beetroot Foam, like a cute little cottage pie, and, Balachao Dusted Pork Belly on Tomato Charasa and Edible Rice Paper, tender, quality pork cubes, in a rich savoury sauce, and yes! edible rice paper!. Treasures of the Sea, £7 consists of Soft Shelled Crabs on Puffed Rice, Prawn Cocktail with Lemon Cloud, a delicately spiced prawn cocktail and Salmon Tikka with Salmon and Mango Caviar. The salmon dissolves in the mouth! Welsh Beef Tamarina @ cloud 9, £6 is juliennes of beef in tamarind and black pepper sauce, served with sugar cloud and Baby Nan, beautifully presented in its own little lidded, circular, metal box, reminiscent of the Daba lunch boxes of Bombay. The beef had been slow-cooked, so was incredibly tender and had absorbed the flavours of the aromatic sauce. The, sugar cloud, was in fact candy floss. Tarik and Hasan from Sylhet, served our main course dishes, which consisted of: Punjabi Butter Chicken, £12, Tikkas in rich tomato, cream and butter finished with fenugreek. Served with cinnamon nitro essence; Ratnagiri Mango Lamb, £13, sweet and spicy lamb and Ratnagiri mango spheres and lamb cooked in coconut milk, mango pulp, spices and chilli and, Drunken Aatish-E-King Prawns, £18, saffron and garlic flavoured king prawns cooked in the Tandoor, served with raspberry foam raita. The prawns came hanging on skewers on a custom-made stand. Should you have room, Death by Chocolate will finish you off! Steven is deservedly proud of his food. Whilst he allows some innovative elements, the main subject is artfully cooked in the traditional manner. He is equally proud of his team. The house is led by GM Atmaram Sahu (Alan), assisted by Adam Sharieff and head waiter Tarik. The brigade is headed Steven, of course and he is hands-on, his deputy is Head Chef Guru Prasad, Sous-Chef Mukesh Josmi. Mon-Sat: 12-2.30, 6-11 (Fri to Sun to 12).

MOWGLIS
151 Crwys Road, Cathays, Cardiff, CF24 4NH
029 2034 3705 www.mowglis.co.uk

Established in 2009 by Zaman Ahmed who says *'the adorable character in the famous jungle book was the inspiration behind our new restaurant.'* Head chef Nurul Ahmed produces all the regular curryhouse dishes and a few of his own such as starters: Tokri Chat Pate, £3.95, spicy popadom filled with onion, chick peas, egg & tamarind. Lemon Rosso £5.50, carved lemon shell filled with chicken tikka, mixed fruit, almond and sweet yogurt dressing and mains such as: Chicken Sagor Ana, £9, Tandoroi chicken, chicken tikka & sheekh kebab prepared with tomato, egg, potato and cinnamon in a bhuna sauce,

Murgh Anarosh £9, strips of chicken marinated in chefs special recipe all stuffed in a melon or pineapple shell. Ducksheri Special £12, grilled duck caramelised in onion & garlic in a tandoori sauce. *'Ostrich is promised in their blurb but was off on the day we went. No matter everything was hunky-dori.'* HEG. Weds & Sun specials £5. Sat-Th:12-l2.30 (booking only). Daily:6-11.

PURPLE POPPADOM
185 Cowbridge Road East, Canton, Cardiff
029 2022 0026 www.purplepoppadom.com

We met Kerala born Chef Anand George on page 33. He was at Mint & Mustard and is now is chef/patron at Purple Poppadom. Raman Bijalwan is GM, also ex Mint & Mustard. Prashant Shankar is Restaurant Manager and gained his spurs at Covent Garden's Moti Mahal. Starters include: Vegetable Variations £5, Ipomea samosa, the eponymous golden pastry triangle with a fusion filling of spiced sweet potato, parsnip and raisins and Beetroot Pattice, a delicately spiced beetroot cake accompanied by fritters of onion and water chestnuts. Crab from the Pot £9.50, is a trio: Crispy soft shell crab dusted with curry leaves and garlic, Nandu Pillow, a spiced cake of crab encased in crispy Japanese breadcrumbs and Warm salad of crab meat and sweetcorn spiked with turmeric and coconut. Boeuf à Trois £7.50, is another trio: dainty spiced beef samosa, Chapli Kebab of minced beef accompanied by our Billimoria beef and Cobra beer pie – two natural allies in one dish. Mains include: Kozhi Melagu Curry £10.50, Chettinad style chicken curry, with black pepper and fennel seeds, from the rice-growing state of southern India; Murgh Chatpata Kolhapur £10.50, boneless chicken with a thick tangy onion, tomato, fenugreek leaves and lemon juice; Kashmiri Roganjosh £11.50, slow-cooked lamb in the authentic Kashmiri style, finished with fennel seeds and saffron; Raan Akbari £16, classic Mughlai dish, slow-braised Welsh lamb shank marinated with spices and finished in the tandoor, served with a curried butternut squash mash, intensely flavoured sauce reduction and mint sorbet; Thoran, £5 a Keralan dish of vegetables tempered with mustard and curry leaves. Leave room for Chocomosa Anand £6, chef's signature dessert of a light crispy pastry parcel filled with a melted Belgian chocolate ganache. Mon-Sat: 12-2:30; Mon-Th 6-11 (Fri to Sun to 12).

Hengoed

VICEROY OF INDIA
2-14 Penallta Road, Ystrad Mynach, Hengoed, CF82 7AP 01443 862894 www.viceroyofindia.info

Owner Mohammed Miah has all your usual kormas, baltis, tandooris, bhoonas and dhansaks on the menu. But he'd like you to try his Bangladeshi family speciality dishes. Mohammed changes these every year but typical are Bhariniah Kadi Murgh £9.50 chicken breast stuffed with mushroom and simmered in a yoghurt-based sauce or Kalapuri Duck £9, in yoghurt, pepper and hot spices. 5.30-12.

Pontyclun

LEGENDS HOTEL & HAVELI RESTAURANT
Cambrian Industrial Estate East Side, Coedcae Lane, Pontyclun, CF72 9EW   01443 449779
www.havelirestaurant.co.uk   Hotel: 01775 843413

Kewal Singh Randeva and his sons Balraj and Shaam have opened their Haveli just off the M4 J34 in the quiet Cardiff area of Pontyclun. Haveli means a 'tranquil home' and despite its unglamourpus address and being plum in the middle of an industrial area, it is tranquil, at any rate at night, and a home at their 12 room two storey motel alongside (£30 per room per night). Haweli has a bar and some al fresco dining tables out front. So park up, check in, wander the few yards to the restaurant, tank up, fill up and have a good night's sleep just a walk away. 6-10.30. *Branch: Haveli, Slough, Berks.*

Swansea

ANARKALI
80 St Helen's Road, Swansea 01792 650549

Fully licensed and air-conditioned 60-seater established by A Rahman way back in 1978. Such long-standing gives it an assurance, experience and confidence with a long list of regulars. Menu Extracts: Crab Malabar, made from flaked fresh crab, sauteed with spices. Mahasha, cabbage leaves stuffed with lamb mince, rice and selected green herbs, sweet and sour flavour. Goan Lamb Vindaloo, marinated lamb with hot chilli, fresh green chilli, paprika, tomato puree, fenugreek & coriander. 12.12-2 & 5-12.

DHONIYA
100 Sterry Road, Gowerton, Swansea, SA4 3BW
01792 879505   www.dhoniya.co.uk

Farhad, Phool Kolis Imran' snephew has opened a takeaway serving the full formula menu. It has a very comfy waiting area complete with sofas, from where you can see your food being prepared in the open kitchen. Most starters are under £3. Try Sardine Puri, spicy sardine with fried bread. Most curries are around £6. Farhad has an extremely hot section offering Phal, Naga and the tamer Vindaloo. Pops 60p. Free del min order £14). 5.30-11.

GARUDA   INDONESIAN   BYO
18 St. Helens Road, Swansea SA1 4AP 01792 653388   www.garudarestaurant.co.uk

We have always dotted the Guide with alternative spice restaurants and this is a good one. Owner chef, Suriyani (Ani) Watcyn-Jones opened in it June 2000 and is still the only Indonesian restaurant in Wales. You rate it no 3 restaurant in Swansea (out of 250). The menu brings you the inexpensive best of cuisine from the *"land of a thousand islands"*. Starter examples: Sate Ayam, chicken satay or Bakwan, deep-fried shredded vegetables in batter, served with a sweet chilli dip. Mains include: Tauco Udang, king prawns cooked in fresh green chilli, ginger, onion, garlic, tomato, lemon grass and lime leaf with a yellow bean sauce; Sambal Ayam is a national dish of chicken cooked in a hot chilli sauce; Krengsengan, is medium spicy lamb curry and Rendang is beef cooked in coconut milk with red chilli, onion, garlic, ginger, galangal, lemon grass and lime leaf. Mie Goreng Telur is egg noodles andNasi Goreng Istimewa is special fried rice with egg, chicken & prawn, etc. Booking advisable. Bring your own wine, beer, no charge. Takeaway service available but only when not busy. At the time of writing Ani is recovering from illness and the hours are limited to Th-Sat: 7-11 (Kitchen closes at 9.20.)

GOVINDAS   VEGETARIAN   NO ALC
8 Cradock Street, Swansea, SA1 3EN
01792 468469   www.govindasswansea.co.uk

Established in 1999 as the Swansea Hare Krishna centre for *'meditation, yoga and kirtan chanting'*, it also has a small shop with Fairtrade goods, books, incense, teas etc. The restaurant is open to all and is has a short *'home-cooked organic'* vegetarian menu. Their special, dhal soup, veg curry, rice, pakora, pop, chutney, salad and soft drink is just £5 and is e-a-m-a-y-l. (Students £4). Veggie Burger with trimmings is £5, Kofta £4.49; Chapati wrap £3.75. Lassi £2. Mon-Sat: 12-5 (Fri-Sat:6-9); Sun Closed.

JUBORAJ   TOP 100
20-21 Wind Street · Swansea SA1 1DY 01792 649944 www.juborajgroup.com/swansea.html

Ana Miah's Juboraj group continues to thrive. See Cardiff for details.

MIAHS   TOP 100
St. Pauls Church, St. Helens Rd, Swansea SA1 4BL
01792 464084   www.miahs.net

Abdul Miah converted this beautiful old church in 2000. It's not the first curryhouse in a church, but done well it does lead interesting venue, and yes, it the décor is done well here. The bar is now the high altar, picked out with gothic arches in its front panels. Over it is a funky modern chandelier. Tables line the blonde wood floor. Your eye is drawn to the sweeping staircase, which shows off the huge stained-glass gothic window, and up to the fabulous vaulted roof. The stairs sweep left and right and take you to the balcony. But you can't eat the décor. We have desisted entering Miah's before because you tell us of uncaring service, excess red colouring and cold food. But of late we have had more cheering reports, and we'd like more please. The menu offers all the .Bangladeshi curryhouse favourites, and there is a section called the 'connoisseur's menu' with a selection of chef's specials. Prices a bit higher than average. Lunch and dinner daily.

MUMTAZ
480 Mumbles Rd, Mumbles, SA3 4BX   01792 367196

Amazing views of the bay as you drive round it. Mumtaz, formerly Lal Quila stands out for its Indian decor and by being a 3 storey building amid the row of 2 storeys. Inside youll get the views if you are lucky enough to get a window table (booking may help). The menu is the full montey of favourites. Mon-Th: 5.30-11.45 (to12.15 Fri-Sat).

PATTI RAJ   PATTI RAJ   TOP 100
Patti Pavilion, Gorse lane Mumbles Road, Victoria Park, Swansea, SA2 4PQ
01792 475444   www.pattipavillion.co.uk/pattiraj

This is a new restaurant in the city's rebuilt Patti Pavilion. In 2008 the Welsh Assembly financed a £1.7m facelift to this Grade II listed building in Victoria Park. It was built in 1800 by opera singer Adelina Patti in the grounds of her Swansea home. On her death in 1920 she bequeathed it to the people of Swansea and it was transported to the citys seafront. It staged many concerts and events before falling into disrepair, despite a superficial attempt to refurb it by Anneka Rice for TV in1994. Part of the 2008 facelift included an extension of a new glass covered wing containing a 110-seat restaurant. The lease has been taken by Mabs Noor, 34, with Amin Shah, Aklis Shah, Monzur Ahmed who describe themselves as Swansea lads. Future plans could extend the restaurant to the first floor, build an outdoor terrace and open, smaller daytime cafe with seating outside. Mr Ahmed is chef and his food has already been widely acclaimed. The numbered menu extends to nearly 200 items, so you have plenty to choose from. 43 starters range in price from £2.50 for soup to £10.95 for a mixed grill. Curries are £7 (CTM) to £13 for KP dishes. The favourites are £6. 20 signature dishes are interesting and theres even an English section, though *quite why anyone would order it, beats me. 'After so many times admiring this impressive place from the road, we ate there last night. What can I say - fantastic! Beautiful location, nice spacious feel inside, staff really friendly but all this is eclipsed by the food. The menu is extensive and our selections were delicious. We will return!'* JWR. 10% Discount on Takeaways. Self Servie Sun e-a-m-a-y-l buffet 12-5. Mon-Th: 5.30-12; Fri-Sat to 1; Sun: 12-10. 30.

We need your opinions please. Welsh reports always welcomed, as they are from anywhere. email to pat@patchapman.co.uk

---

GWENT
Monmouthshire

Area:
Southeast Wales

Adjacent Counties:
Glamorgan, Gloucs, Herefordshire and Powys

In the 1996 county reorganisation, Monmouthshire was restored for some purposes and Gwent for others, including for this Guide. Newport became an independent Unitary Authority, and we retain it here.

Abergavenny

SHAHI BALTI
5 Mill Street Abergavenny, NP7 5HE   01873 792011

'*Having gone to visit friends, they chose the venue and booked a table – good job too – very popular with locals and those from out of town. Had a drink in the tiny bar, whilst table was readied. Chose a rather unimaginative Chicken and Potato Balti, pleasantly surprised, tasty indeed, good value at £6.50. Suggested a vegetable Thali for friend, who is unused to eating spicy food. Very impressed, a very appetising selection with ample portions. One other thing to note - Nans tasty, substantial.*' MD. Hours: 6-11.30.

Caldicot

INDIAN EMPIRE
Park Wall Crick, Caldicot, NP26 5UT
01291 431144   www.indianempire.co.uk

Kazad Uddin's 200 seater is 3 miles from the Welsh border town of Chepstow and 12 miles from Newport. It has ample parking. '*I met Manager Tufayer Ahmed and Chef Abdul Boshor along in the busy kitchen which was clean and tidy and there was always someone with a mop ready to clean up any spillages. All the cooking instruments were cleaned once finished with. Chef showed me how they prepare their bases and rice for the day, which were Masala, Korma, Curry and Pillau Rice. My wife and I ordered Chicken Tikka Masala, a Keema Naan, a plain Naan, Keema fried rice, pillar rice and chips. The food was all I expected it to be hot, fresh and spicy. I highly recommend this restaurant.*' MJ. 12-2 except Fri & daily 6-11.30.

Monmouth

MISBAH TANDOORI   TOP 100
9 Priory Street, Monmouth, NP25 3BR 01600 714940
www.misbahtandoori.co.uk

D Miah opened his 80-seater in 1990 in the historic

market town of Monmouth, alongside the river Monnow, inearMonmouth castle and the ancient Market square. This comfortable venue exudes customer care. Mr Miah's Misbah attracts celebs, and he's delighted to tell you about them (ask him – each one has a tale). Chef A Rahman heads the chef brigade. Menu Snapshot: Sathkora Gosth £14, slightly hot, diced lamb cooked with onions, peppers and sathkora, a unique citrus fruit only grown in Sylhet, served with Pilau Rice; Fish-e-Palok £14, Bangladeshi fresh water fish cooked with spinach, onions, tomatoes and coconut milk, lightly spiced semi dry curry; Monow Valley £9, lamb cooked with green beans; Bangladesh Special £11, lamb cooked with onions, garnished with spinach & lamb mince meat. Modhu-Mothi £9, selection of mixed vegetables, cooked with onions, tomatoes, spinach, coconut; Baigan Bhajee £.5, aubergine; Shahi Rice £3.95, almond, sultanas, peas, onion and spices; Special Nan £2.50, stuffed with vegetables, egg, cheese and spices. *'Clean, friendly, basic menu, good service. Strangely quiet for a Friday night though. Excellent Chicken Jalfrezi and Pullao Rice. Excellent.'* IB. *'Warm, personal welcome. Intimate friendly service. Appealingly presented tables. All senses catered for. Wonderful food, succulent meat, stupendous prawns - all flavours beautifully blended, a richly textured Tarka Dal. Fluffy and exotically flavoured Rice and above all FRESH Mango! Gastronomic excellent.'* GL & DT.

Newport

JUBORAJ   TOP 100
84 Commercial Stret, Risca, Newport, NP20 1LS
01633 262646   www.juborajgroup.com

'Good decor, classy, almost temple-like, very clean and inviting. Welcoming, friendly staff, attentive. Very tasty, fresh Mixed Starter – onion bhajia, meat samosas and chicken pakora, small portion. Lamb and Prawn Madras with Pullao Rice and Aloo Gobi, very good portions with generous sauce, not at all oily, flavoursome. Delicious CTM. All in all very good.' PAH. Menu Extracts: Juboraj King Prawn, cooked in shell; Coriander Chicken, fillets, ground coriander; Kohlapuri, hot and spicy chicken, turmeric, cumin, coriander, green chillies. 12-2 & 6-12. Branches: Cardiff (4), Swansea.

THE KOH I NOOR
164 Chepstow Road, Maindee, Newport, NP19 8EG
01633 258028   www.thekohinoor.net

Mrs L Khanan's venerable 60-seater was established in 1978, and has appeared in most of our Guides. We've said before that nothing on the menu changes. Chef Tahir Ullah's curries are listed under such categories as mild, fruity, fairly hot, very hot, hottest and most-favourite. In other words this is one of the early curryhouses with its clutch of once-a-week regulars. Nothing wrong with that, especially since you might get a disount if you show them this Guide. Mon-Sat: 6-1am. Sun. 6-12.30.

'Have visited for takeaways and sit-down meals for over five years. Consistently, exceptionally high standard. Feels like home.' JT. *'Popadoms and chutneys arrived immediately. Exciting menu with authentic dishes. Clean toilets.'* S&DT. *'Food superb and promptly served.'* HE. *'The quality of the food is a good mix between the comfort blanket of the traditional and the innovative and new.'* AR. *'Delicious, wonderful food, lots of lovely vegetarian dishes.'* J&HA.   Super stuff. Misbah has been in our Guide since it opened. It achieved Best in Wales last time. Restaurants like this are what this Guide is all about. Takeaway: 10% off. Hours: 12-2.30 & 5.30-11.30.

YOU SAY OK, GWENT
You may get a disount if you show them this Guide.

ABERGAVENNY: SHAHI BALTI 5 Mill Street NP7 5HE 01873 859201

CALDICOT: INDIAN EMPIRE Parkwall, Crick · NP26 5UT 01291 431144 www.indianempire.co.uk Kazad Uddin;s 200 seat Indian Empire was established in 1999 has recently undergone a plus refurbishment. Parking is easy in the out of town site. Sat-Th: 12-2; Daily: 6-11.30.

CAERPHILLY: RAJ OF INDIA, 8a Market Street, CF83 1NX 029 2086 8230   www.therajofindia.co.uk   5 course meal £9.95

CRUMLIN: RAJDOOT 17 Main Street Crumlin   01495 243032 *'The Thali was excellent with a very good fruit salad.'* PH. 5.30-12, Friday and Saturday to 12.30.

CYMBRAN: KHAN TANDOORI 4 Commercial St, Pontnewydd NP44 1DZ 01633 867141 www.khan-tandoori.co.uk E-a-m-a-y-l buffet: Lunch £6, Dinner £10. T/a evenings only. Mon-Sat: 12-2 Mon-Th: 5.30-11:30; Fri-Sat to 12; Sun to 11.

Newport

THE 3 MUGHALS www.threemughals.co.uk
Western Valley Road, Pye Corner, Rogerstone,
Newport NP10 9DS   01633 894365

Sazzadur Rahman (Ray) bought the former 3 Salmons pub in 2009 and renamed it the 3 Mughals. It is in Rogerstone west of Newport in a detached building at the end of village-like main road. It has ample parking and an extensive menu in the hands of Master Chef Ataur Rahman includes the ususal starters,'Tandoori 'Sizzlers,' Set-meals (with vegetarian option,) Traditional Thalis, Main Courses, Chef's Specials, Vegetarian Dishes, side orders and rice's, breads and chutneys. *'We liked the '3-2-1-Chilli' pictorial guide to the spiciness of each dish ... I like hot, hubby likes mild .. So choice is easy.'* H&DB. 12-2.30 & 5.30-11.30.

DELHI
131 Cearleon Road, Newport, NP19 7BZ
01633 222281   www.delhi-restaurant.co.uk

Mr Joynal's Delhi is in an attractive corner building just a skip from J25A of the M4. It offers the full menu of favourite curries and sides at good prices. 5:30 till late.

JUBORAJ
Commercial Street, Newport, Gwent NP20 1LS
01633 262646   www.juborajgroup.com

The award winning restaurant group, Juboraj, has opened it's fourth branch at Newport, after refurbishment at The Old Grand Restaurant. Sample the finest Indian/Bangladeshi cuisine in a superb modernised and fully air conditioned atmosphere. Function room available. *Branches: Cardiff & Swansea, Glam. See p 84.*

NEW LAHORE
145 Lower Dock, NP20 1EE   01633
265665   www.newlahore.co.uk

Being established in 1961 makes the 60 seat Lahore a real veteran in the area. Mr. Islam, the original proprietor first started serving high quality authentic Indian meals in 1961. His original head chef Mr. Khan is still involved in the full menu of favourites nearly 50 years later. It includes Tandoori, Baltis and all you expect of a curryhouse of this vintage. 5.30-12.30.

YOU SAY OK, NEWPORT
You may get a disount if you show them this Guide.

BALTINITE TANDOORI 8 Gladstone Street Cross Keys NP11 7PA 01495 271234

KOHINOOR, 164 Chepstow Road, NP19 8EG   01633 258615 www.thekohinoor.net   Regular menu at this old hand (est 1980). 4 Course Dinner Sun & Mon £8.95. Mon-Th: 6 -1am; Fri-Sat to 2; Sun to 12.30am.

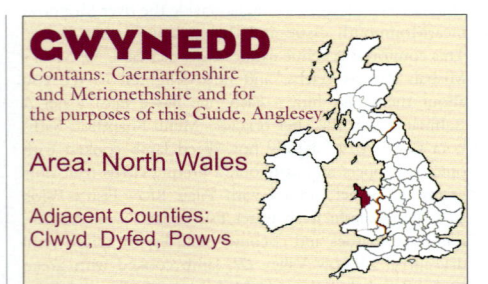

GWYNEDD
Contains: Caernarfonshire and Merionethshire and for the purposes of this Guide, Anglesey

Area: North Wales

Adjacent Counties:
Clwyd, Dyfed, Powys

Barmouth

SAFFRON
Church Street, Snowdonia National Park, Barmouth
LL42 1EW   01341 281102

Malik Allam manages this regular licensed curryhouse. It's on the main street of this stunning seaside town surrounded by Snowdonia National Park, which gets many tourists being on the junction of the sea and the mouth of the river Afton. Lunch & dinner.

Llandudno

BENGAL DYNASTY   AWARD WINNER
Llandudno Bengal Dyn   LL30 2LP
01492 878445   www.thebengaldynasty.com

Manikur Ahmed opened his 86-seat Bengal Dynasty the day before Bangladesh Independence Day, in 1988. Llandudno is a really fabulous seaside town with gorgeous Georgian buildings running in an arch along the waterfront. Lewis Carroll wrote Alice in Wonderland in this seaside resort. The Bengal Dynasty is situated upstairs in three dining rooms in one of these fine buildings. Popular dishes include: Jalfrezi, Masala, and Korai Specials:: Chicken Bondhuk; Lamb Satkora Bangladeshi citrus fruit; and Macher Tarkari, a Bangladeshi fish dish. All Tandoori dishes are served with green salad and mint yoghurt. *'I was about to settle for fish & chips when I saw it, upstairs above a shoe shop. I had Lamb Tikka to start and then Chicken Bhuna, which was excellent.'* AG *'King Prawn Butterfly followed by my usual main courses. A very accomplished meal. Keema Nan was the highlight together with a homemade Kulfi. Gets my vote.'* JL. *'Service was welcoming, prompt and polite. Pops and chuts fresh and crisp. Main meals were large, everything was hot and well presented. An enjoyable experience, but not outstanding.'* SR. *'Menu was wide and varied. Papadoms and chutneys excellent. Raita exceptional. All meals were served piping hot with hot plates and the portions were satisfying. Waiters were very accommodating in making changes to dishes for our individual tastes. Smart, clean and tasteful surroundings. Highly recommended.'* NC. Takeaway: 15% discount.

Cobra, £2.90 a bottle, house wine £8.95 a bottle. You might get a discount if you show Mr Ahmed this Guide. Price Check: Popadom 60p, CTM £7.75, Pullao Rice £1.70. Hours: 12-2.30. (4.30 on Sun.)/6-11.30. Branches: *Bengal Dynasty, Deeside, Clwyd* and *Northwich, Cheshire*

Llanberis

SPICE OF LLANBERIS

32 High Street, Llanberis, Snowdonia National Park LL55 4EU, 01286 871983

Llanberis is at the northern edge of the beautiful Snowdonia National Park. It is alongside lake surrounded by the hills. To the delight of its many tourists, the high street has distinquished itself by the brightly painting many of its buildings,The Spice, near the post office, is a a red brick building with featrues picked out in lilac. It's smallish inside with the standard menu friendly, staff . In 2005 Abdul Jalil owns this 60 seater. Chef Suruk Miah cooks up Bangladeshi styled curries, including Shere e Bangla £6.50 - medium dry spiced chicken and lamb tikka with spring onions, green peppers, herbs, garlic and mushrooms served with vegetable curry sauce; Sylheti Chicken £6.50 - marinated, sliced chicken, lightly spiced, medium hot sauce, boiled eggs, green peppers - recommended with Pullao Rice; Jomuna Issa £6.50 - prawns, medium sauce, garlic, ginger, coriander leaves. You might get a discount if you show Mr Jalil this Guide. Hours: 5 - 11. Branch: *Polash Balti, 28, Penlawst, Pwllheli*.

Porthmadog

PASSAGE TO INDIA

26 Lombard Street · Porthmadog LL49 9AP
01766 512144

Porthmadog is on the western seaborad side of Snowdonia National Park and has the Ffestiniog Railway terminus which makes the town a magnet for on tourists. Passage to India is not far from from the marina and is nestled in a small corner site at the junction of Lombard and Bank Streets where this small curryhouse has done the formula for 20 years or so. Lunch & dinner.

YOU SAY OK GWYNEDD
You may get a disount if you show them this Guide.

CAERNARFON SOPNA, Felin Wen, Pontrug 01286 675222
GARNDOLBENMAEN: MADHIA Caernarfon Rd 01766 530530
LLANDUDNO: ASIA INDIAN, 96 Gloddaeth St 01492 870178
PWLLHELI: POLASH BALTI, 28 Penlan Street 01758 613884
MENAI BRIDGE: SOPNA Pentraeth Road 01248 717778

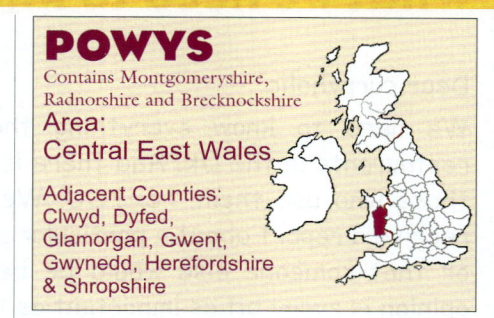

POWYS
Contains Montgomeryshire, Radnorshire and Brecknockshire
Area:
Central East Wales

Adjacent Counties:
Clwyd, Dyfed,
Glamorgan, Gwent,
Gwynedd, Herefordshire
& Shropshire

Brecon

GURKHA CORNER   NEPALESE
12 Glamorgan Street, Brecon LD3 7DW,
01874 610871   www.gurkhacorner.co.uk

a friendly welcome and great, fresh tasting Nepalese food at the small and cosy Gurkha Corner. It's popular too, so booking is wise. The heart of a Nepali meal is "daal bhat" (rice and lentils) and "achar" (chutney) with other main dishes. Menu snapshot: Aloo Tama Bodi £5.40, spiced potatoes with bamboo shoots and black-eyed beans; Misayeko Tarkari £5.40, vegetables in hot spices; Khursani Achaar, 95p, very hot red marble chilli pickle; Momos £4.90, steamed dumplings with chicken, pork or veg filling Mains: Curries, chicken, pork or lamb (KP +£2): Amilo Mitho Piro, sweet & hot stir-fry; Sisnu, cooked with Himalayan nettles; Bhuteko Masu, dry stir-fry; Kaagati Bhat £2.75, wok-fried rice with lemon juice, mustard seeds, onion and vegetables; Kalo Dal £3, is black lentils fried with Jimmu, a Nepalese herb. Set Meal £16. Gurha beer. T/a: 10% discount Tues-Sun; 12-2.30 & 5.30-11. Closed Mon.

YOU SAY OK, POWYS
You may get a disount if you show them this Guide.

LLANDRINDOD WELLS: ZEERA Emporium Building, 2 Temple Street, Llandrindod Wells, LD1 5DL 01597 823843 Take the health-giving waters the curry!
LLANSANTFFRAID: THE PALACE Waterloo House, SY22 6AR 01691 828152 Takeawayonly est 1994 by Shoakoth Ali. Black ash coffee table with red chairs for waiting customers. Menu Extracts: Keema Chana Masala, minced lamb, chick peas, masala sauce; Pista Nan, pistachio nuts; Green Lamb Masala, lamb pieces with peas, green herbs, touch of cream, butter. Credit cards not accepted. Hours: 5-11.30, Fri-Sat to 12.
MONTGOMERY: LIMES COTTAGE INDIAN 1 Long Bridge St, SY18 6EE 01686 411228 Formerly Cottage Inn, it offers thefull menu. 10% disc for t/a; 12-2.30 & 6 till late.
NEWTOWN: PREEM Pool Road, Y16 1DJ 01686 625534 Mehoraz owns this 80 seater. Shamim Uddin. cooks formula curries and specials such as Stuffed Pepper £3, chicken or lamb or vegetable; Tandoori Duck £9; Chicken or Lamb Delight £13, with cointreau, cream and almonds. Min charge: £10. Delivery: 3 m, £15 min. 5-12.
NEWTOWN: SHILAM 49 Broad Street Newtown, SY16 2AU 01686 625333I. *'Good all round menu. Superbly presented, very good food on garnished platters rather than the traditional oval stainless dish. Bangol Maslee £8, Spicy Tandoori Trout starter exceptional.Vindaloo had lots of bite. Loads of green chillies in very hot Jalfrezi. Most impressed.'* KN. 5.30-12, Fri-Sat to 2.

What we need to know

Dear curryholic

We need to know everything there is to know about all curry restaurants in the UK. And there is no one better able to tell us than those who use them, i.e. YOU. We do not mind how many times we receive a report about a particular place, so please don't feel inhibited or that someone else would be better qualified. They aren't. Your opinion is every bit as important as the next person's. Ideally, we'd like a report from you every time you dine out – even on a humble takeaway. We realize this is hard work so we don't mind if your report is very short, and you are welcome to send in more than one report on the same place telling of different occasions. Please cut out the forms alongside. Or you can even use the back of an envelope or a postcard, or we can supply you with more forms if you write in (with an S.A.E., please). Alternatively, you can use the website <**patchapman.co.uk**> Go to **Restaurant Reports** and follow the prompts.

If you can get hold of a menu (they usually have takeaway menus to give away) or visiting cards, they are useful to us too, as are newspaper cuttings, good and bad, and advertisements, scanned or mailed. So, please send anything along with your report.

They are used when preparing the next edition of this Guide. We do not pay for reports but our ever-increasing corps of regular correspondents receive the occasional perk from us. Please join them. Please send us your report after your next restaurant curry.

Thank you and happy curries!

Pat

Pat Chapman
Founder, The Curry Club
PO Box 7, Haslemere
Surrey, GU27 1EP
E-mail it to pat@patchapman.co.uk

Restaurant Report Form

Photocopy or scan this form. Mail it or e-mail it to the address below.
Whenever you have an 'Indian' meal or takeaway, The Curry Club would like to have your opinion.

Your Name and address: ....
....

Your phone number .... Your e-mail address ....

....

Restaurant name: ....
Street no and Streetname: ....
....

Town: .... County: ....
Postcode: .... Telephone: .... e.mail: ....
Website: .... Date Visited: ....

....

REPORT

Please tell us everything – your first impressions, the welcome, cleanliness, your table – was it appealing? Nice things waiting for you on it? The menu, quantities, quality, service, background music, comfort, decor. Irritating or pleasing? The food? How were the toilets? First visit? Been before? Would you go back? recommend to friends? Overall was the restaurant TOP 100, good, bad, indifferent, appaling?

Please continue on separate sheets of paper if required

Please return your info to: The Curry Club, PO Box 7, Haslemere, Surrey. GU27 1EP. <www.patchapman.co.uk>

Restaurant Update Information

Photocopy or scan this form. Mail it or e-mail it to the address below.

Your Name and address ....

....

Your phone number .... Your e-mail address ....

Even if you do not fill in a report overleaf, you may be able to give us vital information, such as that below.

DO YOU KNOW OF ANY: NEW CURRY RESTAURANT OPENINGS:

Restaurant name: ....

Street no and name: ....

Town: .... County: ....

Postcode: .... Telephone: ....

DO YOU KNOW OF ANY: CURRY RESTAURANT CLOSURES OVER THE LAST FEW MONTHS

Including any listed in this Guide

Restaurant name:

....

Street no and name: ....

Town: ....County: ....

Postcode: .... Telephone: ....

DO YOU KNOW OF ANY: HYGIENE OR OTHER OFFENCES

Please back up with a local press cutting if possible

Restaurant name: ....

Street no and name: ....

Town: ....County: ....

Postcode: .... Telephone: ....

YOUR FAVOURITE RESTAURANT(S)

If possible, in descending order, best first

Restaurant name: ....

Street no and name: ....

Town: ....County: ....

Postcode: .... Telephone: ....

ANY OTHER CURRY RESTAURANT INFORMATION

Please continue on separate sheets of paper if required

Please return your info to: The Curry Club, PO Box 7, Haslemere, Surrey. GU27 1EP

Restaurant Report Form

Photocopy or scan this form. Mail it or e-mail it to the address below.
Whenever you have an 'Indian' meal or takeaway, The Curry Club
would like to have your opinion.

Your Name and address: ....
....

Your phone number .... Your e-mail address ....

Restaurant name: ....
Street no and Streetname: ....
....
Town: .... County: ....
Postcode: .... Telephone: .... e.mail: ....
Website: .... Date Visited: ....

REPORT
Please tell us everything – your first impressions, the welcome, cleanliness, your table – was it appealing? Nice things waiting for you on it? The menu, quantities, quality, service, background music, comfort, decor. Irritating or pleasing? The food? How were the toilets? First visit? Been before? Would you go back? recommend to friends? Overall was the restaurant TOP 100, good, bad, indifferent, appaling?

Please continue on separate sheets of paper if required
Please return your info to: The Curry Club, PO Box 7, Haslemere, Surrey. GU27 1EP. <www.patchapman.co.uk>

Restaurant Update Information

Photocopy or scan this form. Mail it or e-mail it to the address below.

Your Name and address ....

....

Your phone number .... Your e-mail address ....

Even if you do not fill in a report overleaf, you may be able to give us vital information, such as that below.

DO YOU KNOW OF ANY: NEW CURRY RESTAURANT OPENINGS:

Restaurant name: ....

Street no and name: ....

Town: .... County: ....

Postcode: .... Telephone: ....

DO YOU KNOW OF ANY: CURRY RESTAURANT CLOSURES OVER THE LAST FEW MONTHS

Including any listed in this Guide

Restaurant name:
....

Street no and name: ....

Town: .... County: ....

Postcode: .... Telephone: ....

DO YOU KNOW OF ANY: HYGIENE OR OTHER OFFENCES

Please back up with a local press cutting if possible

Restaurant name: ....

Street no and name: ....

Town: .... County: ....

Postcode: .... Telephone: ....

YOUR FAVOURITE RESTAURANT(S)

If possible, in descending order, best first

Restaurant name: ....

Street no and name: ....

Town: .... County: ....

Postcode: .... Telephone: ....

ANY OTHER CURRY RESTAURANT INFORMATION

Please continue on separate sheets of paper if required

Please return your info to: The Curry Club, PO Box 7, Haslemere, Surrey. GU27 1EP

Contributors

This Guide contains Britain's top curry restaurants literally as chosen by you. Our sincere thanks to everyone who has sent in report(s) on restaurants. We list you here. (Apologies for any errors, duplications, omissions (tell us if we did), and for the tiny print necessitated by space considerations).

A Martin Abbott, Gloucs; Colin Adam, Kilwinning; Ray Adams, Kimberley; Meena Ahamed, London; F. Ahmed, Salisbury; Stephen Albrow, Norfolk; Diane Aldsworth, email; Alex, email; Paul Allen, Chatham; Maria Allen, Milton Keynes; Tony and Lesley Allen, Rugby; Harri Ahola, Espom, Finland; MF Alsan, Rugby; G Amos, Wirral; Capt R Anclive, BFPO 12; Apryl Anderson, Ponteland; Bill Anderson, Berwick Upon Tweed; Karen Andras, Nottingham; Andy from Aus; Lisa Appadurai, Benfleet; Richard Arch, e-mail; Pete Archer, Tamworth; Robin Arnott, Strafford; Mrs M Asher, Woodford Green; Dave Ashton, Warrington; Jo Ashton, Elland; Allan Ashworth, York; Berry Ashworth, Compton Bassett; Michelle Aspinal, Chester; Darius Astell, Southampton; Rachael Atkinson, Cheshire; Simon Atkinson, N5; Y Atkinson, IOM; Claire Austin, Stoke; Arman Aziz, N4.

B Tom Bailey, Alresford; John Baker, Loughton; Kim Baker, BBC; Raji Balasubramaniam, Bangalore; Mridula Baljekar, Camberley, Jan & Randolph Baller, Nantwich; David Bker, Cranleigh; Kim Baker, Hatfield; Mr & Mrs ML Banks, Enfield; Keith Bardwell, Hertford; Jan Barlex, Ilford; Trevor Barnard, Gravesend; Christopher Barnes, Ashton; Derek Barnett, Colchester; Tony Barrel, Hounslow; R.Barry-Champion, Market Harborough; Joanne Bastock, Saltash; Mike Bates, Radcliffe; Shirley Bayley, Worthing; Karin and Angela, Rugby; Mr MJ Beard, Stafford; Joyce Bearpark, Murcia Spain; Dave Beazer, Cornwall; DJ Beer, Ross-on-Wye; Derick Behrens, Bucks; Ian Bell, Cheshire, Matt Bell, Derbys; P Bell, Carlisle; Sam Bell, Coventry; TW Bennett, Sherborne; Becky Benson, Worcs; John Bentley, Northampton; Ron Bergin, Gerrards Cross; Ian Berry, Goole; Ian and Jan Berry, Sheffield; Martyn Berry, SE3; Michael Berry, email; Shirley and Nick Bertram, London; Kenneth Beswick, Lincoln; DJ Betts, Bexhill; Jonathan Bick, Cardiff; Brian and Anne Biffin, Fleet; BH Birch Hyde; Ed Birch Guildford, Colin Bird; Welwyn Garden City; Jim Birkumshaw, Derby; James Birtles, Manchester; Chris Blackmore, Bristol; David Bolton, Lichfield; Mrs C Bone, Norfolk; A Boughton, SE27; L le Bouochon, Jersey; J Bowden, email; Mrs I Bowman, Rochester; Julie Bowman, email; Robert Box, Knottingley; Alan Boxall, Burwash; Colin Bird, Welwyn Garden City; Sean Boxall, Graham Bowden-Peters email; Andover; F Boyd, Stranraer; Iain Boyd, Wealdstone; Pippa Bradley, Walsall; Roderick Braggins, Peebles; Amanda Bramwell, Sheffield; Susan Brann, Worthing; Dave Bridge, Wallasey; Michael E Bridgstock, Northants; Sandra Brighton, Nelson; Steve Broadfoot, Anfield; John and Susan Brockington, Sutton Coldfield; Paul Bromley, SE13; Robert Brook, London; Rose Brooke, Oakham; Nigel John Brooks, Stoke-on-Trent; David Brown, Leeds; IA Brown, Fernhurst; Janet Brown, email; Mark Brown, Scunthorpe; Steve Brown, Twickenham; DA Bryan, York; Rachel Bryden, email; RC Bryant, Witney; Robert Bruce, Thornaby; Heather Buchanan, Inverness; Dr TM Buckenham, SW11; Mrs J Buffey, Sutton Coldfield; LG Burgess, Berkhamsted, DA Burke, London, A Burton, Weston-super-Mare; Bob Butler & family, email; Sanah Butt, Middlesex.

C A C, email, Dennis C Weymouth, D Cadby, Swindon; Barry Caldwell, Chesterfield; David Caldwell, Brownhills; Stan Calland, Kingsley; Hugh Callaway, Cleethorpes; Duncan Cameron, Fordoun; Frank Cameron, Dundee; HS Cameron, Wirral; Iain Cameron Harley Wintney; Alex Campbell, Ramsey Campbell, Wallasey; Hartley Wintney; Mrs E Campbell, Harrogate; N Campbell, Edinburgh; Josephine Capps, Romford; L Carroll, Huddersfield; James Casey, Wilts; Peter Cash, Liverpool; Mark Caunter, Guildford; TM Chandler, Farnborough; Desmond Carr, N8; J Carr, Birkenhead; TO Carr, Warrington; BR Carrick, Wakefield; DL Carter, Huntingdon; Mrs M Carter, Colchester; Madeline Castro, Bury St Edmunds; Dr WF Cavenagh, Norfolk; Judith Chambers, Heref; Neil Chantrell, Warrington; Hilary J Chapchal, Leatherhead; Mr & Mrs DR Chapchal, Leatherhead; DBA Chapman (Ed), Haslemere; John Chapman, Leics; OD Chapman, e-mail; Paul Chapman, Leighton Buzzard; Charlie and Linda, Zakynthos, Greece; Mr & Mrs Chatfield, Wimborne; Rajender Chatwal, Bicester; Dr GT Cheney, Salhouse; Paul Chester, Cuffley; Kathryn Chitty, Merseyside Quest PR Ltd; Chris Isitt, Cholsey; Dave Christian, IOM; Sqn Ldr PF Christopher, Ferndown; Martin Churchill, Ross-on-Wye; Alexis Ciusczak, Capistrano Beach, CA; Imogen Clist, Les Routiers in Britain, email; Peter Clyne, SW11; VA Coak, Penzance; Alan Coates, Sheffield; Louise Coben-Sutherland, Enfield; Neil Coburn, SW11; CH Coleman, Sussex; Robin Collier, Mid Calder; Chris Coles, Biggin Hill, Billy Collins, Wirral; Glen Collins, Durham; Mrs J Collins, Portsmouth; CJ Comer, Basingstoke; Rhys Compton, Cheltenham; John Conybeare, Cardiff; A Conroy, Durham; Joseph Coohil, Oxford; Neil Cook, Royston; Peter Cookson, Notts; Mr LW Coombes, Devon; Alan & Margaret Cooper, Llansteffan; Kim Cooper, Basildon; DW Cope, Whitchurch; Dr JC Coppola, Woodstock; Will Coppola, Oxford; Nigel Cornwall, Orpington; John Costa, Tunbridge Wells; MJ Cotterill, Bristol; Ron A Couch, email; T.Cowan; Dundee Record; Stephen Cowie, SW16; Steve Cowling, Shrops; Julie Cozens, Oxon; Dr AM Croft, Cornwall; Roderick Cromar, Buckie; Simon Crosby, Kent; C Cross, Poole; Yasmin Cross, Huddersfield; Major & Mrs FJB Crosse, Salisbury; Robert Crossley, Huddersfield; F Croxford, Edinburgh; Frank and Elizabeth Crozier, Redruth; Gordon Cruickshank, Banffshire; R Cuthbertson, Southampton.

D S.Daglish, Scarborough; P Dalton, Wirral; Jan Daniel, Felpham; Mr & Mrs PE Dannat, Eastleigh; Martin Daubney, Hitchin; Gary Davey, W4; Alasdair Davidson, Heswall; Adrian Davies, NW3; Gwyn Davies, Wirral; Mrs JC Davies, Leeds; Josephine Davies, Swansea; Lucy Davies, Essex; Paul Davies, Chiddingfold; Mrs G Davies-GoV, Marlow; Shelley Davies, Bristol; Colin Davis, Tatsfield; Martyn Dawe, London; Ian Dawson, Mirfield; DM Day, Preston; Michael Day, West Bromwich; Angela Dean, Solihull; Peter Deane, Bath; Gary & Katy Debono, High Wycombe; David Dee, Ruislip; Elizabeth Defty, Co. Durham; Neil Denham, The Netherlands; R Dent, Bishop Auckland; Les Denton, Barnsley; Richard Develyn, St Leonards; Nigel Deville, Uttoxeter; Ken Dewsbury, Somerset; Richard Diamond, Romsey; Phil Dicey, Cyprus; RC Dilnot, Broadstairs; Graham Divers, Glasgow; Geof Dixon, Durham; James Dobson, Burscough; S Dolden, Rochester; R Dolley, W11; Donna, Worthing; Clive Doody, Surrey; Keith Dorey, Barnet; Neil Downey, Worthing; Sarah Dowsett, Swindon; Anna Driscoll, Cape Province; Mrs J Driscoll, BFPO; Hazel Drury, Bromborough; Diane Duame, Wicklow; Eric Duhig, Hornchurch; Sheila Dunbar, Pinner; James Duncan, West Kilbride; Jon Dunham, Northants; Mark Dunn, E18; Rachael Dunn, Hemel, Robin Durant, Brighton; Martin Durrant, Chester; Avishek Dutt, London, Mr & Mrs JA Dywer, Birmingham.

E A Edden-Jones, Bristol; Bruce Edwards, Norwich; Dave Edwards, Rugeley; Fred and Hilary Edwards, Worthing; CM Eeley, Witney; Rod Eglin, Whitehaven; Wendy Elkington; Ray Elliott, Worcester; Chris Ellis, email; H Ellis, Worthing; Peter Ellis, London, PT Ellis, W'rtn; Stuart and Christine Ellis, email; Mrs G Elston, Woodley; Tony Emmerton, Chorley; Mark Evans, SW5; Mr & Mrs A Evans, Manchester; Brian Exford, Derbys.

F Colin Fairall, Hants; Gary Fairbrother, Crosby; J.M.Fairhurst, Baldock; Hazel Fairley, Guildford; Chris Farrington, Cherry Hinton; Graham Faulkner, Dorking; Joy Fawcett, Sheffield; John Fearson, Bucks; Denis Feeney, Glasgow; Kevin Fenner, Rothley; Bill and Laraine Field, Newcastle-upon-Lyme; RC Field, Hants; Stephen Field, Norton; Mick Fielden, Glossop; AJ Finch, Enfield Wash; Duncan Finley, Glasgow; Maureen Fisher, Woodford Green; Bernard Fison, Holmrook; John Fitzgerald, Great Missenden; David Flanagan, Orkney; Gerry Flanagan Pepsi Co Germany; Merly Flashman, TN12; Colin & Toni Fleet, Dorset; Dr Cornel Fleming, N6; KD Flint, Kempsey; Fiona Floyd, Truro; Sarah Flynn, Beds; Stephen & Elizabeth Foden, Lynton; Chris Fogarty, Enfield; Gareth Foley, Porthcawl; Neil Foley, Essex; IE Folkard-Evans, Manchester; Jonathan Follows, Wilmslow; SR Tracy Forster, Beds; Rod Fouracres, Glos.; Rosemary Fowler, Midhurst; John R Fox, King's Lynn; John W Fox, Doncaster; Linda Foye, Barry; Theresa Frey, Fareham; Chris Frid, North Shields; Steve Frost, Kingston; Ben Fryer, Worthing; Derek Fulford, York; Alan Furniss, Wraysbury; June Fyall, Bronwydd; Mrs MAJ Fyall, Dyfed.

G Gail & Brendan, Orme; Stephen Gaines, Middlesex; MJ Gainsford, Burbage; Leo Gajsler, Geneva; Harry E Garner, London; Steve Garrod, Hull; Mrs FE Gaunt, Stonehouse; Phillip Gentry, Bexleyheath; Brian George, Wolverton; Nick & Julie Gerrard, Gwynedd; CM Gerry, Cyprus; G Gibb, SE21; Alistair Gibson, East Lothian; Robert (Bob) Giddings, Poole; Michael Gill, Leeds; Emma Gillingham, Huddersfield; Andrew Gillies, Edinburgh; AV Glanville, Windsor; Ms D Glass, Liverpool; A Glenford, Lincoln; Gillian Glover, The Scotsman; Johanne & Mark Glover, Nottiingham; Nick Goddard, Stevenage; Andrew Godfrey, Seer Green; Matthew Goldsmith, Burgess Hill;

Contributors

Mr & Mrs A. Goldthorp, Halstead; John Goleczka, Pensford; Michael Goodband, Perhore; Mrs A Gooding, Aylesbury, email; Bryn Gooding, Corfu; Nigel Goodrich, Thornhill, Scotland; Dr G Gordon, Kidlington; Mrs J Gorman, Strood; Ian Gosden, Woking; Bill Gosland, Camberley; Mr and Mrs J Gough, Brough; Chris Goulden, Andover; David Gramagan, Formby; DC Grant, Enfield; Kathryn Grass, Wigan; Alan Gray, Erskine; DR Gray, sw11; A Greaves, Chester; Andrew Greaves, Derbys; Rachel Greaves, Tavistock; Denise Gregory, Herts; Jonathan Green, Cathays, Michael Green, Leicester; Nigel Green, Orpington; Richard Green, Gerrards Cross; Sheila Green, Barrow; A Gregor, Boston; Frank Gregori, NW10; Andrew Grendale, Ingatestone; A Griffiths, Milton Keynes; JK Greye, Bath; M Griffiths, Northampton; Dave Groves, Walsall; Lynda Gudgeon, Roopa Gulati, London; Willenhall, Louis Gunn, Chelmsford.

H Jackie Hale, e-mail; Karen Haley, Telford; John Hall, Cullercoats; Andrew Halling, Leigh; Stephen Hames, Bewdley; Alan Hamilton, Wakefield; Tina Hammond, Ipswich; Geoff & Janet Hampshire-Thomas, Kirkland; Neil Hancock, Derby; Ray Hancock, Chester; David T. Hanlin, email; Dorothy Hankin, Fordingbridge; David T. Hanlin, Solihull; Sharon Hanson, Derby; Glynn Harby, Knaresborough; Martyn Harding, Powys; Roger Hargreaves, Stoke; J Harman, Brentwood; Gerald Harnden, Westcliff-on-Sea; Justin Harper, Hemel; Dawn Harris, Dubley; Paul Harris, BFPO; David Harrison, Dursley; Mr and Mrs I Harrison, Warwick; Mark Harrison, Oxon; Patrick Harrison, Cambridge; Louise Hartley, Edinburgh; David Harvey, SE24; S Harwood, Lewes; John K Hattam, York; Sally Haseman, Surbiton; Christopher & Linda Haw, Dewsbury; Andy Hayler.com; Ann & David Haynes, Bournemouth; John Haynes, Saffron Walden; DI Hazelgrove, West Byfleet; M Hearle, Tunbridge Wells; Kevin Hearn, Newcastle; Bernice Heath, Nottingham; Jane Helmich, South Wales Argus; Andy Hemingway, Leeds; Terry Herbat, Barnsley; Georgina Herridge, W9; Andy Herrin, yellow fingers.co.uk; T & M Hetherington, Preston; Victoria Heywood, Burton; Roger Hickman, N1; Stuart Hicks email; Pat & Paul Hickson, Chorley; Janet Higgins, Blackburn; Mrs S Higgins, Blackburn; Mrs B Higgs, Cotty; Dave Hignett, Newcastle-upon-Tyne; Alec Hill, Wigan; Carolyn Hill, Nottingham; Stephen Hill, Chesterfield; Barry Hills, Surrey; David Hindle, W5; Bharti Hindocha, Richmond; Daniel Hinge, Bishop Auckland; Mrs MJ Hirst, Kent; SC Hodgon; Daniel Hodson, Abingdon; Peter Hoes, Bingley; Bernard Hofmiester, Berlin; P Hogkinson, Sheffield; Duncan Holloway, Windsor; Kevin Hooper, St Austell; Linda Horan, Wirral; Will H Horley, Barnsley; Peter Hornfleck, Farnborough; Jerry Horwood, Guildford; Dr MP Houghton, Rugby; Neil Houldsworth, Keighley; Nigel & Rev Erika Howard, JK Howard, Enfield Wash; P Howard, Hornchurch; David & Val Howarth, Derbs; Mrs J Howarth, Oldham; Mat Howarth, Burton Upon Trent; Kathy Howe, Carlisle; Simon Howell, Gillingham; Bruce Howerd, Tongham; Lynn Howie, Sanderstead; Deh-Ta Hsiung, London; Jan Hudson, Hemel Hempstead; Tom Hudson, Jarrow; Chris Hughes, Wraysbury; Paul Hughes, Detroit; Paul Hulley, Stockport; SP Hulley, Reddish; HL & S Humphreys, Stoke-on-Trent; AG Hunt, Southend-on-Sea; John & Frances Hunt, Langport; Paul Hunt, Essex; Roger Hunt, Sidmouth; Vince Hunt, Manchester; Penny Hunter, Brighton; Sheila Hunter, Dundee; Humayan Hussain, Journalist; Dr M Hutchinson, Gwynedd; Mike Hutchinson, Stafford; Mrs V Hyland, Manchester; Jeffrey Hyman, email.

I DM Ibbotson, Sheffield; Nick & Mandy Idle, Ossett; Ken Ingram, Leeds; G Innocent, Dawlish; Mrs G Irving, Redditch; Chris Issit, Chosely; Robert Izzo, Horsham.

J Dr AG James, Wigan; O Jarrett, Norwich; Sue Jayasekara, Essex; Sally JeVries, Heathfield; L Jiggins, Dagenham; Bal Johal, email; G John, Wirral; Maxine & Andrew Johnson, Leiden; Colin Johnson, Southall; Peter Johnson, Droitwich; Paul Jolliffe, Exeter; CML Jones, St Albans; Clive Jones, nw; Gareth Jones, Tonypandy; Kate Jones, Leiden; Mark Jones Newport, Gwent; RW Jones, N9; Shirley Jones, SE13; WA Jones, Flintshire; Wendy Jones, Clwyd; Michael Lloyd Jones, Cardiff; Esther Juby, Norwich; Surjit Singh Jutla, Reading.

K Tessa Kamara, W13; Sarah Kaikini, Surrey; AD Kantes, Northants; Chris Keardey, Southampton; Anthony Kearns, Stafford; David R Keedy, T & W; Russ Kelly, Seaforth; Prof. and Mrs Kemp, Royston; D Kennedy, Edinburgh; Mr & Mrs MJB Kendall, Hook; David Kenny, Kenmare; Simon Kerfoot Northampton; David Kerray, Akrotiri; John Kettle, Dover; John Kettle, Crewe; JS Kettle, Banbury; Saul Keyworth, Essex; Horna Khaleeli, The Gurdian; M. Arif Khan, London; Stephen Kiely, N16; John Kilbride, Glasgow; Cleo Kinder and Toby Kinder, SE17; David King, Biggleswade; Mike King, Sussex; John & Jane Kingdom, Plymouth; Alyson Kingham, Oldham; Mark Kirby, Ashtead; Frances Kitchen, Langport; Peter Kitney, Banbury; J & P Klusiatis, Reading; Drs Heather & Mark Knight, Oxford; Ana Knowles, Walton on Thames; Drs MJ & A Krimholtz, SW14.

L Caz Lack, Kent; Martin Lally, Chester; Colin Lambert, Bucks; John Lambourne, Majorca; Mrs Langley, email; Ian Langsdown, Edinburgh; Alan Lathan, Chorley; Clive Lawrence, email; Cass Lawson, Swindon; Ronnie Laxton, London; Jonathan Lazenby, Mamhilad, Gwent; Gary Leatt, St. Brelade, Jersey; Andrew Lecomber, Durham; DH Lee, Waltham Abbey; Mark Lee, e-mail; Jackie Leek, Dartford; Simon Leng, Wakefield; David Leslie, Aberdeen; Russell D Lewin, NW2; A Lewis, Sherborne; CK Lewis, Maidenhead; Margaret Ann Lewis, Ashford; R Lewis, Rayleigh; Pat Lindsay, Hants; David Lloyd Walgrave, N'ton; David Lloyd, Oswestry; Eleanor & Owen Lock, Geneva; Peter Long, Cheltenham; J Longman, Bodmin; John Loosemore, Orpington; DA Lord, Hove; Julia & Philip Lovell, Brighton; AP Lowe, Tolworth; Paul Lowe, Stourbridge; Peter Lowe, Lewes; Mr & Mrs DN Luckman, Horley; Jeremy Ludlow, Dorset; Mrs H Lundy, Wallasey; Graeme Lutman, Herts; Tim Lynch, Romford; Jamie Lyon, Burscough.

Mac/Mc
M Mcbryde, Watford; Loraine McClean, Poole; Alan McIntyre, Northumberland; David Mackay, Twickenham; Darren McKenzie, T&W; David Mackenzie, Darlington; Lin Macmillan, London; Deb McCarthy, E6; Patrick McCloy, N8; Vanessa McCrow, Teddington; David McCulloch, NW11; Michael McDonald, Ellesmere Port; David McDowell, Telford; BJ McKeown, Seaford; Ian McLean, Brighton; Dr and Mrs J McLelland, Mid Calder; Alan & Jean McLucas, Solihull; Dr FB McManus, Lincoln; Alan McWilliam, Inverurie.

M Chris Mabey, Swindon; Fiona Maddock, Guildford; Rakesh Makhecha, Harrow; Paul Lowe, Stourbridge; Chloe Malik, email; Richard Manley, Wirral; Cherry Manners, Hatfield; Emma and Peta Manningham, email; E Mansfield, Camberley; Clive Mantle; Mark of Melbourne; JF Marshall, Bedford; Geraldine Marson, Winsford; Colin Martin, Nuneaton; Derek Martin, Marlow; Jane Martin, SW19; PR Martin, Southend; DH Marston, Southport; Gavin Marwick Tenterden; DJ Mason, Cleveland; LJ Mason, Leeds; John Maundrell, Tunbridge Wells; Gilian May, Hayes; Peter F May, St Albans; Simon Mayo, Farnborough; Simon Meaton, Andover; John Medd, Nottingham; Tim Mee, Harrow; Sue & Alf Melor, Hanworth; Nigel Meredith, Huddersfield; Sujata Mia, Middlesex; Andy Middleton, Rotherham; H Middleton, Coventry; Simon Mighall, St Neots; PJL Mighell, Canterbury; Robert Miles, Herts; Catherine Millar, BFPO; DR Millichap, Horsham; BW Milligan; AJ Millington, Woodford; Sally Millington, N10; Mr & Mrs P Mills, Mold; Mary Mirfin, Leeds; Al Mitchell, Belfast; Jonathon Mitchell, Alton; F Moan, Cuddington; Sarah Moles, Buxton; Jon Molyneaux, Peterborough; Mrs SE Monk, Gisburn; Steven Montgomery, Monash, Australia; AV Moody, Portsmouth; Christy Moore, Dublin; Christy Moore, London; DM Moreland, Willington; S Morgan, Feltham; Tim & Katherine Morgan, Scotland; Ian Morris, Gwynedd; Miranda Mortlock, Suffolk; Peter Morwood, Wicklow; A Moss, Colchester; Caroline Moss, Solihull; K Mosley, email; Paul Motley, Northampton; Mrs L Muirhead, Glasgow; David Muncaster, Stoke; Andy Munro, Balti Brum; Joan Munro, Leyburn; Annette Murray, Thornton Cleveleys; JL Murray, Enfield; RG Murray, Carlisle; Drs Heather & Harry Mycook. **N:** Simon Nash, Cheshire; Mrs PG Naylor, Salisbury; Hugh Neal, Kent; Jeff Neal, Bolton; Marcus Neal, Liss; Rob Neil, Ashford; A Nelson-Smith, Swansea; Liam Nevens, Stockton; Tony Newbold, email; Rebecca Newman, Hayes; Tony Newman, Margate; J Newsom, Lancing; Jan Newson Southgate, N14; Clive Newton, Northwich; John Nicholson, Bromborough; Nick, e-mail; P & D Nixon, Basildon; Mrs DA Nowakowa, Tiverton; Robert Nugent, SE31; Canon Peter Nunn, Glocs; Jody Lynn Nye, Illinois.

O Beverley Oakes, Essex; AM O'Brien, Worthing; Eamon O'Brien, Holland; Pauline O'Brien, London; DC O'Donnell, Wetherby; Elise O'Donnell, Wolverhampton; Mary O'Hanlon, Dr M. Ogden, Barnsley; Ann Oliver nee Cridland, email; N Oliver, London; Helensburgh; Sheila Openshaw, Hants; David O'Regan, Leeds; Joanne Osborne, Bromborough; Steve Osborne, Bucks; Chris Osler, email; Jan Ostron, Felpham; Judith Owen, SW6; William & Sue Oxley, Southampton.

P Trevor Pack, Rushden; RH Paczek, Newcastle; M Padina, Mattingley; Mr & Mrs GG Paine, Coventry; Keith Paine, Tilbury; GJ Palmer, Gainsborough; RS Palmer, Norfolk; Mrs A Parker, Birmingham; Mr GM Parker, Birmingham; John MF Parker, North Yorks; Philip Parker, Matlock; Roger Parkes, Petersfield Curry Club; Bill Parkes-Davies, Tunbridge Wells; Angela Parkinson, Clitheroe; Nick Parrish; Brian Parsons, email; M Parsons, Fareham; Roy Parsons, Richmond; Donald

SPLENDIDLY INDIAN, SUPERBLY SMOOTH

Paterson, East Grinstead; GM Patrick, London; Paul, email; Mrs PA Pearson, Bristol; Mrs G Pedlow, Hitchin; David and Dandra Peet, Surrey; Mrs Barrie Penfold, Bourne End; J Penn, Southampton; Elaine & Martin Perrett, Dorchester; AJW Perry, Bristol; Graham Perry, Truro; Ian Perry, Essex; MJ Perry, E17; Ian Pettigrew, Edinburgh; J Pfeffer, Manchester; Christopher Phelps, Gloucester; Adrian & Angela Phillips, Ammanford; Diane Phillips, Hyde; John Phillips, Wrexham; Jonathan Phillips, Saffron Walden; Steve Phillips, Wokingham; Colin Phipps, Scarborough; Sara Pickering, Northolt; Jack Pievsky, Pinner; Dr Dirk Pilat, e-mail; Mike Plant, Essex; Susan Platt, Bury; Rod Plinston, Reading; D Pool, SE2; K Pool, Leyland; SR Poole, Runcorn; Tony Pope, Derbys; Steve Porter, Walsall; Julia Pounds, Brighton; RL Power, Sutton Coldfield; Dave Prentice, Dartmouth; Steve Prentice, Devon; Tim Preston, Barrow; Alison Preuss, Glencarse; Jeff Price, Bristol; Mr J Priest, Sawbridgeworth; Dr John Priestman, Huddersfield; D Pulsford, Marford; Janet Purchon, Bradford; John Purkiss, Stourbridge; Steve Puttock, Chatham; Julie Pyne, County Down.

Q Sheila Quince, E11.

R Jon R, W5; Diane Radigan, Welling; Harish B Raichura, Reading; Rohit Rajput, email; Kevin Ramage, Berwick; Clive Ramsey, Edinburgh; Pradeep Rao, Derby; Alison Ratcliff, Halstead; KJ Rayment, Hertford; RC Raynham, Chelmsford; CR Read, Epsom; Mark Read, Romford; Guy Reavely, Surrey; Kim Reeder, South Shields; Debbie Reddy, W12; Francis Redgate, Nottingham; Steven Redknap, Ashford; I Reid, Fife; Lorraine Reid, Edinburgh; Duncan Renn, Dursley; Jon Restall, Ealing W5; Sam Revel Bournemouth Echo; Kevin Rhodes, Largo Florida; Richard, email; Derek Richards, Bewdley; Sean Richards, Dover; Michael & June Richardson, Hull; Simon Richardson, Gainsborough; Steve Ridley, email; Mike Ridgway, Buxton; Mathew Riley, SE3; Laurence Ritchie, Ilkeston; David Roberts, Northampton; Lindsay Roberts, Lancaster; Margaret Roberts, Rubery; Peter Roberts, Shipston; Gary Robertson, Edinburgh; Stewart & Anne Robertson, Leamington; Simon Roccason, Willenhall; Pat Roche, Chislehurst; J & P Rockery, Leicester; KG Rodwell, Harston; Mike Roebuck, Dewsbury; R Ronan, IOW; John Roscoe, Stalybridge; Brian Roston, Pontefract; John Rose, Hull; WJ Rowe; Steve Rowland, Matlock; Gareth Rowlands, email; the Royston family, East Sussex; Mrs EM Ruck, Darlington; DC Ruggins, Chalfont; JA Rumble, Rochford; Sue & Mike Rumfitt, Bedford; Paul Rushton, Nottingham; K Ruth, W1; Bob Rutter, Blackpool; EJ Ryan, Effingham; N Ryer, Mansfield.

S George and Mrs J Sadler, Thetford; MB Samson, Herts; Pauline Sapsford, Milton Keynes; MR Sargeant, Cornwall; Mark Sarjant, Guildford; GM Saville, Egremont; Mike Scotlock, Rayleigh; Mike Scott, Holmer Green; MJ Scott, SE26; Nicky & Don Scowen, Romford; Tim Sebensfield, Beeston; L Segalove, SN2; M Seefeld, W5; Patrick Sellar, Maidstone; Richard Sellers, East Yorks; Philip Senior, Liverpool; N Sennett, Hull; David Sewell, Aldershot; Mrs DA Seymour, Burnham-on-Sea; Richard Shackleton, Wakefield; Brian Shallon, Camberley; Sarah Shannon, B'hm; Jeane Sharp, St Albans; Mark Shaw, Swindon; Michelle Shaw, Ilford; Mrs Loraine Shaw, West Yorks; Deborah Shent, Nottingham;

Barrie Shepherd, Bishopston; Howard & Mary Sherman, Upton-by-Chester; Theresa Shilcock, Derbs; Stephen Shooman, Bolton; Ewan Sim, Leeds; Carolyn Simpson, SE13; P Simpson, Livingstone; Timo Sinclair, Hartley Wintney; Jennifer Singh, Enfield; Jeff Slater, e6; John G Slater, Hants; Joy Slater, Northum; William P Sloan, Camberley; Else & Harald Smaage, Sauvegny; David Smith, Norwich; David Smith, Swindon; Denis Smith, Swindon; EK Smith, Edinburgh; Gillian Smith, St Andrews; Hazel Smith, Llandrinio; Howard Smith, Cardiff; Jim Smith, Cork; LP & A Smith, Gibraltar; Mark Smith, Lancs; Nora Smith, Cardiff; Peter Smith-Cullen Islington; RB Smith, BFPO; Sue Smith, Northampton; Susan Smith, Devon; Sylvia Smith, Northum; Tim Smith, e-mail; Colin Snowball, Cheltenham; Tim Softly, Leigh; Robert Solbe, Surrey; Peter Soloman, Middlesbrough; M Somerton- Rayner, Cranwell; Maurice Southwell, Aylesbury; Gill Sparks, Halifax; Andrew Speller, Harlow; GD Spencer, Stonehaven; Mrs P Spencer, Norwich; Andy Spiers, Brighton; R Spiers, Wolverhampton; CP Spinks, Church Langley; Chris Spinks, Ilford; John Spinks, Hainault; Martin Spooner, Wallsend; DJ Stacey, Cambridge; David Stagg, Andover; Mrs WL Stanley-Smith, Belper; Mr & Mrs M Stanworth, Haywards Heath; John Starley, Birdingbury; Nigel Steel, Carlisle; Avril Steele, Crossgar; Bob Stencill, Sheffield; John Stent, Liss; Ian Stewart, Potters Bar; Tim Stewart, Norfolk; Roger Stimson, email; Susie Stockton-Link, Powys; Tina Stone, Illford; Barry Strange, Kent; Rob Struthers, Brighton; Mrs MB Such; Hazel Sugarman, Harlow; Steve Sumner, W.Yorks; FD Sunderland, Plympton; FC Sutton, Poole; Andrew Swain, Sudbury; Carolyn Swain, Leeds; Gary Swain, Coventry; DL Swann, Parbold; Frank Sweeney, Middlesbrough; Dennis Swift, Atherton; Gill & Graham Swift, Beeston; MS Sykes, Dorrington; Dr John Szewczyk, Lincs.

T Richard Tamlyn, Bovey Tracey; Nigel & Gill Tancock, Newbury; Steve Tandy, Cleveleys; Janet Tansley, Liverpool Echo; Bernard Tarpey, Failsworth; Bob Tarzey, email; Andrew Tattersall, North Yorks; CB Taylor, Wolverhampton; Colin Taylor, Preston; Darren Taylor, Som; Jeremy Taylor, Newport, Gwent; Kevin Taylor, Sevenoaks; Ken Taylor, Sevenoaks; Mick and Penny Taylor, email; Peter Taylor, Kingston-upon-Hull; Philip & Vivien Taylor, Cromer; Roger Taylor, Hamela; Len Teff, Whaddon; Mrs PF Terrazzano, Leigh-on-Sea; RL Terry, Kent; Michael Third, Nothum; André Thomas, Stoke; Christopher & Niamh Thomas, Barnet; DGThomas, Glocs; DL Thomas, Peterborough; Mrs J Thomas, Cumbria; Mark Thomas, Exeter; Nigel Thomas, Lincoln; Dr DA & AHE Thombs, Slimbridge; Alan Thompson, Clwyd; David & Lisa Thompson, SE10; Richard Thompson, Rainham; Bill Thomson, Ramsgate; Paul Thomson, Salford; J Thorne, South Benfleet; Penny Thurston, Buckingham; Ric & Nicky Tilbe, Wokingham; Mrs BM Clifton Timms, Chorley; Joan & Ken Timms, West Sussex; Mrs M Tindale, Beverley; Alan Tingle, Hayling Island; Graham Todd, Crawley; Tom and Charlotte, Leeds; Joan Tongue, Huddersfield; Tom and Charlotte, Leeds; Alex & Sarah Torrence, Cleveland; SR Tracey-Forster, Bronham; Bernard Train, Barton; Leigh Trevitt, Bishops Stortford; Jonathan Trew, Metro.co.uk; R Trinkwon, Ferring; Kevin & Sarah Troubridge,

Chelmsford; Dr JG Tucker, SW17; Paul Tunnicliffe, Cleveland; Martin Turley, Belgium; Don Turnbull, Geneva; Mrs SM Turner, Stroud; R Twiddy, Boston; S Twiggs, Lower Kingswood; Jeremey Twomey, Leamington; John Tyler, Romford.

V David Valentine, Forfar; Alan & Lesley Vaughan, Paington; Dorothy (Dot) Vaughan-Williams, Penyffordd; Puja Vedi, London; Mrs B Venton, Chipstead; Richard Vinnicombe, Camberley; Mr & Mrs T Vlismas, Crymoyh; Sarah Vokes, Dorking; Gordon Volke, Worthing.

W Phil Wain, Merseyside; PM Waine, Manchester; R Waldron, Oxon; Alison Walker, Droitwich; Andrew Walker, Aklington; Katherine Walker, London; Dr JB Walker, Burnham; John Walker, Chorley; Dr PAW Walker, Wirral; Si Walker Maidenhead; William Wallace, West Kilbride; Alison Walton, North Shields; Brian and Maureen Walsh, Market Harborough; Jennie Want, SW20; Mrs J Ward, Wakefield; Cathy Ward, Slough; Pamela Ward, Birmingham; Simon Ward, Croydon; John Warren, Lancs; Mrs G. Warrington, Hyde; Nicholas Watt, Houghton; RG Watt, Bromyard; Rod Watts, St Helier; Duncan Weaver, Bury St Edmunds; Stephanie Weaver, Northants; Andy Webb, Aberdeen; Peter Webb, West Byfleet; TG Webb, Peterborough; Nick Webley, Llandeilo; Dave Webster, Gateshead; Harry and Marina Webster, Nottingham; Andrew Wegg, SW16; Michael Welch, Reading; J Weld, Eastleigh; Dave Weldon, Hale; Mr and Mrs Wellington, Market Harborough; John Wellings, Edinburgh; AD West, Leics; Laurence West, Torquay; Dr PJ West, Warrington; Joyce Westrip, Perth, Australia; Sarah Wheatley, Leavesden; James and Bethan Whitelaw, Market Harborough; George Whilton, Huddersfield; Andy Whitehead, Swindon; Mr & Mrs DW Whitehouse, Redditch; George Whitton, Huddersfield; Peter Wickendon, East Tilbury; Jennette Wickes, Fleet; PM Wilce, Abingdon; Malcolm Wilkins, Gravesend; Chris Wilkinson, Cumbria; Geoffrey Wilkinson, Orpington; Babs Williams, Bristol; Mark P Williams, Bromley; P Williams, St Austell; Raoul Williams, Cambridge; Ted Williams, Norwich; David Williamson, NW3; David Williamson, Stamford; Rob Willis Leighton Buzzard; BP and J Willoughby, Devizes; Bob & Eve Wilson, NW2; David Wilson, Sunderland, Garry Wilson, e-mail; Dr Michael Wilson, Crewe; Major Mike Wilson, BFPO 140; John Wirring, Swindon; Mrs AC Withrington, Hindhead; David Wolfe, SW1, Douglas Wood; Hugh Wood, Brough; W Wood, Hornsea; Vilna Woolhead, Sussex; John Woolsgrove, Enfield; JL Wormald, Leeds; Geof Worthington, Handforth; Howard Worton, email ; Mrs C Wright, Glasgow; Mrs CF Wright, Stockport; Clive Wright, Halesowen; D Wright, Rotherham; John D Wright, St Ives; Georgina Wright, Nottingham; Lynn Wright, Newark; Mick Wright, Beds.

Y Tracy Yam, USA; Stephen Yarrow, Stanmore; EJ Yea, Cambs; Rev. Can. David Yerburgh, Stroud; Andrew Young, Cumbria; Andy Young, Penrith; Mrs B Young, Basildon; Carl Young, Nottingham; Mrs E Young, Ilmington.

Town Index

A
Aberdeen	350
Abergavenny	370/1
Abingdon	278
Addlestone	288
Alderney	348
Alfreton	208
Alton	285
Altrincham	244
Amersham	195
Arlesey	189
Ashtead	288
Ashton-Under-Lyne	245
Aston Clinton	195
Atherton, M46	246
Aylesbury	195

B
Banbury	278
Barking	215
Barmouth	372
Barnard Castle	213
Barnet (GL):	232
Barra	346
Barrow-In-Furness	206
Basildon	215
Basingstoke	220
Bath	281
Batley	336
Beaconsfield	195
Bedford	189
Bedlington	272
Beer	210
Beeston	276
Benfleet:	215
Berkhamsted	232
Berwick-on-Tweed	271
Beverley	332
Bewdley	329
Bicester	278
Birmingham Balti	315
Birmingham Central	311
Bishop Auckland	214
Bishops Stortford	232
Blackpool	239
Bodmin	204
Bolton	246
Bolton Le Sands	240
Borders, Scottish	**356**
Boston:	244
Boscombe	212
Bourne Lincs	244
Bourne End	195
Bournemouth	212
Bovey Tracey:	210
Bowmore	347
Brackley	268
Bradford	336
Braintree:	215
Brandon	288
Brecon	373
Brentford	254
Bridgend	365
Bridgnorth	281
Bridlington	332
Bridgwater	285
Brighton	298
Bristol	193
Bromborough	254
Bromley (GL)	230
Bromsgrove	327
Bromyard	227
Buckingham	195
Burnham-On-Crouch	215
Burton-On-Trent	208
Bury-St-Edmonds	287
Byfleet	291

C
Caernarfon	373
Caerphilly	371
Caldicot	370/1
Calne	325/8
Camberley	291
Cambridge	201
Cannock	285
Cardiff	367
Carlisle	206
Carmarthen	365
Carshalton	291
Castle Donnington	209
Caversham	190.
Chadsmoor	285
Channel Isles	**348**
Cheam Village	289
Cheddar	285
Chelmsford	216
Cheltenham	218
Cheshunt	232
Chester	202
Chester-Le-Street	214
Chesterfield	209
Chinnor	278
Chippenham	325/8
Chipstead	291
Cholsey	278
Christchurch	212
Church Stretton	281
Clacton-On-Sea	215
Clayton Brook	240
Cleethorpes	242
Clevedon	285
Clwyd	**364**
Coatbridge	357
Cobham	289
Cockermouth:	207
Colchester	216
Coleshill	308
Cockermouth	206
Cookham	190/5
Corbridge	272
Corby	269
Coventry	321
Cowes	347
Cranleigh	290
Crawley	299
Crewe	203
Crowthorne:	190
Croydon	290
Crumlin	371
Cupar	349
Cymbran	371

D
D & G	**349**
Dagenham (GL)	216
Dalkeith	351
Darlington	214
Deeside	**364**
Derby	209
Devizes	328
Didcot	279
Diss	268
Doncaster	333
Dorking	291
Douglas	347
Downham	268
Dudley	322
Dukinfield	246
Dumfries	349
Dumfries & Galloway	**349**
Dundee	363
Dunfermline	350
Dunmow	215
Durham	214
Dyfed	**365**

E
Earls Barton	270
East Molesey	296
East Yorkshire	**332**
Eastbourne	301
Eastcote	255
Eccleshall	285
Edgbaston	321
Edgware	255
Edinburgh	352-356
Ellesmere Port, Wirral	202
Elgin	351
Ellon	351
Enfield	256
Epping	215/6
Epsom	292
Esher	292
Eton	190
Everleigh	325
Evesham	327
Ewell	292
Exeter	210
Eyemouth	356

F
Fareham	220
Faringdon	279
Farnham	222
Farnham	292
Faversham	232
Felixstowe	288
Feltham, Middx	256
Fetcham	293
Fife	349
Findon	301
Fleet	221
Flint	364
Folkestone	232
Freshwater	347

G
Galashiels	356
Gants Hill GL	216
Garndolbenmaen	373
Gateshead	304
Gatwick (nr)	293 & 299
Gillingham	232
Glamorgan	**365**
Glenrothes	349
Gloucester	219
Gloucestershire	**218**
Gerrards Cross	197
Glasgow	358-363

382

SPLENDIDLY INDIAN, SUPERBLY SMOOTH

Glossop	210	I		Leicestershire	240	Mitcham	294
Gosforth	305	Ilford (GL)	216/8	Leigh, Mcr	247	Monmouth	371
Grampian	**350**	Ilfracombe:	210/211	Leigh-on-Sea	218	Montgomery	373
Grantham	243/4	Innerleithen	356	Leighton Buzzard	189	Morden	294
Great Malvern	329	Inverness	351	Leominster	227	Moreton	254
Great Yarmouth	267	Ipswich	288	Lerwick	346	Morpeth	272
Greater Manchester	**244**	Ironbridge	280	Letchworth	232	Mull	347
Grimsby	243/44	Islay	347	Lewes	302		
Guernsey	348	Isle of Barra	346	Lincoln	243/4	**N**	
Guildford	293	Isle of Islay	347	**Lincolnshire**	**243**	Nairn	351
Gwent	**370**	Isle of Lewis	347	Liskeard:	205	Neston	203
Gwynedd	**372**	Isle of Man	347	Liss	222	New Malden	295
		Isle of Mull	347	Lichfield	286	Newark	276
H		Isle of Skye	347	Linwood	358	Newcastle-u-Lyme	287
Haddenham	197	Isle of Wight	347	Liverpool	252/4	Newcastle-on-Tyne	305
Hale, Mcr	246	**Isles & Islands**	**346**	Llanberis	373	Newdigate	294
Halesowen	322			Llandrindod Wells	373	Newhaven	302
Halstead, Essex	218	**J**		Llandudno	372/3	Newmarket	288
Halstead Kent	232	Jersey	348	Llanelli	365	Newport, IOW	347
Hampshire	**220**			Llangollen	365	Newport, Gwent	370/2
Hampton Court	296	**K**		Llansantffraid	373	Newport Pagnell	201
Hampton, Middx	258	Keele	286	**Lothian**	**351**	Newton Abbot	210
Hampton Wick	296	Kegworth	240	Lowestoft	288	Newtown	373
Hanley, Stoke	287	Keighley	341	Ludlow	281	Norfolk	267
Harlow	218	Kendal	207	Luton	189	North Walsham	288
Harrow	256/8	Kenilworth	309	Lye	322	Northampton	270
Hatfield	232.	Kensham	284	Lyndhurst	222	**Northamptonshire**	**268**
Hawick	356	**Kent**	**230**			Northumberland	271
Hebrides Isles	346	Keswick	207	**M**		Northwich	203
Hednesford	287	Kettering	269/70	Maidstone	232	Norwich	267
Helensburgh	357	Kidderminster	329	Malvern	328	Nottingham	273
Hemel Hempstead	228	Kidlington	278	Manchester East	249	**Nottinghamshire**	**273**
Henley-in-Arden	310	Kingsthorpe	269	Manchester M1-M4	247	Nuneaton	309
Henley-on-Thames	278	Kingston-(GL)	293	Manchester North	249		
Hertfordshire	**227**	Kingston-Upon-Hull	332	Manchester Rusholme	250	**O**	
Hereford	226/7	Kings Langley	228	Manchester South	249	Oldbury	322
Herefordshire	**226**	King's Lynn	268	Manchester West	250	Oldham	251
Hersham	296	Kington	227	Mansfield	273	Ongar	218
Hexham	272	Kirby West	254	Marden	232	**Orkney Isles**	**346**
Heybridge:	218	Kirkcaldy	350	Margate	233	Orpington (GL)	232
High Wycombe	197	Kirkby Stephen	206	Market Drayton	281	Oswestry	281
Highland	**351**	Kirkwall	346	Marlborough	325	Oxford	278
Hengoed	368	Knowle	322	Marlow	197	**Oxfordshire**	**278**
Hinchley Wood	296	Knutsford	203	Matlock Bath	210	Oxted	295
Hitchin	232	Kyleakin	347	Menai Bridge	373		
Horley	293			**Merseyside**	**252**	**Q**	
Hornchurch (GL)	218	**L**		Meriden	322	Quinton	321
Hounslow	258	L'Eree	348	Middlesex	**254**		
Hove	301	**Lancashire**	**238**	Middlewich:	203	**P**	
Huddersfield	341	Leamington Spa	308	Milton Keynes	197	Paddock Wood,	234
Hull	332	Leeds	342	Minehead	285	Padstow	204
Hungerford	190	Leek	286	Minster, Isle of Sheppey	232	Peacehaven	302
Hyde, Mcr	246	Leicester	240	Minster, Thanet	232	Penzance	204

Town Index

Penrith	207	SCOTLAND	349	Sussex	298	Waterlooville	222
Peterborough:	202	Seaton	211	Sutton, Surrey	296	Wembley	266
Plymouth	211	Seven Kings (GL)	218	Sutton-in-Ashfield	276	West Kingsdown	235
Pontyclun	369	Sevenoaks:	235	Swanley	235	**West Midlands**	**311**
Poole	212	Shanklin	347	Swansea	369	West Yorkshire	336
Port Ellen	347	Sheffield	334	Swindon	328	West Wickham:	235
Port St Mary	347	Sherborne	212			Westcliff-on-Sea	218
Portree	347	Sheringham	288	T		Westerham	235
Porthmadog	373	**Shetland Isles**	**346**	**T &W**	**304**	Weston-super-Mare	285
Portsmouth	222	Shifnall	280	Tarporley	203	Weymouth	212
Powys	**373**	Shipley	344	Taunton	284	Whitehaven	207
Princess Risborough	201	Shrewsbury	281	**Tayside**	**363**	Whitley Bay	308
Purley	296	**Shropshire**	**280**	Tenbury Wells	328	Wigan	252
Pwllheli	373	Shoreham-by-Sea	302	Tenby	365	Wilmslow Road	250
		Sidcup (GL)	235	Tenterden	234	Williton	285
R		Sidmouth	211	Tewkesbury	220	**Wiltshire**	**328**
Ramsbottom	251	Skegness	244	Thatcham	192	Windsor	192
Ramsgate	232	Skye	347	Thornbury	220	Winlaton	308
Rayleigh	218	Sleaford	243	Thornton Heath	296	Winsford	203
Reading	190	Slough	191	Tolworth (GL)	296	Winslow	201
Redditch	327/9	Smethwick	321	Tonbridge:	235	Wirral	254
Redhill	296	Solihull	323	Tring	232	Wisbech	202
Reigate	296	**Somerset**	**281**	Thornton Heath	296	Warlingham	297
Richmond (GL)	296	South Shields	308	Tobermory	347	Wokingham	193
Ripley, Derbs	210	**South Yorkshire**	**333**	Torquay	211	Wolverhampton	324
Rochdale	251	Southall	259-264	Tow Law	214	Worcester	328/9
Rochester	232/4	Southampton	223	Truro	205	Worcester Park, Surrey	298
Romford (GL)	218	Southend-on-Sea	217	Tunbridge Wells	235	**Worcestershire**	**327**
Ross-on-Wye	227	Southsea	224	Twickenham	264	Worthing	303
Rotherham	334	Southport	254	Twyford	192/3	Wrexham	365
Rugby	310	Stafford	286	**Tyne &Wear**	**304**	Wrightington	240
Rugeley	287	**Staffordshire**	**285**				
Ruislip	258	Staines	296	U		Y	
Rusholme	250	Stamford	244	Uttoxeter	287	Yeovil	284
Rutland	**279**	Stapleford	276	Uckfield	303	**Yorkshire East**	**332**
Ryde	347	Staveley	207	Upton-on-Severn	328	**Yorkshire South**	**333**
Rye	302	Stevenage	232			**Yorkshire West**	**336**
		Stockport	251	V			
S		Stoke-on-Trent	287	Virginia Water	296		
St Albans	230	Stornoway	347				
St Andrews	349	Stourbridge	323	W			
St Aubin	348	Stratford-on-Avon	310	Wakefield	345		
St Austell	205	**Strathclyde**	**357**	**WALES**	**364**		
St Brelade	348	Stretford,	249	Wallasey	254		
St Helier	348	**Stirling**	**357**	Wallington	296		
St Ives, C'wall	205	Stourport-on-Severn	329	Walsall	324		
St Peter Port	348	**Suffolk**	**287**	Waltham Cross	232		
Salisbury	326	Sunderland	308	Wareham	213		
Sandbach	203	Sunbury-on-Thames	264	Warley, B66	324		
Sandown	347	Sunderland	308	Warlingham	297		
Sandwich	235	Suningdale	192	Warrington	203		
Scottish Borders	**356**	Surbiton	296	Warwick	310		
Scottish Isles	**346**	**Surrey**	**288**	**Warwickshire**	**308**		